Fodor's

COLORADO

8th Edition

**Where to Stay and Eat
for All Budgets**

**Must-See Sights
and Local Secrets**

Ratings You Can Trust

Fodor's Travel Publications New York, Toronto, London, Sydney, Auckland
www.fodors.com

FODOR'S COLORADO
Editors: Joanna G. Cantor, Salwa Jabado

Editorial Production: Astrid deRidder
Editorial Contributors: John Blodgett, Jad Davenport, Lois Friedland, Debbie Harmsen, Ann Miller, Molly Moker, Gregory Robl, Kyle Wagner
Maps & Illustrations: David Lindroth, Ed Jacobus, Mark Stroud, Henry Colomb, *cartographers*; William Wu; Robert Blake and Rebecca Baer, *map editors*
Design: Fabrizio LaRocca, *creative director*; Guido Caroti, Siobhan O'Hare, *art directors*; Tina Malaney, Chie Ushio, Ann McBride, *designers*; Melanie Marin, *senior picture editor*; Moon Sun Kim, *cover designer*
Cover Photo (Cumbres and Toltec Railroad): Ron Ruhoff/Index Stock/Photolibrary
Production/Manufacturing: Matthew Struble

Eighth Edition

ISBN 978–14000–1909–0

ISSN 0276–9018

SPECIAL SALES
This book is available at special discounts for bulk purchases for sales promotions or premiums. Special editions, including personalized covers, excerpts of existing books, and corporate imprints, can be created in large quantities for special needs. For more information, write to Special Markets/Premium Sales, 1745 Broadway, MD 6-2, New York, New York 10019, or e-mail specialmarkets@randomhouse.com.

AN IMPORTANT TIP & AN INVITATION
Although all prices, opening times, and other details in this book are based on information supplied to us at press time, changes occur all the time in the travel world, and Fodor's cannot accept responsibility for facts that become outdated or for inadvertent errors or omissions. So **always confirm information when it matters,** especially if you're making a detour to visit a specific place. Your experiences—positive and negative— matter to us. If we have missed or misstated something, **please write to us.** We follow up on all suggestions. Contact the Colorado editor at editors@fodors.com or c/o Fodor's at 1745 Broadway, New York, NY 10019.

PRINTED IN THE UNITED STATES OF AMERICA
10 9 8 7 6 5 4 3 2 1

Be a Fodor's Correspondent

Your opinion matters. It matters to us. It matters to your fellow Fodor's travelers, too. And we'd like to hear it. In fact, we need to hear it.

When you share your experiences and opinions, you become an active member of the Fodor's community. That means we'll not only use your feedback to make our books better, but we'll publish your names and comments whenever possible. Throughout our guides, look for "Word of Mouth," excerpts of your unvarnished feedback.

Here's how you can help improve Fodor's for all of us.

Tell us when we're right. We rely on local writers to give you an insider's perspective. But our writers and staff editors—who are the best in the business—depend on you. Your positive feedback is a vote to renew our recommendations for the next edition.

Tell us when we're wrong. We're proud that we update most of our guides every year. But we're not perfect. Things change. Hotels cut services. Museums change hours. Charming cafés lose charm. If our writer didn't quite capture the essence of a place, tell us how you'd do it differently. If any of our descriptions are inaccurate or inadequate, we'll incorporate your changes in the next edition and will correct factual errors at fodors.com immediately.

Tell us what to include. You probably have had fantastic travel experiences that aren't yet in Fodor's. Why not share them with a community of like-minded travelers? Maybe you chanced upon a beach or bistro or B&B that you don't want to keep to yourself. Tell us why we should include it. And share your discoveries and experiences with everyone directly at fodors.com. Your input may lead us to add a new listing or highlight a place we cover with a "Highly Recommended" star or with our highest rating, "Fodor's Choice."

Give us your opinion instantly at our feedback center at www.fodors.com/feedback. You may also e-mail editors@fodors.com with the subject line "Colorado Editor." Or send your nominations, comments, and complaints by mail to Colorado Editor, Fodor's, 1745 Broadway, New York, NY 10019.

You and travelers like you are the heart of the Fodor's community. Make our community richer by sharing your experiences. Be a Fodor's correspondent.

Tim Jarrell, Publisher

CONTENTS

CLOSE UPS

ABOUT THIS BOOK

Our Ratings

Sometimes you find terrific travel experiences and sometimes they just find you. But usually the burden is on you to select the right combination of experiences. That's where our ratings come in.

As travelers we've all discovered a place so wonderful that its worthiness is obvious. And sometimes that place is so unique that superlatives don't do it justice: you just have to be there to know. These sights, properties, and experiences get our highest rating, **Fodor's Choice,** indicated by orange stars throughout this book.

Black stars highlight sights and properties we deem **Highly Recommended,** places that our writers, editors, and readers praise again and again for consistency and excellence.

By default, there's another category: any place we include in this book is by definition worth your time, unless we say otherwise. And we will.

Disagree with any of our choices? Care to nominate a place or suggest that we rate one more highly? Visit our feedback center at *www. fodors.com/feedback.*

Budget Well

Hotel and restaurant price categories from ¢ to $$$$ are defined in the opening pages of each chapter. For attractions, we always give standard adult admission fees; reductions are usually available for children, students, and senior citizens. **AE, D, DC, MC, V** following restaurant and hotel listings indicate whether American Express, Discover, Diner's Club, MasterCard, and Visa are accepted.

Restaurants

Unless we state otherwise, restaurants are open for lunch and dinner daily. We mention dress only when there's a specific requirement and reservations only when they're essential or not accepted—it's always best to book ahead.

Hotels

Hotels have private bath, phone, TV, and air-conditioning and operate on the European Plan (aka EP, meaning without meals), unless we specify that they use the Continental Plan (CP, with a continental breakfast), Breakfast Plan (BP, with a full breakfast), or Modified American Plan (MAP, with breakfast and dinner) or are all-inclusive (AI, including all meals and most activities). We always list facilities but not whether you'll be charged an extra fee to use them, so when pricing accommodations, find out what's included.

Many Listings
- ★ Fodor's Choice
- ★ Highly recommended
- ⊠ Physical address
- ✛ Directions
- ⌂ Mailing address
- ☎ Telephone
- 🖷 Fax
- ⊕ On the Web
- ✉ E-mail
- 🎫 Admission fee
- ☉ Open/closed times
- Ⓜ Metro stations
- ▭ Credit cards

Hotels & Restaurants
- 🏨 Hotel
- ⤴ Number of rooms
- ⌂ Facilities
- ❍ Meal plans
- ✕ Restaurant
- ⌂ Reservations
- ⤡ Smoking
- 🆒 BYOB
- ✕🏨 Hotel with restaurant that warrants a visit

Outdoors
- 🏌 Golf
- ⛺ Camping

Other
- ♨ Family-friendly
- ⇨ See also
- ⊠ Branch address
- ☞ Take note

WHEN TO GO

The Colorado you experience will depend on the season of your visit. Summer is a busy time. Hotels in tourist destinations book up early, especially in July and August, and hikers crowd the backcountry from June through Labor Day. Ski resorts buzz from December to early April, especially around Christmas and Presidents' Day. Many of the big resorts are becoming popular summer destinations as well.

If you don't mind capricious weather, spring and fall are opportune seasons to visit. Rates drop and crowds are nonexistent. Spring's pleasures are somewhat limited, since snow usually blocks the high country—and mountain-pass roads—well into June. But spring is a good time for fishing, rafting on rivers swollen with snowmelt, birding, and wildlife viewing. In fall, aspens splash the mountainsides with gold, and wildlife come down to lower elevations. The fish are spawning, and the angling is excellent.

Climate

Summer in the Rocky Mountains begins in late June or early July. Days are warm, with highs often in the 80s; nighttime temperatures fall to the 40s and 50s. Afternoon thunderstorms are common over the higher peaks. Fall begins in September, often with a week of unsettled weather around mid-month, followed by four to six gorgeous weeks of Indian summer—frosty nights and warm days. Winter creeps in during November, and deep snows arrive by December. Temperatures usually hover near freezing by day, thanks to the surprisingly warm mountain sun, dropping considerably overnight, occasionally as low as -60°F. Winter tapers off in March, though snow lingers into

April on valley bottoms and into July on mountain passes.

At lower elevations (Denver, the eastern plains, and the southwestern corner of the state), summertime highs above 100°F are not uncommon, and winters are still cold, with highs in the 20s and 30s at the height of winter. The entire state sees snowy winters, even on the plains—where some of the most powerful blizzards hit. Colorado has a reputation for extreme weather, to be sure, but that cuts two ways: No condition ever lasts for long.

Forecasts Weather Channel Connection (⊕ www.weather.com).

Aspen, CO

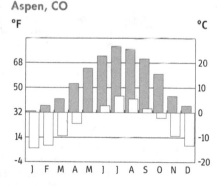

WHAT'S WHERE

DENVER	Denver is Colorado's capital and largest city, with 2.7 million residents in the metro area. The lively downtown area has a baseball stadium, an amusement park, historic neighborhoods, and a vast park system. Denver also claims the Denver Art Museum, the Denver Museum of Nature & Science, and the Denver Performing Arts Complex. The true beauty of Denver, however, is the combination of urban pleasures with easy access to all sorts of outdoor recreation.
THE ROCKIES NEAR DENVER	One of the country's most-scenic highways, Interstate 70 cuts through the heart of Colorado's high country. En route from Denver, I–70 ascends into the foothills through the onetime mining hub of Idaho Springs and on to another historic gem in Georgetown before cruising through the Eisenhower Tunnel towards serious ski country, starting with Loveland on the east end and then Winter Park. For those who'd rather try Lady Luck than tumble down the slopes, there are the neighboring gaming towns of Central City and Black Hawk.
SUMMIT COUNTY	Expansive Summit County encompasses the highly regarded ski-resort towns of Keystone, Breckenridge, and Copper Mountain, along with local favorite Arapahoe Basin. The towns of Dillon, Silverthorne, and Frisco cluster around Dillon Reservoir, connected by an extensive paved bike path and rimmed by the looming peaks of the Continental Divide that border the east and south of the county. The old mining town of Leadville, with its exceptional greenway and historic buildings, has become a destination for families.
VAIL VALLEY	The next stop on I–70's westward trek from Denver is the so-called Vail Valley. Vail, the world's largest single-mountain ski resort, is neatly situated along the interstate. Also in the valley are Beaver Creek and Minturn, a study in opposites: Beaver Creek is an upscale ski area noted for its tony restaurants and hotels, while Minturn is a sleepy old railroad town with a handful of antiques stores and diner-style eateries.
ASPEN & THE ROARING FORK VALLEY	Glitzy Aspen, well known as the playland of the rich and famous, is a serious skiing draw. Farther west (but closer to I–70) is Victorian charmer Glenwood Springs, centered on a massive pool fed by mineral hot springs.

BOULDER & NORTH CENTRAL COLORADO	At the foot of the Rocky Mountains, the college town of Boulder balances a bohemian philosophy with a largely high-tech economy. Estes Park, on the banks of the Big Thompson and Fall rivers, abuts Rocky Mountain National Park's eastern entrance, while Grand Lake is its considerably less-developed western gateway.
ROCKY MOUNTAIN NATIONAL PARK	The wildlands and alpine tundra of Rocky Mountain National Park are home to black bear, elk, bighorn sheep, and outdoor nuts. The park's 355 mi of trails, high-alpine lakes, snow-capped peaks, and wildflower-covered meadows lend themselves to an abundance of outdoor activities year-round.
NORTHWEST COLORADO & STEAMBOAT SPRINGS	Northwest Colorado is where the Rockies transition into an arid desert. Grand Junction is the region's hub farther east, Palisade is Colorado's fruit and wine capital. Nearby are the Colorado National Monument and Dinosaur National Monument. Also in the northwest corner is Steamboat Springs, a ski resort that blends the luxury of Vail and Aspen with a dollop of cowboy charm and fewer crowds.
SOUTHWEST COLORADO	Colorado's southwest quadrant descends from evergreen-clad peaks to red desert speckled with impressive sandstone formations. Black Canyon of the Gunnison offers fishing, rafting, hiking, and other outdoor pursuits. Mountain biking mecca Crested Butte has a bevy of Victorian buildings. Telluride is nestled in an idyllic box canyon rife with trails and waterfalls. Durango has a delightful historic downtown and lively nightlife, as well as the Silverton Narrow Gauge Railroad, which winds through spectacular scenery to artsy Silverton, a onetime mining town.
MESA VERDE NATIONAL PARK	Designated as a park in 1906, this protected series of canyons provides a peek into the lives of the Ancestral Puebloan people who made their homes among the cliffs. Drive through the 80-square-mi park, stopping along the way to climb down into the dwellings, which tuck into the dramatic formations.
SOUTH CENTRAL COLORADO	Colorado Springs was Colorado's first resort town, luring Easterners in the late 1800s to its mineral springs. Pikes Peak looms a few miles west of town. Cañon City is one white-water hub (and also the closest city to the 1,000-foot-deep Royal Gorge); farther north, Buena Vista and Salida, fast becoming Colorado's artists' colony, are two more. To the south, explore Great Sand Dunes National Park.

QUINTESSENTIAL COLORADO

Green Chile

Not the pepper itself but a gravylike stew is what Coloradans refer to when they talk about *chile verde*, the heady mixture that migrated with families who made their way from Mexico up through New Mexico and Texas and over from California to settle the high country. Its recipes vary as much across the state as minestrone does across Italy and pot-au-feu across France, but you can usually count on a pork-based concoction with jalapeños, sometimes tomatoes, and maybe tomatillos, with the heat ranging from mellow to sinus-clearing. Arguments rage over the best Mexican joints for a proper bowl, but most agree that Federal Boulevard in Denver is the place for the most *auténtico*. Green chile can smother just about anything—from enchiladas to huevos—but a plain bowlful with a warmed tortilla is all the purist requires, and it's the best hangover cure ever.

The Great Outdoors

Colorado gets more than 300 sunny days per year, and that's a big part of why the natives get restless when forced to spend too much time inside. The state is tailor-made for outdoor activities. On any given day you'll find folks figuring out ways to get out there, from biking to work along the intricate veins of multiuse paths to hiking with the dog around expanses of open space to soccer and jogging at the well-planned parks scattered around cities. Even cafés and coffeehouses are in on the action—alfresco dining is known to be pushed well into the cooler month of November in some places. In fact, Coloradans talk about the outdoors the way some people elsewhere talk about meals. They want to know where you just skied, hiked, biked, or rafted, and then, while they're in the middle of those adventures themselves, they'll discuss in-depth the next places on the list.

Colorado is famous as one big playground, from snowcapped ski resorts and biking and hiking trails to white-water rivers and mineral-fed hot springs. Not surprisingly, energy is required to fuel all of this play in the outdoors, and folks wind up or down with their nourishment of choice.

Hot Springs

In the late 1800s, people came to Colorado not for gold or skiing, but for the legendary magical restorative powers of the mineral-rich hot springs that had been discovered all over the state. Doc Holliday was one such patient. Suffering from consumption, he spent his final days breathing the sulfurous fumes in Glenwood Springs. To this day nearly two dozen commercial hot springs resorts exist, most with lodging or other activities attached, and many more pools have been identified where people can hike in for the private backcountry experience. Some hot springs have been left in their natural state, while others are channeled into Olympic-size swimming pools and hot tubs. Either way, they have become destinations for all who long to take advantage of the therapeutic benefits.

Microbrews

Although fancy cocktails and wine continue to make headway against beer elsewhere in the country, Colorado is still the land of microbrews. Pool tables, multiple televisions for sports viewing, and live music make the brewpub an essential part of the weekend scene in most major cities and towns, all of which have at least one outpost of a Denver microbrewery along with a homegrown offering. Many of the best Denver brewpubs are in LoDo, or lower downtown. These offer tasting flights much like wineries, served with food that runs the gamut from pub grub to upscale. Many microbreweries also have tasting rooms open to the public, where glass jugs of fresh beer can be purchased for takeout, perfect for picnics and tailgate parties.

IF YOU LIKE

Horseback Riding

Horseback riding in the Rocky Mountains can mean a quick trot on a paved trail through craggy red rocks or a week-long stay at a working dude ranch where guests rise at dawn and herd cattle from one snowcapped mountain range to another.

Horse-pack trips are great ways to visit the backcountry, since horses can travel distances and carry supplies that would be impossible for hikers. Although horsemanship isn't required for most trips, it's helpful, and even an experienced rider can expect to be a little sore for the first few days. June through August is the peak period for horse-pack trips; before signing up with an outfitter, inquire about the skills they expect.

Dude ranches fall roughly into two categories: working ranches and guest ranches. Working ranches, where guests participate in such activities as round-ups and cattle movements, sometimes require experienced horsemanship. Guest ranches offer a wide range of activities in addition to horseback riding, including fishing, four-wheeling, spa services, and cooking classes. At a typical dude ranch, guests stay in log cabins and are served meals family style in a lodge or ranch house; some ranches now have upscale restaurants on-site, too. For winter, many ranches have added such snow-oriented amenities as sleigh rides, snowshoeing, and cross-country skiing.

When choosing a ranch, consider whether the place is family oriented or adults only, and check on the length-of-stay requirements and what gear, if any, you are expected to bring. Working ranches plan around the needs of the business, and thus often require full-week stays for a fixed price, while regular guest ranches operate more like hotels.

Academy Riding Stables, Colorado Springs. Ideal for those who have only a short time in the area but long to do a half-day trail ride, Academy brings red-rock country up close via the Garden of the Gods, with pony rides for kids and hay wagon or stagecoach rides for groups.

C Lazy U Guest Ranch, Granby. One of the finest ranches in the state, C Lazy U offers a relaxing upscale experience, from daily horseback rides with a horse chosen for the duration of the visit to supervised kids' activities and chef-prepared meals, deluxe accommodations, a spring-fed pool, and an on-site spa.

Colorado Cattle Company & Guest Ranch, New Raymer (near Fort Collins). The real deal, the adults-only Colorado Cattle Company is two hours from Denver International Airport and seconds from turning guests on to a true Western experience, with continual cattle drives, branding, fencing, and roping on a 7,000-acre ranch with 1,000 head of cattle.

Devil's Thumb Ranch, Tabernash (near Winter Park). Their commitment to the environment, use of renewable resources, and focus on the finest quality, from the organic ingredients in the restaurant to the luxurious bed linens in the rustic yet upscale cabins, make Suzanne and Bob Fanch's spread a world-class getaway. They continue to update the ranch, with a new spa and lodge added to the superior horseback-riding, cross-country skiing, and ice-skating programs already in place.

Skiing & Snowboarding

The champagne powder of the Rocky Mountains can be a revelation for newcomers. Forget treacherous sheets of rock-hard ice, single-note hills where the bottom can be seen from the top, and mountains that offer only one kind of terrain from every angle. In the Rockies, the snow builds up quickly, leaving a solid base that hangs tough all season, only to be layered upon by thick, fluffy powder that holds an edge, ready to be groomed into rippling corduroy or left in giddy stashes along the sides and through the trees. Volkswagen-size moguls and half-pipe–studded terrain parks are the norm, not the special attractions.

Skiing the Rockies means preparing for all kinds of weather, sometimes in the same day, because the high altitudes can start a day off sunny and bright but kick in a blizzard by afternoon. Layers help, as well as plenty of polypropylene to wick away sweat in the sun, and a water-resistant outer layer to keep off the powdery wetness that's sure to accumulate—especially if you're a beginner snowboarder certain to spend time on the ground. Must-haves: plenty of sunscreen, because the sun is closer than you think, and a helmet, because so are the trees.

The added bonus of Rocky Mountain terrain is that many resorts have a wide variety of terrain at all levels, from beginning (green circle) to expert (double black diamond). Turn yourself over to the rental shops, which are specialized enough at each resort to offer expert help in planning your day and outfitting you with the right equipment. Renting is also a great chance for experienced skiers and snowboarders to sample the latest technology.

Shop around for lift tickets before you leave home. Look for package deals, multiple-day passes, and online discounts. Call the resort and ask if there are any off-site locations (such as local supermarkets) where discount tickets can be purchased. The traditional ski season usually runs from mid-December until early April, with Christmas, New Year's, and the month of March being the busiest times at the resorts.

Aspen. Part "Lifestyles of the Rich and Famous" and part sleepy ski town, picturesque Aspen offers four mountains of well-varied terrain within easy access and some of the best dining in the state.

Breckenridge. Four terrain parks, each designed to target a skill level and promote advancement, give snowboarders the edge at this hip resort, which manages to make skiers feel just as welcome on its big, exposed bowls.

Keystone. The family that does winter sports together stays together at Keystone, which is small enough to navigate easily. Nestled neatly near Breckenridge and Copper Mountain and not too far from Vail, Keystone has a high percentage of beginner and intermediate offerings.

Vail. Those looking for the big-resort experience head to Vail, where modern comforts and multiple bowls mean a dizzying variety of runs and every possible convenience, all laid out in a series of contemporary European-style villages.

Winter Park. Winter Park has retained the laid-back feel of a locals' mountain and is still one of the better values on the Front Range. Mary Jane offers a mogul a minute while the gentler Winter Park side gives cruisers a run for their money.

Hiking

Hiking is easily the least-expensive and most-accessible recreational pursuit. Sure, you could spend a few hundred dollars on high-tech hiking boots, a so-called personal hydration system, and a collapsible walking staff made of space-age materials, but there's no need for such expenditure. All that's really essential are sturdy athletic shoes, water, and the desire to see the landscape under your own power.

Hiking in the Rockies is a three-season sport that extends as far into fall as you're willing to tromp through snow, though in the arid desert regions of southwestern Colorado it's possible to hike year-round without snowshoes. One of the greatest aspects of this region is the wide range of hiking terrain, from high-alpine scrambles that require stamina to flowered meadows that invite a relaxed pace to confining slot canyons where flash floods are a real danger.

There are few real hazards to hiking, but a little preparedness goes a long way. Know your limits, and make sure the terrain you are about to embark on does not exceed your abilities. It's a good idea to check the elevation change on a trail before you set out—a 1-mi trail might sound easy, until you realize how steep it is—and be careful not to get caught on exposed trails at elevation during afternoon thunderstorms in summer. Bring layers of clothing to accommodate changing weather, and always carry enough drinking water. Make sure someone knows where you're going and when to expect your return.

Bear Lake Road, Rocky Mountain National Park. A network of trails crisscross among the alpine lakes, waterfalls, aspens, and pines. Stroll 1 mi to Sprague Lake on a wheelchair-accessible path or take a four-hour hike past two waterfalls to Mills Lake with its views of mighty Longs Peak.

Black Canyon of the Gunnison National Park. These are serious trails for serious hikers. There are six routes down into the canyon, which can be hot and slippery, and super steep. But the payoff is there: a rare look into the heart of a stunning canyon and the fast-moving Gunnison River.

Chautauqua Park, Boulder. Meet the locals (and their dogs) as you head up into the mountains to look back down at the city or to get up close and personal with the Flatirons. There's even a grassy slope perfect for a picnic.

Colorado National Monument, Grand Junction. Breathe in the smell of sagebrush and juniper as you wander amid red-rock cliffs, canyons, and monoliths.

The Colorado Trail. The beauty of this epic hike, which starts just north of Durango and goes all the way to Denver, is that you can do it all or just pieces of it. As the route ascends and drops back down, there are plenty of places to duck in and out, as well as views of a variety of climates and mountain ranges.

Green Mountain Trail, Lakewood. Part of Jefferson County Open Space, the easy, mostly exposed trail affords panoramic views of downtown Denver, Table Mesa, Pikes Peak, and the Continental Divide from the top. You must share with bikers and dogs, as well as other critters.

Maroon Bells, Aspen. Bring your camera and take your shot at the twin, mineral-streaked peaks that are one of the most-photographed spots in the state.

Bicycling

The Rockies are a favorite destination for bikers. Wide-open roads with great gains and losses in elevation test (and form) the stamina for road cyclists, while riders who prefer pedaling fat tires have plenty of mountain and desert trails to test their skills. Unmatched views often make it difficult to keep your eyes on the road.

Thanks to the popularity of the sport here, it's usually easy to find a place that rents bicycles, both entry level and high end, if you'd prefer to leave yours at home. Bike shops are also a good bet for information on local rides and group tours.

The rules of the road are the same here as elsewhere, though some areas are less biker-friendly than others. On the road, watch for trucks and stay as close as possible to the side of the road, in single file. On the trail, ride within your limits and keep your eyes peeled for hikers and horses (both of which have the right of way), as well as dogs. Always wear a helmet and carry plenty of water.

Breckenridge. Groups of mixed-skill level bikers make for Summit County, where beginners stick to the paved paths, the buff take on Vail Pass, and single-track types test their technical muscles in the backcountry.

Cherry Creek Bike Path, LoDo, and Cherry Creek. The ultimate urban trek, the paved trail runs along the burbling creek from Cherry Creek Shopping Center to Larimer Square. It's part of 400 mi of greenway the Denver Parks Department has linked for folks to get around the area.

Crested Butte. Pearl Pass is the storied birthplace of the mountain-biking craze in Colorado (be sure to check out the museum devoted to it in town). If your legs are not quite ready for that 40-mi, 12,700-foot challenge, there are plenty of paths more suitable to mere mortals.

Durango. Bikes seem to be more popular than cars in Durango, another fabled biking mecca. You can bike around town or into the mountains with equal ease, and there are plenty of locals ready to advise you as to their favorite routes.

Grand Junction/Fruita. With epic rides such as Over the Edge and the famous Kokopelli Trail, these two areas beckon single-track fanatics with their wavy-gravy loop-de-loops and screaming downhill payoffs. Beware: The heat can get you, so plan accordingly.

Keystone. Serious downhillers head to Keystone's Drop Zone, the resort's new expert section packed with rock gardens and high-speed jumps. Don't like the grunt-filled climb? Hop on a chairlift and smile away the sweet downhill.

Rangely. The Raven Rims are also known as the Rangely Rims, because you can see the town from nearly every point along this fun mountain-bike ride that starts in the corrals at Chase Draw.

Steamboat Springs. Yes, it is a cowboy town. But the backcountry is also laced with miles of jeep trails and single-track perfect for the solitude-seeking cyclist.

Winter Park. Home to the fabled Fat Tire Classic bike ride, Winter Park features tree-lined single-track trails that vary from gentle, meandering jaunts to screaming roller-coaster rides.

Rafting

Rafting brings on emotions as varied as the calm induced by flat waters surrounded with stunning scenery and backcountry beauty and wildlife and the thrill and excitement of charging a raging torrent of foam.

For the inexperienced, the young, and the aged, dozens of tour companies offer relatively mundane floats ranging from one hour to one day starting at $20. Others fulfill the needs of adventure tourists content only with chills, potential spills, and the occasional wall of water striking them smack-dab in the chest. Beginners and novices should use guides, but experienced rafters may rent watercraft.

Seasoned outfitters know their routes and their waters as well as you know the road between home and work. Many guides offer multiday trips in which they do everything, including searing your steak, setting up your tent, and rolling out your sleeping bag. Select an outfitter based on recommendations from the local chamber, experience, and word of mouth.

The International Scale of River Difficulty is a widely accepted rating system that ranks waters from Class I (the easiest) to Class VI (think Niagara Falls). Ask your guide about the rating on your route before you book. Remember, ratings can vary greatly throughout the season due to runoff and weather events.

Wear a swimsuit or shorts and sandals and bring along sunscreen and sunglasses. Outfitters are required to supply a life jacket for each passenger; although most states don't require that it be worn, it's the law in Colorado. Early summer, when the water is highest, is the ideal time to raft in the West, although many outfitters will stretch the season, particularly on calmer routes.

Animas River, Durango. Even at high water, the Lower Animas stays at Class III, which makes for good times and a great way to see the Durango area (try it on an inflatable kayak). Meanwhile, the Upper Animas runs between Class III and Class IV, hits a few at V, and gives little time to appreciate the mountain scenery, old railroad beds, and canyon views that race by.

Arkansas River, Buena Vista & Salida. The Arkansas rages as a Class V or murmurs as a Class II, depending on the season. It's *the* white-water rafting destination in the state.

Blue River, Silverthorne. The Class I–III stretches of the Blue that run between Silverthorne and Columbine Landing make for an ideal paddle for first-timers. Be sure to check the flows; this is a short-season spot.

Colorado River in Glenwood Canyon, Glenwood Springs. Take your pick—a wild ride through the Shoshone Rapids (Class IV in peak season) or a mellow float down the lower Colorado, with a dip in the nearby hot springs to warm you up.

Gunnison River, north of Black Canyon of the Gunnison National Monument. Packhorses carry your equipment into this wild area that leads into Gunnison Gorge, where Class I–III waters take the group past granite walls while bald eagles fly overhead.

Yampa & Green Rivers, Grand Junction. Ride the Yampa and Green rivers through the remote, rugged canyons of Dinosaur National Monument.

Fishing

Trout do not live in ugly places.

And so it is in Colorado where you'll discover unbridled beauty, towering pines, rippling mountain streams, and bottomless pools. It's here that blue-ribbon trout streams remain much as they were when Native American tribes, French fur trappers, and a few thousand faceless miners, muleskinners, and sodbusters first placed a muddy footprint along their banks.

Those early-day settlers had one advantage that you won't—time. To make the best use of that limited vacation in which fishing is a preferred activity, consider the following advice:

Hire a guide. You could spend days locating a great fishing spot, learning the water currents and fish behavior, and determining what flies, lures, or bait the fish are following. A good guide will cut through the options, get you into fish, and turn your excursion into an adventure complete with a full creel.

If you're comfortable with your fishing gear, bring it along, though most guides loan or rent equipment. Bring a rod and reel, waders, vest, hat, sunglasses, net, tackle, hemostats, and sunscreen. Always buy a fishing license.

If you're not inclined to fork over the $250-plus that most quality guides charge per day for two anglers and a boat, your best bet is a stop at a reputable fly shop. They'll shorten your learning curve, tell you where the fish are, what they're biting on, and whether you should be "skittering" your dry fly on top of the water or "dead-drifting" a nymph.

Famed fisherman Lee Wolff wrote that "catching fish is a sport. Eating fish is not a sport." Most anglers practice "catch and release" in an effort to maintain productive fisheries and to protect native species.

Seasonality is always a concern when fishing. Spring runoffs can cloud the waters; summer droughts may reduce stream flows; and fall weather can be unpredictable. But, as many fishing guides will attest, the best time to come and wet a line is whenever you can make it.

Arkansas River, Buena Vista. Fly-fish for brown or rainbow trout through Browns or Bighorn Sheep Canyon, or combine white-water rafting with fishing by floating on a raft through the Royal Gorge.

Gunnison River, Almont. In a tiny hamlet near Crested Butte and, more importantly, near the headwaters of the Gunnison, they *live* fly-fishing.

Lake Dillon, Dillon. Pick your spot along 26 mi of shoreline and cast away for brown and rainbow trout and kokanee salmon. The marina offers rentals for those who want to get out on the water and a fully stocked store.

Lake Granby, Grand Lake. Can't wait for summer? Try ice fishing on Lake Granby, on the western side of Rocky Mountain National Park.

Roaring Fork River, Aspen. Uninterrupted by dams from its headwaters to its junction with the Colorado, the Roaring Fork is one of the last free-flowing rivers in the state, plus it has a healthy population of 12- to 18-inch trout.

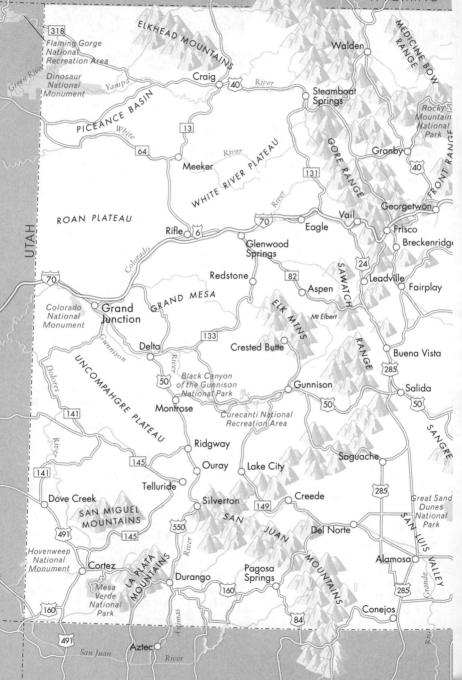

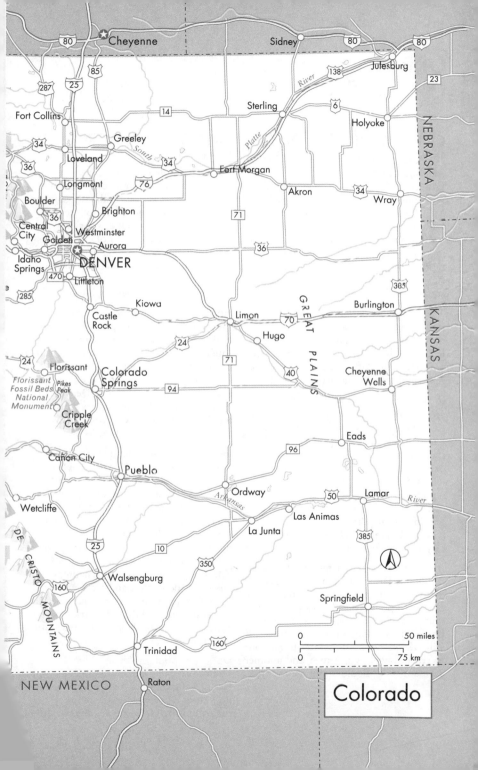

Colorado

GREAT ITINERARIES

CONNECTING THE DOTS IN COLORFUL COLORADO

Arriving in Denver

Denver is filled with folks who stopped to visit and never left. After a few days in the Mile High City and surrounding metro area, it's easy to see why: Colorado's capital has much to recommend it, including a thriving cultural scene, restaurants representing every ethnicity, plenty of sunshine, outdoor options galore, and snowcapped peaks for visual variety.

The Old West still holds sway in visitors' imaginations, and there are plenty of throwback trappings to check out, but the reality is that Denver is a modern metropolis that offers cosmopolitan amenities and state-of-the-art amusements.

Logistics: There are myriad well-marked ground transportation options near baggage claim at the sprawling Denver International Airport (DEN). Head to the taxi stand to pay about $50 to get downtown, or visit the RTD desk for bus schedules (SkyRide operates multiple routes starting at $8 one-way). Several independent companies operate shuttles from desks within the airport for about $19 one-way, and many hotels offer complimentary shuttles for their guests.

All of the major car-rental companies operate at DEN. The rental-car counters that you see in the main terminal are there merely to point you toward the shuttles that take you to the car-rental center. Depending on time of day and traffic, it will take between 30 minutes to an hour to reach downtown Denver and another 30 minutes for Boulder and the foothills.

DAYS 1–2: DENVER & BOULDER

Option 1: Metro Denver

After you've settled into your hotel, head downtown, or if you're already staying there—always a good option to truly explore the city—make your way to Lower Downtown, or LoDo. The historic district is home to many of the city's famous brewpubs, art galleries, and Coors Field, as well as popular restaurants and some of the area's oldest architecture.

Hop on the free MallRide, the shuttle bus run by RTD, to head up the 16th Street Mall, a pedestrian-friendly, shopping-oriented strip that runs through the center of downtown. From there you can walk to Larimer Square for more shopping and restaurants, as well as the Denver Art Museum, the Colorado History Museum, the Colorado State Capitol, the Molly Brown House, and the U.S. Mint.

Logistics: Vending machines at each station for TheRide, Denver's light-rail, show destinations and calculate your fare ($1.50–$2.75 depending on the number of zones crossed). The machines accept bills of $20 or less and any coin except pennies. Children under age five ride free when accompanied by a fare-paying adult. RTD buses also provide an excellent way to get around; schedules are posted inside shelters and are available at Civic Center Station at the south end of the 16th Street Mall and Market Street Station toward the north end. Fares are $1.50 one-way.

Option 2: Boulder

Boulder takes its fair share of ribbing for being a Birkenstock-wearing, tofu-eating, latter-day hippie kind of town, but the truth is that it is one healthy, wealthy area, exceedingly popular and rapidly heading toward overdevelopment. For now, though, it's still a groovy place to visit. Stroll along the Pearl Street Mall and sample the excellent restaurants and shops, catching one of the dozens of street performers; or head just outside the city to tour Celestial Seasonings, the tea manufacturer; or to Chautauqua Park to hike in the shadow of the dramatic Flatiron Mountains. In winter, Eldora Mountain Resort is a 21-mi jaunt up a steep, switchback-laden road with no lift lines as payoff. The University of Colorado campus here means there is a high hip quotient in much of the nightlife.

Logistics: You can take an RTD bus to Boulder from Denver, but it's just as easy to drive up U.S. 36, and if you're going to go beyond the Pearl Street Mall, it's nice to have a car once you're there. Parking, though, can be quite tight.

DAYS 3–7: THE ROCKIES
Option 1: Estes Park, Rocky Mountain National Park & Grand Lake
Rocky Mountain National Park (RMNP) is a year-round marvel, a park for every season: summer's hiking, fall's elk-mating ritual, winter's snowcapped peaks, and spring's wildflowers. Estes Park is the gateway to RMNP but a worthwhile destination itself, a small town swelling to a large one with the tourists who flock to its Western-theme shops and art galleries. The alpine surrounded Grand Lake is a rustic charmer, a mecca for the sports person, and an idyllic locale for a family vacation.

Logistics: Estes Park is a hop-skip from Denver and Boulder, about 65 mi northwest of Denver via Interstate 25 and then

CO–66 and U.S. 36. To get to RMNP, simply take U.S. 34 or U.S. 36 into the park. Grand Lake is on the other side of RMNP via U.S. 34, or from Denver, it's 100 mi by taking Interstate 70 to U.S. 40 over Berthoud Pass through Winter Park, Fraser, and Granby, and then turning onto U.S. 34 to Grand Lake. It can be a bit more challenging in winter.

Option 2: Aspen & the Roaring Fork Valley
The drive to Aspen sends you straight through the heart of the Rocky Mountains, from the foothills to the peaks, with plenty of highs and lows between. Along the way, there are several possible stops, including small-town diversions in places such as Idaho Springs and Georgetown, outlet shopping in Silverthorne, high-alpine mountain biking and hiking in Vail, and a dip in the hot springs in Glenwood Springs. Once in Aspen, world-class dining, upscale shopping, and celebrity-sighting await, while, depending on the season, the slopes will serve up wildflower-covered meadows or some of the best skiing in North America. Do not miss a pilgrimage to the Maroon Bells Wilderness area for a glimpse of the famous peaks.

Logistics: There are several flights in and out of Aspen/Pitkin County Airport daily, most routing through Denver. Many travelers drive to Aspen, however, making the 220-mi journey west on I–70 from Denver to Glenwood Springs, then taking U.S. 82 to Aspen. From May until about mid-October, Independence Pass, a more-scenic option, is open; from I–70 take U.S. 91 at Copper Mountain south through Leadville to U.S. 82 and then use Independence Pass.

Option 3: Colorado Springs, Manitou Springs & Cripple Creek

The Pikes Peak area may be dominated by 14,110-foot Pikes Peak itself—long ago the inspiration for "America the Beautiful"—and certainly getting to its summit, whether by cog railway, foot, or car, is a worthy goal. But there are other options along this popular corridor, such as strolling through the red rocks of the Garden of the Gods, peeking at the tunnel in Cave of the Winds, checking out the animals at the Cheyenne Mountain Zoo, taking advantage of the healing vibes in the artists' community that is Manitou Springs, or exploring the old gold-mining town of Cripple Creek.

Logistics: Colorado Springs sits 70 mi south of Denver on Interstate 25. You'll enjoy mountain views on most of the drive; Pikes Peak is visible on clear days. Take U.S. 24 west from Interstate 25 to reach Manitou Springs; follow CO–67 south from U.S. 24 west to visit Cripple Creek.

DAYS 8–14: THE SOUTHWEST

Option 1: Salida & Buena Vista

The way the Collegiate Peaks open up in magnificent panorama as you come around the bend on U.S. 285 is only one of the draws of a trip from Denver to Buena Vista and Salida. The plethora of outdoor activities available in this mountain- and river-rich region adds to the appeal. Salida has become a haven for its bevy of artists making a national name for their Western-oriented themes and grassroots sensibilities, and the banana-belt weather makes it all the more alluring.

Logistics: Take U.S. 285 south to Buena Vista. To reach Salida, continue on to Poncha Springs, then follow U.S. 50 east. Winter sports enthusiasts will want to make a side trip to Monarch Mountain, while mountain bikers won't want to miss the Monarch Crest Trail at Monarch Pass, both about 18 mi west of Salida on U.S. 50.

Option 2: Alamosa, San Luis Valley & Great Sand Dunes National Park

The Sand Dunes dominate this sleepy, agriculturally abundant area, though they are only one of the natural playgrounds available to visitors. Alamosa National Wildlife Refuge is famous for its crane migrations, the fishing is superior in the Rio Grande, and the Sangre de Cristo Wilderness has its peaks and trails. Hop aboard the Cumbres & Toltec Scenic Railroad for a 64-mi trip back in time; the area, not to mention the train itself, has changed little since the 1880s.

Logistics: The round-trip is a worthwhile excursion alone, because the corridor between the Sangre de Cristo Mountains and the San Juans is one of the largest intermountain valleys in the world. Take Interstate 25 south to Walsenburg, then west on U.S. 160 to Alamosa, and then north on CO–150.

Option 3: Telluride, Mesa Verde & Durango

Durango is about an eight-hour drive from Denver, and well worth the effort. Mountain bikers make it a mission to try their mettle on the tough trails, and the Old West feel and small-town charm put this energetic spot high on the list for tourists. Telluride, though second home to several notable celebrities and famous for its film festival and other national

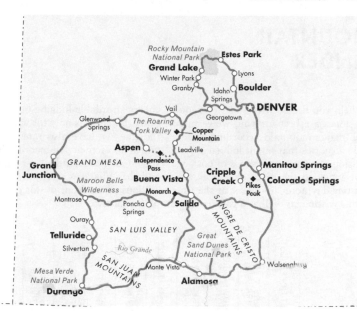

events, sports a less-glitzy face than other ski resorts like Aspen; and the San Juan Skyway, a 236-mi loop that connects Durango, Telluride, Ouray, and Silverton, is a gloriously scenic tour of mountains, alpine forests, and wildflower meadows. Mesa Verde National Park, meanwhile, safeguards the 1,400-year-old cliff dwellings of the Ancestral Puebloans.

Logistics: To go straight to Durango, take U.S. 285 southwest to Monte Vista and then head west on U.S. 160. Mesa Verde is a one-and-a-half-hour drive from Durango, heading west on U.S. 160. For Telluride, take I–70 to Grand Junction and go south on U.S. 50 to Montrose; continue south on CO–550 to Ridgway, then turn right onto CO–62. Follow this to CO–145 and turn left. Follow the signs into Telluride. Telluride and Durango also have regional airports with limited service from major carriers.

TIPS

■ Guard against the effects of altitude. Drink lots of water, slather on the sunscreen, and watch your alcohol intake. And pace yourself, especially when hiking or engaging in other outdoor pursuits.

■ Pack a lunch for your day in Rocky Mountain National Park. You'll have your pick of jaw-droppingly gorgeous spots for a picnic.

■ For the night in Aspen, consider reserving a room down valley in Basalt or Carbondale if the rates in Aspen proper look too steep.

■ Denver and Aspen are the places to splurge on meals.

■ If you have a morning flight, consider staying the final night in Denver.

MOUNTAIN FINDER

To help you decide which of Colorado's ski slopes are best for you, we've rated each major mountain according to several categories that might influence your decision. To give some sense of cost, we have included the price of a peak season one-day adult lift ticket at the time of this writing, as well as a category that covers affordable lodging options. Don't think this chart is only for winter visitors though—we have also rated the mountain areas on their summer offerings. You should also consult the regional chapters and the What's Where and If You Like sections at the front of this guide as you plan your trip.

	LIFT TICKET COST	VARIETY OF TERRAIN	SNOWBOARDER FRIENDLY	OTHER SNOW SPORTS	FAMILY FRIENDLY	DINING VARIETY	NIGHTLIFE	AFFORDABLE LODGING	OFF-SLOPE ACTIVITIES	SUMMER ACTIVITIES	CONVENIENCE FACTOR
Arapahoe Basin	$58	◑	●	○	◑	○	○	○	○	○	●
Aspen	$87	●	◑	●	◑	●	●	○	●	●	◑
Beaver Creek	$92	◑	◑	◓	●	◑	◓	○	◓	◑	◑
Breckenridge	$86	◑	●	●	●	◑	◑	◑	●	●	◑
Copper Mountain	$86	●	●	◓	●	◓	◑	◑	◓	○	◑
Crested Butte	$79	◑	●	◓	●	○	◑	◓	◑	●	○
Purgatory at Durango	$65	◓	◑	●	◑	○	○	●	○	○	○
Eldora	$59	◓	●	◓	◑	○	○	○	○	○	◓
Keystone	$86	●	◑	◑	●	◓	◑	◑	◑	◓	●
Loveland	$54	◓	●	○	●	○	○	○	○	○	●
Monarch	$52	◑	◑	○	●	○	○	○	○	○	○
Ski Cooper	$39	○	◑	○	●	○	○	○	○	○	◓
Snowmass	$87	◑	◓	◓	●	◓	◓	○	◑	◓	◓
Steamboat	$85	◑	●	●	●	◓	◓	◑	●	●	◓
Telluride	$85	◑	◑	◑	◑	◑	◑	◓	◑	●	○
Vail	$92	●	◑	◑	●	●	●	◓	◓	●	◑
Winter Park	$86	●	●	◓	●	○	○	●	○	◓	●
Wolf Creek	$48	◑	◑	○	●	○	○	●	○	○	○

KEY: ○ few or none   ◓ moderate   ◑ substantial   ● noteworthy

Denver

WORD OF MOUTH

"Tops on my list would be Red Rocks Amphitheatre and Park. It's a short drive out I–70, then south to Morrison. It's open and free to go around the theatre and enjoy the marvelous view of the plains and the incredible rock formations. The visitor center is a virtual museum of the famous bands who have played there. There's a short trail for hiking as well."

—tekwriter

"Do go to the Art Museum—the new wing opened [in 2007] and is gorgeous."

—martym

Revised &
Updated by
Kyle Wagner

YOU CAN TELL FROM ITS skyline alone that Denver is a major metropolis, with a major league–baseball stadium in the center of downtown and parking-meter rates that rival even Chicago and New York. But look to the west to see where Denver distinguishes itself. You'll be driving along Interstate 70, contemplating the industrial warehouses on the way back from Denver International Airport, and suddenly the Rocky Mountains, snow-peaked and breathtakingly huge, appear in the distance. This combination of urban sprawl and proximity to nature is what gives the city character. People spend their weeks commuting to LoDo, the business district and historic downtown, and their weekends reveling in the multitude of skiing, camping, hiking, bicycling, and fishing areas surrounding the city limits.

Throughout the 1960s and 1970s, when the city mushroomed on a huge surge of oil and energy revenues, Denver worked on the transition from Old West "cowtown" to a comfortable, modern place to live. The city demolished its large downtown "Skid Row" area, paving the way for developments such as the Tabor Center and the Auraria multicollege campus. In the early '90s Mayors Federico Peña and Wellington Webb championed a massive new airport to replace the rickety Stapleton. Then the city lured major-league baseball, in the form of the purple-and-black Colorado Rockies, and built Coors Field in the heart of downtown. Around the stadium, planners developed LoDo, a business-and-shopping area including hip nightclubs, Larimer Square boutiques, and bike and walking paths.

Since the mid-1990s, Denver has caught the attention of several major national corporations looking to move their operations to a thriving city that enjoys a relatively stable economy and a healthy business climate. The fact that the Democratic National Party chose Denver for the 2008 national convention made it clear that the city had finally arrived. And although the sports teams have yet to regain the top status that they enjoyed in the past—the Broncos have not revisited their two Super Bowl championships, while the initial promise of the Rockies has yet to be fulfilled—they nonetheless continue to imbue the city with a sense of pride.

Many Denverites are unabashed nature lovers who can also enjoy the outdoors within the city limits, walking along the park-lined river paths downtown. (Perhaps as a result of their active lifestyle, Denverites are the "thinnest" city residents in the United States, with only 20% of the adult population overweight.) For Denverites, preserving the environment and the city's rich mining and ranching heritage are of equally vital importance to the quality of life. LoDo buzzes with jazz clubs, restaurants, and art galleries housed in carefully restored century-old buildings. The culturally diverse populace avidly supports the Denver Art Museum, the Denver Museum of Nature & Science, the Colorado History Museum, and the Museo de las Americas. The Denver Performing Arts Complex is the nation's second-largest theatrical venue, bested in capacity only by New York's Lincoln Center. An excellent public transportation system, including a popular, growing light-rail and 400 mi of bike paths, makes getting around easy.

TOP REASONS TO GO

Denver Art Museum: Designed by architect Daniel Libeskind, the new Hamilton Building wing is an architectural work of art itself, but is only one of the many attractions. Visitors are treated to Asian, pre-Columbian, and Spanish Colonial works along with a world-famous collection of Native American pieces.

Red Rocks Amphitheatre: Even if you aren't attending a concert, the awe-inspiring red rocks of this formation-turned-venue are worth a look. There are hiking trails nearby, and the visitor center displays photographs and memorabilia from concerts past.

Denver Botanic Gardens: Brilliant and creatively arranged displays of more than 15,000 plant species from around the world draw garden enthusiasts throughout summer, and in the off-season the tropical conservatory is a warm, welcoming haven. Tea ceremonies and world-renowned musicians add an extra spark.

Larimer Square: Specialty stores, superior people-watching, and some of the city's top restaurants bring tourists and locals alike to one of Denver's liveliest sections. Located on the city's oldest street, it is also home to red brick–lined Writer Square, a charming courtyard area of boutique stores and coffee shops.

LoDo: Lower downtown's appeal lies in its proximity to Coors Field, its navigational ease thanks to the free Mall shuttle and its plethora of great restaurants, nightclubs, and art galleries. A busy area for shopping and spa-hopping by day, it is the hot spot of choice for the city's hipsters by night.

EXPLORING DENVER

For many out-of-state travelers, Denver is a gateway city, a transitional stop before heading into the nearby Rocky Mountains. Often, visitors will simply fly into Denver International Airport, rent a car, ask for directions to I–70 and head west into the mountains. But it's worth scheduling an extra few days, or even a few hours, to delve into the city itself. The city is a fairly easy place to maneuver, with prominent hotels such as the Brown Palace, excellent shopping at Cherry Creek and Larimer Square, sporting events ranging from the fabulous Avalanche to the ever-improving Nuggets, and plenty of (expensive) parking.

GETTING YOUR BEARINGS

Interstate 25 bisects Denver north to south. University Boulevard is a north–south road that runs from Cherry Creek up to City Park, and Speer Boulevard is a diagonal street that runs along Cherry Creek and up into the Platte River valley area. Most Denverites are tied to their vehicles and for good reason; the RTD bus system, though reliable, is confusing until you're well versed in its schedule, and light-rail only works if you're going to certain areas.

If you are staying downtown, it's easy to travel from one end to the other by walking or using light-rail or the free Mall shuttle. You can visit LoDo, Capitol Hill, and Larimer Square this way. The Platte River valley can be accessed by taking the Mall shuttle all the way north to

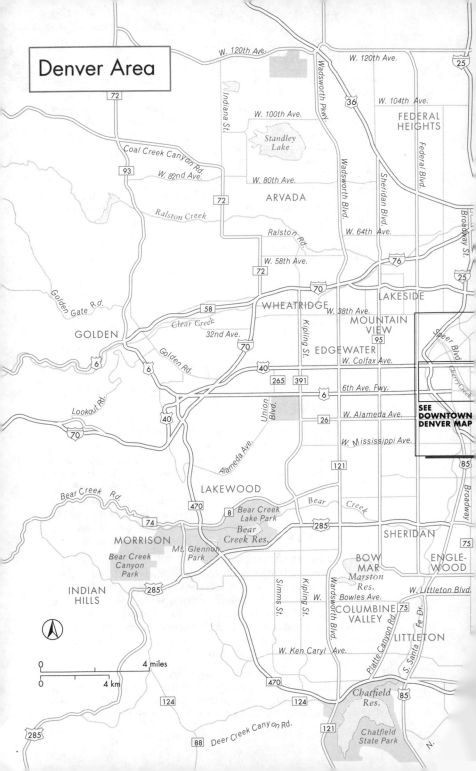

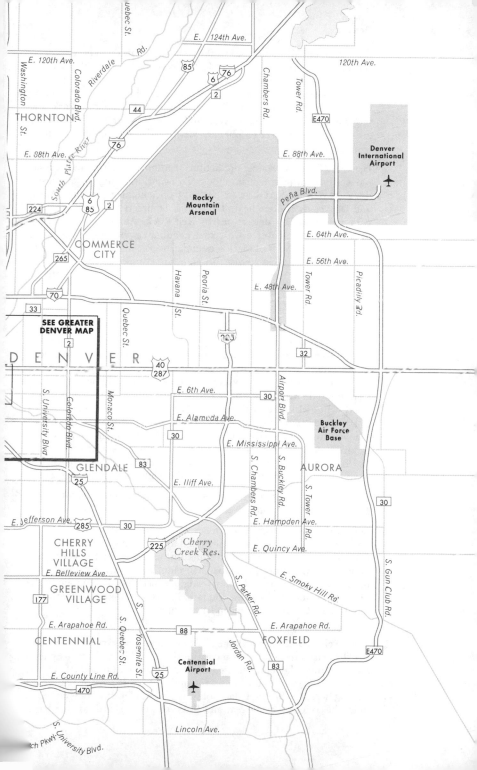

the end and then walking across the footbridge. You will need a car to get out to Cherry Creek or City Park, however, but once there, those sections also are easy to explore on foot. Driving to Cherry Creek is a 10- to 15-minute proposition, and parking can be a hassle. A cab ride will cost about $12 to $15. The restaurants in Washington Park, the Highland, and central, east, west, and south Denver require a 10- to 20-minute drive or $12 to $20 cab ride. Morrison is a 25-minute drive from downtown.

Denver defies easy weather predictions. Although its blizzards are infamous, snowstorms are often followed by beautiful spring weather just a day or two later. Ski resorts are packed from roughly October to April, and Denver itself often bears the traffic. Summers are festival-happy, with a rock-concert slate at nearby Red Rocks Amphitheatre and big names at the tent-covered Universal Lending Pavilion (also known as CityLights), in the parking lot outside the Pepsi Center downtown. Perhaps the best times to visit, though, are spring and fall, when the heat isn't so hot, the snow isn't so plentiful, and crowds are relatively thin. Ski resorts are still as scenic, but less expensive.

DOWNTOWN

Denver's downtown is an intriguing mix of well-preserved monuments from the state's frontier past and modern high-tech marvels. You'll often catch the reflection of an elegant Victorian building in the mirrored glass of a skyscraper. Hundreds of millions of dollars were poured into the city in the '90s in such projects as Coors Field, the downtown home of Denver's baseball Rockies; the relocation of Elitch Gardens, the first amusement park in the country to move into a downtown urban area; and an expansion of the light-rail system to run from downtown into the southern suburbs. Lower downtown, or LoDo, is a Victorian warehouse district revitalized by the ballpark, loft condominiums, and numerous brewpubs, nightclubs, and restaurants.

Numbers in the text correspond to numbers in the margin and on the Downtown Denver map.

TIMING   Downtown is remarkably compact and can be toured on foot in an hour or less, but a car is recommended for exploring outside of downtown proper. The Denver Art Museum merits at least two to three hours and the Colorado History Museum can be covered in an hour or two. Save some time for browsing and people-watching along the 16th Street Mall and Larimer Square. LoDo is a 30-block-square area that takes a few hours to meander through.

WHAT TO SEE

⑩ Brown Palace. The grande dame of Denver hotels was built in 1892 and is still considered the city's most prestigious address. Famous guests have included Dwight D. Eisenhower, Winston Churchill, Beyoncé, President George W. Bush, and Shaquille O'Neal. Even if you aren't staying here, the Brown Palace lobby is a great place to sit on comfortable old couches, drink tea, and listen to piano standards (or harp, during afternoon tea). Reputedly this was the first atrium hotel in the United States; its ornate lobby and nine stories are crowned by a Tiffany stained-glass window. ✉*321 17th St., LoDo* ☎*303/297–3111* ⊕*www.brownpalace.com.*

❻ **Byers-Evans House Museum.** Sprawling and detailed, red and black, this elaborate Victorian went up in 1883 as the home of *Rocky Mountain News* publisher William Byers. (He sold it in 1889 to William Evans of the Denver Tramway Company.) Restored to its pre–World War I condition, the historic landmark has occasional exhibitions and regular tours. Its main appeal is the glimpse it provides into Denver's past, specifically 1912 through 1924. The furnishings are those the Evans family acquired over the 80-some years they lived here. ✉*1310 Bannock St., Civic Center* ☎*303/620–4933* ⊕*www.coloradohistory.org* ✉*$5* ⊗*Tues.–Sun. 11–3.*

> ### FISH OUT OF WATER
>
> President Eisenhower was a frequent guest at the Brown Palace, using the hotel as his summer headquarters. He also was an avid fisherman, and during one of his visits, the kitchen created an elaborate ice carving of a Colorado mountain scene, complete with pine trees and a lake, in which they placed tiny live trout. The diorama was a huge hit and had Ike completely enthralled, until one of the trout leaped out of the lake and onto the floor, whereupon the president jumped up from his chair so abruptly to save the fish he nearly overturned a whole table.

❶ **Civic Center.** A peaceful respite awaits in this three-block park in the cultural heart of downtown, site of the State Capitol. A 1919 Greek amphitheater is in the middle of one of the city's largest flower gardens. Two of the park's statues, *Bronco Buster* and *On the War Trail,* depicting a cowboy and an Indian on horseback, were commissioned in the '20s. Festivals such as Cinco de Mayo, Taste of Colorado, and the People's Fair keep things lively here in spring and summer. The park was born in 1906, when Mayor Robert Speer asked New York architect Charles Robinson to expand on his vision of a "Paris on the Platte." ⊹*Bannock St. to Broadway south of Colfax Ave. and north of 14th Ave., Civic Center.*

❸ **Colorado History Museum.** The state's frontier past is vibrantly depicted in this flagship of the Colorado Historical Society. Changing exhibits highlight eras from the days before white settlers arrived to the boom periods of mining. General exhibit themes include the growth of historic preservation and black cowboys in the American West. Permanent displays include Conestoga wagons, old touring cars, and an extraordinary time line called "The Colorado Chronicle 1800–1950," which covers the state's history in amazing detail. The museum is easy to spot by its huge, colorful mural of Native Americans, miners, and red rocks. The large brick area outside the front door, complete with grassy strip, is a great place to relax if you're walking through downtown. ✉*1300 Broadway, Civic Center* ☎*303/866–3682* ⊕*www.coloradohistory.org* ✉*$7* ⊗*Mon.–Sat. 10–5, Sun. noon–5.*

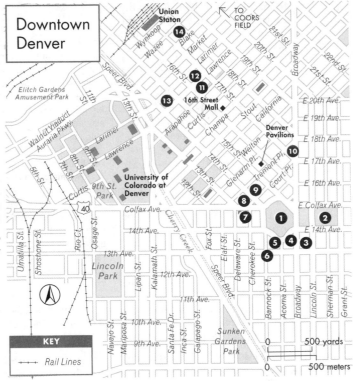

⓫ Daniels and Fisher Tower. This 330-foot-high, 20-floor structure emulates the campanile of St. Mark's Cathedral in Venice, and it was the tallest building west of the Mississippi when it was built in 1909. William Cooke Daniels originally commissioned the tower to stand adjacent to his five-story department store. In the '70s, when the city razed the department store during an urban-renewal project, preservationists saved and renovated the tower. It reopened in 1981 as an office building. Today, it's the city's most convenient clock tower and is particularly striking—the clock is 16 feet high—when viewed in concert with the fountains in the adjacent Skyline Park. ⊠*16th and Arapahoe Sts., LoDo.*

🖐 **❺ Denver Art Museum.** Unique displays of Asian, pre-Columbian, Spanish
Fodor's Choice Colonial, and Native American art are the hallmarks of this model
★ of museum design. Among the museum's regular holdings are John DeAndrea's sexy, soothing, life-size polyvinyl painting *Linda* (1983); Claude Monet's dreamy flowerscape *Le Bassin des Nymphéas* (1904); and Charles Deas' red-cowboy-on-horseback *Long Jakes, The Rocky Mountain Man* (1844). The works are thoughtfully lighted, though dazzling mountain views through hallway windows sometimes steal your attention. Imaginative hands-on exhibits and video corners will appeal to children; the Adventures in Art Center has hands-on art

classes and exploration for children and adults. With the opening of the $90.5 million Frederic C. Hamilton building in October 2007, the museum doubled in size. Designed by architect Daniel Libeskind, the 146,000-square-foot addition prompts debate: Some to say the glass and titanium design has ruined the view, while others think the building is a work of art in its own right. To the east of the museum is an outdoor plaza—you'll know it by the huge, orange metal sculpture—that leads to the Denver Public Library next door. ⊠ *100 W. 14th Ave. Pkwy., Civic Center* ☎ *720/865–5000* ⊕ *www.denverartmuseum.org* ⊠ *$13, free Sat. for Colorado residents* ⊙ *Tues., Thurs., Sat. 10–5; Fri. 10–10; Sun. noon–5.*

NEED A BREAK?

The Denver Art Museum's restaurant, Palettes (⊠ **100 W. 14th Ave. Pkwy.** ☎ **303/534–0889**) is the product of another kind of artist. Chef Kevin Taylor, a local fixture who also runs Prima Ristorante and Restaurant Kevin Taylor, fills the menu with colorful dishes like fruit-stuffed pork and flash-fried calamari. There's also a coffee shop, Novo Coffee, on the second floor of the museum, as well as Mad Greens Inspired Eats, a sandwich and salad spot on Martin Plaza across from the museum's main entrance, with outdoor tables on the plaza between the museum and the Denver Public Library.

☟ ⑧ **Denver Firefighters Museum.** Denver's first firehouse was built in 1909 and now serves as a museum where original items of the trade are on view, including uniforms, nets, fire carts and trucks, bells, and switchboards. Artifacts and photos document the progression of firefighting machinery, from horses and carriages in the early 1900s to the flashy red-and-white trucks of today. The museum rents out its second floor for weddings and parties; climbing in and out of fire trucks for hours at a time while eating cake is particularly exciting for kids. ⊠ *1326 Tremont Pl., LoDo* ☎ *303/892–1436* ⊕ *www.denverfirefightersmuseum.org* ⊠ *$6* ⊙ *Mon.–Sat. 10–4.*

❹ **Denver Public Library's Central Library.** A life-size horse on a 20-foot-tall chair and other sculptures decorate the expansive lawn of this sprawling complex with round towers and tall, oblong windows. Originally built in the mid-'50s, the Central Library underwent a massive, Michael Graves–designed renovation in 1995. The map and manuscript rooms, Gates Western History Reading Room (with amazing views of the mountains), and Schlessman Hall (with its three-story atrium) merit a visit. The library houses a world-renowned collection of books, photographs, and newspapers that chronicle the American West, as well as original paintings by Remington, Russell, Audubon, and Bierstadt. The children's library is notable for its captivating design and its unique, child-friendly multimedia computer catalog. ⊠ *10 W. 14th Ave. Pkwy., Civic Center* ☎ *720/865–1111* ⊕ *www.denver.lib.co.us* ⊙ *Mon. and Tues. 10–8, Wed.–Fri. 10–6, Sat. 9–5, Sun. 1–5.*

OFF THE BEATEN PATH

Forney Museum of Transportation. Inside a converted warehouse are an 1898 Renault coupe, Teddy Roosevelt's tour car, Amelia Earhart's immaculately maintained "Goldbug," and a Big Boy steam locomotive, among other former vehicles of the country's railroads and highways.

Other exhibits in this eccentric museum consist of antique bicycles, cable cars, experimental car-planes, and even "Zabeast," a 1975 Pontiac entirely covered in bumper stickers. This trivia-laden gem is outside of the downtown loop: Go north on Brighton Boulevard; the museum is adjacent to the Denver Coliseum on the south side of I–70. ⊠*4303 Brighton Blvd., Globeville* ☎*303/297–1113* ⊕*www.forneymuseum. org* ⊠*$7* ⊙*Mon.–Sat. 9–5.*

⑬ Larimer Square. Larimer Square is on the oldest street in the city, immor-
Fodor'sChoice talized by Jack Kerouac in his seminal book, *On the Road.* It was
★ saved from the wrecker's ball by a determined preservationist in the 1960s, when the city went demolition-crazy in its eagerness to present a more-youthful image. Much has changed since Kerouac's wanderings; Larimer Square's rough edges have been cleaned up in favor of upscale retail and chic restaurants. The Square has become a serious late-night party district thanks to spillover from the expanded LoDo neighborhood and Rockies fans flowing out from the baseball stadium. Shops line the arched redbrick courtyards of **Writer Square,** Denver's most charming shopping district. ⊠*Larimer and 15th Sts., LoDo* ☎*303/685–8143* ⊕*www.larimersquare.com.*

★ ⑭ LoDo. The Lower Downtown Historic District, the 25-plus square-block area that was the site of the original 1858 settlement of Denver City, is nicknamed LoDo. It's home to art galleries, chic shops, nightclubs, and restaurants ranging from Denver's most upscale to its most downhome. This part of town was once the city's thriving retail center, then it fell into disuse and slid into slums. Since the early 1990s, LoDo has metamorphosed into the city's cultural center, thanks to its resident avant-garde artists, retailers, and loft dwellers who have taken over the old warehouses and redbricks. The handsome **Coors Field** (⊠*Blake and 20th Sts., LoDo*), home of baseball's Colorado Rockies, has further galvanized the area. Its old-fashioned brick and grillwork facade was designed to blend in with the surrounding Victorian warehouses. As with cuddly Wrigley Field, on the north side of Chicago, Coors Field has engendered a nightlife scene of sports bars, restaurants, and dance clubs. *From Larimer St. to South Platte River, between 14th and 22nd Sts., LoDo* ⊕*www.lodo.org.*

OFF THE BEATEN PATH

Museo de las Americas. The region's first museum dedicated to the achievements of Latinos in the Americas has a permanent collection as well as rotating exhibits that cover everything from Hispanics in the state legislature to Latin American women artists in the 20th century. Among the permanent pieces are the oil painting *Virgin of Solitude* (circa 1730) and a Mayan polychrome jar (circa 650–950), in addition to contemporary works. Admission is free the first Friday of each month. ⊠*861 Santa Fe Dr., Lincoln Park* ☎*303/571–4401* ⊕*www. museo.org* ⊠*$5* ⊙*Tues.–Fri. 10–5, weekends noon–5.*

★ 16th Street Mall. Outdoor cafés and tempting shops line this pedestrians-only 12-block thoroughfare, shaded by red-oak and locust trees. The Mall's businesses run the entire socioeconomic range. There are high-class joints like Bravo Ristorante, in the Adam's Mark hotel, where the waitstaff sings show tunes; decent tavern food at the Paramount Cafe, around the corner from the Paramount Theatre; and plenty of fast-food chains. Although some Denverites swear by the higher-end Cherry Cheek Shopping District, the 16th Street Mall covers every retail area and is a more-affordable, diverse experience. You can find Denver's best people-watching here. Catch one of the free shuttle buses that run the length of downtown. Pay attention when you're wandering across the street, as the walking area and bus lanes are the same color and are hard to distinguish. ✉ *From Broadway to Wynkoop St., LoDo.*

② **State Capitol.** Built in 1886, the capitol was constructed mostly of materials indigenous to Colorado, including marble, granite, and rose onyx. Especially inspiring is the gold-leaf dome, a reminder of the state's mining heritage. The dome is once again open for tours by appointment only weekdays 9 AM–2 PM every hour on the hour; 30 people at a time can go to the top (using a staircase, not an elevator) to enjoy the 360-degree view of the Rockies. The 18th step is exactly 1 mi high (above sea level). The legislature is generally in session from January through May, and visitors are welcome to sit in third-floor viewing galleries above the House and Senate chambers. ✉ *200 E. Colfax Ave., Capitol Hill* ☎ *303/866–2604, 303/866–3834 for dome tours* ⊕ *www.colorado-dome.org* ✉ *Free* ⊙ *Bldg. weekdays 7–5:30. Tours, Sept.–May, weekdays 9–2:30; June–Aug., weekdays 9–3:30.*

⑫ **Tabor Center.** This festive shopping mall has about 55 stores (mostly chains such as Casual Corner and Petite Sophisticate) and attractions, including fast-food eateries, strolling troubadours, jugglers and fire-eaters, and splashing fountains. A concierge desk at the Lawrence Street entrance is staffed with friendly people who lead free walking tours around the city. Horse-drawn carriages are usually waiting out front, unless weather is inclement or the drivers have been called away for an event, to give rides around downtown (be aware that they do not follow any predictable schedule). ✉ *Larimer and Lawrence Sts. on 16th St., LoDo* ☎ *303/572–6868* ⊕ *www.taborcenter.com.*

⑨ **Trianon Museum and Art Gallery.** This tranquil museum houses a collection of 18th- and 19th-century European furnishings and objets d'art dating from the 16th century onward. Guided tours are on the hour. ✉ *335 14th St., LoDo* ☎ *303/623–0739* ✉ *$1* ⊙ *Mon.–Sat. 10–4.*

⑦ **U.S. Mint.** Tour this facility to catch a glimpse of the coin-making process, as presses spit out thousands of coins a minute. There are also exhibits on the history of money and a restored version of Denver's original mint, prior to numerous expansions. More than 14 billion coins are minted yearly, and the nation's second-largest hoard of gold is stashed away here. To arrange a visit and schedule a tour, contact your U.S. congressperson's office (the Mint's Web site provides a link with contact information). The gift shop, which sells authentic coins and currency, is in the Tremont Center, across Colfax Avenue from the Mint. ✉ *320 W. Colfax Ave., Civic Center* ☎ *303/405–4761* ⊕ *www.usmint.gov* ✉ *Free* ⊙ *Gift shop, weekdays 9–3:30, tours by reservation only* ⚐ *Same-day walk-up tours on a limited space-available basis, weekdays 8–2, excluding federal holidays and Code Orange–security level days.*

PLATTE RIVER VALLEY

Less than a mile west of downtown is the booming Platte River valley. Once the cluttered heart of Denver's railroad system, it's now overflowing with attractions. The imposing glass facade of the NFL Broncos' new Invesco Field at Mile High, the stately Pepsi Center sports arena, the Downtown Aquarium, and the flagship REI outdoors store are but four more crowd-pleasers to add to the growing list in Denver. New restaurants, a couple of coffeehouses, and a few small, locally owned shops, including some that sell sporting goods and a wine boutique, make it appealing to wander around. The sights in this area are so popular that the city plans to complete a light-rail system that will connect the attractions with downtown by the end of the decade.

The South Platte River valley concrete path, which extends several miles from downtown to the east and west, snakes along the water through out-of-the-way parks and trails. The 15th Street bridge is particularly cyclist- and pedestrian-friendly, connecting LoDo with growing northwest Denver in a seamless way. The most relaxed, and easiest, way to see the area is on one of the half-hour or hour-long trolley tours, which can be accessed by parking at the Children's Museum and catching the streetcar east of the lot by the Platte River.

Numbers in the text correspond to numbers in the margin and on the Greater Denver Area map.

WHAT TO SEE

★ ☺ ⑮ **Children's Museum of Denver.** This is one of the finest museums of its kind in North America, with constantly changing hands-on exhibits that engage children (up to about age eight) in discovery. The Maze-eum is a walk-through musical maze. Children can build a car on an assembly line and send it careening down a test ramp at the Inventions display. One of the biggest attractions is the Center for the Young Child, a 3,700-square-foot playscape aimed at newborns through four-year-olds and their caregivers. (Don't worry, the museum contains "wash this toy" buckets to keep slobbery artifacts from infecting other children.) A trolley ($2) clatters and clangs the 2 mi down the South Platte River from the museum to the REI flagship store. The trolley also connects to the Downtown Aquarium. Older kids tend to blaze through this museum in a morning or afternoon, but the under-six set can spend all day here. ⊠ *2121 Children's Museum Dr.,* ✛ *off Exit 211 of I–25, Jefferson Park* ☎ *303/433–7444* ⊕ *www.mychildsmuseum.org* ✉ *$7.50* ☺ *Weekdays 9–4, weekends 10–5.*

★ ☺ ⑯ **Downtown Aquarium.** On the north side of the Platte River across from Elitch Gardens, the Downtown Aquarium, formerly Colorado's Ocean Journey, is the only million-gallon aquarium between Chicago and the West Coast. It has four sections that show water and aquatic life in all its forms, from the seas to the river's headwaters in the Colorado mountains. Houston-based Landry's Restaurants, Inc., bought the facility in early 2003 and has added enough attractions, including the 250-seat Aquarium Restaurant built around a 150,000-gallon tank filled with sharks and fish, to make this a good four- to six-hour stop. The

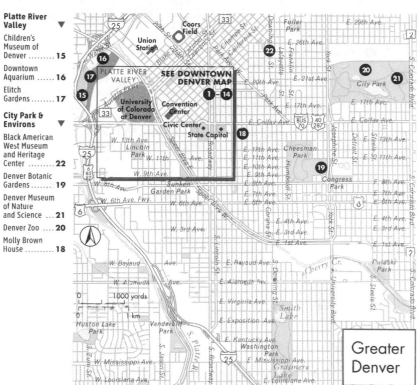

Greater Denver

new highlights include an expanded stingray touch pool, a gold-panning area, animatronic creatures, and an interactive shipwreck. The aquarium also has a lounge with a weeknight happy hour. ⊠*700 Water St.,* ✛*off Exit 211 of I–25, Jefferson Park* ☎*303/561–4450* ⊕*www. downtownaquariumdenver.com* ⊠*$13.75; $9.95 after 6* PM ⊙*Sun.– Thurs. 10–10, Fri. and Sat. 10–11.*

NEED A BREAK?

Down the street from the REI store, along the bicycle path on 15th Street, My Brother's Bar (⊠ **2376 15th St.** ☎ **303/455–9991**) **is a homey neighborhood tavern that serves different microbrews, burgers—buffalo and beef— and sandwiches of all kinds. The bar's name isn't on the facade, so you might wander by once or twice before figuring out where it is.**

Platte River Greenway. Just behind the REI flagship store, this serene park is at the center of the South Platte River valley path. Its rocks and rapids are especially attractive in summer for kayakers, bicyclists, and hikers. Sidewalks extend down the Platte River to the east (toward the suburbs) and west (toward Invesco Field at Mile High). A pathway in yet another direction leads to LoDo. From the park, it's about a 20-minute walk to the 16th Street Mall and Coors Field, which makes it a healthy way to sightsee when the weather is good. Or you can rent a kayak from nearby **Confluence Kayaks** (☎*303/433–3676* ⊕*www.confluencekayaks.*

com) and take a quick lesson before paddling yourself down the river. ✉*1615 Platte St., Jefferson Park.*

★ ☕ **⑰ Elitch Gardens.** This elaborate and thrilling park was a Denver family tradition long before its 1995 relocation from northwest Denver to its current home on the outskirts of downtown. The park's highlights include hair-raising roller coasters and thrill rides; for younger kids and squeamish parents, there are also plenty of gentler, Bugs Bunny–hosted attractions. Twister II, an update of the classic, wooden Mister Twister, is from the original Elitch Gardens, as is a 100-foot-high Ferris wheel that provides sensational views of downtown. A 10-acre water-adventure park is included in the standard entry fee. You can spend a whole day at either the water park or the main park, so if you want to do both, plan on spending around 8 to 10 hours there. Locker and stroller rentals are available. ✉*I–25 and Speer Blvd., Auraria* ☎*303/595–4386* ⊕*www.sixflags.com/elitchgardens* ✉*$44.99 unlimited-ride pass* ☽*June–Labor Day, daily; Apr., May, Sept., and Oct., Fri.–Sun.; hrs vary so call ahead.*

CITY PARK & ENVIRONS

Acquired by the city in 1881, City Park, Denver's largest public space (370 acres), contains rose gardens, lakes, a golf course, tennis courts, and a huge playground. A shuttle runs between two of the city's most popular attractions: the Denver Zoo and the Denver Museum of Nature & Science, both on the premises. If you have children or are an animal lover, you could easily spend half a day in City Park. The park is east of downtown Denver and runs from East 17th Avenue to East 26th Avenue, between York Street and Colorado Boulevard.

Numbers in the text correspond to numbers in the margin and on the Greater Denver Area map.

IN CITY PARK

☕ **㉑ Denver Museum of Nature & Science.** Over the past 100 years, the museum
Fodor's Choice has amassed more than 775,000 objects, making it the largest natural
★ history museum in the western United States. It houses a rich combination of traditional collections—dinosaur remains, animal dioramas, a mineralogy display, an Egyptology wing—and intriguing hands-on exhibits. In the Hall of Life, you can test your health and fitness on a variety of contraptions and receive a personalized health profile. The Prehistoric Journey exhibit covers the seven stages of Earth's development. The massive complex also includes an IMAX movie theater and a planetarium whose Space Odyssey exhibit simulates a trip to Mars and thoroughly annotates the stars in the night sky. The impressively refurbished eating-and-relaxation area has a full-window panoramic view of the Rocky Mountains. ✉*2001 Colorado Blvd., City Park* ☎*303/322–7009 or 800/925–2250* ⊕*www.dmns.org* ✉*Museum $10, IMAX $8; $15 for combined pass* ☽*Daily 9–5, IMAX shows at 6 and 7:40* PM *on Fri. and Sat.*

BORN AND RAISED IN DENVER

Every city likes to claim inventions, and Denver is no different. At the top of the city's list of accomplishments is the cheeseburger, for which resident Louis Ballast received a patent in 1935 after he accidentally spilled cheddar on his grill at the Humpty-Dumpty Drive-In on Speer Boulevard. The Denver boot, a bright yellow lock that attaches to a car tire and can only be removed with a special key, was invented by Frank Marugg as a way to keep people from stealing tires during World War II, when rubber snagged big bucks; in 1955, the boot came back to halt scofflaws. The Barnes Dance, a way for pedestrians to cross a four-way street diagonally, was named after Denver traffic engineer Henry Barnes in the 1930s, and although he didn't invent it, he was the first to use it on a large scale. And the Denver omelet, with green peppers, onions, and diced ham, has so many theories of inception it's almost impossible to track, but the best explanation is its evolution from the Western sandwich, with similar ingredients slapped inside bread by Chinese cooks who translated egg foo yung while working on the railroads.

NEED A BREAK? An old-fashioned greasy-spoon diner that specializes in huge pancakes and spicy huevos rancheros, **Pete's Kitchen** (✉ *1962 E. Colfax Ave.* ☎ *303/321–3139*) is just a few minutes by car from the Denver Museum of Nature & Science. It's often packed, particularly on Sunday morning, so prepare to fight for parking, wait for a table, and resign yourself to a seat at the counter.

★ ☾ ⑳ **Denver Zoo.** A bright peacock greets you at the door of the nation's fourth-most-visited zoo, whose best-known exhibit showcases man-eating Komodo dragons in a lush re-creation of a cavernous riverbank. The **Conservation Carousel** ($1) rotates in the center of the 80-acre zoo, with handcrafted endangered species as mounts. Also of note is the 7-acre Primate Panorama, which houses 31 species of primates in state-of-the-art environments that simulate the animals' natural habitats. Other highlights include a nursery for baby animals; seal shows; the world's only painting rhinoceros, Mshindi; the electric Safari Shuttle, which snakes through the property as you are treated to a lesson on the zoo's inhabitants; and the usual lions, tigers, bears, giraffes, monkeys, and one extremely hairy elephant. The exhibits are spaced far apart along sprawling concrete paths, so build in enough time to visit everything. ✉ *E. 23rd Ave. between York St. and Colorado Blvd., City Park* ☎ *303/376–4800* ⊕ *www.denverzoo.org* 🎫 *$9 Oct.–Mar., $11 Apr.–Sept.* ☉ *Oct.–Mar., daily 10–5; Apr.–Sept., daily 9–6.*

NEAR CITY PARK

㉒ **Black American West Museum.** The revealing documents here depict the vast contributions that African-Americans made to opening up the West. Nearly a third of the cowboys and many pioneer teachers and doctors were African-Americans. One floor is devoted to black cowboys; another to military troops such as the Buffalo Soldiers. Changing exhibits focus on topics such as the history of black churches in the West. ✉ *3091 California St., Five Points* ☎ *303/292–2566* ⊕ *www.*

blackamericanwestmuseum.com
✉*$8* ⊙ *Sept.–May, Tues.–Sat. 10–2; June–Aug., Tues.–Sat. 10–5.*

★ ⑲ **Denver Botanic Gardens.** The horticultural displays in thoughtfully laid-out theme gardens—more than 15,000 plant species from Australia, South Africa, and the Himalayas, and especially the western United States—are at their peak in summer, when garden enthusiasts could spend half a day here. The tropical conservatory alone is worth an hour's visit in the off-season. Spring brings a brilliant display of wildflowers to the world-renowned rock alpine garden. Tea ceremonies take place some summer weekends in the tranquil Japanese garden, and artists such as folk–rocker Richard Thompson, singer–songwriter Jewel, and bluegrassy jazzman Bela Fleck have performed as part of the summer concert series. ✉*1005 York St., Cheesman Park* ☎*720/865-3500* ⊕*www.botanicgardens.org* ✉*$13 May–Sept., $12 Sept.–Feb., $7.50 Mar and Apr.* ⊙*May–mid-Sept., Sat.–Tues. 9–8, Wed.–Fri. 9–5; mid-Sept.–Apr., daily 9–5.*

⑱ **Molly Brown House.** This Victorian celebrates the life and times of the scandalous, "unsinkable" Molly Brown. The heroine of the *Titanic* courageously saved several lives and continued to provide assistance to survivors back on terra firma. Costumed guides and period furnishings in the museum, including flamboyant gilt-edge wallpaper, lace curtains, tile fireplaces, and tapestries, evoke bygone days. The museum collects and displays artifacts that belonged to Brown, as well as period items dating to 1894–1912, when the Browns lived in the house. A bit of trivia: Margaret Tobin Brown was known as Maggie, not Molly, during her lifetime. Meredith Willson, the composer–lyricist of the musical, *The Unsinkable Molly Brown,* based on Brown's life, thought Molly was easier to sing. Tours run every half hour; you won't need much more than that to see the whole place. ✉*1340 Pennsylvania St., Capitol Hill* ☎*303/832–4092* ⊕*www.mollybrown.org* ✉*$6.50* ⊙*June–Aug., Mon.–Sat. 10–3:30, Sun. noon–3:30; Sept.–May, Tues.–Sat. 10–3:30, Sun. noon–3:30.*

WHERE TO EAT

As befits a multiethnic crossroads, Denver lays out a dizzying range of eateries. Head for LoDo, 32nd Avenue in the Highland District, or south of the city for the more-inventive kitchens. Try Federal Street for cheap ethnic eats—especially Mexican and Vietnamese—and expect more-authentic takes on classic Italian, French, and Asian cuisines than the city has offered in the past. Throughout Denver, menus at trendy restaurants are pairing international flavors with regional products in unique ways; Denver's top chefs are gaining the attention of national food magazines and winning culinary competitions.

WHAT IT COSTS					
	¢	$	$$	$$$	$$$$
AT DINNER	under $8	$8–$12	$13–$18	$19–$25	Over $25

Prices are per person for a main course, excluding 8.22% tax.

LODO

AMERICAN

$$ ✕Wynkoop Brewing Co. This trendy yet unpretentious local institution was Denver's first brewpub, and now its owner, John Hickenlooper, is Denver's mayor. Different crowds frequent its pool hall, cabaret, and dining room levels—with the younger crowd on the top floor enjoying drinks and bar snacks during happy hour or down in the lower cabaret level for improv or live music, and families and urban professionals dining on the main level. Try the terrific shepherd's pie or charbroiled venison medallions with oven-roasted red potatoes and caramelized shallot sauce. Wash it down with one of the Wynkoop's trademark microbrews—try either the exemplary Railyard Ale or the spicy chili beer. ⊠ *1634 18th St., LoDo* ☎ *303/297–2700* ▭*AE, D, DC, MC, V.*

INDIAN

$$$ ✕India House. Diners get to see their food being prepared in the tandoor in this handsome renovation—complete with luxurious wall treatments, comfy upholstery, and interesting art—of the longtime Denver Indian eatery Delhi Darbar. The spicing is gentle and the preparations skillful on the lengthy, well-chosen menu, which includes vegetarian options. A local favorite is the *shahi sabz,* vegetables in a nut-strewn cream sauce, and the house-made ice creams are delicious. The market-price lobster dishes are standouts, too. ⊠ *1514 Blake St., LoDo* ☎ *303/595–0680* ▭*AE, D, DC, MC, V.*

JAPANESE

$$$ ✕Sonoda's. In the below-street-level dining room and sushi bar, the blue colors, aquariums, and colorful fish hanging everywhere make you feel as though *you're* inside a fish tank. Instead, you're just getting to take advantage of the creations of some savvy sushi chefs who match pace with a kitchen that puts out great grilled fish, teriyaki, and tempura, too. The meals all come with sides of salad, vegetables, and rice, and the sake selection is competitive. The staff is eager to turn first-timers on to entry-level sushi, and the sushi chefs themselves are unusually friendly. ⊠ *1620 Market St., LoDo* ☎ *303/337–3800* ▭*MC, V* ⊗*No lunch Sun.*

NEW AMERICAN

$$$ ✕1515 Restaurant. Owner Gene Tang seems to be one of the hardest working men in the restaurant business, judging by the personal attention he gives the tables in his two-story place. Walking past the first-floor bar gives diners the feeling of being someplace important (although the smokiness gives some pause), as locals hang out and

Where to Eat in Denver

Denver Zoo

City Park

E. 36th Ave.
E. 35th Ave.
E. 33rd Ave.
E. 31st Ave.
E. 30th Ave.
E. 28th Ave.
E. 27th Ave.
E. 25th Ave.
E. 23rd Ave.
E. 22nd Ave.
Montview Blvd.
E. 17th Ave.
17th Ave. Pkwy
E. 16th Ave.
E. 14th Ave.
E. 13th Ave.
E. 12th Ave.
E. 11th Ave.
E. 10th Ave.
E. 9th Ave.
E. 8th Ave.
E. 7th Ave.
E. 6th Ave.
E. 5th Ave.
E. 4th Ave.
E. 3rd Ave.
E. 2nd Ave.
E. 1st Ave.
E. Ellsworth Ave.
E. Cedar Ave.
E. Alameda Ave.

Denver Botanic Gardens
Congress Park
Pulaski Park
Burns Park
Union Station
Coors Field
Tabor Center
Larimer Square

take in the scene. Once upstairs, though, it's all business, with efficient servers bringing a succession of world-beat fare that's highly structural and eminently flavorful. Braised lamb shank shares space on the menu comfortably with sake-glazed ahi, and trendy foams complement textbook crab cakes. The menu includes a few vegetarian options, meat lovers have several impressively prepared steaks from which to choose, and the wine list is a wonder—affordable and daring. ⊠ *1515 Market St., LoDo* ☎ *303/571–0011* ⌖ *Reservations essential* ⊟ *AE, D, DC, MC, V* ⊘ *Closed Sun. No lunch Sat.*

★ **$$$** ✕ **Vesta Dipping Grill.** Both the remodeled building and the interior space designed to house this modern grill, named after Vesta, the Roman hearth goddess, have won national architectural awards, and it's easy to see why: The sensual swirls of fabric and copper throughout the room make diners feel as though they're inside a giant work of art, and the clever, secluded banquettes are among the most sought-after seats in town. The menu is clever, too, and the competent grill masters in the kitchen put out expertly cooked meats, fish, and vegetables, all of which can be paired with some of the three dozen dipping sauces that get their inspiration from chutneys, salsas, mother sauces, and barbecue. The wine list is as cool as the clientele. ⊠ *1822 Blake St., LoDo* ☎ *303/296–1970* ⌖ *Reservations essential* ⊟ *AE, D, DC, MC, V* ⊘ *No lunch.*

SEAFOOD

$$$ ✕ **Jax Fish House.** A popular oyster bar serves as the foyer to the ever-busy Jax, whose brick-lined back dining room packs in the crowds, especially when there's a ball game at Coors Field three blocks away. A dozen different types of oysters are freshly shucked each day, and they can be paired with one of the house-made, fruit-infused vodkas or chili-fired shooters. Main courses make use of fresh catches flown in from both coasts such as ahi, scallops, snapper, and shrimp, and although there are a couple of meat dishes, only the truly fish-phobic should go there. The sides are fun, too: beignets, succotash, frittatas. ⊠ *1539 17th St., LoDo* ☎ *303/292–5767* ⌖ *Reservations essential* ⊟ *AE, DC, MC, V* ⊘ *No lunch.*

STEAK HOUSE

$$$$ ✕ **Morton's of Chicago.** The Denver outpost of this nationally revered steak house is as swanky and overwhelming as the rest, with dark woods, white linens, and the signature steak knives at each place setting. Diners are greeted by expert staff wielding the cuts of the day and their accompaniments, and once choices are made the experience is almost always seamless. The steaks themselves are superb—prime, well aged, and unadorned. All sides cost extra, but they're big enough

1

to feed two or three. The extensive wine list is pricey, and the delicious desserts are enormous. ⊠ *1710 Wynkoop St., LoDo* ☎ *303/825–3353* ⚘ *Reservations essential* ▤ *AE, DC, MC, V* ⊙ *No lunch.*

$$$$ ✕ **Sullivan's Steakhouse.** Sullivan's bills itself as a more-affordable steak house, and although technically that may be true, it's easy to spend just as much here as at any other top-tier steak joint. Still, it's worth it, because the hand-carved, aged Black Angus beef is of high quality, well grilled, and accompanied by stellar sides such as grill-greasy onion rings and chunky mashed potatoes. The wood-lined barroom is filled with high tables and makes for a fun gathering place, especially when there's live jazz. It's reminiscent of a 1940s club. ⊠ *1745 Wazee St., LoDo* ☎ *303/295–2664* ⚘ *Reservations essential* ▤ *AE, D, DC, MC, V* ⊙ *No lunch weekends.*

$$$ ✕ **Denver ChopHouse & Brewery.** This is the best of the LoDo brewpubs and restaurants surrounding the Coors Field ballpark. Housed in the old Union Pacific Railroad warehouse, the restaurant, similar to the ones in Washington, D.C., Cleveland, and Boulder, is clubby, with dark-wood paneling and exposed brick. The food is basic American, and there's plenty of it: steaks, seafood, pizzas, and chicken served with hot corn bread and honey butter, and "bottomless" salads tossed at the table. ⊠ *1735 19th St., LoDo* ☎ *303/296–0800* ▤ *AE, DC, MC, V.*

LARIMER SQUARE

MEDITERRANEAN

★ $$$ ✕ **Rioja.** When chef Jennifer Jasinski left Panzano to open her own place, Denver nearly salivated with anticipation over what she would do. Rioja, a tribute to Mediterranean food with contemporary flair, is the result of Jasinski's intense attention to detail. Her partners in this venture are all women: Beth Gruitch runs the front of the house while sous chef Dana Rodriguez helps in the back, and together this trio makes Gorgonzola ravioli with sugary pears and walnuts in browned butter sing, and crispy angel hair–wrapped shrimp so well melded you can't tell where pasta ends and shrimp begins. The restaurant is hip and artsy, with exposed brick and blown-glass lighting, arched doorways, and textured draperies. The wine list presents riojas galore, and is very well priced for Larimer Square. ⊠ *1431 Larimer St., Larimer Square* ☎ *303/820–2282* ⚘ *Reservations essential* ▤ *AE, DC, MC, V.*

MEXICAN

$$$ ✕ **Tamayo.** Chef–owner Richard Sandoval brought his popular concept of modern, upscale Mexican cuisine from New York to Denver, and it's just as welcome here. The food is classic Mexican with a twist, such as seafood tacos, *huitlacoche* (edible fungus) soup, elaborate moles, and chocolate tamales for dessert. The tequila flights are a favorite at the large, inviting bar, which is highlighted by a mural made of semiprecious stones (made by artist and restaurant namesake Rufino Tamayo). In season, the outdoor patio supplies a rare view of the mountains, and the interior is filled with screens made from blond wood and Spanish art. ⊠ *1400 Larimer St., Larimer Square* ☎ *720/946–1433* ⚘ *Reservations essential* ▤ *AE, MC, V* ⊙ *No lunch weekends.*

$ ✗ **Lime.** A basement-level hidden gem, Lime is green and white, gently lighted, ultracasual, and always happening, especially for the younger, hipper crowd whose pockets aren't deep enough for more-upscale LoDo spots. The made-to-order deep-fried tortilla chips arrive at the table when you do, and the salsas are zippy and well crafted. Imbibers are treated to a half-shot in a lime shell, and the Mighty Margarita is the only way to go from there. Shrimp stuffed with jalapeños and cream cheese, the tamales, and chiles rellenos are all winners, and the bar is a fun place for late-night snacking. ✉ *1424-C Larimer St., Larimer Square* ☎ *303/893–5463* ▤ *AE, MC, V* ⊗ *Closed Sun. No lunch.*

STEAK HOUSE

$$$$ ✗ **Capital Grille.** In a town that loves its steaks, the Rhode Island–based chain was taking a chance moving in and pretending to offer anything different from the other high-end big-boy steak houses. That said, Capital Grille—housed in a dark, noisy, broodingly decorated room typical of the genre—has much to recommend it, including a drop-dead Delmonico, textbook French onion soup, and terrific skin-on mashed potatoes. If you were ever to try steak tartare, this would be the place to do it, and the lobster is one of the best in town. The wine list is long, important, and expensive, but the service is remarkably fresh-faced and eager to please. ✉ *1450 Larimer St., LoDo* ☎ *303/539–2500* ⟐ *Reservations essential* ▤ *AE, D, DC, MC, V* ⊗ *No lunch Sun.*

DOWNTOWN

DELI

¢   ✗ **Spicy Pickle Sub Shop.** A spicy pickle does indeed come with every order at this hopping deli, which makes giant subs and panini, all filled with Boar's Head meats and house-made spreads. The breads are baked locally, and the side salads are good quality. Sit and eat in the casual space or take it to go. ✉ *988 Lincoln St., Downtown* ☎ *303/860–0730* ⟐ *Reservations not accepted* ▤ *AE, MC, V.*

DINER

$$ ✗ **Rocky Mountain Diner.** In the heart of the downtown business district, you can come in to this Western-theme diner, complete with cigar store Indian, plenty of horse paraphernalia, and red-and-white checked napkins—and sample all-American fill-ups of cowboy steak, pan-charred rib eye served with crisp onions, or the very popular buffalo meat loaf. Don't miss the real mashed potatoes, gravy, and all the fixings. ✉ *800 18th St., Downtown* ☎ *303/293–8383* ⟐ *Reservations not accepted* ▤ *AE, D, DC, MC, V.*

$ ✗ **Sam's No. 3.** Greek immigrant Sam Armatas opened his first eatery in Denver in 1927, and his three sons use the same recipes Pop did in their updated version of his all-American diner, from the famous red and green chilies to the Coney Island–style hot dogs and the creamy rice pudding. The room is a combination of retro diner and a fancy Denny's, and the bar is crowded with theatergoers and hipsters after dark. Good luck choosing: The menu is 10 pages long, with Greek and Mexican favorites as well as diner classics. The chunky mashed potatoes rule, and breakfast, which is served all day, comes fast. ✉*1500 Curtis St., Downtown* ☎*303/534–1927* ⚓*Reservations not accepted* ▱*AE, D, DC, MC, V.*

GERMAN

$$ ✕**Cafe Berlin.** New owners and a new location have transformed this beloved German eatery into an even more-inviting spot, with an updated, somewhat contemporary feel and a small bar. But the traditional German fare remains the same. No fake beer-house stuff here: The potato pancakes taste like your (German) grandma made them, and the liver pâté and homemade German bread are as authentic as it gets. The kitchen attempts to lighten up heavy items such as dumplings, spaetzle, and Wiener schnitzel, and the sweet-and-sour cabbage is amazing. Check out the German beer roster, and finish off with an apple strudel. ✉*323 14th St., Downtown* ☎*303/377–5896* ▱*D, MC, V* ⊗*Closed Sun. No lunch weekends.*

ITALIAN

$$$ ✕**Prima.** The less-expensive, whimsically decorated little sister of the upscale Restaurant Kevin Taylor also resides in the Hotel Teatro. With its Italian opera prints, curvaceous mezzanine, and black-granite bar, Prima appeals to lovers of modern Italian fare. The menu focuses on upscale renditions of contemporary classics, such as charbroiled swordfish with Sicilian couscous stew and roasted bass with farro and tomato ragout, and theatergoers love the one-block proximity to the Denver Performing Arts Complex. The weekend champagne brunch, which begins with a full line of crudo and continues through an astounding selection of northern Italian specialties such as crispy roasted fluke, draws a crowd. ✉*1106 14th St., Downtown* ☎*303/228–0770* ⚓*Reservations essential* ▱*AE, DC, MC, V.*

MEDITERRANEAN

$$$$ ✕**Restaurant Kevin Taylor.** Elegant doesn't do justice to this restaurant's
Fodor'sChoice dining room, a classy, soothing room done in tones of gold and hunter
★ green. Exclusive upholstery, flatware, and dishes add to the upscale attitude, as does the formal service style and a top-shelf wine list. The contemporary menu has an updated Mediterranean bent underscored by French techniques, with such classics as braised short ribs sharing space with antelope strudel and black truffle baked potatoes. The tasting menu, geared to theatergoers heading to the Denver Performing Arts Complex a block away, gives a rare chance to try chef Taylor's eclectic creations, and the stone-lined wine cellar makes for intimate private dining. ✉*1106 14th St., Downtown* ☎*303/820–2600* ⚓*Reservations essential* ▱*AE, DC, MC, V* ⊗*Closed Sun. No lunch.*

PIZZA

¢ ✕**Anthony's Pizza.** This two-story dive, with a standing counter as well as a sit-down dining area upstairs crammed with ramshackle chairs and tables in various stages of disrepair is the closest Denver gets to a New York slice. Fold each triangle in half, tilt it to let it drip, and inhale. ✉*1550 California St., Downtown* ☎*303/573–6236* ▱*MC, V* ⊗*Closed Sun.*

STEAK HOUSE

$$$$ ✕**Palm Restaurant.** This Denver outpost of the longtime New York steak house serves meat, seafood, pork chops, and other American dishes à la carte. The walls are bedecked with caricatures of local celebrities, and there's a chance you might see one in person—the restaurant is a favorite of local politicians, executives, and athletes, and with good reason: The steaks and the portions are both superlative. ⊠*1672 Lawrence St., Downtown* ☎*303/825–7256* ▭*AE, D, DC, MC, V* ⊘*No lunch weekends.*

SWISS

$$$ ✕**La Fondue.** Each table has its own stove setup that allows diners to cook the foods they choose, and the choices are what makes the experience so one of a kind. Sit in an elegant, warmly colored space that manages to be casual and classy at the same time, all the while simmering seafood, beef, and chicken to your liking in one of the flavored broths. You can then dip the foods into seasoned sauces while savvy servers keep an eye on the proceedings. Don't be alarmed by the seemingly high prices: All of the fondue meals are for two, and include a starter of cheese as well as salads and dessert, the latter of which involves decadent chocolate. ⊠*1040 15th St., Downtown* ☎*303/534–0404* ⌂*Reservations essential* ▭*AE, D, DC, MC, V* ⊘*No lunch.*

CAPITOL HILL

AMERICAN

$ ✕**CityGrille.** Politicians and construction workers rub shoulders while chowing down on the well-crafted sandwiches, soups, and salads at this casual eatery across the street from the State Capitol. CityGrille has won numerous local awards and national attention for both the burger, a half-pounder of ground sirloin, and the chili, a gringo stew of pork, jalapeños, and tomatoes that's spicy and addictive. The three-martini lunch lives on in this power-packed spot, and you can get a meal here until midnight (1 AM on weekends). ⊠*321 E. Colfax Ave., Capitol Hill* ☎*303/861–0726* ▭*AE, DC, MC, V.*

DINER

¢ ✕**Hotcakes Diner.** This jumping Capitol Hill spot is a breakfast and lunch hangout. Weekend brunch draws crowds of bicyclists and newspaper readers in search of the croissant French toast, "health nut" pancakes, and colossal omelets. Even bigger are the scrumptious one-dish skillets; a popular one tops grilled pork chops with home fries, chili, cheddar, and eggs. ⊠*1400 E. 18th Ave., Capitol Hill* ☎*303/832–4351* ▭*D, MC, V* ⊘*No dinner.*

CENTRAL DENVER

AMERICAN

$$ ✕**Dazzle Restaurant and Lounge.** If it's martinis and jazz you're after, come to this art deco space that allows for a groovy bar scene on one side and groovy dining on the other. The menu is as retro as the atmo-

sphere, with an emphasis on comfort foods with a twist (check out the gourmet macaroni and cheese or the baked casserole dips), and live music most nights makes this a laid-back spot. The cocktail roster, printed inside old jazz albums, is one of the most intricate around, and the Sunday jazz brunch swings. ✉*930 Lincoln St., Central Denver* ☎*303/839–5100* ☰*AE, DC, MC, V* ☺*No lunch.*

BARBECUE

$$ ✕**Brother's BBQ.** Two brothers from England traveled the southern United States on a quest to learn everything there is to know about barbecue, and they decided to share the information with Denver. The result is some of the best 'cue in town, from St. Louis–style ribs to beef brisket, pulled pork, and chicken. The sauces are a mishmash of their favorites, including a vinegary one and a sweet one, and the baked beans use their smoked meats for extra flavor. Eat at one of the metal tables amid license plates and knickknacks from the boys' travels, or get it packed up nicely to go. ✉*568 N. Washington St., Central Denver* ☎*720/570–4227* ⌣*Reservations not accepted* ☰*MC, V.*

FRENCH

$$$ ✕**Aix.** The foods of Provence are showcased in a small, whimsically chic eatery that is part urban hipster and part auberge. Dishes include a Napoleon made from crab and zucchini, a French olive–stuffed quail, herb-lacquered salmon, and a clam-risotto appetizer that's to die for. The room can get noisy once it's full, but the black-clad staff tries hard and the wine list is decidedly French. The menu changes weekly, and Sunday brunch is a hit. ✉*719 E. 17th Ave., Central Denver* ☎*303/831–1296* ☰*AE, D, DC, MC, V* ☺*Closed Mon. No dinner Sun. No lunch.*

$$ ✕**Le Central.** A real find, this homey bistro serves excellent mussel dishes and provincial French specialties, including beef bourguignonne (braised in red wine and garnished with mushrooms and onions), salmon *en croûte* (wrapped in pastry and baked), and steak au poivre. You can depend on Le Central for fabulous food, great service, and a surprisingly low tab. ✉*112 E. 8th Ave., Central Denver* ☎*303/863–8094* ☰*AE, D, DC, MC, V.*

INDIAN

$$ ✕**Little India.** The all-you-can-eat lunch buffet ($6.50), with dozens of well-prepared Indian dishes, is the big draw for Denverites at this casually elegant restaurant between downtown and Cherry Creek. Little India's menu has nearly 100 items, but it specializes in curries, vindaloos, and *biryanis,* all of which are expertly spiced. Be sure to try one of the specialty naans (tandoori-baked flat bread). The sweet mango *lassi,* a yogurt drink, is delightfully rich. ✉*330 E. 6th Ave., Central Denver* ☎*303/871–9777* ☰*MC, V.*

ITALIAN

$$$$ ✕**Barolo Grill.** This restaurant looks like a chichi Italian farmhouse, with dried flowers in brass urns, hand-painted porcelain, and straw baskets everywhere. The food isn't pretentious in the least, however. It's more like Santa Monica meets San Stefano—bold, yet classic, healthful, yet flavorful. Duckling stewed in red wine; fresh pastas, including spaghetti tossed with shrimp, octopus, and arugula; and gnocchi with ricotta, kalamata olives, and fresh basil, are all well made and fairly priced. ⊠*3030 E. 6th Ave., Central Denver* ☎*303/393–1040* ⚛*Reservations essential* ☰*AE, D, DC, MC, V* ☉*Closed Sun. and Mon. No lunch.*

$$$$ ✕**Luca d'Italia.** The restaurant's steel-gray, orange-and-red contemporary decor belies the fact that it's one of the most authentic Italian restaurants in the city. Chef–owner Frank Bonanno summons the memory of his Italian grandmother to re-create small-town Italy through wild boar with pappardelle, duck liver–stuffed ravioli, and house-cured capocollo and homemade cheeses. His tiramisu and chocolate sorbet have to be tasted to be believed. Service is as impeccable as at Bonanno's other restaurant, Mizuna, and the wine list is agreeably priced and heavy on interesting Italians. ⊠*711 Grant St., Central Denver* ☎*303/832–6600* ⚛*Reservations essential* ☰*AE, D, DC, MC, V* ☉*Closed Sun. and Mon. No lunch.*

$$$ ✕**Panzano.** This dining room in Hotel Monaco is filled with fresh flowers and windows that let in natural light, making the space cheerful and bright. Three meals a day are served, but it's lunch and dinner that focus on true Italian cuisine. Everything on the menu is multilayered, such as white asparagus salad with basil aioli, watercress, and endive; or risotto made with caramelized acorn squash and foie gras mousse. The breads are baked in-house. The superior service and accommodating staff make for a pleasant dining experience. The large, roomy bar is available for dining, too. ⊠*909 17th St., Central Denver* ☎*303/296–3525* ⚛*Reservations essential* ☰*AE, D, DC, MC, V.*

JAPANESE

$$$ ✕**Domo.** Domo's owners pride themselves on fresh flavors and the painstaking preparation of Japanese country foods, as well as one of the largest sake selections in town. Everything is prepared to order, and it's worth the wait: this is where you can find some of Denver's best seafood, curry dishes, and vegetarian fare. The house specialty is *wanko-sushi*—three to five courses of sushi accompanied by rice, soup, and six of Domo's tantalizing side dishes. The restaurant also houses a cultural-education center, a museum, and a Japanese garden. ⊠*1365 Osage St., Central Denver* ☎*303/595–3666* ☰*MC, V* ☉*Closed Sun.*

NEW AMERICAN

$$$$ ✕**Mizuna.** Chef–owner Frank Bonanno knows how to transform butter and cream into comforting masterpieces at this cozy, charming eatery with warm colors and intimate seating. His menu is reminiscent of California's French Laundry, with quirky dishes such as "liver and onions" (foie gras and a sweet-onion tart), and his Italian heritage has given him the ability to work wonders with red sauce, such as in his inimitable ragout. Be sure to try the griddle cakes for dessert, and expect to be served by the most professional staff in town. ⊠*225 E. 7th Ave., Central Denver* ☎*303/832–4778* ⚛*Reservations essential* ☰*AE, DC, MC, V* ☉*Closed Sun. and Mon. No lunch.*

Fodor's Choice
★

$$$ ✗**Fruition.** In the two buildings that once held the popular restaurant Somethin' Else, a group of veteran restaurateurs have opened a charming eatery to rave reviews. Fruition features well-crafted, elegant comfort food made from seasonal ingredients in compelling combinations, like warm king crab with crispy artichokes and capers and duck breast paired with smoked duck prosciutto and grilled arugula. The two small but nicely spaced dining rooms are gently lighted for a warm-toned atmosphere that fades into the background, allowing the evening to focus on the food and the expertly chosen and fairly priced wine list. ✉*1313 E. 6th Ave., Central Denver* ☎*303/831–1962* ▤*AE, MC, V, D* ⊘*Closed Mon.*

$$$ ✗**Potager.** The menu changes monthly at this industrial-designed restaurant, whose name, French for "kitchen garden," refers to the herb-rimmed back patio. Exposed ducts and a high ceiling give the dining room a trendy feel, and the floor-to-ceiling front windows allow the hip to be seen and the twinkling lights outside and in to be reflected for a warm glow. The menu always includes a risotto of the day along with fish dishes and the ever-popular goat cheese soufflé. The wine list is all over the map but well priced, and the servers are among the most savvy in town. ✉*1109 Ogden St., Central Denver* ☎*303/832–5788* ⚖*Reservations not accepted* ▤*AE, MC, V* ⊘*Closed Sun. and Mon. No lunch.*

$$$ ✗**Strings.** This light, airy restaurant with its wide-open kitchen resembles an artist's loft. It's a preferred hangout for Denver's movers and shakers as well as for visiting celebs, whose autographs on head shots, napkins, and program notes hang on the walls. The specialties include seafood dishes such as brown sugar–spiced sea scallops and pasta such as the popular lobster ravioli in a Grand Marnier cream sauce, and the desserts are amazingly intricate and well crafted. ✉*1700 Humboldt St., Central Denver* ☎*303/831–7310* ⚖*Reservations essential* ▤*AE, D, DC, MC, V* ⊘*No lunch weekends.*

STEAK HOUSE

$$$$ ✗**Buckhorn Exchange.** If hunting makes you queasy, don't enter this Denver landmark and taxidermy shrine, where 500 pairs of eyes stare down at you from the walls. The handsome men's-club decor—with pressed-tin ceilings, burgundy walls, red-checker tablecloths, rodeo photos, shotguns, and those trophies—probably hasn't changed much since the Buckhorn first opened in 1893. Rumor has it Buffalo Bill was to the Buckhorn what Norm Peterson was to *Cheers*. The dry-aged, prime-grade Colorado steaks are huge, juicy, and magnificent, as is the game. Try the smoked buffalo sausage or navy bean soup to start. ✉*1000 Osage St., Central Denver* ☎*303/534–9505* ▤*AE, D, DC, MC, V* ⊘*No lunch weekends.*

VEGETARIAN

$ ✗**WaterCourse Foods.** In a town known for its beef, WaterCourse stands out as a devoted vegetarian eatery, and now that it's moved to new, more-spacious digs uptown, even more herbivores are able to access its delectable creations. This casual, low-key place serves three meals a day, most of which are based on fruits, vegetables, whole grains, and meatlike soy substitutes. There are vegan and macrobiotic dishes available, along with items for those who eat cheese and eggs. The Reuben, with sauerkraut, portobellos, and Swiss on grilled rye, is amazing. ✉*837 E. 17th Ave., Central Denver* ☎*303/832–7313* ▤*MC, V.*

HIGHLAND

BRAZILIAN

$$ ✕**Café Brazil.** This always-packed spot is still worth the trip to Highland for shrimp and scallops sautéed with fresh herbs, coconut milk, and hot chilies; *feijoda completa*, the Brazilian national dish of black-bean stew and smoked meats, accompanied with fried bananas; or grilled chicken breast in a sauce of palm oil, red chili, shallots, and coconut milk. There's a party style in this festive café with its vivid paintings and colorful traditional masks, and it's frequented by locals in the know. ✉*4408 Lowell Blvd., Highland* ☎*303/480–1877* ◬*Reservations essential* ▤*MC, V* ⊘*Closed Sun. and Mon. No lunch.*

MEXICAN

★ $$$ ✕**LoLa Mexican Seafood.** The move to the Highland 'hood was a smart one for this casual seafood eatery, bringing in a younger, hipper clientele and providing a spectacular view of the city skyline from most of the sunny dining room, the bar, and the patio. Tableside guacamole, more than 90 tequilas, superior margaritas, and a clever, glass-lined bar area are just a few of the reasons the lovely LoLa remains a locals' hangout. The food is modern Mexican, with fresh seafood in *escabeche* (marinated, poached fish), *ceviche* (lime-cooked fish), and salads, as well as smoked rib eye and chicken *frito* (fried chicken). A Mexican-style brunch is served Saturday and Sunday. ✉*1575 Boulder St., Highland* ☎*720/570–8686* ◬*Reservations essential* ▤*AE, DC, MC, V* ⊘*No lunch.*

NEW AMERICAN

★ $$$$ ✕**Highland's Garden Café.** Chef–owner Pat Perry follows the philosophy of Alice Waters and her infamous Chez Panisse: Use what's fresh that day. The result is an ever-changing menu that takes advantage of Colorado's unique produce and meats, and Perry puts them together in interesting and refreshing ways, like in her pan-seared trout with sautéed apples and sweet potatoes in rum-cider sauce. And as the name implies, the outdoor patio is surrounded by elaborate gardens, and the inside dining rooms, which occupy two Victorian houses, are painted with trompe l'oeil views into gardens, as well. ✉*3927 W. 32nd Ave., Highland* ☎*303/458–5920* ◬*Reservations essential* ▤*AE, D, DC, MC, V* ⊘*No lunch.*

SOUTHWESTERN

$$ ✕**Julia Blackbird's.** Julia Blackbird herself cooks the food at this tiny eatery that specializes in cooking from northern New Mexico. The narrow space feels like Blackbird's home, and her staff is so welcoming you'd think it was theirs, too. Baked goods are made from blue corn, stews of hominy and beans abound, and the chilies are stuffed with goat cheese and smothered in a thick, chili-spiked sauce. Fabulous

margaritas, beer, and wine complement the meals. ✉*3434 W. 32nd Ave., Highland* ☎*303/433–2688* ⚞*Reservations not accepted* ▭*MC, V* ⊘*Closed Sun.*

NORTH DENVER

MEXICAN

$ ✗ **Jack 'n' Grill.** The friendly family that runs this small, pepper-decorated place moved to Denver from New Mexico, and they brought their love of chilies with them. The green chile is fire-breathing spicy, and the red is a smoky, complex brew. The best item, though, is the plate of chicken or beef *vaquero* tacos, slathered with a sticky-sweet barbecue sauce and served on buttery tortillas. Get it with a bowl of freshly roasted corn off the cob. Lunch is always packed, so arrive early, and don't be afraid to tackle a gigantic breakfast burrito, either. There's a mean margarita and there are cervesas, too. ✉*2424 Federal Blvd., North Denver* ☎*303/964–9544* ⚞*Reservations not accepted* ▭*MC, V* ⊘*Closed Mon.*

CHERRY CREEK

CHINESE

$$$ ✗ **Little Ollie's.** Black dominates the glossy interior of the swank Ollie's, which has a large outdoor patio and exceptionally well-crafted Chinese food. The whole steamed sea bass in black-bean sauce is one of the menu's highlights, along with mu shu pork and crispy duck. Lunch specials make this a popular midday spot, and the wine list is unusually well chosen for a Chinese restaurant. Reservations are taken for parties of six or more. ✉*2364 E. 3rd Ave., Cherry Creek North* ☎*303/316–8888* ▭*AE, MC, V.*

ITALIAN

$$$ ✗ **Campo de Fiori.** As bright and airy as the marketplace this Italian eatery is named for, Campo serves fresh cuisine from northern Italy that makes it one of the busiest spots in town. Some come for the spacious, see-and-be-seen bar scene, some for the simple but flavorful fare, but all are treated well by the experienced staff. The food includes fried calamari, bruschetta, and grilled fresh vegetables as starters, and the entrées are a mix of pastas and grilled meats. The room is filled with tile-top tables and surrounded by wall murals evocative of the Italian countryside. ✉*300 Fillmore St., Cherry Creek North* ☎*303/377–7887* ⚞*Reservations essential* ▭*AE, DC, MC, V* ⊘*No lunch.*

$$$ ✗ **NoRTH.** The beautiful people of Cherry Creek, young and old, flock to this jazzy space, the entire front of which opens to the sidewalk in nice weather. The space is decorated in what sound like food-themed Crayola colors: vanilla white and sherbet orange, lime green and cocoa brown, all setting diners up for a parade of savory dishes. Start with the paper-thin zucca chips—faintly oily, addictively crispy, deep-fried zucchini—and then move on to an entrée; pasta, fish, and meat are each kissed with just the right amounts of Mediterranean herbs and sauces. The staff is smiley and reflects the cheerful exuberance of the

atmosphere, and the lively bar is usually packed three deep. ⊠*190 Clayton La., Cherry Creek* ☎*720/941–7700* ⚑*Reservations essential* ▤*AE, D, DC, MC, V.*

STEAK HOUSE

$$$$ ✕**Elway's.** You won't see the big guy here very often, but that doesn't keep hopeful sports fans from packing it in. But when the toothy-grinned former Broncos QB John Elway doesn't show, diners console themselves with some of the best steak-house fare in town, particularly the porterhouse (big enough for half a football team) and the huge side of chunky-creamy Yukon gold mashed potatoes. While you eat, ease back into the intimately set-up, camel-color suede booths and watch waterfalls cascade over granite slabs, choose from the pricey but appealing wine list, and save room for make-your-own s'mores. ⊠*2500 E. 1st Ave., Cherry Creek* ☎*303/399–5353* ⚑*Reservations essential* ▤*AE, D, DC, MC, V.*

WASHINGTON PARK

ITALIAN

$$$ ✕**Carmine's on Penn.** It's hard to pick out this house from the ones that surround it in this cozy neighborhood, but the steady crowds streaming in and out of its art-lined dining rooms are a sure sign that this isn't a private residence. They come for the family-style servings of outstanding Italian fare. Tomatoes, garlic, basil, and good-quality olive oil make up the basis of many of the meals, and the sauces are superb: puttanesca, Bolognese, *boscaiolo* (a rich mushroom sauce). The menu is written out on chalkboards, and there's a private back room for big groups. ⊠*92 S. Pennsylvania St., Washington Park* ☎*303/777–6443* ⚑*Reservations essential* ▤*AE, D, DC, MC, V* ◷*Closed Mon. No lunch.*

SOUTH DENVER

CHINESE

$$$ ✕**Imperial Chinese.** Papier-mâché lions greet you at the entrance of this sleek Szechuan stunner, which is probably the best Chinese restaurant in a 500-mi radius. Seafood is the specialty. Try the steamed sea bass in ginger or the spicy, fried Dungeness crab, or spring for the Peking duck. The elegantly appointed dining room, filled with gleaming, lacquered furniture, is spacious and usually filled with families and large groups. ⊠*431 S. Broadway, South Denver* ☎*303/698–2800* ▤*AE, DC, MC, V* ◷*No lunch Sun.*

JAPANESE

★ **$$$** ✕**Sushi Den.** With a sister restaurant in Japan and owners who import sushi-grade seafood to the United States, it's easy to see why this chic sushi bar is the one Denverites count on to provide the best quality available. The sushi chefs here can meet your every request, and the cooked dishes are just as well prepared (don't miss the steamed fish baskets). Check out the tony crowd and feast your eyes on the luxurious fabrics and well-designed furniture. There's almost always a wait to get in and parking can be a hassle, but for serious sushi-heads, this is the place to be. From Sunday through Thursday, they'll accept a reservation for parties of five or more. ✉ *1487 S. Pearl St., South Denver* ☎ *303/777–0826* ☲ *AE, D, MC, V* ☹ *No lunch weekends.*

MEXICAN

$$ ✗ **Blue Bonnet Cafe and Lounge.** Its location out of the tourist loop, in a fairly seedy neighborhood southeast of downtown, doesn't stop the crowds (mostly tourists) from lining up early for this restaurant. The early Western, Naugahyde decor and fantastic jukebox set up an upbeat mood for killer margaritas and some of the best burritos and green chile in town. ✉ *457 S. Broadway, South Denver* ☎ *303/778–0147* ⌂ *Reservations not accepted* ☲ *MC, V.*

PIZZA

$ ✗ **Pasquini's Pizzeria.** Come to this informal, popular spot, which recently expanded to add much-needed tables to its once-cramped space but still offers the comforting bustle of a New York–style pizzeria, to indulge in fresh, homemade pastas, pizzas, and calzones. Individual pizzas are the house specialty. Don't miss the bakery's fresh Italian breads, and end with the warm, dense, chocolate truffle cake. ✉ *1310 S. Broadway, South Denver* ☎ *303/744–0917* ☲ *AE, D, DC, MC, V* ☹ *No lunch Sun.*

EAST DENVER

ECLECTIC

$$$ ✗ **Cork House.** Two veteran Denver restaurateurs took over the beloved, 30-year-old Tante Louise and turned it into a popular small-plate place (they also offer plenty of large plates, too), gently renovating the romantic restaurant into a slightly more-contemporary space that invites snacking with a glass of wine from the lengthy, well-priced roster. The wine bar offers 25 to 30 cheeses a night, with fresh breads, pâtés, and other appetizers, and the staff is adept at matching the international vino with the eclectic victuals. ✉ *4900 E. Colfax Ave., East Denver* ☎ *303/355–4488* ☲ *AE, D, MC, V* ☹ *No lunch.*

WEST DENVER

CHINESE

$$ ✗ **King's Land Seafood Restaurant.** Like a Chinese eatery in New York or San Francisco, King's Land does dim sum to perfection, serving it daily during the week for lunch and during their crazy, jam-packed weekends. Choose from dozens of dumplings, buns, and steamed dishes that are wheeled to you on carts, or go with the regular menu, also available at night, which includes delectable duck and seafood specialties. The dining room is huge and always noisy, and the staff doesn't speak much English. Just close your eyes and point. Reservations are accepted for parties of six or more. ✉ *2200 W. Alameda Ave., West Denver* ☎ *303/975–2399* ☲ *AE, MC, V.*

VIETNAMESE

$$ ✕**New Saigon.** Picked as Denver's best Vietnamese by every local publication for more than a decade, New Saigon is always crowded with folks trying to get at their crispy egg rolls, shrimp-filled spring rolls, and cheap but hefty noodle bowls. With nearly 200 dishes on the menu, this vast, avocado-color eatery has everything Vietnamese covered, including 30-some vegetarian dishes and 10 with succulent frogs' legs. Service can be spotty and not much English is spoken, but the staff goes overboard trying to help and never steers anyone wrong. It's best to go at off times to ensure a seat. Reservations are accepted for parties of six or more. ✉*630 S. Federal Blvd., West Denver* ☎*303/936–4954* ▭*MC, V.*

> **BEAR IN MIND**
>
> In 1963, through a series of odd circumstances that never were fully explained, the Fort Restaurant's owner, the late Sam Arnold, came into possession of an abandoned four-month-old black bear cub named Sissy. For the next few years Sissy became a beloved part of the place, sidling up next to patrons at the bar—her beverage of choice was root beer—gently pulling cocktail cherries from the lips of schoolchildren and celebrities, and generally being charming. Stuffed-animal versions of Sissy, and Arnold's tales about living with a 500-pound animal, are available at the restaurant.

MORRISON

STEAK HOUSE

$$$$ ✕**The Fort Restaurant.** This adobe structure, complete with flickering
Fodor'sChoice luminarias and a pinyon pine bonfire in the courtyard, is a perfect
★ reproduction of Bent's Fort, a Colorado fur-trade center. Buffalo meat and game are the specialties; the elk with huckleberry sauce and tequila-marinated quail are especially good. Intrepid eaters might try the buffalo bone-marrow appetizer, peanut-butter–stuffed jalapeños, or Rocky Mountain oysters. Costumed characters from the fur trade wander the restaurant, playing the mandolin and telling tall tales. ✉*19192 Hwy. 8, Morrison 80465* ☎*303/697–4771* ▭*AE, D, DC, MC, V* ☉*No lunch.*

WHERE TO STAY

Denver has lodging choices ranging from the stately Brown Palace to the commonplace YMCA, with options such as bed-and-breakfasts and business hotels in between. Unless you're planning a quick escape to the mountains, consider staying in or around downtown, where most of the city's attractions are within walking distance. Many of the hotels cater to business travelers, with accordingly lower rates on weekends (many establishments slash their rates in half on Friday and Saturday). The three hotels in the vicinity of Cherry Creek are about a 10- to 15-minute drive from downtown.

1

WHAT IT COSTS				
	¢	$	$$	$$$	$$$$
AT DINNER	under $80	$80–$120	$121–$170	$171–$230	over $230

Prices are for two people in a standard double room in high season, excluding service charges and 14.85% tax.

DOWNTOWN

$$$$ **Brown Palace.** This grande dame of Colorado lodging has hosted
Fodor's Choice public figures from President Eisenhower to the Beatles since it first
★ opened its doors in 1892. The details are exquisite: A dramatic nine-story lobby is topped with a glorious stained-glass ceiling, and the Victorian rooms have sophisticated wainscoting and art deco fixtures. The hotel pays equal attention to modern necessities, such as high-speed Web access and cordless telephones. The Churchill cigar bar sells rare cigars and single-malt scotches. In 2005 a $2 million spa was added (in a space that originally held a spa when the hotel first opened), with Swiss showers and a natural rock waterfall that draws from the hotel's artesian well. **Pros:** sleeping here feels like being part of history, exceptional service, spacious and comfortable rooms. **Cons:** one of the most expensive hotels in Denver, parking costs extra. ⊠ *321 17th St., Downtown, 80202* ☎*303/297–3111 or 800/321–2599* ⊕*www. brownpalace.com* ⊅*230 rooms, 25 suites* ⊟*In-room: refrigerator (some), VCR (some), ethernet. In-hotel: 4 restaurants, room service, bars, gym, spa, concierge, laundry service, public Wi-Fi, parking (fee), no-smoking rooms* ⊟*AE, D, DC, MC, V.*

$$$ **Magnolia Hotel.** The Denver outpost of this Texas-based chain has spacious, elegant rooms with sophisticated furnishings (some with fireplaces) and warm colors, all built within the confines of the 1906 former American Bank Building. Breakfast is included, as is an evening guest reception; drink coupons for the jazzy, retro-hip Harry's Bar; and late-night cookies and milk. One block off the 16th Street Mall, the Magnolia is well situated for downtown and LoDo conveniences. There's also an on-site Starbucks. **Pros:** pretty, comfortable rooms, nice complimentary breakfast, good restaurants. **Con:** although classy, can feel like a generic chain hotel. ⊠ *818 17th St., Downtown, 80202* ☎*303/607–9000 or 888/915–1110* ⊕*www.magnoliahoteldenver.com* ⊅*246 rooms, 119 suites* ⊟*In-room: ethernet, Wi-Fi. In-hotel: room service, bar, gym, concierge, laundry service, public Wi-Fi, parking (fee), no-smoking rooms* ⊟*AE, D, DC, MC, V* ⊺*BP.*

$$$ **Adam's Mark.** The city's largest hotel for conventions is composed of two distinct structures: a former Radisson designed by I. M. Pei and the onetime May D&F Department Store across the street. The glittering glass hotel—among the 25 largest in the country—includes more than 1,000 rooms and 130,000 square feet of meeting space. The location, at one end of the 16th Street Mall, is ideal. **Pros:** great location, many amenities. **Cons:** huge hotel means a lot of people, can be noisy, staff not so helpful. ⊠ *1550 Court Pl., Downtown, 80202* ☎*303/893–3333 or 800/444–2326* ⊕*www.adamsmark.com/denver* ⊅*1,133 rooms, 92*

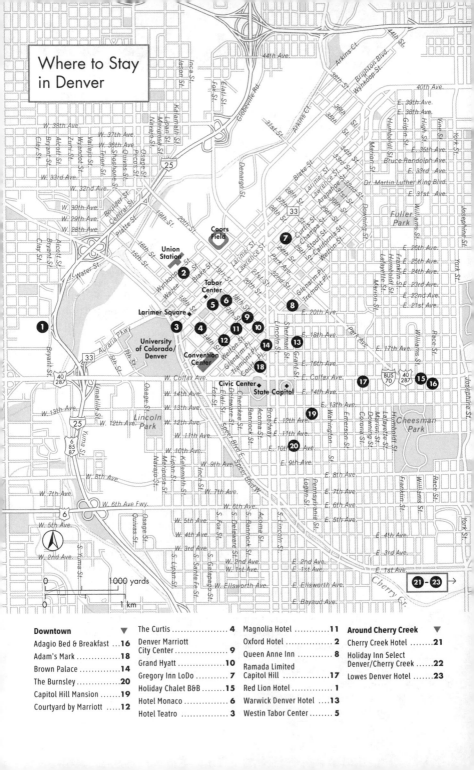

Where to Stay in Denver

1

suites ⟨⟩ *In-room: ethernet. In-hotel: 3 restaurants, room service, bars, pool, gym, concierge, laundry service, public Wi-Fi, parking (fee), no-smoking rooms* ⊟ *AE, D, DC, MC, V.*

$$$ ⊡ **Courtyard by Marriott.** This stunning building (it used to be Joslins Department Store) sits right on the 16th Street Mall, which means everything downtown is a few blocks or a free Mall shuttle away. The lobbies and public spaces are modern Western in theme, and the cream-color, sparsely decorated rooms have city and mountain views. There's a Starbucks on-site. **Pros:** great location and views. **Cons:** pricey, rooms nothing fancy. ✉ *934 16th St., Downtown, 80202* ☎ *303/571–1114 or 888/249–1810* ⊕ *www.marriott.com* ⟲ *177 rooms, 15 suites* ⟨⟩ *In-room: ethernet, Wi-Fi. In-hotel: restaurant, room service, bar, pool, gym, concierge, laundry service, parking (fee), public Wi-Fi, no-smoking rooms* ⊟ *AE, D, DC, MC, V.*

$$$ ⊡ **Grand Hyatt.** The Grand Hyatt (formerly the Hyatt Regency) is close to Larimer Square, the theaters, the 16th Street Mall, and the Colorado Convention Center. A stone fireplace makes for an inviting lobby and the roomy quarters are done in beige-and-violet tones with black accents. The Colorado-theme eatery 1876 (named for the year Colorado became a state) is decorated in wrought iron and cherrywood and serves contemporary Front Range favorites. The fitness center is one of the best equipped of any hotel in town. **Pros:** great views from top floors, prime location, top-notch gym. **Con:** restaurants inconsistent. ✉ *1750 Welton St., Downtown, 80202* ☎ *303/295–1234 or 800/233–1234* ⊕ *www.grandhyattdenver.com* ⟲ *526 rooms, 30 suites* ⟨⟩ *In-room: ethernet. In-hotel: 2 restaurants, room service, pool, gym, concierge, laundry service, public Internet, parking (fee), no-smoking rooms* ⊟ *AE, D, DC, MC, V.*

$$$ ⊡ **Gregory Inn LoDo.** Decorated to resemble an old English inn, the Gregory in the Curtis Park neighborhood captures old-world charm through the use of mossy colors and exquisite linens and accents. All of the rooms, each distinctive and luxurious, have private baths, and many have small sitting rooms. There's also a sumptuous carriage house, which contains a full kitchen, washer and dryer, and dining and living areas. Breakfast is served each morning in the dimly lighted, soothing Gathering Room. **Pros:** a few blocks removed from downtown's bustle, pretty setting, excellent breakfasts. **Cons:** extra blocks from downtown center mean more walking, no young children. ✉ *2500 Arapahoe St., LoDo, 80205* ☎ *303/295–6570 or 800/925–6570* ⊕ *www.gregoryinn. com* ⟲ *8 rooms, 1 suite* ⟨⟩ *In-room: refrigerator, Wi-Fi. In-hotel: no elevator, public Wi-Fi, no kids under 12, no-smoking rooms* ⊟ *AE, D, DC, MC, V.*

★ $$$ ⊡ **Hotel Monaco.** Celebrities and business travelers check into this hip property, which occupies the historic 1917 Railway Exchange Building and the 1937 Art Moderne Title Building, for the modern perks and art deco–meets–classic French style. The unabashedly colorful guest rooms, in vivid reds and yellows, have original art, custom headboards, glass-front armoires, and CD players. The service is similarly a cut above: Room service is available around the clock, pets are welcome, and guests without pets are given the complimentary company of a goldfish.

The hotel's mascot, a Shih Tzu named Hercules, hangs out in the lobby during the day. **Pros:** one of the pet-friendliest hotels in town, welcoming complimentary wine hour, central location. **Con:** pricier than some options. ⊠*1717 Champa St., Downtown, 80202* ☎*303/296–1717 or 800/397–5380* ⊕*www.monaco-denver.com* ☞*157 rooms, 32 suites* ♨*In-room: refrigerator, ethernet, Wi-Fi. In-hotel: restaurant, room service, bar, gym, spa, concierge, laundry service, public Internet, parking (fee), some pets allowed, no-smoking rooms* ⊟*AE, D, DC, MC, V.*

★ **$$$** ⊞**Hotel Teatro.** Black-and-white photographs, costumes, and scenery from plays that were staged in the Denver Performing Arts Complex across the street decorate the grand public areas of this hotel. With 12-foot ceilings, the earth-tone rooms are sleek and stylish, featuring Frette linens, the latest technology, and spacious bathrooms with soaking tubs and rain forest showers. The ninth-floor rooms have balconies. The two restaurants here—contemporary and elegant Restaurant Kevin Taylor and its casual Italian kid sister Prima—are both highly regarded. **Pros:** great location for theater and other downtown pursuits, excellent restaurants, lovely rooms and hotel spaces. **Cons:** the area can be noisy and chaotic, parking is costly, some of the rooms are tiny. ⊠*1100 14th St., Downtown, 80202* ☎*303/228–1100 or 888/727–1200* ⊕*www. hotelteatro.com* ☞*110 rooms, 6 suites* ♨*In-room: ethernet, Wi-Fi. In-hotel: 2 restaurants, room service, bar, gym, concierge, laundry service, parking (fee), no-smoking rooms* ⊟*AE, D, DC, MC, V.*

$$$ ⊞**Oxford Hotel.** During the Victorian era this hotel was an elegant fix-
Fodor's Choice ture on the Denver landscape, and civilized touches like complimentary
★ shoe shines, afternoon sherry, and morning coffee remain. The charming and comfortable rooms are furnished with French- and English-period antiques and the Cruise Room bar re-creates an art deco ocean liner. Art galleries are nearby. The popular McCormicks Restaurant ($$$) serves excellent seafood and a delicious Sunday brunch. **Pros:** prime LoDo location, beautiful historical setting, great restaurants on-site and nearby. **Con:** noisy, ballpark crowds in-season turn LoDo area into a big party. ⊠*1600 17th St., LoDo, 80202* ☎*303/628–5400 or 800/228–5838* ⊕*www.theoxfordhotel.com* ☞*80 rooms* ♨*In-room: VCR (some), ethernet, Wi-Fi. In-hotel: restaurant, room service, bars, gym, spa, public Wi-Fi, parking (fee), no-smoking rooms* ⊟*AE, D, DC, MC, V.*

★ **$$$** ⊞**Westin Tabor Center.** This sleek, luxurious high-rise opens right onto the 16th Street Mall and all the downtown action. Rooms are oversize and done in grays and taupes, with white duvets, piles of cushy pillows, and contemporary prints on the walls. The fourth-floor pool has one of the best views of the Rockies in all of downtown. The hotel buys blocks of tickets for weekend shows at the Denver Performing Arts Complex for guests' exclusive use. The Palm, a branch of the Manhattan-based steak house, is a favorite eating and drinking spot for local luminaries. **Pros:** convenient location on Mall, contemporary rooms, nice pool. **Cons:** the Palm is pricey, other restaurant not great for breakfast. ⊠*1672 Lawrence St., Downtown, 80202* ☎*303/572–9100 or 800/937–8461* ⊕*www.westin.com* ☞*430 rooms* ♨*In-room: ethernet. In-hotel: 2 restaurants, room service, bars, pool, gym, concierge,* *laundry service, public Internet, parking (fee), no-smoking rooms* ▤*AE, D, DC, MC, V.*

$$ ⚑ **The Burnsley.** This 16-story Bauhaus-style tower is a haven for executives seeking peace and quiet; it's a few blocks south of the State Capitol. The tastefully appointed suites have balconies and full kitchens. Marble foyers and old-fashioned riding prints decorate the rooms. Many suites have a sofa bed, making this a good bet for families. The swooningly romantic restaurant is a perfect place to pop the question. **Pros:** family-friendly, good for business travelers, convenient location. **Con:** rooms are somewhat plain. ✉*1000 Grant St., Downtown, 80203* ☎*303/830–1000 or 800/231–3915* ⊕*www.burnsley.com* ⇲*80 suites* ⚑*In-room: kitchen, ethernet. In-hotel: restaurant, room service, bar, pool, concierge, laundry service, public Internet, parking (no fee), some pets allowed, no-smoking rooms* ▤*AE, D, DC, MC, V.*

$$ ⚑ **Capitol Hill Mansion Bed & Breakfast Inn.** The dramatic turret and intense rust color of this Richardson Romanesque Victorian mansion built in 1891 is enough to draw you in. Inside are eight elegantly appointed rooms done in varying themes, such as Rocky Mountain, Victorian, and Colonial. The Gold Banner suite is cheerfully yellow, with a separate sitting room and gas-log fireplace, and it, along with other rooms, has a view of the Rockies. Breakfast and afternoon refreshments are included, along with samplings of Colorado wines. **Pros:** charming hosts, inviting rooms. **Cons:** walls are thin, place feels remote compared to rest of downtown. ✉*1207 Pennsylvania St., Capitol Hill, 80203* ☎*303/839–5221 or 800/839–9329* ⊕*www.capitolhillmansion. com* ⇲*8 rooms, 3 suites* ⚑*In-room: refrigerator, ethernet, Wi-Fi. In-hotel: no elevator, public Wi-Fi, no-smoking rooms* ▤*AE, D, DC, MC, V* ❍❙*BP.*

$$ ⚑ **The Curtis.** In the renovated former Executive Tower Hotel, each floor has a pop-culture theme, from classic cars to TV to science fiction. Don't be surprised when the elevator doors close and you feel like you are in a shark cage—the space is decorated like one. The setting takes you back to a happier, gentler time, when bubbly music made you feel good (it plays in the hallways) and robots were going to take away some of our work instead of add to it (one roams the halls). The rooms are spacious and groovy, with speakers for your MP3 player and comfy, mod furnishings. The Corner Office Restaurant and Martini Lounge ($$) is a retro eatery and popular local happy-hour joint that serves gourmet comfort food such as lobster mac and cheese, French fries, and even Captain Crunch (yes, for dinner). The Oceanaire ($$$) is a tonier seafood restaurant. **Pros:** across the street from Denver Performing Arts Complex, kid-friendly, very reasonably priced considering location. **Cons:** can be pretty noisy, lots of traffic in area. ✉*1405 Curtis St., Downtown, 80202* ☎*303/571–0300 or 800/525–6651* ⊕*www. exectowerhotel.com* ⇲*334 rooms, 2 suites* ⚑*In-room: ethernet, Wi-Fi. In-hotel: 2 restaurants, room service, bar, pool, concierge, laundry service, public Wi-Fi, parking (fee), no-smoking rooms* ▤*AE, D, DC, MC, V.*

$$ ⚑ **Denver Marriott City Center.** The Denver Marriott is definitely geared toward the business traveler; it's a three-block walk to the Denver

Convention Complex and has 25,000 square feet of meeting space of its own. Rooms are small but classy, with a strong "executive" look (many stripes, much leather). The cozy, fall-color Great Divide Lounge and the savvy American fare at Allies American Grille are worthwhile whether you have an expense account or not. The on-site, full-service City Spa offers massages and facial treatments. **Pros:** reasonable rates for location, nice gym and pool. **Con:** not much maneuvering space in the rooms. ✉*1701 California St., Downtown, 80202* ☎*303/297–1300 or 800/228–9290* ⊕*www.denvermarriott.com* ⌦*613 rooms, 14 suites* ♿*In-room: ethernet, Wi-Fi. In-hotel: restaurant, room service, bar, pool, gym, spa, concierge, laundry service, public Wi-Fi, parking (fee), no-smoking rooms* ☐*AE, D, DC, MC, V.*

$$ ⬚**Holiday Chalet B&B.** Stained-glass windows and homey accents throughout make this 1896 Victorian brownstone exceptionally charming. It's also in Capitol Hill, the neighborhood immediately east of downtown. Many of the rooms have overstuffed Victorian arm-chairs and such historic touches as furniture once owned by Baby Doe Tabor. Some units have tile fireplaces, others have small sitting rooms. Each room has a full kitchen, a holdover from the building's days as an apartment building, and full breakfast is included. Across a serene courtyard, the B&B serves a light lunch with tea Thursday through Sunday. **Pros:** charming staff, teas are delightful, enchanting decor. **Con:** parking can be a challenge. ✉*1820 E. Colfax Ave., Capitol Hill, 80218* ☎*303/321–9975 or 800/626–4497* ⊕*www.holidaychalet.net* ⌦*10 rooms* ♿*In-room: kitchen, VCR, ethernet, Wi-Fi. In-hotel: no elevator, public Wi-Fi, some pets allowed, no-smoking rooms* ☐*AE, D, DC, MC, V* ⑩*BP.*

$$ ⬚**Queen Anne Inn.** Just north of downtown in the regentrified Cle-ments historic district (some of the neighboring blocks have yet to be reclaimed), this inn made up of adjacent Victorians is a delightful, romantic getaway. Both houses have handsome oak wainscoting and balustrades, vaulted ceilings, numerous bay or stained-glass windows, and period furnishings like brass and canopy beds, cherry and pine armoires, and oak rocking chairs. The best accommodations are the four "gallery suites" dedicated to Audubon, Rockwell, Calder, and Remington. A full breakfast and afternoon tastings of Colorado wines are offered daily. **Pros:** lovely rooms, welcoming hosts, hearty fare. **Con:** not right downtown. ✉*2147 Tremont Pl., Central Denver, 80205* ☎*303/296–6666 or 800/432–4667* ⊕*www.queenannebnb.com* ⌦*10 rooms, 4 suites* ♿*In-room: ethernet. In-hotel: no elevator, public Wi-Fi, no-smoking rooms* ☐*AE, D, DC, MC, V* ⑩*BP.*

$$ ⬚**Warwick Denver Hotel.** This stylish midsize business hotel, ideally located on the edge of downtown, underwent a monumental $20 million renovation that was completed in 2001. The oversize rooms and suites are some of the best in town, with brass and mahogany furnishings and the latest in high-tech perks. All rooms contain wet bars and private terraces with exceptional city views. The restaurant, Randolph's, serves contemporary American cuisine three meals daily, with a recent noticeable upgrade in the caliber of its cuisine. **Pros:** rea-sonable rates, friendly staff, spacious rooms. **Con:** food at Randolph's

inconsistent. ✉*1776 Grant St., Downtown, 80203* ☎*303/861–2000 or 800/525–2888* ⊕*www.warwickdenver.com* ↩*161 rooms, 58 suites* ♿*In-room: safe, Wi-Fi. In-hotel: restaurant, room service, bars, pool, gym, concierge, public Wi-Fi, parking (fee), some pets allowed, no-smoking rooms* ⊟*AE, D, DC, MC, V.*

$–$$ ⚐**Adagio Bed & Breakfast.** The music room of this 1892 Victorian mansion has a grand piano and rooms are named after composers. The theme continues with breakfast, served *adagio*—or at your leisure. Guest rooms have lace-trim linens, period furniture, and different color schemes and special amenities; the Copland Suite has a living room, a working gas fireplace with original mantel, and a whirlpool bath. Convenient to both downtown and Cherry Creek, this B&B also stands out because of modern conveniences such as in-room Wi-Fi and cable television. The hired chef is restaurant quality, and you can choose a full-meal plan for an additional cost. **Pros:** breakfast available when you want it; pretty, cozy rooms; within driving distance of major attractions. **Con:** not within walking distance of downtown or Cherry Creek. ✉*1430 Race St., Capitol Hill, 80206* ☎*303/370–6911 or 800/533–3241* ⊕*www.adagiobb.com* ↩*6 rooms, 1 suite* ♿*In-room: ethernet, Wi-Fi. In-hotel: no elevator, public Wi-Fi, no-smoking rooms* ⊟*AE, MC, V* ⦿*BP, MAP.*

$ ⚐**Ramada Limited Capitol Hill.** As the name suggests, this Ramada is within walking distance of the State Capitol, as well as nine blocks east of downtown and the 16th Street Mall. A Southwestern flair pervades the leather couch–dominated Western-style lobby and lounge area. The somewhat dated but reasonably spacious rooms have dark carpeting and red and rose colors. **Pros:** very reasonable rates, easy to get downtown. **Con:** not the safest part of Colfax Avenue. ✉*1150 E. Colfax Ave., Capitol Hill, 80217* ☎*303/831–7700 or 800/272–6232* ⊕*www. ramada.com* ↩*143 rooms, 8 suites* ♿*In-room: safe, ethernet, Wi-Fi. In-hotel: restaurant, room service, bar, pool, gym, laundry service, parking (no fee), no-smoking rooms* ⊟*AE, D, DC, MC, V.*

$ ⚐**Red Lion Hotel.** A stone's throw from Invesco Field at Mile High, the Red Lion provides free parking and complimentary shuttles to downtown (half a mile away). Visitors and locals alike hang out at the Skybox Grill and Sports Bar on the 14th floor, which has a panoramic view of the Denver skyline and surrounding attractions. Rooms are done in red, white, and warm-yellow colors, with plenty of space to maneuver and an oversize desk. **Pros:** reasonable rates, easy highway access, spacious rooms good for business travelers. **Cons:** rooms feel dated, traffic during rush hours can be a nightmare. ✉*1975 Bryant St., Downtown, 80203* ☎*303/433–8331 or 800/388–5381* ⊕*www.redliondenverdowntown.com* ↩*171 rooms* ♿*In-room: Wi-Fi. In-hotel: restaurant, room service, bar, pool, gym, concierge, laundry service, parking (no fee), no-smoking rooms* ⊟*AE, D, DC, MC, V.*

AROUND CHERRY CREEK

$$ ▫️ **Cherry Creek Hotel.** Mountain views, proximity to Cherry Creek shopping, and a complimentary shuttle service to anywhere within a 5-mi radius count among this former Sheraton outpost's advantages. Rooms are forest green and brown, with modern art and oversize chairs. Not only is the outdoor pool area attractively landscaped, but the pool itself is heated. You receive a daily pass to Bally's Total Fitness Center next door. **Pros:** nice views, shuttle service, great pool. **Con:** not near downtown. ✉️*600 S. Colorado Blvd., Glendale, 80246* ☎️*303/757–3341* ☞*210 rooms* ♿*In-room: ethernet. In-hotel: restaurant, room service, bar, pool, gym, laundry service, parking (no fee), some pets allowed, no-smoking rooms* ▤*AE, D, DC, MC, V.*

$$ ▫️ **Holiday Inn Select Denver/Cherry Creek.** The Cherry Creek shopping district is 4 mi away and the major museums and the zoo a five-minute drive from this bustling hotel, which provides coveted mountain views from many of its rooms. The entrance is impressive, with stone-supported pillars and Southwestern effects, whereas the rooms are decorated in autumn tones with velvety upholstery and leather chairs. At night, Olives Martini Bar brings in Denverites, as well. **Pros:** good location for business travelers, Starbucks on-site, location bridges gap for folks who want to museums and hit downtown. **Cons:** not walking distance to any attractions, not near downtown. ✉️*455 S. Colorado Blvd., Cherry Creek, 80246* ☎️*303/388–5561 or 888/388–6129* ⊕*www.cherrycreekhoteldenver.com* ☞*276 rooms, 7 suites* ♿*In-room: ethernet. In-hotel: restaurant, room service, bar, pool, gym, concierge, laundry service, parking (no fee), no-smoking rooms* ▤*AE, D, DC, MC, V.*

$$ ▫️ **Loews Denver Hotel.** The 12-story steel-and-black-glass facade conceals the unexpected and delightful Italian baroque motif within. Spacious rooms are done in earth tones and blond wood and garnished with fresh flowers, fruit baskets, and Renaissance-style portraits. The formal Tuscany restaurant ($$$) serves sumptuous Italian cuisine. Use of a nearby health club and a continental breakfast are included. If downtown or the Denver Tech Center are your primary destinations, this location is a drawback, but Cherry Creek fans will find its proximity a plus. **Pros:** gorgeous rooms and public spaces, wonderful restaurant, gracious staff. **Con:** not near downtown. ✉️*4150 E. Mississippi Ave., Southeast Denver, 80222* ☎️*303/782–9300 or 800/345–9172* ⊕*www.loewshotels.com* ☞*183 rooms, 17 suites* ♿*In-room: safe, ethernet. In-hotel: restaurant, room service, bar, gym, concierge, laundry service, public Internet, parking (no fee), no-smoking rooms* ▤*AE, D, DC, MC, V* ⏐○⏐*CP.*

SPORTS & THE OUTDOORS

Denver is a city that can consistently, enthusiastically support three professional sports teams. Unfortunately, it has four (not counting soccer)—the Colorado Rockies, Colorado Avalanche, Denver Broncos, and Denver Nuggets. In recent years, the Nuggets have been the odd team out, as the Rockies, Avalanche, and Broncos have all reached or won championships in their respective sports. But the Nuggets may be about to catch up, given a nucleus of new, young players.

What's great about Denverites is that most aren't just spectators. After a game, they go out and do stuff—hiking, bicycling, kayaking, and, yes, playing the team sports themselves. The city and its proximity to outdoor pursuits encourage a fit lifestyle.

BASEBALL

The Colorado Rockies, Denver's National League baseball team, play April–October in **Coors Field** (⊠ *2001 Blake St., LoDo* ☎ *303/292–0200 or 800/388–7625* ⊕ *www.coloradorockies.com*). Because of high altitude and thin air, the park is among the hardest in the major leagues for pitchers—and the Rockies have had a tough time preserving young arms. But each year they manage to finish on a high enough note to bring the fans back into the stands the next season.

BASKETBALL

The Denver Nuggets of the National Basketball Association have been the ugly duckling in Denver's professional-sports scene for years. However, they continue to raise expectations with top-draft picks and exciting young players. From November to April, the Nuggets play at the **Pepsi Center** (⊠ *1000 Chopper Circle, Auraria* ☎ *303/405–8555* ⊕ *www.nba.com/nuggets*). The 19,000-seat arena, which opened in 1999, is also the primary spot in town for large musical acts such as Bruce Springsteen and Christina Aguilera.

BICYCLING & JOGGING

The **Denver Parks Department** (☎ *720/913–0696* ⊕ *www.denvergov.org/parks*) has suggestions for bicycling and jogging paths throughout the metropolitan area's 250 parks, including the popular Cherry Creek and Chatfield Reservoir State Recreation areas. With more than 400 mi of off-road paths in and around the city, cyclists can move easily between urban and rural settings.

Just south of downtown, the **Bicycle Doctor/Edgeworks** (⊠ *860 Broadway, Golden Triangle* ☎ *303/831–7228* ⊕ *www.bicycledr.com*) repairs street and mountain bikes, and rents them for $15 to $50 a day.

The well-kept **Cherry Creek Bike Path** (⊠ *Cherry Creek, LoDo*) runs from Cherry Creek Shopping Center to Larimer Square downtown alongside the peaceful creek of its name. The scenic **Highline Canal** (⊠ *Auraria, Cherry Creek, LoDo*) has 70 mi of mostly dirt paths through the metro area running at almost completely level grade. **Platte River Greenway** (⊠ *Auraria, Cherry Creek and LoDo*) is a 20-mi-long path for in-line skating, bicycling, and jogging that runs alongside Cherry Creek and the Platte River. Much of it runs through downtown Denver. There are 12 mi of paved paths along the **South Platte River** (⊠ *Platte River valley, LoDo*) heading into downtown. West of the city, paved paths wind through **Matthews/Winters Park** (⊕ *South of I–70 on CO 26, Golden*) near both Golden and Morrison. It's dotted with plaintive pioneer graves amid the sun-bleached grasses, thistle, and columbine. The **Deer Creek Canyon** (⊠ *Littleton* ⊕ *www. co.jefferson.co.us/opens-*

CLOSE UP

Staking Out the Stock Show

Thousands of cowpokes retrieve their string ties and worn boots and indulge in two weeks of hootin', hollerin', and celebratin' the beef industry during the National Western Stock Show every January.

Whether you're a professional rancher or bull rider, or just plan to show up for the people-watching, the Stock Show is a rich, colorful glimpse of Western culture. The pros arrive to make industry connections, show off their livestock, and perhaps land a few sales. The entertainment involves nightly rodeo events, presentations of prized cattle (some going for thousands of dollars), and "Mutton Bustin'." The latter is one of those rowdy rodeo concepts that usually has no place in a genteel metropolis like Denver:

Kids, six years and younger, don huge hockey-goalie helmets and hold for dear life on to the backs of bucking baby sheep. At the trade show you can buy hats and boots, of course, but also yards of beef jerky and quirky gift items like caps from the Universal Semen Sales company.

The yearly event is held at the **Denver Coliseum** (✉ *4655 Humboldt St., ⊹ east of I–25 on I–70 Elyria* ☎ *303/297–1166 Ext. 810* ⊕ *www.nationalwestern.com*). Just be sure to call first and ask for directions; although parking is plentiful, the Coliseum, usually home of straightforward sporting and entertainment events, becomes a labyrinth of lots and shuttles during the Stock Show.

---

pace) trail system is popular with mountain bikers, running through forested foothills southwest of Denver near the intersection of C–470 and Wadsworth Avenue.

FOOTBALL

The National Football League's Denver Broncos play September–December at **Invesco Field at Mile High** (✉ *1701 Bryant St., ⊹Exit 210B off I–25, Sun Valley* ☎ *720/258–3000* ⊕ *www.denverbroncos.com*). Every game has sold out for 30 years, so tickets are not easy to come by, despite the Broncos' tepid success in the post–John Elway world.

GOLF

With their sprawling layouts and impressively appointed greens, these four private clubs, all of which were awarded four stars from *Golf Digest,* merit a special look over their city-operated counterparts simply because of their more-rural settings. On any Denver-area course, though, out-of-town golfers should keep in mind that the high altitude affects golf balls like it does baseballs—which is why the Rockies have so many more home runs when they bat at home. It's generally agreed that your golf ball will go about 10%–15% farther in the thin air here than it would at sea level.

Arrowhead Golf Club. Designed by Robert Trent Jones Jr., this course is set impressively among red sandstone spires. It's 45 minutes from downtown in Roxborough State Park, which means any members of your group who don't want to golf can hike nearby. ✉ *10850 W. Sundown Trail, Littleton* ☎ *303/973–9614* ⊕ *www.arrowhead*

colorado.com ⚓*18 holes. Yards: 6,682/5,465. Par: 70/72. Green Fee: $49/$129.*

Buffalo Run. A Keith Foster–designed course and the site for the 2004 Denver Open, the bargain-priced Buffalo Run counts wide-open views of the plains surrounding its lake-studded course among its charms, which also include streams running through it and the Bison Grill Restaurant. ✉*15700 E. 112th Ave., Commerce City* ☎*303/289–1500* ⊕*www.buffalorungolfcourse.com* ⚓*18 holes. Yards: 7,411/5,277. Par: 72/71. Green Fee: $25/$44.*

Ridge at Castle Pines North. Tom Weiskopf designed this 18-hole course with great mountain views and dramatic elevation changes. It's ranked among the nation's top 100 public courses. It's in Castle Rock, about 45 minutes south of Denver on I–25. ✉*1414 Castle Pines Pkwy., Castle Rock* ☎*303/688–0100* ⊕*www.theridgecpn.com* ✍*Reservations essential* ⚓*18 holes. Yards: 7,013/5,001. Par: 71/71. Green Fee: $55/$100.*

Riverdale Golf Courses. It's two golf courses in one: Riverdale has the Dunes, a Scottish-style links course designed by Pete and Perry Dye that sits on the South Platte River and offers railroad ties, plenty of bunkers, and water, while the Knolls has a more-gnarly, park-inspired layout. Both courses are shaded by plenty of trees, and you can't beat the green fee. ✉*13300 Riverdale Rd., Brighton* ☎*303/659–6700* ⊕*www.riverdalegolf.com* ⚓*Knolls: 18 holes. Yards: 6,771/5,891. Par: 71/72. Dunes: 18 holes. Yards: 7,064/4,903. Par: 73/70. Green Fee: $19/$43.*

Six courses, City Park, Evergreen, Kennedy, Overland Park, Wellshire, and Willis Case, are operated by the City of Denver and are open to the public. Green fee for all range from $10 to $24. For same-day tee times, you can call the starters at an individual course (*City Park* ☎*303/295–2096* ✉*Evergreen* ☎*303/674–6351* ✉*Kennedy* ☎*303/751–0311* ✉*Overland Park* ☎*303/698–4975* ✉*Wellshire* ☎*303/692–5636* ✉*Willis Case* ☎*303/458–4877*), but for advance reservations golfers must call the **main reservation system** (☎*303/784–4000*) up to three days in advance.

HIKING

Mount Falcon Park looks down on Denver and across at Red Rocks. It's amazingly tranquil, laced with meadows and streams, and shaded by conifers. The trails are very well marked. ✛*Off Rte. 8, Morrison exit, or U.S. 285, Parmalee exit, Aurora.*

Fodor'sChoice
★ Fifteen miles southwest of Denver, **Red Rocks Park and Amphitheatre** is a breathtaking, 70-million-year-old wonderland of vaulting oxblood-and-cinnamon-color sandstone spires. The outdoor music stage is in a natural 9,000-seat amphitheater (with perfect acoustics, as only nature could have designed). The Trading Post loop hiking trail, at 6,280 feet, is 1.4 mi long and quite narrow with drop-offs and steep grades. Allow about two hours. The trail closes one-half hour before sunset. The park

is open from 5 AM to 11 PM daily. *Morrison I–70 west to Exit 259, turn left to park entrance ⊕www.redrocksonline.com.*

Roxborough State Park has an easy 2-mi loop trail through rugged rock formations, offering striking vistas and a unique look at metro Denver and the plains. This trail is wheelchair accessible. ⊠*Littleton,* ⊹*I–25 south to Santa Fe exit, take Santa Fe Blvd. south to Titan Rd., turn right and follow signs.*

Green Mountain is the first named foothill as you head west from Denver toward the mountains. Part of Jefferson County Open Space and a piece of William Frederick Hayden Park (City of Lakewood), the easy, mostly exposed trail affords panoramic views of downtown Denver, Table Mesa, Pikes Peak, and the Continental Divide from the top (895 feet in elevation gain). You must share with bikers and dogs, as well as other critters. There are multiple trails from several trailheads, including a 6.4-mi loop and a 3.1-mi loop. Allow one to two hours. Open 5 AM to 10 PM daily. ⊠*Lakewood,* ⊹*I–70 west to C–470 to W. Alameda Pkwy., turn left to trailhead entrance ⊕www.lakewood.org.*

HOCKEY

The Colorado Avalanche of the National Hockey League are wildly popular in Denver; the team won the Stanley Cup in 1996 and beat the New Jersey Devils for an encore in 2001. Although they've been relatively disappointing since, and legendary goalie Patrick Roy retired after the 2003 season, the still-exciting team plays October to April at the **Pepsi Center** (⊠*1000 Chopper Pl., Auraria* ☎*303/405–8555* ⊕*www.coloradoavalanche.com*), a 19,000-seat arena.

NIGHTLIFE & THE ARTS

Friday's *Denver Post* and *Rocky Mountain News* both publish calendars of the week's events, as does the slightly alternative *Westword,* which is free and published on Thursday. Downtown and LoDo are where most Denverites go at night. Downtown has more-mainstream entertainment, whereas LoDo is home to fun, funky rock clubs and small theaters. Remember that Denver's altitude can intensify your reaction to alcohol.

The ubiquitous **TicketMaster** (☎*303/830–8497*) is Denver's prime agency, selling tickets to almost all concerts, sporting events, and plays that take place in the Denver area. On the theatrical side of the spectrum, the **Ticket Bus** (☎*No phone*), on the 16th Street Mall at Curtis Street, sells tickets from 10 until 6 weekdays, and half-price tickets on the day of the performance.

THE ARTS

PERFORMANCE VENUES

★ The **Denver Performing Arts Complex** is a huge, impressively high-tech group of theaters connected by a soaring glass archway to a futuristic symphony hall. The complex, which occupies a four-block area, hosts more events than any other performing arts center in the world. Run by the 35-year-old Denver Center for the Performing Arts, the complex's anchors are the round, relaxing Temple Hoyne Buell Theatre, built in 1991, and the more-impressive, ornate Auditorium Theatre, built in 1908. Both host large events, from classical orchestras to comedian Jerry Seinfeld to country singer Lyle Lovett. Some of the other five theaters include the small Garner Galleria Theatre, where the comedy *I Love You, You're Perfect, Now Change* once packed the house for more than four years running, and the midsize Space Theatre. Both the ballet and opera have their seasons here. Guided tours for groups of five or more are available by appointment only. ⊠ *Box office, 14th and Curtis Sts., LoDo* ☎*303/893–4000* ⊕*www.denvercenter.org.*

Downtown, the **Paramount Theatre** (⊠*1631 Glenarm Pl., LoDo* ☎*303/623–0106* ⊕*www.theparamount.net*) is the venue for large-scale rock concerts. Designed by renowned local architect Temple H. Buell in the art deco style in 1930, the lovingly maintained Paramount is both an elegant place to see shows and a rowdy, beer-serving party location for rock fans.

Fodor'sChoice
★

The exquisite 9,000-seat **Red Rocks Amphitheatre** (⊠*Morrison ⊹ off U.S. 285 or I–70* ☎*303/640–2637* ⊕*www.redrocksonline.com*), amid majestic geological formations in nearby Morrison, is renowned for its natural acoustics, which have awed the likes of Leopold Stokowski and the Beatles. Although Red Rocks is one of the best places in the country to hear live music, be sure to leave extra time when visiting—parking is sparse, crowds are thick, paths are long and extremely uphill, and seating is usually general admission.

SYMPHONY, OPERA & DANCE

Colorado's premier orchestra, opera company, and ballet company are all in residence at the Denver Performing Arts Complex.

The **Colorado Symphony Orchestra** performs September to June in the **Boettcher Concert Hall** (⊠*13th and Curtis Sts., LoDo* ☎*303/640–2862* ⊕*www.coloradosymphony.org*).

Opera Colorado (☎*303/778–1500* ⊕*www.operacolorado.org*) has a spring season, often with internationally renowned artists, in the magnificent new Ellie Caulkins Opera House in the renovated Newton Auditorium. Already world-renowned for its superior acoustics and a Figaro seat-back titling system, which allows attendees to follow the text of the opera, the cherrywood-accented theater sports red-velvet seating and a lyre shape, ideal for full-bodied sound travel.

The **Colorado Ballet** (☎*303/837–8888* ⊕*www.coloradoballet.org*) specializes in the classics with performances from September to April.

THEATER

The **Bug Theatre Company** (⊠*3654 Navajo St., Highland* ☎*303/477–9984*) produces primarily cutting-edge, original works in Denver's Highland neighborhood. **Denver Center Attractions** (⊠*14th and Curtis Sts., at DPCA's Temple Hoyne Buell and Auditorium theaters, LoDo* ☎*303/893–4100*) brings Broadway road companies to town. The **Den-**

ver Center Theater Company (⊠*14th and Curtis Sts., LoDo* ☎*303/893–4100*) presents high-caliber repertory theater, including new works by promising playwrights, at the Bonfils Theatre Complex (part of the Denver Performing Arts Complex). **El Centro Su Teatro** (⊠*4725 High St., Elyria* ☎*303/296–0219*) is a Latino-Chicano company that puts on mostly original works and festivals during its May to September season. **Hunger Artists Ensemble Theater** (⊠*Denver Civic Theater, 721 Santa Fe Dr., Civic Center* ☎*303/893–5438*) presents dramas, comedies, and adaptations of works from the likes of Shakespeare, James Joyce, and Tom Stoppard.

NIGHTLIFE

BARS & BREWPUBS

The **Denver ChopHouse & Brewery** (⊠*1735 19th St., LoDo* ☎*303/296–0800*) is a high-end microbrewery on the site of the old Union Pacific Railroad headhouse—with the train paraphernalia to prove it. It's a bit expensive for a brewpub, but if you hang out after Broncos games you might encounter local sports celebrities celebrating or commiserating. **Mynt Lounge** (⊠*1424 Market St., LoDo* ☎*303/825–6968*) has established a chichi reputation with its fruity martinis (try the Strawberry Banana) and Miami-style pastel colors. Considered by some Denverites as the best bar in town, the laid-back, casual, slightly divey **PS Lounge** (⊠*3416 E. Colfax Ave., Capitol Hill* ☎*303/320–1200*) has a well-stocked jukebox and an owner, known to all simply as Pete, who hands out a free shot to anyone who behaves and seems to be having a good time. **Rock Bottom Brewery** (⊠*1001 16th St., LoDo* ☎*303/534–7616*) is a perennial favorite, thanks to its rotating special brews and reasonably priced pub grub. A new vintage-style poolroom is yet another reason to stop by the beloved **Skylark Lounge** (⊠*140 S. Broadway, South Denver* ☎*303/722–7844*), which counts live music, pinball machines, comfortable seating, and friendly staffers among its many charms. The **Wynkoop Brewing Co.** (⊠*1634 18th St., LoDo* ☎*303/297–2700*) is now more famous for its owner—Denver Mayor John Hickenlooper—than for its brews, food, or ambience. But it remains one of the city's best-known bars—a relaxing, slightly upscale, two-story joint filled with halfway-decent bar food, the usual pool tables, and

> ### AND THE AWARD GOES TO...
>
> Though it's a title many have tried to usurp, only one person (at a time) can truly be the Beerdrinker of the Year, as determined by Wynkoop Brewing Company and its panel of local and national judges (read: serious beer drinkers), who wear British wigs and robes during the finals. Begun in 1997 by then-owner and current Denver mayor John Hickenlooper, the annual contest is extremely competitive and draws contestants from all over the country, who are required to submit beer résumés and undergo a rigorous battery of tests and contests to determine their beery worthiness. Winners receive free beer for life at Wynkoop, not to mention bragging rights.

games and beers of all types. It has anchored LoDo since it was a pre-Coors Field warehouse district.

CABARET

Downstairs in the Wynkoop brewpub, the **Impulse Theater** (✉ *1634 18th St., LoDo* ☎ *303/297–2111* ⊕ *www.impulsetheater.com*) hosts everything from top-name jazz acts to up-and-coming stand-up comedians to cabaret numbers.

COMEDY CLUBS

Three area improv groups make their home at **Bovine Metropolis Theater** (✉ *1527 Champa St., LoDo* ☎ *303/758–4722* ⊕ *www.bovinemetropolis.com*), which also stages satirical productions. Denver comics have honed their skills at **Comedy Works** (✉ *1226 15th St., LoDo* ☎ *303/595–3637* ⊕ *www.comedyworks.com*) for 20 years. Well-known performers often drop by.

COUNTRY MUSIC CLUBS

The **Grizzly Rose** (✉ *5450 N. Valley Hwy.,* ⊕ *I–25 at Exit 215, Globeville* ☎ *303/295–1330*) has miles of dance floor, national bands, and gives two-step dancing lessons—and sells plenty of Western wear, from cowboy boots to spurs. This club, in an old far-north Denver neighborhood, boomed in the early '90s, when Garth Brooks and Billy Ray Cyrus were huge, and has settled into its solidly popular incarnation. Classic-rock bands are big, in addition to country acts big and small. The suburban **Stampede Grill & Dance Emporium** (✉ *2430 S. Havana St., Aurora* ☎ *303/337–6909*) is another cavernous boot-scooting spot, with dance lessons and a restaurant.

DANCE CLUBS

The **Funky Buddha Lounge** (✉ *776 Lincoln St., Capitol Hill* ☎ *303/832–5075*) distinguishes itself with the Ginger Bar, an upstairs outdoor dance area with live DJs six nights a week. **Midtown Beat** (✉ *4040 E. Evans Ave., Virginia Village* ☎ *303/759–5302*), a cavernous building south of Glendale with three dance floors, a fireplace lounge, six bars, and a killer patio, is where the cool college crowd goes to get carded. The venerable dance club the **Snake Pit** (✉ *608 E. 13th Ave., Capitol Hill* ☎ *303/831–1234*) caters to a well-varied crowd.

GAY BARS

Charlie's (✉ *900 E. Colfax Ave., Capitol Hill* ☎ *303/839–8890*) has country-western atmosphere and music. **JR's Bar & Grill** (✉ *777 E. 17th Ave., Central Denver* ☎ *303/831–0459*) features theme nights (retro, trivia), a raucous atmosphere, and a huge, long patio—with neighborhood people-watching—in nice weather.

JAZZ CLUBS

El Chapultepec (✉ *1962 Market St., LoDo* ☎ *303/295–9126*) is a cramped, fluorescent-lighted, bargain-basement Mexican dive. Still, the limos parked outside hint at its enduring popularity: This is where Ol' Blue Eyes used to pop in, and where visiting musicians, including the Marsalis brothers, continue to jam after hours. **Dazzle Restaurant and Lounge** (✉ *930 Lincoln St., Central Denver* ☎ *303/839–5100*) is a

CLOSE UP

Denver Rocks

Colorado's moments of pop-music history have been spectacular. Many happened at Red Rocks Amphitheatre, where the Beatles performed in 1964 and U2's Bono made his famous "this song is not a rebel song—this song is 'Sunday Bloody Sunday'" speech in 1983. The Denver–Boulder area was a huge hub for country-rock in the '70s, and members of the Eagles, Poco, Firefall, and others lived here, at least briefly. Some of the most famous spots have closed, but rock fans can tour the hallowed ground—Ebbets Field, where Steve Martin and Lynyrd Skynyrd made early-career appearances in the '70s, at 15th and Curtis; and the original Auditorium Theatre, where Led Zeppelin performed its first U.S. show in 1968, at 14th and Curtis. The local scene remains strong, with the Samples, Big Head Todd and the Monsters, Leftover Salmon, String Cheese Incident, Apples In Stereo, and Dressy Bessy attracting audiences. Check *Westword* for show listings.

cozy, casual spot for nightly live jazz in the Golden Triangle. *Downbeat* magazine has named it one of the 100 best jazz clubs in the world; it offers acoustically treated walls in the dining room and the lounge, where the audience is up close and personal with the musicians. Hidden in the back of a parking lot, the hipster favorite **Herb's Hideout** (⊠ *2057 Larimer St., LoDo* ☎ *303/299–9555*) is a gloriously nostalgic bar with dim lighting and checkerboard floors.

ROCK CLUBS

Of Denver's numerous smoky hangouts, the most popular is the regally restored **Bluebird Theater** (⊠ *3317 E. Colfax Ave., Capitol Hill* ☎ *303/322–2308*), which showcases local and national acts, emphasizing rock, hip-hop, ambient, and the occasional evening of cinema. **Cricket on the Hill** (⊠ *1209 E. 13th Ave., Capitol Hill* ☎ *303/830–9020*) is a somewhat seedy Denver institution, presenting a mix of rock, blues, acoustic, and alternative music. The **Fillmore Auditorium** (⊠ *1510 Clarkson St., Capitol Hill* ☎ *303/837–1482*), Denver's classic San Francisco concert hall spin-off, looks dumpy on the outside but is elegant and impressive inside. Before catching a big-name act such as Coldplay, LL Cool J, or Snoop Dogg, scan the walls for color photographs of past club performers.

The **Gothic Theatre** (⊠ *3263 S. Broadway, Englewood* ☎ *303/830– 8397*) came to age in the early '90s, with a steady stream of soon-to-be-famous alternative-rock acts such as Nirvana and the Red Hot Chili Peppers. It has since reinvented itself as a community venue for theater, music, and charity events, and sits south of downtown. Down-home **Herman's Hideaway** (⊠ *1578 S. Broadway, Overland* ☎ *303/777–5840*) showcases mostly local rock in a south Denver neighborhood, with a smattering of reggae and blues thrown in. The **Lions Lair** (⊠ *2022 E. Colfax Ave., Capitol Hill* ☎ *303/320–9200*) is a beautiful dive where punk-rock bands and occasional name acts (like British rocker Graham Parker) perform on a tiny stage just above a huge, square, central bar. The **Mercury Café** (⊠ *2199 California St., Five Points* ☎ *303/294–9281*) triples as a health-food restaurant (sublime tofu fettuccine), fringe theater, and rock club in a downtown neighborhood specializing in acoustic sets, progressive, and newer wave music. The **Ogden Theatre** (✉ *935 E. Colfax Ave., Capitol Hill* ☎ *303/830–2525*) is a classic old theater that showcases alternative-rock acts such as the Breeders and the Flaming Lips.

SHOPPING

Denver may be the best place in the country for shopping for recreational gear. Sporting-goods stores hold legendary ski sales around Labor Day. The city's selection of books and Western fashion is also noteworthy.

MALLS & SHOPPING DISTRICTS

The **Denver Pavilions** (✉ *16th St. Mall between Tremont and Welton Sts., LoDo* ☎ *303/260–6000* ⊕ *www.denverpavilions.com*) is downtown Denver's newest shopping and entertainment complex, a three-story, open-air structure that houses national stores like Barnes & Noble, NikeTown, Ann Taylor, Talbot's, and a Virgin Records Megastore. There are also restaurants, including Denver's Hard Rock Cafe, and a 15-screen movie theater, the UA Denver Pavilions. Most of the restaurants and theaters are national chains, so don't expect distinctive local flavor, but it's a practical complement to Larimer Square a few blocks away. When attending a movie here, build in extra minutes to locate sparse downtown parking (Pavilions also has its own lots behind the mall) and maneuver the steps and escalators leading to the box office.

Historic **Larimer Square** (✉ *14th and Larimer Sts., LoDo*) houses distinctive shops and restaurants. Some of the square's retail highlights are the Vespa scooter dealership; Earthzone, a gallery of art fashioned from fossils and minerals; and John Atencio Designer Jewelry. **Tabor Center** (✉ *16th St. Mall, LoDo*) is a light-filled atrium whose 20 specialty shops and restaurants include the ESPN Zone–theme restaurant and the Shirt Broker. Others, such as the Colorado Baggage store, showcase uniquely Coloradan merchandise and souvenirs. **Writer Square** (✉ *1512 Larimer St., LoDo*) has Tiny Town—a doll-size village inhabited by Michael Garman's inimitable figurines—as well as shops and restaurants.

In a pleasant, predominantly residential neighborhood 2 mi from downtown, the **Cherry Creek** shopping district has retail blocks and an enclosed mall. At Milwaukee Street, the granite-and-glass behemoth **Cherry Creek Shopping Mall** (✉ *3000 E. 1st Ave., Cherry Creek* ☎ *303/388–3900*) holds some of the nation's top retailers. Its 160 stores include Abercrombie & Fitch, Eddie Bauer, Banana Republic, Burberry's, Tiffany & Co., Macy's, Nordstrom, Louis Vuitton, Neiman Marcus, Polo–Ralph Lauren, and Saks Fifth Avenue. Just north of the Cherry Creek Shopping Mall is the district **Cherry Creek North** (✉ *Between 1st and 3rd Aves. from University Blvd. to Steele St., Cherry Creek* ☎ *303/394–2904*), an open-air development of tree-lined streets and shady plazas, with art galleries, specialty shops, and fashionable restaurants.

The upscale **Park Meadows** (⊹*I–25, 5 mi south of Denver at County Line Rd., Littleton*) is a mall designed to resemble a ski resort, with a 120-foot-high log-beam ceiling anchored by two massive stone fireplaces. The center includes more than 100 specialty shops. On snowy days, "ambassadors" scrape your windshield while free hot chocolate is served inside.

Between Denver and Colorado Springs, **Prime Outlets at Castle Rock** (⊹*Exit 184 off I–25, Castle Rock*) attract shoppers with 25%–75% savings on everything from appliances to apparel at its more than 50 outlets.

SPECIALTY SHOPS

ANTIQUES DEALERS
South Broadway between 1st Avenue and Evans Street, as well as the side streets off this main drag, is chockablock with dusty antiques stores. Patient browsing could net some amazing bargains.

Antique Mall of Lakewood. More than 80 dealer showrooms make for one-stop shopping. ⊠*9635 W. Colfax Ave., Lakewood* ☎*303/238–6940.*

BOOKSTORES
Fodor'sChoice **Tattered Cover.** A must for all bibliophiles, the Tattered Cover may be the
★ best bookstore in the United States, not only for the near-endless selection of volumes (more than 400,000 on two floors at the new Colfax Avenue location and 300,000 in LoDo) and helpful, knowledgeable staff, but also for the incomparably refined atmosphere. Treat yourself to the overstuffed armchairs, reading nooks, and afternoon readings and lectures, but be prepared for a less cozy environment at the Capitol Hill site in the renovated historic Lowenstein Theater than at the original Cherry Creek location. ⊠*2526 E. Colfax Ave., Capitol Hill* ☎*303/322–7727* ⊠*1628 16th St., LoDo* ☎*303/436–1070.*

CRAFTS & ART GALLERIES
LoDo has the trendiest galleries, many in splendidly and stylishly restored Victorian warehouses.

Camera Obscura Gallery. One of the oldest and best photography galleries between the east and west coasts, Camera Obscura carries both contemporary and vintage images. ⊠*1309 Bannock St., Capitol Hill* ☎*303/623–4059.*

David Cook–Fine American Art. David Cook specializes in historic Native American art and regional paintings, particularly Santa Fe modernists. ⊠*1637 Wazee St., LoDo* ☎*303/623–8181.*

Mudhead Gallery. This gallery sells museum-quality Southwestern art, with an especially fine selection of Santa Clara and San Ildefonso pottery, and Hopi kachinas. ⊠*555 17th St., across from the Hyatt,*

LoDo ☎*303/293–0007* ✉*321 17th St., in Brown Palace, LoDo* ☎*303/293–9977.*

Native American Trading Company. The collection of weavings, pottery, jewelry, and regional paintings is outstanding. ✉*213 W. 13th Ave., Golden Triangle* ☎*303/534–0771.*

Old Santa Fe Pottery. The 20 rooms are crammed with Mexican masks, pottery, rustic Mexican furniture—and there's even a chip dip and salsa room. ✉*2485 S. Santa Fe Dr., Overland* ☎*303/871–9434.*

Pismo. Cherry Creek has its share of chic galleries, including Pismo, which showcases exquisite handblown-glass art. ✉*235 Fillmore St., Cherry Creek* ☎*303/333–2879.*

SPORTING GOODS

★ **REI.** Denver's REI flagship store, one of three such shops in the country, is yet another testament to the city's adventurous spirit. The store's 94,000 square feet are packed with all stripes of outdoors gear and some special extras: a climbing wall, a mountain-bike track, a white water chute, and a "cold room" for gauging the protection provided by coats and sleeping bags. There's also a Starbucks inside. Behind the store is the Platte River Greenway, a park path and water area that's accessible to dogs, kids, and kayakers. ✉*1416 Platte St., Jefferson Park* ☎*303/756–3100.*

Sports Authority. At this huge, multistory shrine to Colorado's love of the outdoors, entire floors are given over to a single sport. There are other branches throughout Denver. ✉*1000 Broadway, Civic Center* ☎*303/861–1122.*

WESTERN PARAPHERNALIA

Cry Baby Ranch. This rambunctious assortment of 1940s and '50s cowboy kitsch is at Larimer Square. ✉*1422 Larimer St., LoDo* ☎*303/623–3979.*

DENVER ESSENTIALS

TRANSPORTATION

BY AIR

Denver International Airport (DEN) is 15 mi northeast of downtown. It's served by most major domestic carriers and many international ones. Arrive at the airport with plenty of time before your flight, preferably two hours; the airport's check-in and security-check lines are particularly long.

Information Denver International Airport (DEN) (☎*800/247–2336* ⊕*www.flydenver.com*).

TRANSFERS Between the airport and downtown, Super Shuttle makes door-to-door trips. The region's public bus service, Regional Transportation District (RTD), runs SkyRide to and from the airport; the trip takes 50 minutes, and the fare is $8–$10 each way. There's a transportation center in the airport just outside baggage claim. A taxi ride to downtown costs $55–$60.

Contact Regional Transportation District/SkyRide (☎ *303/299–6000 for route and schedule information* ⊕ *www.rtd-denver.com*).**Super Shuttle** (☎ *303/370–1300*).

TO AND FROM DENVER **BY BUS**
Contact Greyhound Lines (✉ *1055 19th St., LoDo* ☎ *800/231–2222* ⊕ *www. greyhound.com*).

WITHIN DENVER In downtown Denver, free shuttle-bus service operates about every 10 minutes until 1 AM, running the length of the 16th Street Mall (which bisects downtown) and stopping at two-block intervals. If you plan to spend much time outside downtown, a car is advised, although Denver has one of the best city bus systems in the country and taxis are available.

The region's public bus service, RTD, is comprehensive, with routes throughout the metropolitan area. The service also links Denver to outlying towns such as Boulder, Longmont, and Nederland. You can buy bus tokens at grocery stores or pay with exact change on the bus. Fares vary according to time and zone. Within the city limits, buses cost $1.75.

Contact RTD (☎ *303/299–6000 or 800/366–7433* ⊕ *www.rtd-denver.com*).

BY CAR
Rental-car companies include Advantage, Alamo, Avis, Budget, Dollar, Enterprise, Hertz, and National. All have airport and downtown representatives.

Reaching Denver by car is fairly easy, except during rush hour when the interstates (and downtown) get congested. Interstate highways 70 and 25 intersect near downtown; an entrance to I–70 is just outside the airport.

When you're looking for an address within Denver, make sure you know whether it's a street or avenue. Speer Boulevard runs alongside Cherry Creek from northwest to southeast through downtown; numbered streets run parallel to Speer and most are one-way. Colfax Avenue (U.S. 287) runs east–west through downtown; numbered avenues run parallel to Colfax. Broadway runs north–south. Other main thoroughfares include Colorado Boulevard (north–south) and Alameda Avenue (east–west). Try to avoid driving in the area during rush hour, when traffic gets heavy. Interstates 25 and 225 are particularly slow going given the long-term Transportation Expansion Project (T-REX), which will eventually add a light-rail system along the highways, plus bicycle lanes and other improvements.

PARKING Finding an open meter has become increasingly difficult in downtown Denver, especially during peak times such as Rockies games and weekend nights. Additionally, most meters have two-hour limits until 10 PM, and at 25¢ for 10 minutes in some downtown areas, parking in Denver is currently more expensive than in New York or Chicago. However, there's no shortage of pay lots ($5 to $25 per day).

BY TAXI

Cabs are available by phone and at the airport and can generally be hailed outside major hotels for $1.60 minimum, $2 per mile. However, at peak times—during major events and at 2 AM when the bars close—taxis are very hard to come by.

Contacts **Freedom Cab** (☎ *303/292-8900*). **Metro Taxi** (☎ *303/333-3333*). **Yellow Cab** (☎ *303/777-7777*).

BY TRAIN

Union Station, a comfortable old building in the heart of downtown, filled with vending machines and video games, has Amtrak service.

RTD's Light Rail service's original 5.3-mi track links southwest and northeast Denver to downtown. RTD extended the tracks down to the city's southern suburbs; the peak fare is $1.25 within the city limits.

Contacts **Amtrak** (☎ *800/872-7245* ⊕ *www.amtrak.com*). **RTD Light Rail** (☎ *303/299-6000* ⊕ *www.rtd-denver.com*). **Union Station** (✉ *17th Ave. at Wynkoop St., LoDo* ☎ *303/534-2812*).

CONTACTS & RESOURCES

EMERGENCIES

Concentra Medical Center is a full medical clinic. HealthOne and Health Advisors have a free referral service. Rose Medical Center refers patients to doctors from 8 to 5:30 and is open 24 hours for emergencies. Exempla St. Joseph Hospital is open 24 hours. Walgreens and King Soopers pharmacies are both open around the clock.

Ambulance or Police (☎ *911*).

Dentists **American Dental Referral** (☎ *888/657-6453*). **Dental Referral Service** (☎ *800/428-8773*).

Hospitals **Concentra Medical Center** (✉ *1860 Larimer St., Suite 100, LoDo* ☎ *303/296-2273*). **Exempla St. Joseph Hospital** (✉ *1835 Franklin St., Capitol Hill* ☎ *303/837-7111*). **Health Advisors** (☎ *303/777-6877*). **HealthOne** (☎ *877/432-5846*). **Rose Medical Center** (✉ *4567 E. 9th Ave., Hale* ☎ *303/320-2121*).

24-Hour Pharmacies **King Soopers** (✉ *3100 S. Sheridan Blvd., Bear Valley* ☎ *303/937-4404*). **Walgreens** (✉ *2000 E. Colfax Ave., City Park* ☎ *303/331-0917*).

MEDIA

NEWSPAPERS & MAGAZINES The *Denver Post* and the *Rocky Mountain News,* now under a joint operating agreement, are Denver's two daily newspapers. *Westword* is an alternative, liberal-leaning weekly that's published every Thursday, focusing on local politics, media, and entertainment. *5280* is a light arts and entertainment magazine that's published nine times a year.

TOURS

BUS TOURS Actually Quite Nice Brew Tours' 23-seat Brewmobile hauls beer aficionados to the best microbreweries in Metro Denver, which it touts as the
"Napa Valley of Brewing."

Gray Line offers the usual expansive and exhaustive coach tours of
anything and everything, from shopping in Cherry Creek to visiting
Rocky Mountain National Park. Fees range from $35 to $95.

Contacts **Actually Quite Nice Brew Tours** (☎ *303/431–1440*). **Gray Line**
(☎ *800/348–6877* ⊕ *grayline.com*).

WALKING Lower Downtown District, Inc., runs guided tours of historic Den-
TOURS ver. Self-guided walking-tour brochures are available from the Denver
Metro Convention and Visitors Bureau.

Contact **Lower Downtown District, Inc.** (☎ *303/628–5428*).

VISITOR INFORMATION

The Denver Metro Convention and Visitors Bureau, open weekdays
9–5 and Saturday 9–2, is downtown above the Wolf Camera store on
California Street. They also offer free guided walking tours at 9:30 AM
on Thursday and Saturday June–August.

Contact **Denver Metro Convention and Visitors Bureau** (✉ *1600 California St.,
LoDo, 80202* ☎ *303/892–1112 or 800/393–8559* ⊕ *www.denver.org*).

The Rockies
Near Denver

2

WORD OF MOUTH

"[My favorite day trips include:]
—A day at Idaho Springs … and a drive back home up 'Oh My God' road, with a stop in Nederland for a wonderful Italian dinner.
—A day in Georgetown—walking, eating, browsing, maybe taking the [Georgetown Loop] narrow gauge railroad."

—seasweetie

"seasweetie… DON'T tell anyone about the 'Oh My God Road.' That is one of my favorite places when I am working in Denver and I love it because in all the times I have done the trip I have only seen 2 or 3 people total."

—TxTravelPro

Revised &
Updated by
Lois Friedland

IF YOU EVER WONDERED WHY folks living along the Front Range (as the area west of Denver and east of the Continental Divide is known) continually brag about their lifestyles, you need only look at the western horizon where the 14,000-foot snowcapped Rocky Mountains rise a 35-minute drive from downtown. For those drawn to the Front Range, a morning workout might mean an hour-long single-track mountain bike ride at Meyer Ranch Park, a half-hour kayak session in Golden's Clear Creek, or a 40-minute hike in Mount Falcon Park. The allure of this area, which rises from the dusty foothills cloaked in mountain mahogany and ponderosa pine to shaded spruce forests and summer snowfields, has brought increasing recreational pressures as mountain bikers, equestrians, hikers, dog lovers, hunters, and conservationists all vie for real estate that is increasingly gobbled up by McMansion sprawl. On the Front Range the days of the elitist "Native" bumper stickers are long since gone; almost everyone here is from somewhere else. Finding an outdoor paddling, climbing, or skiing partner is about as difficult as saying hello to the next person you meet on the trail.

EXPLORING THE ROCKIES NEAR DENVER

The Front Range Mountains are the easternmost mountains in Colorado and run more than 180 mi from the Wyoming border to Cañon City. The Continental Divide flows along much of the northern portion of this spine, which includes several "Fourteeners," 14,000-foot peaks, among them the famed Longs Peak (14,255 feet), fifth highest in the state. A boon for high-country lovers, the Front Range is easily accessed from the metro area via Interstate 70, Colorado's major east–west interstate, or Colorado Highway 285, the major route heading southwest into the mountains toward Fairplay in the now infamous South Park. On I–70, it's less than an hour's drive from downtown Denver to the St. Mary's Glacier trailhead, where you can take an exhilarating 20-minute hike to an alpine lake. I–70 stitches together Denver, Golden, Idaho Springs, and Georgetown before crossing the Continental Divide near Loveland Ski Resort.

The Gore Range, with steep, rugged peaks, intersects the Front Range just west of Loveland Pass and runs northwest toward Steamboat Springs before petering out into low rolling summits. Highway 40 climbs northwest from I–70, west of Idaho Springs, making a switchback ascent up Berthoud Pass before dropping into Winter Park and continuing on to Steamboat Springs.

Water is sparse in this arid land. Although the Front Range is a luminous green in May and early June, by midsummer, if rain is scarce, fire danger signs begin flashing. Currently, large swaths of mountainside throughout the Front Range and Summit County look brown because the lodgepole pines are dying from a pine beetle epidemic. What little water reaches the eastern slope comes from the South Platte River; the mighty Colorado gathers its waters on the western side of the Divide.

TOP REASONS TO GO

Exploring the Rockies: This section, called the Front Range by locals, butts up against the Denver metro area, so it's easy to explore interesting towns and enjoy the mountain lifestyle.

Coors Brewery: An entertaining tour ending in a sudsy stop at the Coors Tavern for an informal (and free) tasting of up to three brews. You'll see the steeping, roasting, and milling of the barley, then tour the Brew House where the "malt mash" is cooked in massive copper kettles.

Georgetown Loop Railroad: Peering out the window at the raw, steep mountainside and the rickety trestle

bridge on the vintage train ride from Georgetown to Silverplume provides an eye-opening lesson in the way miners traveled to work in the 1800s. Take a tour of the mine at the midway point of the route.

Winter Park: The variety of slopes offers something for everyone: a blocked-off area for beginners and chutes and inbounds off piste–style terrain for experts. The resort has an outstanding children's program

St. Mary's Glacier: It's a relatively easy hike up, albeit at a high altitude, to a spectacular, often year-round glacier.

ABOUT THE PARKS & RECREATION AREAS

Most recreational lands in the foothills west of Denver, including Mount Falcon, Meyer Ranch, and Elk Meadow parks, are protected by **Jefferson County Open Space Parks** (☎303/271–5925 ⊕*www. co.jefferson.co.us/openspace/index.htm*). These relatively small county parks are heavily used and have excellent hiking, mountain biking, and horse-riding trails. **Golden Gate Canyon State Park** (☎303/582–3707 ⊕*www.parks.state.co.us*), just west of Golden, has great hiking and wildlife viewing. For Class II to IV rafting and kayaking, try **Clear Creek** (☎800/353–9901 ⊕*www.clearcreekrafting.com*), which offers rafting on Clear Creek near Idaho Springs and on the Arkansas during the early spring snowmelt season and throughout the summer.

Much of the northern Front Range region is within **Arapaho-Roosevelt National Forest** (☎303/541–2500 ⊕*www.fs.fed.us*). The **Indian Peaks Wilderness Area** is northwest of Denver and encompasses a rugged area of permanent snowfields, alpine lakes, and 13,000-foot peaks. Although it is the most-often-visited-wilderness area in Colorado, it is a good choice for overnight trips. Some of the trailheads on the eastern side are about one hour from Boulder and almost two hours from Denver. Because 90% of the people enter from the east side of the forests, visitors entering from the west side will find more solitude. *For more information about the Indian Peaks, see the Boulder & North Central Colorado chapter in this book.*

ABOUT THE RESTAURANTS

Front Range dining draws primarily from the Denver metro area; you'll mostly find standard chains with the occasional Middle Eastern or Thai restaurant thrown in. With the region's large Hispanic population, a sure bet for tasty and fresh food is a cantina; you'll find one in almost every burg. The Front Range is best known for Coors beer (brewed in Golden). Tommyknockers in Idaho Springs has an odd but tasty special—maple beer.

ABOUT THE HOTELS

Unlike other areas in the Colorado Rockies, which cater to throngs of winter and summer visitors, the Front Range is largely a locals playground. The exception is Winter Park where more than half of the skiers and snowboarders come from out of state for multiday visits. In the summertime, out-of-state and regional visitors flock to Georgetown and Idaho Springs to explore the rustic ambience, tour a mine, and hike or mountain bike on trails that thread the mountainsides; or to Golden to tour the Coors Brewery. You won't find megaresorts or grand old lodges; but there are bed-and-breakfasts, condominiums, a few nice hotels in Golden, and some chain hotels.

WHAT IT COSTS					
	¢	$	$$	$$$	$$$$
RESTAURANTS	under $8	$8–$12	$13–$18	$19–$25	over $25
HOTELS	under $80	$80–$120	$121–$170	$171–$230	over $230

Restaurant prices are for a main course at dinner, excluding 7.1%–8.9% tax. Hotel prices are for two people in a standard double room in high season, excluding service charges and 8.9% tax.

TIMING

Summers are hot along the Front Range, especially in the lower foothills. It's a time of year when many hikers and bikers head for the higher peaks. Heavy traffic on I–70 has become a sad fact of life for those wanting to explore the Front Range and Colorado's High Country. Slowdowns correspond with normal morning and afternoon rush hours, but peak on Friday and Sunday afternoons when stop-and-go jams are the norm, particularly around Idaho Springs and Georgetown. Winter traffic fares little better with regular slowdowns in the morning rush to the Summit County ski resorts, and afternoon returns. Many locals claim the best seasons in Colorado are the spring and fall "mud seasons" when the tourists are gone and the trails are empty. In spring the Front Range is carpeted with fresh new growth, while late September brings the shimmering gold of turning aspens. The interstate is well maintained, but it can see snow any time of the year at the Eisenhower Tunnel. Drive defensively, especially downhill to Denver and Dillon where runaway truck ramps see a fair bit of use.

GOLDEN

15 mi west of Denver via I–70 or U.S. 6 (W. 6th Ave.).

Golden was once the territorial capital of Colorado. City residents have smarted ever since losing that distinction to Denver by "dubious" vote in 1867, but in 1994, then-Governor Roy Romer restored "cer-

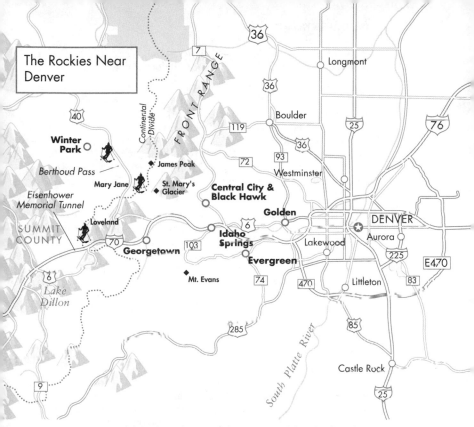

The Rockies Near Denver

emonial" territorial-capital status to Golden. Today the city is one of Colorado's fastest growing, boosted by the high-tech industry as well as longtime employers Coors Brewery and Colorado School of Mines.

Golden is a 25-minute drive from downtown Denver via Colorado Highway 6. You can explore downtown and the Coors Brewery in three hours or so.

COORS & DOWNTOWN GOLDEN

Thousands of beer lovers make the pilgrimage to the venerable **Coors Brewery** each year. One of the world's largest breweries, it was founded in 1873 by Adolph Coors, a 21-year-old German stowaway. The free tour lasts 45 minutes and explains the brewing process. Informal tastings are held at the end of the tour for those 21 and over, which can take another 45 minutes; souvenirs are available at the gift shop. ⊠ *13th and Ford Sts.* ☎ *303/277–2337* ⊕ *www.coors.com* ✉ *Free* ⊙ *Mon.– Sat. 10–4* ☞ *Children under 18 must be accompanied by adult.*

Golden's **12th Street,** a National Historic District, has a row of handsome 1860s brick buildings. In a restored late Victorian–era Western hotel and boardinghouse is the **Astor House Museum** (⊠ *11th and Arapahoe Sts.* ☎ *303/278–3557* ✉ *$3; $4.50 for museum and Clear Creek*

History Park ⊙ *Tues.–Sat. 10–4:30; June–Aug., also Sun. 11–3*), which explores the material culture and local life of the era.

Clear Creek History Park, in the National Historic District, interprets the Golden area circa 1843–1900 via restored structures and reproductions, including a tepee, prospector's camp, one-room schoolhouse, and cabins, and is populated with live chickens and bees. Guides in period clothing lead 45-minute tours. ✉*11th and Arapahoe Sts.* ☎*303/278– 3557* ✇*$3; $4.50 for park and Astor House* ⊙ *June–Aug., Tues.– Sat. 10–4:30, Sun. 11–3; May and Sept., Sat. 10–4:30; Oct.–Apr., by appointment only, 2 wks notice required for tours; Apr–mid-May, Sat. 10–4:30.*

★ The drive up **Lookout Mountain** to the **Buffalo Bill Museum and Grave** provides a sensational panoramic view of Denver that alone is worth the price of admission. It was this view that encouraged Bill Cody, Pony Express rider, cavalry scout, and tireless promoter of the West, to request Lookout Mountain as his burial site. Adjacent to the grave is a small museum with art and artifacts detailing Cody's life and times, as well as a souvenir shop. The grave is 100 yards past the gift shop on a paved walkway. ✛*Rte. 5 off I–70 Exit 256, or 19th Ave. out of Golden* ☎*303/526–0747* ⊕*www.buffalobill.org* ✇*$3* ⊙ *Museum, May–Oct., daily 9–5; Nov.–Apr., Tues.–Sun. 9–4; grave, daily until 6:30* PM.

ALSO WORTH SEEING
The **Colorado School of Mines,** the nation's largest and foremost school of mineral engineering, has a lovely campus containing an outstanding **geology museum** with minerals, gemstones, and fossils from around the world and a reproduction of a gold mine. Also on campus is the prominent **U.S.G.S. National Earthquake Information Center** (✉*1711 Illinois St.* ☎*303/273–8500* ⊙ *Tours, Tues.–Thurs. by appointment only, for 6th grade and above*), which is responsible for pinpointing seismic activity all over the country. Geology museum ✉*1310 Maple St.* ☎*303/273– 3815* ⊕*www.mines.edu* ✇*Free* ⊙ *Mon.–Sat. 9–4, Sun. 1–4; closed Sun. mid-May–late Aug.*

Just outside Golden is a must-visit for any choo-choo lover. More than ♻ 100 vintage locomotives and cars are displayed outside the **Colorado Railroad Museum.** Inside the replica-1880 masonry depot are historical photos and memorabilia of Puffing Billy (the nickname for steam trains), along with an astounding model train set that steams through a miniature-scale version of Golden. In the Roundhouse you can witness a train's restoration in progress. ✉*17155 W. 44th Ave.* ☎*303/279– 4591* ⊕*www.crrm.org* ✇*$7* ⊙ *Daily 9–5.*

♻ **Heritage Square,** a colorful re-creation of an 1880s frontier town, has an opera house, a narrow-gauge railway train ride, a Ferris wheel, a waterslide, a bungee-jumping tower, and specialty shops. A vaudeville-style review ends each evening's entertainment. ✛*Off the Golden I–70 exit on U.S. 40 north 1 mi* ☎*303/279–2789* ⊕*www.heritagesquare. info* ✉*Entrance to park is free; admission varies per ride* ⊙ *Shops: Memorial Day–Labor Day, Mon.–Sat. 10–8, Sun. noon–8; Labor Day–*

Memorial Day, Tues.–Fri. noon–5, weekends noon–6. Rides: June–Sept., daily, hrs vary.

SPORTS & THE OUTDOORS

HIKING **Turkey Trot Trail, in Mount Falcon Park,** is a great way to explore the true foothills of the Front Range, and the trail's comparatively low elevation makes it a good warm-up for higher ventures. Early in the morning mule deer can be seen grazing on the adjacent slopes. Take the Turkey Trot Trail from the east parking lot in the Morrison Town Park marked with a "hikers only" sign. The trail winds 1.7 mi up the east face of Mount Falcon through brushy slopes before curving behind the mountain up a forested draw to top out at around 7,000 feet. The trail loops back around and connects to the Castle Trail for a 1.3-mi easy return to the parking lot. Allow about 90 minutes. ⚠CAUTION: **Stay on the path to avoid critters, including rattlesnakes, that lie in the grass.** ⊠*Jefferson County Open Space, start at east parking lot* ⊕*www.co.jefferson.co.us/ext/dpt/comm_res/openspac/falcon.htm.*

KAYAKING **Kayaking on Clear Creek.** Locals love to kayak along Clear Creek as it runs through Golden; there's even a racecourse on the water.

GOLF **Fossil Trace Golf Club.** Created by James Engh, this spectacular 18-hole course is set into an old quarry. Along the way, players can stop to look at fossils of triceratops' footprints in an aeons-old rock wall. The course was ranked among the "Best Places to Play" by *Golf Digest* in 2006/2007. ⊠*3050 Illinois St.* ☎*303/277–8750* ⊕*www.fossiltrace.com* 🏌*Yards: 6,831; Green Fee: $41/$58 for 18 holes plus $17 per rider for cart with GPS.*

WHERE TO EAT

$–$$ ✕**Woody's Wood Fired Pizza.** Choose the $8.99 all-you-can-eat pizza, FodorsChoice soup, and salad bar. The choices on the pizza bar range from classic ★ to It's Greek to Me and Margherita, and the place is so popular that the choices are always just out of the oven. ⊠*1305 Washington Ave. 80401* ☎*303/277–0443* ▤*AE, D, MC, V* ☉*Closed Mon. No lunch.*

EVERGREEN

20 mi west of Golden via U.S. 6 east, C–470, I–70 west, and CO Hwy. 74 (Evergreen Pkwy.); 28 mi west of Denver.

Once a quiet mountain town 45 minutes from downtown Denver, today Evergreen is a tony community filled with upscale to extravagantly designed homes. The core of this mountain—where Colorzado Highway 74 and County Highway 73 meet—remains rustic in feel, however, and on warm-weather weekends is filled with tourists and Denverites escaping the city heat. Visitors browse the eclectic mix of shops and mingle with locals walking their dogs on the path, which circles Lake Evergreen. The annual multiday Evergreen Jazz Fest in July features musicians from around the country.

The **Hiwan Homestead Museum** is a restored 17-room log cabin built between 1880 and 1942 that shows a popular and relaxed mountain summertime lifestyle. The museum, which includes three other buildings, has an exceptional collection of Southwestern Indian artifacts. ✉4208 S. Timbervale Dr. ☎303/674–6262 ⊕www.co.jefferson.co.us/openspace/openspace_T56_R10.htm 🎟Free.

WHERE TO STAY

$–$$
Fodor'sChoice
★

🛏**Highland Haven Creekside Inn.** Walking distance from downtown Evergreen, the inn has a combination of luxurious rooms, suites, and cottages ($$$$) set alongside Bear Creek, where guests can go trout fishing. Look for amenities such as flat-screen TVs, gourmet breakfasts, fireplaces, and Jacuzzis in the luxury rooms and cabins which offer a lot of privacy. Denverites have rated Highland Haven as "the top place to pop the question" and "the top mountain secret" in different issues of *5280,* the main Denver magazine. **Pros:** ideally located for travelers who want to stay in a mountain town, but be 35 minutes from downtown Denver or Georgetown; quiet; you might even see a celebrity or two. **Con:** you'll have to stroll into Evergreen or drive for dinner. ✉4395 Independence Trail 80439 ☎303/674–3577 or 800/459–2406 ⊕www.highlandhaven.com ⊲4 rooms, 4 junior suites, 3 large suites, 6 cottages ♿In-room: kitchen (some), DVD, VCR, Wi-Fi. In-hotel: no elevator, some pets allowed, no-smoking rooms ☰AE, D, DC, MC, V ⦿BP.

SHOPPING

Evergreen Art Gallery (✉28195 Hwy. 74 ☎303/674–4871), owned by local artist Meryl Sabeff, has an excellent collection of both decorative and useful ceramics, art glass, photographs, and other fine craft work.

CENTRAL CITY & BLACK HAWK

18 mi west of Golden via U.S. 6 and Rte. 119; 38 mi west of Denver.

When limited-stakes gambling was introduced in 1991 to the beautifully preserved old mining towns of Central City and Black Hawk, howls of protest were drowned out by cheers from struggling townspeople. Strict zoning laws were legislated to protect the towns' architectural integrity, and by and large the laws have successfully handled the steady stream of tour buses. Because buses and cars reached Black Hawk first, while driving up Colorado Highway 119, and the traffic crawled in the narrow road connecting the two towns, Black Hawk thrived while the casinos in Central City languished. In response, wide Central City Parkway was built from I–70 directly to Central City, and it's a much easier route to drive.

Both towns are about a 45-minute drive from Denver. Bus transportation is also available from Denver and Golden through most of the casinos and the Opera House. You can cover Central City and Black Hawk's main attractions in a few hours on foot. If you're the gaming type, set aside extra time to try your luck. Although the casinos are open year-round, the museums are open only in summer.

CASINOS

There are nearly 40 casinos in Black Hawk and Central City. Many of the casinos in Central City are in buildings dating from the 1860s—from jails to mansions—and their plush interiors have been lavishly decorated to re-create the Old West era—a period when this town was known as the "Richest Square Mile on Earth." Virtually every casino has a restaurant with the usual all-you-can-eat buffets. The biggest casinos are in newer buildings in Black Hawk. Hotel deals are prevalent, but this is no Las Vegas.

Gaming here is restricted to blackjack, poker, and slots, and the maximum bet is $5. The casinos all close at 2 AM. One of Colorado's largest casinos is the **Isle of Capri Casino and Hotel** (⊠ *401 Main St., Black Hawk* ☎ *303/998–7777* ⊕ *www.isleofcapricasino.com*). **Doc Holliday Casino** (⊠ *131 Main St., Central City* ☎ *303/582–1400*) is also worth checking out.

ALSO WORTH SEEING

★ Opera has been staged at the **Central City Opera House**, the nation's fifth-oldest opera, almost every year since opening night in 1878. Lillian Gish has acted, Beverly Sills has sung, and many other greats have performed in the Opera House. Performances are held in summer only. ⊠ *124 Eureka St., Central City* ☎ *303/292–6700, 800/851–8175 Denver box office* ⊕ *www.centralcityopera.org* ☉ *Late June–early Aug.*

Teller House was once one of the West's ritziest hotels. Built in 1872, the first $30,000 for this hotel and its name came from Senator Henry Teller, the first U.S. Secretary of the Interior from Colorado. Adorning the floor of the famous Face Bar within the house is a portrait of a woman. Despite rumors about her identity, she is none other than the wife of the painter, Herndon Davis. He painted the portrait in 1936. Teller House serves box lunches during the six-week summer opera season. Tours are available. ⊠ *120 Eureka St., Central City* ☎ *303/582–5283* ⊟ *AE, D, MC, V* ☉ *Memorial Day–Labor Day 11–4.*

The **Thomas House Museum**, built in 1874, is an example of Victorian mountain elegance. It depicts the life of a middle-class turn-of-the-20th-century family through family photos and heirlooms such as period quilts and feather hats. ⊠ *209 Eureka St., Central City* ☎ *303/582–5283* ⊕ *www.gilpinhistory.org* ⊠ *$5* ☉ *By appointment only.*

At the **Gilpin History Museum**, photos and reproductions, as well as vintage pieces from different periods of Gilpin County history, paint a richly detailed portrait of life in a typical rowdy mining community. ⊠ *228 High St., Central City* ☎ *303/582–5283* ⊕ *www.gilpinhistory. org* ⊠ *$5; $8 includes admission to Thomas House Museum* ☉ *Late May–early Sept., daily 11–4; Mid Sept.–late May, by appointment only.*

Apart from the casinos, **Mountain City Historic Park** is the prime attraction in Black Hawk, consisting of a dozen homes and commercial structures from the town's heyday. It's an interesting stroll that takes you past

intermingling Victorian and Gothic architectural styles. ⊠*Gregory St.,*
Black Hawk.

WHERE TO STAY & EAT

$$–$$$ ✕**White Buffalo Grille.** The focus here is on steaks, seafood such as
honey-glazed salmon, and Colorado rack of lamb. The atmosphere is
upscale and the views from the all-glass enclosure on a bridge above
Richmond Street are divine. ⊠*Lodge Casino, 240 Main St., Black
Hawk 80422* ☎*303/582–6375* ▤*AE, D, DC, MC, V* ⊘*Closed Mon.
No lunch.*

$$ ⛺**Chase Creek B&B.** This historic house was nearly a casualty of Black
Hawk Casino by Hyatt construction, before owners Hal and Karen Mid-
cap had it moved to the banks of namesake Chase Creek. The Yankee
and Sleepy Hollow rooms are done up in contemporary Victorian style
with lace curtains and pastel walls, while the attic Polar Star room has
Mission-style furniture. There's also a gas fireplace and access to a pri-
vate hot tub on the first floor. **Pro:** get a real feel for life in miners' times.
Con: almost all of the nearby restaurants are in big casinos. ⊠*250 Chase
St., Black Hawk 80422* ☎*303/582–3550* ⊕*www.chasecreekinn.com*
🛏*3 rooms* ♿*In-room: no a/c. In-hotel: no elevator, no kids under 21,
no-smoking rooms* ▤*MC, V, D* ❑*BP.*

IDAHO SPRINGS

*11 mi south of Central City via Central City Pkwy. and I–70; 33 mi
west of Denver via I–70.*

Colorado prospectors struck their first major vein of gold here on Janu-
ary 7, 1859. That year local mines dispatched half of all the gold used
by the U.S. Mint—ore worth a whopping $2 million. Today the quaint
town recalls its mining days, especially along downtown's **Miner Street,**
where pastel Victorians will transport you back to a century giddy with
all that glitters.

During gold-rush days, the **Argo Gold Mill** processed more than $100
million worth of the precious metal. To transport the ore from mines in
Central City, workers dug through solid rock to construct a tunnel to
Central City, 4.5 miles away. When completed in 1910 the Argo Tunnel
was the longest in the world. During a tour of the mine and mill, guides
explain how this monumental engineering feat was accomplished.
Admission includes the small museum and a gold-panning lesson. This
tour focuses more on the processing of gold than visiting a gold mine.
⊠*2350 Riverside Dr.* ☎*303/567–2421* ⊕*www.historicargotours.com*
🎟*$15* ⊘*Mid-Apr.–mid-Oct., daily 9–6, weather permitting.*

Just outside town is the **Phoenix Gold Mine,** still operating today. A sea-
soned miner leads tours underground, where you can wield 19th-cen-
tury excavating tools or pan for gold. Whatever riches you find are
yours to keep. ⊠*Off Trail Creek Rd.* ☎*303/567–0422* 🎟*$10; $5 for
gold panning only* ⊘*Daily 10–6, weather permitting.*

Idaho Springs presently prospers from the hot springs at **Indian Springs Resort.** Around the springs, known to the Ute natives as the "healing waters of the Great Spirit," are geothermal caves that were used by tribes as a neutral meeting site. The hot springs, a translucent dome-covered mineral-water swimming pool, mud baths, and geothermal caves are the primary draws for the resort. You don't need to be an overnight guest to soak in the mineral-rich waters; day rates start at $18 for the geothermal cave baths (depending on type of bath and day of week) and $14 for the pool. ⊠*302 Soda Creek Rd.* ☏*303/989–6666* ⊕*www.indianspringsresort.com* ⊡*Varies according to whether one uses the bath, pool,* ☉ *Daily 7:30* AM*–10:30* PM.

Within sight of Indian Springs Resort is a 600-foot waterfall, Bridal Veil Falls. The imposing **Charlie Tayler Water Wheel**—the largest in the state—was constructed in the 1890s by a miner who attributed his strong constitution to the fact that he never shaved, took baths, or kissed women. ⌖*South of Idaho Springs on I–70.*

Fodor'sChoice **St. Mary's Glacier** is a vision of alpine splendor. From the exit, it's a beau-
★ tiful 10-mi drive up to a forested hanging valley to the glacier trailhead. The glacier, technically a large snowfield compacted in a mountain saddle at the timberline, is thought to be the southernmost glacier in the United States. During drought years it all but vanishes; a wet win-ter creates a wonderful Ice Age playground throughout the following summer. Most visitors are content to make the steep 0.75-mi hike on a rock-strewn path up to the base of the glacier to admire the snowfield and sparkling sapphire lake. The intrepid hiker can climb up the rocky right-hand side of the snowfield to a plateau less than a mile above for sweeping views of the Continental Divide. Because of its proximity to Denver, St. Mary's Glacier is a popular weekend getaway for summer hikers, snowboarders, and skiers. There are no facilities or parking, except for a rough pull-out area near the base of the trail, and you risk a ticket if you park on private property. Don't look for a St. Mary's Gla-cier sign on I–70; it has been replaced with the Fall River Road/Alice sign. ⌖*I–70 Exit 238, west of Idaho Springs.*

Fodor'sChoice The incomparable **Mount Evans Scenic and Historic Byway**—the highest
★ paved road in the United States—leads to the summit of 14,264-foot-high Mount Evans. This is one of only two Fourteeners in the United States that you can drive up (the other is her southern sister, Pikes Peak). The pass winds past placid lakes and through stands of tower-ing Douglas firs and bristlecone pines. This is one of the best places in the state to catch a glimpse of shaggy white mountain goats and regal bighorn sheep. Small herds of the nimble creatures stroll from car to car looking for handouts. Feeding them is prohibited, however. Keep your eyes peeled for other animals, including deer, elk, and feather-footed ptarmigans. From Idaho Springs, State Road 103 leads south 15 mi to the entrance to the road. ⊠*State Rd. 3* ☏*303/567–3000* ⊕*www.mountevans.com* ⊡*$10* ☉*The road is only open when road condi-tions are safe. Generally, the last 5 mi to summit, Memorial Day–Labor Day.*

★   Although most travelers heading to Central City take the new highway from I–70, adventurous souls can take the **Oh-My-Gawd Road.** Built in the 1870s to transfer ore, this challenging drive climbs nearly 2,000 feet above Idaho Springs to Central City. After traveling along a series of hairpin curves you arrive at the summit, where you are treated to sweeping views of Mount Evans. The dusty road is often busy with mining traffic, so keep your windows up and your eyes open. From Idaho Springs (Exit 240), drive west through town on Colorado Boulevard. Turn right on 23rd Avenue, left on Virginia Street, and right at Virginia Canyon Road (279). ⊠*Hwy. 279.*

WHERE TO STAY & EAT

$–$$ ✗**Beau Jo's Pizza.** This always-hopping pizzeria is the area's original après-ski destination. Be prepared for a wait on winter weekends because Denverites often stop in Idaho Springs for dinner until the traffic thins down. Topping choices for the famous olive oil–and-honey pizza crust range from traditional to exotic. ⊠*1517 Miner St., 80452* ☎*303/567–4376* ▭*AE, D, MC, V.*

$–$$ ✗**Buffalo Bar & Restaurant.** No surprise as to the specialties here: burgers, fajitas, chili, and steak sandwiches, all made with heart-healthy bison meat. A Western theme dominates the dining room, where the walls are jam-packed with frontier memorabilia. The ornate bar dates from 1886. ⊠*1617 Miner St., 80452* ☎*303/567–2729* ▭*AE, D, DC, MC, V.*

$–$$ ✗**Tommyknocker Brewery & Pub.** Harking back to gold-rush days, this casual bar and restaurant is usually filled with skiers in winter and travelers or Denverites year-round who want to meet High Country friends halfway. The suds have a distinctly local flavor and sporty names like Glacier Ale and Pick Axe Pale Ale. In addition to fare such as buffalo burritos, the brewery has plenty of vegetarian options. ⊠*1401 Miner St., 80452* ☎*303/567–2688* ▭*AE, D, MC, V.*

$$$ ✗▥**Peck House.** A 10-minute drive from either Georgetown or Idaho Springs via I–70, this red-roof inn is Colorado's oldest continually operating hostelry. The dining room ($$$–$$$$) is crammed with period antiques, including tinted lithographs and etched-glass shades for the gas lamps that once hung in the state capitol. Game is the house specialty: expertly prepared quail and venison (perfect with the hearty cabernet sauce) are among the standouts. The charming rooms are awash in Victorian splendor. **Pro:** a quaint, old lodging experience. **Con:** you'll have to drive to see the sights—the inn is on U.S. 40, 2 mi north of I–70. ⌂*Box 428, Empire 80438* ☎*303/569–9870* ⊕*www.thepeckhouse.com* ⤴*11 rooms, 10 with bath* ⚲*In-room: no a/c, no phone, no TV. In-hotel: restaurant, no elevator, no-smoking rooms* ▭*AE, D, DC, MC, V* ⏅*CP.*

SHOPPING

Ramblin' Rose Ranch (⊠*1430 Miner St.* ☎*303/567–1582*) sells all things Western from attractive clothing to housewares.

WINTER PARK

36 mi west of Idaho Springs; 67 mi west of Denver via I–70 and U.S. 40.

WORD OF MOUTH

"We went to Winter Park last weekend. The weather was great and we saw little kids and college kids alike skiing bare chested as well as men skiing in kilts and clover-decorated boxers on St. Paddy's Day. I forgot how big that mountain is. And getting better all the time with the addition of new lifts."   —amwosu

Denverites have come to think of Winter Park as their own personal ski area—and understandably so, as it's owned by the City of Denver and is only a 1½-hour drive from downtown Denver. But, the reality is that about 60% of the visitors come from out of state. Once the most affordable "large" ski area in Colorado, today's lift-pass pricing is similar to those of other resorts with slopes of similar size. Winter Park is equally popular in summer with hikers, bicyclists, and golfers, but has few tourist attractions besides its natural beauty. Change is rampant, though, as development of Winter Park continues. Anchored by the existing Zephyr Mountain Lodge and Fraser Crossing and Founders Pointe condominiums, a large slope-side village of condos, restaurants, bars, and shops is on the horizon.

DOWNHILL SKIING & SNOWBOARDING

★ **Winter Park** is really two interconnected ski areas: Winter Park and Mary Jane, both open to skiers and snowboarders. Between the two peaks there are four distinct skiable sections: Winter Park; the "Jane"; Vasquez Ridge, which is primarily intermediate cruising; and Vasquez Cirque, which has seriously steep inbounds off-piste terrain.

Mary Jane is famous for her bumps and chutes, while Winter Park's runs promise lots of learning terrain for beginners and easy cruising for intermediates. Pick a meeting place for lunch in case you and your friends get separated.

The skiing on the Winter Park and Vasquez Ridge trails is generally family friendly and there are segregated areas for beginners. On busy weekends Vasquez Ridge is a good place for escaping crowds, partly because this area is a bit more difficult to find, but the runouts can be long.

Mary Jane delivers 2,610 vertical feet of unrelenting moguls on a variety of trails, although there are a couple of groomed intermediate runs. Experts gravitate toward the far end of the Jane to runs like Trestle and DeRailer, or to Hole-in-the-Wall, Awe, and other chutes. Expert skiers and riders seeking inbound off piste–style terrain hike over the Vasquez Cirque.

The resort has also recently developed the Eagle Wind terrain, which has advanced steeps and deeps. The panoramic Express behind Mary Jane provides access to above-the-tree-line skiing at Parsenn Bowl. The pitch is moderate, making the bowl a terrific place for intermediate skiers to try powder and crud-snow skiing.

The resort's Rail Yard, with its superpipe and two terrain parks, is specially designed for freestylers. The Rail Yard, a 4,200-foot 15-acre park, is one of Colorado's largest and has a number of progressive rails designed by Planet Snowtools and the local Bent Metal Crew. For the amusement and enjoyment of shredders and skiers, the resort created replicas of famous Colorado street rails, including ones from Coors Field, Mile High Stadium, Red Rocks, and the state capital. ☎*800/729–5813 or 970/726–5587* ⊕*www.skiwinterpark.com.*

FACILITIES   3,060-foot vertical drop; 2,886 skiable acres; 145 trails; 8% beginner, 17% intermediate, 19% advanced, 56% expert; 25 lifts; 6 six-person chairs, 7 high-speed quad chairs, 4 triple chairs, 6 double chairs, 5 surface lifts.

LESSONS   For adult skiers and snowboarders, the **Winter Park Ski and Snowboard**
& PROGRAMS   **School** (⊠*Balcony House* ☎*800/729–7907*) has half-day lessons starting at $49. Daylong children's programs, which include lunch, start at $105. Winter Park is home to the **National Sports Center for the Disabled** (⊡*Box 1290, Winter Park 80482* ☎*303/726–1540*), one of the country's best program for skiers with disabilities.

LIFT TICKETS   The walk-up rate is $86, but you can save 25% on multiday tickets.

RENTALS   **Slopeside Mountain Adventure Center** (⊠*Zephyr Mountain Lodge* ☎*970/726–1664*) rents skiing and snowboarding gear. Winter Park Resort has rental packages starting at $35 at **West Portal Boots and Boards** (⊠*West Portal Station* ☎*970/726–1665*). Rental equipment is also available from shops downtown.

NORDIC SKIING

TRACK SKIING   About 7 mi northwest of Winter Park, **Devil's Thumb Ranch** grooms about 80 mi of cross-country trails. Some skiing is along fairly level tree-lined trails; some is with more ups and downs and wide-open views. The ranch has rentals, lessons, and backcountry tours. ⊠*3530 County Rd. 83, Tabernash* ☎*970/726–5632 or 800/933–4339* ⊕*www.devilsthumbranch.com* ⊠*Trail fee $15.*

Snow Mountain Ranch, 12 mi northwest of Winter Park, has a 62-mile track system that includes almost 3 mi of trails lighted for night skiing. The ranch is a YMCA facility (with discounts for members) and has added bonuses such as a sauna and an indoor pool. Lessons, rentals, and on-site lodging are available. ⊠*1101 County Rd. 53, Granby* ☎*970/887–2152 or 800/777–9622* ⊕*www.ymcarockies.org* ⊠*Trail fee $15.*

BACKCOUNTRY   South of Winter Park, **Berthoud Pass** (⊠*Hwy. 40* ⊕*www.berthoud-*
SKIING   *pass.com*) is a hard place to define. A former downhill skiing area—its lifts have been removed—it's now one of the Front Range's premier backcountry skiing areas. There's no regular avalanche control here, so skiers and snowboarders venturing in must have their own rescue equipment including beacons, shovels, and probes. Berthoud is well worth a visit but only for very experienced, well-conditioned skiers and riders. You must check avalanche conditions before starting out.

OTHER SPORTS & THE OUTDOORS

GOLF **Pole Creek Golf Club.** Designed by Denis Griffiths, Pole Creek has three 9-hole par-36 courses and fantastic views of the mountains. You can play any combination of 18 holes, but try and get on the Ridge 9, which has particularly challenging holes with slippery greens. One year, the readers of *Colorado Avid Golfer* magazine voted Pole Creek the state's second-best public mountain course. ⊠*5827 County Rd. 51* ☎*970/887–9195* ⊕*www.polecreekgolf.com* ⬥.*Meadow: Yards: 3,497/2,476. Ranch: Yards: 3,609/2,532. Ridge: Yards: 3,603/2,526. Green Fee: $59/$82 for 18 holes.*

Headwaters is an 18-hole course laid out through a natural landscape and passes very few buildings. The original course by Micheal Asmundson is being redesigned by the Nicklaus Design firm to turn it into a more-walkable course. The back nine is fraught with interesting challenges and fast greens. ⊠*1000 Village Rd, Granby* ☎*888/850–4615* ⊕*www.granbyranch.com/golf* ⬥.*7,210 from the golds. Green Fee: $80 peak/$60 nonpeak for 18 holes and cart with GPS.*

HIKING If you aren't used to it, high altitude can catch you off guard. Take plenty of water with you and slather on the sunscreen. In summer, an early morning start is best. Afternoon thunderstorms are frequent and you should never be above the tree line during a storm with lightning.

At 12,804 feet, **Byers Peak** is one of the tallest mountains overlooking Fraser and the highest point in the Byers Peak Wilderness Area. The trail climbs the northern ridge of Byers through lodgepole pine and Engelmann spruce forests before entering the spaciousness of the alpine tundra at around 11,200 feet. Climbers are rewarded with views of the Indian Peaks Wilderness, the Gore Range, and Middle Park. The trail is an easy 1.5 mi, but it climbs 2,400 feet so it can pose a problem for hikers who are not used to high altitudes. Plan on three hours for the round-trip hike. ⊠*Sulphur Ranger District, Arapaho-Roosevelt National Forest* ☎*970/887–4100* ⊕*www.fs.fed.us/r2/arnf.*

HORSEBACK RIDING For leisurely horseback riding tours of the Fraser Valley, your best bet is **Cabin Creek Stables at Devil's Thumb Ranch** (⊠*3530 County Rd. 83, Tabernash* ☎*800/933–4339).*

MOUNTAIN BIKING Winter Park is one of the leading mountain-biking destinations in the Rockies, with some 50 mi of trails crisscrossing the main part of the resort and 600 more mi off the beaten path.

★ **Vazquez Creek** (⚐*Trailhead: parking garage next to the visitor center at the junction of U.S. 40 and Vazquez Rd.*) is an easy but fun 4.5-mi trail that runs along a forest of blue spruce, fir, and aspen. The trail sticks to dirt roads with easy grades; the elevation gain is barely 600 feet. For more-serious bikers, the side trails have challenging climbs and rewarding vistas.

SNOW-MOBILING Rentals and guided tours are available from **Trailblazer Snowmobile Tours** (⊠*County Rd. 50 S* ☎*970/726–8452 or 800/669–0134).* Rates range from $55 per hour to $200 for a full-day tour.

SNOW TUBING   Two lifts, groomed trails, and a warming hut at **Fraser Snow Tubing Hill** (⊠*County Rd. 72 and Fraser Valley Pkwy.* ☎*970/726–5954*) make your tubing most enjoyable. And the hill is lighted at night, no less. The rate is $17 per hour.

WHERE TO STAY & EAT

★ $$$$ ✕**Dining Room at Sunspot.** Reached via gondola, this log-and-stone structure is a real stunner. Douglas fir beams and Southwestern rugs on the walls add to the rustic charm. The real draw is the view, but be sure to arrive early enough to catch a glimpse of it. The five-course prix-fixe menu includes game and fish paired with side dishes such as wild rice and potatoes roasted in olive oil and herbs. ⊠*Top of Zephyr Express Lift* ☎*970/726–1446* ⌕*Reservations essential* ⊟*AE, D, DC, MC, V* ⊗*Hrs vary with the season.*

$$ ✕**Carver's.** Long a local and Denverite favorite for breakfast, the Belgian waffles are delicious as are the variety of Benedicts and scrambles with fresh orange or grapefruit juice. Lunch and dinner are also served in this casual joint with a bar. ⊠*93 Cooper Creek Way, behind Cooper Creek Sq.* ☎*970/726–8202* ⊟*AE, D, MC, V.*

$$ ✕**Deno's Mountain Bistro.** A sizable selection of beers from around the world helps make this casual establishment the liveliest spot in town. But what sets it apart is a wine list that's comprehensive and fairly priced—a rarity in low-key Winter Park. The cellar full of fine vintages is a labor of love for Deno and his son, the powerhouse duo behind the restaurant. The menu ranges from sesame-crusted seared ahi tuna to the best burgers in town, all expertly prepared and served by friendly staffers who know their stuff. ⊠*78911 U.S. 40* ☎*970/726–5332* ⊟*AE, D, MC, V.*

$$–$$$ ✕⊡ **Gasthaus Eichler.** Antler chandeliers cast a cheery glow as Strauss waltzes lilt softly in the background at this quaint little guesthouse. Here you'll find two of Winter Park's most romantic dining spots ($$–$$$): Fondue Stube, where dinner and dessert fondues bubble, and Dezeley's, where veal and other meats are grilled to perfection. **Pro:** the cozy guest rooms charm you with their lace curtains, wooden armoires, and beds piled high with down comforters. **Con:** you're right in the middle of town and on busy weekends the streets in front of the hotel can rock with action. ⊠*78786 U.S. 40, 80482* ☎*970/726–5133 or 800/543–3899* ⊕*www.gasthauseichler.com* ↩*15 rooms* ⌂*In-hotel: 2 restaurants, no elevator, no-smoking rooms* ⊟*AE, MC, V* ⊙|*BP, MAP.*

$$$$ ⊡ **Zephyr Mountain Lodge.** This ski-out lodging in Winter Park Village is a short walk from the express lift. The one-, two-, and three-bedroom units are compact but comfortable and nicely equipped. **Pros:** it's a nice place to stay in the wintertime, because it's so close to the lifts, and there are fireplaces in most units. **Con:** choose other lodging in the summertime because there is no air-conditioning and no circulation in the units. ⊠*201 Zephyr Way, 80482* ☎*866/433–3908* ⊕*www.zmlwp.com* ↩*175 rooms* ⌂*In-room: no a/c, kitchen, Wi-Fi. In-hotel: restaurant, gym, laundry facilities, no-smoking rooms* ⊟*AE, D, DC, MC, V.*

2

$$$–$$$$ 🖼**Iron Horse Resort.** On the banks of the Fraser River, this was the first ski-in ski-out facility in Winter Park. From the fifth floor you can ski about three blocks right into a Winter Park lift line. This condo complex is one of the most popular lodgings in the area. There are studios for couples, and the one- and two-bedroom apartments for families. Most apartments have full kitchens and balconies with views of a grove of aspen. **Pro:** truly ski-in ski-out. **Con:** isolated area, so you must drive to town for all the restaurants and shops. ⌂*101 Iron Horse Way, Box 1286, Winter Park 80482* ☎*970/726–8851 or 800/621–8190* 🖷*970/726–2321* ⊕*www.ironhorse-resort.com* 🛏*85 rooms* ⏦*In-room: kitchen, Wi-Fi. In-hotel: restaurant, bar, pool, gym, no-smoking rooms* ☰*AE, D, DC, MC, V.*

★ $$$–$$$$ 🖼**Wild Horse Inn.** Tucked into the woods on the way to Devil's Thumb Ranch, this rustic retreat is a bit off the beaten path. Your reward, however, is complete relaxation. The lodge rooms, many with beamed ceilings and four-poster beds, have private balconies overlooking the forest; breakfast—perhaps peach-and-pecan pancakes or an apple, bacon, and brie frittata—is served in the handsome lodge or in bed. The secluded cabins—stylish, not rustic—have a fireplace and small kitchenette. **Pro:** after an exhausting day of skiing you can book an hour with the on-site massage therapist. **Con:** it's a 10- to 15-minute drive to get into Winter Park. ✉*1536 County Rd. 83, 80482* ☎*970/726–0456* ⊕*www.wildhorseinncolorado.com* 🛏*7 rooms, 3 cabins* ⏦*In-room: no a/c, Wi-Fi. In-hotel: no elevator, no kids under 12, no-smoking rooms* ☰*AE, D, DC, MC, V* ⏹*BP.*

$$$ 🖼**Vintage Hotel.** This is the most pet-friendly place in town. Spacious, comfortable rooms look out onto the mountains. The hotel has nine room configurations, from standard rooms to lofted studios. **Pro:** pet-friendly property. **Con:** though very close to the slopes, you'll still need to take a shuttle. ✉*100 Winter Park Dr., 80482* ☎*970/726–8801 or 800/472–7017* ⊕*www.vintagehotel.com* 🛏*118 rooms* ⏦*In-room: kitchen (some), dial-up. In-hotel: no a/c, restaurant, bar, pool, gym, laundry facilities, concierge, some pets allowed, no-smoking rooms* ☰*AE, D, DC, MC, V.*

GUEST RANCH   🖼 **Devil's Thumb Ranch.** Many visitors initially come to this 5,000-acre
$$$$ ranch outside Winter Park for the unrivaled cross-country skiing, with
FodorsChoice   100 kmof groomed trails. But they wind up staying for the luxury and
★   privacy this resort affords. Spacious cabins set in a semiprivate wood are heated using eco-friendly geothermal springs, as is the pool. The on-site Ranch House restaurant ($$$) also uses sustainable and organic ingredients. Take in a yoga class at the recently renovated, full-service spa or horseback ride, fly fish, mountain bike, and hike in the surrounding area. Working with cattle is also an option. A newly constructed main lodge, opening in 2008, promises 52 hotel-style rooms. **Pros:** cabins are remarkably comfortable, the restaurant is top-notch, feels like a real getaway. **Cons:** in winter, getting there can be rough; one of the pricier properties in the state; must drive to eat in any other restaurant or cook your own meals. ✉*3530 County Rd. 83, Tabernash, 80478* ☎*800/933–4339* ⊕*www.devilsthumbranch.com* 🛏*16 cabins* ⏦*In-room: no a/c, kitchen, no TV. In-hotel: restaurant, bar, pool, spa,*

CLOSE UP

Eisenhower Memorial Tunnel

As you travel west along I–70 you'll reach one of the world's engineering marvels, the 8,941-foot-long Eisenhower Memorial Tunnel. Most people who drive through take its presence for granted, but until the first lanes were opened in 1973, the only route west through the mountains was the perilous Loveland Pass, a heart-pounding roller-coaster ride. Snow, mud, and a steep grade proved the downfall of many an intrepid motorist. In truly inclement weather the eastern and western slopes were completely cut off from each other. Authorities first proposed the tunnel in 1937. Geologists warned about unstable rock; through more than three decades of construction, their direst predictions came true as rock walls crumbled, steel girders buckled, and gas pockets caused mysterious explosions. When the project was finally completed, more than 500,000 cubic yards of solid granite had been removed from Mount Trelease. The original cost estimate was $1 million. By the time the second bore was completed in 1979, the tunnel's cost had skyrocketed to $340 million. Today, there can be a long wait during busy weekends because so many travelers use I–70.

public Internet, parking (no fee), some pets allowed, no-smoking rooms ⊟AE, D, DC, MC, V.

CONDOS

Fodor'sChoice

★

Destinations West is the premier source for luxury condos, townhomes, and multi-bedroom, million-dollar homes on the fairways at Pole Creek, at the base of Winter Park, and in Granby by the lake. Price-wise, if you're bringing a family or a group of friends it's worth comparing these luxury homes against regular condos. Concierge services are available. *⌂Box 3478, Winter Park 80482 ☎800/545–9378 🖷970/726–4534 ⊕www.toski.com/destinations.*

NIGHTLIFE

For a bit of local color, head down the road a few miles to Fraser and the **Crooked Creek Saloon** (⊠*401 Zerex St.* ☎*970/726–9250*). The motto here is "Eat till it hurts, drink till it feels better." Locals show up for the cheap beer during happy hour. The under-30 crowd hangs out at the **Pub** (⊠*78260 Hwy. 40* ☎*970/726–4929*), grooving to local bands.If you've never done your laundry while sipping a brew, don't miss **Buckets** (⊠*78415 Hwy. 40* ☎*970/726–3026*), a combination bar and coin laundry in the basement of the Winter Park Movie Theater. This friendly place seems to attract as many tourists as locals.

SHOPPING

Cooper Creek Square (⊠*47 Cooper Creek Way* ☎*970/726–8891*) is filled with inexpensive souvenir shops and fine jewelers, upscale eateries and local cafés, plus live entertainment all summer in the courtyard.

GEORGETOWN

32 mi southwest of Winter Park via U.S. 40 and I–70; 50 mi west of Denver via I–70.

Georgetown rode the crest of the silver boom during the second half of the 19th century. Most of the impeccably maintained brick buildings that make up the town's historic district date from that period. Georgetown hasn't been tarted up, so it provides a true sense of what gracious living meant in those rough-and-tumble times. Just west of where I–70 and U.S. 40 intersect, Georgetown is close enough to attract day-trippers from Denver, but its quiet charms warrant more than a hurried visit. It's a popular tourist stop in the summertime and be sure to keep an eye out for the state's largest herd of rare bighorn sheep when driving on I–70.

Hop on the **Georgetown Loop Railroad,** a 1920s narrow-gauge steam train that connects Georgetown with the equally historic community of Silver Plume. The 6-mi round-trip excursion takes about 70 minutes and winds through vast stands of pine and fir before crossing the 95-foot-high Devil's Gate Bridge, where the track actually loops back over itself as it gains elevation. You can add on a tour of the **Lebanon Silver Mill and Mine,** which is a separate stop between the two towns. ⊠*100 Loop Dr.* ☎*888/456–6777* ⊕*www.georgetownlooprr.com* ✉*$18.75 for train; $26.75 for train ride and mine tour* ⊙*May–Oct., daily 10–3:45.*

South of Georgetown, the **Guanella Pass Scenic Byway** treats you to marvelous views of the Mount Evans Wilderness Area. The road over the pass has a lot of hairpin turns. Make sure to park at Georgetown Lake, where you can catch a glimpse of the state's largest herd of rare bighorn sheep. ⊠*Rte. 381.*

Dating from 1867, **Hamill House** once was the home of silver magnate William Arthur Hamill. The Gothic Revival beauty displays most of its original wall coverings and furnishings. Don't miss the gleaming white structure's unique curved-glass conservatory. ⊠*3rd and Argentine Sts.* ☎*303/569–2840* ⊕*www.historicgeorgetown.org* ✉*$5* ⊙*June–Aug., daily 10–4; Sept.–Dec., weekends noon–4; Jan.–May, by appointment.*

The elaborate **Hotel de Paris,** built almost single-handedly by Frenchman Louis Dupuy in 1878, was one of the Old West's preeminent hostelries. Now a museum, the hotel depicts how luxuriously the rich were accommodated: Tiffany fixtures, lace curtains, and hand-carved furniture re-create an era of opulence. ⊠*409 6th St.* ☎*303/569–2311* ⊕*www.hoteldeparismuseum.org* ✉*$5* ⊙*June–Aug., daily 10–4:30; May and Sept.–Dec., weekends noon–4.*

SKIING & SNOWBOARDING AT LOVELAND

Because of its proximity to Denver (an hour's drive), lack of resort facilities and hotels, and seemingly small area, **Loveland Ski Area** is one of the most overlooked ski areas in the rush to hit the monster resort slopes in Summit and Eagle counties. And that's just the way locals

Hiking to the Continental Divide

The Continental Divide, that mythical geographic division that sends raindrops to either the Atlantic or Pacific oceans, makes a worthy pilgrimage for day hikers and backpackers alike in summer. Although it doesn't look dangerous to the untrained eye, the slopes off the Divide are avalanche prone, so it is an extremely dangerous place to ski in winter. The easiest way to reach the divide is to drive up U.S. Highway 6 over Loveland Pass at the Eisenhower Tunnel on I–70 and park on top of the divide. Hiking trails lead both east and west along the divide. If you feel like breaking a sweat, hike to the summit of James Peak from the base of St. Mary's Glacier. This 4-mi round-trip hike rewards you with views of almost the entire Front Range as well as staggered mountain ranges farther west. Take I–70 west just past Idaho Springs and get off at Exit 238 (St. Mary's and Fall River Road). Follow the road until you see the trailhead on the left. It takes an hour to reach the trailhead from Denver.

like it. Loveland has some of the highest and hairiest runs in Colorado spread across a respectable 1,365 acres serviced by 11 lifts. It's split between Loveland Valley, a good place for beginners, and Loveland Basin, a good bet for everyone else. Loveland Basin has excellent glade and open-bowl skiing and snowboarding, especially on the 2,410-foot vertical drop. Best of all, it opens early and usually stays open later than any other ski area except Arapahoe Basin. ⌖ I–70 Exit 216, 12 mi west of Georgetown ☎ 303/571–5580 or 800/736–3754 ⊕ www. skiloveland.com ⊘ Mid-Oct.–May, weekdays 9–4, weekends 8:30–4.

FACILITIES   2,410-foot vertical drop; 1,365 skiable acres; 80 runs; 13% beginner, 41% intermediate, 46% advanced; 11 lifts; 4 doubles, 2 triples, 3 quads, 1 surface, and 1 tow.

LESSONS & PROGRAMS   **Loveland Ski School** (☎ 303/571–5580) offers 2½-hour group "Newcomer Packages" beginning at 10 AM and 1 PM for $72 including all rental gear and an all-day lift ticket; advanced half-day lessons (a maximum of four people per group) are $55 or $85 with rental gear.

LIFT TICKETS $54. In the early season, from opening to December 14, tickets are $45. Discount tickets are on sale at local Safeway and King Soopers stores.

RENTALS   **Loveland Rentals** (☎ 303/569–3203) has two on-mountain locations. Sport packages are $29, and performance packages are $39. Snowboard packages are $34; helmets run $10.

WHERE TO STAY & EAT

$$$ ✕ **New Prague.** A surprising find in this mountain town, New Prague's chef does come from the Czech Republic and the food is authentic. The pork with a light gravy is delicious, and among the side dishes you'll find the best red cabbage you've ever tasted. ✉ 511 Rose St. ☎ 303/569–2861 ▭ AE, D, MC, V.

$–$$ ✕ **Red Ram.** This Georgetown landmark has been serving up some of the region's tastiest meals since the 1950s. The secret is keeping the menu simple: burgers, ribs, and south-of-the-border favorites such as fajitas. Black-and-white photos of the town's heyday bedeck the walls. Stop by on weekends when there's live entertainment. ⊠ *606 6th St.* ☎*303/569–2300* ▤*AE, D, MC, V.*

$ ⛰ **Georgetown Mountain Inn.** The Georgetown Mountain Inn, next door to the Old Georgetown Railroad, provides a quiet haven. The rooms are a step up from a basic motel, decorated with Western-style wood furniture and Southwestern blankets. A stone fireplace crowned with an elk rack greets you in the lobby and a small indoor pool is a great place to soak after a day of skiing or exploring the High Country. **Pro:** right by the station for the Georgetown Loop railroad. **Con:** several blocks away from the historic downtown. ⊠ *1100 Rose St., 80444* ☎*303/569–3201 or 800/884–3201* ⊟*303/569–3407* ⊕*www.georgetownmountaininn. com* ⊠*33 rooms* ⛁*In-room: Wi-Fi. In-hotel: pool, no elevator, some pets allowed, no-smoking rooms* ▤*AE, D, MC, V.*

SHOPPING
Georgetown Antique Emporium (⊠*501 Rose St.* ☎*303/569–2727*) specializes in oak and brass antiques. The **Grizzley Creek Gallery** (⊠*510 6th St.* ☎*303/569–0433*) has wonderful scenic large-scale photographs of the Rockies and wildlife.

THE ROCKIES NEAR DENVER ESSENTIALS

TRANSPORTATION

BY AIR
Denver International Airport (DEN) is east of Denver, about a 20-minute taxi ride from the city center and a 1 hour and 14-minute drive from the Continental Divide when the roads are clear and traffic is normal.

Information Denver International Airport (DEN) (☎*800/247–2336* ⊕*www. flydenver.com*).

BY BUS AND SHUTTLE
Greyhound Lines has regular service from Denver to several towns along I–70. The company also runs intercity bus service. Winter Park has a shuttle between the village and the slopes.

Contacts Home James (☎*800/359–7503 shuttle service from Denver International Airport to Winter Park and Grand County* ⊕*www.ridehj.com*).

BY CAR
The most convenient place to rent a car is at Denver International Airport.

The hardest part about driving in the High Rockies is keeping your eyes on the road, what with canyons, mountain ridges, and animals to distract your attention. Some of the most scenic routes aren't necessarily the most direct, like the spectacular Loveland Pass.

Although it is often severely overcrowded, I–70 is still the quickest and most direct route from Denver to the High Rockies. It slices through the state, separating it into northern and southern halves. Idaho Springs is along I–70. Winter Park is north of I–70, on U.S. 40 and over Berthoud Pass, which is has gorgeous views but also has several hairpin turns. Berthoud Pass can be treacherous when a winter storm blows in.

Gasoline is readily available along I–70 and its arteries, but not so in more-remote areas like Mount Evans and Guanella Pass. Blinding snowstorms can appear out of nowhere on the high passes at any time of the year. It's a good idea to bring chains and a shovel along. Road reports and signage on the highways will indicate if chains or four-wheel-drive vehicles are required. Keep your eyes peeled for wildlife, especially along the stretch of I–70 from Idaho Springs to the Eisenhower Tunnel. Bighorn sheep, elk, and deer frequently graze along the north side of the highway.

Information **Colorado Road Condition Hotline** (☎ *303/639–1111 statewide*). **Colorado State Patrol** (☎ *303/239–4500* ⊕ *www.csp.state.co.us*).

BY TRAIN

Amtrak has service from Denver's Union Station to the Winter Park Ski Area station in nearby Fraser (where shuttles to the area are available). The nonstop Ski Train leaves Denver's Union Station most Saturday and Sunday mornings during ski season.

Contacts **Amtrak** (☎ *800/872–7245* ⊕ *www.amtrak.com*).

CONTACTS & RESOURCES

EMERGENCIES
Ambulance or Police (☎ *911*).

Clinic **Seven Mile Medical Clinic** (⊠ *Base of Winter Park Ski Area, Winter Park* ☎ *970/887–7470*).

TOURS

Mad Adventures has Continental Divide van tours from Winter Park. If rafting is your choice, Mad Adventures can help you shoot the rapids of the North Platte, Colorado, and Arkansas rivers.

Contact **Mad Adventures** (⌂ *Box 650, Winter Park, 804827* ☎ *970/726–5290 or 800/451–4844* ⊕ *www.madadventures.com*).

VISITOR INFORMATION
Snow Reports **Loveland** (☎ *800/736–3SKI Ext 221* ⊕ *www.skiloveland.com*). **Winter Park** (☎ *970/726–7669* ⊕ *www.skiwinterpark.com*).

Contacts **Chamber and Tourism Bureau of Clear Creek County** (⌂ *Box 100, Idaho Springs 80452* ☎ *303/567–4660 or 866/674–9237* ⊕ *www.clearcreekcounty. org*). **Greater Golden Chamber of Commerce** (⊠ *1010 Washington Ave., Golden 80402* ☎ *303/279–3113* ⊕ *www.ingolden.com*). **Winter Park/Fraser Valley Chamber of Commerce** (⌂ *Box 3236, Winter Park 80482* ☎ *970/726–4118 or 800/903–7275* ⊕ *www.winterpark-info.com*).**Winter Park Resort** (⌂ *Box 36, Winter Park 80482* ☎ *800/729–5813 or 970/726–5587* ⊕ *www.skiwinterpark.com*).

Summit County

WORD OF MOUTH

"Leadville and Breck are two very different places. Leadville is a rustic old mining town. There are some great little B&Bs, and an old historic hotel there. Breck is more modern [with] trendy-type restaurants [and] more bars. My pick is Leadville—I like the quaint, mountain-town feeling. But I guess it depends on what kinds of things you like!"

—seasweetie

"Summit County is one of my favorite places in any season. There are tons of great places to snowshoe and cross country ski in the area. We like snowshoeing around Frisco because you get some wonderful views of the lake."

—sundown

Revised &
Updated by
Jad Davenport

SUMMIT COUNTY, A MERE HOUR drive from the Denver Metro Area on a straight shot up Interstate 70, is Denver's playground. The wide-open mountain park ringed by 13,000-foot peaks greets westbound travelers minutes after they pop out the west portal of the Eisenhower Tunnel. The sharp-toothed Gore Range rises to the northwest and the Tenmile Range gathers up behind Breckenridge. Resting in the center of this bowl are the sapphire waters of Dillon Reservoir, an artificial lake fed by Blue River.

In winter Summit County is packed with tourists and Front Range day-trippers skiing the steeps at Arapahoe Basin, Breckenridge, Keystone, or Copper Mountain. The high density of first-rate ski resorts generally keeps lift lines low, particularly on weekdays. In summer the steady westbound traffic is mostly four-wheel drives stacked with lake kayaks and mountain bikes.

Summit County, as its name implies, is relatively high. The town of Breckenridge sits at 9,603 feet (Aspen by comparison is at 7,908 feet), and the resort's newest ski lift tops out just shy of 13,000 feet. Visitors from sea level should take their time getting acclimated. Even Denverites find themselves breathless in the thin air. Drink lots of water and rest your first few days. There will be plenty of time to play.

EXPLORING SUMMIT COUNTY

The great east–west Colorado corridor I–70 cleaves through the heart of Summit County, punching west from Denver past Idaho Springs and Georgetown. The traffic here can be heavy and fast; everyone is in a hurry to make it through the Eisenhower Tunnel, the traditional gate-way to Summit County. Those with an extra half hour and a yearning for hairpin turns, shaggy mountain goats, and hundred-mile views opt for Highway 6 over Loveland Pass and the Continental Divide. As it drops into the Summit County Basin on the west side of the divide, Highway 6 passes Arapahoe Basin and Keystone Ski Resort before merging with I–70. Both roads skirt Dillon Reservoir with its shoreline communities of Dillon and Frisco. The highway quickly disappears back into a narrow mountain valley and climbs to Copper Mountain and then up and over Vail Pass. Highway 9 quarters Summit County, running north along the lazy Blue River to Kremmling and south past Breckenridge to its headwaters near Hoosier Pass.

ABOUT THE PARKS & RECREATION AREAS

Summit County is perched in a 9,000-foot-high park (a wide valley surrounded by peaks) with Lake Dillon at its recreational heart. It's sur-prising that, given the natural beauty and heavy use this area sees, none of it falls inside a national park. The lodgepole pine forests and alpine tundra in the wild Gore Range northwest of Lake Dillon are protected within the Eagles Nest Wilderness Area, administered by the **Arapaho National Forest** (☎ *970/295–6600* ⊕ *www.fs.fed.us*) and the **White River National Forest** (☎ *970/945–2521* ⊕ *www.fs.fed.us*). These two forestry units encompass most of Summit County, including large parts of all the ski resorts. Like all wilderness areas in Colorado, motorized or

TOP REASONS TO GO

Skiing: You won't find more choices to ski and ride within snowball-throw's distance of one another than in Summit County, a mere hour-drive from the Denver Metro Area. With five ski resorts ringing the mountains—A-Basin, Breck, Cooper, Copper, and Keystone—Summit County is a skier's and rider's Valhalla with everything from the easy beginner glades at Copper to backcountry cat skiing at Keystone.

Leadville: It was gold that built Colorado in the 1800s, and this legacy is alive and well in the rejuvenated mining town of Leadville Walk the small downtown of our country's highest city—a breath-sapping 10,430 feet—and visit some of the local museums like the National Mining Hall of Fame and Museum.

Lake Dillon: Nothing beats a day of lake kayaking or fishing among the many wooded islets on Lake Dillon, the reservoir that is the heart of Summit County.

Party Towns: If you're looking for a reason to party surrounded by white-capped mountains, Breckenridge hosts numerous festivals including the aptly named Spring Massive Festival in April, and the weeklong Ullr Festival in January.

Trail Biking: Sure, there are plenty of beautiful single tracks for mountain bikers, but the real draw in Summit County is the glorious paved bike trail that runs from Dillon all the way up and over Vail Pass down into that ski town. Bring your helmet and your wallet—you can stop off for refreshments at Copper Mountain Resort.

mechanized vehicles (forestry-speak for mountain bikes) are prohibited. You can tackle the backcountry peaks with your own two feet or on horseback. The Blue River, which bisects the county south to north and is the lifeblood of Lake Dillon, offers gold-medal fishing beginning below Lake Dillon to the Green Mountain Reservoir.

ABOUT THE RESTAURANTS

Whereas the restaurants in the celeb resorts of Aspen and Vail mimic the sophistication and style of New York and Los Angeles, Summit County eateries specialize in pub food and Mexican cuisine for calorie-hungry hikers, skiers, and boaters. You won't find much sushi here, but you will find fish tacos, shepherd's pies, and burgers with every imaginable topping. Hearty, reasonably priced pub fare is served at a number of cozy brewpubs along with handcrafted local suds like Dam Straight Lager, Avalanche Amber, and Ptarmigan Pilsner.

ABOUT THE HOTELS

Summit County is a great place for history buffs looking for redone Victorian mining mansions–cum–bed-and-breakfasts and budget hunters who want affordable rooms close to the slopes. The county probably has the highest density of condominium units in the state. The competition tends to keep prices lower than in other resort towns. Note that staff at hotels in the region are sometimes young and inexperienced, which may result in less-than-desirable service at some otherwise excellent properties. Also note that many accommodations do

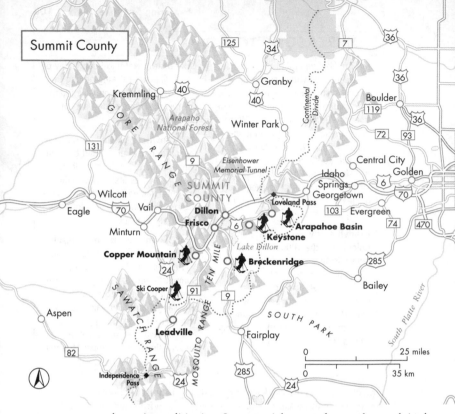

Summit County

not have air-conditioning. Summer nights are often cool enough in the mountains that opening the windows will do the trick.

	WHAT IT COSTS				
	¢	$	$$	$$$	$$$$
RESTAURANTS	under $8	$8–$12	$13–$18	$19–$25	over $25
HOTELS	under $80	$80–$120	$121–$170	$171–$230	over $230

Restaurant prices are for a main course at dinner, excluding 7.75%–12.7% tax. Hotel prices are for two people in a standard double room in high season, excluding service charges and 8.8%–12.1% tax.

TIMING

Summit County is a haven for winter enthusiasts: The resorts of Arapahoe Basin and Breckenridge—and nearby Loveland in Clear Creek County—are so high that the ski season often dawns here weeks before it does in the rest of the state, with Arapahoe Basin and Loveland competing to see who has the longest season. The altitude also means that it can snow on any day of the year, so be prepared. Traffic, particularly on the I–70 approaches to the Eisenhower Tunnel and the Georgetown-to-Idaho Springs stretch, moves at a snail's pace around weekend rush hours—3 to 10 PM on Friday and all day Sunday.

DILLON

73 mi west of Denver via I–70.

Dillon can't seem to sit still. Founded in 1883 as a stagecoach stop and trading post for men working in the mines, Dillon has had to pack up and move three times since its conception. It was first relocated to be closer to the Utah and Northern Railroad, and

then to take advantage of the nearby rivers. Finally, in 1955, bigwigs in Denver drew up plans to dam the Blue River so they could quench the capital's growing thirst. The reservoir would submerge Dillon under more than 150 feet of water. Once again the town was dismantled and moved, this time to pine-blanketed hills mirrored in sapphire water. Residents agreed that no building in the new location would be higher than 30 feet so as not to obstruct the view of the reservoir, which is appropriately called Lake Dillon.

Dillon now blends with neighboring Silverthorne, where dozens of factory outlets are frequented by locals and travelers vying for bargains. Combined, the two towns have hotels, restaurants, and stores galore.

Fodor's Choice Resting in the heart of Summit County at 9,017 feet is the Front
★ Range's answer to a day at the beach—beautiful **Lake Dillon** and her two ports, Dillon, just off I–70 on the south, and Frisco, off I–70 and Highway 9 on the west. The lake is actually a 231-foot earth-filled dam that fills the valley where Dillon once sat. During the frequent western droughts, when water levels can drop dramatically, collectors wander along the exposed shores hunting for artifacts from this Rocky Mountain Atlantis.

It was these droughts that inspired the Denver Water Board to construct the reservoir and divert the water through the Harold D. Roberts Tunnel, beneath the Continental Divide. Below the mile-long dam the Blue River babbles past the outlet shopping haven and turns into miles of gold-medal fly-fishing waters on its journey north.

The lake has been an aquatic boon to both the Front Range and the exploding Summit County population. There are more than 27 mi of gravel beaches, marshes, peninsulas, and wooded islets for picnickers to enjoy, many accessible from a 7.5-mi paved trail along the northern shores, or from the informal dirt paths elsewhere. Gaze out at the deep blue waters from Sapphire Point Lookout (a short ½-mi hike on the south side of the lake) any nice day and you'll see a flotilla of motorboats, sailboats, canoes, kayaks, and sailboarders dancing in the waves. In winter the frozen waters are enjoyed by ice anglers and cross-country skiers.

Because the lake is considered a drinking-water source, swimming is not permitted and the lake is patrolled vigorously by Summit County sheriffs. Just because you don't see a patrol boat doesn't mean they can't see you; their surveillance is done with binoculars.

SPORTS & THE OUTDOORS

BICYCLING
Fodor'sChoice
★
☺
Summit County attracts cyclists with its 40 mi of paved bike paths and extensive network of backcountry trails. There are dozens of trailheads from which you can travel through gentle rolling terrain, up the sides of mountains, and along ridges for spectacular views. Starting in Dillon, you could bike around the reservoir to Frisco. From there you could ride the Blue River Pathway, largely along the river, to Breckenridge. Or you could ride through beautiful Tenmile Canyon all the way to Copper Mountain. If you're really fit, you could even continue your ride over Vail Pass and down into Vail Village. The **Summit County Chamber of Commerce Information Center** (⊠246 *Rainbow Dr., Silverthorne* ☎800/530–3099 ⊕*www.experiencethesummit.com*) has detailed information about bike trails in the area. Ask for a free Summit County Bike Trail Guide that outlines, with great detail, your options. Listings include distance, difficulty, and elevation changes.

BOATING
☺
The **Frisco Bay Marina** (⊠*Frisco* ☎970/668–4334 ⊕*www.friscobay-marina.com*) is less crowded than Dillon and offers quick access to the numerous pine-cloaked islands along the western shores. Here you can rent powerboats, canoes, and kayaks. Take I–70 Exit 203 to Highway 9 to Main Street and follow signs to the marina. At **Dillon Marina** (⊠*Lake Dillon* ☎970/468–5100 ⊕*www.dillonmarina.com*) you can rent a rowboat, sailboat, or just about anything else that floats. Reserve ahead in high season. Take I–70 Exit 205 to Highway 6, and follow the signs to the marina.

Boats rented from the Frisco Bay and Dillon marinas are not permitted to beach; the aluminum pontoons are easily damaged on the rock and gravel shores.

FISHING
A favorite with locals, **Cutthroat Anglers** (⊠*400 Blue River Pkwy., Silverthorne* ☎ 970/262–2878 or 888/876–8818 ⊕*www.fishcolorado.com*) has a pro shop chock-full of gear for avid fly fishermen. Their wade trips are best for beginners; float-trip adventures are for those with a bit more experience. Both come in half-day and full-day versions.

GOLF
Raven Golf Club at Three Peaks. *Colorado Avid Golfer* magazine named this 18-hole beauty the best mountain course and the best golf experience in Colorado. Each hole on the par-72 course has dramatic views of the Gore Mountain range. ⊠*2929 N. Golden Rd., Silverthorne* ☎970/262–3636 ⊕*www.ravengolf.com* ⚞*Reservations essential* 🏌*18 holes. Yards: 7,413/5,235. Par: 72/72. Green Fee: $65/$140.*

WHERE TO EAT

$$ ✕**Dillon Dam Brewery.** Belly up to the horseshoe-shape bar and sample the ales and lagers while you munch on burgers, sandwiches, or pub grub. The menu is steps above average bar food. Try the pan-seared salmon encrusted with sesame seeds or the crispy San Luis pepper duckling with peppercorn demi-glace and wild rice pilaf. Carnivores

Golf

3

It isn't easy to define "golf" in Colorado because the topography varies so dramatically, from the rolling plains near the Kansas state line to the flat-top buttes and mesas at the western end of the state. In the Rockies, the state's central spine, the courses climb up and down mountainsides; in the foothills the fairways roll over more-gentle terrain and over canyons; and down in the cities many layouts march back and forth in confined spaces.

Mountain golf has unique challenges, but vacationers flock to the high-country golf courses because of their dramatic scenery. "Aim for that peak" is an oft-repeated phrase. It doesn't matter whether you are playing the Jack Nicklaus–designed 27-hole municipal course in Breckenridge, the Club at Crested Butte, or the golf course at the Snowmass Club, there's bound to be a hole where that description fits.

Resort courses, available to guests staying at certain lodgings, are spread around mountain towns from Snowmass and Steamboat to Vail and Telluride. For example, guests staying at certain properties in Vail and Beaver Creek get access to the Tom Fazio course (woven through sagebrush-covered hills) and the Greg Norman course (spread around a broad valley with shots across ravines) at the posh, private Red Sky Golf Club in Edwards, 15 minutes west of Beaver Creek. Even if you're not staying in a hotel that has preferred tee times at specific resort courses, a good concierge (or your own Web search) will obtain tee times at many entertaining courses, such as the Raven at Three Peaks in Summit County and Sheraton Steamboat Golf Club in Steamboat.

When playing high-altitude golf, you do have to deal with mountain lies and illusions. The thrill of a clean hit and watching the ball fly 300 yards downhill may be deflected by the agony of seeing a putt topple off the back edge of a green because you "knew" that the green tilted left, although it actually sloped right. Low-land golfers who come to the mountains to play golf quickly learn they may have to change club lengths and lofts, because balls fly 10%–15% farther in the thinner air and land on never-level terrain. Greens are especially difficult to read, because the ball will try to roll from the highest mountain peak to the nearest valley—unless the course architect foxes players by building up the green's lower end to counterbalance that pull. Ask the pro in the golf shop for tips before setting out.

If you aren't heading up to the mountains, there are plenty of public and semiprivate courses in and around the bigger cities. Some city-owned courses in Denver proper tend to be unimaginative layouts in confined spaces, but there's a variety of challenging and award-winning courses in the surrounding burbs, especially in Lakewood, Littleton, and Parker.

On the western slopes, a big standout is the Golf Club at Redland Mesa in Grand Junction. This award-winning Jim Engh public course is woven among mesas and sand-color flat-top buttes.

Here in Colorado there's an array of golf courses designed to offer you entertaining challenges in a spectacular setting.

—Lois Friedland

and vegetarians alike have a big selection, including the Ptarmigan Portobello, a char-grilled mushroom-stuffed wrap on a whole-wheat bun topped with melted pepper jack. ⊠*100 Little Dam St., Dillon* ☎*970/262–7777* ⊟*AE, D, DC, MC, V.*

$$ ✕**Historic Mint.** Built in 1862, this raucous eatery originally served as a bar and brothel. The olden days are still evident in the bar's brass handles and hand-carved wood, as well as in the antiques and vintage photographs covering the walls of the dining area. Red meat reigns supreme, although you'll also find chicken and fish on the menu. Either way, you cook your own meal on lava rocks sizzling at 1,100°F. If you prefer to leave the cooking to the chef, there's a prime rib special. A well-stocked salad bar complements your entrée. ⊠*347 Blue River Pkwy., Silverthorne* ☎*970/468–5247* ⊟*MC, V* ☉*No lunch.*

NIGHTLIFE

The bars and clubs in Dillon rock well after midnight, especially on winter nights when the towns are packed with skiers and snowboarders.

Across from the post office, **Pug Ryan's Steak House & Brewery** (⊠*104 Village Pl.* ☎*970/468–2145*) is a popular brewpub that attracts villagers and vacationers. The **Tiki Bar** (⊠*Dillon Marina* ☎*970/262–6309*) has the best sunset views in Summit County. Enjoy them from the deck overlooking Lake Dillon while you sip your rumrunner and munch on peel-and-eat shrimp. **Wild Bill's Pizza Saloon** (⊠*119 La Bonte* ☎*970/468–2006*) serves pizzas, grinders, and some of the area's best buffalo wings.

SHOPPING

Factory Stores (⊕*I–70 Exit 20* ☎*970/468–9440*) is a sprawling complex with more than 50 discount outlets. Clusters of shops are color-coded for your shopping convenience. The Red Village has **Tommy Hilfiger, Eddie Bauer,** and other upscale clothing shops. If you need sneakers, the Blue Village is home to the **Nike Factory Store.** For dishes, head to the **Kitchen Collection** in the Green Village.

KEYSTONE

8 mi southeast of Dillon via U.S. 6.

Fodor'sChoice ★ One of the region's most laid-back destinations, Keystone is understandably popular with families and, as the state's only large resort to offer night skiing (with lifts running until 9 PM), has long been a local favorite. Its trails are spread across three adjoining peaks: Dercum Mountain, North Peak, and the Outback. Through the years, as the resort added more runs, it morphed from a beginner's paradise on Keystone Mountain to an early-season training stop for the national ski teams that practice on the tougher and bumpier terrain on North Peak. During the 2006–07 season, Keystone even added full-day guided snowcat tours ($100; backcountry ski gear like avalanche beacons, shovels, and probes are provided for those without). Today it's a resort for all types of skiers and riders, whether they prefer gentle slopes, cruising, or high-adrenaline challenges on the Outback's steep bowls.

The planners were sensitive to the environment, favoring colors and materials that blend inconspicuously with the natural surroundings. Lodging, shops, and restaurants are in Lakeside Village, the older part of the resort, and in River Run, a newer area at the base of the gondola that has become the heart of Keystone. Everything at the resort is operated by Keystone, which makes planning a vacation here one-stop shopping. Keystone is quickly becoming a magnet in summer, with a small lake for water sports, mountain biking and hiking trails, two golf courses that have been ranked highly by golf magazines, and outdoor concerts and special events.

3

DOWNHILL SKIING & SNOWBOARDING

What you see from the base of the mountain is only a fraction of the terrain you can enjoy when you ski or snowboard at Keystone. There's plenty more to Keystone Mountain, and much of it is geared to novice and intermediate skiers. The Schoolmarm Trail has 3.5 mi of runs where you can practice turns. Dercum Mountain is easily reached from the base via high-speed chairs or the River Run gondola. You can ski or ride down the back side of Dercum Mountain to reach North Peak, a mix of groomed cruising trails and ungroomed bump runs.

If you prefer to bypass North Peak, the River Run gondola is a short walk from the Outpost gondola, which takes you to the Outpost Lodge (home to the Alpenglow Stube, which at 11,444 feet above sea level is advertised as the "highest gourmet restaurant in the country"). From here it's an easy downhill run to the third mountain, appropriately named the Outback because of its wilderness setting. Some glades have trees thinned just enough for skiers and riders who are learning to explore gladed terrain; other sections are reserved for advanced skiers. Weather permitting, the resort also has snowcat tours that whisk you up to powder skiing on some of the state's steepest terrain.

One of the most popular nonskiing or boarding sports at Keystone is **tubing.** Both Adventure Point at the summit of Dercum Mountain (Wednesday–Sunday noon–4 PM and noon–8 PM on night-skiing days) and the Keystone Nordic Center have tube rentals and runs, but reserve a day or two ahead of time. Personal sleds and tubes are not allowed. ⊠ *Hwy. 6* ☎ *970/468–2316 or 800/239–1639* ⊕ *www.keystoneresort. com* ⊙ *Skiing: late Oct.–late Apr.; call for hrs.*

FACILITIES   3,128-foot vertical drop; 3,148 skiable acres; 19% beginner, 32% intermediate, 49% advanced; 20 lifts; 2 gondolas, 1 super six lift, 5 high-speed quad chairs, 1 quad chair, 1 triple chair, 3 double chairs, 7 surface lifts and carpets.

LESSONS & PROGRAMS   Keystone has a variety of instructional programs, from half-day group lessons to specialty clinics, including mogul classes and women's seminars. A notable special program is the Mahre Training Center with intensive three- and five-day clinics hosted by Phil or Steve Mahre, both Olympic medalists.

LIFT TICKETS   With prices at $86 for a lift ticket, few skiers pay the walk-up rate. Season passes, which range from 10 days of skiing to unlimited access, are available through Vail Resorts, which owns Keystone, Breckenridge, Vail, and Beaver Creek. Most vacationers purchase lift-and-lodging packages or multiday lift passes at discounted rates online and at local Safeway and King Soopers grocery stores.

RENTALS Rental packages (skis, boots, and poles, or snowboards and boots) start at around $35 per day for a basic package but increase quickly for high-performance gear. Cheaper ski and snowboard stores are found in Breckenridge, Dillon, and Frisco.

> **BREATHLESS?**
>
> Feeling breathless, nauseous, and crummy? Fifteen percent of skiers in Colorado and Utah experience some degree of altitude sickness if they arrive from sea level. Indulge in wakeful resting, avoid alcohol and high-carbohydrate food, drink plenty of water, and take aspirin for headaches. If your body doesn't adapt within a day or two, or if your symptoms worsen, consult a doctor. The only remedy may be to descend.

CHILD CARE Keystone has Children's Centers at the base of River Run and at the Mountain House for children three months to six years. The resort also has private classes for families.

NORDIC SKIING

The **Keystone Cross-Country Center** (✉ *River Course Clubhouse* ☎ *800/354–4386*) has 35 mi of trails available for track skiing, skate skiing, and snowshoeing. Lessons and rentals of cross-country skis and snowshoes are available.

OTHER SPORTS & THE OUTDOORS

FISHING **Summit Outdoor Sports** (✉ *Lakeside Village at Keystone* ☎ *970/468–8945* ⊕ *www.summitoutdoorsports.com*) is a fly shop that has full- and half-day fishing trips throughout Summit, Grand, and Eagle counties. This company also leads fly-fishing float trips on several rivers.

GOLF **Keystone Golf.** With 36 challenging holes, Keystone lures golfers as soon as the snow melts. **Keystone Ranch,** designed by Robert Trent Jones Jr., has a links-style front nine; the back nine has a traditional mountain-valley layout. Holes play past lodgepole pines, meander around sage meadows, and include some carries across water. **The River Course** is a par-71 stunner designed by Michael Hurdzan and Dana Fry. The front nine runs around the Snake River, whereas the back nine threads through a stand of lodgepole pines. Dramatic elevation changes, bunkers, and water hazards combine to test golfers of all levels. Add magnificent views of the Continental Divide and Lake Dillon and it's easy to see why this course is so popular. ✉ *1239 Keystone Ranch Rd.* ☎ *970/496–4250* ⊕ *www.golfkeystone.com* ⚐ *Reservations essential* ⚑ *Keystone Ranch: 18 holes. Yards: 7,090/5,596. Par: 72/72. Green Fee: $75/$130. The River Course: 18 holes. Yards: 6,886/4,762. Par: 71/70. Green Fee: $85/$160.*

ICE SKATING In winter Keystone Lake freezes to become the country's largest outdoor **ice-skating rink** (✉ *Lakeside Village* ☎ *970/496–4386 or 800/354–4386*). You can rent skates, sleds, or even hockey sticks for an impromptu game. Lessons in figure skating and hockey are available. Weather permitting, skating runs from late November to early March.

WHERE TO STAY & EAT

★ **$$$$** ✕**Alpenglow Stube.** The competition has heated up in recent years, but Alpenglow Stube remains among the finest mountaintop restaurants in Colorado. The exposed wood beams, a stone fireplace, and floral upholstery make it elegant and cozy. At night, the gondola ride you take to get here alone is worth the cost of the meal. Dinner is a six-course extravaganza, starting with the signature pinecone pâté, followed perhaps by rack of caribou in a pear–liqueur sauce. Lunch is equally delectable, with excellent pasta specials. Remove your ski boots and put on the plush slippers reserved for diners. ☒*North Peak* ☏*970/496–4386 or 800/354–4386* ⚷*Res ervations essential* ▬*AE, D, DC, MC, V* ☉*Closed late Apr.–early June and mid-Sept.–late Nov.*

$$$$ ✕**Keystone Ranch.** This 1930s homestead was once part of a working cattle ranch, and cowboy memorabilia is strewn throughout, nicely blending with stylish throw rugs and Western crafts. The gorgeous and massive stone fireplace is a cozy backdrop for sipping an aperitif or after-dinner coffee. Chef David Welch's seasonal six-course menu emphasizes local ingredients, including farm-raised game and fresh fish. You're in luck if the menu includes elk with wild mushrooms in juniper sauce with quince relish or Gorgonzola flan. ☒*Keystone Ranch Golf Course, 1239 Keystone Ranch Rd.* ☏*970/496–4386 or 800/354–4386* ⚷*Reservations essential* ▬*AE, D, DC, MC, V* ☉*No lunch Oct.–May.*

$$$$ ✕**Ski Tip Lodge.** In this ski lodge dating from the 1800s, almost every-
Fodor's Choice thing on the menu will melt in your mouth. The four-course, prix-fixe
★ dinner is a favorite in the area for its American cuisine with a Colorado twist. The main course may be wood-grilled pork tenderloin, a roast pheasant with game sausage, or seafood fricassee with coconut and lime. The delicious homemade bread and soup are a meal in themselves. Adjourn to the cozy lounge for the decadent desserts and specialty coffees. The restaurant is open during ski season, typically late October through mid-April. ☒*764 Montezuma Rd.,* ✛*1 mi off U.S. 6* ☏*970/496–4386 or 800/354–4386* ▬*AE, D, DC, MC, V* ☉*Closed Tues. and Wed. No lunch.*

$$ ✕**Kickapoo Tavern.** This rustic bar and grill in Jackpine Lodge has local microbrews on tap and big portions of home-style dishes such as chunky beef stew, hearty sandwiches, and burritos said to be "as big as a barn." The central location, pleasant outdoor patio, and TVs tuned to sporting events keep the place hopping both après ski and après night ski. ☒*River Run Plaza* ☏*970/496–4386 or 800/354–4386* ▬*AE, MC, V.*

¢ ✕**Cala Inn.** A street sign noting the distance to Galway is the first clue that you've entered an Irish pub. It's a scruffy but entertaining place

3

where diners and drinkers sit around wood tables inhaling pub fries, bangers and mash, and steak-and-kidney pie. If you're brave enough, down a "Nessie" shot—layered Midori and Bailey's with a floater of Jägermeister. ✉ *40 Cove Blvd.* ☎ *970/468–1899* ▤ *MC, V.*

$$$$ ▦ **Keystone Lodge & Spa, a Rock Resort.** The cinder-block structure gives no hint of the gracious, pampered living just inside the door. Rooms with king-size beds are on the small side, whereas rooms with two queen-size beds tend to be more generously proportioned. Many rooms have terraces overlooking the trees. The lodge is next to the tiny lake in Keystone Village, and close to several restaurants and shops. Perhaps best of all, a short shuttle ride delivers you directly to the slopes. After skiing, the resort spa provides a welcome respite. Choose from traditional massages, or opt for a more-exotic treatment like the arctic algae facial. **Pros:** one of larger properties in the resort, spa, ski valet. **Cons:** iffy service, rooms are small, hot tubs get crowded. ⌂ *Keystone Resort, Box 38, Keystone 80435* ☎ *970/496–2316 or 866/455–7625* ✇ *www. keystonelodge.rockresorts.com* ⇱ *152 rooms* ⌂ *In-room: no a/c, dial-up. In-hotel: 3 restaurants, room service, bar, tennis courts, pool, gym, spa, concierge, children's programs (ages 6 mos–6 yrs), laundry facilities, laundry service, public Internet, public Wi-Fi, airport shuttle, parking (fee), no-smoking rooms* ▤ *AE, D, DC, MC, V.*

$ ▦ **Ski Tip Lodge.** Opened as a stop along the stagecoach route back in the 1880s, this property was turned into the state's first ski lodge in the 1940s by skiing pioneers Max and Edna Dercum. The rooms in this charming log cabin have been given quaint names like Edna's Eyrie. Homespun furnishings and accessories, such as quilts and hand-knitted throw rugs, make each unit distinct. Some rooms have dramatic four-poster beds. In winter you can relax in the sitting room in front of a wood-burning fireplace. In summer retreat to the patio for a view of the surrounding mountains. A delicious breakfast is included in the room rate. **Pros:** good location for the price, rustic. **Cons:** small rooms, outdated bathrooms, hit-or-miss service. ⌂ *Keystone Resort, Box 38, Keystone 80435* ☎ *970/496–4500 or 877/753–9786* ✇ *www.keystoneresort.com* ⇱ *11 rooms, 2 suites* ⌂ *In-room: no a/c, no phone, no TV, Wi-Fi. In-hotel: restaurant, bar, no elevator, concierge, airport shuttle, parking (no fee), no-smoking rooms* ▤ *AE, D, DC, MC, V* ⊘*BP.*

CONDOS **Keystone Resort Corporation** (☎ *877/753–9786*) operates most of the lodgings at the resort, which range from hotel-style rooms at Keystone Lodge and the Inn at Keystone to a wide range of apartments. The condos are in Lakeside Village, River Run, and Ski Tip. Free shuttles ferry visitors to other parts of the resort.

NIGHTLIFE

Across from Mountain View Plaza, the **Goat Soup and Whiskey** (✉ *U.S. 6* ☎ *970/513–9344*) has two bars filled with twenty- and thirtysomethings drinking whiskey and beer. There's live music during ski season. Live music with rockabilly leanings makes the **Snake River Saloon** (✉ *23074 U.S. 6* ☎ *970/468–2788*) a good spot to stop for a beer. The fun-loving crowd is mostly under 35.

ARAPAHOE BASIN

6 mi northeast of Keystone via U.S. 6.

Arapahoe Basin was the first ski area to be built in Summit County. It has changed—but not a lot—since its construction in the 1940s, and most of A-Basin's dedicated skiers like it that way. It's America's highest ski area, with a base elevation of 10,780 feet and a summit of 13,050 feet. Many of the runs start above the timberline, ensuring breathtaking views (and the need for some extra breaths). Aficionados love the seemingly endless intermediate and expert terrain and the wide-open bowls that stay open into June (sometimes July). "Beachin' at the Basin" has long been one of the area's most popular summer activities. If you've got your heart set on slope-side accommodations or fine dining, look elsewhere: A-Basin has no rooms and serves only the most basic cafeteria food. You'll have to set up your base camp in nearby Keystone, Breckenridge, Frisco, or Dillon and shuttle in for the day.

DOWNHILL SKIING & SNOWBOARDING

What makes **Arapahoe Basin** delightful is also what makes it dreadful in bad weather: its elevation. Much of Arapahoe's skiing is above the tree line and when a storm moves in, you can't tell up from down.

If that sounds unpleasant, consider the other side of the coin: On sunny spring days, Arapahoe is a wonderful place because the tundra surrounded by craggy peaks is reminiscent of the Alps. Intermediate-level skiers can have a great time here on the easier trails. But A-Basin is best known for its expert challenges: the East Wall, a steep face with great powder-skiing possibilities; Pallavicini, a wide tree-lined run; and the West Wall, from which skiers of varying degrees of bravado like to launch themselves. After a long battle with the U.S. Forest Service, A-Basin won permission to install a snowmaking machine for certain trails. In 2006, the resort opened October 13, the earliest opening ever. ✆ *Box 5808, 80435* ☎ *970/468–0718 or 888/272–7246* ⊕ *www. arapahoebasin.com* ☉ *Late Oct.–mid-June or early July.*

FACILITIES 2,270-foot vertical drop; 900 skiable acres; 10% beginner, 40% intermediate, 25% advanced, 25% expert; 1 quad, 2 triple chairs, 3 double chairs, 1 carpet.

LESSONS & PROGRAMS Contact **Arapahoe Basin Central Reservations** (☎*970/468–0718*) for information on regular classes and ski clinics.

LIFT TICKETS $58, depending on the season. Multiday tickets can save you as much as 20%.

RENTALS Daily ski rental packages (skis, boots, and poles) start at $29, and snowboard packages at $35. Ski stores in Breckenridge, Dillon, and Frisco are even cheaper.

BRECKENRIDGE

22 mi southwest of Keystone via U.S. 6, I–70, and Rte. 9.

Breckenridge was founded in 1859, when gold was discovered in the surrounding hills. For the next several decades the town's fortunes rose and fell as its lodes of gold and silver were discovered and exhausted. Throughout the latter half of the 19th century and the early 20th century, Breckenridge was famous as a mining camp that "turned out more gold with less work than any camp in Colorado," according to the *Denver Post*. Dredging gold out of the rivers continued until World War II. Visitors today can still see evidence of the gold-dredging operations in the surrounding streams.

At 9,603 feet above sea level and surrounded by peaks that climb much higher, Breckenridge is the oldest continuously occupied town on the western slope. The town was originally dubbed Breckinridge, but the spelling was changed after its namesake, a former U.S. vice president, became a Confederate brigadier general in the Civil War. Due to an error by a cartographer, Breckenridge wasn't included on the official U.S. map until 1936, when the error was discovered by a member of the Breckenridge Women's Club.

Much of the town's architectural legacy from the mining era remains, so you'll find stores fit into authentic Victorian storefronts, restaurants, and bed-and-breakfasts tucked into Victorian homes. Surrounding the town's historic core, Breckenridge is packed with condos and hotels both in the woods and along the roads threading the mountainsides toward the base of the Peak 8.

Downtown Breckenridge has one of Colorado's largest historic districts, with about 250 buildings in the National Register of Historic Places. The district is roughly a compact 12 square blocks, bounded by Main, High, and Washington streets and Wellington Road. There are ★ some 171 buildings with points of historical interest. The **Breckenridge Historical Alliance** leads 90-minute walking tours past prominent structures, from simple log cabins to Victorians with lacy gingerbread trim, all lovingly restored. ⊠*203 S. Main St.* ☎*800/980–1859* ⊕*www. breckheritage.com* ☞*$5* ⊙*Year-round by appointment.*

Dating from 1875, the **Edwin Carter Museum** is dedicated to the "log cabin naturalist" who helped to create Denver's Museum of Nature and Science. Look for realistic stuffed animals, including a large buffalo and a burro carrying a miner's pack. ⊠*111 N. Ridge St.* ☎*800/980–1859* ⊕*www.breckheritage.com* ☞*Free* ⊙*Daily 11–4.*

A century ago the **Washington Gold Mine** was one of the area's largest producers of gold and silver. Five shafts burrowed deep underground. Tours include a visit to the mine and to a prospector's cabin. ⊠*469 Illinois Gulch Rd.* ☎*970/453–9022* ☞*$5* ⊙*June–mid-Sept., tours by appointment.*

At **Lomax Placer Gulch** you can learn how chemists determined the quality of the ore from nearby mines and discover the uses of tools such as sluices, riffles, and flumes. You can also pan for gold. ✉ *301 Ski Hill Rd.* ☎ *800/980–1859* 💲 *$8* ☉ *June–mid-Sept., tours by appointment.*

Since gold was discovered here in 1887, the **Country Boy Mine** has been one of the region's top producers. During tours of the facility you can belly up to the stove in the restored

WORD OF MOUTH

"Because it is closer to Denver, Breck will also have a lot of 'day-trippers' (skiers that come up from Denver on weekends), making the weekends and holidays much more crowded." —furledleader

blacksmith shop. The mine has hayrides in summer and romantic dinner sleigh rides in winter. ✉ *0542 French Gulch Rd.* ☎ *970/453–4405* ⊕ *www.countryboymine.com* 💲 *$18 for mine tours, $82 for dinner sleigh rides* ☉ *Days and hrs vary seasonally; call ahead.*

FESTIVALS   Festivals run rampant here, and it's rare to show up when locals aren't celebrating. Among the best festivals are the annual Chevy Truck U.S. Snowboard Grand Prix and the International Snow Sculpture championships in winter, the Spring Massive Festival in April, and Genuine Jazz in Breckenridge in June. Summer events include the Toast of Breckenridge food and wine festival; and the National Repertory Orchestra, which performs at the Riverwalk Center near the center of town.

DOWNHILL SKIING & SNOWBOARDING

With plenty of facilities for snowboarders, **Breckenridge** is popular with young people. There are several terrain parks and an area where you can learn to freeride. The resort's slopes are spread across four interconnected mountains in the Tenmile Range, named Peaks 7, 8, 9, and 10. The highest chairlift in North America—a high-speed quad lift on Peak 8 tops out at an air-gulping 12,840 feet. Peak 7 and Peak 8 have above-the-timberline bowls and chutes. The lower reaches of Peak 7 have some of the country's prettiest intermediate-level terrain accessible by a lift. Peak 8 and Peak 9 have trails for all skill levels. Peak 10 has long trails with roller-coaster runs.

Owing to the town's proud heritage, some runs are named for the old mines, including Bonanza, Cashier, Gold King, and Wellington. During one week each January the town declares itself an "independent kingdom" during the wild revel called Ullr Fest, which honors the Norse god of snow. ☎ *970/453–5000* ⊕ *www.breckenridge.com* ☉ *Nov.–Apr., daily 8:30–4.*

FACILITIES   4,337-foot vertical drop; 2,358 skiable acres; 14% beginner, 50% intermediate, 36% advanced; 29 lifts; 1 gondola, 2 high-speed six-person lifts, 7 high-speed quad chairs, 1 triple chair, 6 double chairs, 12 surface lifts.

LESSONS &   Contact the **Breckenridge Ski & Ride School** (☎ *888/576–2754*) for infor-
PROGRAMS   mation about lessons and specialty clinics. The Children's Ski and Ride School at Peak 8 has its own lift.

LIFT TICKETS   Few skiers and riders pay the mid-season walk-up rate of $86 for a one-day lift ticket. Breckenridge skiers use a variety of season passes sold by Vail Resorts, which owns Breckenridge, Beaver Creek, Keystone, and Vail. Most vacationers purchase lift and lodging packages, or buy advance multiday lift passes at discounted rates online.

RENTALS Rental packages (skis, boots, and poles; snowboards and boots) start at $30 per day. Prices vary, but not dramatically. If you can't find your brand of high-performance equipment in the first store you try, you're sure to find it elsewhere.

> **THAT'S NOT MY WIFE!**
>
> Lift lines dragging? Pull the local skip and hop in the singles line with your significant other. You might get lucky and ride together, or you might get even luckier and meet some new friends.

CHILD CARE Breckenridge has a variety of child-care programs. All-day classes or half-day classes for kids are available. Early drop-off is an option if you want to get to the slopes before everyone else. Classes meet at the Kids' Castle at Peak 8, and Beaver Run and the Village on Peak 9.

NORDIC SKIING

BACKCOUNTRY SKIING They don't call this place Summit County for nothing—mountain passes above 10,000 feet allow for relatively easy access to high-country terrain and some of the area's best snow. But remember this word of caution: Avalanche-related deaths are all too common in Summit County (more often involving snowmobilers than skiers). Don't judge an area solely on appearances, as slopes that look gentle may slide. Never head into the backcountry without checking weather conditions, without wearing appropriate clothing, or without carrying survival gear. For information on snow conditions and avalanche dangers, contact the **Dillon Ranger District Office of the White River National Forest** (☎970/468–5400).

One popular touring route is the trip to Boreas Pass, just south of Breckenridge. The 12-mi-long trail follows the route of a former railroad, with good views of distant peaks along the way. The **Summit County Huts Association** (✉Box 2830, Breckenridge 80424 ☎970/453–8583 ⊕www.summithuts.org) has four backcountry cabins where skiers can spend the night (two are open for summer hikers). If you're traveling farther afield, there are also cabins available through the **10th Mountain Division Hut Association** (☎970/925–5775 ⊕www.huts.org).

TRACK SKIING The **Breckenridge Nordic Center** (☎970/453–6855 ⊕www.breckenridge nordic.com) has 18.5 mi of groomed tracks for classic and skate skiing, as well as ungroomed trails in the Golden Horseshoe. There are also 6 mi of marked snowshoe trails.

OTHER SPORTS & THE OUTDOORS

Alpine Events (✉1516 Blue Ridge Rd. ☎970/262–0374) has a full range of summer and winter activities. In warm weather there are tours of the backcountry in all-terrain vehicles, cattle drives, and "saddle and paddle" days (combining horseback riding and rafting). In winter there's snowmobiling, dogsledding, and sleigh rides.

FISHING **Mountain Angler** (☎970/453–4665 or 800/453–4669 ⊕*www.moun-tainangler.com*) organizes fishing trips, including float trips on the Colorado River, half-day trips on streams near Breckenridge, and all-day trips on rivers farther away.

GOLF **Breckenridge Golf Club.** This is the world's only municipally owned course designed by Jack Nicklaus. You may play any combination of the three 9-hole sets: the Bear, the Beaver (with beaver ponds lining many of the fairways), or the Elk. The course resembles a nature reserve as it flows through mountainous terrain and fields full of wildflowers. ⊠*200 Clubhouse Dr.* ☎970/453–9104 ⊕*www.breckenridgegolfclub.com* ⅃27 *holes. Yards: 7,276/5,063. Par: 72/72. Green Fee: $53/$99.*

RAFTING **Breckenridge Whitewater Rafting** (⊠*842 N. Summit Blvd., Frisco* ☎800/370–0581 or 970/423–7031 ⊕*www.breckenridgewhitewater.* ☾ *com*) runs stretches of the Colorado, Arkansas, and Eagle rivers. The company also has guided fishing trips on the Colorado River and white-water rafting through Gore Canyon.

Performance Tours (☎800/328–7238 ⊕*www.performancetours.com*) leads expeditions on the Arkansas, Blue, and the upper Colorado rivers for newcomers looking for some action and experienced rafters ready for extremes. The company is based in Buena Vista, but will pick up groups in Breckenridge for all-day trips.

☾ **Whitewater Kayak Park** (⊠*880 Airport Rd.* ☎970/453–1734) is a play-ground for kayakers, with splash rocks, eddy pools, and S-curves. This public park on the Blue River behind the Breckenridge Recreation Department is free and open from April through August.

SNOW-MOBILING **Good Times Adventures** (⊠*6061 Tiger Rd.* ☎970/453–7604 or 800/477–0144 ⊕*www.snowmobilecolorado.com*) runs snowmobile trips on more than 40 mi of groomed trails, through open meadows, and along the Continental Divide to 11,585-foot-high Georgia Pass.

WHERE TO STAY & EAT

$$$ ✕**Café Alpine.** With stained-glass windows set high on white walls, this romantic restaurant is one of the prettiest in town. The menu, which changes daily, focuses on foods found in the region. Entrées include Asian-style seared jumbo sea scallops, Creole-seasoned tender-loin medallions, and grilled ruby-red trout. At the tapas bar (after 5 PM) you can sample specialties like coriander-and black-pepper–crusted tuna sashimi, garlic herb Brie, and truffled white bean hummus. Café Alpine serves more than a dozen wines by the glass. ⊠*106 E. Adams Ave.* ☎970/453–8218 ⊟*AE, D, MC, V* ⊗*No lunch.*

$ ✕**Blue Moose.** Locals flock here for the hearty breakfasts of eggs, oat-meal, pancakes, and much more. At lunch, there are satisfying sand-wiches, burritos, pastas, or salads. Neither the food nor the decor is fancy, but a meal here will hit the spot. ⊠*540 S. Main St.* ☎970/453–4859 ⊟*MC, V* ⊗*No dinner.*

$ ✕**Downstairs at Eric's.** Loud, dark, and lots of fun for young partiers, this place is video-game central. Kids hang out in the arcade while their folks watch sports on the big-screen TVs. Pizzas are popular here—try them topped with veggies, seafood, or "garbage" (the management's colorful term for everything). The sandwiches are just as good. The Avalanche Burger is smothered with pizza sauce and mozzarella cheese, and the Philly Burger is topped with sautéed green peppers, onions, and melted Swiss cheese. ⊠*111 S. Main St.* ☎*970/453–1401* ▤*DC, MC, V.*

☺ $ ✕**Giampietro Pasta & Pizzeria.** The smell of freshly baked pizza will draw families to the door of this Italian eatery. Peek through the window and you'll see families gathered around tables covered with the ubiquitous red-checked tablecloths. There are lots of pastas on the menu, from classic baked ziti to tasty spaghetti with shrimp and pesto. Hungry diners gravitate toward the New York–style pizza with the works and the Sicilian-style deep-dish pizza. You can also build your own calzone or pizza from the huge list of ingredients. A take-out menu is available. ⊠*100 N. Main St.* ☎*970/453–3838* ▤*MC, V.*

$ ✕**Quandry Grille.** Overlooking pretty Maggie Pond, this barn-size place in Main Street Station serves classic Western cuisine. Grab a seat at one of the rough-hewn wooden tables and enjoy a burger made with a half pound of beef or buffalo meat, chicken breast, or even black beans. Other choices include burritos, bourbon chicken, and fresh White River trout. ⊠*505 S. Main St.* ☎*970/547–5969* ▤*AE, DC, MC, V.*

$$$$ ⊡**Main Street Station.** One of the newer properties in Breckenridge, Main Street Station is actually a complex of four buildings. Resort Quest manages Grand Central, East, and West, all of which have condos on the upper floors above retail outlets that sell everything from ski gear to fresh flowers. The fourth building is a members-only Hyatt Vacation Club. The units, which are furnished and decorated by their individual owners, range from studios to four bedrooms. There are plenty of amenities, including concierge grocery delivery, gas fireplaces, and stereo systems. Some rooms overlook Maggie Pond, a popular gathering spot in summer. The hustle and bustle of Main Street is just outside. **Pros:** spa next to the hotel, free underground parking, good location between the town and lifts. **Cons:** views vary greatly, so-so service. ⊠*505 S. Main St., 80424* ☎*970/453–4000 or 800/525–2258* ⊕*www.resortquestbreckenridge.com* ↩*32 rooms* ⚘*In-room: no a/c, kitchen (some), refrigerator (some), DVD (some), VCR (some), ethernet (some), Wi-Fi. In-hotel: room service, bar, pool, gym, concierge, laundry facilities, laundry service, airport shuttle, parking (no fee), no-smoking rooms* ▤*AE, MC, V.*

$$$$ ⊡**Mountain Thunder Lodge.** Rising above the trees, this lodge constructed from rough-hewn timber brings to mind old-fashioned ski lodges. But the property, which opened in 2003, has modern amenities such as Internet access and a state-of-the-art gym. The studio and one-, two-, and three-bedroom condos all have fully furnished kitchens, fireplaces, balconies, and snug living rooms where chairs are pulled up to rock fireplaces. The property is tucked into the woods on the road leading up to Peak 8, but it's less than a five-minute walk to Main Street. The lodge has shuttle service to the slopes for guests. **Pros:** clean, close to ski lifts. **Cons:** short walk to main street, no Wi-Fi. ⊠*50 Mountain Thunder Dr., 80424* ☎*888/989–1233* ⊕*www.mtnthunderlodge.com*

~88 *rooms* � *In-room: no a/c, kitchen (some), refrigerator (some), DVD (some), ethernet. In-hotel: pool, gym, spa, concierge, laundry facilities, laundry service, public Internet, airport shuttle, parking (fee and no fee), no-smoking rooms* ☰AE, D, DC, MC, V.

$$ 🏨**Allaire Timbers Inn.** Nestled in a wooded area, this stone-and-timber log cabin has a living room dominated by a stone fireplace, as well as a reading loft and a sunroom with a green slate floor and handcrafted log furniture. The main deck has a hot tub and spectacular views of the Tenmile Range. The cozy rooms look rustic, with wood furniture and beds piled with handmade duvets. Two larger rooms (not quite accurately called suites) have king-size four-poster beds, two-person hot tubs, and river-rock fireplaces. A hearty breakfast is included, as are afternoon sweets and hot drinks. It's a 10-minute walk to Main Street. **Pros:** great mountain views, friendly owners, tasty homemade breakfast. **Cons:** downstairs rooms can be noisy, no elevator. ✉*9511 S. Main St., 80424* ☎*970/453–7530 or 800/624–4904* ⊕*www.allairetimbers. com* ~*8 rooms, 2 suites* � *In-room: no a/c, Wi-Fi. In-hotel: no elevator, public Wi-Fi, parking (no fee), no-smoking rooms* ☰AE, D, MC, V ⎟O⎟BP.

★ **$$** 🏨**Barn on the River Bed and Breakfast.** Innkeepers Fred Kinat and Diane Jaynes run this modern, timber-frame B&B. The five country-style bedrooms have fireplaces and private decks or patios overlooking the willow-lined river and the mountains. Rooms are loaded with antiques, and one has extra-long beds. **Pros:** all rooms are within earshot of the river, gas fireplaces, friendly owners. **Cons:** rooms fill fast, reservations are essential. ✉*303B N. Main St., 80424* ☎*970/453–5258* ⊕*www. breckenridge-inn.com* ~*5 rooms* � *In-room: no a/c, Wi-Fi. In-hotel: no elevator, parking (no fee), no-smoking rooms* ☰AE, D, DC, MC, V ⎟O⎟BP.

$$ 🏨**Lodge & Spa at Breckenridge.** Although it has the disadvantage of
Fodor's Choice being on a mountainside beyond the downtown area, this lodge more
★ than compensates with breathtaking views of the Tenmile Range from nearly every angle. There's regular shuttle service to the town and the ski area. The place resembles a cozy chalet. Well-lighted spacious rooms are comfortable with feather duvets and pillows. Upgrade to a suite and you'll also have a fireplace and a kitchenette. The full-service spa and health club is a great place to relax after a morning of skiing. **Pros:** great mountain views, fresh cookies and brownies in the lobby, Aveda bathroom products. **Cons:** young, sometimes disinterested staff; no room service; slack maintenance. ✉*112 Overlook Dr., 80424* ☎*970/453–9300 or 800/736–1607* ⊕*www.thelodgeatbreck. com* ~*45 rooms, 1 house* � *In-room: no a/c, kitchen (some), refrigerator (some), Wi-Fi. In-hotel: restaurant, bar, pool, gym, spa, parking (no fee), some pets allowed, no-smoking rooms* ☰AE, D, DC, MC, V ⎟O⎟CP.

$ 🏨**Great Divide Lodge.** Close to the ski areas and dozens of shops and restaurants, this lodge is in the middle of it all. Planned as a condominium, the complex has enormous studio and one-bedroom apartments, all of which have sophisticated Southwestern style. There are thoughtful touches, such as plush robes in the baths and gourmet coffee for the coffeemakers. The one surprising omission is air-conditioning. **Pros:** close to Peak 9 lift, one block off main street, free Wi-Fi. **Cons:** disinterested service, needs refurbishing. ⊠*550 Village Rd., 80424* ☎*970/547–5725 or 888/906–5698* ⊕*www.greatdividelodge.com* ⤳*208 rooms* ⅄*In-room: no a/c, refrigerator (some), Wi-Fi. In-hotel: restaurant, room service, bar, pool, gym, spa, concierge, laundry service, public Internet, public Wi-Fi, airport shuttle, parking (fee and no fee), some pets allowed, no-smoking rooms* ▭*AE, D, DC, MC, V.*

$ ⚏ **Village at Breckenridge.** The word "village" puts it mildly, as this sprawling resort is spread over 14 acres of mountainous terrain. Accommodations range from lodge-style rooms to three-bedroom condos, and from Southwestern chic to gleaming chrome-and-glass units. All rooms are ski-in ski-out. Studios and efficiencies all have kitchenettes. **Pros:** great concierge, ski-in and ski-out. **Cons:** some rooms have better decor than others, no on-site restaurant. ⊠*535 S. Park Ave., 80424* ☎*970/453–2000 or 800/800–7829* ⊕*www.breckresorts.com* ⤳*295 rooms* ⅄*In-room: no a/c, kitchen (some), refrigerator (some), DVD (some), VCR (some), Wi-Fi. In-hotel: bar, pool, gym, spa, concierge, laundry facilities, laundry service, public Wi-Fi, airport shuttle, parking (fee and no fee), some pets allowed, no-smoking rooms* ▭*AE, D, DC, MC, V.*

CONDOS Several companies handle condominiums in the area. **Breckenridge Central Lodging** (☎*970/453–2160 or 800/858–5885* ⊕*www.skibcl.com*) has more than 60 condo complexes in and around Breckenridge. **Resort Quest** (☎*800/525–2258* ⊕*www.resortquest.com*) manages Main Street Station and other complexes.

NIGHTLIFE

Breckenridge attracts an international clientele. The town has long been popular with a young, lively crowd that stays out until early morning.

BARS & LOUNGES **Breckenridge Brewery** (⊠*600 S. Main St.* ☎*970/453–1550*) serves eight microbrews, from Avalanche Amber Ale to Oatmeal Stout. It's a great après-ski spot. On the lower level of La Cima Mall, **Cecilia's** (⊠*520 S. Main St.* ☎*970/453–2243*) is a lounge with mouthwatering martinis. Smokers head to the cigar patio. **Downstairs at Eric's** (⊠*111 S. Main St.* ☎*970/453–1401*) is standing room only when there's a game. There are 4 big-screen TVs and 34 smaller ones scattered around the bar, so you don't have to worry about missing a touchdown. More than 120 brands of bottled beers (another 21 on tap) make this a favorite of aficionados. With maroon velour wallpaper and lacy curtains, **Hearthstone** (⊠*130 S. Ridge St.* ☎*970/453–1148*) hints at its roots as a bordello. Skiers and locals scarf down the happy-hour specials, including jalapeño-stuffed shrimp.

MUSIC CLUBS **Base 9 Bar** (⊠*620 Village Rd.* ☎*970/453–6000 Ext. 8754*) is a lively après-ski destination with two pool tables, three high-definition TVs and a martini bar.

SHOPPING

Main Street, stretching the entire length of Breckenridge, has an abundance of shopping. There's everything from T-shirt shacks to high-end boutiques to art galleries. It's a good idea to spend an evening window-shopping before breaking out your wallet.

In a quaint Victorian house, the **Bay Street Company** (⊠*232 S. Main St.* ☎*970/453–6303*) carries colorful hand-painted furniture and collectibles. At **Images of Nature** (⊠*505 S. Main St.* ☎*970/547–2711*), the walls are covered with outstanding photographs by Thomas D. Mangelsen, who documents the great outdoors. Western paintings, Navajo weavings, and cowboy memorabilia are on display at the **Paint Horse Gallery** (⊠*104 Towne Square Mall, 100 N. Main St.* ☎*970/453–6813*).

FRISCO

9 mi north of Breckenridge via Rte. 9.

Keep going past the hodgepodge of strip malls near the interstate and you'll find that low-key Frisco has a downtown district trimmed with restored B&Bs. The town is a low-cost lodging alternative to pricier resorts in the surrounding communities.

Frisco Historic Park re-creates the boom days. Stroll through 10 buildings dating from the 1880s, including a fully outfitted one-room schoolhouse, a trapper's cabin with snowshoes and pelts, the town's original log chapel, and a jail with exhibits on mining and skiing. ⊠*Main and 2nd Sts.* ☎*970/668–3428* ⊠*Free* ☉*Tues.–Sun. 10–5.*

FISHING **Blue River Anglers** (⊠*209 N. Main St.* ☎*888/453–9171* ⊕*www.blueriver anglers.com*) runs fly-fishing tours on the Blue, South Platte, and Williams Fork rivers, as well as various lakes and streams in the area. You can expect to catch 18- to 20-inch rainbow and brown trout.

WHERE TO STAY & EAT

★ $$$ ✗**Silverheels at the Ore House.** At this longtime favorite, you can join the locals who gather around the bar for margaritas and appetizers from 11 AM to 11 PM. The selection of tapas varies with the season, but may include such *bocadillos* (sandwiches) as seared ahi tuna with ginger, and Brie with sweet chili relish. Entrées range from a south-of-the-border combo that includes enchiladas and chiles rellenos to paella made with hot sausage. ⊠*603 Main St.* ☎*970/668–0345* ▱*AE, MC, V.*

★ $ ✗**Fiesta Jalisco.** With a sunny deck overlooking Tenmile Creek, this casual eatery serves great margaritas and south-of-the-border specialties such as blackened fish tacos. The Taos tacos with cheese, pinto beans, and roasted vegetables are especially tasty. ⊠*450 W. Main St.* ☎*970/668–5043* ▱*AE, DC, MC, V.*

¢ ✗**Log Cabin Café.** The is the best breakfast spot in Frisco, and arguably in the county. Basics such as eggs and bacon are most popular, but you can also chow down on biscuits and gravy with hash browns or *huevos rancheros* (Mexican-style scrambled eggs) with green chile. Amazingly, you can also get heart-healthy selections. Photographs depicting historic Frisco hang on the walls. ✉ *121 Main St.* ☎ *970/668–3947* ☐ *MC, V* ⊘ *No dinner.*

★ **$$$$** 🏨 **Hotel Frisco.** This Main Street hostelry is a great home base for skiers wanting to hit Breckenridge, Copper, Keystone, and Arapahoe Basin. After a long day of skiing you can relax in front of the two-story riverstone fireplace, complete with trophy bull moose mount, or warm up in the outdoor hot tub. Owners Mark and Mary Waldman are gracious with advice about the best hiking trails and least-crowded ski runs. The hotel mascot, a yellow lab named Hannah, is equally friendly. You can rent her out for a walking fee of one dog biscuit per hour. The rooms are done in pastel colors with wood accents, and the bedding is plush—down comforters and 300-thread-count sheets. One room has a private hot tub, another has a fireplace. During high season, the free parking lot behind the hotel is a godsend. **Pros:** centrally located, friendly owners, rent-a-dog service. **Con:** small bathrooms. ✉ *308 Main St., 80443* ☎ *970/668–5009 or 800/262–1002* ⊕ *www.hotelfrisco.com* ⟿ *11 rooms, 2 suites* ⚏ *In-room: no a/c, kitchen (some), refrigerator (some), DVD (some), Wi-Fi. In-hotel: no elevator, public Wi-Fi, parking (no fee), some pets allowed, no-smoking rooms* ☐ *AE, MC, V.*

$$$ 🏨 **Woods Inn.** The rooms are as distinctive as their names in this cedar-frame house one block from Frisco's Main Street. The Columbine is a nod to romance with a canopied queen bed and private kitchenette, while the Arboretum, within earshot of a nearby waterfall, is lush with potted and hanging plants. Alpine fans will enjoy the Winterhausen Room with its queen-size four-poster bed and electric fireplace. Best of all, the outdoor hot tub bubbles 24 hours a day. The breakfast buffet is hearty and inexpensive. **Pros:** natural setting, outdoor hot tub. **Cons:** could be cleaner, needs maintenance. ✉ *205 S. 2nd Ave., 80443* ☎ *970/668–2255 or 877/664–3777* ⊕ *www.woodsinn.biz* ⟿ *12 rooms* ⚏ *In-room: no a/c, no phone, kitchen (some), refrigerator (some), DVD (some) Wi-Fi. In-hotel: no elevator, laundry facilities, parking (no fee), some pets allowed, no-smoking rooms* ☐ *AE, MC, V.*

$$ 🏨 **Frisco Lodge.** In 1885 this was a stagecoach stop. Today it has morphed into a European-style boutique hotel complete with a chalet façade and a garden courtyard. The rooms are cozy, dressed with Victorian wallpaper and trimmed in dark woods. Antique lamps cast a warm glow on the wrought-iron beds draped with beautiful quilts. A delicious buffet breakfast of eggs, sausage, fruit, fresh breads, and Belgian waffles is included. **Pros:** great location on Main Street, outdoor hot tub and fireplace, courtyard garden. **Cons:** street noise audible, thin walls. ✉ *321 Main St., 80443* ☎ *970/668–0195 or 800/279–6000* ⊕ *www.friscolodge.com* ⟿ *19 rooms, 13 with bath* ⚏ *In-room: no a/c, VCR, dial-up. In-hotel: some pets allowed, no-smoking rooms* ☐ *AE, MC, V* ⦿ *BP.*

CONDOS **Summit Mountain Rentals** (⌖ *308 Main St., 80443* ☎ *970/668–5009 or 800/262–1002* ⊕ *www.summitmountainrentals.com*), run by the owners of the Hotel Frisco, has a collection of medium and high-end condos throughout Summit County.

NIGHTLIFE

Boisterous **Backcountry Brewery** (⊠ *Main St. between 2nd and 3rd* ☏ *970/668–2337*) is home to Great American Beer Festival gold medal–winner Telemark IPA and other homemade brews. The **Moose Jaw** (⊠ *208 Main St.* ☏ *970/668–3931*) is a locals' hangout. Pool tables beckon, and a plethora of old-time photographs, trophies, and newspaper articles makes the barn-wood walls all but invisible.

SHOPPING

Odds and ends fill the **Junk-Tique Inc.** (⊠ *313 Main St.* ☏ *970/668– 3040*). Don't miss the 1881 narrow-gauge mail car on display.

3

COPPER MOUNTAIN

7 mi south of Frisco via I-70.

Skiers who haven't driven past Copper Mountain within the last few years won't recognize the resort. Once little more than a series of strip malls strung along the highway, Copper Mountain is now thriving. The resort's heart is a pedestrian-only village, anchored by Burning Stones Plaza, which is prime people-watching turf. High-speed ski lifts march up the mountain on one side of the plaza, and the other three sides are flanked by condominiums with retail shops and restaurants on the ground floors. Lodgings extend westward toward Union Creek and eastward to Copper Station, where a six-pack high-speed lift ferries skiers uphill.

In winter Burning Stones is filled with skiers on their way to and from the slopes and shoppers browsing for gifts to give to those left at home. In summer people relax on condo balconies or restaurant patios as they listen to free concerts on the plaza or watch athletes inch up the 37-foot-high climbing wall. Kids can also learn to kayak or float in paddleboats.

DOWNHILL SKIING & SNOWBOARDING

Copper Mountain has been voted the "locals' favorite" in the *Summit Daily* Readers' Poll for five years running. The resort's 2,450 acres are spread across several peaks where the terrain is naturally separated into areas for beginners, intermediates, and expert skiers and snowboarders. The Union Creek area contains gentle, tree-lined trails for novices. The slopes above the Village at Copper and Copper Station are an invigorating blend of intermediate and advanced trails. Several steep mogul runs are clustered on the eastern side of the area, and have their own lift. At the top of the resort, and in the vast Copper Bowl, there's challenging above-tree-line skiing. Freeriders gravitate to the super pipe and the Catalyst Terrain Park. Weather permitting, several days each week beginning in mid-February, expert skiers can grab a free first-come, first-served snowcat ride up Tucker Mountain for an ungroomed, wilderness-style ski experience. ☏ *970/968–2882 or 800/458– 8386* ⊕ *www.coppercolorado.com* ⊗ *Nov.–mid-Apr., daily 9–4.*

CLOSE UP

Colorado's Fragile Wilderness

More than 1,500 peaks pierce the Colorado skyline, creating one of the most extensive and pristine alpine landscapes in the United States. It is a treeless landscape that has changed little in thousands of years; summer storms bury prehistoric glaciers, colorful wildflowers push up through snowy meadows, and ice-covered mountains fill 100-mi views.

But time is catching up with this ice-age wilderness. The very characteristics that once preserved the panoramic heights from human impact—rugged peaks, polar weather, barren vistas—are the same ones that today threaten it. Growing environmental pressures from recreational use, industrial pollution, and changing land-use patterns are taking a toll on this surprisingly fragile ecosystem.

Colorado's burgeoning population is increasing at an annual rate of 3%, a rate not seen since the gold-rush days of 1859. Many who move to the Mile High State enjoy an outdoor lifestyle that includes hiking. A popular pastime for many has been tackling the Fourteeners, the state's 54 peaks that top 14,000 feet. As more and more hikers trample up these mountains, they gouge new trails, compact thin soil, and crush root systems. This damage can take a surprisingly long time to heal. Trails across the tundra near Rocky Mountain National Park that were carved out by Ute and Arapaho scouts hundreds of years ago are still visible today.

Less subtle than erosion, and equally devastating, is the harm caused by industrial pollution. Western Slope power plants in Craig and Hayden burn low-sulfur coal. Scientists believe the resulting sulfur and nitrogen emissions may be creating acid snow in the alpine watersheds, the same watersheds that pour forth several of the great American rivers, including the Colorado, Rio Grande, and Arkansas.

Ironically one of the greatest threats to the alpine tundra comes from attempts at preserving native wildlife. With wolves and grizzlies extinct in Colorado and hunting banned in Rocky Mountain National Park, the elk population has exploded from a handful of over-hunted animals to more than 2,500. Their sharp hooves trample summer pastures above the timberline and destroy many of the arctic willow stands that provide food and shelter for other wildlife, including the white-tailed ptarmigan.

Despite tales told to the tourists who admire its raw beauty in record numbers, Colorado's alpine wilderness is not the land that time forgot. In an amazing wilderness that has been around for more than 100 centuries, the clock is still ticking.

—Jad Davenport

FACILITIES   2,601-foot vertical drop; 2,450 skiable acres; 21% beginner, 25% intermediate, 36% advanced, 18% expert; 1 high-speed six-person chair, 4 high-speed quad chairs, 5 triple chairs, 5 double chairs, 4 surface lifts, 3 conveyor lifts.

LESSONS &   Copper Mountain's **Ski and Ride School** (☎ *970/968–2318*) has classes
PROGRAMS   for skiers and snowboarders, private lessons, men- and women-only
ↄ   groups, and special sessions such as Level Busters (to help you make a quantum leap in skills). Copper's Kids Sessions, divided into groups

based on age and skill level, are designed to both teach and entertain. There's also Kids' Night Out, popular among parents who want an evening without the children.

LIFT TICKETS Early-season window tickets (through mid-December) are $51 and then jump to $86 in high season. Few people, however, pay the walk-up rate. Vacationers usually purchase lift-and-lodging packages, which include discounted lift rates. Copper Mountain has last minute deals online at ⊕ *www.coppersavers.com.* Passes can save skiers and riders 20% or more. The best deal is Copper's four-pass program for $99 (with some blackout dates). If you want to short-circuit lift lines during busy times (like Christmas week and spring break, try the Bee Line Advantage—for $20 a day you can get on the lifts 15 minutes earlier in the morning and use a dedicated (and shorter) lift line. Ask about it when you book your hotel or condo; many properties offer this as a free bonus.

RENTALS Rental packages (skis, boots, and poles) start at $30 per day for sport ski packages and go as high as $45 per day for high-performance equipment. Snowboard rental packages (snowboard and boots) start at $42 for adults. Helmet rentals begin at $10.

CHILD CARE Copper Mountain Resort has ski-school options for older kids, and child care for youngsters. The smell of chocolate-chip cookies wafts from the Belly Button Bakery, day care for those two to four years old. Belly Button Babies accepts kids six weeks to two years old. Children's programs are based in the Mountain Plaza at Center Village.

OTHER SPORTS & THE OUTDOORS

BICYCLING Hundreds of miles of bike paths weave around the resort, leading up and down mountainsides and through high-country communities. In summer there are weekly group rides for early risers. **Gravitee** (⊠ *The Village at Copper* ☎*970/968–0171)* has all the gear you need for cycling in the area.

For serious cyclists, Olympic medalists Connie Carpenter and Davis Phinney of the **Carpenter/Phinney Bike Camps** (☎*303/442–2371* ⊕*www.bikecamp.com)* conduct private camps in Summit County. Camps focus on riding technique, training methods, and bicycle maintenance.

GOLF Copper Mountain has reasonably priced golf and lodging packages. You can also take a shuttle from the resort to the Raven Golf Club at Three Peaks, about 15 minutes away in Dillon.

Copper Creek Golf Club. Right at the resort is a par-70, 6,057-yard course designed by Pete and Perry Dye. The highest-elevation 18-hole golf course in North America, it flows up and down some of the ski trails at the base of the mountain and between condos and town homes in the resort's East Village. ⊠*104 Wheeler Pl.* ☎*970/968–3333* ⊕*www.coppercolorado.com* ⚐*Reservations recommended* ⚑*18 holes. Yards: 6,057 and down (depending on selected tees). Par: 70. Green Fee: $89/$55.*

WHERE TO STAY & EAT

$ ✗**Endo's Adrenaline Café.** Enjoy rock music as you climb atop one of the high bar stools at this high-energy establishment. Try a grilled turkey melt or a mountainous plate of nachos. This place is easy to find at the base of the American Eagle lift. ⊠*The Village at Copper* ☎*970/968–3070* ⊟*AE, MC, V.*

$ ✗**JJ's Rocky Mountain Tavern.** You have to love a tavern right at the base of a ski lift (the Super Bee) with a 52-foot-long bar and 10 draft beers on tap. And people do, which is why this loud little pub on the first floor of Copper Station always seems like it's shoulder-to-shoulder. Many hungry skiers have stopped in for a quick lunch of Buffalo quesadillas with chipotle sauce only to find themselves lingering over a dinner of homemade tomato fennel soup and wasabi pea–encrusted salmon. ⊠*102 Wheeler Circle* ☎*970/968–3062* ⊟*AE, D, DC, MC, V.*

☾ $$$ 🏨**Copper Mountain Resort.** The resort runs the majority of lodging in the area, ranging from standard hotel rooms to spacious condos and town homes. No matter where you stay, you have use of the beautiful Copper Mountain Racquet & Athletic Club. The Village at Copper is the center of activity, as it's close to most of the shops and restaurants. The complex has studios and one- to four-bedroom units, many with fireplaces and balconies. East Village is not as centrally located, but provides easier access to the mountain's more-challenging terrain. **Pros:** centrally located, wide range of accommodations. **Cons:** Village can be noisy, quality of rooms varies greatly. ⊠*209 Tenmile Circle, 80443* ☎*970/968–2882 or 800/458–8386* ⊕*www.coppercolorado. com* ⌨*800 rooms* ⌂*In-room: no a/c, safe (some), kitchen (some), refrigerator (some), DVD (some), VCR (some), ethernet (some), Wi-Fi (some). In-hotel: 16 restaurants, bars, golf course, tennis courts, pool, gym, children's programs (ages 2–4), airport shuttle, parking (no fee), some pets allowed, no-smoking rooms* ⊟*AE, D, DC, MC, V.*

NIGHTLIFE

Whether it's a warm afternoon in winter or a cool evening in summer, one of the best places to kick back is at one of the tables spreading across Burning Stones Plaza. At the base of the American Eagle lift, **Endo's Adrenaline Café** (⊠*The Village at Copper* ☎*970/968–3070*) is the place to be for après-ski cocktails. In the evenings there's live music and a raucous crowd. The East Village is home to **JJ's Rocky Mountain Tavern** (⊠*102 Wheeler Circle* ☎*970/968–3062*), the best place for a beer after a long day on the bumps. Musician Moe Dixon, a favorite with the locals, has people dancing on the tables when he covers everyone from John Denver to Jimmy Buffett Wednesday through Sunday during ski season. **Pravda** (⊠*The Village at Copper* ☎*970/968–2222*), a Russian-theme night spot, rocks all night long. Doormen are clad in KGB-style trench coats and fur hats, and bartenders aren't stingy with the vodka.

SHOPPING

Retail shops fill the ground floors of the Village at Copper, a pedestrians-only plaza.

Visit the **Copper Clothing Company** (✉ *The Village at Copper* ☎ *970/968–2318*) for a fleece pullover to keep you warm on the slopes, a baseball cap to shade your face, and beer mugs and other remembrances of your trip—all with Copper Mountain logos. Shop for ski and snowboard gear, book your ski lessons, and reserve rental equipment at **Mountain Adventure Center** (✉ *The Village at Copper* ☎ *970/968–2318*).

LEADVILLE

24 mi south of Copper Mountain via Rte. 91.

Sitting in the mountains at 10,430 feet, Leadville is America's highest incorporated city. The 70 square blocks of Victorian architecture and adjacent mining district hint at its past as a rich silver-mining boomtown. In the history of Colorado mining, perhaps no town looms larger. Two of the state's most fascinating figures lived here: mining magnate Horace Tabor and his second wife, Elizabeth Doe McCourt (nicknamed Baby Doe), the central figures in John LaTouche's Pulitzer prize–winning opera *The Ballad of Baby Doe.*

The larger than life Tabor amassed a fortune of $12 million, much of which he spent building monuments to himself and his ambitious mistress "Baby Doe." His power peaked when his money helped him secure a U.S. Senate seat in 1883. He married Baby Doe, after divorcing his first wife, the faithful Augusta. The Tabors incurred the scorn of high society by throwing their money around in what was considered a vulgar fashion. In 1893 the repeal of the Sherman Act caused the price of silver to plummet, and Tabor was penniless. He died a pauper in 1899, admonishing Baby to "hang on to the Matchless," his most famous mine, which he was convinced would restore her fortunes. It never did. Baby Doe became a recluse, rarely venturing forth from her tiny unheated cabin beside the mine entrance. She froze to death in 1935.

FESTIVALS Eccentricity is still a Leadville trait, as witnessed by the **International Pack Burro Race.** The annual event is part of **Leadville Boom Town Days** (⊕ *www.leadville.com/boomdays*), held the first weekend of August. The race takes man and beast over Mosquito Pass. The event is immortalized with thousands of T-shirts and bumper stickers that read, "Get Your Ass Over the Pass."

The three-story **Tabor Opera House** opened in 1879, when it was proclaimed the "largest and best west of the Mississippi." It hosted luminaries such as Harry Houdini, John Philip Sousa, and Oscar Wilde. Shows on the current schedule, like *Million Dollar Baby* and *A Portrait of Molly Brown*, revisit the rags-to-riches characters of the Colorado golden days. ✉ *308 Harrison St.* ☎ *719/486–8409* ⊕ *www.taboroperahouse.net* 💲 *$5* ☺ *Memorial Day–Labor Day, Mon.–Sat. 10–5.*

The **Matchless Mine** and Baby Doe's cabin are 1 mi east of downtown. Peer into the dark shaft, then pay a visit to the small museum with its tribute to the tragic love story of Horace and Baby Doe Tabor. ✉ *E.*

7th St. ☎*719/486–1229* ⊕*www.*
matchlessmine.com ✉*$7* ☉*Daily*
9–5.

☺ ★ The **National Mining Hall of Fame
and Museum** covers virtually every
aspect of mining, from the discovery of precious ore to fashioning it
into coins and other items. Dioramas in the beautiful brick building explain extraction processes.

✉*120 W. 9th St.* ☎*719/486–1229* ⊕*www.mininghalloffame.org*
✉*$7* ☉*Daily 9–5.*

On a tree-lined street in downtown Leadville you'll find the **Healy House
and Dexter Cabin,** an 1878 Greek Revival house and an 1879 log cabin—
two of Leadville's earliest residences. The lavishly decorated rooms of
the clapboard house yield clues as to how the town's upper crust, such
as the Tabors, lived and played. ✉*912 Harrison St.* ☎*719/486–0487*
✉*$5* ☉*Memorial Day–Labor Day, daily 10–4:30.*

The **Heritage Museum** paints a vivid portrait of life in Leadville at the
turn of the last century, with dioramas depicting life in the mines. There's
also furniture, clothing, and toys from the Victorian era. ✉*120 E. 9th St.*
☎*719/486–1878* ✉*$4* ☉*Memorial Day–late Oct., daily 10–4.*

☺ Still chugging along is the **Leadville, Colorado & Southern Railroad Company,** which can take you on a breathtaking trip to the Continental
Divide. The train leaves from Leadville's century-old depot and travels
beside the Arkansas River to its headwaters at Freemont Pass. The
return trip takes you down to French Gulch for views of Mount Elbert,
Colorado's highest peak. ✉*326 E. 7th St.* ☎*719/486–3936* ⊕*www.
leadville-train.com* ✉*$28.50* ☉*Memorial Day–early Oct., daily; call
for hrs.*

★ The massive, snowcapped peak watching over Leadville is **Mount Elbert.**
At 14,433 feet, it's not only the highest mountain in Colorado, but
the tallest peak in the entire Rocky Mountain Range, second in height
in the contiguous 48 states only to California's 14,495-foot Mount
Whitney.

DOWNHILL SKIING & SNOWBOARDING

☺ Located 9 mi west of Leadville, **Ski Cooper** is one of those undiscovered
boutique ski areas in the Rockies. It has 400 acres skiable via lift and
another 2,400 acres of backcountry powder accessible by snowcat.
The 26 groomed runs are perfect for beginning or intermediate skiers.
✉*Rte. 24* ☎*719/486–3684 or 800/707–6114* ⊕*www.skicooper.com*
☉*Late Nov.–early Apr., daily 9–4.*

FACILITIES   1,200-foot vertical drop; 400 skiable acres; 30% beginner, 40% more
difficult, 30% advanced; 5 lifts; 1 triple chair, 1 double chair, 3 surface lifts.

LESSONS &
PROGRAMS

The **Ski Cooper Ski School** (☎ *719/486–8114*) covers the gamut for skiers and snowboarders. A "Never Ever" two-hour lesson with full lift ticket and rental gear is $60, or you can join a two-hour group lesson for $45. You can also book private lessons, race and telemark clinics, and lessons for your children, which can be extended as part of the all-day child-care programs. Lessons for handicapped skiers are available by appointment.

Ski Cooper offers a number of options for children, including their popular Panda Patrol for children ages 5 to 11. A full-day package (from 10 AM to 3 PM) includes a group ski lesson, equipment rental, lunch, and full mountain lift ticket for $75. The Panda Cub program caters to four-year-olds and provides a two-hour lesson, lift ticket, and rental package for $47.

Chicago Ridge Snowcat Tours (☎ *719/486–2277*) are for expert backcountry skiers who want the off-piste adventure of scripting their signature across acres of untracked powder. Tickets are $275 but you'll get your fill of phat snow. The terrain has tree glades and open bowls. You must be over 18 (or be accompanied by an adult) and fit; the runs are up to 10,000 feet long and some vertical drops top 1,400 feet. Wide powder skis are available for rent for those who really want to float.

LIFT TICKETS

At $39 for a full-day lift ticket, you'll be hard-pressed to find cheaper powder. Vacationers should still shop around for discounted rates at King Soopers and Safeway stores.

RENTALS

Rental packages (skis, boots, and poles) start at $15 per day, among the cheapest in the state. Snowboarding packages start at $25. Performance packages and backcountry ski gear rentals are also available and start at $25.

OTHER SPORTS & THE OUTDOORS

CANOEING &
KAYAKING

There's no better way to see the high country than by exploring its lakes and streams. **Twin Lakes Canoe & Kayak** (⊠ *6451 State Hwy. 82, ✛about 20 mi south of Leadville* ☎ *719/251–9961*) supplies equipment to beginners who just want to stay cool and to experts wanting to run the rapids.

GOLF
★

Mt. Massive Golf Course. Play North America's highest 9-hole green at 9,680 feet—and watch your distance increase in the thin mountain air. Just west of Leadville in the Arkansas River valley, this public golf course was opened in the 1930s to the delight of the mining community. True green fairways replaced sagebrush flats after a $50,000 grant in the 1970s heralded an automated irrigation system. ⊠ *259 County Rd. 5* ☎ *719/486–2176* ⊕ *www.mtmassivegolf.com* ✍ *Reservations essential* ♣ *9 holes. Yards: 6,170. Par: 36. Green Fee: $20/$32.*

HORSEBACK
RIDING

If you're feeling like it's time to hit the trail, contact **George's Wild West Horseback Rides** (⊠ *225 Harrison Ave.* ☎ *719/486–0739*). Rides can be tailored to all skill levels. **Mega Mountain Magic** (⊠ *1100 County Rd. 18* ☎ *719/486–4570*) has a stable of horses ready for the trail.

SNOW-
MOBILING

Skiing extreme slopes isn't the only way to feel the blast of powder on your face. Fire up your own mechanical beast with **Alpine Snowmobiles** (⊠*4037 Hwy. 91* ☎*719/486–9899*). Snowmobiling fans often head to **2 Mile Hi Ski-Doo** (⊠*1719 Poplar* ☎*719/486–1183*).

WHERE TO STAY & EAT

☾ $ ✕**The Grill.** Run by the Martinez family since 1965, this locals' favorite draws a standing-room-only crowd. The service is sometimes slow, but that leaves time for another of the marvelous margaritas. Tex-Mex dishes are the specialty here, including the hand-roasted green chilies. In summer you can retreat to the patio to toss horseshoes. The restaurant is open for lunch on summer weekends only. ⊠*715 Elm St.* ☎*719/486–9930* ⚑*Reservations essential* ▤*AE, MC, V* ☾*No lunch except summer weekends.*

★ $$ ▦**Delaware Hotel.** This beautifully restored 1886 hotel is one of the best examples of high Victorian architecture in the area, so it's no surprise it's listed in the National Register of Historic Places. The columned lobby has brass fixtures, crystal chandeliers, and rich oak paneling. The comfortable rooms have graceful touches like lace curtains and antique heirloom quilts. **Pros:** loaded with gold-rush character, great mountain views, very friendly staff. **Cons:** lobby is like a crowded antiques store, the altitude in Leadville can be tough for guests arriving from sea level. ⊠*700 Harrison Ave., 80461* ☎*719/486–1418 or 800/748–2004* ᖴ*719/486–2214* ⊕*www.delawarehotel.com* ⇱*32 rooms, 4 suites* ⚘*In-room: no a/c. In-hotel: restaurant, bar, public Wi-Fi, parking (no fee), no-smoking rooms* ▤*AE, D, DC, MC, V* �ⓘⓞⓘ*CP.*

★ $ ▦**Ice Palace Inn Bed & Breakfast.** Rooms in this lovingly restored Victorian—some with jetted tubs for two—have period antiques and luxurious featherbeds. Innkeepers Sherry Randall and Marcie Stassi are just as inviting. A full breakfast is included in the room rate. Don't forget your slippers; no shoes are allowed on the inn's plush carpets. **Pros:** easy access to trailheads, gracious owners, romantic. **Cons:** short walk to the main street, adults only. ⊠*813 Spruce St., 80461* ☎*719/486–8272 or 800/754–2840* ⊕*www.icepalaceinn.com* ⇱*5 rooms* ⚘*In-hotel: no elevator, public Wi-Fi, no kids, no-smoking rooms* ▤*AE, D, DC, MC, V* ⓘⓞⓘ*BP.*

SUMMIT COUNTY ESSENTIALS

TRANSPORTATION

BY AIR

Denver International Airport (DEN) is the gateway to the attractions and ski resorts in Summit County. The airport is an hour's drive from the Continental Divide along I-70.

Information Denver International Airport (DEN) (☎*800/247-2336* ⊕*www. flydenver.com*).

TRANSFERS   To and from Summit County (Breckenridge, Copper Mountain, Dillon, Frisco, and Keystone), use Colorado Mountain Express and 453 Taxi, which have regular service to and from the Denver airport.

Contacts Colorado Mountain Express (☎ *970/949-4227 or 800/525-6353*). **453 Taxi** (☎ *970/453-8294*).

BY BUS OR SHUTTLE
Greyhound Lines serves Frisco.

All the resorts run free or inexpensive shuttles between the ski villages and the slopes. Summit Stage provides free public transportation to town and ski areas, in and between ski areas in Summit County.

Contacts Breckenridge Free Shuttle (☎ *970/547-3140*). **Greyhound Lines** (☎ *800/231-2222* ⊕ *www.greyhound.com*). **Keystone Resort Transportation** (☎ *970/468-4200*). **Summit Stage** (☎ *970/668-0999*).

BY CAR
The most convenient place for visitors to rent a car is at the Denver International Airport.

The hardest part about driving in the High Rockies is keeping your eyes on the road. A glacier carved canyon off to your left, a soaring mountain ridge to your right, and there, standing on the shoulder, a bull elk. Some of the most scenic routes aren't necessarily the most direct. The Eisenhower Tunnel sweeps thousands of cars daily beneath the mantle of the Continental Divide, whereas only several hundred drivers choose the slower, but spectacular, Loveland Pass. Some of the most beautiful byways, like the Mount Evans Scenic and Historic Drive, are one-way roads.

Although it severely overcrowded, I–70 is still the quickest and most direct route from Denver to Summit County. The interstate slices through the state, separating it into northern and southern halves. Breckenridge is south of I–70 on Route 9; Leadville and Ski Cooper are south of I–70 along U.S. 24 and Route 91.

Gasoline is readily available along I–70 and its arteries, but when venturing into more-remote areas be sure you have enough fuel to get there and back. Blinding snowstorms can appear out of nowhere on the high passes at any time of the year. Chains aren't normally required for passenger vehicles on highways, but it's a good idea to carry them in bad weather. A shovel isn't a bad idea, either. Keep your eyes peeled for wildlife, especially along the stretch of I–70 from Idaho Springs to the Eisenhower Tunnel. Large herds of bighorn sheep frequently graze along the north side of the highway.

Information Colorado Road Condition Hotline (☎ *303/639–1111 near Denver, 303/639–1234 statewide* ⊕ *www.cotrip.org*). **Colorado State Patrol** (☎ *303/239–4500* ⊕ *www.csp.state.co.us*).

CONTACTS & RESOURCES

EMERGENCIES
Ambulance or Police (☎ *911*).

24-Hour Medical Care Summit Medical Center (✉ *340 Peak One Dr., Rte. 9 and School Rd., Frisco* ☎ *970/668-3300*).

TOURS
The Breckenridge Heritage Alliance leads lively 90-minute tours of downtown Breckenridge, Colorado's largest National Historic District; the schedule varies seasonally.

Contact Breckenridge Heritage Alliance (☎ *800/980-1859* ⊕ *www.breck heritage.com*).

VISITOR INFORMATION
If you're ready to take to the slopes, the first thing you will need to know is whether there is plenty of snow. Each resort has its own hotline with the latest on weather conditions.

Snow Reports Arapahoe Basin (☎ *970/468-0718*). **Breckenridge** (☎ *970/496-4111 or 800/934-2485*). **Copper Mountain** (☎ *970/968-2100*). **Keystone** (☎ *970/496-4111 or 800/934-2485*).

Contacts Arapahoe Basin Ski Area (✎ *Box 5808, Dillon 80435* ☎ *970/468-0718 or 888/272-7246* ⊕ *www.arapahoebasin.com*). **Breckenridge Resort Chamber** (✉ *311 S. Ridge St., Breckenridge 80424* ☎ *970/453-2913* ⊕ *www.gobreck.com*). **Copper Mountain Resort** (✎ *Box 3001, Copper Mountain 80443* ☎ *970/968-2882 or 800/458-8386* ⊕ *www.coppercolorado.com*). **Keystone Resort** (✎ *Box 38, Keystone 80435* ☎ *970/468-2316* ⊕ *www.keystoneresort.com*). **Leadville Chamber of Commerce** (✉ *809 Harrison St., Leadville 80461* ☎ *719/486-3900* ⊕ *www. leadvilleusa.com*). **Summit Information Center** (✎ *246 Rainbow Dr., Silverthorne 80498* ☎ *800/530-3099* ⊕ *www.summitchamber.org*).

Vail Valley

WORD OF MOUTH

"Vail local responding here: You could ski Vail all week and never sky the same run twice. Why go anywhere else? But if you MUST you can take the bus over to Beaver Creek (10 minutes away) or since Vail Resorts also owns Breckenridge and Keystone, your pass is good there and there is a shuttle (about 40 minutes). For those small, fun restaurants, most locals eat in Edwards (15 miles west of Vail)—Fiesta's for Mexican can't be beat. Lots more to choose from. Vail is famous for its fabulous dining."

—localgal

Revised &
Updated by
Jad Davenport

IF ASPEN IS COLORADO'S HOLLYWOOD East, then her rival Vail is Wall Street West. So popular is this ski resort with the monied East Coast crowd that locals sometimes refer to particularly crowded weeks as "212" weeks, in reference to the area code of their visitors.

The attraction for vacationers from all over is the thin, aspen-cloaked Vail Valley, a narrow corridor slit by Interstate 70 and bounded by the rugged Gore Range to the north and the tabled Sawatch escarpments to the south. Through it all runs the sparkling Eagle River.

The resorts begin just west of Vail Pass, a saddle well below tree line, and stretch 20 mi through the communities of Vail Village, Eagle-Vail, Minturn, Avon, Beaver Creek, Arrowhead, and Edwards. The hub of activity in winter and summer revolves around Vail Village, but many vacationers will spend time dining, skiing, and shopping in the other towns. The vibe in these places varies dramatically, from Beaver Creek, a gated community of second (and probably third) megahomes; to Edwards, a rapidly growing worker town; to Vail Village, filled with styles of lodging, dining, and shopping appealing to a wide range of tastes.

In winter, this region is famous for the glittering resorts of Vail and Beaver Creek. Between these two areas, skiers and snowboarders have almost 7,000 acres at their disposal including the unforgettable Back Bowls far beyond the noise of I–70 traffic.

In summer, these resorts are great bases from which you can explore the high country by foot, horseback, raft, or bike. But take heed: all trails go up. Some trails are designated for bikers, others for hikers, and many for both. Always remember that bikers should yield to hikers, though in practice it's considered courteous to let them blow by. In addition, there are hundreds of miles of trails weaving through the White River National Forest. Warm-weather weekends are filled with an exciting range of cultural events, including performances by groups such as the New York Philharmonic and the Bolshoi Ballet.

EXPLORING THE VAIL VALLEY

Finding your way around the Vail Valley is relatively easy; the valley runs east and west, and everything you need is less than a mile or two off the I–70 corridor (and the constant drone of traffic), which parallels the Eagle River. The Gore Range to the north is one of the most rugged wilderness areas in Colorado—the peaks are jagged and broken, and any hiking here immediately involves a steep and sustained climb. To the south the tabled heights of the Sawatch Mountain are gentler and give Vail her superb skiing, particularly in the famed Back Bowls. Beaver Creek feels more isolated, being set off the highway behind a series of gates that control access to the posh communities within.

ABOUT THE PARKS & RECREATION AREAS
The Vail Valley has two wilderness areas in close proximity—the truly untrampled Eagle's Nest Wilderness Area to the northeast in the Gore Range, and the more-popular Holy Cross Wilderness to the southwest.

TOP REASONS TO GO

The Slopes: Despite the somewhat corny faux-Tyrolean ambience of the village, Vail has as real and challenging a ski mountain as you will find anywhere in the western United States, with the steeps and back bowls to prove it.

Romantic Meals: The art of romantic dining has been perfected here. Both Vail and Beaver Creek have a number of intimate restaurants hidden away among the peaks reachable by ski, on horseback, and even by horse-drawn sleighs (van shuttles are also available).

Rugged Scenery: If you're expecting the Alps—sheer, glacier-scraped peaks—you might be disappointed with much of Colorado's High Country, which tends toward rounded summits and eroded ridges. But not in the Vail Valley. The Gore Range to the north sports some of the most rugged and sharp-spined backcountry in the state with ice-cold tarns and sheer cliffs. Not surprisingly, shaggy white mountain goats are frequently seen here.

Golfing: The thin air at this altitude lets your Titleist fly much farther than in the denser air at sea level. And you'll have plenty of venues—more than a dozen—to play on, so enjoy those hero swings.

Festivals: If hiking the steeps in summer doesn't appeal to you, check out some of Vail's many cultural activities—summer is full of music and dance festivals.

The land in between, including much of the ski resorts' slopes, is part of the **White River National Forest** (☎970/945–3255 ⊕ *www.fs.fed.us/r2/ whiteriver*). The Eagle River, whose headwaters are on the north side of Tennessee Pass, is an excellent fishing stream, mostly for brook and brown trout in the 6- to 12-inch range. Public access is easiest upriver of Red Cliff on Forest Service land. There's some superb rafting in Gore Canyon on the Colorado River west of Vail, particularly in spring when the river is boiling with snow runoff.

ABOUT THE RESTAURANTS

Unlike the nearby Summit County ski resorts, which pride themselves on standard "mining fare" like surf and turf, Vail offers a distinctly European dining experience. This is the town in which to sample creamed pheasant soup or bite into a good cut of venison.

ABOUT THE HOTELS

Vail and Beaver Creek are purpose-built resorts, so you won't find any quaint historic Victorians converted into bed-and-breakfasts here like you will in Breckenridge and Aspen. Instead, Vail lodgings come in three flavors—European chalets that blend with the Bavarian architecture, posh chain resorts tucked up side canyons, and loads of small but serviceable condominiums perfect for families.

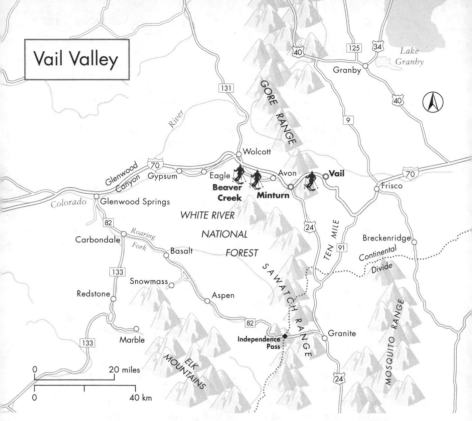

Vail Valley

	¢	$	$$	$$$	$$$$
WHAT IT COSTS					
RESTAURANTS	under $8	$8–$12	$13–$18	$19–$25	over $25
HOTELS	under $80	$80–$120	$121–$170	$171–$230	over $230

Restaurant prices are for a main course at dinner, excluding 4.4%–8.4% tax. Hotel prices are for two people in a standard double room in high season, excluding service charges and 5.4%–9.8% tax.

TIMING

Winter is by far the most crowded time in Vail, with the early spring seeing the highest number of visitors hoping to catch that blissful blend of thick powder and china-blue skies. Naturally, prices are highest then as well. Although summer is quickly gaining in popularity, the real deals can be had in the mud seasons—late autumn and late spring when the ski slopes are closed. Restaurants will often offer two-for-one entrées with a bottle of wine, and hotels run deeply cut rates. Traffic through the I–70 corridor moves at a good clip unless snows have stacked up truckers putting on chains on either side of Vail Pass. The pass itself is low, and stays below tree line, affording it some protection from drifting and blowing snow.

VAIL

100 mi west of Denver via I–70.

Consistently ranked as one of North America's leading ski destinations, Vail has a reputation few can match. The four-letter word means Valhalla for skiers of all skill levels. Vail has plenty of open areas where novices can learn the ropes. It can also be an ego-building mountain for intermediate and advanced skiers who hit the slopes only a week or two a season. Some areas, like Blue Sky Basin, make you feel like a pro.

Vail is one of the least likely success stories in skiing. Seen from the village, the mountain doesn't look at all imposing. There are no glowering glaciers, no couloirs, and no chutes slashed from the rock. Even local historians admit that the Gore Creek valley in which Vail sits was an impoverished backwater, too isolated to play a prominent or colorful role in Colorado history, until the resort opened its gates in 1962.

In truth, the men who lent their names to the valley and resort deserve more notoriety than notice. Sir St. George Gore was a wealthy, swaggering, drunken lout of a baronet who went on a three-year bacchanal in the 1850s and butchered every herd of elk and buffalo in sight. Charles Vail, the otherwise obscure chief engineer of the Colorado Highway Department from 1930 to 1945 was—according to townspeople who dealt with him—an ornery cuss who was rumored to accept kickbacks from contractors.

Then two visionaries appeared on the scene: Pete Seibert, a veteran of the 10th Mountain Division that prepared for alpine warfare in the surrounding Gore and Sawatch ranges during World War II, and Earl Eaton, a uranium prospector who had grown up in and surveyed these ranges. In 1957 they ascended the mountain now known as Vail, and upon attaining the summit discovered what skiers and riders salivate over: the Back Bowls, more than 3,000 acres of open glades formed when the Ute Indians set "spite fires" to the timberland in retaliation for being driven out by ranchers and miners. After five years of bureaucratic red tape and near financial suicide, Seibert's dream became reality, and the resort known as Vail was created.

Vail wasn't much to look at in the early years—at the base of the mountain there were a handful of buildings vaguely resembling a Bavarian hamlet. Today's visitors only get a sense of that ambience in the heart of the village, now surrounded by condo complexes, hotels, and upscale homes in a large village that sprawls for miles along both sides of I–70 and climbs up the sides of the mountains. It's informally sectioned into residential East Vail, upscale Vail Village, and more-modest and utilitarian Lionshead.

The 1990s were an era of consolidation in the ski industry, and many of the major resorts were snapped up by companies that were, or shortly became, publicly traded. In 1996, in a move that surprised the ski industry, Vail purchased Breckenridge and Keystone resorts, then began selling stock as Vail Resorts. Since then, the company has purchased Heavenly in California, Snake River Lodge & Spa in Wyoming, and lodges at several other resorts. Among the positive aspects of this consolidation was the creation of flexible passes allowing skiers to use the lifts on nearly all the company's properties.

Vail, along with most savvy ski resorts, actively courts families through special packages, classes for youngsters, and activities geared to people of all ages. At Vail, kids can play in specially designed ski parks like Chaos Canyon and Fort Whippersnapper. After a day on the slopes, the whole family can get in on the action at Adventure Ridge, where activities range from snowmobile rides to laser tag.

In terms of size, Vail overwhelms nearly every other ski area in North America. There are 5,289 acres popular with skiers and riders of all skill levels. Areas are clearly linked by a well-placed network of lifts and trails. The Front Side is draped with long trails; the infamous Back Bowls beckon powder skiers. A few hours of adventure skiing in Blue Sky Basin is a must for intermediate to advanced skiers and riders.

When the snows melt and two-for-one dinners are advertised in restaurant windows, you can be sure of two things—Vail is in the heart of the mud season, and the tranquillity won't last long. With the blooming of summer columbines come the culture crowds for music festivals and self-enrichment in writing workshops and health-food seminars. While the valley teems with visitors, hikers and mountain bikers stream up the steep slopes, on foot and via ski lifts, to head into the network of trails that web the seemingly endless backcountry.

★ Vail is only a few decades old, so there aren't many sights. But there are two places worth a visit. The **Betty Ford Alpine Gardens,** open daily from snowmelt (around Memorial Day) to snowfall (Labor Day or a bit later), are an oasis of forsythia, heather, and wild roses. These are the highest public botanical gardens in North America. ⊠ *Ford Park* ☎ *970/476–0103* ⊕ *www.bettyfordalpinegardens.org* ⊠ *Free* ◷ *May– Sept., daily dawn–dusk.*

The **Colorado Ski Museum/Ski Hall of Fame** traces the development of the sport throughout the world, with an emphasis on Colorado's contributions. On display are century-old skis and tows, early ski fashions, and an entire room devoted to the 10th Mountain Division, an Army division that trained nearby. ⊠ *231 S. Frontage Rd.* ☎ *970/476–1876* ⊕ *www.skimuseum.net* ⊠ *$1* ◷ *Tues.–Sun. 10–5.*

FESTIVALS   Vail Village hosts a wide variety of festivals, starting with the Teva Mountain Games, showcasing such sports as kayaking, rafting, and mountain biking. Then there are the Big Wheels, the Brews and Chili Festival, the Vail Wine and Food Festival, and the Annual Vail Jazz Party, to name just a few. There are also free outdoor concerts by up-and-coming musicians, as well as concerts by some of the biggest names in the business.

Fodor'sChoice   Stretching from late June through early August, the annual **Bravo!** ★   **Vail Valley Music Festival** (⊠ *Box 2270, Vail 81658* ☎ *877/812–5700* ⊕ *www.vailmusicfestival.org*) is a month-and-a-half-long celebration of music. Among the performers that are in residence for a few days or more than a week are the New York Philharmonic and the Dallas Symphony Orchestra. Chamber-music concerts, many performed by the ensemble-in-residence, are popular events. There's also music from an American composer-in-residence.

★ Held early in August, the annual **Vail International Dance Festival** (☎970/949-1999 ⊕*www.vvf. org*) hosts an unparalleled collection of ballet and modern dance groups from around the globe. The

> **KNOW YOUR SNOW**
>
> Vail is known for its "powder": slopes puffed with light, fluffy flakes that make you feel like you are gliding on silk. Ungroomed runs, however, can quickly turn to "crud" as they get "tracked out" (scarred with deep tracks). That's when it's time to hunt up the "corduroy"--freshly groomed runs.

performers vary from year to year, but frequently include guest artists from the American Ballet Theatre, the Pacific Northwest Ballet, and other world-class companies. In recent years, visitors enjoyed Savion Glover of the Tony Award–winning "Bring in Da Noise, Bring in Da Funk." Most of the performances are at the Vilar Center for the Arts and the Gerald R. Ford Amphitheater, an outdoor venue where some people sit in the seats, but many more recline on blankets on the surrounding lawn.

DOWNHILL SKIING & SNOWBOARDING

Year after year, **Vail** logs more than a million "skier days" (the ski industry's measure of ticket sales), perpetuating its ranking as one of the top two or three most popular resorts in North America. From the top of China Bowl to the base of the Lionshead Gondola, the resort is more than 7 mi across. The vast acreage is roughly divided into three sections: the Front Side, the Back Bowls, and Blue Sky Basin. Snowboarders will find plenty of steeps on the Front Side, and technical challenges at the Golden Peak Terrain Park, but they should avoid the Back Bowls, where long catwalks can get slow in the afternoon sun.

Vail is perhaps best known for its legendary **Back Bowls,** more than 3,000 acres of wide-open spaces that are sensational on sunny days. Standing in any one of them, it's difficult to get a visual perspective, as skiers on the far side resemble Lilliputians. These bowls stretch from the original Sun Up and Sun Down to Game Creek on one side and Teacup, China, Siberia, and Outer Mongolia bowls on the far side. The terrain ranges from wide, groomed swatches for intermediate skiers to seemingly endless bump fields to glades so tight that only an expert boarder can slither between the trees. When there's fresh powder, these bowls beckon to skiers intermediate and above. But after the fresh snow has been tracked up by skiers and pummeled by wind and sun, it may be wise for less-than-expert skiers to stay in the groomed sections of the bowls.

The **Front Side** of Vail Mountain delivers a markedly different experience. Here there's lots of wide-trail skiing, heavily skewed toward groomed intermediate runs, especially off the Northwood Express, Mountaintop Express, and Avanti Express lifts, as well as the slopes reachable via the Eagle Bahn Gondola. Pockets of advanced and expert terrain are tucked in and around the blue-marked slopes. The upper parts of Riva Ridge (the Glade) and the top of Prima (the Cornice) are just a few of the places you'll find skilled skiers. The best show in town is on Highline (you can see it while riding Chair 10), where the experts groove through the moguls and those with a bit less experience career around the bumps. The other two extremely difficult double-black-diamond trails off this slow lift are the best cruisers on the mountain for skilled skiers.

It takes time (as long as 45 minutes) to reach **Blue Sky Basin,** made up of three more bowls, but it's worth the effort. Tucked away in a secluded corner of Vail, this 645-acre area has been left in a wilder state, and the majority of the terrain is never groomed. Intermediate skiers will find a few open trails with spectacular views of rugged mountain peaks. For advanced and expert skiers, the real fun is playing in glades and terrain with names such as Heavy Metal, Skree Field, the Divide, and Champagne Glade. ☎ *800/404–3535* ⊕ *www.vail.com* ⊙ *Mid-Nov.–mid-Apr., daily 9–4.*

FACILITIES 3,450-foot vertical drop; 5,289 skiable acres; 18% beginner, 29% intermediate, 53% expert (the majority of this terrain is in the Back Bowls); 1 gondola, 16 high-speed quads, 1 regular quad, 2 triples, 3 doubles, 9 surface lifts.

LESSONS & PROGRAMS The **Vail and Beaver Creek Ski and Snowboard School** (☎ *970/479–4330*) runs classes for skiers of all levels. The school at Vail has almost 1,000 instructors who teach in 30 languages. Afternoon-only group lessons are $80 to $90, depending on the season. All-day lessons are $120. Special workshops and clinics are offered throughout the year. Beginners take three-day courses that include equipment rental and lift passes. Workshops for women, teen sessions, and telemark courses are among the programs targeting specific groups.

LIFT TICKETS Few skiers pay the walk-up rate of $92 for a one-day lift ticket. Colorado's Front Range skiers purchase a variety of season passes. Most vacationers purchase lift-and-lodging packages, or go online to buy multiday lift passes at discounted rates. A lift ticket purchased at either Vail or Beaver Creek may also be used at Breckenridge, Keystone, and Arapahoe Basin.

RENTALS **Vail Sports** (✉ *600 Lionshead Pl.* ☎ *970/479–0600* ⊕ *www.vailsports.com*) is within steps of the lifts. The shop rents a wide range of ski gear, including high-end equipment. Prices for skis range from $35 to $55 a day. Book online and save up to 10% on daily rentals and up to

20% for rentals of five days or more. At Lionshead, at **One Track Mind Snowboard Shop** (⌧492 E. *Lionshead Circle* ☎970/476–1397) you can rent everything you need for snowboarding.

NORDIC SKIING

BACKCOUNTRY SKIING

Fodor'sChoice

★

The **10th Mountain Division Hut and Trail System** is one of Colorado's outdoor gems. This network of 29 huts is set in the mountains near Camp Hale where the decorated namesake World War II division trained. Skiers and snowshoers in winter (snowmobiles are not permitted to approach the huts) and hikers and mountain bikers in summer tackle sections of the more than 350 mi of trails linking new and rustic cabins on day trips or weeklong expeditions. Apart from the joy of a self-reliant adventure among rugged mountains, travelers enjoy the camaraderie of communal living (there are very few private rooms in the huts), and evenings spent swapping stories by the glow of a wood-burning stove or the twinkle of summer stars. Maps and other information are available through the **10th Mountain Division Hut Association** (⌧1280 Ute Ave., Aspen 81611 ☎970/925–5775 ⊕www.huts.org). Hut reservations should be made at least a month in advance.

If you aren't familiar with the area's backcountry trails, hiring a guide is a good idea. In Vail, contact **Paragon Guides** (⌧Box 130, Vail 81658 ☎970/926–5299).

TRACK SKIING

The cross-country skiing at the **Vail Nordic Center** (⌧1778 Vail Valley Dr. ☎970/476–8366) is on a golf course. It's not the most beautiful route, but it's free.

OTHER SPORTS & THE OUTDOORS

Activities Desk of Vail (☎970/476–9090) has the lowdown on events in the area. In summer, **Adventure Ridge** (⌧600 Lionshead Circle ☎970/476–9090), at the top of Lionshead, is the hub of Vail Mountain activities. It's cool and high, and it has the views. It also has tons of activities like Friday afternoon club bands, beer, sunset watching, the Dino Dig (a large sandbox with buried plastic dinosaur bones for kids), a gravity trampoline, horseshoe pits, volleyball nets, Frisbee golf, and mountain-bike rentals. In winter, you can go tubing, play laser tag, ice-skate, or try a ski bike.

BICYCLING

A popular summer destination for both road bikers and mountain bikers, Vail has a variety of paved bike paths (including one that leads up to Vail Pass), plus dozens of miles of dirt mountain-bike trails. You can take bikes on lifts heading uphill, then head downhill on an array of routes. **Vail Bike Tech** (⌧555 E. Lionshead Circle ☎800/525–5995 ⊕www.vailbiketech.com) rents and repairs bikes. Best of all, they are only steps from the Eagle Bahn Gondola, a summer gateway to the ski slope trails.

Each summer, riders from around the region participate in races sponsored by the **Beaver Creek & Vail Summer Adventure Ridge Mountain Challenge** (⌧700 S. Frontage Rd. E ☎970/479–2280 ⊕www.vailrec.com).

FITNESS & SPAS

Deciding to get a massage or spa treatment is the easy part—deciding where to get it is a bigger problem, because there are many outstanding spas and health clubs in the area. The **Aria Spa & Health Club** (✉ *1300 Westhaven Dr.* ☎ *970/476–7400* ⊕ *www.vailcascade.com*) is one of the best places to be pampered. If you're up for a full-spa experience, ask about the Symphony for the Senses packages. This huge facility in the Vail Cascade Resort & Spa also has racquetball, basketball, and tennis courts. In the Sonnenalp Resort, the lovely **Sonnenalp Spa** (✉ *20 Vail Rd.* ☎ *970/476–5656* ⊕ *www.sonnenalp.com*) is a Euro-

---

WORD OF MOUTH

"As a fairly good skier, it would still take several days to ski MOST of Vail, so staying there is the best option. I would check into lodging ASAP, though. If price and availability are tough, check out Avon and Edwards—cheaper but, of course, not as convenient."

—BLYVAIL

---

pean-style facility where you can relax on one of the lounge chairs around a big fireplace as you sip juice from the nearby bar.

GOLF   Golfers who love to play mountain courses know that some of the best are in Vail Valley. These courses meander through the valleys dividing the area's soaring peaks. The region is home to more than a dozen courses, and there are another half dozen within easy driving distance. It's all just a matter of where you're staying and how much you want to spend. Some courses are only open to members and to guests at certain lodges.

Sonnenalp Golf Course. This Robert Cupp–Jay Morrish design threads through an upscale neighborhood 13 mi west of Vail. There are some serious elevation changes. Guests at the Sonnenalp Resort get preferred tee times. ✉ *1265 Berry Creek Dr., Edwards* ☎ *907/477–5371* ⊕ *www.sonnenalpgolfclub.com* ⚒ *Reservations essential* ⛳ *18 holes. Yards: 7,059/5293. Par: 71/71. Green Fee: $75/$175.*

Vail Golf Club. The area's municipal course rolls along between homes and condominiums in East Vail. ✉ *1778 Vail Valley Dr.* ☎ *970/479–2260* ⊕ *www.vailgolfclub.com* ⚒ *Reservations essential* ⛳ *18 holes. Yards: 6,740/5,277. Par: 71/71. Green Fee: $45/$80.*

HIKING   If you aren't used to it, high altitude can catch you off guard. Drink plenty of water to help stave off the effects of altitude sickness—dizziness, shortness of breath, headache, and nausea. Slather on the sunscreen—it's easy to get sunburned up here. And, in summer, an early morning start is best, as afternoon thunderstorms are frequent and a danger above the tree line.

Eagle's Loop (⊹ *Trailhead: Top of Eagle Bahn Gondola*) starts at 10,350 feet, but it's a mellow, 1-mi stroll along the mountaintop ridge with panoramic views of the Mount of the Holy Cross. Allow about half an hour.

Fodor'sChoice   **Booth Lake** is one of Vail's most popular hikes, so get on the trail early ★   or pick a weekday during the summer high season. This is a sustained 6-mi one-way climb from 8,400 feet to Booth Lake at 11,500 feet, right above the tree line. Fit hikers can do this in about seven hours.

En route, hikers can cool off at the 60-foot Booth Creek Falls; at only 2 mi in, this is also a great spot to turn around if you're feeling winded (this should take about two to three hours round-trip and is a great option for an easier hike). The reward for pushing on is a nice view of Booth Lake cradled among the alpine tundra. ✣ *Trailhead: Take Exit 180 from I–70 to end of Booth Falls Rd.*

Paragon Guides (✉ *Box 130, Vail 81618* ☎ *970/926–5299* ⊕ *www. paragonguides.com*) offers backcountry adventures. In summer, there's rock climbing, mountain biking, and day and overnight llama treks in and around Vail Valley. In winter, the company runs daylong ski trips through the backcountry, and three- to six-day trips along the 10th Mountain Division Hut System.

HORSEBACK RIDING
One of the best ways to see Vail Valley is from the back of a horse. On scenic Sweetwater Lake, **A. J. Brink Outfitters** (✉ *3406 Sweetwater Rd., Sweetwater* ☎ *970/524–9301*) has day and overnight horseback excursions high in the Flat Tops Wilderness.

About 12 mi north of Vail, **Piney River Ranch** (✉ *Piney Lake* ☎ *970/477–1171*) has pony rides for kids and guided one-hour horseback rides for adults.

NATURE CENTERS
The **Vail Nature Center** (✉ *Adjacent to Ford Park* ☎ *970/476–2291*) occupies an old homestead just across from the Betty Ford Alpine Gardens. You can sign up for half-day and full-day backcountry hikes, wildflower walks, morning birding expeditions, and evening beaver pond tours. ★ winter, backcountry snowshoe excursions and photography classes are available at the **Vail Nordic Center** (✉ *1778 Vail Valley Dr.* ☎ *970/476–8366*).

SNOW-MOBILING
Adventure Ridge (✉ *600 Lionshead Circle* ☎ *970/476–9090*), at the top of Lionshead, leads twilight snowmobile excursions, as well as snowshoe, snow inner-tubing, and ice-skating trips. **Nova Guides** (✉ *7088 U.S. Hwy. 24, Red Cliff* ☎ *970/827–4232*) has snowmobile rentals and guided tours.

WHERE TO EAT

★ $$$$ ✕**Chap's Grill & Chophouse.** This steak house in the Vail Cascade Resort earned its reputation by serving only the most-tender cuts of meat. Locals rave about the dry-aged beef rib eye and the Blackfoot buffalo rib eye. But Chap's is also a well-regarded seafood restaurant, which is why you'll find tempting entrées like seared ahi and 1½-pound Nova Scotia lobsters. Savory soups, such as caramelized lobster and corn bisque, are good starters. Finish the meal with chocolate-lava cake—it has a molten-truffle center that melts in your mouth. ✉ *Vail Cascade Resort, 1300 Westhaven Dr., Cascade Village* ☎ *970/479–7014* ▭ *AE, D, DC, MC, V.*

$$$$ ✕**Game Creek Club.** Getting to this private club is certainly half the
Fodor's Choice fun, as you must catch a gondola up the mountain, then hop on a
★ snowcat to get across Game Creek Bowl. The Bavarian-style lodge is members-only for lunch, but open to the public for dinner all year and for an outstanding Sunday brunch in summer. Be prepared to linger

over a multicourse prix-fixe meal as you enjoy spectacular views of the slopes and the mountains beyond. You might start with a house-cured gravlax and mesclun salad with toasted goat cheese, followed by grilled venison strip loin or a porcini-crusted dry-aged sirloin. ⊠ *278 Hanson Ranch Rd.* ☎ *970/479–4275* ⚇ *Reservations essential* ▭ *AE, D, DC, MC, V* ⊗ *No lunch.*

$$$$ ✕ **La Bottega.** This casual, small restaurant has a loyal following who appreciates the creative northern Italian fare. Customers especially love the lunch specials, which include creative pizzas from the stone ovens and delicious pastas. Some people turn out for a glass of vino in the wine bar, which takes up one side of the establishment. The cellar is one of the best in town. ⊠ *100 E. Meadow Dr., Vail Village* ☎ *970/476–0280* ▭ *D, MC, V.*

$$$$ ✕ **Larkspur.** An open kitchen bustling with activity is the backdrop at Larkspur, popular with a parka-clad crowd at lunch and well-dressed diners in the evening. Owner and chef Thomas Salamunovich has a talent for blending cuisines, so the menu is filled with creative entrées such as pumpkin seed–crusted salmon with wild mushroom–potato ravioli and duck breast with foie gras and duck-confit stuffing. Leave room for decadent desserts such as warm chocolate spice cake and petite doughnuts with chocolate and espresso sabayon. ⊠ *Golden Peak Lodge, 458 Vail Valley Dr., Vail Village* ☎ *970/479–8050* ⚇ *Reservations essential* ▭ *AE, MC, V.*

$$$$ ✕ **Sweet Basil.** The decor may be understated—blond-wood chairs and buff-color walls—but chef Bruce Yim's contemporary cuisine is anything but. He uses the freshest ingredients available, so the menu changes several times each season. You might find coriander-rubbed venison, seared Hawaiian ahi, or a Colorado lamb trio of rib chop, bacon, and lamb shank ragout. Pair these entrées with one of the hundreds of wines from the restaurant's award-winning cellar. Leave room for luscious desserts such as hot sticky toffee pudding cake. ⊠ *193 E. Gore Creek Dr., Vail Village* ☎ *970/476–0125* ▭ *AE, MC, V.*

★ $$$$ ✕ **Terra Bistro.** With dark furniture and walls hung with black-and-white photographs, this sleek, sophisticated space looks as if it belongs in a big city. Only the fireplace reminds you that this is Vail. The menu focuses on contemporary American cuisine that throws in a few Asian, Mediterranean, and Southwestern influences. Seared bone-in Colorado lamb loin in Indian spices and salted Amish beef filled with mashed Yukon gold potatoes are headliners. The restaurant is in the Vail Mountain Lodge & Spa, so it's no surprise that organic produce and free-range meat and poultry are used whenever possible. ⊠ *Vail Moun-*

tain Lodge & Spa, 352 E. Meadow Dr., Vail Village ☎*970/476–6836* ⊟*AE, D, MC, V.*

$$ ✕**Bart & Yeti's.** Grilled portobello-mushroom sandwiches, spicy South western green chili, and Irish stew are among the choices at this laid-back restaurant. Pictures of cowboys on horseback, wagon wheels, and other odds and ends line the rough log walls. If you want a full meal, entrées include favorites like barbecued baby back ribs and crispy fried chicken. The deck is a popular gathering spot in warm weather. The place is in Lionshead, just north of the Eagle Bahn gondola. ⊠*553 E. Lionshead Cir., Lionshead* ☎*970/476–2754* ⊟*AE, D, MC, V.*

$ ✕**Pazzo's Pizzeria.** This hole-in-the-wall is right in the heart of Vail Village. It serves some of the best pizzas in the area, ready to eat in the dining room or to take to one of the tables outside. Create your own masterpiece from a list of more than 20 ingredients, or opt for the cheesy lasagna, the chicken parmigiana, or one of the chubby calzones. Ask about the happy-hour specials. ⊠*122 E. Meadow Dr., Vail Village* ☎*970/476–9026* ⊠*82 E. Beaver Creek Blvd., Avon* ☎*970/949–9900* ⊠*0500 Chambers Ave., Eagle* ☎*970/337–9900* ⊟*D, MC, V.*

WHERE TO STAY

At this writing, Lionshead, a concrete and-steel portion of the resort built in the 1970s, is undergoing a major reconstruction project to bring it more in line with the Bavarian look of Vail Village. In the meantime, Vail Village will be the quieter—and prettier—place to stay. Beyond Vail, Beaver Creek tends to be a quiet, family-oriented resort without the rollicking nightlife. Down valley in Edwards and Minturn you'll find that accommodation prices drop, but so does the accessibility to the slopes.

$$$$ 🏨**Galatyn Lodge.** This luxury lodge in a quiet part of Vail Village maintains a low profile, which is just the approach its hard-core skiing regulars prefer. A staff is on call 24 hours a day to see to your every need. There are a handful of four-bedroom apartments that can be partitioned off into smaller spaces. All of these apartments are spacious, luxuriously decorated, and have kitchens with all the latest gadgets. **Pros:** indoor/outdoor heated pool, high percentage of return guests, apartments. **Cons:** no children's programs, no restaurant or bar. ⊠*365 Vail Valley Dr., Vail Village, 81657* ☎*970/479–2418 or 800/943–7322* ⌐*3 4-bedroom apartments* ⌂*In-room: safe (some), kitchen (some), refrigerator (some), DVD, Wi-Fi. In-hotel: pool, concierge, laundry facilities, laundry service, public Internet, public Wi-Fi, airport shuttle, parking (no fee), no-smoking rooms* ⊟*AE, MC, V.*

$$$$ 🏨**Gasthof Gramshammer.** Pepi Gramshammer, a former Austrian Olympic ski racer who runs some of the country's best intensive ski programs, operates this guesthouse. The charming rooms, all done up in pastels, are filled with original oil paintings and fluffy down comforters. In keeping with the theme, the waitresses are done up in dirndls. **Pros:** European flavor, location in Village. **Cons:** no room service, fewer amenities than larger properties. ⊠*231 E. Gore Creek Dr., Vail Village, 81657* ☎*970/476–5626 or 800/610–7374* ⊕*www.pepis.com* ⌐*30 rooms, 9 suites and apartments* ⌂*In-room: no a/c, safe (some),* kitchen (some), refrigerator, DVD (some), VCR (some), Wi-Fi (some). In-hotel: restaurant, bar, pool, laundry facilities, laundry service, public Wi-Fi, airport shuttle, parking (no fee), no-smoking rooms ▤AE, D, MC, V.

$$$$ 🏨 **Lodge at Vail.** The first facility to open in Vail in 1962, the sprawling lodge—modeled after the Lodge at Sun Valley—is popular with skiers and families because of its fabulous location only 150 feet from the village's main lift, the Vista Bahn. Ski valets ready your skis every morning (after the complimentary wax, of course) and collect your gear for drying in the evening. The quality and size of the rooms varies tremendously. The older wing has smaller, individually decorated rooms with a homey feel, while the newer wing has larger suites with modern touches like heated marble floors in the bathrooms and gas fireplaces. Mickey's piano bar is a favored après-ski spot. **Pros:** on-mountain ski storage, located near main ski lift. **Cons:** can get noisy with partiers, quality of rooms varies. ⊠174 E. Gore Creek Dr., Vail Village, 81657 ☎970/476–5011 or 877/528–7625 ⊕www.lodgeatvail.rockresorts. com ⇌79 rooms, 46 suites, 44 1-, 2-, and 3-bedroom condos ⚙In-room: no a/c (some), safe (some), kitchen (some), refrigerator (some), DVD (some), Wi-Fi. In-hotel: 2 restaurants, room service, bar, golf course, pool, gym, spa, concierge, laundry facilities, laundry service, public Internet, public Wi-Fi, airport shuttle, parking (fee), some pets allowed, no-smoking rooms ▤AE, D, DC, MC, V.

$$$$ 🏨 **Sitzmark Lodge.** This cozy lodge buzzes with a dozen languages, thanks to the international guests who return year after year. Rooms, which range from moderate to large, have balconies that look out onto Vail Mountain or Gore Creek. Some have gas-burning fireplaces to keep things comfortable. The decor is a blend of light woods and cheerful floral fabrics. The staff is extremely friendly, encouraging guests to congregate in the sunny, split-level living room on winter afternoons for complimentary mulled wine. The lodge is only 75 yards from the lifts, and a continental breakfast is served in winter. **Pros:** easy access to ski lifts, international ambience, great views. **Cons:** breakfasts are standard, customer service varies. ⊠183 Gore Creek Dr., Vail Village, 81657 ☎970/476–5001 or 888/476–5001 ⊕www.sitzmarklodge.com ⇌35 rooms ⚙In-room: no a/c, safe (some), kitchen (some), refrigerator (some), DVD (some), Wi-Fi (some). In-hotel: restaurant, bar, pool, concierge, laundry facilities, laundry service, public Internet, public Wi-Fi, parking (no fee), no-smoking rooms ▤AE, MC, V.

$$$$
Fodor'sChoice
★
🏨 **Sonnenalp Resort.** It's the sense of family tradition and European elegance that makes the Sonnenalp Resort the most Tyrolean and romantic of all hotels in the faux-Tyrolean village of Vail. Four generations of the Fassler family have worked in the hotel business, and the Sonnenalp showcases their expertise not only in the Bavarian architecture and decor (stucco walls hatched with wood beams and balconies with flower boxes) but also in the impeccable manners of everyone from front-desk receptionists to the waiters at Ludwig's. Room configurations vary from two-story suites to cozy rooms barely bigger than the overstuffed beds. The first-floor spa is set around an alcove fireplace, but the indoor heated pool flows outdoors and fronts a beautiful gar-

den beside Gore Creek. **Pros:** classic alp architecture and ambience, incredible breakfasts, spa. **Cons:** removed from lifts, tough to regulate room temperature in winter. ✉*20 Vail Rd., Vail Village, 81657* ☎*970/476–5656 or 800/654–8312* ⊕*www.sonnenalp.com* ⛛*12 rooms, 128 suites* ♿*In-room: safe (some), kitchen (some), refrigerator (some), DVD (some), Wi-Fi. In-hotel: 3 restaurants, room service, bar, golf course, pool, gym, spa, concierge, children's programs (ages 5–12), laundry service, public Internet, public Wi-Fi, airport shuttle, parking (fee), some pets allowed, no-smoking rooms* ☐*AE, D, DC, MC, V.*

$$$$ 🏨**Vail Cascade Resort & Spa.** Down-to-earth yet luxurious is the best way to describe this family-oriented ski-in ski-out hotel. Despite its size, it manages to maintain an intimate feel. Rooms reflect a "mountain eclectic" decor, with rich plaid and floral fabrics, wicker furniture, and wrought-iron lamps. The restaurant has garnered acclaim for its outstanding grilled foods and fine selection of wines. Guests have access to the adjoining Aria Spa & Club and the full-service health club with racquetball, squash, and basketball courts. The best deals at any time of year are the packages, which might include lift tickets in winter or sports massages in summer. **Pros:** right on the slope, spa and health club, nice views of creek. **Cons:** staff can be hard to find, concrete exterior, expensive parking. ✉*1300 Westhaven Dr., Cascade Village, 81657* ☎*970/476–7111 or 800/420–2424* ⊕*www.vailcascade.com* ⛛*292 rooms, 27 suites, 78 condominiums* ♿*In-room: no a/c, safe (some), kitchen (some), refrigerator (some), DVD (some), ethernet, Wi-Fi. In-hotel: restaurant, room service, bars, tennis courts, pool, gym, spa, concierge, children's programs (ages 3 months–12), laundry facilities (some), laundry service, public Internet, public Wi-Fi, airport shuttle, parking (fee), no-smoking rooms* ☐*AE, D, DC, MC, V.*

CONDOS **Vail/Beaver Creek Reservations** (☎*800/525–2257*) is the place for one-stop shopping. You can buy lift tickets, arrange ski and snowboard lessons, get updates on events and activities, and book lodging at many of the hotels and condominium properties in the Vail Valley. **Vail Valley Chamber and Tourism** (☎*800/824–5737*) operates a central reservations service for properties in Vail, Avon, and Beaver Creek. It also gives out information on events and activities and reports on snow conditions.

NIGHTLIFE

In the heart of Vail Village, **FuBar** (✉*333 Bridge St.* ☎*970/476–0360*) is hopping all night. There are several theme rooms, including one with a 1950s-style jukebox that cranks out classic rock. Then there's the Red Room, a smoking lounge, and a dance club with a disco ball and a floor with glow-in-the-dark stars. Near the gondola in Lionshead, **Garfinkel's** (✉*536 W. Lionshead Mall* ☎*970/476–3789*) has plenty of televisions where you can catch the game. It's open late, especially on weekends. In the Lodge at Vail, **Mickey's** (✉*174 E. Gore Creek Dr.* ☎*970/476–5011*) attracts the après-ski crowd. A pianist plays soothing standards. The **Red Lion** (✉*304 Bridge St.* ☎*970/476–7676*) is a tradition in Vail. It's standing-room only in the afternoon, and a bit mellower in the evening. Most nights there's guitar or piano music.

Sarah's (✉ *356 E. Hanson Ranch Rd.* ☎970/476–5641) showcases Helmut Fricker, a Vail institution who plays accordion while yodeling up a storm. You can catch him during the ski season Tuesday and Friday evenings. A young crowd scarfs down excellent late-night pizzas at **Vendetta's** (✉ *291 Bridge St.* ☎970/476–5070).

SHOPPING

Shopping options in the pedestrian-only streets of Vail Village include high-end boutiques, ski and snowboard shops, art and crafts galleries, and stores filled with T-shirts and other souvenirs.

BOUTIQUES
Across from the Children's Fountain, **Axel's** (✉ *201 Gore Creek Dr.* ☎970/476–7625) carries high-end European fashions including Italian suede pants, riding boots, and shearling coats.For years, a golden bear (papa-, mama-, or baby-size) on a chain has been a popular souvenir from this ski resort. The **Golden Bear** (✉ *286 Bridge St.* ☎970/476–4082 ✉*Village Hall, Beaver Creek* ☎970/845–7881) makes many versions of its namesake, as well as other popular items such as hammered gold necklaces and bracelets. You can also purchase fashionable clothes and accessories. Stocking everything from buffalo-hide coats to bowls filled with potpourri, **Gorsuch** (✉ *263 Gore Creek Dr.* ☎970/476–2294 ✉*70 Promenade, Beaver Creek* ☎970/949–7115) is an odd combination of an upscale boutique and a sporting-goods store. **Pepi's Sports** (✉ *231 Bridge St.* ☎970/476–5202) sells chic ski clothing and accessories from designers such as Bogner, Skea, Descente, and Spyder.

GALLERIES
The **Claggett/Rey Gallery** (✉ *100 E. Meadow Dr.* ☎800/252–4438) is the place to purchase canvases and sculptures by well-known Western artists. You'll be dazzled by handblown creations at the **Pismo Gallery** (✉ *122 E. Meadow Dr.* ☎970/476–2400). The outstanding collection of handblown glass ranges from perfume bottles to paperweights.

MINTURN

5 mi west of Vail; 105 mi west of Denver via I–70.

The Vail Valley stretches far beyond the town of Vail. As you travel west along I–70, Exit 171 leads to this quaint community. Minturn began to thrive in 1987, when the Rio Grande Railway extended a narrow-gauge line into town to carry away the zinc, copper, silver, and lead extracted from nearby mines. The main street has an eclectic collection of antiques, curio, and other shops, plus popular restaurants tucked into the old buildings. You might begin a sojourn here by visiting **Minturn Cellars Winery** (✉ *107 Williams St.* ☎970/827–4065), a wine-tasting room featuring some of the finest local wines.

WHERE TO STAY & EAT

$$$ ✕ **Minturn Country Club.** This homey hangout is one of those "you've gotta go" places people talk about after returning home. Steaks, fish, and chicken are all delicious. You have only yourself to blame if you wanted your meat medium rare and it came out well done, as you grill

your meal yourself. ⊠*131 Main St.* ☎*970/827–4114* ⏦*Reservations not accepted* ☰*MC, V* ⊗*No lunch.*

$$ ✕**The Saloon.** After a day on the slopes, reward yourself with margaritas made with real lime juice and baskets of tortilla chips served with homemade salsa. No wonder the place is always packed with locals. In a dining room that calls to mind the Old West, you can chow down on such specialties as *chiles rellenos* (stuffed peppers) and a steak-and-quail plate. There's even a children's menu. ⊠*146 N. Main St.* ☎*970/827–5954* ⏦*Reservations not accepted* ☰*AE, MC, V* ⊗*No lunch.*

$ ⬚**Minturn Inn.** This three-story 1915 log home, one of the town's oldest residences, was converted into a charming inn with theme rooms popular with couples. When business became brisk, the owners added the neighboring Eagle Street Bed & Breakfast and the Grouse Creek Inn. These properties have two-person hot tubs, river-rock fireplaces, and private decks or patios overlooking the Eagle River. Hearty breakfasts are included. **Pros:** historic lodgings, view of the river, fireplaces. **Cons:** removed from the ski resort, few room and hotel amenities. ⊠*442 Main St., 81645* ☎*970/827–9647 or 800/646–8876* 🖷*970/827–5590* ⊕*www.minturninn.com* ⮒*18 rooms, 1 cabin* ⬚*In-room: no a/c, Wi-Fi. In-hotel: no elevator, parking (no fee), no-smoking rooms* ☰*AE, D, MC, V* ⦿*BP.*

POUNDING SWORDS INTO SKIS

A pair of red-crossed swords on a blue shield is the familiar insignia of the famed 10th Mountain Division, created to train soldiers in mountain and winter warfare during World War II. One of their first training centers, Camp Hale, was opened in 1942 in a small park between Red Cliff and Leadville. The high valley must have borne at least a passing resemblance to the Himalayas because before it closed in 1966, the CIA also secretly trained Tibetan guerrillas there to wage a war of independence in their Chinese-occupied homeland.

BEAVER CREEK

12 mi west of Vail; 110 mi west of Denver via I–70.

As with the majority of the area's resorts, the heart of Beaver Creek is a mountainside village. What sets Beaver Creek apart is that it's a series of cascading plazas connected by escalators. In this ultraposh enclave, even boot-wearing skiers and snowboard-hauling riders ride the escalators from the hotels and shuttle stops on the lower levels. Opened in 1980 as a smaller version of Vail, Beaver Creek has overshadowed its older sibling. In fact, its nearest rival in the luxury market is Utah's Deer Valley.

Locals know that Beaver Creek is the best place to ski on weekends when Vail is too crowded, or anytime there's fresh powder. Beaver Creek is just far enough from Denver that it doesn't get the flood of day-trippers who flock to Vail and the other Front Range resorts. The slopes of Beaver Creek Mountain are connected to those of even ritzier Bachelor Gulch. These are close to Arrowhead, creating a village-to-village ski experience like those found in Europe.

Savvy travelers have learned that Beaver Creek is even lovelier in summer, when diners can enjoy a meal on a spacious patio, mountain bikers can hitch a ride uphill on the chairlift, and golfers can play on the beautiful Beaver Creek Course or on one of the dozen others in the Vail Valley. On special evenings you can attend concerts, get tickets to the theater, or head to a performance at the Beaver Creek Vilar Center for the Arts. In Beaver Creek you have easy access to all of the activities in Vail Valley.

Beaver Creek speaks loudly and clearly to a settled and affluent crowd, but visitors on a budget can also enjoy the resort's many attractions. Just drive past the pricier lodgings in the village and opt instead for a room in nearby Avon, Edwards, or even Vail.

DOWNHILL SKIING & SNOWBOARDING
Beaver Creek is a piece of nirvana, partly because of its system of trails and partly because of its enviable location two hours from Denver. Although only a third the size of Vail, Beaver Creek is seldom crowded. The skiable terrain extends from the runs down Beaver Creek to the slopes around Bachelor Gulch to the network of trails at Arrowhead. You can easily ski from one village to another.

Beaver Creek has a little of everything, from smoother slopes for beginners to difficult trails used for international competitions. Grouse Mountain, in particular, is famed for its thigh-burning bump runs. Beginners have an entire peak, at the summit of Beaver Creek Mountain, where they can learn to ski or practice on novice trails. (And newcomers can return to the village on one of the lifts if they are too tired to take the long trail all the way to the bottom.) Intermediate-level skiers have several long cruising trails on the lower half of Beaver Creek Mountain and in Larkspur Bowl. Both locations also have black-diamond trails, so groups of skiers and snowboarders of varying abilities can ride uphill together. The Birds of Prey runs, like Peregrine and Redtail, are aptly named, because the steepness of the trails can be a surprise for skiers who mistakenly think they are skilled enough to take on this challenging terrain. The days of snowboarders getting snubbed in Beaver Creek are long gone, and shredders can tackle a series of terrain parks with increasing difficulty from Park 101 to the Zoom Room and on to the Moonshine half-pipe.

The slopes of neighboring **Bachelor Gulch** are a mix of beginner and intermediate trails. Here you can often find fresh powder hours after it's gone elsewhere. Many of the open slopes weave past multimillion-dollar homes where the cost of real estate is even higher than in Beaver Creek. The Ritz-Carlton Bachelor Gulch, which sits at the base of the lift, is one of the region's most beautiful hotels. A stop here is a must for any architecture buff. Many skiers plan to arrive in time for a hearty lunch at Remington's or an après-ski cocktail in the Buffalo

CLOSE UP

Hitting the Slopes

Although downhill skiing has long been the classic winter activity, snowboarding—once the bastion of teenage "riders" in baggy pants—is fast catching up as a mainstream sport. Telemarking and cross-country skiing still have loyal followings, though these skiers tend to prefer the wide-open backcountry to the more-populated resorts.

Although it snows somewhere in the Colorado high country every month—and resorts can open their lifts as early as October and close as late as the fourth of July—the traditional ski season usually runs from December until early April. Christmas through New Year's Day and the month of March (when spring breakers arrive) tend to be the busiest periods for most ski areas. The slower months of January and February often yield good package deals, as do the early and late ends of the season.

EQUIPMENT RENTAL

Rental equipment is available at all ski areas and at ski shops around resorts or in nearby towns. It's often more expensive to rent at the resort where you'll be skiing, but then it's easier to go back to the shop if something doesn't fit. Experienced skiers can "demo" (try out) premium equipment to get a feel for new technology before upgrading.

LESSONS

In the United States, the Professional Ski Instructors of America (PSIA) has devised a progressive teaching system that is used at most ski schools. This allows skiers to take lessons at different ski areas. Classes range in length from hour-long skill clinics to half- or full-day workshops. Deals can be had for first-time and beginner skiers and snowboarders who attend morning

clinics and then try out their new skills on beginner and intermediate slopes for the remainder of the day.

Most ski schools follow the PSIA teaching approach for children, and many also incorporate SKIwee, another standardized teaching technique. Classes for children are arranged by ability and age group; often the ski instructor chaperons a meal during the teaching session. Children's ski instruction has come a long way in the last 10 years; instructors specially trained in teaching children, and equipment designed for little bodies, mean that most children can now begin to ski successfully as young as three or four. Helmets are often de rigueur.

The Winter Park National Sports Center for the Disabled, the largest such center in the world, specializes in teaching skiers with disabilities and has welcomed more than 50,000 new aficionados to the winter recreational world.

LIFT TICKETS

With some lift ticket prices increasing every year, the best advice is to shop around. Single-day, adult, holiday-weekend passes cost the most, but better bargains can be had through off-site purchase locations (check newspaper Sunday sections and local supermarkets, such as King Soopers and Safeway), multiple-day passes, and season passes. You can always call a particular resort's central reservations line to ask where discount lift tickets can be purchased. With a little leg work, you should never have to pay full price.

TRAIL RATING

Ski areas mark and rate trails and slopes—Easy (green circle), Intermediate (blue square), Advanced (black diamond), and Expert (double black diamond). —Jad Davenport

4

Bar or the Fly Fishing Library. There are shuttles handy to take you back to Beaver Creek.

The third village in the area, **Arrowhead,** has the best and usually the least crowded intermediate terrain. Locals take advantage of sunny days by sitting on the spacious deck at the Broken Arrow Café. It's not much more than a shack, but the burgers can't be beat. The European concept of skiing from village to village was introduced here in 1996 when the new owners, Vail Associates, decided to connect Arrowhead, Beaver Creek, and Bachelor Gulch via lifts and ski trails. ☎ *800/404–3535* ⊕ *www.beavercreek.com* ⊘ *Late Nov.–mid-Apr., daily 9–4.*

FACILITIES 4,040-foot vertical drop; 1,805 skiable acres; 19% beginner, 43% intermediate, 38% advanced; 2 gondolas, 10 high-speed quads, 2 triples, 2 doubles, 1 surface lift.

LESSONS & PROGRAMS The **Vail and Beaver Creek Ski and Snowboard School** (☎ *970/476–3239*) runs classes at both resorts. At Beaver Creek there are about 600 instructors; lessons are offered in more than 20 languages. Afternoon-only group lessons are $80 to $90, depending upon the season. All-day lessons are $120. Special workshops and clinics are offered throughout the year. Beginners take three-day courses that include equipment rental and lift passes. Workshops for women, teen sessions, and telemark courses are among the programs targeting specific groups of skiers.

LIFT TICKETS Few skiers pay the walk-up rate of approximately $92 for a one-day lift ticket. Most vacationers purchase lift-and-lodging packages for Beaver Creek, or go online to ⊕ *www.snow.com* and purchase multiday lift passes at discounted rates. A lift ticket purchased at Beaver Creek may also be used at Vail, Breckenridge, Keystone, and Arapahoe Basin.

RENTALS **Beaver Creek Sports** (⊠ *Beaver Creek Village* ☎ *970/754–5418*) rents ski equipment for $45 to $60, depending upon whether you choose regular or high-performance gear.

NORDIC SKIING

TRACK SKIING The prettiest place for cross-country skiing is **McCoy Park,** with more
★ than 19 mi of trails groomed for traditional cross-country skiing, skate skiing, and snowshoeing, all laid out around a mountain peak. To reach McCoy Park, take the Strawberry Park chairlift—a plus because it gets you far enough from the village that you're in a pristine environment. The groomed tracks have a fair amount of ups and downs (or perhaps because the elevation rises to 9,840 feet, it just seems that way).

Lessons, equipment rentals, and guided tours are available through **Beaver Creek Nordic Sports Center** (⊠ *Strawberry Park Condo Bldg.* ⊹ *at the bottom of Chair 12* ☎ *970/845–5313* ⊘ *9–4*).

OTHER SPORTS & THE OUTDOORS

The **Activities Desk of Vail** (☎ *970/476–9090*) gives you the lowdown on many of the activities in the region, summer or winter.

BICYCLING **Colorado Bike Services** (⊠ *41149 U.S. Hwy. 6 and 24* ☎ *970/949–4641*) is the place to get more information about the trails around Beaver Creek.

Each summer, riders from around the region participate in races sponsored by the **Beaver Creek & Vail Summer Adventure Ridge Mountain Challenge** (⊠ *700 S. Frontage Rd. E, Vail* ☎*970/479–2280* ⊕*www.vailrec.com*).

FITNESS & SPAS   Whether you're looking for a full-body massage or a workout on state-of-the-art equipment, it's easy to find in Beaver Creek. In the Park Hyatt Beaver Creek, the **Allegria Spa** (⊠ *136 E. Thomas Pl.* ☎*970/748–7500* ⊕*www.allegriaspa.com*) has a full range of services, including a wonderful "barefoot" massage.

GOLF   If you're serious about improving your game, check into the **David Leadbetter Golf Academy** (⊠ *376 Red Sky Rd., Wolcott* ☎*970/477–8350*). Named number-one golf instructor by *Golf Digest*, Leadbetter has coached U.S. PGA tour players over the past 30 years. His instructors use high-tech tools at the academy's intense two- and three-day sessions. For example, they employ four cameras to record your swing so they can analyze everything from your stance to your grip.

The Club at Cordillera. The Lodge & Spa at Cordillera has three 18-hole courses and a 10-hole course. Hotel guests can play the Jack Nicklaus–designed Summit Course, which surrounds a peak like a string of pearls. The Hale Irwin Mountain Course runs through aspen groves, past lakes, and through meadows surrounded by luxury homes. The Dave Pelz–designed 10-hole course lets you show off (or makes you practice) your short-game skills. ⊠ *2205 Cordillera Way, Edwards* ☎*970/926–5100* ⊕*www.cordillera-vail.com* ⚑*Reservations essential* ⚑ *Mountain: 18 holes. Yards: 7,416/5,226. Par: 72/72. Green Fee: $237. Short: 10 holes. Yards: 1,252/592. Par: 27/27. Green Fee: $55. Summit: 18 holes. Yards: 7,441/5,425. Par: 72/72. Green Fee: $235.*

★ **Eagle Ranch Golf Club.** This 6,600-foot-high course was landscaped in the lush wetlands of the Brush Creek valley. Caddies like to joke that the perfect club might actually be a fly rod. Arnold Palmer, who designed the 18-hole course, said, "The fairways are very playable and the roughs are not extremely rough." ⊠ *Sylvan Lake Rd., Eagle* ☎*970/328–2882 or 866/328–2882* ⊕*www.eagleranchgolf.com* ⚑*Reservations essential* ⚑ *18 holes. Yards: 7,500. Par: 72. Green Fee: $89/$99.*

Red Sky Golf Club. At this tony private course a few miles west of Beaver Creek, members alternate with guests on two courses designed by Tom Fazio and Greg Norman. The Tom Fazio Course's front nine are laid out on sagebrush-covered hills, but the back nine flows up and down a mountainside covered with groves of junipers and aspens. The Greg Norman Course sprawls through a broad valley. Some shots require carries across jagged ravines. Norman's signature bunkers abound, guarding slippery greens. In order to play at Red Sky Golf Club, you must be staying in the Lodge at Vail, the Pines Lodge in Beaver Creek, the Ritz-Carlton Bachelor Gulch, other hotels owned by Vail Resorts, or other partner properties. ⊠ *376 Red Sky Rd., Wolcott* ☎*970/477–8400* ⊕*www.redskygolfclub.com* ⚑*Reservations essential* ⚑ *Greg Norman: 18 holes. Yards: 7,580/5,269. Par: 72/72. Green Fee: $225/$240. Tom Fazio: 18 holes. Yards: 7,113/5,265. Par: 72/72. Green Fee: $100/$200.*

HIKING   The **Holy Cross Wilderness Area** is southwest of Beaver Creek. **Eagle Lake** is a great trail for hikers who want to test their bodies out at altitude without overdoing it. The trail starts at 9,100 feet (just slightly higher than Beaver Creek's base at 7,400 feet) and contours through a glacial valley for almost 2.5 mi around Woods Lake to Eagle Lake at 10,000 feet. Plan on a five-hour round-trip journey. You can continue up the valley to explore more lakes if you're feeling fit. ✉ *Holy Cross Ranger District, White River National Forest* ☎ *970/827–5715* ⊕ *www.fs.fed. us/r2/whiteriver/recreation/wilderness/holycross.*

The **Beaver Creek Hiking Center** (✉ *Beaver Creek Village* ☎ *970/754– 5373*) arranges everything from easy walks to difficult hikes. If you're traveling with kids, ask about educational programs.

HORSEBACK   **Beaver Creek Stable** (✉ *Box 2050, Eagle* ☎ *970/845–7770*) arranges
RIDING   outings ranging from one-hour rides to all-day excursions. Many trips include a tasty picnic lunch. In the evenings there are hayrides and sunset rides.

WHERE TO EAT
A dinner for two in Vail or Beaver Creek in one of the upscale joints will likely cost you more than a pair of lift tickets, so choose wisely. For the most-romantic options look into a slope-side restaurant like Beano's where the fixed-course menus and unique transportation (horses in summer and sleighs in winter) make the experience more than just a meal. If you're just after some quick and tasty carbs, however, there are still bargains to be had, particularly at Mexican food restaurants where the portions are generous and the prices reasonable. The farther down valley you move, the more the prices drop. It's still possible to find a hearty meal in Edwards for under $10.

$$$$ ✗ **Beano's Cabin.** One of the memorable experiences during a trip to Beaver Creek is traveling in a sleigh to this former hunting lodge. (In summer you can get here on horseback or by shuttle van.) During the journey, your driver will undoubtedly fill you in on some local history. The pine-log cabin, warmed by a crackling fire, is an unbeatable location for a romantic meal. Choose from among the entrées that change with the seasons. Pair pan-seared buffalo carpaccio with wood-grilled venison, then top it all off with a bourbon pecan torte. ✉ *Larkspur Bowl* ☎ *970/845–9090 or 866/395–3185* ⚛ *Reservations essential* ☰ *AE, MC, V.*

$$$$ ✗ **Mirabelle.** Set in a restored farmhouse at the entrance to Beaver Creek, Mirabelle is one of the area's loveliest restaurants. Owner and chef Daniel Joly serves superb Belgian–French cuisine. His preparations are a perfect blend of colors, flavors, and textures. The menu changes regularly, but if available try hot foie gras with caramelized golden apples, and roasted elk medallions in a red-wine sauce accompanied by poached baby pear, potato gnocchi, and rhubarb coulis. Depending on your point of view, the elaborate desserts are either heavenly or sinful. The extensive wine list has garnered notice from *Wine Spectator.* ✉ *55 Village Rd., Avon* ☎ *970/949–7728* ☰ *AE, D, MC, V* ☙ *Closed Sun. No lunch.*

$$$$ ✗ **Spago.** The newest outpost of Wolfgang Puck's Spago, located at the Ritz Carlton, Bachelor Gulch, is housed in an expansive, recently-redone dining room whose decor—vegetable-dyed wood paneling and enlarged black-and-white photographs of the surrounding mountain peaks—achieves a sleekly modern look without contradicting the resort's rustic mountain sensibility. Puck's seasonal menu often favors Asian accents and regional ingredients. In late autumn, the menu featured a pumpkin soup deliciously intensified with cardamom cream, and Colorado lamb chops spiced with Hunan eggplant and cilantro-mint vinaigrette. The pumpkin and mascarpone *agnolotti* with sage butter is not to be missed, and for dessert, the *kaiserschmarren,* a souffléd crème fraîche pancake with strawberry sauce, is otherwordly. Service is impeccable, if a touch formal; those who prefer a low key (or less bank-breaking) meal might consider dining in the bar area. ⊠ *0130 Daybreak Ridge, Avon, Colorado 81620 (At the Ritz Carlton, Bachelor Gulch).* ☎ *970/343-1555. Reservations essential.* ⊟ *AE, D, DC, MC, V.*

$$$$ ✗ **Splendido.** With elegant marble columns and custom-made Italian linens, this posh eatery is the height of opulence. Owner and chef David Walford is a master of New American cuisine, and he borrows freely from many traditions. He is equally adept at turning out rack of lamb with rosemary as he is grilling up an elk loin with braised elk osso buco. Retire for a nightcap to the classically elegant piano bar, where Peter Vavra tickles the ivories. ⊠ *17 Chateau La., Beaver Creek Village* ☎ *970/845–8808* ⊟ *AE, D, DC, MC, V* ⊗ *No lunch.*

$$$$ ✗ **Toscanini.** You have a ringside seat at the ice rink in the heart of Beaver Creek when you dine at this casual eatery. The menu is authentic Italian, starting with a variety of dipping oils for the fresh bread, then beef tenderloin carpaccio with Kalamata olives and shaved Parmesan. Entrées include pan-seared diver scallops with roasted fennel mashed potatoes. Don't pass up the rosemary and garlic marinated lamb chops with basil risotto. ⊠ *Market Sq., Beaver Creek Village* ☎ *970/845–5590* ⊟ *AE, D, DC, MC, V.*

$$$$ ✗ **traMonti Ristorante.** This breezy trattoria in the Charter at Beaver Creek showcases the vibrant cuisine of chef Dustin Aipperspach. He loves experimenting with bold juxtapositions of flavors and is most at home with creative pizzas, such as spicy shrimp with fennel, roasted peppers, basil, feta, and infused garlic oil. Try lobster ravioli in Olathe sweet corn puree, or the osso buco. ⊠ *The Charter at Beaver Creek, 120 Offerson Rd., Beaver Creek Village* ☎ *970/949–5552* ⊟ *AE, MC, V* ⊗ *No lunch.*

$$$ ✗ **The Gashouse.** This longtime hangout set inside a 1930s-era log cabin has walls covered with hunting trophies. (If stuffed animal heads aren't your thing, think twice about eating here.) Locals swear by the steak, prime rib, and fresh salmon. Stop in for a brew and some buffalo wings and watch how some of the Vail Valley residents kick back. ⊠ *34185 U.S. Hwy. 6, 4 mi west of Beaver Creek, Edwards* ☎ *970/926–3613* ⊟ *AE, MC, V.*

$$ ✗ **Gore Range Brewery.** After a morning on the slopes or an afternoon playing a few rounds of golf, locals gravitate here for a burger or spicy ribs and a locally brewed beer. In the Edwards Village Center, the brewery blends high-tech styling with a laid-back aura on its spacious outdoor patio and comfortable indoor booths. ✉ *0105 Edwards Village Blvd., Edwards* ☎ *970/926–2739* ▤ *AE, MC, V.*

$ ✕ **Fiesta's.** The Marquez sisters, Debbie and Susan, use old family recipes brought to Colorado by their great-grandparents to create great Southwestern cuisine. Among the favorites are chicken enchiladas in a white jalapeño sauce and blue-corn enchiladas served Santa Fe style with an egg on top. Handmade corn tamales are stuffed with pork and smothered in a classic New Mexican–chili sauce. The eatery in Edwards Plaza is brightly decorated with New Mexican folk art and paintings. More than 20 tequilas keep the bar—and patrons—hopping. ✉ *57 Edwards Access Rd., Edwards* ☎ *970/926–2121* ▤ *AE, D, MC, V.*

WHERE TO STAY

Most mid-range properties can be found in Beaver Creek Village close to the ski resort, while Bachelor Gulch is a posh hideaway for those staying at the Ritz-Carlton or in upscale condos. Avon and Edwards are the bedroom communities that support the resort.

★ $$$$ 🛏 **Beaver Creek Lodge.** A central atrium grabs all the attention at this European-style lodge a few hundred yards from the lifts. Rooms are generously proportioned—you'll probably get more space for your money here than at most other properties in the heart of the village, which makes it great for families. The decor is mountain chic—polished leather furniture, original art, sleek cabinets, flat-screen TV in the bedroom, and beds plumped with pillow-top mattresses. **Pros:** right next to the lifts, large rooms, attractively decorated. **Cons:** fee for parking, no spa. ✉ *26 Avondale La., Beaver Creek Village, 81620* ☎ *970/845–9800* ⊕ *www. beavercreeklodge.net* ➾ *72 suites* ⌂ *In-room: safe, kitchen (some), refrigerator (some), DVD, Wi-Fi. In-hotel: 2 restaurants, room service, bar, pool, gym, concierge, children's programs (ages 3–12), laundry facilities, laundry service, public Internet, public Wi-Fi, airport shuttle, parking (fee), no-smoking rooms* ▤ *AE, D, DC, MC, V.*

$$$$ 🛏 **Lodge & Spa at Cordillera.** An aura of quiet luxury prevails at this mountaintop lodge, with a decor that calls to mind the finest alpine hotels, and is popular with return guests. The rooms vary quite a bit in size; those in the newer wing tend to be larger. There are wood-burning fireplaces in some of the older rooms, whereas the newer rooms have gas fireplaces. The indoor pool has a view of the mountains through the wall of windows. The lodge is in the gated community of Cordillera, 15 minutes from Beaver Creek. The lodge operates a shuttle to the lifts. **Pros:** spa, fireplaces in rooms. **Cons:** must take shuttle to lifts, pools crowded with children. ✉ *2205 Cordillera Way,* ✉ *Box 1110, Edwards 81632* ☎ *970/926–2200 or 800/877–3529* ⊕ *www.rockresorts.cordillera.com* ➾ *56 rooms* ⌂ *In-room: refrigerators (some), DVD (some), VCR (some), Wi-Fi. In-hotel: 4 restaurants, room service, bars, golf courses, pool, gym, spa, concierge, laundry service, public Internet, public Wi-Fi, airport shuttle, parking (no fee), no-smoking rooms* ▤ *AE, D, DC, MC, V.*

$$$$ ⬚ **Park Hyatt Beaver Creek Resort & Spa.** With a magnificent antler chandelier and towering windows opening out onto the mountain, the lobby of this ski-in ski-out hotel manages to be both cozy and grand. Rooms are designed with skiers in mind, so they have nice touches like heated towel racks. Perhaps the ultimate in pampering is stepping into your warmed and waiting ski boots. Once the boots are off, enjoy a hot toddy by the outdoor fire pit. The on-site Allegria Spa and the nearby Beaver Creek Golf Club (with preferred tee times for guests) make this hotel popular with nonskiers. **Pros:** cozy Colorado mountain feel, ski-in ski out. **Cons:** fee for parking, views vary, uninterested staff. ✉ *136 E. Thomas Pl., Beaver Creek Village, 81620* ☎ *970/949–1234 or 800/233–1234* ⊕ *www. beavercreek.hyatt.com* ⏎ *190 rooms, 15 suites* ⬚ *In-room: safe, kitchen (some), refrigerator, DVD (some), VCR (some), Wi-Fi. In-hotel: 2 restaurants, room service, bars, golf course privileges, tennis courts, pool, gym, spa, concierge, children's programs (ages 3–12), laundry facilities, laundry service, public Internet, public Wi-Fi, airport shuttle, parking (fee), no-smoking rooms* ▭ *AE, D, DC, MC, V.*

$$$$ ⬚ **Pines Lodge.** This ski-in ski-out lodge is a winner for skiers, combining upscale accommodations with an unpretentious atmosphere. The aura of laid-back luxury comes from little extras such as afternoon tea by the fireplace in the lobby and a ski concierge who can arrange a complimentary guided tour. Rooms vary in size, so ask for one at the end facing the mountain, which have an extra sofa for contemplating the views from the large windows. Some rooms have balconies overlooking the ski area. **Pros:** slope-side, ski concierge. **Cons:** valet parking only, staff sometimes difficult to locate, gym needs updating. ✉ *141 Scott Hill Rd., Beaver Creek Village, 81620* ☎ *970/754–7200 or 866/859–8242* ⊕ *www.pineslodge.rockresorts.com* ⏎ *60 rooms, 12 condos* ⬚ *In-room: no a/c, safe, kitchen (some), refrigerator (some), DVD (some), VCR (some), Wi-Fi. In-hotel: restaurant, room service, bar, golf course, pool, gym, spa, concierge, laundry facilities, laundry service, public Internet, public Wi-Fi, airport shuttle, parking (fee), no-smoking rooms* ▭ *AE, D, MC, V.*

$$$$ ⬚ **Ritz-Carlton, Bachelor Gulch in Beaver Creek.** The stone-and-timber Ritz-
★ Carlton at Bachelor Gulch crowns Beaver Creek mountain above the bustle of Vail Valley like one of King Ludwig's Bavarian castles. Inside this imposing hotel are all the amenities any royal might desire—panoramic views from most of the rooms, stone fireplaces in more than a third, and high, plush beds in all. Guests can borrow Bachelor, the resident yellow Lab, for company on hikes (Bachelor's tips go to the Eagle Valley Humane Society). When you're finished hiking or skiing (or grow tired of gazing out at your kingdom from a balcony), head to the 21,000-square-foot spa and fitness center for a dose of bottled oxygen at the fresh-air salon or a dip in the cascading grotto hot tub. Wolfgang Puck opened a fourth location of his famous restaurant Spago here in late 2007. **Pros:** The most luxurious property on the mountain, excellent guest service, ski-in ski-out. **Cons:** High altitude (9,000 feet), removed from the Village. ✉ *0130 Daybreak Ridge, Bachelor Gulch Village, 81620* ☎ *970/748–6200, 800/241–3333* ⊕ *www. ritzcarlton.com* ⏎ *140 rooms, 40 suites* ⬚ *In-room: safe, kitchen (some), refrigerator (some), DVD, Wi-Fi. In-hotel: 4 restaurants, room service,*

4

bars, golf course, tennis courts, pool, gym, spa, bicycles, concierge, children's programs (ages 5–12), laundry service, executive floor, public Internet, public Wi-Fi, airport shuttle, parking (fee), some pets allowed, no-smoking rooms ⊟*AE, D, DC, MC, V.*

$$$ ☷ **Charter at Beaver Creek.** With its elegantly angled blue-slate roof, this sprawling property is one of the area's handsomest accommodations. Wisps of smoke from the fireplaces found in many rooms rise above, giving the place a homey feel perfect for families. There are plenty of choices for rooms, including one- to five-bedroom condominiums catering to families, many with balconies that let you gaze over the tops of the trees. The location is perfect—the ski-in ski-out hotel is a short walk from the main plaza at Beaver Creek. **Pros:** attractive architecture, ski-in ski-out. **Cons:** mediocre breakfasts, pools can be noisy with children. ⊠*120 Offerson Rd., Beaver Creek Village, 81620* ☎*970/949–6660 or 800/525–2139* ⊕*www.thecharter.com* ⊲*65 rooms, 156 condominiums* ⅋*In-room: no a/c, safe (some), kitchen (some), refrigerator (some), DVD (some), VCR (some), Wi-Fi. In-hotel: 2 restaurants, room service, bar, pools, gym, spa, concierge, laundry facilities, laundry service, public Internet, public Wi-Fi, airport shuttle, parking (no fee), no-smoking rooms* ⊟*AE, MC, V.*

CONDOS **Vail/Beaver Creek Reservations** (☎*800/525–2257*) lets you book ahead at properties all over Vail Valley. You can also buy lift tickets, arrange ski lessons, and get updates on events and activities. **Vail Valley Chamber and Tourism** (☎*800/824–5737*) operates a central reservations service for properties in Vail, Avon, and Beaver Creek. It also gives out information on events and activities and reports on snow conditions in winter.

NIGHTLIFE & THE ARTS

THE ARTS **Vilar Center for the Arts** (⊠*68 Avondale La.* ☎*970/845–8497 or* ★ *888/920–2787*) is an artwork in itself, with gold-color wood paneling and an etched-glass mural re-creating with bold strokes the mountains outside. Seating more than 500, the horseshoe-shape auditorium has great views from just about every seat. Throughout the year there's a stellar lineup of events, including concerts by orchestras and pop stars, great theater, and even a circus. In the surrounding plazas you'll find many art galleries. Just walking around Beaver Creek is a feast for the eyes, because sculptures are set almost everywhere you look.

NIGHTLIFE The boisterous **Coyote Café** (⊠*210 The Plaza* ☎*970/949–5001*) is a kick-back-and-relax sort of place where locals hang out in the after-

---

THE MYTH OF MUD

It's called the "mud season"—that quiet time between when the ski lifts clatter to a stop in April and the summer festivals open in June—a rainy, muddy May full of mosquitoes and boredom. At least that's what the locals would have you believe. Longer days, warmer nights, and less-crowded mountains mean mud season is the perfect time to enjoy Vail Valley. Backpack on trails emerging from snowdrifts, kayak rivers swollen to Class V white water from snowmelt, and mountain bike without breaking too much of a sweat.

noon and evening. If you're into local brews or giant margaritas, head to the **Dusty Boot Saloon** (⊠ *St. James Pl.* ☎ *970/748–1146*). At the base of the mountain, **McCoy's Café** (⊠ *Village Hall* ☎ *970/845–7808*) draws crowds most afternoons in the winter months with live music. After attacking the moguls, unwind with a glass of wine or a single-malt scotch in the **Whiskey Elk** (⊠ *136 E. Thomas Pl.* ☎ *970/949–1234*). You can relax on overstuffed sofas and chairs placed around the fireplace at this lounge in the Park Hyatt Beaver Creek. There's quieter music during après-ski hours and more-raucous entertainment several evenings each week.

SHOPPING

Christopher & Co. (⊠ *Edwards Village Center, Edwards* ☎ *970/926–8191*) has vintage poster art dating from the 1890s to the 1950s. Depictions of American and European ski resorts are found among the more than 3,000 posters on display. Walk carefully around the **Pismo Gallery** (⊠ *Village Hall* ☎ *970/949–0908*), as there's an outstanding collection of handblown glass. Look for the fragile, colorful creations by Dale Chihuly. There are lamp shades, perfume bottles, and other gorgeous items. Although the **Shaggy Ram** (⊠ *Edwards Village Center, Edwards* ☎ *970/926–7377*) sounds like it would stock mostly Western items, this shop is a large treasure trove of French and English antiques. Items range from fringed lamps to crystal decanters to elegant old desks. Look for the shop near the Gore Range Brewery.

VAIL VALLEY ESSENTIALS

TRANSPORTATION

BY AIR

Denver International Airport (DEN), the gateway to the High Rockies, is 119 mi east of Vail. It's a 90-minute drive from Vail, but if you get caught in ski traffic, it could take two hours (and much longer if a blizzard hits). The Vail Valley is served by Eagle County Airport (EGE), 34 mi west of Vail. During ski season, American, Continental, Delta, Northwest, United, and US Air have nonstop flights to Eagle County from several gateways. United and American fly here year-round.

If possible, try snagging a direct flight straight into the Eagle County Airport from your hometown. But if your trip involves a connection through Denver or another hub, it is often faster to rent a car and make the scenic 90-minute drive through the mountains or catch one of the many shuttle services. Although winter mountain weather can be fickle and delay flights, the two high passes on I–70 between Denver–Loveland and Vail are rarely closed, though traffic might slow to a creep.

Information Denver International Airport (DEN) (☎ *800/247-2336* ⊕ *www.flydenver.com*). **Eagle County Airport (EGE)** (☎ *970/524-9490* ⊕ *www.eagle-county.us/airport*).

TRANSFERS **Contacts Colorado Mountain Express** (☎ *970/949-4227 or 800/525-6353*). **Vail Valley Taxi** (☎ *970/476-8294 or 877/829-8294*).

BY BUS & SHUTTLE
Greyhound Lines serves Vail.

All the resorts run free or inexpensive shuttles between the ski villages and the slopes. Locals and visitors alike hop the free Town of Vail buses up and down from the East Village to the West Village (a distance of nearly 6 mi with Vail Village at the center). For trips to Beaver Creek, catch the ECO Transit bus from the Vail Transportation Center in Vail Village (beside the Vail Information Center). A one-way fare is $5.

Contacts Avon Beaver Creek Transit (☎ *970/748–4120*). **Colorado Mountain Express** (☎ *800/525–6363 or 970/468–7600* ⊕ *www.ridecme.com*). **Greyhound Lines** (☎ *800/231–2222* ⊕ *www.greyhound.com*). **Town of Vail** (☎ *970/479–2100*). **Village Transportation** (☎ *970/949–1938*).

BY CAR
The most convenient place for visitors to rent a car is at the Denver International Airport. Alamo, Avis, Budget, Dollar, Enterprise, Hertz, and National have offices in Eagle County Airport as well.

Although it is often severely overcrowded, I–70 is still the quickest and most direct route from Denver to Vail. For the first 45 minutes, it climbs gradually through the dry Front Range Mountains before ducking beneath the Eisenhower Tunnel. The last 45 minutes are through the high Summit County Basin and up and over the mellow grade of Vail Pass.

Information Colorado Road Condition Hotline (☎ *303/639–1111*).**Colorado State Patrol** (☎ *303/239–4500* ⊕ *www.csp.state.co.us*).

CONTACTS & RESOURCES

EMERGENCIES
Ambulance or Police (☎ *911*).

24-Hour Medical Care Beaver Creek Village Medical Center (✉ *1280 Village Rd., Beaver Creek* ☎ *970/949–0800*). **Vail Valley Medical Center** (✉ *181 W. Meadow Dr., Vail* ☎ *970/476–2451*).

TOURS
Vail's Nova Guides runs jeep and all-terrain-vehicle tours, as well as rafting, fishing, snowmobiling, and hiking expeditions.

Contacts Nova Guides (✉ *Red Cliff* ☎ *970/827–4232*). **Timberline Tours** (✉ *Vail* ☎ *970/476–1414*).

VISITOR INFORMATION
Snow Reports Vail (☎ *970/476–4888*).

Contacts Vail Resorts, Inc. (✉ *Box 7, Vail 81658* ☎ *970/476–5601* ⊕ *vail.com*). **Vail Valley Partnership** (✉ *100 E. Meadow Dr., Vail 81657* ☎ *970/476–1000 or 800/653–4523* ⊕ *www.visitvailvalley.com*).

Aspen & the Roaring Fork Valley

WORD OF MOUTH

"I personally prefer Aspen over Vail, so I'd give it the entire visit, or at least more than just one night. If you've already been to Vail, why not just choose Aspen this time? There's so much to do there. And it's prettier, I think, because it doesn't sit right on an interstate highway, like Vail does."

—MaureenB

". . . stay in Aspen. It has more atmosphere than Snowmass and is a classic old Western town. Snowmass lacks the feel of being in a real town— it is more condos and hotels that are built around the mountain."

—MarieF

Revised &
Updated by
Jad Davenport

FOREVER HONORED IN THE LYRICS of John Denver, the Roaring Fork Valley—and Aspen, its crown jewel—is the quintessential Colorado Rocky Mountain High. A rampart of the state's famed Fourteeners (peaks over 14,000 feet) guard this valley. There are only two ways in or out: over the precipitous Independence Pass or up the four-lane highway through the booming Roaring Fork Valley that stretches nearly 50 mi, from Glenwood Springs to Aspen.

Outside Aspen, Colorado natives regard the city and its eclectic populace of longtime locals, newly arrived ski bums, hard-core mountaineers, laser-sculpted millionaires, and tanned celebs with a mixture of bemusement and envy. The "real Aspenites," who came for the snow and stayed for summers, are slowly getting squeezed out by seven-digit housing prices. Many have migrated down valley to the bedroom communities of Basalt and Carbondale. In the words of one refugee, "the Aspen millionaires are making room for the billionaires."

The quest for wealth in the valley dates back to the mid-1800s, when the original inhabitants, the Ute people, were supplanted by gold prospectors and silver miners, who came to reap the region's mineral bounty. The demonetization of silver in 1893 brought the quiet years, as the population dwindled and ranching became a way of life. Nearly half a century later, the tides turned again as downhill skiing gave new life to Aspen. Today the Roaring Fork Valley weaves together its past and present through a unique blend of small-town charm and world-class amenities, all surrounded by the majestic beauty of central Colorado's 2-million-acre White River National Forest.

EXPLORING ASPEN & THE ROARING FORK VALLEY

Wedged in a valley between the Elk Mountain palisades to the southwest and the high-altitude massifs of the Sawatch Range in the east, the Roaring Fork Valley is a Rocky Mountain Shangri-la with Aspen at the headwaters. The charm and beauty of this isolation can make reaching Aspen both a scenic and frustrating journey.

The only way in or out of Aspen is Highway 82—either up the Roaring Fork Valley from Glenwood Springs or over Independence Pass in summer from the eastern side of the mountains (the pass begins at the junction of U.S. 24 and Highway 82). Aspen's explosive growth hasn't come without some headaches. Despite ongoing improvements and expanded lanes, Highway 82 can quickly clog with weekend skiers and day commuters. Still, you'll have some gorgeous scenery to distract you.

ABOUT THE PARKS & RECREATION AREAS

The Roaring Fork Valley is ringed by recreational land, checkerboarded between wilderness areas and national forests. To the southeast in the Collegiate Peaks Wilderness area, more 14,000-foot summits beckon peak baggers and day hikers than anywhere else in the Lower 48.

The often-overlooked Hunter-Fryingpan Wilderness Area is one of Colorado's hidden gems—a thin-air spine of unnamed peaks and excellent

TOP REASONS TO GO

The Scene: You'll see it all in Aspen: Hollywood celebs in cowboy boots elbowed up to the J-Bar, glamorous wives of Saudi royalty shopping for $500 jeans, and tanned European ski instructors leading parades of children down the slopes. But don't let the surreal flash keep you from enjoying the warmth and sincerity of the town; for all the glitz, Aspen is still full of fascinating and friendly locals.

Historic Hotels: Along with such luxurious properties as the St. Regis Resort in Aspen and the hip Sky Hotel, there are plenty of other, more-sentimental lodging choices in the valley. Thanks to moneyed preservationists the Roaring Fork Valley is home to several of Colorado's finest historic hotels including the Victorian Hotel Jerome in Aspen, the Medici-inspired Hotel Colorado in Glenwood Springs, and the elegant Redstone Inn in Redstone.

The Maroon Bells: If you're looking for postcard Colorado, you'll find it in the 14,000-foot Maroon Bell peaks. Visit on a quiet autumn morning when the aspen are turning and the steep-faced pyramid peaks reflect a dusting of snow in Maroon Lake, and don't be surprised if you hum a John Denver tune.

Fine Fare: From Matsuhisa sushi to lobster strudel, Aspen, Carbondale, and Glenwood Springs have just about any dish you can imagine due to the world-class chefs drawn to the region's blizzard of tourist dollars. It's possible to dine like a king (and pay a king's ransom), but there are also tasty and affordable options to be found.

Hot Springs: You'll find modern spas galore in Aspen, but the authentic and natural treat can be found down valley at Glenwood Springs where the 90°F mineral-water pool has been a therapeutic retreat since the Ute Indians knew it as *Yampah* or "healing waters."

trout rivers in the Williams Mountains just east of Aspen. On the other side of the Continental Divide, the Hunter-Fryingpan becomes the Mount Massive Wilderness Area, named for Colorado's second-highest peak, which stands 14,421 feet tall. Most of these wilderness areas are encompassed within the much larger—and more-fragmented—White River National Forest.

ABOUT THE RESTAURANTS

Sushi? Coconut curry? Bison and lobster? Colorado's culinary repertoire reaches its zenith in Aspen. With all the Hummers and designer handbags comes a certain gourmet sophistication that eclipses the rest of the state. Plates can be pricey, particularly in Aspen, but many eateries offer several moderately priced entrées (usually pastas) as a nod to the budget-conscious. For those who want a break from Aspen, there are good dining options down valley in Basalt and Carbondale as well.

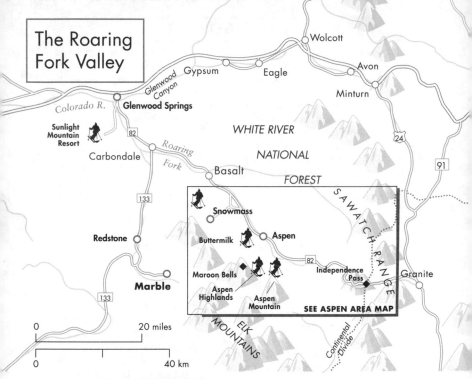

The Roaring Fork Valley

Wolcott
Gypsum
Glenwood Canyon
Eagle
Avon
Minturn
Colorado R. Glenwood Springs
WHITE RIVER
Sunlight Mountain Resort
82
Roaring
Carbondale
Fork
Basalt
NATIONAL
FOREST
133
SAWATCH RANGE
Snowmass
Redstone
Buttermilk
Aspen
82
Marble
Maroon Bells
Independence Pass
Granite
Aspen Highlands
Aspen Mountain
SEE ASPEN AREA MAP
0   20 miles
ELK MOUNTAINS
Continental Divide
0   40 km
24
91

ABOUT THE HOTELS

There's no shortage of lodging in Aspen and the Roaring Fork, however you'll pay the highest rates in the state. Downriver alternatives like Carbondale and Glenwood Springs are attractive for budget hunters—but you'll face a surprising amount of traffic when commuting to Aspen. With seven drive-in campsites around the city, tenting it is also an option; make sure you reserve a site early, though, as summer campgrounds fill before noon. If you're staying for more than a weekend or are traveling with a large group, condominiums offer an affordable option and the added bonus of a kitchen.

WHAT IT COSTS					
	¢	$	$$	$$$	$$$$
RESTAURANTS	under $8	$8–$12	$13–$18	$19–$25	over $25
HOTELS	under $80	$80–$120	$121–$170	$171–$230	over $230

Restaurant prices are for a main course at dinner, excluding 8.2%–8.6% tax. Hotel prices are for two people in a standard double room in high season, excluding service charges and 8.6%–10.7% tax.

TIMING

Aspen and the Roaring Fork Valley are increasingly a year-round destination. If it's skiing you're after, February and March have the best snow and warmest winter weather. Aspen's summers are legendary for

CLOSE UP

Independence Pass

From Memorial Day to Labor Day, the most beautiful route to Aspen is over Independence Pass. From the Vail-Leadville–Buena Vista corridor on the east side of the Sawatch Mountains, Highway 82 climbs up and over 12,080-foot Independence Pass and switchbacks down to Aspen along the way passing above tree line and making some spectacular white-knuckle hairpin turns (drive slowly to appreciate the scenery and also because you might have to yield to oncoming traffic in narrow, one-lane sections).

The pass divides the Mount Massive Wilderness to the north and the Collegiate Peaks to the south and is not for the fainthearted, given the long exposed drops and the possibility for snow at any time of the year. Elk and mule deer herds can sometimes be seen at dawn and dusk grazing in the willow thickets beside Lake Creek as it cascades down the eastern flank of the pass. As soon as the autumn snow flies, however, the pass closes and Aspen becomes a cul-de-sac town accessible only via Glenwood Springs.

5

their food, art, and music festivals. Although only 6,000 locals call Aspen home, the population more than quadruples to 27,000 in summer and winter high seasons. Traffic and parking during both times can try your patience; if you're in town, it's best to explore on foot. June is best for rafting (snowmelt spawns high-octane rapids), but many high-country hiking and mountain-biking trails are buried under snowdrifts until July when the wildflowers peak. Mid-September brings cooler days, photogenic snow dustings in the Maroon Bells, and flame-orange aspen groves.

ASPEN

220 mi west of Denver via I–70 and Hwy. 82.

One of the world's fabled resorts, Aspen practically defines glitz, glamour, and glorious skiing. To the uninitiated, Aspen and Vail are synonymous. To residents, a rivalry exists, with locals of each claiming to have the state's most epic skiing, finest restaurants, and hottest nightlife. The most obvious distinction is the look: Vail is a faux-Bavarian development, whereas Aspen is an overgrown mining town. Vail is full of politicians—it's where Gerald Ford, Dan Quayle, and John Sununu fled to escape the cares of state—whereas Aspen is popular with singers and movie stars. Don Johnson and Melanie Griffith married (and divorced) here, and this is where Barbra Streisand took a stand against state legislation that discriminated against gay people.

Between the galleries, museums, music festivals, and other glittering social events, there's so much going on in Aspen that even in winter

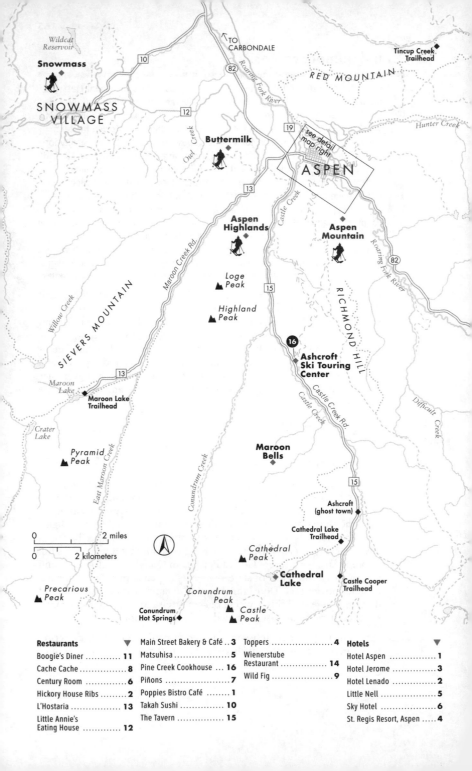

Restaurants ▼

Boogie's Diner **11**

Cache Cache **8**

Century Room **6**

Hickory House Ribs **2**

L'Hostaria **13**

Little Annie's
Eating House **12**

Main Street Bakery & Café .. **3**

Matsuhisa **5**

Pine Creek Cookhouse ... **16**

Piñons **7**

Poppies Bistro Café **1**

Takah Sushi **10**

The Tavern **15**

Toppers **4**

Wienerstube
Restaurant **14**

Wild Fig **9**

Hotels ▼

Hotel Aspen **1**

Hotel Jerome **3**

Hotel Lenado **2**

Little Nell **5**

Sky Hotel **6**

St. Regis Resort, Aspen **4**

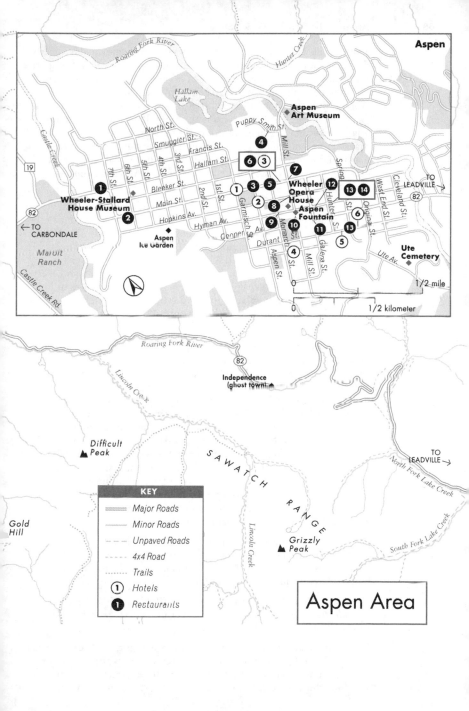

many people come simply to "do the scene" and never make it to the slopes. High-end boutiques have been known to serve free Campari-and-sodas après-ski, a practice so over the top that there's a certain charm to it. At the same time, Aspen is a place where people live fairly average lives, sending their children to school and working at jobs that may or may not have to do with skiing. It is, arguably, America's original ski-bum destination, a fact that continues to give the town's character an underlying layer of humor and texture. You can come to Aspen and have a reasonably straightforward, enjoyable ski vacation, because once you've stripped away the veneer, Aspen is simply a great place to ski.

Aspen has always been a magnet for cultural and countercultural types. The late bad-boy gonzo journalist Hunter S. Thompson was one of the more-visible citizens of the nearby community of Woody Creek. One of Aspen's most amusing figures is Jon Barnes, who tools around in his "Ultimate Taxi" (it's plastered with 3-D glasses, crystal disco balls, and neon necklaces and is redolent of dry ice and incense). You'll find everyone from socialites with *Vogue* exteriors and vague interiors to long-haired musicians in combat boots and fatigues. Ultimately, it doesn't matter what you wear here, as long as you wear it with conviction.

Originally called Ute City (after its displaced former residents), Aspen was founded in the late 1870s during a silver rush. The most prominent early citizen was Jerome Wheeler, who opened two of Aspen's enduring landmarks, the Hotel Jerome and the Wheeler Opera House. The silver market crashed in 1893, and Aspen's population dwindled from 15,000 to 250 by the end of the Depression. In the late 1930s the region struck gold when Swiss mountaineer and ski consultant Andre Roche determined that Aspen Mountain would make a prime ski area. By 1941 it had already landed the U.S. Nationals, but Aspen was really put on the world map by Walter Paepcke, who developed the town as a cultural mecca. In 1949 he helped found the Aspen Institute for Humanistic Studies, and subsequently organized an international celebration to mark Johann Wolfgang von Goethe's 200th birthday. This event paved the way for such renowned annual festivities as the Aspen Music Festival and the International Design Conference.

Downtown Aspen is easily explored on foot. It's best to wander without a planned itinerary. You can spend an afternoon admiring the sleek window displays and graceful Victorian mansions, many of which now house fine boutiques and restaurants.

Fodor'sChoice   The **Aspen Music Festival and School** (☎970/925–3254 ⊕*www.aspen*
★   *musicfestival.com*), focusing on chamber music to jazz, runs from late June to mid-August.

☾   In summer, grab a bench near the town's focal point, the **Aspen Fountain** (⊠*Mill St. and Hyman Ave*). Jets of water shoot up at random, soaking anyone who happens to be in the way. It's a great spot for people-watching during the day and listening to musicians in the evening.

Many of Aspen's beautiful buildings were constructed in the 1880s, when the surrounding mines were overflowing with silver. Jerome Wheeler, one of the town's most prominent citizens, constructed the 1889 **Hotel Jerome** (⊠ *330 E. Main St.* ☎ *970/920–1000*). Peek into the ornate lobby to get a sense of turn-of-the-20th-century living.

Built in the same year, the elegant **Wheeler Opera House** (⊠ *320 E. Hyman Ave.* ☎ *970/920–5770*) still serves as a concert venue.

NEED A BREAK? Follow the locals to **Ink! Coffee** (⊠ *520 E. Durant Ave.* ☎ *970/544-0588*) where you can sample hot and cold coffee, tea, and other drinks, including their signature Blended Black and White—iced espresso mixed with black and white chocolate ($5). The café also serves pastries and snacks. In summer the patio is a nice place to relax.

You can get a taste of Victorian high life at the Queen Anne–style **Wheeler-Stallard House Museum**, which displays memorabilia collected by the Aspen Historical Society. While you're there, ask about the organization's newest endeavor, the Holden–Marolt Ranching and Mining Museum, a hands-on exploration of Aspen's past, housed in an old barn on the western edge of town. ⊠ *620 W. Bleeker St.* ☎ *970/925–3721* ⊕ *www.aspenhistory.org* ☐ *$6* ☉ *Tues.–Sat. 1–5.*

Works by top regional and national artists are exhibited at the **Aspen Art Museum.** The complimentary wine-and-cheese reception held every Thursday from 5 to 7 is the best time to visit. ⊠ *590 N. Mill St.* ☎ *970/925–8050* ⊕ *www.aspenartmuseum.org* ☐ *$5, free on Fri.* ☉ *Tues., Wed., Fri., and Sat. 10–6; Thurs. 10–7; Sun. noon–6.*

With a trail that winds through gravestones dating to the 1800s, **Ute Cemetery** (✛ *Next to Ute Park off Ute Ave.*) is a reminder that Aspen's roots go back deep into the nation's history.

The majestic **Maroon Bells** (⊠ *White River National Forest,* ⊠ *Maroon Creek Rd.,* ✛ *10 mi west of Aspen*) are twin peaks more than 14,000 feet high. The colorful peaks, thanks to mineral streaking, are so vivid you'd swear they were blanketed with primrose and Indian paintbrush. It's one of the most-photographed spots in the state. Cars are allowed only partway, but the Roaring Fork Transportation Authority provides shuttle buses that leave regularly in summer months from the Rubey Park Transportation Center in downtown Aspen. A convenient pass, available for $18.50, includes one trip to the Maroon Bells and one ride up Aspen Mountain's Silver Queen Gondola, where concerts, nature walks, amazing hiking, and other activities await you.

Fodor's Choice ★

DOWNHILL SKIING & SNOWBOARDING

Aspen is really four ski areas rolled into one resort. Aspen Highlands, Aspen (or Ajax) Mountain, Buttermilk, and Snowmass can all be skied with the same ticket. Aspen, Aspen Highlands, and Buttermilk are clustered close to downtown Aspen, whereas Snowmass is down the valley near Snowmass Village. A free shuttle system connects the four.

Locals' favorite **Aspen Highlands** is essentially one long ridge with trails dropping off either side. Over the past few years the antiquated lift system has been replaced by three high-speed quads, and a massive base-area village has risen, turning the maverick ski hill into a destination in and of itself. Aspen Highlands has thrilling descents at Golden Horn, Olympic Bowl, and now, Highland Bowl, a hike-in experience unlike any in Colorado. The steep and often bumpy cluster of trails around Steeplechase and Highland Bowl makes this mountain one of the best places to be on a good-powder day. Aspen Highlands has a wide-open bowl called Thunder that's popular with inter-

> ### WHERE HAVE ALL THE FLOWERS GONE?
>
> The Maroon Bells Snowmass Wilderness Area southwest of Aspen is famed for dramatic escarpments and alpine meadows. But knowing how to find the best wildflower displays means understanding the relationship between temperature and elevation: The higher you go, the colder it gets. The bloom will start first in the valleys and eventually climb above the 11,200-foot tree line. Most Colorado wildflowers will reach their peak from just before the summer solstice until mid-July.

mediate skiers, as well as plenty of lower-mountain blue runs. The best overall downhill run is Highland Bowl. Besides the comparatively short lift lines and some heart-pounding runs, a highlight of Aspen Highlands is your first trip to the 12,500-foot summit. The view, which includes the Maroon Bells and Pyramid Peak, is the most dramatic in the area and one of the best in the country. ⊠ *Maroon Creek Rd.* ☏*970/925–1220 or 800/525–6200* ⊕*www.aspensnowmass.com* ⊘*Early Dec.– early Apr., daily 9–4.*

Open since 1947, **Aspen Mountain** is a dream destination for mogul and steep skiers. Nearby Bell Mountain provides some of the best bump skiing anywhere, followed by Walsh's (also a favorite for snowboarders), Hyrup's, and Kristi's. Those wanting long cruisers head to the ridges or valleys: Ruthie's Run, Ridge of the Bell, and International are the classics. Newcomers should note that there are no novice-level runs here. This is a resort where nearly half the trails are rated advanced or expert, and a black-diamond trail here might rank as a double-black diamond elsewhere. The narrow ski area is laid out on a series of steep, unforgiving ridges with little room for error. Most skiers spend much of the morning on intermediate trails off the upper-mountain quad. Then they head for lunch on the deck of Bonnie's, the mid-mountain restaurant that on sunny days is one of the great people-watching scenes in the skiing world. After a big storm, there's snowcat skiing on the back side of the mountain. The biggest drawback to skiing at Aspen Mountain is that too many trails funnel into Spar Gulch, making the end-of-day rush to the bottom chaotic and often dangerous—a situation that has become increasingly tense because snowboarders are now part of the mix. ⊠ *Durant St.* ☏*970/925–1220 or 800/525–6200* ⊕*www. aspensnowmass.com* ⊘*Late Nov.–mid-Apr., daily 9–4.*

If you're looking for an escape from the hustle and bustle of Aspen, spend a day at **Buttermilk**—a family-friendly place where it's virtually impossible to get into trouble. Buttermilk is terrific for novices, intermediates, and, thanks to its half-pipe and 2-mi-long Crazy T'rain Park, snowboarders. It's a low-key, lighthearted sort of place, and an antidote to the kind of hotdogging you might encounter at Aspen Mountain. Sterner Run is a favorite for its length and curves, while Racer's Edge appeals to speed demons. Among the featured attractions is a hangout for children named Fort Frog. The Tiehack section to the east, with sweeping views of Maroon Creek valley, has several advanced runs (though nothing truly expert). It also has superb powder, and the deep snow sticks around longer because many serious skiers overlook this mountain. Buttermilk's allure hasn't been lost on pros, however; it now hosts the Winter X Games. ⊠ *W. Buttermilk Rd.* ☎*970/925–1220 or 800/525–6200* ⊕*www.aspensnowmass.com* ☉*Early Dec.–mid-Apr., daily 9–4.*

> ## WORD OF MOUTH
>
> "The town of Aspen sits at the base of Aspen Mountain (some call it Ajax Mountain). Good intermediate skiers should have no trouble getting around on it at all. I'd suggest checking into an "Ambassador" tour of the mountain. It's free, and it's led by a local volunteer...they will take you on a "blue run only" tour around the mountain. The ambassadors will show you the best ways to get around the mountain, the best runs at certain times of the day, and other little gems (ask them to take you to some of the memorials on the mountain—there's one for John Denver, Marilyn Monroe, Elvis, and others)." —Furledleader

FACILITIES **Aspen Highlands:** 3,635-foot vertical drop; 790 skiable acres; 131 trails; 18% beginner, 30% intermediate, 16% advanced, 36% expert; 3 high-speed quad chairs, 2 triple chairs.

Aspen Mountain: 3,267-foot vertical drop; 673 skiable acres; 76 trails; 48% intermediate, 26% advanced, 26% expert; 1 6-passenger gondola, 1 high-speed quad chair, 2 quad chairs, 1 high-speed double chair, 3 double chairs.

Buttermilk: 2,030-foot vertical drop; 435 skiable acres; 44 trails; 35% beginner, 39% intermediate, 26% advanced; 2 high-speed quad chairs, 3 double chairs, 4 surface lifts.

LESSONS & **Aspen Skiing Company** (☎*970/925–1220 or 800/525–6200*) gives les-
PROGRAMS sons at all four mountains. Half-day group lessons start at $74, and a private half-day lesson will cost you $329. A noteworthy deal is the three-day guaranteed learn-to-ski or learn-to-snowboard package at Snowmass or Buttermilk, which includes lessons, rental gear, and lift tickets for $327. The company also runs snowcat trips on Aspen Mountain.

Aspen Mountain Powder Tours (☎*970/925–1220*) provides access to 1,500 acres on the back side of Aspen Mountain via snowcats. Most of the terrain is negotiable by confident intermediates, with about

10,000 vertical feet constituting a typical day's skiing. Reservations are required at least a day in advance, but you should book as early as possible. Trips cost $335.

LIFT TICKETS   Lift tickets are $87, but almost nobody pays full price thanks to multi-day savings, early- and late-season specials, and other discounts.

RENTALS   Numerous ski shops in Aspen rent equipment. Rental packages (skis, boots, and poles) start at around $40 per day and rise to $50 or more for the latest and greatest equipment. Snowboard packages (boots and boards) run about $40. Bargain shopping at stores around town may turn up better deals. **Aspen Sports** (⊠*408 E. Cooper Ave.* ☎*970/925–6331*) has plenty of gear to choose from. **Durrance Sports** (⊠*414 E. Cooper Ave.* ☎*970/429–0101*), in Aspen Highlands Village, has equipment from many companies. **Pomeroy Sports** (⊠*614 E. Durrant Ave.* ☎*970/925–7875*), at the base of Aspen Mountain gondola, has good deals on equipment.

NORDIC SKIING

BACKCOUNTRY   The **Alfred A. Braun Hut System** is one of Aspen's major backcountry
SKIING   networks. The trailhead leads from the Ashcroft Ski Touring Center into the Maroon Bells–Snowmass Wilderness. Take the usual precautions, because the trails cover terrain prone to avalanche. Huts sleep 7 to 14 people. They're open in winter only, and reservations can be made beginning May 1. ⌂*Box 7937, Aspen 81612* ☎*970/925–5775* ⊕*www.huts.org* ⊠*$25 per person per night, 4-person minimum.*

★   The **10th Mountain Hut & Trail System,** named in honor of the U.S. Army's 10th Mountain Division, includes 10 huts along the trail connecting Aspen and Vail. The main trail follows a generally avalanche-safe route in altitudes from 8,000 feet to 12,000 feet. This translates to a fair amount of skiing along tree-lined trails and a good bit of high-alpine ups and downs. You must be in good shape, and some backcountry skiing experience is extremely helpful. Accommodations along the trail vary, but this system does include the Ritz-Carltons of backcountry huts, supplied with mattresses and pillows, precut logs for wood-burning stoves, and utensils for cooking. Huts sleep from 6 to 16 people (more if you're willing to cuddle). For a $25 membership fee, you can enter a reservation lottery in March. Otherwise, reservations are accepted beginning in April; weekends in peak ski season fill up quickly. ⊠*1280 Ute Ave., 81611* ☎*970/925–5775* ⊕*www.huts.org* ⊠*$28 and up per person per night.*

If you're either unfamiliar with the hut system or inexperienced in backcountry travel, you should hire a guide. One reliable company is **Aspen Alpine Guides** (⌂*Box 659, Aspen 81612* ☎*970/925–6618 or 800/643–8621* ⊕*www.aspenalpine.com*). In Aspen, the best place for backcountry-gear rentals (including ski equipment, climbing skins, packs, sleeping bags, and mountaineering paraphernalia) is the **Ute Mountaineer** (⊠*308 S. Mill St.* ☎*970/925–2849*).

TRACK SKIING   There is something to be said for maintaining a wealthy tax base. Subsidized by local taxes, the **Aspen/Snowmass Nordic Council** (⌂*Box 10815,*

Aspen 81612 ☎*970/429–2039* ⊕*www.aspennordic.com*) charges no fee for the 48 mi of maintained trails in the Roaring Fork Valley, making it the largest free groomed Nordic-trail system in North America. For a longer ski try the Owl Creek Trail, connecting the Aspen Cross-Country Center trails with the Snowmass Club trail system. More than 10 mi long, the trail leads through some lovely scenery.

Lessons and rentals are available at the **Aspen Cross-Country Center** (⊠*39551 Hwy. 82* ☎*970/925–2145*). Diagonal, skating, racing, and light-touring setups are available.

About 12 mi from Aspen, the **Ashcroft Ski Touring Center** (⊠*11399 Castle Creek Rd.* ☎*970/925–1971*) is sequestered in a high-alpine basin up Castle Creek, which runs between Aspen Mountain and Aspen Highlands. The 25 mi of groomed trails are surrounded by the high peaks of the Maroon Bells–Snowmass Wilderness, and crisscross the ghost town of Ashcroft. This is one of the most dramatic cross-country sites in the High Rockies.

SPORTS & THE OUTDOORS

★ ☾ **Aspen Center for Environmental Studies** (⊠*100 Puppy Smith St.* ☎*970/ 925–5756* ⊕*www.aspennature.org*) is a research center and wildlife sanctuary where children and adults alike can take refuge. The facility sponsors snowshoe walks with naturalist guides in winter, and wildlife workshops that teach everything from how to create a small wildlife sanctuary in your own backyard to what animals you might find on local trails. In summer there are bird-watching hikes and "special little naturalist" programs for four- to seven-year-olds, which include nature walks and arts and crafts. A permanently injured golden eagle is kept on the premises.

FISHING The **Roaring Fork River,** fast, deep, and uninterrupted by dams from its
★ headwaters to its junction with the Colorado, is one of the last free-flowing rivers in the state. The healthy populations of rainbow and brown trout—of the hefty 12- to 18-inch variety—make the Roaring Fork a favorite with anglers. From the headwaters at Independence Pass to within 3 mi of Aspen, most of the river access is on public lands and is best fished in summer and early fall. Downstream of Aspen the river crosses through a checkerboard pattern of private and public land; it's fishable year-round. The river's rounded stones make felt soles or studs a good idea for waders. See ⊕*www.wildlife.state.co.us/fishing.* for more information.

Aspen Trout Guides (⊠*520 E. Durant Ave.* ☎*970/379–7963* ⊕*aspen-troutguides.com*) runs fly-fishing tours of local waterways. The company is located in the Hamilton Sports Pro Shop. **Taylor Creek Fly Shop** (⊠*408 E. Cooper Ave.* ☎*970/920–1128*) has the town's best selection of flies and other supplies.

FITNESS The upscale **Aspen Club & Spa** (⊠*1450 Crystal Lake Rd.* ☎*970/925– 8900*) has plenty of weight-training and cardiovascular equipment, as well as indoor courts for squash, basketball, and other sports. It's also home to John Clendenin's Ski Doctor indoor ski simulator. When you're finished getting all sweaty, relax in the luxurious full-service spa.

HIKING   If you aren't used to it, high altitude can catch you off guard. Drink plenty of water to help stave off the effects of altitude sickness—dizziness, shortness of breath, headache, and nausea. Slather on the sunscreen—it's easy to get sunburned at altitude. And, in summer, an early morning start is best, as afternoon thunderstorms are frequent and can be dangerous above the tree line.

> **GETTING HIGH IN ASPEN**
>
> Surrounded by 14,000-foot peaks, Aspen almost demands to be appreciated from a bird's-eye view. Old-fashioned foot power can take you up any of the numerous peak trails while the lazy can simply enjoy the ski lifts, both summer and winter. If you're looking for a boost of adrenaline, try a morning balloon flight. Real thrill seekers will opt for paragliding.

Fodor'sChoice   Aspen excels at high-altitude scenery (seven of the state's 54 Fourteeners are in the Elk Mountain range) and nowhere is the iconic image of the Colorado Rockies more breathtaking than in the **Maroon Bells–Snowmass Wilderness Area.** In summer, shuttle buses take visitors up Maroon Creek Road to Maroon Lake at the base of the peaks from 8:30 AM until 5 PM. Private cars are allowed at all other times (there is a $10 recreational fee). More-ambitious sightseers can select from a number of trails. ⊠*Sopris Ranger District, White River National Forest* ✛*Maroon Creek Rd. 10 mi west of Aspen* ☎*970/963–2266* ⊕*www.fs.fed.us/r2/whiteriver.*

★   You'll get a taste of several ecozones as you tackle **Cathedral Lake,** a 5.6-mi round-trip trail. The trail starts gently in aspen and pine groves but earns sweat quickly in a long, steep climb into a high valley. Another series of steep, short switchbacks ascend a headwall. From there it's a short stroll to a shallow alpine lake cupped by a wall of granite cliffs. When the high-country snows melt off in mid-July, the meadows and willow thickets surrounding the lake are colored with blooming mountain lupine, columbine, and Indian paintbrush. ⊠*Sopris Ranger District, White River National Forest* ☎*970/963–2266* ⊕*www.fs.fed. us/r2/whiteriver.*

HORSEBACK   For day or overnight horseback tours into the spectacular Maroon
RIDING   Bells–Snowmass Wilderness, try **Maroon Bell Outfitters** (⊠*3129 Maroon Creek Rd.* ☎*970/920–4677*).

ICE SKATING   The **Aspen Recreation Center** (⊠*0861 Maroon Creek Rd.* ☎*970/544–4100*) is home to an indoor ice rink big enough for National Hockey League games. There's also an Olympic-size swimming pool. If you prefer outdoor skating, try the **Silver Circle** (⊠*433 E. Durant Ave.* ☎*970/925–6360*).

MOUNTAIN   **Crystal and Lead King Basin** is a scenic 16-mi loop on four-wheel-drive
BIKING   roads surrounded by the Maroon Bells–Snowmass Wilderness. The first
★   6 moderate mi get you to the ghost mine of Crystal. You can turn back here, or tackle the rugged, remaining 2 mi and enjoy views from the 10,800-foot summit. Keep your eyes out for bouncing jeeps behind

you. ⚓*Trailhead: From north side of Beaver Lake in Marble, continue driving up Forest Service Rd. 314 (Daniel's Hill). The ride begins wherever you park.*

Aspen Sports (⊠*408 E. Cooper Ave.* ☎*970/925–6331*) has the area's widest selection of rental bikes, including tandems and all types of carriers for kids. **Blazing Adventures** (⊠*555 E. Durant Ave.* ☎*970/923–4544 or 800/282–7238*) leads downhill bicycle tours through Aspen and the surrounding valleys. **Hub of Aspen** (⊠*315 E. Hyman Ave.* ☎*970/925–7970*) offers rental bikes.

PARAGLIDING It seems a pity to enjoy Aspen only from a horizontal viewpoint when so much of its scenery is vertical. If you've ever considered **paragliding**, Aspen—with its shining river and black-diamond ski slopes—is the place to do it. Though they look like rectangular parachutes, paragliders are actually classed as aircraft and can fly high on warm thermals. After a short safety briefing, you'll be harnessed to an instructor for a mad dash down one of the steep ski slopes until the wind fills the "wing" and you are airborne. The ride along the ridges and over the valley can last anywhere from 10 minutes to over an hour, depending on the weather. Mornings are best; gusty afternoon winds can sometimes ground flights until the following day. **Aspen Expeditions** (⊠*426 S. Spring St.* ☎*970/925–7625* ⊕*www.aspenexpeditions.com*) provides everything you'll need for a safe and memorable flight.

Fodor'sChoice
★

WHITE-WATER
RAFTING For the truly adventurous, **Blazing Adventures** (⊠*48 Upper Village Mall, Snowmass Village* ☎*970/923–4544 or 800/282–7238* ⊕*www.blazingadventures.com*) runs mild to wild excursions on the Shoshone, Upper Roaring Fork, and lower Colorado rivers.

WHERE TO EAT
Surprisingly, in a resort where jeans can cost four figures and mortgages would bankrupt small cities, eating out in Aspen—even in the finer establishments—can be done on a budget. Virtually all of the trendiest spots in town offer a couple of reasonably priced entrées, usually a basic burger or pasta dish. If you have the cash, nothing beats a romantic Aspen dinner; if not, lunch can be a good time to sample equally delicious cuisine at more-affordable prices.

★ $$$$ ✕**Century Room.** Everything about the Hotel Jerome is exquisite, and dinner in this dining room is no exception; with its high, vaulted ceilings, massive stone-and-marble fireplace, and comfortable wingback chairs, it is at once impressive and intimate. Chef Todd Slossberg's signature dishes—try the lobster-and-crab cakes—complement more-traditional fare, such as Colorado rack of lamb. ⊠*330 E. Main St.* ☎*970/920–1000* ⚑*Reservations essential* ⊟*AE, DC, MC, V* ⊗*No lunch.*

★ $$$$ ✕**Matsuhisa.** Renowned in Los Angeles, New York, London, and Tokyo, Nobu Matsuhisa has brought his nouveau-Japanese cuisine to Aspen. Although you shouldn't expect to see Nobu in the kitchen, his recipes and techniques are unmistakable. His jalapeño yellowtail is scrumptious, his *anticucho* beef (skewered and grilled beef hearts) is delicious, his new-style sashimi marvelous, and his prices astronomical. Check out Matsuhisa Lounge upstairs (or outdoors in warm weather) for cocktails and a limited but still superb menu. ⊠ *303 E. Main St.* ☎ *970/544–6628* ⚑ *Reservations essential* ☰ *AE, MC, V* ✆ *No lunch.*

$$$$ ✕ **Pine Creek Cookhouse.** Strap on cross-country skis or board a horse-drawn sleigh (or hike in summer) to get to this homey log cabin. The emphasis is on game specialties, including quail, elk, and wild boar. Lunch offerings include hot smoked-salmon salad, spinach crepes, and Hungarian goulash. In winter or summer, shoot for a seat on the deck for breathtaking views of the Elk Mountains. ⊠ *11399 Castle Creek Rd.* ☎ *970/925–1044* ⚑ *Reservations essential* ☰ *AE, MC, V.*

$$$$ ✕ **Piñons.** The Southwestern ranch–style dining room has leather-wrapped railings, a teal-green ceiling, and upholstered walls. The contemporary American menu scores high on creativity. Try the lobster strudel appetizer, a mainstay of chef–owner Rob Mobillian, or the foie gras–topped beef fillet entrée. The service and wine list are impeccable. ⊠ *105 S. Mill St.* ☎ *970/920–2021* ⚑ *Reservations essential* ☰ *AE, MC, V* ✆ *No lunch.*

$$$$ ✕ **Poppies Bistro Cafe.** Ask 20 Aspenites where to find the most romantic meal in Aspen, and 19 of them will tell you to go to Poppies (the other one probably works at the competition). Its out-of-the-way location, on the tranquil, westernmost edge of town, makes it feel like a secret retreat, and the intimate atmosphere—lace curtains, faded antiques, and beautiful paintings—give it loads of Victorian charm, perfect for a romantic rendezvous. The cuisine ranges from classic bistro entrées such as steak au poivre in a cognac cream sauce to house specialties like spicy Anaheim peppers stuffed with lobster and goat cheese. It's cozy in winter, but even better in summer after an afternoon concert at the nearby music tent. ⊠ *834 W. Hallam St.* ☎ *970/925–2333* ☰ *AE, MC, V* ✆ *No lunch.*

$$$$ ✕ **Wild Fig.** A friendly establishment with an unbeatable location right
Fodor's Choice off the pedestrian mall, this cozy restaurant—there are only 10 tables—
★ and bar offer light Mediterranean dishes in a Jazz-era room with a faux tin ceiling, yellow walls with dark wood, and tile trim. The restaurant has one of Aspen's more- unusual plates: "fish in the bag" (fish of the night is cooked and served in a brown paper bag). For dessert try the warm figs, of course, and a cup of amante coffee, custom-roasted in the northern Italian tradition. ⊠ *315 E. Hyman Ave.* ☎ *970/925–5160* ⚑ *Reservations essential* ☰ *AE, MC, V.*

$$$–$$$$ ✕ **Cache Cache.** The sunny flavors of Provence explode on the palate thanks to chef Christopher Lanter's savvy use of garlic, tomato, eggplant, fennel, and rosemary. The osso buco in marsala sauce is sublime; salads and rotisserie items are sensational; desserts are worth leaving room for. The bar menu offers a budget-conscious way to sample this outstanding cuisine. ⊠ *205 S. Mill St.* ☎ *970/925–3835 or 888/511–3835* ☰ *AE, DC, MC, V* ✆ *No lunch.*

★ $$$–$$$$ ✕ **Takah Sushi.** In a town with several sushi haunts, locals will tell you that Takah Sushi has the best plates and prices (a bento box with miso soup and hot sake runs $36). It has an outdoor patio right off the pedestrian mall for the see-and-be-seen crowd, and a rowdy basement for larger parties. The large and tasty appetizers include *gyoza* (pork and vegetable pot stickers) and Takah's terrific egg roll. Those who are sushied-out might like straight seafood plates such as blackened tuna steak in Cajun spices and baked black cod fillets. ⊠ *320 S. Mill St.* ☎ *970/925–8588 or 877/925–8588* ⊟ *AE, MC, V.*

$$$ ✕ **L'Hostaria.** This subterranean hot spot is sophisticated yet rustic, with an open-beam farmhouse ceiling, sleek blond-wood chairs, contemporary art, and a floor-to-ceiling glass wine cooler in the center of the room. The menu relies on simple, subtle flavors in specialties such as goat-cheese flan on mixed greens, gnocchi with duck ragout, risotto with veal sauce, and a delectable veal Milanese. For a change of pace, check out the carpaccio bar, which features wonderful cured meats and fish. ⊠ *620 E. Hyman Ave.* ☎ *970/925–9022* ⊟ *AE, MC, V.*

$$$ ✕ **The Tavern.** The brains behind Mustards Grill and Tra Vigne, two of Napa Valley's finest cateries, have created this bright, pleasant restaurant, with mahogany paneling, diamond-pattern floors, leather banquettes, open kitchen, and an eager, unpretentious waitstaff. Try the grilled lamb chops with seasonal vegetables. The wine list, showcasing Napa's best, is almost matched by the fine selection of microbrews. Enjoy outstanding lunch offerings on the spacious, sunny patio, which abuts Aspen Mountain. ⊠ *685 E. Durant Ave.* ☎ *970/920–9333* ⌂ *Reservations essential* ⊟ *AE, D, DC, MC, V.*

$$ ✕ **Little Annie's Eating House.** Everything at this casual charmer is simple, from the wood paneling and red-and-white checked tablecloths to the fresh fish, barbecued ribs and chicken, and Colorado lamb. Annie's is a big favorite with locals, who like the relaxed atmosphere, dependable food, and reasonable prices, not to mention the Bundt cake and "shot and a beer" special at the noisy bar. ⊠ *517 E. Hyman Ave.* ☎ *970/925–1098* ⊟ *AE, DC, MC, V.*

$$ ✕ **Toppers.** Cheerful Greg Topper has opened a fuss-free café and take-out shop with first-rate American food. He serves fresh salads, soups, and fancy pizzas (think truffle oil), and the best sandwiches in town. Locals love the Aspen Bowls: You mix and match main items, such as fennel-spiced pork stew, red snapper, and rock shrimp vegetable curry, with various sides. If you come for dinner, try the succulent, slow-braised short ribs. Also popular are venison chili, rotisserie chicken, trout puttanesca, and Colorado lamb. ⊠ *300 Puppy Smith St.* ☎ *970/920–0069* ⊟ *MC, V.*

$ ✕ **Boogie's Diner.** This cheerful spot filled with diner memorabilia resounds with rock-and-roll faves from the 1950s and '60s. The menu has true diner range—from vegetarian specialties to grilled cheese and half-pound beef or turkey burgers. Other items are excellent soups, a monster chef salad, meat loaf and mashed potatoes, and a hot turkey sandwich. There's even a potato bar with 1-pound taters and many toppings. Save room for a gigantic milk shake, malted, or float. ⊠ *534 E. Cooper Ave.* ☎ *970/925–6610* ⊟ *AE, MC, V.*

$ ✕ **Hickory House Ribs.** Tie on your bib and dig in. No one will mind if your hands and face are covered in the secret sauce that tops the slow-cooked meats and chicken at this rustic, log cabin–style joint. These hickory-smoked baby back ribs have won more than 40 national competitions. The rustic Hickory House is also home to Aspen's only Southern-style breakfast, grits and all. And after a late night on the town, nothing beats a breakfast of ribs and eggs. ✉ *730 W. Main St.* ☎ *970/925–2313* ▭ *D, MC, V.*

$ ✕ **Main Street Bakery & Café.** Perfectly brewed coffee and hot breakfast buns and pastries are served at this café, along with a full breakfast menu that includes homemade granola. On sunny days, head out back to the deck for the mountain views. This is also a good spot for lunch and dinner (it's a quiet respite during the heart of the season). Try the Yankee pot roast, chicken potpie, and homemade soups. ✉ *201 E. Main St.* ☎ *970/925–6446* ▭ *AE, MC, V* ☉ *No dinner Apr.–June and Sept.–Nov.*

$ ✕ **Wienerstube Restaurant.** *Wienerstube* means "living room" in Austrian German, and that's exactly what this modest breakfast eatery feels like. Founder Gerhard grew up in Villach, Austria, and brought some Bohemian flair to the Aspen restaurant scene in 1965. In one corner is the *Stammtisch*, a large community table where old-time ski legends pass the syrup and spin tall tales of skiing in Aspen "before it was Aspen." Ski patrollers claim the Wienerstube has the best Bloody Marys in town, and the eggs Benedict menu features four versions including the famed West Coaster—avocado, bacon, asparagus, and hollandaise sauce over eggs and an English muffin. ✉ *633 E. Hyman Ave.* ☎ *970/925–3357* ▭ *AE, MC, V.*

WHERE TO STAY

It's no surprise that in Aspen, where starter homes round out in the low millions, accommodations are among the priciest in the state. As in other resort towns, the nightly rates climb the closer you get to the slopes with ski-in ski-out properties commanding a premium. Before booking down valley, however, look for special deals in town that might include lift tickets and parking. Out-of-town bargains might wind up costing more than a lower-end condo.

$$$$ ⬚ **Hotel Jerome.** One of the state's truly grand hotels since it opened in
Fodor's Choice 1889, Hotel Jerome is an romantic treasure trove of Victoriana. The
★ sumptuous public rooms have five kinds of wallpaper, antler sconces, and rose damask curtains, as well as crystal chandeliers, intricate woodwork, and gold-laced floor tiling. Guest rooms are generously sized, with high ceilings, sprawling beds, and huge bathtubs. The restaurants are held in high regard, and the J-Bar is legendary. Ask about "ski free" packages. **Pros:** most exclusive address in Aspen, great bar, summer music in the gardens. **Cons:** street facing rooms can be noisy, only valet parking. ✉ *330 E. Main St., 81611* ☎ *970/920–1000 or 800/331–7213* ⬤ *www.hoteljerome.rockresorts.com* ➥ *92 rooms, 8 suites* ⬦ *In-room: safe, refrigerator (some), DVD, dial-up. In-hotel: 2 restaurants, room service, bar, pool, gym, concierge, laundry service, public Internet, public Wi-Fi, airport shuttle, parking (fee), some pets allowed, no-smoking rooms* ▭ *AE, DC, MC, V.*

★ $$$$ ⬚ **Hotel Lenado.** The focal point of this dramatic inn, a favorite with couples, is a very modern, 28-foot-tall stone-and-concrete fireplace. The smallish but quaint rooms contain either intricate carved applewood or hickory beds (*lenado* is Spanish for wood, and much of it appears throughout the hotel). You'll also find antique armoires and wood-burning stoves, in addition to modern amenities such as cable TV. Rates include a full breakfast, served in the urbane bar area, which is also a great place to enjoy an evening aperitif. **Pros:** romantic ambience, great break-

fast cooked to order. **Cons:** no restaurant, rooms facing street can be noisy. ⊠*200 S. Aspen St., 81611* ☎*970/925–6246 or 800/321–3457* ⊕*www.hotellenado.com* ⇄*19 rooms* ☼*In-room: refrigerator (some), Wi-Fi. In-hotel: bar, concierge, laundry service, public Internet, public Wi-Fi, parking (fee), some pets allowed, no-smoking rooms* ⊟*AE, DC, MC, V* ⦿|*BP.*

★ **$$$$** ⃞**Little Nell.** This hotel is the only true ski-in ski-out property in Aspen. Belgian wool carpets and overstuffed couches distinguish the lobby. The luxurious rooms have fireplaces, beds piled with down comforters, and large marble baths. Equally superior is the staff, who anticipate your needs. The Montagna restaurant ($$$$) serves delicious farmhouse fare. In summer the most sought after tables are on the patio with views of Aspen Mountain; even your dog can enjoy a gourmet meal from the doggie menu. The bar hosts one of town's most fashionable après-ski scenes. **Pros:** ski-in and ski-out, great people-watching. **Cons:** expensive, difficult to get a room in high-season. ⊠*675 E. Durant Ave., 81611* ☎*970/920–4600 or 888/843–6355* ⊕*www.thelittlenell.com* ⇄*78 rooms, 14 suites* ☼*In-room: safe (some), DVD (some), Wi-Fi. In-hotel: 2 restaurants, room service, bars, pool, gym, concierge, laundry service, public Internet, public Wi-Fi, airport shuttle, parking (fee), some pets allowed, no-smoking rooms* ⊟*AE, D, DC, MC, V.*

$$$$ ⃞**St. Regis Resort, Aspen.** This hotel is a memorable one, even by Aspen's
Fodor'sChoice exacting standards. The posh reception area is comfortably furnished
★ with overstuffed chairs, soft suede pillows, leather-top tables, and rawhide lamp shades. The rooms follow suit with dark-wood furniture, muted colors, and signature touches like bowls of fresh fruit. Luxurious baths are stocked with Remède toiletries. The new Remède Spa has 15 treatment rooms and a reclining oxygen bar. **Pros:** one of Aspen's most luxurious properties, close to the slopes, world-class spa. **Cons:** expensive, rooms are small, only valet parking. ⊠*315 E. Dean St., 81611* ☎*970/920–3300 or 888/454–9005* ⊕*www.stregisaspen.com* ⇄*155 rooms, 24 suites* ☼*In-room: safe, DVD, Wi-Fi. In-hotel: restaurant, room service, bars, pool, gym, spa, concierge, laundry service, public Internet, public Wi-Fi, airport shuttle, parking (fee), some pets allowed, no-smoking rooms* ⊟*AE, D, DC, MC, V.*

$$$$ ⃞**Sky Hotel.** Aspen's trendiest hotel attracts a young, hip couples crowd. The Sky has a sleek style and slope-side locale that make it ideal for those in search of something a bit different. The lobby, with its black walls and oversize white leather chairs—think *Alice in Wonderland*—leads to the ultracool and ultracrowded 39 Degrees bar and the daily "altitude adjustment" happy hour with complimentary wine. The rooms, with yellow walls, white headboards, and black accents, are small but unforgettable. Signature touches like high-definition TVs, L'Occitane bath products, and your own bottle of oxygen make this hotel stand out from the rest. **Pros:** young crowd, great location for skiers. **Cons:** can be noisy, valet parking only. ⊠*709 E. Durant Ave., 81611* ☎*970/925–6760 or 800/882–2582* ⊕*www.theskyhotel.com* ⮐*90 rooms* ⟐*In-room: safe, refrigerator, DVD (some), Wi-Fi. In-hotel: restaurant, room service, bar, pool, gym, concierge, laundry service, public Internet, public Wi-Fi, airport shuttle, parking (fee), some pets allowed, no-smoking rooms* ▤*AE, D, DC, MC, V.*

$$$ 🛏 **Hotel Aspen.** Just a few minutes from the mall and the mountain, this hotel on the town's main drag is a good, if sometimes noisy, find. The modern exterior opens up with huge windows that take full advantage of the spectacular view; the lobby has a sleek Southwestern influence. Rooms are comfortable, if not luxurious, with plenty of down pillows and comforters. Most have balconies or terraces, and a few have hot tubs. A continental breakfast is included in the room rate, as is après-ski wine and cheese. **Pros:** affordable, great location, free parking. **Cons:** traffic can be noisy, no restaurant. ⊠*110 W. Main St., 81611* ☎*970/925–3441 or 800/527–7369* ⊕*www.hotelaspen.com* ⮐*37 rooms, 8 suites* ⟐*In-room: kitchen (some), refrigerator, DVD, Wi-Fi. In-hotel: pool, laundry service, public Internet, public Wi-Fi, airport shuttle, some pets allowed, no-smoking rooms* ▤*AE, D, DC, MC, V* ⏍❶*CP.*

CONDOS **Aspen Alps** (⊠*700 Ute Ave., 81611* ☎*970/925–7820 or 800/228–7820* ⊕*www.aspenalps.com*) has nicely appointed condos at the base of Aspen Mountain. **Coates, Reid & Waldron** (⊠*720 E. Hyman Ave., 81611* ☎*970/925–1400 or 800/222–7736* ⊕*www.resortquest.com*) rents everything from studios to large homes. **Frias Properties** (⊠*730 E. Durant Ave., 81611* ☎*970/920–2010 or 800/633–0336* ⊕*www.friasproperties.com*) has lavish homes in the mountains.**The Gant** (⊠*610 W. End St., 81611* ☎*970/925–5000 or 800/345–1471* ⊕*www.gantaspen.com*) has impressive accommodations with an excellent pool and meeting space.

NIGHTLIFE & THE ARTS

The **Aspen Writers' Foundation** (☎*970/925–3122*) has everything from a weekly writers' group (visitors welcome) to a summer literary festi-

THE ARTS ★ val.**Jazz Aspen Snowmass** (☎*970/920–4996*) has festivals in June and September, and also sponsors free Thursday-night concerts in summer. **Wheeler Opera House** (⊠*320 E. Hyman Ave.* ☎*970/920–5770*) presents big-name classical, jazz, pop, and opera performers, especially in summer.

BARS & LOUNGES East Hyman Avenue is the best place for barhopping—a cluster of four nightspots share the same address and phone number. **Aspen Billiards** (⊠*315 E. Hyman Ave.* ☎*970/920–6707*) is the town's most upscale pool hall. Challenge the locals to a game of eight ball. The smoky

CLOSE UP

The Sound of Music

Aspen's venerated Music Festival and School founded in 1949 is one of the most popular reasons to visit this mountain town in summer. From June through August, famous musicians like Joshua Bell and Sarah Chang make pilgrimages here to perform at more than 350 events held at the 2,050-seat Benedict Music Tent, the Victorian Wheeler Opera House, and the Harris Concert Hall. Tickets ($10–$80) are readily available online. A quarter of the performances are free and one of the great pleasures of the festival is showing up on the free-seating lawn outside the Benedict Music Tent with some friends, a blanket, and a bottle of shiraz.

If you're visiting in winter, you may not have to miss out on the tunes entirely; check the festival's Web site for information about the winter artist recital series. ⊕ *www.aspenmusicfestival.com*

5

Cigar Bar (⊠*315 E. Hyman Ave.* ☎*970/920–6707*) is a dimly lighted joint straight from Humphrey Bogart movies. Overstuffed chairs and sofas and velvet curtains set the mood. Whiskey—and lots of it—is the claim to fame of **Eric's Bar** (⊠*315 E. Hyman Ave.* ☎*970/920–6707*), a hip little watering hole that attracts a rowdy crowd. There's a varied lineup of imported beers on tap. Inside Hotel Jerome, the **J-Bar** (⊠*330 E. Main St.* ☎*970/920–1000*) is a fun, lively spot. You can't say you've seen Aspen until you've set foot in this place. **Su Casa** (⊠*315 E. Hyman Ave.* ☎*970/920–6707*) is the place to get your fill of margaritas or sangria.

Woody Creek Tavern (⊠*2 Woody Creek Plaza, Woody Creek* ☎*970/923–4585*) is a great place to socialize. Atmosphere, assorted bar games, and notable visitors such as Don Johnson attract crowds. Hunter S. Thompson was a regular. Join the masses by riding your bike here in summer via the Rio Grande Trail.

CABARET The **Crystal Palace** (⊠*300 E. Hyman Ave.* ☎*970/925–1455*) is an Aspen fixture, offering one seating nightly with fine food and fiercely funny political and social satire.

Once a country-and-western saloon and now a full-on disco, **Bar Aspen** (⊠*220 S. Galena St.* ☎*970/925–4567*) is the only place in town to MUSIC & shake it up on the dance floor. Jazz is all that's needed to draw crowds DANCE CLUBS to the cozy but crowded bar at **Little Nell** (⊠*675 E. Durant Ave.* ☎*970/920–4600*). For late-night jazz of truly astounding quality, head to **Syzygy** (⊠*520 E. Hyman Ave.* ☎*970/925–3700*).

SHOPPING
Downtown Aspen is an eye-popping display of conspicuous consumption. For an eclectic mix of glitz and glamour, T-shirts, and trinkets, stroll past the shops lining Cooper Street.

★ Show up on Hunter and Hopkins streets any Saturday from mid-June to late October and you can enjoy the **Aspen Saturday Market,** a sort of farmers' market–meets-arts fair.

Saturday Market

Get a taste of daily life in Aspen every Saturday from mid-June though late October at the Aspen Saturday Market on Hopkins Avenue next to City Hall. This is an arts fair masquerading as a farmers' market, but the real fun is the people-watching. Women in $1,200 designer jeans chat on cell phones beneath rumpled cowboy hats, off-duty waiters stroll muddy mountain bikes past, and the vendors and artists hope to mine the new Aspen wealth. You can buy ceramic plates, mugs, and serving dishes from a number of local potters—be sure to take a look at Alleghany Meadows—some of whom also supply flatware to local restaurants. For beautiful rings and dangling earrings, try Cathleen Crenshaw or Harmony Scott. There's even a blacksmith, Stephen Bershenyi, who crafts delicate flowers out of iron. Hungry? Don't forget the food vendors, including Jack Rabbit Hill Winery, Cloud Nine Brownie, and the Haystack Goat Dairy.

For chic boutiques, check out the **Brand Building** (⊠*Hopkins Ave. between Mill and Galena Sts.*). This edifice is home to Gucci, Louis Vuitton, and Christian Dior, as well as local lions like Cashmere Aspen. For something silly for the folks back home, your best bet is the **Hyman Avenue Mall** (⊠*Hyman Ave. between Mill and Galena Sts.*).

ART GALLERIES **Baldwin Gallery** (⊠*209 S. Galena St.* ☎*970/920–9797*) is the place to see and be seen at receptions for nationally known artists. **David Floria Gallery** (⊠*525 E. Cooper Ave.* ☎*970/544–5705*) exhibits the hottest new artists. **Galerie Maximillian** (⊠*602 E. Cooper Ave.* ☎*970/925–6100*) is the place to find high-quality paintings and sculpture. **Magidson Fine Art** (⊠*525 E. Cooper Ave.* ☎*970/920–1001*) is known for its well-rounded collection of contemporary art. **Soroka Gallery** (⊠*400 E. Hyman Ave.* ☎*970/920–3152*) specializes in rare photos.For offbeat exhibits, including works by such notables as Hunter S. Thompson and Andy Warhol, drive to the **Woody Creek Store** (⊠*6 Woody Creek Plaza, Woody Creek* ☎*970/922–0990*).

BOOKS **Explore Booksellers and Bistro** is an independent bookstore located in a beautiful Victorian house. The store stocks more than 100,000 books and is particularly noted for its political, travel, and literature sections. Upstairs, the all-vegetarian bistro is a perfect place for a light meal or snack. ⊠*221 E. Main St.* ☎*970/925–5336 bookstore, 970/925–5338 bistro* ⊙*Bookstore, daily 10–10; bistro, early Sept.–Nov., daily 11:30–9; Dec.–Aug., daily 11:30–10.*

BOUTIQUES In downtown Aspen, **Boogie's** (⊠*534 E. Cooper Ave.* ☎*970/925–6111*) sells everything from jeans to jewelry. **Chepita's** (⊠*525 E. Cooper Ave.* ☎*970/925–2871*) calls itself a "toy store for adults," which means it sells kinetic clothing and designer watches and jewelry. **Pitkin County Dry Goods** (⊠*520 E. Cooper Ave.* ☎*970/925–1861*) has a good selection of men's and women's apparel. **Scandinavian Designs** (⊠*675 E. Cooper Ave.* ☎*970/925–7299*) features some of Aspen's finest hand-knit sweaters, as well as everything Scandinavian, from Swedish clogs to Norwegian trolls.

CRAFTS **Aspen Potters** (⊠*231 E. Main St.* ☎*970/925–8726*) sells the latest designs from local artisans. To create your own art, contact the **Kolor-on-Wheels** (☎*970/544–6191*), a paint-it-yourself mobile pottery studio that will come to you.

SPORTING **Aspen Sports** (⊠*408 E. Cooper Ave.* ☎*970/925–6331*) is the biggest GOODS sporting-goods store in town. It stocks a full line of apparel and equipment for all sports. **Ute Mountaineer** (⊠*308 S. Mill St.* ☎*970/925–2849*) has mountaineering clothes and equipment.

SNOWMASS VILLAGE

10 mi northwest of Aspen via Hwy. 82.

Heading east along Highway 82 toward Aspen you'll spot the turnoffs (Brush Creek and Owl Creek roads) to the Snowmass Ski Area, one of four ski mountains owned by Aspen Skiing Company. The town at the mountain's base, Snowmass Village, has a handful of chic boutiques and eateries, but it's more down-to-earth and much slower-paced than Aspen.

Snowmass Village was built in 1967 as Aspen's answer to Vail—a ski-specific resort—and although it has never quite matched the panache or popularity of Vail, it has gained a certain stature with age. But the town struggles with finding its identity, a difficult proposition since it often calls itself Snowmass Village at Aspen. And the town's most recent battle—what to do with its outdated base area—has been another problem.

Still, an effort has been made to breathe new life into Snowmass Village to the tune of $25.5 million in village improvements for the 2007–08 season, including the Treehouse Kid's Adventure Center (full of fun activities for children ages eight weeks and up) and new restaurants and shops. In general, Snowmass is the preferred alternative for families with young children, leaving the town of Aspen to a more up-at-the-crack-of-noon crowd. Snowmass, one of the best intermediate hills in the country, has more ski-in ski-out lodgings and a slower pace than Aspen.

OFF THE
BEATEN
PATH

Basalt. As you drive down Highway 82 through the bedroom communities of Carbondale and El Jebel on the way to Aspen and Snowmass, a detour through this old railroad town is well worth the trouble. Basalt, at the confluence of the Fryingpan and Roaring Fork rivers, has the feeling of a ski town without the lift. Walking down its main drag, Midland Avenue, you get a hint of what Aspen must have been like years ago. Browse the town's quaint shops and surprisingly upscale galleries, then dine at one of several new and impressive restaurants. Or, at the gateway to Ruedi Reservoir, take to the water for a day of fishing, boating, or just relaxing away from the hustle and bustle of the town's noisy neighbors.

DOWNHILL SKIING & SNOWBOARDING

Snowmass is a sprawling ski area, the biggest of the four Aspen–area mountains. Aspen Highlands, Aspen Mountain, Buttermilk, and Snowmass can all be skied with the same ticket. A free shuttle system connects all four. Snowmass now includes 64,000 square feet of new shops and restaurants, the new Elk Camp Gondola, and Elk Camp Meadows Activity Center. There are six distinct sectors: Elk Camp, High Alpine–Alpine Springs, Big Burn, Sam's Knob, Two Creeks, and Campground. Except for the last two, all these sectors funnel into the pedestrian mall at the base. Snowmass is probably best known for Big Burn, itself a great sprawl of wide-open, intermediate skiing. Experts head to such areas as Hanging Valley and the Cirque for the best turns.

At Snowmass 50% of the 3,128 skiable acres are designated for intermediate-level skiers. The route variations down Big Burn are essentially inexhaustible, and there are many other places on the mountain for intermediates to find entertainment. The novice and beginning-intermediate terrain on the lower part of the mountain makes Snowmass a terrific place for younger children.

But don't overlook the fact that Snowmass is four times the size of Aspen Mountain, and has triple the black- and double-black-diamond terrain of its famed sister, including several fearsomely precipitous gullies at Hanging Valley. Although only 32% of the terrain is rated advanced or expert, this huge mountain has enough difficult runs, including the consistently challenging Powderhorn and the more-relaxed Sneaky's Run, to satisfy all but the most demanding skiers.

Snowboarders take note: This mountain has one of the most comprehensive snowboarding programs in the country, with the heart of the action in the Headwall Cirque. A special terrain map points out the numerous snowboard-friendly trails and terrain parks while steering riders away from flat spots. You'll want to visit Trenchtown in the Coney Glade area, which has two lift-accessed pipes, video evaluation, piped-in music, and a yurt hangout complete with couches and snacks. ✛ *West of Aspen via Brush Creek Rd. or Owl Creek Rd.* ☎*970/925–1220 or 800/525–6200* ⊕*www.aspensnowmass.com* ☉*Late Nov.–mid-Apr., daily 9–4.*

FACILITIES   4,406-foot vertical drop; 3,100 skiable acres; 88 trails; 6% beginner, 50% intermediate, 12% advanced, 32% expert; 24 lifts, 1 8-passenger gondola, 1 high-speed 6-passenger chair, 1 6-passenger gondola, 6 high-speed quad chairs, 2 quads, 4 double lifts, 5 magic carpets, 2 school lifts, 2 platter pulls.

LESSONS &   **Aspen Skiing Company** (⊠*Snowmass Village Mall* ☎*970/925–1220*
PROGRAMS   *or 800/525–6200*) gives lessons at Snowmass and Aspen's other mountains.

LIFT TICKETS   Lift tickets are $87, but almost nobody pays full price thanks to multi-day savings, early- and late-season specials, and other discounts.

RENTALS   Snowmass has numerous ski shops offering rental packages (skis, boots, and poles). **Aspen Sports** (⊠*70 Snowmass Village Mall* ☎*970/*

923–6111) is one of the best-known outfitters in Snowmass. **Incline Ski Shop** (⊠*1 Snowmass Village Mall* ☎*970/923–4726*) is just steps from the shuttle-bus stop.

NORDIC SKIING

TRACK SKIING **Aspen/Snowmass Nordic Council** (⌖*Box 10815, Aspen 81612* ☎*970/429–2039*) has 48 mi of maintained trails in the Roaring Fork Valley. Probably the most varied, in terms of scenery and terrain, is the 18-mi Snowmass Club trail network. For a longer ski, try the Owl Creek Trail, connecting the Snowmass Club trail system and the Aspen Cross-Country Center trails. More than 10 mi long, the trail provides both a good workout and a heavy dosage of woodsy beauty, with many ups and downs across meadows and aspen-gladed hillsides. Best of all, you can take the bus back to Snowmass Village when you're finished. Nordic-skiing equipment is available at the **Snowmass Cross-Country Center** (⊠*239 Snowmass Village Circle* ☎*970/923–3148*).

OTHER SPORTS & THE OUTDOORS

BALLOONING **Unicorn Balloon Company** (☎*970/925–5752*) flies you over the slopes of Aspen, and gives you a personal flight video as a keepsake.

DOGSLEDDING With about 200 dogs ready to go, **Krabloonik** (⊠*4250 Divide Rd.*
★ ☎*970/923–3953*) can always put together a half-day ride. These trips, beginning at 8:30 AM and 12:30 PM, include lunch or dinner at the Krabloonik restaurant, one of the best in the area. In summer, meet the dogs during daily kennel tours.

FISHING **Aspen Skiing Company** (⊠*97 Lower Mall, Snowmass Village Mall* ☎*970/ 923–8647*) can hook you up with outfitters that lead trips on the Colorado, Roaring Fork, and Fryingpan rivers.

MOUNTAIN **Aspen Skiing Company** (⊠*97 Lower Mall, Snowmass Village Mall*
BIKING ☎*970/925–1220*) can give you a map of area trails, including the terrain park accessed by the Burlingame Lift. The company can also sell you a lift ticket so you won't have to ride uphill. **Aspen Sports** (⊠*70 Snowmass Village Mall* ☎*970/923–6111*) has the widest selection of rental bikes in town, plus carriers for the kids.

WHERE TO STAY & EAT

$$$$ ✕**Il Poggio.** In the cutthroat competition between resort-town restaurants, this unassuming Italian place is smart enough to let the big boys duke it out. It wins in the end; it's quite possibly the best casual restaurant in the village. The classic Italian food is well received by the après-ski crowd. Try one of the hearth-baked pizzas, a hearty pasta dish, or any beef or chicken entrée. ⊠*73 Elbert La.* ☎*970/923–4292* ⊟*AE, DC, MC, V* ⊗*No lunch.*

$$$$ ✕**Krabloonik.** Owner Dan MacEachen has a penchant for dogsled racing, and Krabloonik (Eskimo for "big eyebrows," and the name of

5

his first lead dog) helps subsidize his expensive hobby. This rustic yet elegant log cabin is on the slopes, which means you'll be treated to wonderful views on your way there. Although you can drive to the restaurant, the best—and most memorable—way to arrive is by dogsled. You'll dine sumptuously on some of the best game in Colorado, like caribou, elk, and wild boar, as well as house-smoked trout and signature wild mushroom soup. Wash it all down with a selection from Snowmass's most extensive wine list. ⊠ *4250 Divide Rd.* ☎ *970/923–3953* ⚞ *Reservations essential* ⊟ *AE, MC, V.*

$$$ ✕ **Butch's Lobster Bar.** Once a lobsterman off Cape Cod, Butch Darden knows his lobster, and serves it up countless ways. The menu includes plenty of other seafood favorites, including crab legs, shrimp, and steamers. There are also the obligatory steak and chicken dishes. Although the atmosphere isn't fancy and the service isn't doting, this is the best place in town to get your finny fix. ⊠ *Timberline Condominiums, 2nd fl., 264 Snowmelt Rd.* ☎ *970/923–7311* ⚞ *Reservations essential* ⊟ *AE, MC, V* ⊗ *No lunch.*

$ ✕ **The Stewpot.** There's a lot more than stew on the menu here, but stick to the namesake dish; a hearty bowl of beef or chicken stew with homemade bread is hard to beat. This is an ideal spot for lunch after a long morning on the slopes. Daily soup specials—tomato cheddar is a winner, as is chicken vegetable barley—and a selection of sandwiches are also on the menu. The two-story restaurant has windows overlooking the mall and walls hung with photographs by local artists. ⊠ *62 Snowmass Village Mall* ☎ *970/923–2263* ⊟ *MC, V.*

★ $$$$ ⬚ **Stonebridge Inn.** Slightly removed from the hustle and bustle of the Village Mall, this inn hides its true character behind a boxy exterior. It's one of the nicest lodging options in Snowmass. The lobby and bar are streamlined and elegant with mood lighting and contemporary furniture. The cozy, window-ringed Artisan restaurant offers simple, hearty preparations of the freshest regional ingredients. There's also an inexpensive bar menu. A continental breakfast is included. Rooms, all with two queen beds, aren't fancy, but are comfortably appointed; the adjacent two- and four-bedroom Tamarack Townhouses are also available. Ask about "stay and ski" packages. **Pros:** quiet location, good on-site restaurant, town-house options for families. **Con:** must catch a shuttle to lifts. ⊠ *300 Carriage Way, 81615* ☎ *970/923–2420 or 800/922–7242* ⊕ *www.stonebridgeinn.com* ⬪ *90 rooms, 5 suites, 28 condos* ⚬ *In-room: DVD. In-hotel: restaurant, bar, pool, gym, concierge, laundry facilities, laundry service, public Internet, public Wi-Fi, airport shuttle, parking (fee), no-smoking rooms* ⊟ *AE, D, DC, MC, V* ⦿*CP.*

$$$–$$$$ ⬚ **Silvertree Hotel.** This ski-in ski-out property, under the same management as the Wildwood Lodge next door, is built into Snowmass Mountain. It's a sprawling complex—virtually everything you need is under one roof. After a morning on the slopes, warm up in one of the hot tubs or in the steam room. Rooms and suites are small but attractively decorated in subdued colors, with all the expected amenities. Condos are also available, with full use of hotel facilities. **Pros:** ski-in, ski-out, steam room. **Cons:** self-parking is removed from hotel, rooms get hot in

summer. ✉*100 Elbert La., 81615* ☎*970/923–3520 or 800/525–9402* ⊕*www.silvertreehotel.com* ⤳*262 rooms, 15 suites, 200 condos* ⅏*In-room: safe (some), refrigerator (some), DVD, Wi-Fi. In-hotel: 2 restaurants, room service, bars, pools, gym, spa, concierge, laundry facilities, laundry service, executive floor, public Internet, airport shuttle, parking (fee), some pets allowed, no-smoking rooms* ☰*AE, D, DC, MC, V.*

$$ 🏨 **Snowmass Inn.** This family-owned lodge is one of Snowmass's original digs; it commands a prime location in the middle of the Snowmass Village Mall. It's also a short stroll from the slopes. Rooms are spacious and comfortable, although some are showing signs of wear. Still, this is the perfect place for those on a budget or looking to be in the middle of the action. **Pros:** good location for skiers, big rooms, moderately priced for Snowmass. **Cons:** poor customer service, few room or hotel amenities. ✉*67 Daily La., 81615* ☎*970/923–4204 or 800/635–3758* ⊕*www.snowmassinn.com* ⤳*39 rooms* ⅏*In-room: no a/c, refrigerator (some). In-hotel: no elevator, laundry facilities, laundry service, public Internet, airport shuttle, parking (fee in winter), no-smoking rooms* ☰*AE, D, DC, MC, V* �🍴*CP.*

CONDOS **Snowmass Lodging Company** (⌖*425 Wood Rd., 81615* ☎*970/923–3232 or 800/365–0410* 🖷*970/922–4992*) rents a wide variety of condominiums. **Stay Aspen Snowmass** (☎*888/290–1325* ⊕*www.stayaspensnowmass.com*) is the central lodging service for the area. **Village Property Management** (⌖*100 Elbert La., 81615* ☎*970/923–3520 or 800/525–9402* 🖷*970/923–5192*) has everything from studio apartments to fully stocked homes.

NIGHTLIFE

BARS & The **Cirque Cafe** (✉*105 Snowmass Village Mall* ☎*970/923–8686*) has
LOUNGES the most happening après-ski scene, with live music most evenings. The sun-soaked deck is a popular place in summer. For a mellow experience, try the **Conservatory** (✉*100 Elbert La.* ☎*970/923–3520*). It has a dark, moody atmosphere and occasional live music. **Zane's Tavern** (✉*10 Snowmass Village Sq.* ☎*970/923–3515*) is your classic mountain-town bar, with loud music, pool tables, and beer by the pitcher.

SHOPPING

Anderson Ranch Arts Center (✉*5263 Owl Creek Rd.* ☎*970/923–3181*) exhibits the work of resident artists. It also hosts lectures, workshops, and other special events. **Aspen Sports** (✉*70 Snowmass Village Mall* ☎*970/923–6111*) is the biggest store around, with a full line of apparel and equipment for all sports.

GLENWOOD SPRINGS

27 mi northwest of Aspen via Hwy. 82; 159 mi west of Denver via I–70.

Once upon a time, Glenwood Springs, the famed spa town that forms the western apex of a triangle with Vail and Aspen, was every bit as tony as those chic resorts are today, attracting a faithful legion of the pampered and privileged who came to enjoy the waters of the world's largest natural hot springs, said to cure everything from acne to rheumatism.

Today the town feels more like a bedroom community for Aspen workers; it's marred by the proliferation of strip malls, chain motels, and fast-food outlets. Remnants of her glory days can still be seen in the grand old **Hotel Colorado** (⊠ *526 Pine St.*), regally commanding the vaporous pools from a patrician distance. Modeled after the Villa de Medici in Italy, the property opened its doors in 1893. Teddy Roosevelt even made it his unofficial "Little White House" in 1905.

★ ℭ **Hot Springs Pool,** formerly called Yampah Hot Springs, was discovered by the Utes ("Yampah" is Ute for "big medicine"). Even before the heyday of the hotel, Western notables from Annie Oakley to Doc Holliday came to take the curative waters. In Doc's case, however, the cure didn't work, and six months after his arrival in 1887 he died—broke, broken down, and tubercular. (He lies in Linwood Cemetery, 0.5 mi east of town.) The smaller pool is 100 feet long and maintained at 104°F. The larger is more than two city blocks long (405 feet), and contains more than a million gallons of constantly filtered water that is completely refilled every six hours and maintained at a soothing 90°F. ⊠ *401 N. River St.* ☎ *970/945–6571 or 800/537–7946* 🖷 *970/947–2950* ⊕ *www.hotspringspool.com* ⊠ *$17* ⊙ *Late May–early Sept., daily 7:30 AM–10 PM; mid-Sept.–mid-May, daily 9 AM–10 PM.*

The **Yampah Spa & Salon** is a series of three natural underground steam baths. The same 120°F-plus springs that supply the pool flow under the floors of the only known natural vapor caves in North America. Each chamber is successively hotter than the last, and with 15 minerals in the waters, you can purify your body (and soul, according to Ute legend) in a matter of minutes. A variety of spa treatments, from massages to body wraps, are also available. ⊠ *709 E. 6th St.* ☎ *970/945–0667* ⊕ *www.yampahspa.com* ⊠ *$12 for caves, additional cost for treatments* ⊙ *Daily 9–9.*

ℭ Glenwood is home to many caves, including **Fairy Caves and Glenwood Caverns,** whose subterranean caverns, grottoes, and labyrinths are truly a marvel of nature (the area was touted as the "Eighth Wonder of the World" upon its public opening in 1887). Now part of the Glenwood Caverns Adventure Park (think tourist trap), the still-amazing caves are easily accessible via the Iron Mountain Tramway, a seven-minute gondola ride affording a bird's-eye view of Glenwood Springs and the surrounding landscape. You can take one of two cavern tours: a two-hour, family-friendly walk; or a more-extensive, crawl-on-your-belly spelunking adventure. For a second helping of adrenaline, try the gravity-powered alpine coaster that drops 3,400-feet, ride the 50-mph zip line, or sail out over 1,300 feet above the Colorado River cliffs on a giant swing. ⊠ *51000 Two Rivers Plaza Rd.* ☎ *800/530–1635* ⊕ *www.glenwoodcaverns.com* ⊠ *$10 and up* ⊙ *Late May–late Sept., daily 9 AM–10 PM; Oct.–mid-May, daily 10–6. Times may vary, so call ahead to check.*

CLOSE UP

Doc Holliday

John Henry "Doc" Holliday was a gun-slinger with an attitude. Part scholar, part rebel, he was often only one step ahead of the law. Born on August 14, 1851, in Griffin, Georgia, Holliday went to dental school. Shortly after opening his practice, he was diagnosed with tuberculosis. On the advice of his doctor, Holliday moved west in 1873 in search of a drier climate.

While living in Texas, Holliday took up gambling, which became his sole means of support. His violent temper turned him into a killer: After shooting a prominent citizen and leaving him for dead, Holliday had to flee Texas. Carrying one gun in a shoulder holster, another on his hip, and a long-bladed knife (just in case), he blazed a trail of death across the Southwest. It's not known just how many men died at his hands, but some have estimated the number to be as high as 25 or more. However, historians generally believe the true number is considerably less. Holliday's reasons for killing run the gamut from fights over cards to self-defense—or so he claimed. He will forever be known for his role in one of the most famous gunfights in the history of the Wild West: a 30-second gunfight at the O.K. Corral, in Tombstone, Arizona.

In May of 1887 Holliday moved to Glenwood Springs, hoping that the sulfur vapors of the hot springs there would help his failing lungs. He lived out his dying days at the Hotel Glenwood. On the last day of his life, Holliday knocked back a glass of whiskey and remarked, "This is funny." A few minutes later he was dead. Holliday was 36 years old.

Along I–70 east of town is the 15-mi-long **Glenwood Canyon.** Nature began the work as the Colorado River carved deep granite, limestone, and quartzite gullies—buff-tint walls brilliantly streaked with lavender, rose, and ivory. This process took a half billion years. Then man stepped in, seeking a more-direct route west. In 1992 the work on I–70 through the canyon was completed, at a cost of almost $500 million. Much of the expense was attributable to the effort to preserve the natural landscape as much as possible. When contractors blasted cliff faces, for example, they stained the exposed rock to simulate nature's weathering. Biking trails were also created, providing easy access to the hauntingly beautiful **Hanging Lake Recreation Area.** Here Dead Horse Creek sprays ethereal flumes from curling limestone tendrils into a startlingly turquoise pool, as jet-black swifts dart to and fro. It's perhaps the most transcendent of several idyllic spots in the canyon reachable on bike or foot. The intrepid can scale the delicate limestone cliffs, pocked with caverns and embroidered with pastel-hue gardens.

DOWNHILL SKIING & SNOWBOARDING

Sunlight Mountain Resort, 20 minutes south of Glenwood Springs, is affordable Colorado skiing at its best. Overshadowed by world-class neighbors, the resort sees far less traffic than typical Colorado slopes. Fresh powder, typically skied off at Aspen within an hour, can last as long as two days here on classic downhill runs like Sun King and steeps like Beaujolais; you won't stand in any lines at the four lifts. The resort has 67 trails including the super-steep glades of Extreme Sunlight, with a drop of 2,010 vertical feet. The varied terrain, sensational views, and lack of pretension make this a local favorite. Snowboarders even have a dedicated feature—the Peace Pipe. Families will appreciate that every child under 12 skis free with an adult and every slope meets at the bottom. For winter sports enthusiasts who don't want to ride a chairlift, there's a 20-mi network of cross-country ski and snowshoe trails just off the slopes. The cafeteria has cold sandwiches, burgers, and pizzas. ⊠*10901 County Rd. 117* ☎*970/945–7491 or 800/445–7931* ⊕*www. sunlightmtn.com* ☯ *Late Nov.–early Apr., daily 9–4.*

FACILITIES 2,010-foot vertical drop; 475 skiable acres; 67 trails; 20% beginner, 55% intermediate, 20% advanced, 5% expert; 4 lifts, 1 triple chair, 2 double chairs, 1 surface lift.

LESSONS & Two-hour ski lessons (including gear rental and lift ticket) cost $75;
PROGRAMS snowboarding is $80. Five-hour ski lessons are $115, $120 for snowboarding.

The resort offers exciting half- and full-day backcountry skiing courses for skiers who want an off-piste adventure. The courses are conducted on nearby Williams Peak. All rescue gear—avalanche beacon, probes, and shovels—are included in the price ($75 for half day; $110 for full day) and instructors teach basic route-finding, avalanche awareness, and backcountry skiing techniques.

The resort, in conjunction with Glenwood Springs, also offers a ski-stay-swim package for $60. It includes one night's lodging, a big breakfast, a full-day ski pass, and a full-day at the Glenwood Hot Springs Pool.

LIFT TICKETS Lift tickets are the second cheapest in the state, only $45 at the window. But, as at all Colorado ski resorts, no one ever needs to pay full price. Purchase a discounted pass at the Safeway or King Soopers grocery store in Glenwood Springs.

RENTALS **Sunlight Mountain Ski Resort** (⊠*10901 County Rd. 117* ☎*970/945– 7491 or 800/445–7931*) has complete rental gear setups on shaped skis. Rentals of the latest snowboards are available for as little as $20. The resort's retail outlet, **Sunlight Ski and Bike Shop** (⊠*309 9th St.,* ☎*970/945–9425*), is in Glenwood Springs.

OTHER SPORTS & THE OUTDOORS

BIKING Though it's a shame that I–70 heads through the spectacular depths of Glenwood Canyon, the busy corridor has opened up this gorge to
★ biking. The **Glenwood Canyon Bike Path,** a concrete path sandwiched between the Colorado River and the freeway traffic, runs 34.6 mi from Dotsero east to Glenwood Springs. Fortunately, the path generally runs below, and out of sight of, the interstate and the roar of the river drowns out the sound of traffic. Because of the mild climate on Colorado's Western Slope, the trail can be ridden almost year-round. The concrete path also has several dirt spurs that head up into White River National Forest for hikers and mountain bikers. A choice ride is the 18-mi round-trip from Glenwood Springs east up to Hanging Lake where you can leave your bike and hike a steep mile (climbing 900 feet)

to the beautiful lake. Horseshoe Bend, 2 mi from the Vapor Caves, is a perfect picnic spot since the highway ducks out of sight into a series of tunnels. ✛*Trailhead: enter path from either Yampah Hot Springs Vapor Caves in Glenwood Springs or farther west on I–70 at the Grizzly Creek rest area.*

Sunlight Ski and Bike Shop (✉*309 9th St.,* ☎*970/945–9425*) rents mountain and comfort bikes; $5 per hour, $15 for four hours, or $20 for the day.

FISHING **Roaring Fork Anglers** (✉*2205 Grand Ave.* ☎*970/945–0180*) leads wade and float trips throughout the area. **Roaring Fork Outfitters** (✉*2022 Grand Ave.* ☎*970/945–5800*) has a huge selection of flies, and guides who'll make sure you find the right ones.

GOLF **River Valley Ranch Golf Club.** Jay Moorish designed this course on the banks of the Crystal River. There is lots of water, a constant breeze, and superb—if not distracting—views of Mount Sopris. The course is in Carbondale, 15 mi from Glenwood Springs. ✉*303 River Valley Ranch Dr., Carbondale* ☎*970/963–3625* ⊕*www.rvrgolf.com* ⚑*18 holes. Yards: 7,348/5,168. Par: 72/72. Green Fee: $75/$85.*

WHITE-WATER RAFTING When the ski season is over and Colorado's white gold starts to melt, many ski instructors swap their sticks for paddles and hit the mighty

★ **Colorado River** for the spring and summer rafting seasons. Stomach-churning holes, chutes, and waves beckon adrenaline junkies, while calmer souls will revel in the shade of Glenwood Canyon's towering walls. All the outfitters below offer a basic half-day raft trip on the Colorado for $43.

☾ **Blue Sky Adventures** (✉*319 Hwy. 6* ☎*970/945–6605 or 877/945–6605*) offers a unique "pedal and paddle" deal with a half-day raft trip followed by a half-day bike tour. If you're the independent type, lead your own white-water rafting adventure by putting in at the boat ramp operated by the **Colorado Division of Wildlife** (✉*County Rd. 106* ☎*970/947–2920*). It's on the Roaring Fork River, just east of town.**Colorado Whitewater Rafting** (✛*I–70 at Exit 114* ☎*970/945–8477 or 800/993–7238*) is home of the "Double Shoshone," a round-trip through the area's most hair-raising rapids.**Rock Gardens Rafting** (✉*1308 County Rd. 129* ☎*970/945–6737 or 800/958–6737*) runs trips down the Colorado and Roaring Fork rivers, and operates a full-service campground on the banks of the Colorado.

WHERE TO STAY & EAT

$$ ✗**Florinda's.** The peach walls of this handsome space are graced by constantly changing art exhibits. The chef has a deft hand with northern and southern Italian dishes. Try the double-cut veal chops served with a shiitake mushroom sauce or the nightly specials, which are always extensive and superb. And don't miss homemade Italian desserts like tiramisu, zabaglione, and cannoli. ✉*721 Grand Ave.* ☎*970/945–1245* ▤*MC, V* ☾*Closed Sun. No lunch.*

$ ✗**The Bayou.** "Food so good you'll slap yo' mama," trumpets the menu at this casual Cajun eatery, whose most distinctive attribute is its frog

CLOSE UP

Rafting the Roaring Fork Valley

The key to understanding white-water rafting is the rating system. Rivers are rated from Class I (small waves where you really don't need to paddle to avoid anything) to Class VI (almost impossible to run, a mistake can be fatal). To confuse matters, rivers change classes depending on how fast they are flowing (measured in cubic feet of water per second). May and June are peak rafting seasons for those who want the adrenaline rush of fighting spring runoff. By mid-August many rivers are little more than lazy float trips.

The Roaring Fork, a free-flowing river (no dams), is regularly considered a Class III. Because it runs away from major highways through the heart of ranch country, you're liable to see more wildlife than on the Colorado; in June your guides may point out a nest full of croaking bald eaglets. Cemetery

Rapids, a half-mile churning stretch of white water, is the most exciting run.

The stretch of the mighty Colorado that runs through the steep, spectacular walls of Glenwood Canyon alongside I-70 is divided into two sections: the rough and tumble Shoshone below the dam, and the wider, mellower regions beyond. During the peak runoff season, the Shoshone is considered a Class IV river with aptly named rapids like Maneater and Baptism. The lower Colorado still has some exciting stretches, including Maintenance Shack, a Class III rapid that can flip a large raft. By July and August, you can hit the same rapid sideways or backward and barely get wet. The lower stretches of the Colorado pass by several hidden, and not-so-hidden, shallow hot springs. If you'd like to warm up in them, ask your guides.

---

awning (two bulbous eyes beckon you in). Choose from "pre-stuff, wabbit stuff, udder stuff," such as lip-smacking gumbo that looks like mud (and is supposed to), étouffée and blackened fish, or lethal Cajun martinis. And when the menu labels an item "hurt me" hot, it's no joke. On summer weekends musicians perform on the patio. ⊠*919 Grand Ave.* ☎*970/945–1047* ▤*AE, MC, V.*

$ ✕ **Daily Bread.** For years, locals have been packing this little café, where you can get some of the best food at the best prices in town. Hearty breakfasts such as the veggie skillet, breakfast burrito, and cinnamon-roll French toast are served until noon, and lunch features creative sandwiches, soups, and burgers. Many items are low-fat or vegetarian. The bakery also sells goodies to go. ⊠*729 Grand Ave.* ☎*970/945–6253* ▤*D, MC, V* ☽*Closed Sun. No dinner.*

$ ✕ **Narayan's Nepal Restaurant.** In a cow town like Glenwood Springs, finding good foreign fare is no easy feat, but this little eatery, tucked into a strip mall beside the highway, has tasty Nepalese food. The chef, a former Sherpa who now owns this restaurant and its twin in Aspen, serves up dishes so authentic that you'll swear you're in the high Himalayas. Try fish *kawab* (marinated overnight and then baked in a tandoor) with a side of garlicky *naan* (spongy flat bread) if you're skeptical. ⊠*6824 Hwy. 82* ☎*970/945–8803* ▤*AE, MC, V* ☽*No lunch Sun.*

$$$ 🛁 **Hot Springs Lodge.** This lodge is perfectly located, just steps from the Hot Springs Pool (which is used to heat the property). The attractive rooms, decorated in jade, teal, buff, and rose, have a Southwestern flavor. Deluxe rooms have small fridges and tiny balconies in addition to standard conveniences such as cable TV. Breakfast is included. **Pros:** right next to the hot springs, comfortable rooms. **Con:** no bar. ✉*415 E. 6th St., Glenwood Springs 81601* ☎*970/945–6571 or 800/537–7946* ⊕*www.hotspringspool.com* ➣*107 rooms* ⚒*In-room: refrigerator (some), safe (some), Wi-Fi. In-hotel: restaurant, pool, gym, laundry facilities, public Internet, public Wi-Fi, airport shuttle, parking (no fee), no-smoking rooms* ▭*AE, D, DC, MC, V* ⦿*CP.*

$$$ 🛁 **Hotel Colorado.** When you catch sight of the graceful sandstone colonnades and Italianate campaniles of this exquisite building, you won't be surprised that it's listed in the National Register of Historic Places. The impression of luxury continues in the imposing yet gracious marble lobby and public rooms. The sunny rooms and suites—most with high ceilings, fireplaces, gorgeous period wainscoting, marble bathrooms, and balconies affording gorgeous vistas—are designed to match. The notable (Teddy Roosevelt) and notorious (Al Capone) stayed here in the hotel's halcyon days. The on-site bike shop and white-water rafting outfitter can get you geared up for adventures outside the hotel. **Pros:** One of the most historic properties in the valley, large rooms, great views. **Cons:** no air-conditioning, some rooms need refurbishing. ✉*526 Pine St., 81601* ☎*970/945–6511 or 800/544–3998* ⊕*www.hotelcolorado.com* ➣*130 rooms, 30 suites* ⚒*In-room: no a/c, kitchen (some), refrigerator (some), DVD, Wi-Fi. In-hotel: restaurant, room service, bar, gym, spa, concierge, laundry service, executive floor, public Wi-Fi, parking (no fee), some pets allowed, no-smoking rooms* ▭*AE, D, DC, MC, V.*

$$ 🛁 **Hotel Denver.** Although this hotel was built in 1914, its most striking features are the numerous art deco touches throughout. Most rooms open onto a view of the nearby springs or a three-story New Orleans–style atrium bedecked with colorful canopies. The accommodations are a bit dated, but comfortable, and so quiet it's hard to believe you're only footsteps from the train station. Glenwood's only microbrewery—the Glenwood Canyon Brewing Company—is the hotel restaurant. **Pros:** right downtown, romantic decor, on-site brewpub. **Cons:** no concierge, no room service. ✉*402 7th St., 81601* ☎*970/945–6565 or 800/826–8820* ⊕*www.thehoteldenver.com* ➣*72 rooms* ⚒*In-room: kitchen (some), refrigerator (some), DVD (some), Wi-Fi. In-hotel: restaurant, bar, gym, laundry facilities, laundry service, public Wi-Fi, parking (no fee), some pets allowed, no-smoking rooms* ▭*AE, D, DC, MC, V.*

$$ 🛁 **Sunlight Mountain Inn.** This charming traditional ski lodge, perfect for couples and families, is a few hundred feet from the Sunlight Mountain Resort lifts. It brims with a country ambience, from the delightful lounge (with a carved fireplace and wrought-iron chandeliers) and Western-flair restaurant to the cozily rustic rooms, all with pine-board walls and rough-hewn armoires. The restaurant, open in winter only, specializes in apple dishes made with local fruit; the bar is a perfect

place to end your day. This is a true get-away-from-it-all place, so there are no TVs to distract you. A full breakfast is included year-round. **Pros:** a wonderfully remote getaway, delicious meals, no distractions. **Cons:** no cell phone service, limited room and hotel amenities, restaurant open seasonally. ⊠ *10252 County Rd. 117, 81601* ☎ *970/945–5225 or 800/733–4757* ⊕ *www.sunlightinn.com* ⇌ *20 rooms* ⚬ *In-room: no a/c, refrigerator (some), no TV. In-hotel: restaurant, bar, no elevator, parking (no fee), some pets allowed, no-smoking rooms* ☰ *AE, D, MC, V* ⚬*BP.*

REDSTONE & MARBLE

29 mi south of Glenwood Springs via Hwy. 82 and Hwy. 133.

Redstone is a charming artists' colony whose streets are lined with pretty galleries and boutiques, and whose boundaries are ringed by the impressive sandstone cliffs from which the town draws its name. Summer sees streams of visitors strolling the main drag, Redstone Boulevard; in winter, horse-drawn carriages carry people along the snow-covered road.

Redstone's history dates to the late 19th century, when J. C. Osgood, director of the Colorado Fuel and Iron Company, built Cleveholm Manor, now known as **Redstone Castle** (⊠ *58 Redstone Blvd.* ☎ *970/963–2526*). Here he entertained other titans of his day, such as John D. Rockefeller, J. P. Morgan, and Teddy Roosevelt. Among the home's embellishments are gold-leaf ceilings, maroon velvet walls, silk brocade upholstery, marble and mahogany fireplaces, Persian rugs, and Tiffany chandeliers. Although the Castle has been closed as a public lodge for several years, Redstone Historical Society is overseeing operations so that you can still catch a glimpse of the baronial splendor during sporadic tours.

A few miles up Highway 133 is **Marble,** a sleepy town that's undergoing a small renaissance as seekers of rural solitude are making it their summer residence and winter retreat. Incorporated in 1899 to serve workers of the Colorado Yule Marble Quarry, the tiny hamlet includes many historic sites, including the old quarry (marble from this spot graces the Lincoln Memorial and Tomb of the Unknowns in Washington, D.C.), a one-room schoolhouse that houses the Marble Historical Society Museum, and the quaint Marble Community Church. Marble is also the gateway to one of Colorado's most-photographed places: the **Crystal Mill.** Set on a craggy cliff overlooking the river, the 1917 mill harkens back to the area's mining past; it's also the perfect place to enjoy a picnic lunch in the solitude of the Colorado Rockies. A four-wheel-drive vehicle is needed to get you here in good weather (your feet will have to do on rainy days when the road isn't passable).

SPORTS & THE OUTDOORS

FISHING Often overlooked by anglers anxious to cast their lines in the Roaring Fork, the Crystal River runs for more than 35 mi from its headwaters near the town of Marble to its junction with the Roaring Fork in

Carbondale. In spring and fall, this junction offers excellent fishing for brown and rainbow trout as they attempt a run up the Crystal to spawn. Mountain whitefish can also be hooked. The upper reaches of the river traverse public land in the White River National Forest, but the last 6 mi are mostly private property. Be sure to check signage. Near the confluence public fishing is possible at the Days Inn in Carbondale, Satank Road, and the Division of Wildlife Fish Hatchery on Highway 133, 1 mi south of Carbondale. Redstone Lodge offers fishing for a fee.

The riverscape ranges from deep boulder pools and white-water rapids to slow, flat sections. Because of the steep shore terrain, storm runoff can sometimes cloud the river, making sight-casting difficult.

Roaring Fork Anglers (⊠*2205 Grand Ave., Glenwood Springs* ☎*970/ 945–0180*) has everything you need to get started. See ⊕*www.wildlife. state.co.us/fishing* for more fishing information.

HORSEBACK
RIDING

Chair Mountain Stables (⊠*17843 Hwy. 133, Redstone* ☎*970/963–1232*) offers daily one-hour rides, as well as dinner tours, all-day adventures, and overnight stays in the surrounding backcountry.

NORDIC
SKIING

Ute Meadows Nordic Center (⊠*2880 County Rd. 3* ☎*970/963–5513, 970/948–1895 snow conditions*) is a winter playground with 10 mi of groomed cross-country trails and countless miles of ungroomed skiing and snowshoe trails set in the remote reaches of the Crystal River valley. A complete rental shop, with services including waxing and tune-ups, is on the premises. Dogs are welcome to accompany skiers and snowshoers (there's a nominal fee).

WHERE TO STAY & EAT

Drifting down valley can save you plenty when it comes to accommodations, but the options are limited to several boutique inns and lodges and a handful of mom-and-pop motels. Fortunately for the palate and purse, as the wealth shifts down valley in the Roaring Fork, so, too, do the more-creative and less-expensive menus. Dining options in Basalt and Carbondale range from traditional American and Mexican eateries to Asian fusion restaurants and boutique cafés.

$$$
FodorsChoice
★

✕**SIX89.** Locals might argue that the best food in the valley is not served in the posh eateries of Aspen, but in this Carbondale favorite. The irreverent menu and whimsical lexicon (a glossary is provided for your reference), superb service, and inventive preparations of excellent local produce, game, and fish create a downright delightful dining experience. Try the salad with seared chèvre gnocchi or the Black Angus fillet with lobster tater tots. There's an extensive wine list (and a knowledgeable sommelier) to complement your meal. If you're feeling adventurous, put yourself in chef Mark Fischer's capable hands with "Random Acts of Cooking," a family-style tasting menu. ⊠*689 Main St., Carbondale* ☎*970/963–6890* ⌂*Reservations essential* ▭*AE, D, MC, V* ⊗*No lunch.*

$$–$$$

▭**Redstone Inn.** The inn was originally designed as an elegant lodge for the bachelor employees of the Colorado Fuel and Iron Company.

(Owner J. C. Osgood also constructed one of the region's first planned communities, a utopian model in its day.) Eat in the casual poolside Grill or the more-formal Redstone Dining Room, where people from miles around come for Sunday brunch. Many of the rooms have verandas with views. Don't pass up the complimentary wine-and-cheese receptions every afternoon. **Pros:** beautiful and romantic inn, pretty location. **Cons:** no air-conditioning, no elevator. ⊠*82 Redstone Blvd., Redstone 81623* ☎*970/963–2526 or 800/748–2524* ⊕*www.redstone-inn.com* ⟿*35 rooms* ⚲*In-room: no a/c, Wi-Fi. In-hotel: 2 restaurants, bar, tennis court, pool, gym, no elevator, public Internet, public Wi-Fi, parking (no fee), some pets allowed, no-smoking rooms* ▭*AE, D, MC, V.*

THE ARTS

The studio gallery and sculpture garden at the **Redstone Arts Center** (⊠*173 Redstone Blvd.* ☎*970/963–3790*) display such art and crafts as sculpture, painting, jewelry, and pottery.

ASPEN & THE ROARING FORK VALLEY ESSENTIALS

TRANSPORTATION

BY AIR

Aspen-Pitkin County Airport (ASE) is 3 mi from Aspen. It is served daily by United Express, America West Express/Mesa, and Northwest Express/Mesaba, and has nonstop United service to Los Angeles in ski season.

Information **Apen-Pitkin County Airport (ASE)** (☎*970/920–5384* ⊕*www.aspenairport.com*). **Denver International Airport (DEN)** (☎*800/247–2336* ⊕*www.flydenver.com*).

TRANSFERS Your best bet for traveling to and from Aspen and Snowmass Village is Roaring Fork Transit Agency, which provides bus service from Aspen-Pitkin County Airport to the Rubey Park bus station right at the base of the ski mountain. Colorado Mountain Express connects Aspen with Denver, Grand Junction, and the Eagle County airport. High Mountain Taxi will also provide charter service outside the Roaring Fork Valley.

Contacts **Colorado Mountain Express** (☎*970/949–4227 or 800/525–6353*). **High Mountain Taxi** (☎*970/925–8294 or 800/528–8294*). **Roaring Fork Transit Agency** (☎*970/925–8484*).

BY BUS AND SHUTTLE

Greyhound Lines serves Glenwood Springs. The Roaring Fork Transit Agency provides bus service up and down the valley.

Contacts **Greyhound Lines** (☎*800/231–2222*). **Roaring Fork Transit Agency** (☎*970/925–8484*).

BY CAR

If you are flying into Aspen, you can rent a car from Alamo or National at the airport.

The hardest part about driving in the High Rockies is keeping your eyes on the road. A glacier-carved canyon off to your left, a soaring mountain ridge to your right, and there, standing on the shoulder, a bull elk. Some of the most scenic routes aren't necessarily the most direct. In summer, the 160-mi, three-hour drive from Denver to Aspen is a delightful journey up the I–70 corridor and through the Continental Divide at the Eisenhower Tunnel (or over the slower, but more-spectacular, Loveland Pass), down along the eastern ramparts of the Collegiate Peaks along State Highway 91 and U.S. Highway 24, with a final push on serpentine State Highway 82 up and over 12,095-foot Independence Pass.

The scenery, particularly south of Leadville on U.S. 24, is among the best in Colorado, with western views of 14,433-foot Mount Elbert, the highest mountain in the state. Independence Pass is closed in winter (timing depends on snowfall, typically late October–late May), but motorists should always drive cautiously. Blinding snowstorms—even in July—can erase visibility and make the pass treacherously icy. Be especially careful on the western side where the road narrows and vertigo-inducing drop-offs plunge thousands of feet from hairpin curves. Both Route 82 and I–70, like all Colorado roads, should be driven with caution, especially at night when elk, bighorn sheep, and mule deer cross without warning.

Generally speaking, driving to Aspen from Denver in winter is more trouble than it's worth, unless you plan to stop along the way. The drive west on I–70 and east on Route 82 takes more than three hours at best, depending on weather conditions and increasingly, ski traffic. On the other hand, the 3-mi drive from the Aspen-Pitkin County Airport is a breeze along the flat valley floor.

Information Colorado Road Condition Hotline (☎ *303/639–1111 near Denver, 303/639–1234 statewide*).**Colorado State Patrol** (☎ *303/239–4500* ⊕ *www.csp. state.co.us*).

BY TRAIN

Glenwood Springs is on Amtrak's *California Zephyr* route, which runs from Emeryville California to Chicago.

Contact Amtrak (☎ *800/872-7245* ⊕ *www.amtrak.com*).

CONTACTS & RESOURCES

EMERGENCIES
Ambulance or Police (☎ *911*).

24-Hour Medical Care Aspen/Snowmass: Aspen Valley Hospital (✉ *0401 Castle Creek Rd.* ☎ *970/925–1120*).**Glenwood Springs: Valley View Hospital** (✉ *1906 Blake St.* ☎ *970/945–6535*).

LODGING

CAMPING Despite the abundant federal and state land that checkerboards the High Rockies, finding an established campsite is surprisingly difficult along the I–70 corridor. From Memorial Day to Labor Day campsites fill up quickly, especially on weekends and holidays. To improve your chances, call to reserve a campsite or arrive early in the day. Established car-camping sites generally have restrooms, water pumps, trash cans, and fire pits. Open fires are only allowed when the danger of wildfires is low. Wilderness devotees who don't relish the idea of a neighborhood of tents can escape into the vast backcountry. The Indian Peaks Wilderness Area—a string of 13,000-foot-high peaks that brace the Continental Divide north of I–70—offers limitless opportunities. As long as you are 200 feet away from a water source, you can pitch your tent anywhere.

Contact **Colorado Campground and Lodge Owners Association** (☎ *970/259–1899* ⊕ *www.campcolorado.com*).

TOURS

In Aspen, a romantic way to orient yourself to the backcountry is by taking the T Lazy Seven Ranch private sleigh ride. Aspen Carriage Company has stagecoach tours around downtown and the historic West End. From the beginning of summer through mid-October, narrated bus tours from Aspen to the Maroon Bells are available.

Contacts **Aspen Carriage Co.** (✉ *Aspen* ☎ *970/925–3394* ⊕ *www.aspencarriages.com*). **Maroon Bells bus tour** (✉ *Aspen* ☎ *970/925–9000 or 888/649–5982* ⊕ *www.rfta.com*). **T Lazy Seven Ranch** (✉ *Aspen* ☎ *970/925–4614* ⊕ *www. tlazy7.com*).

VISITOR INFORMATION

Snow Reports **Aspen** (☎ *907/925–1221*).

Contacts **Aspen Chamber Resort Association** (✉ *425 Rio Grande Pl., 81611* ☎ *970/925–1940 or 888/290–1324* ⊕ *aspenchamber.org*). **Glenwood Springs Chamber Resort Association** (✉ *1102 Grand Ave., 81601* ☎ *970/945–6589 or 800/221–0098* ⊕ *glenwoodchamber.com*).

Boulder & North Central Colorado

WITH ESTES PARK & GRAND COUNTY

WORD OF MOUTH

"Boulder is well worth seeing and exploring . . . you could go hiking in the Flatirons, the hills above the city, spend time on the Pearl St. Mall, a pedestrian shopping area, visit a very cool restaurant, the Dushanbe Teahouse, stroll around the Colorado University campus . . ."

—tekwriter

"[S]tay in Estes Park. This location puts you very close to Rocky Mountain National Park. Great hiking, biking, horseback riding. Estes Park is also a very cute town with lots of charm, shops, and restaurants."

—sweetsailing

Revised &
Updated by
Gregory Robl

THE ENVIABLE LIFESTYLE OF NORTH central Colorado is set up by the region's geography and climate. Where else does a string of sophisti-cated yet laid-back cities parallel a mountain chain that offers such a plethora of outdoor activities? It's all here: Restaurants serving nearly every cuisine from around the world, universities, eclectic shopping, high-tech industries, ranching, breweries, bustling nightlife, and con-certs are mere minutes from the idyll of the mountains and wilderness with the endless hiking, fishing, rock climbing, cycling, skiing, and kayaking. Toss more than 300 sunny days per year and views of the towering mountains into the equation, and you can see why residents relish it all with hedonistic abandon.

Boulder is the region in a nutshell. Every conceivable trend in food, alternative health care, education, and personal style has come through town, and yet, with its commitment to preserving open space and wil-derness, the city abuts so many nonurbanized zones that you can be on a trail to a mountain peak in no time. In Grand County, where ranching is still a livelihood for many, guest ranches and golf courses provide an indulgent retreat. Waterskiing, sailing, canoeing, ice fishing, and snowmobiling have made Grand Lake Village and Colorado's "Great Lakes" a destination even for vacationing Coloradans.

North central Colorado became part of the United States in 1803 through the Louisiana Purchase—hence towns with names like La Porte, Platteville, and La Salle, as well as the river named Cache la Poudre. Coal mines between Boulder and Broomfield attracted settlers and many Italian immigrants in the late 1800s and early 1900s, but the region grew mostly on agriculture and ranching. Out-of-state leisure travelers first came in the early 20th century to benefit from both the curative qualities of the dry air and the waters of spas like Eldorado Springs and Hot Sulphur Springs. Reminders of a grand style of touring exist in resort towns such as Estes Park and Grand Lake, the gateways to Rocky Mountain National Park.

EXPLORING NORTH CENTRAL COLORADO

Boulder and Fort Collins are the two most prominent and characteristic cities of the region. Between these two energetic university towns, you'll find the sprawling cities of Loveland and Longmont and a few former coal mining towns with homey, small-town character like Marshall, Louisville, Lafayette, and Erie. To the west are the proud, independent mountain hamlets of Lyons, Nederland, Ward, and Jamestown. Beyond the high peaks are broad valleys dotted with unpretentious ranching communities like Granby and Kremmling, and right in the middle of it all is the area's crown jewel, Rocky Mountain National Park, and its resorts, Grand Lake and Estes Park. Despite their proximity, each town in the region has its own milieu—a distinct character and a unique his-tory—as though hundreds of miles separated them. Throughout the region are never-ending vistas of green pastures and fields of grain, snowcapped granite peaks, pine- and aspen-forested valleys, raging

TOP REASONS TO GO

The local breweries: The Front Range is home to many small breweries, and a vacation could be filled by touring and sampling myriad ales, stouts, and lagers. In late June the state's small brewers congregrate in Fort Collins for the Colorado Brewers' Festival to show off their pride and joy.

Hiking near Boulder and in the Indian Peaks Wilderness: On weekends year-round you'll find the trails packed. Whether an easy jaunt or a strenuous climb, none disappoint. The views are singularly spectacular, especially in midsummer when the wildflowers bloom.

Boulder Dushanbe Teahouse: This traditional Central Asian teahouse was given to Boulder by the city of Dushanbe, Tajikistan. Master artisans in Tajikistan carved and painted everything right down to the tables and chairs.

Chautauqua Park: Open since July 4, 1898, you can still attend a lecture, a silent film, or a classical concert here much like visitors did 100 years ago. Enjoy a picnic on the green or dine in the hall before the event.

The Arts: Theater buffs have enjoyed the Colorado Shakespeare Festival for 50 summers with a picnic on the lawn before a performance in the outdoor theater. The Grammy- and Grammophone–Award winning Takács Quartet is beloved for its stunning performances of music by Beethoven, Bartók, and Brahms.

rivers and meandering streams, deep canyons, and manicured greenbelts—all shared by wildlife and humans.

ABOUT THE PARKS & RECREATION AREAS

Rocky Mountain National Park is known for its scenery, hiking, wildlife watching, camping, and snowshoeing. *See the Rocky Mountain National Park chapter in this book.*

Spanning the Continental Divide between Grand Lake and Nederland just south of Rocky Mountain National Park is the **Indian Peaks Wilderness,** a favorite for hiking and backcountry camping. The **Arapaho National Recreation Area** (⊠*Sulphur Ranger District, Granby* ☏*970/887–4100* ⊕*www.fs.fed.us/r2/arnf/recreation/anra/index. shtml*), near the national park's west entrance, has fishing, boating, sailing, and waterskiing, all on Lake Granby and Shadow Mountain Reservoir, as well as hiking, mountain biking, birding, and camping.

North central Colorado has five state parks, each popular for different activities. **Eldorado Canyon State Park** (☏*303/494–3943*) is known mainly for rock climbing. Six miles south of downtown Boulder, it's also popular with hikers, stream anglers, and picnickers.

State Forest State Park (☏*970/723–8366*) is the most remote park in the region (about 75 mi west of Fort Collins or 75 mi north of Granby) and is great for hiking, camping, sailing, lake and stream fishing on Michigan Creek and North Michigan Reservoir, and snowmobiling or hut-to-hut skiing in winter.

In Boulder and Fort Collins you can literally walk out your door, up the street, and into the mountains or foothills on a hiking trail, but plenty of riparian trails and open-space paths within the city limits can take you for miles and have plenty of access points. **City of Boulder Open Space & Mountain Parks** is best known for the hiking and bicycling trails. **Horsetooth Mountain Park** in Fort Collins is also a destination for hikers.

The northern Front Range has only one downhill ski resort, **Eldora Mountain Resort**, a few miles west of Nederland and 30 minutes west of Boulder.

ABOUT THE RESTAURANTS

Thanks to the influx of people from around the world, and their willingness and means to pay for quality food, diners here have curious and educated palates. Restaurants in north central Colorado run the gamut from simple diners with tasty, homey basics to elegant establishments with wine lists numbering hundreds of wines. Increasingly, eateries are featuring organic ingredients and several serve exclusively organic meals and locally produced foods. Even places catering to college students know that their existence depends on good meals made and priced honestly. Some restaurants take reservations, but many, particularly in the middle range, seat on a first-come, first-served basis.

ABOUT THE HOTELS

Bed-and-breakfasts and small inns in north central Colorado vary from old-fashioned fluffy cottages to modern, sleek buildings with an understated lodge theme. Ever-popular guest ranches and spas are places to escape and be pampered after having fun outdoors. In the high-country resorts of Estes Park and Grand Lake and in towns nearby, the elevation keeps the climate cool, and you'll have a tough time finding air-conditioned lodging. The region is also full of franchise motels and hotels, often at the access points to cities.

WHAT IT COSTS				
	¢	$	$$	$$$	$$$$
RESTAURANTS	under $8	$8–$12	$13–$18	$19–$25	over $25
HOTELS	under $80	$80–$120	$121–$170	$171–$230	over $230

Restaurant prices are for a main course at dinner, excluding 5.75%–8.46% tax. Hotel prices are for two people in a standard double room in high season, excluding service charges and 5.75%–10.25% tax.

TIMING

Visiting the Front Range is pleasurable in any season. Wintertime in the urban corridor can be mild, but the mountainous regions are cold and snowy. Snowfall along the Front Range is highest in spring, particularly March, making for excellent skiing, but poor car travel. Spring is capricious—75°F one day and a blizzard the next—and June can be hot or cool and rainy. July typically ushers in high summer, which can last through September, although most 90-plus–degree days occur in July and early August. In the higher mountains, summer temperatures are generally 15–20 degrees cooler than in the urban corridor. After-

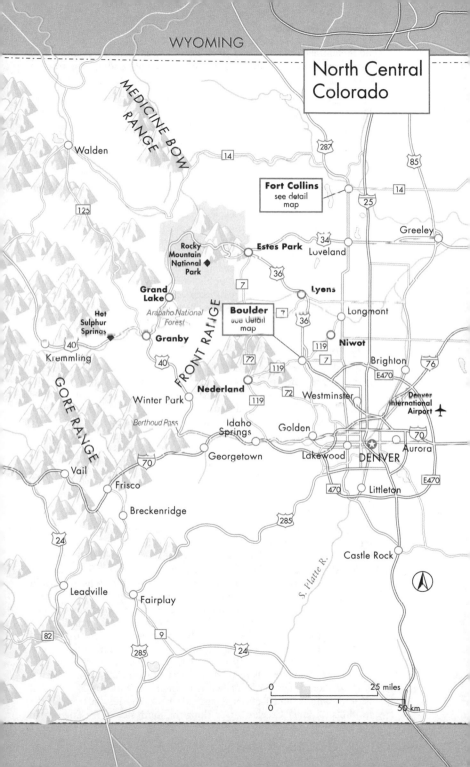

noon summer thunderstorms can last 30 minutes or all evening. Fall has crisp sunny days and cool nights, some cold enough for frost in nonurban areas.

Art and music festivals start up in May and continue through September. With them comes an increase in tourist traffic. Spring and summer are the best times to watch for wildlife or fish.

BOULDER

No place in Colorado better epitomizes the state's outdoor mania than Boulder, where sunny weather keeps locals busy through all seasons. There are nearly as many bicycles as cars in this uncommonly beautiful and beautifully uncommon city embroidered with 30,000 acres of parks and greenbelts and laced with more than 200 mi of trails for hiking, walking, jogging, and bicycling. Boulder started taxing itself in 1967 in order to buy greenbelts and in 2000 had a referendum (failed) on the ballot to provide free public transportation for city residents. Even in winter, residents cycle to work and jog on the open-space paths. It's nearly a matter of civic pride to spend a lunch hour playing Frisbee, in-line skating, hiking with the family dog, and even rock climbing on the Flatirons. The proverbial Boulder three-piece suit is a T-shirt, fleece vest, and shorts, completed by Birkenstock sandals.

EVENTS   The **Boulder Creek Festival** (☎ *303/652–4942* ⊕ *www.bouldercreekevents. com*) lasts all Memorial Day weekend: you can feast at the pancake breakfast, browse the bazaar, learn about alternative healing, and see regional artistic talent at the art show and the artists' marketplace. Children have fun with dance, theater, and hands-on activities at the Kids' Place. Live music runs the gamut: Irish, Senegalese, John Philip Sousa, and jazz. Don't miss the **Great Rubber Duck Race** on Memorial Day afternoon. Get a rubber duck and compete against hundreds of others in Boulder Creek.

EXPLORING BOULDER

Boulder is beautiful, and the best place to take a first look is from the scenic overlook on Davidson Mesa (it's on U.S. 36 south of town). On the left you'll see Bear Mountain and the obvious Devil's Thumb on its left slope marking the entrance to Eldorado Canyon. To the right is Green Mountain and its trademark red sandstone Flatirons that you'll be able to see from almost every vantage point in town. These massive rock upthrusts, so named for their flat faces, are popular among rock climbers and hikers. Flagstaff Mountain, Bald Mountain, and Lee Hill are to the right, and at the horizon behind them you'll see the Indian Peaks. Meeker and Longs Peak, both in Rocky Mountain National Park, tower above them all nearly straight ahead of you in the distance. The red-tile roofs of the University of Colorado at Boulder are easy to spot, and the downtown is to the right with the Red Rocks, Mount Sanitas, and Dakota Ridge as a backdrop just in front of the foothills. Boulder Creek courses along the south side of the downtown area at the bottom of "the Hill" on which both the university and its companion off-beat neighborhood are located.

Although 10 minutes of walking separate downtown and the Hill, the milieus seem miles and ages apart; downtown bustles with families, buskers, the arts, classy boutiques, and eateries, while the Hill pulsates with trendy shops, packed coffeehouses, bars, and restaurants geared more to students. Parking and driving in these sections of Boulder can be cumbersome and time-consuming. Leave your car at the hotel and try the Hop, a bus that circulates in both directions between downtown, the Hill, and the university for about the cost of an hour at a parking meter.

> ## WHAT IS THE FRONT RANGE, ANYWAY?
>
> Geographically, the Front Range comprises the mountains that slope down east from the Continental Divide to the foothills along the high plains. Demographically, it is the heavily populated corridor between Fort Collins and Pueblo, Colorado. Locals say that, except for Denver, eastern Colorado begins on the east side of I-25. The Front Range in north central Colorado is a blend of cities with historic downtowns, verdant buffers full of recreational opportunities, farms, ranches, and suburbs.

Historic Boulder (✉ *1123 Spruce St.* ☎ *303/444–5192* ⊕ *www.historic boulder.org*) sells brochures ($1.50) for seven self-guided walking tours, including the University of Colorado at Boulder, the Hill, Chautauqua Park, the Mapleton Historic District, and the Downtown Boulder Historic District. The annual Tour of Homes (early May) and the Historic Homes for the Holidays (first weekend of December) tours are highly popular with locals. Be sure to reserve tickets for the holiday tour ($15).

Banjo Billy's Bus Tours (✉ *Tour starts from Hotel Boulderado at 13th and Spruce Sts.* ☎ *720/938–8885* ⊕ *www.banjobilly.com* ♿ *Reservations essential* 💲 *$16* ⊘ *Closed Mon.*)offers a 90-minute tour of downtown Boulder, part of the University of Colorado, Chautauqua Park, and "the Hill," aboard a bus that has been built to look like a log cabin. Everyone on the bus gets to vote on the topic of the tour: ghost stories, history, folklore, or crime stories. Your seat may be a saddle or a recliner, or you can opt to sit on the couch.

DOWNTOWN

Pearl Street, between 8th and 20th streets, is the city's hub, an eclectic collection of classy boutiques, consignment shops, eccentric bookstores, art galleries, cafés, bars, and restaurants. A few national chains have hung out their signs among the home-grown businesses along the four-block pedestrian mall, but beyond 11th Street to the west and 15th Street to the east, the milieu evokes the early days of the Pearl Street Mall.

The late-19th- and early-20th-century commercial structures of the **Downtown Boulder Historic District** once housed mercantile stores and saloons. The period architecture—including Queen Anne, Italianate, and Romanesque styles in stone or brick—has been preserved, but stores inside cater to modern tastes, with gourmet coffees and Tibetan prayer flags. The area is bounded by the south side of Spruce Street between 10th and 16th streets, Pearl Street between 9th and 16th streets, and the north side of Walnut Street between Broadway and 9th Street.

Three blocks north of Pearl Street and west of Broadway is **Mapleton Historic District.** This neighborhood of turn-of-the-20th-century homes shaded by old maple and cottonwood trees is bounded roughly by Broadway, the alley between Pearl and Spruce streets, 4th Street, and the alley between Dewey Street and Concord Avenue.

The **Boulder Museum of Contemporary Art** hosts local and national contemporary art exhibits, performance art, dance, experimental film, and poetry readings. In summer when the farmers' market takes place in front of the museum, hours are extended: Wed. 11–8 and Sat. 9–4. ⊠ *1750 13th St.* ☎ *303/443–2122* 🖃 *$5* ◎ *Tues.–Fri. 11–5, Sat. 11–4, Sun. noon–3.*

THE UNIVERSITY & THE HILL

South of downtown is the **University of Colorado at Boulder.** Red sandstone buildings with tile roofs (built in the "Rural Italian" architectural style that Charles Z. Klauder created in the early 1920s) outline the campus's green lawns and small ponds. The original campus began in 1875 with the construction of Old Main, which borders the **Norlin Quadrangle** (on the National Register of Historic Places), a broad lawn where students sun themselves or play a quick round of Frisbee between classes. The **CU Heritage Center** (⊠ *Old Main Bldg. on Norlin Quadrangle* ☎ *303/492–6329* 🖃 *Free* ◎ *Weekdays 10–4*) preserves the history of the university—including notable student pranks and a lunar sample on long-term loan from NASA. Also displayed are the personal memorabilia of alumni such as Marilyn Van Derbur, Robert Redford, and Glenn Miller. One room is devoted to CU's 17 astronauts, including Ellison Onizuka, who was killed aboard the *Challenger* space shuttle in 1986, and Kalpana Chawla, who died on the *Columbia* in 2003. The natural history collection at the **University of Colorado Museum** (⊠ *Henderson Bldg.* ☎ *303/492–6892* ⊕ *http://cumuseum.colorado. edu* 🖃 *Free* ◎ *Weekdays 9–5, Sat. 9–4, Sun. 10–4*) includes dinosaur relics and has permanent and changing exhibits. ⊠ *University Memorial Center* ☎ *303/492–1411, 303/492–6301 to reserve tour* ⊕ *www. colorado.edu* 🖃 *Free* ◎ *Campus tours year-round, weekdays 9:30 and 1:30* ☞ *Reservations essential.*

Star shows and laser shows set to classic compositions like *Peter and the Wolf* or the music of well-known rock bands entertain at the university's **Fiske Planetarium/Sommers-Bausch Observatory.** During the academic year, shows begin Friday at 9:30 PM. "Star Talks" are at 8 PM on Thursday and Friday. Matinees take place in summer on Tuesday, Wednesday, and Thursday at 10 AM and 1 PM. ⊠ *Regent Dr.* ☎ *303/492–5002* ⊕ *fiske.colorado.edu* 🖃 *Laser shows and matinees $5; Star Talks $6;*

observatory free ⊗ *Planetarium, year-round, days vary. Observatory, Fri. 9 PM–11 PM. Closed on university holidays.*

A favorite college student hangout is the bohemian neighborhood **University Hill** (*The Hill* ⊠ *13th St. between Pennsylvania St. and College Ave.*), which is home to eateries, music and dance venues, record shops, bars, coffeehouses, and hip boutiques.

NEED A BREAK?

The actor Robert Redford worked at The Sink (⊠ *1165 13th St.* ☎ *303/444-7465***) during his years as a student at the University of Colorado at Boulder. The restaurant has served great pizza, burgers, beer, and other student dietary staples since 1949.**

Housed in the 1889 Harbeck-Bergheim mansion, the **Boulder Museum of History** documents the history of Boulder and the surrounding region from 1858 to the present. If you're interested in the sartorial styles of the 19th century (whether rugged cowboy and miner duds or high-society finery), this museum will delight. It's home to one of Colorado's largest clothing collections, with items dating as far back as 1820. ⊠ *1205 Euclid Ave.* ☎ *303/449-3464* ⊕ *www.boulderhistorymuseum. org* 🎫 *$5* ⊗ *Tues.–Fri. 10–5, weekends noon–4.*

The scent of hops fills the air during free one-hour tours and ale and lager tastings at the **Boulder Beer Company,** Colorado's first microbrewery. The brew house's own pub is open weekdays 11 AM–9 PM. ⊠ *2880 Wilderness Pl.* ☎ *303/444-8448* ⊕ *www.boulderbeer.com* 🎫 *Free* ⊗ *Tours weekdays 2 PM.*

☾ Talking about the weather is *not* boring at the **National Center for Atmospheric Research,** where the hands-on exhibits, video presentation, and one hour tour fires up kids' enthusiasm for what falls out of the sky. I. M. Pei's famous buildings stand majestically on a mesa at the base of the mountains, where you can see mule deer and other wildlife. After browsing the field guides and science kits in the gift shop, follow the interpretive Walter Orr Roberts Nature and Weather Trail to learn about the mesa's weather, climate, plants, and wildlife. The 4-mi loop is wheelchair accessible. If you can't make the guided tour, self-guided and audio tours are available during regular hours. Reservations are required for large groups. ⊠ *1850 Table Mesa Dr., 80305* ✛ *From southbound Broadway turn right on Table Mesa Dr.* ☎ *303/497-1174* ⊕ *www.ncar.ucar.edu* 🎫 *Free* ⊗ *Weekdays 8–5, weekends 9–4. Tour daily at noon.*

PARKS & GREENBELTS

★ For the prettiest views of town, follow Baseline Drive (west from Broadway) up to **Chautauqua Park** (⊠ *900 W. Baseline Rd.*), site of the Colorado Music Festival, and a favorite oasis of locals on weekends. Continue farther up Flagstaff Mountain to Panorama Point and Boulder Mountain Park, where people jog, bike, and climb.

North Boulder Creek drops into Middle Boulder Creek at **Boulder Falls** (✛ *Drive west from Broadway on Canyon Blvd., Rte. 119, 8.5 mi into Boulder Canyon. Watch for a sign marking the falls. Parking is on left*).

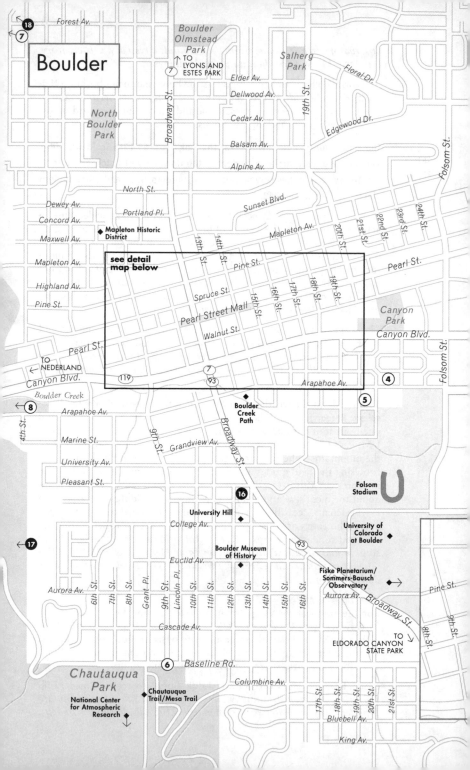

6

The walk to the 70-foot-high falls is less than 0.25 mi round-trip, and it's a spectacular place to take a break and admire the grand scenery.

★ **Eldorado Canyon State Park,** with its awe-inspiring canyon of steep walls and pine forests, offers outdoor activities for everyone—even bird-watchers and artists. Kayakers get adrenaline rushes on the rapids of South Boulder Creek, while rock climbers scale the world-renowned, vertical, granite canyon walls. Picnickers can choose from 42 spots, and anglers' catches average 8 inches. Hikers have 12 mi of trails to wander. The **Streamside Trail** (1 mi round-trip) is mostly level and parallels South Boulder Creek 0.5 mi to West Ridge; 300 feet of the trail are wheelchair accessible. Half of **Fowler Trail** (1.5 mi round-trip) is wheelchair accessible. The trail has interpretive signs about the wildlife. For the best views of the canyon and the Front Range plains, head up **Rattlesnake Gulch Trail.** The 3-mi (round-trip) switchback trail ends at an overlook 800 feet higher in elevation than the trailhead, where you can see the high Rockies of the Continental Divide. Snowshoeing is popular here in winter. Mountain bikers crank on Rattlesnake Gulch Trail and Fowler Trail. **Eldorado Canyon Trail** is open to horseback riding. ⊕ *Drive south on Broadway (Hwy. 93) 3 mi to Eldorado Canyon Dr. (Rte. 170). The paved road ends at village of Eldorado Springs. Drive through town to park entrance* ☎*303/494–3943* ⊕*www.parks.state. co.us* ✉*$7 per vehicle.*

SPORTS & THE OUTDOORS

RACES   Early May finds Boulderites at the Boulder Reservoir for the annual **Kinetic Challenge** (⊕*www.kbco.com/kinetics [works seasonally]*). The competition requires each team to build a craft that can race over the land, slog through the mud, and not sink in the water. Teams are allowed to provide their own judges and bribe other judges. Speed is not necessarily the determining criterion—creativity and onboard sculpture count, too.

Fodor's Choice   Memorial Day brings the annual 10-km **Bolder Boulder** (☎*303/444–* ★   *7223* ⊕*www.bolderboulder.com*), when top international runners, along with 45,000 other citizens, run the country's fourth-largest race. About 100,000 spectators line the route and fill CU's Folsom Stadium to cheer on the participants. Along the racecourse rock bands, jazz musicians, African drumming groups, Elvis impersonators, belly dancers, and classical quartets spur on the runners. The race ends in Folsom Stadium for a ceremony that includes a flyover by U.S. Air Force fighter jets and skydivers who parachute onto the stadium field.

BICYCLING
IN & EAST OF   The **Boulder Creek Path** winds through town for about 9 mi from the
BOULDER   mouth of Fourmile Canyon west of Boulder to the intersection of Arapahoe Avenue and Cherryvale Road, connecting to more than 200 mi of city and greenbelt trails and paths. ⊕*Trailheads: You can access paths from nearly every cross street in town, but don't always count on parking nearby. From downtown the best access points are behind the public library parking lot on south side of Canyon Blvd. between*

9th St. and Broadway or in Central Park on 13th St. between Canyon Blvd. and Arapahoe Ave.

If bicycling on flatter, less-rugged terrain with views of the mountains entices you more than bicycling in them, a few trails will not disappoint. The Community Ditch portion of the **Marshall Mesa/Community Ditch Trail** (⚓*Trailhead: Drive south on Broadway to Marshall Dr. and turn left. Parking is on right*) is open to mountain bikers. The 8-mi round-trip ride takes you up through pine stands and over a plateau where you can look down on Boulder, with the Flatirons and the Rockies in full view. The trail continues across Highway 93 almost to Eldorado Springs.

IN THE
MOUNTAINS
For more-strenuous mountain biking, head west out of town to **Walker Ranch** (✉*Flagstaff Rd.* ⚓*8 mi west of town*); the 7.5-mi loop has great views of the Indian Peaks. For less-challenging bicycling but a scenic 7.2-mi, two-hour ride nonetheless, the **Betasso Preserve Loop** is 4 mi west of Broadway on Canyon Boulevard in Boulder Canyon. Look for the trailhead turnout on the left. The **Foothills Trail,** accessed either off North 4th Street or from the intersection of Linden Street and Wonderland Hill Avenue, offers a somewhat technical 8-mi ride out to Boulder Reservoir. You'll have mountain views on the way back to Boulder. Add on another 6-mi jaunt to Lefthand Valley Reservoir by taking the Lefthand Trail from the north side of the Sage/Eagle Trail loop.

To test your quadriceps, take the **Switzerland Trail,** a 9- to 13-mi ride with a nice drop to the hamlet of Sunset, and a climb up to Gold Hill. ⚓*Trailhead: From Broadway drive west 5 mi on Canyon Blvd./Hwy. 119 and turn right onto Sugarloaf Rd. After 5 mi turn right at Sugarloaf Mountain Rd. Parking area is 1 mi farther.*

BICYCLE
SHOPS
Full Cycle (✉*1795 Pearl St.* ☎*303/440–1002*) rents mountain bikes with helmets and locks for four-hour, one-day, and multiple-day biking adventures.

University Bicycles (✉*839 Pearl St.* ☎*303/444–4196*) rents mountain and town bikes (helmet, lock, and map included) for four hours to one week.

BIRD-WATCHING
Ornithologists have spotted kestrels, falcons, and the occasional bald eagle in the steep cliffs of **Eldorado Canyon State Park.** Owls, chickadees, nuthatches, and woodpeckers are at home in the pine forests along South Boulder Creek in the park.

Walden Ponds and Sawhill Ponds, formerly a gravel quarry, are now home to songbirds, waterfowl, and raptors. More than 3 mi of groomed paths encircle and connect the ponds and lead into wooded areas along Boulder Creek, where owls roost. April to May is when most birds migrate through the Front Range, although the ponds are home to plenty of year-round residents. ⚓*Drive north on 28th St. (U.S. Hwy. 36) and turn right at Valmont Rd. Drive east 4 mi and turn left at 75th St. The sign marking the ponds is about 0.5 mi farther* ☉*Dawn–dusk.*

FISHING

Eldorado Canyon State Park ranger Craig Preston has published a pamphlet describing both fly- and baited-hook fishing in the park. It's available at the visitor center. Anyone older than 16 needs a Colorado fishing license, which you can obtain at local sporting-goods stores. See ⊕*www.wildlife.state.co.us/fishing* for more information.

Kinsley Outfitters (⊠*2070 Broadway* ☎*303/442–6204 or 800/442– 7420* ⊕*www.kinsleyoutfitters.com*) provides Orvis-endorsed guides for the world-class waters of the Colorado and South Platte rivers. You can arrange a personalized half- or full-day guided fishing trip that includes transportation, lunch, and Orvis equipment. Your fishing license will cost extra.

Rocky Mountain Anglers (⊠*1904 Arapahoe Ave.* ☎*303/447–2400* ⊕*www.rockymtanglers.com*) can sell you a few flies or set up a guided tour. The guides have access to private ranches and know where to find secluded fishing holes on public lands. Fees include transportation, gear, and lunch.

GOLF

Indian Peaks Golf Course. This local favorite has views of the Continental Divide, including some of the "Fourteeners" (mountain peaks over 14,000 feet) not visible from Boulder. The excellently tended course boasts low scores and has tee boxes for all skill levels. ⊠*2300 Indian Peaks Trail, Lafayette* ✥*Baseline Rd. to Indian Peaks Trail, 10 mi east of Boulder* ☎*303/666–4706* ⊕*www.indianpeaksgolf.com* ⚐*18 holes. Yards: 7,083/5,468. Par: 72/72. Green Fee: $37/$45.*

HIKING

The **City of Boulder Open Space & Mountain Parks** administers all of the trails described here. They sell an excellent water- and tear-resistant map of hiking, bicycling, and equestrian trails and can give you information on the easy-to-moderate hiking in the area parks. Many trails are open to dogs, provided they are leashed. Be prepared for short thunderstorms during summer afternoons. A parking permit ($3 per vehicle) is required for all non-Boulder County vehicles. You can purchase a daily pass either at self-serve kiosks in the mountain parks or at the office. ⊠*66 S. Cherryvale Rd.* ☎*303/441–3440* ⊕*www. ci.boulder.co.us/openspace* ☉*Weekdays 8–5.*

IN BOULDER For a relaxing amble through a riparian environment, take the **Boulder Creek Path** Trailheads (*see Bicycling, above*), which wind from west of Boulder through downtown and past the university to the eastern part of the city. Within the eastern city limits are ponds, gaggles of Canada geese, and prairie dog colonies. People-watching is half the fun: you'll see cyclists, joggers, and rollerblading dads and moms with their babies in jogging strollers. You'll have great views of the mountains as you walk back toward downtown. Walk west along the path from Broadway to Boulder Canyon and you'll see kayakers negotiating the boulders and inner-tubers cooling off in the summer heat.

CHAUTAUQUA PARK Even a short walk up the grassy slope between Chautauqua Park and the base of the mountains brings out hikers and their dogs to take in some sun. After an early-morning hike, the dining hall at Chautauqua Park fills with hungry people ready to tuck into a hearty breakfast. Afternoon walkers relax on the park's gently sloping lawn with a picnic and gaze up at the foothills stretching along the Front Range. To reach the parking lot, take Baseline Road west from Broadway. The park is on the left just past the intersection with 9th Street.

★ Locals love the **Chautauqua Trail/Mesa Trail** (⊠ *Trailhead: Main parking lot*), a 1.6-mi round-trip loop, for its great views of the city as well as for offering a few peeks at the rock climbers on the Flatirons. From the trailhead go up the Chautauqua Trail 0.6 mi to the Bluebell/Baird trail. Go left 0.4 mi and then left again onto the Mesa Trail, which takes you the 0.6 mi back to the parking area. The trail is a long slope at the beginning, but once in the trees you won't gain much more elevation. Allow a couple of hours for a leisurely walk on this easy hike. The 4-mi round-trip **Royal Arch Trail** (⊠ *Trailhead: Main parking lot*) leads to Boulder's own rock arch. Although it's far from equaling the famous rock formations in Utah, the Royal Arch is worth the steep hike, as are the views of the foothills and cities of the Front Range. The trail spurs off the Chautauqua/Mesa Trail loop and follows along the base of the Flatirons. You'll climb 1,270 feet in 2 mi. Go under the arch to the precipice for the views. If you turn around, the arch frames a couple of Flatirons for a good photo.

IN THE MOUNTAINS Two popular trails on the edge of town get you into the mountains quickly. The parking areas are across the street from each other and fill fast. Go early in the morning or later in the afternoon. Carry a picnic on the **Red Rocks Loop** (⊠ *Trailhead: Mapleton Ave., ✛1 mi west of Broadway on left*) and enjoy the mountain and city views. The Red Rocks Trail goes to the right from the parking lot and takes you through wildflowers and grassy meadows on the way up to the rock outcropping. The 0.5-mi round-trip takes about 20 minutes and gains 340 feet. If you have time for the full 2.3-mi loop allow one hour. You'll gain most of the 600 feet in elevation change on the way back. **Sanitas Valley Loop** (⊠ *Trailhead: Mapleton Ave., ✛1 mi west of Broadway on right*)*known locally as Mount Sanitas,* is an easy 3.5-mi hike and provides constant mountain scenery in Sunshine Canyon while you climb 540 feet going up the west flank of Mount Sanitas. From the trailhead head left onto the Mount Sanitas Trail, which becomes the East Ridge Trail as it wraps around the north side of the mountain. From here you can descend to the right on either the Sanitas Valley Trail back to the parking area or along the Dakota Ridge Trail if you want more city views. Be sure not to take the sharp left at the Dakota Ridge intersection, which leads straight downhill to town. Boulder will be on your left all the way back to the trailhead. Allow two hours to walk and take in the scenery.

★ Flagstaff Mountain offers hikers several easy-to-strenuous hikes. An easy walk along the **Boy Scout Trail** to May's Point offers glorious views of the city and Boulder Valley along the way and exceptional views of the Indian Peaks from May's Point. The 1.5-mi round-trip trail starts at Sunrise Amphitheater where it goes to the left into the spruce forest. After about 0.75 mi and only 140 feet elevation gain, head to the right at the fork in the trail. It's a short distance to May's Point. ⚓*Trailhead: Drive west on Baseline Rd. to sharp curve to right that is Flagstaff Rd., then turn right at Summit Rd. The trail starts from parking area about 0.5 mi in. It's a few hundred ft out to amphitheater.*

Green Mountain Loop rewards ambitious hikers with beautiful vistas of the Front Range and the Indian Peaks. The Gregory Canyon, Ranger, E. M. Greenman, and Saddle Rock trails create a 5.5-mi loop that takes three to four hours to hike. It's a 2,344-foot gain in elevation to Green Mountain's summit (8,144 feet). Follow the Gregory Canyon Trail to the Ranger Trail, and go left. Stay to the right at the E. M. Greenman Trail. At the intersection with Green Mountain West Ridge Trail, turn left. Go on to the summit and descend along the E. M. Greenman and Saddle Rock trails after taking in the view. ⚓*Trailhead (Gregory Canyon Trail): Drive west on Baseline Rd. to sharp curve that is Flagstaff Rd., and then turn left immediately after curve. Parking area is at end of short road where trail starts.*

INNER-TUBING

In July and August, when the daytime temperatures can reach the 90s, Boulderites take to tubing in Boulder Creek—especially near Eben G. Fine Park at the mouth of Boulder Canyon (Junction of Arapahoe and Canyon boulevardslvds.). The **Conoco** (✉*1201 Arapahoe Ave., at Broadway* ☎*303/442–6293*) gas station sells inner tubes ($12) and Boulder Creek is less than a block away. The station is open from 10 AM until 9 PM weekdays and Saturday, and 10 AM–8 PM Sunday.

KAYAKING & CANOEING

Kayakers run the slaloms in Clear Creek, Lefthand Canyon, and the South Platte, but Boulder Creek from within Boulder Canyon midway into the city is one of the locals' favorites. Water in the creek can create Class II–III rapids when summer conditions are right. If calmer waters suit your watercraft-handling style, you can take a canoe to or rent one at the **Boulder Reservoir** and paddle about while taking in great views of the Rockies. ⚓*6 mi northeast of downtown. Drive northeast on Rte. 119 and turn left at Jay Rd. Turn right immediately onto 51st St. and drive on to sign that marks entrance station* ☎*303/441–3468* 🔲*$6.*

Alpine Sports (✉*2707 Spruce St.* ☎*303/325–3231 or 877/325–3231*) rents touring and sit-on-top kayaks, canoes, and rafts for $25–$35 per day. Gear packages, which include helmets, oars, and life preservers, rent for $25 a day. Multiday discounts apply.

Boulder Outdoor Center (✉*2525 Arapahoe Ave., Suite E4–228* ☎*303/ 444–8420 or 800/364–9376* ⊕*www.boc123.com*) organizes group rafting trips to rivers on the Front Range and group kayaking instruction.

SNOWSHOEING

Winter sports in Colorado are not limited to skiing. You can strap on a pair of snowshoes and tramp along trails you would walk in summer. Snowshoers pack a lunch and a thermos of hot cocoa, soy chai, or tea, and take in stunning views while getting a bit of exercise. Even in January, the Front Range has milder daytime temperatures and lots of sunny days. Don't forget the sunscreen—at this altitude, you can sunburn quickly in winter. Dressing in layers is advisable; in the forests, you'll be warm, but out in the open, the wind can be frigid.

For $15 per day you can rent snowshoes from **Alpine Sports** (✉2707 *Spruce St.* ☎303/325–3231 or 877/325–3231). Multiday discounts apply.

Brainard Lake has well-marked trails and gorgeous views of the snow-covered Indian Peaks and the Continental Divide. ✛ *5 mi west of Rte. 72 (Peak-to-Peak Hwy.) on Brainard Lake Rd. (Rte. 102) at Ward. Drive west on Rte. 119 to Nederland and turn north at Rte. 72.*

On sunny winter days, snowshoers head to **Peaceful Valley Campground** for crisp pine forest–scented air and plenty of powder. ✛ *Drive 14 mi north from Boulder on U.S. Hwy. 36 to Lyons and turn left at Rte. 7. Continue 12 mi on Rte. 7, then 4 mi south on Rte. 72 (Peak-to-Peak Hwy.).*

6

WHERE TO EAT

★ $$$$ ✗ **Flagstaff House.** Sit on the patio at one of Colorado's finest restaurants and drink in the sublime views of Boulder from the side of Flagstaff Mountain. Executive Chef Mark Monette has fresh fish flown in daily, grows some of the herbs for his cuisine, and is noted for his exquisite combinations of ingredients—some organic—and fanciful, playful presentations. The menu changes daily, but sample inspirations include ruby red trout with salmon and scallops in caviar butter and watercress sauce; buffalo filet mignon and foie gras Wellington; and Tasmanian king salmon with spicy mustard glaze. The wine list is remarkably comprehensive. ✉*1138 Flagstaff Rd.* ☎303/442–4640 ⌖*Reservations essential* ▤*AE, D, DC, MC, V* ☉*No lunch.*

★ $$$$ ✗ **Frasca Food and Wine.** In the Friuli region of Italy, the *frasca* (tree branch) is a historic marker for a neighborhood eatery. At this sign of the frasca, you are warmly welcomed into a friendly, low-key restaurant with impeccable service. Start with the salumi, a platter of northern Italian cured meats: *prosciutto daniele, speck,* and *salumeria biellese coppa,* all sliced in-house at the salumi bar. Entrées include sliced Quebec veal loin salad, house-made tagliatelle, and butter-roasted Atlantic halibut. The extraordinary wine list focuses on Italian regional wines. ✉*1738 Pearl St.* ☎303/442–6966 ⊕*www.frascafoodandwine.com* ⌖*Reservations essential* ▤*AE, D, MC, V* ☉*Closed Sun. No lunch.*

$$$$ ✗ **Gold Hill Inn.** This humble log cabin on the dirt road going through the former mining town of Gold Hill hardly looks like a bastion of haute cuisine, but the six-course, $31 prix-fixe dinner is something to rave about. Entrées may include roast duck with raspberry sauce

or leg of lamb marinated for four days in buttermilk, juniper berries, and cloves. The inn also hosts occasional "murder mystery" nights with professional actors. ⊠ *401 Main St., Gold Hill ⊹ Sunshine Canyon, 10 mi from Boulder, take Mapleton Ave. west from Broadway. It becomes Sunshine Canyon Rd.* ☎ *303/443–6461* ⚠ *Reservations essential* ⊟ *MC, V* ⊘ *Closed Tues. June–Sept., and Mon. and Tues. May and Oct. No lunch.*

$$$$
Fodor's Choice
★

✕ **The Kitchen.** The menu, which highlights seasonal produce, changes almost daily at this casual restaurant. Professionals just off work and those out for an unpretentious evening gather here for an elegant yet relaxed dinner with great service. The ambience is a combination of bistro and New York hot spot and can be a bit loud. Exceptional entrées like the house-made gnocchi in bacon and Parmesan and the pan-seared ahi tuna with mustard vinaigrette and cherry tomatoes are composed from free-range meats and organic and local produce. Don't overlook dessert: peach crumble with a glass of muscatel or the sticky toffee pudding with vanilla ice cream and a cup of robust coffee are heavenly. ⊠ *1039 Pearl St.* ☎ *303/544–5973* ⚠ *Reservations essential* ⊟ *AE, D, MC, V.*

$$$$

✕ **Q's.** Coffered ceilings, half-moon stained-glass windows, and mosaic-style tile floors create a classy feel at this quiet century-old hotel-restaurant, making it ideal for a celebration or romantic evening. The excellent international wine list features a few Colorado wines as well. Colorado peach bruschetta or Hawaiian tuna tartare are delightful starters before entrées like bacon-wrapped pork tenderloin or olive-crusted wild king salmon. If you're in the mood to be surprised try the three-course prix-fixe menu ($35) or the five-course chef's tasting menu ($60). End on a sweet note with a plate of chocolate truffles or a seasonal stone-fruit crisp. ⊠ *2115 13th St., in Hotel Boulderado* ☎ *303/442–4880* ⊟ *AE, D, DC, MC, V.*

$$$

✕ **Aji.** Enjoy a South American cocktail like a *caiparinha, mojito,* or *pisco sour* before dinner in this busy restaurant. The storefront windows let in plenty of light, the seating is spacious, and the service is great. Try *ceviche* (seafood or fish marinated in lime juice and served with fun accompaniments like banana, pickled peppers, mango, or popcorn) or empanadas to start. The presentation of entrées such as the pecan- and chile-crusted catfish, grilled beef short ribs, or the coffee-rubbed beef tenderloin is innovative and stunning. A Chilean walnut tart or a chocolate empanada and a cup of French-press coffee round out a meal here wonderfully. ⊠ *1601 Pearl St.* ☎ *303/442–3464* ⊟ *AE, D, MC, V.*

$$

✕ **Brasserie 1010.** Diners who appreciate great food head here for the casual and spirited atmosphere starting at happy hour from 3 to 6. The formality of the dining room contrasts slightly with the good-time vibe. The bar's backdrop is a huge mirror reminiscent of a certain famous painting by Renoir. The martini list is 20 variations strong, and the wine list features mostly California and French wines. The menu is predominantly French. If you eat here on a Friday, don't miss the bouillabaisse; the broth is buttery smooth and rich with saffron, the seafood melts in your mouth, and the vegetables are crisp-tender.

✉ *1011 Walnut St.* ☎ *303/998–1010* ⟨ *Reservations essential* ▭ *AE, D, DC, MC, V.*

★ $$$ ✗ **Chez Thuy.** The mussels in coconut-and-lemongrass sauce and the soft-shell crabs are wonderful starters before an entrée of seafood or tofu pad thai, frogs' legs in garlic and ginger, grilled quail, or lamp chops. The well-lighted dining room fills up every night with families, students, and those out purely for excellent food, though the relief murals and wallpaper leave something to be desired in ambience. Everything is made fresh to order, portions are ample, and the service is fast and friendly. ✉ *2655 28th St.* ☎ *303/442–1700* ⟨ *Reservations essential* ▭ *AE, D, MC, V.*

★ $$$ ✗ **L'Atelier.** Chef Radek Cerny, who trained with Paul Bocuse, creates delicious French meals lightly influenced by Spanish cuisine. Seafood entrées are his forte, and the red Tasmanian crab salad with oranges is a wonderful starter before an entrée of duck breast rose with cherries. Be sure to save a crust of bread to use as a sippet in the savory sauces before ending with a crunchy Florentine garnished with fresh berries. The extraordinary wine list covers all price ranges and vintages. ✉ *1739 Pearl St.* ☎ *303/442-7233* ▭ *AE, D, MC, V* ⊘ *No lunch weekends.*

$$$ ✗ **Mediterranean Café.** After work, when all of Boulder shows up to enjoy tapas, "the Med" becomes a real scene. If the crowd gets to be too much, try a table on the patio. The decor is Portofino meets Santa Fe, with abstract art, terra-cotta floors, and brightly colored tile. The open kitchen turns out daily specials such as pork saltimbocca, halibut puttanesca, and horseradish-crusted tuna—dishes complemented by an extensive, well-priced wine list. ✉ *1002 Walnut St.* ☎ *303/444–5335* ▭ *AE, D, DC, MC, V.*

$$$ ✗ **Sunflower.** Storefront-size windows allow plenty of light into the colorfully painted dining room where chef and owner Jon Pell serves savory meals based on fresh, organic ingredients, such as tempeh scaloppine in a bamboo steamer. Entrées, like the New York strip steak frites and grilled elk, are exclusively organic and free-range. End your lunch or dinner with chocolate raspberry mousse, creamy and decadent without any dairy product, refined sugar, or eggs (Mr. Pell spent 16 years developing the dessert; he won't share the recipe). Brunch is served on weekends from 10 to 3. ✉ *1701 Pearl St.* ☎ *303/440–0220* ▭ *AE, MC, V* ⊘ *Closed Mon.*

$$ ✗ **Boulder Dushanbe Teahouse.** Unique to Colorado, this teahouse is a gift from Boulder's sister city, Dushanbe, Tajikistan. Tajik artisans hand-crafted the building in a traditional style that includes ceramic Islamic art and a carved, painted ceiling. The menu presents a culinary cross section of the world; your meal could include such dishes as Spanish seafood paella, Burmese coconut curry, or Tabrizi *kooftah* balls (Persian meatballs with dried fruits, nuts, and herbs in a tomato sauce). The house-tea gingerbread is a favorite. Relax during high tea at 3 PM (reservations required) with one of more than 80 varieties of tea. Creekside patio tables have views of Central Park. Brunch is served on weekends. ✉ *1770 13th St.* ☎ *303/442–4993* ▭ *AE, D, MC, V.*

FodorsChoice
★

★ $$ ✕**Kasa Japanese Grill.** Architect Edward Suzuki designed this elegant and understated restaurant for his friend, Mr. Kim, the owner. Black granite tables, wooden flooring, an entryway made with imported Japanese tiles, and inverted white umbrellas hanging from the ceiling create a bright, stylish dining room filled with everyone from the young and hip to professionals. Kim is unwaveringly fastidious about the quality of both his food and his chefs, and the authentic Japanese kushi (meat and vegetable skewers), sushi, and sashimi are the evidence. For a starter, try the "Monkey Brains," avocado tempura with tuna and crab filling topped with roe. Don't miss the Yuzu (a native Japanese citrus fruit) yogurt for dessert. ✉*1468 Pearl St.* ☎*303/938–8888* ⊟*AE, D, MC, V* ⊘*Closed Mon.*

$$ ✕**Sushi Zanmai.** The delicious seafood is prepared fresh, and the wasabi is zesty at Boulder's perennial favorite sushi restaurant, a bright, open place that fills early. Enjoy dinner at a table or sit at the sushi bar and watch the chefs' intricate artwork with food. The miso soup is salty and tangy, and the mochi-ice dessert (a truffle-size bite of ice cream wrapped in a fruit or chocolate-flavored rice paste) is not to be missed. Happy hour for sushi and drinks is Monday–Saturday from 5 to 6:30 and all night on Sunday. The official karaoke night is Saturday (10 to midnight). ✉*1221 Spruce St.* ☎*303/440–0733* ⊟*AE, MC, V* ⊘*No lunch weekends.*

$ ✕**Efrain's.** It's worth the drive to Lafayette for the savory *chile verde* (green chile) that Efrain cooks every day for the burritos. His family's homey café has simple, green-painted arbors and hand-painted tables. The porch is great for relaxing before dinner with a margarita, served in a pint-size mason jar. Efrain prepares low-fat, authentic entrées with fresh beef and succulent pulled chicken. The large-grain rice is light, and refried beans are creamy but not greasy. Finish your meal with a crisp, hot *sopapilla* (a light, fried pastry served hot with honey). Expect to wait for a table on a weekend night. ✉*101 E. Cleveland St., Lafayette* ✛*Drive 11 mi east on Baseline Rd. to Lafayette and turn right on Public Rd.* ☎*303/666–7544* ⊟*AE, D, MC, V* ⊘*Closed Tues.*

¢   ✕**Bliss Organic Ice Cream.** Pick up a pint of Honey Lavender or Lemon Raspberry to take on a picnic, or cool off on a hot day with a scoop in an organic waffle cone while you admire the local artwork for sale on the shop walls. Bliss also serves sandwiches, soups, salads, and coffee. ✉*2425 Canyon Blvd., Suite B* ☎*303/443–9596* ⊟*D, MC, V.*

¢   ✕**Burnt Toast Restaurant.** The hearty breakfasts served until 3 PM are the reason to eat at this homey café in a 100-year-old, four-square house. The restaurant advertises COLD COFFEE AND SURLY SERVICE, but it exceeds expectations. Omelets are hot and fluffy, potatoes savory and crisp, and the buttery coffee cake is laced with spices and nuts. The cappuccinos are crafted carefully, with perfectly frothy caps. Have a light breakfast of home-baked pastries at the coffee bar, or eat in the sunny dining room, which houses an eclectic collection of antique wooden tables. Don't miss the humorous black-and-white photographs of toasters. ✉*1235 Pennsylvania Ave.* ☎*303/440–5200* ⊟*AE, D, DC, MC, V* ⊘*No dinner Mon.*

Quick Bites in Boulder

Healthy, inexpensive, and prepared-to-order food is readily available in Boulder.

For breakfast try a crisp, light brioche or buttery croissant at **Breadworks** (✉ 2644 Broadway ☎ 303/444–5667). Lunch is casseroles or mac and cheese, meat or vegetarian panini—made with one of their artisan breads—or pizza, a savory soup, and a saucer-size cookie. The ginger snaps are spicy and rich. **Illegal Pete's** (✉ 1447 Pearl St. ☎ 303/440–3955 ✉ 1320 College Ave. ☎ 303/444–3055) serves hefty wrap-style burritos made to order with fresh ingredients and a choice of three salsas. If you're hankering for a delicious Philly-style steak-and-cheese sandwich or a New York–style deli sandwich, **Salvaggio's Italian Delicatessen** (✉ 2609 Pearl St. ☎ 303/938–1981 ✉ 1107 13th St. ☎ 303/448–1200 ✉ 1397 Pearl St. ☎ 303/545–6800) will make one to order with your choice of deli meats and cheeses. **Falafel King** (✉ 1314 Pearl St. ☎ 303/449–9321) has excellent pita pockets of hot and crispy falafel, spicy gyros, or marinated grilled chicken breast. Get an order of tabouli, hummus, or dolmas to round out lunch and finish it off with a piece of sweet and gooey baklava. The thin and crispy pizzas at **Abo's** (✉ 637 S. Broadway ☎ 303/494–1274 ✉ 2761 Iris Ave. ☎ 303/443–1921 ✉ 1110 13th St. ☎ 303/443–3199) will not disappoint. Get just a slice or two, or you can order a whole pizza for a family lunch in the park. **Whole Foods** (✉ 2905 Pearl St. ☎ 303/545–6611) has a sushi bar, a deli with ready-made sandwiches, panini, pizza, and a salad bar. **Wild Oats** (✉ 1651 Broadway, at Arapahoe Ave. ☎ 303/442–0909) has glorious produce and picnic supplies. The café has a self-serve salad bar, a juice bar, and a coffee bar, as well as pizza, panini, sandwiches, and baked goods.

¢ ✕**The Laughing Goat.** This bohemian-style café serves bagels, muffins, cinnamon rolls, and granola for breakfast, and sandwiches and soups for lunch. The excellent lattes made with cow, goat, or soy milk have an artistic pattern drawn in the crema. Students like to take up table space with laptops and textbooks, but they'll happily make room for you. Evenings may include live music by local performers. ✉ 1709 Pearl St. ☎ 303/440–4628 ▭ AE, D, MC, V.

WHERE TO STAY

★ $$$$ ▦ **Gold Lake Mountain Resort & Spa.** At this casual resort you can dip into one of four lakeside hot pools, canoe, fly-fish, snowshoe, horseback ride, hike, and partake in luxurious spa treatments while still staying near Eldora Ski Resort and Estes Park. You'll slumber peacefully on luxurious linens in a rustic, 1920s lakeside cabin with a stylish mix of contemporary and antique furnishings. The chef at Alice's Restaurant ($$$$) has a gift for drawing savory and indulgent three- or seven-course meals out of whole, organic ingredients and bakes all pastries and breads on the premises. The rustic, mountain-style dining room has a large stone fireplace and leather chairs for relaxing after dinner. **Pros:** well situated for hiking, professional and attentive staff, closer to

Estes Park than Boulder. **Con:** somewhat remote from Boulder. ✉*3771 Gold Lake Rd., Ward 80481* ✛*32 mi northwest of Boulder (about 45 mins)* ☎*303/459–3544 or 800/450–3544* ⊕*www.goldlake.com* ⤺*19 cabins* ✚*In-room: no a/c, no TV. In-hotel: restaurant, bar, spa, parking (no fee), no-smoking rooms* ▤*AE, D, MC, V.*

$$$$ 🛏 **St. Julien Hotel & Spa.** Unwind in the indulgent luxury of this classy yet casual hotel. The Colorado red-sandstone structure has hardwood walnut floors, marble staircases, and a golden onyx bar. Most rooms have stunning mountain views, and all have custom-made beds with European pillow tops and duvets, photography by local artists, and oversize slate bathrooms with soaking tubs and seamless walk-in showers. The martini bar, T-Zero, is cozy and intimate, or you can stay in with 24-hour room service. The hotel is downtown, minutes by foot from the Boulder Creek Path. **Pros:** convenient downtown location, close to outdoor activities and mountains. **Cons:** large hotel, books early, quite busy. ✉*900 Walnut St., 80302* ☎*720/406–9696 or 877/303–0900* ⊕*www.stjulien.com* ⤺*201 rooms, 11 suites* ✚*In-room: safe, ethernet. In-hotel: restaurant, room service, bar, pool, gym, spa, parking (fee), no-smoking rooms* ▤*AE, D, DC, MC, V.*

★ $$$ 🛏 **The Bradley Boulder Inn.** Elegant and contemporary, this downtown inn has a spacious great room with warm tones and an inviting stone fireplace. Local artwork is on display throughout. Each room is individually decorated, but all have flat-screen TVs, 400-thread-count cotton duvets and bed linens, and Aveda products. Some rooms have Jacuzzi tubs, fireplaces, and/or balconies. Breakfasts feature fresh fruit parfaits, French toast casserole, quiche, and excellent coffee. **Pros:** quiet inn one block from Pearl Street shopping and dining, wine-and-cheese hour daily, privileges at nearby gym. **Cons:** books early, no young children. ✉*2040 16th St., 80302* ☎*303/545–5200 or 800/858–5811* ⊕*www. thebradleyboulder.com* ⤺*12 rooms* ✚*In-room: DVD, ethernet, Wi-Fi. In-hotel: no elevator, parking (no fee), no kids under 12, no-smoking rooms.* ▤*AE, MC, V* ❏*BP.*

$$$ 🛏 **Hotel Boulderado.** The gracious lobby of this elegant 1909 beauty has a soaring stained-glass ceiling, and the mezzanine beckons with romantic nooks galore. When choosing a room, opt for the old building, with spacious quarters filled with period antiques and reproductions. The new wing is plush and comfortable but has less Victorian character. Rooms with mountain views are available on request. The restaurant, Q's ($$$$), is found within. The Catacombs Blues Bar is always hopping and has live music three nights a week. Guests have access to the nearby health club, One Boulder Fitness. **Pros:** well-maintained historic building, downtown location, good restaurants. **Cons:** on busy and noisy streets; large, busy hotel. ✉*2115 13th St., 80302* ☎*303/442–4344 or 800/433–4344* ⊕*www.boulderado.com* ⤺*160 rooms* ✚*In-room: Wi-Fi. In-hotel: 3 restaurants, bars, public Wi-Fi, no-smoking rooms* ▤*AE, D, DC, MC, V.*

Fodor's Choice
★

$$ 🛏 **Briar Rose B&B.** Innkeeper Gary Hardin warmly welcomes guests to his ecologically sound B&B. The inn has received accolades for its commitment to zero waste. The full breakfast is exclusively organic, and the homemade granola is a guest favorite. Tea trays with homemade shortbread cookies are available anytime during the day. There are six rooms in the sturdy, 1890s brick main house and four in the adjacent carriage house. The individually decorated rooms have down comforters, floral carpeting, and flowers stenciled above the headboards, some have wood-burning fireplaces. **Pros:** the only B&B in central Boulder, close to downtown shopping and dining, extensive selection of fine teas. **Cons:** on a busy and noisy street, small inn that books early. ⊠*2151 Arapahoe Ave., 80302* ☎*303/442–3007* ⊕*www.briarrosebb. com* ⌦*10 rooms* ⌂*In-room: no TV (some), Wi-Fi. In-hotel: parking (no fee), no-smoking rooms* ⊟*AE, DC, MC, V* ⦿*BP.*

$$ 🔲**Quality Inn & Suites Boulder Creek.** Just a 10-minute walk from downtown Pearl Street and 5 minutes from the University of Colorado, this hotel provides the personal attention and services of a B&B, including a free hot-breakfast buffet. The caring staff has been known to scrape ice off guests' car windshields. The well-lighted, spacious rooms, with custom iron lamps and wood and leather furniture in rich earth tones, create a sophisticated yet comfortable feel. **Pros:** friendly and personable staff, free off-street parking, close to sights and activities. **Con:** on busy street. ⊠*2020 Arapahoe Ave., 80302* ☎*303/449–7550* ⊕*www. qualityinnboulder.com* ⌦*40 rooms, 6 suites* ⌂*In-room: refrigerator, Wi-Fi. In-hotel: pool, gym, laundry service, public Internet, parking (no fee), no-smoking rooms* ⊟*AE, D, MC, V* ⦿*BP.*

$ 🔲**Colorado Chautauqua Association.** The association was founded in 1898 as part of the Chautauqua movement and still fulfills its charge to provide a venue for recreation and cultural and educational enrichment. The upgraded, fully furnished lodge rooms and cottages retain their unique historic charm and include linens and cooking utensils (in rooms with kitchens), but do not include daily housekeeping. The lawn is a terrific spot for a picnic on a sunny afternoon. The property is in Chautauqua Park at the foot of the Flatirons; myriad hiking trails take you into the mountains right from your front door. **Pros:** unique lodging; arts, dining, and recreation on property; well-kept cabins; amazing views of town and mountains. **Cons:** books very early, facilities fill with nonresidents for various events and dining. ⊠*900 Baseline Rd., 80302* ☎*303/442–3282* ⊕*www.chautauqua.com* ⌦*22 rooms, 60 cottages* ⌂*In-room: no a/c, no phone, no TV, Wi-Fi. In-hotel: restaurant, tennis courts, some pets allowed, no-smoking rooms* ⊟*AE, MC, V.*

$ 🔲**Foot of the Mountain.** This series of tidy connecting rooms with the red doors and colorful flower boxes under the windows is near the mouth of Boulder Canyon and the Boulder Creek Path. It seems far from Boulder's bustle, yet it's only a few minutes' walk from downtown. Each cozy cabin-style room has either a mountain or stream view. Pets can board, too, for an extra charge. **Pros:** excellent value for the area, quiet neighborhood, close to recreation. **Con:** no on-site restaurant. ⊠*200 Arapahoe Ave., 80302* ☎*303/442–5688 or 866/773–5489* ⊕*www. footofthemountainmotel.com* ⌦*18 rooms, 2 suites* ⌂*In-room: no a/c, refrigerator. In-hotel: parking (no fee), some pets allowed, no-smoking rooms* ⊟*AE, D, MC, V.*

NIGHTLIFE & THE ARTS

THE ARTS

FESTIVALS Between late June and early August the **Colorado Music Festival** (✉ *Chautauqua Park, 900 Baseline Rd.* ☎ *303/440–7666 or 303/449–1397* ⊕ *www.coloradomusicfest.org*),30 years old in 2007, brings classical music to Chautauqua Auditorium. Visiting artists have included the Santa Fe Guitar Quartet and the Takács Quartet, as well as plenty of international talent such as William Barton, a didgeridoo performer from Australia, and Lynn Harrell, who plays a 1673 Stradivarius. Evening meals are available in the dining hall, or pack a picnic and settle in on the Green to take in views of the mountains before the concert.

> ### COLORADO CHAUTAUQUA MOVEMENT
>
> The Colorado Chautauqua National Historic Landmark is on 26 acres in Boulder at the base of the foothills. It opened on July 4, 1898, and is the only remaining Chautauqua west of the Mississippi River in continuous operation with its original buildings. One of only three in the United States today, it was once one of 12,000 venues on the national circuit where educational speeches and artistic performances took place. You can still attend concerts, lectures, and a silent film series as well as eat year-round in the Chautauqua in Boulder.

Fodor'sChoice
★ CU's Mary Rippon Outdoor Theater is the venue for the annual **Colorado Shakespeare Festival** (☎ *303/492–0554* ⊕ *www.coloradoshakes.org*), presenting the bard's comedies and tragedies from early July to mid-August.

THEATER, **Boulder Philharmonic** (✉ *2995 Wilderness Pl., Suite 100, 80301* ✉ *University of Colorado, Macky Auditorium and Old Main Theatre* ☎ *303/449–1343* ⊕ *www.boulderphil.org*) presents its own concert season, as well as chamber music concerts, the Boulder Ballet Ensemble, and performances by visiting divas such as Kathleen Battle.

At the University of Colorado, the superb **College of Music** (☎ *303/492–8008* ⊕ *www.cuconcerts.org*) presents concerts year-round, including chamber music by the internationally renowned Takács String Quartet.

The **Department of Theater and Dance** (☎ *303/492–8181* ⊕ *www.colorado.edu/theatredance*) stages excellent student productions throughout the year.

The **Dairy Center for the Arts** (☎ *303/440–7826* ⊕ *www.thedairy.org*) hosts art shows in the gallery featuring local painters. The center is also a venue for locally produced plays; music, ballet, and dance performances; and film.

Concerts take place throughout summer at Boulder's peaceful **Chautauqua Community Hall** (✉ *900 Baseline Rd.* ☎ *303/442–3282* ⊕ *www.chautauqua.com*). Performers have included Branford Marsalis, Hot Rize, k.d. lang, and the Afro Celt Sound System.

The art deco **Boulder Theater** (✉ *2032 14th St.* ☎ *303/786–7030* ⊕ *www. bouldertheater.com*) is a venue for top touring bands and movies as well as for the radio show *E-Town* (*www.etown.org*). E-Town emcees Helen and Nick Forster host musical talent and discuss environmental and community issues.

Dine while you catch a popular Broadway musical at **Boulder's Dinner Theater** (✉ *5501 Arapahoe Ave.* ☎ *303/449–6000* ⊕ *www.theatrein boulder.com*).

NIGHTLIFE

BARS & LOUNGES Business lunches and after-work gatherings take place at the **Corner Bar** (✉ *2115 13th St.* ☎ *303/442–4344*) in the Hotel Boulderado. It's a contemporary American pub with outdoor seating. **Foundry** (✉ *1109 Walnut St.* ☎ *303/447–1803*) is where the hip of all ages hang out; in back is a cigar bar and smoking parlor, and above is a rooftop deck with its own bar. The main bar has 11 pool tables and a mezzanine overlooking all the action. The cozy **Pearl Street Pub** (✉ *1108 Pearl St.* ☎ *303/939–9900*), with its long brick wall and sports pictures, is a great place to chat over a quiet drink. There's pool and darts downstairs if you're in the mood for a game. Bartenders at **Rio Grande Mexican Restaurant** (✉ *1101 Walnut St.* ☎ *303/444–3690*) make Boulder's best margaritas (no frilly variations—just classic margs).

The **West End Tavern** (✉ *926 Pearl St.* ☎ *303/444–3535*), with its rooftop deck, is a popular after-work hangout serving good pub grub.

BREWPUBS & BREWERIES The **Mountain Sun Pub & Brewery** (✉ *1535 Pearl St.* ☎ *303/546–0886*) crafts 57 beers throughout the year, and there are always about 18 on tap. A favorite of Boulderites is the Colorado Kind, a nicely hopped amber. Tours are available upon request. Stay to have a burger or for the live music Sunday nights. **RedFish FishHouse and Brewery** (✉ *2027 13th St.* ☎ *303/440–5858* ⊕ *www.redfishbrewhouse.com*) has some sidewalk seating and is always busy serving its own beers to wash down tasty appetizers at happy hour. The **Walnut Brewery** (✉ *1123 Walnut St.* ☎ *303/447–1345* ⊕ *www.walnutbrewery.com*) always has seven brews and two cask-conditioned ales on tap. A new seasonal is tapped each month, and every season sees a new wheat beer on tap. Try the Buffalo Gold ale or the malty St. James Irish Red Ale. The excellent beer goes well with the upscale pub fare like mahi tacos, smoked salmon fish-and-chips, and the buffalo fajitas. Tours are available anytime.

MUSIC & DANCE CLUBS The art deco **Fox Theater** (✉ *1135 13th St.* ☎ *303/443–3399*) movie palace hosts touring music talent. Whether DJs are spinning for '80s or hip-hop night, there's dancing every night Wednesday through Sunday at **Round Midnight** (✉ *1005 Pearl St.* ☎ *303/442–2176*) and live music every Friday. There's live music, from reggae to samba, every night and dancing Wednesday through Sunday at the **Trilogy Wine Bar** (✉ *2017 13th St.* ☎ *303/473–9463*). **Rock 'n Soul Cafe** (✉ *5290 Arapahoe Ave.* ☎ *303/443–5108* ⊕ *www.rocknsoulcafe.com* ◷ *Mon. –Sat. 8* AM *–11* PM) serves up live music six nights per week accompanied by espresso drinks and wine by the glass. The café does serve some food: soups, teriyaki, and pastries.

SHOPPING

SHOPPING NEIGHBORHOODS

Boulder's **Pearl Street Mall** (⊠ *Pearl St. between 11th and 15th Sts.*) is a shopping extravaganza, with upscale boutiques, art galleries, bookstores, shoe shops, and stores with home and garden furnishings. Street musicians and magicians, caricaturists, and buskers with lovebirds are magnets for locals and visitors. Stroll along **Twenty-Ninth Street** (⊠ *29th St. between Arapahoe Ave. and Pearl St.*), Boulder's newest area to shop, and pick up a pair of shoes, some outdoor gear, a funny greeting card, or a present to bring home for your pooch. The mall has plenty of nationally known clothiers, a bookstore, a stationer, coffee shops, and eateries. **University Hill** (or "the Hill"), centered around 13th Street between College Avenue and Pennsylvania Street, is a great place for hip duds, new and used CDs, and CU apparel." One of the metropolitan area's most popular shopping centers is **Flatiron Crossing** (⊠ *U.S. 36 between Boulder and Denver* ☎ *720/887–9900*) in Broomfield. Shoppers can hit stores such as Nordstrom, Coach, Borders, and Sharper Image; browse at a few locally owned jewelers and galleries; and take a break in the food court or in one of the restaurants.

ANTIQUES

Serendipitous discoveries and glorious antique furniture, jewelry, and silver services move fast at the **Amazing Garage Sale** (⊠ *4919 N. Broadway* ☎ *303/447–0417*), so it's worth a couple of visits while you're in Boulder.

BOOKSTORES

Boulder has one of the largest concentrations of used-book sellers in the United States. Most shops are on Pearl Street between 8th and 20th streets. Some specialize in titles such as computer books, works of the beat generation, or mysteries.

★ **Boulder Bookstore** (⊠ *1107 Pearl St.* ☎ *303/447–2074*) has thousands of new and used books in all genres, including a great selection of photography, history, and art books about Colorado. It also carries a few out-of-town and foreign newspapers and periodicals.

Mystery fans will find just the right thriller from the huge selection at **High Crimes** (⊠ *946 Pearl St.* ☎ *303/443–8346*).

Sip a robust latte from the in-house café at **Trident Booksellers** (⊠ *940 Pearl St.* ☎ *303/443–3133*) while browsing the eclectic collection of mostly used books—including foreign language, but also many new books at mark-down prices.

Word Is Out (⊠ *2015 10th St.* ☎ *303/449–1415*) carries an excellent collection of gay and lesbian fiction and nonfiction as well as titles on feminism and women's studies. The shop also sells music CDs and some gift items.

CHILDREN'S ITEMS

Boulder kids' favorite store to buy new toys is **Grandrabbit's Toy Shoppe** (⊠*2525 Arapahoe Ave.* ☎*303/443–0780*). **Into the Wind** (⊠*1408 Pearl St.* ☎*303/449–5906* ⊕*www.intothewind.com*) sells traditional and creatively designed kites, imaginative wind decorations, flags, and boomerangs.**Little Mountain** (⊠*1136 Spruce St.* ☎*303/443–1757*) carries outdoor clothing for children, and rents child-carrier backpacks and all-terrain strollers.**Play Fair Toys** (⊠*1690 28th St.* ☎*303/444–7502*)sells Lego and Brio brands as well as books for various ages, puzzles, and fun items like robotic tarantulas and "brain kits.""

CLOTHING BOUTIQUES

Alpaca Connection (⊠*1326 Pearl St.* ☎*303/447–2047*) offers Indian silks, Bolivian alpaca, and Ecuadorian merino-wool garments. **Fresh Produce** (⊠*1218 Pearl St.* ☎*303/442–7507*) is a Boulder-based company that makes brightly colored and whimsically designed cotton clothing for women and children. **Jacque Michelle** (⊠*2670 Broadway* ☎*303/786–7628*) has fashionably casual yet unpretentious women's clothing. The store also sells fun greeting cards and cutting edge gifts.

CRAFTS & ART GALLERIES

Art Source International (⊠*1237 Pearl St.* ☎*303/444–4080*) is Colorado's largest antique print and map dealer. **Boulder Arts & Crafts Cooperative** (⊠*1421 Pearl St.* ☎*303/443–3683*), owned by 45 artists, is popular for pottery and photography. The 150-odd Colorado artists represented create everything from hand-painted silk scarves and hand-woven garments to glass art and furniture. **Hangouts** (⊠*1328 Pearl St.* ☎*303/442–2533*) carries Mayan- and Brazilian-design handmade hammocks. **Middle Fish** (⊠*1500 Pearl St.* ☎*303/443–0835*) has quirky one-of-a-kind clocks crafted from a combination of metals, locally made jewelry, mosaic mirrors, and unusual gifts. **SmithKlein Gallery** (⊠*1116 Pearl St.* ☎*303/444–7200*) showcases beautiful modern art—glass and bronze sculpture, jewelry, and paintings.

FARMERS' MARKET
GIFT STORES

Belvedere Chocolate Shop (⊠*1468 Pearl St., No. 120* ☎*303/447–0336*)makes and sells chocolates. Pick up "three hearts in a heart" for your own sweetheart (three heart-shape chocolates inside a chocolate heart) at home. The hot chocolate is made to order with melted Belgian chocolate and can become a "Belvedere Bliss" by adding hazelnut paste. **Paper Doll** (⊠*1141 Pearl St.* ☎*303/449–1661*) is an eclectic and original gift shop of usual and unusual items—something for everyone from classy stationery and wrapping paper to jewelry and porcelain teapots shaped like cats. **Two Hands Paperie** (⊠*803 Pearl St.* ☎*303/444–0124*) carries elegant European stationery, handmade paper, and handcrafted, leather-bound journals. Try out a stylish, European fountain pen, and select a well of emerald or havana ink to fill it. **Where the Buffalo Roam** (⊠*1320 Pearl St.* ☎*303/938–1424*) sells quirky T-shirts, CU and Colorado souvenirs, and tacky trinkets.

HOME & GARDEN

The store to visit for the finest selection in crockery, cookware, table linen, and kitchen utensils (many from Europe), as well as gourmet food items and cookbooks, is **Peppercorn** (⊠ *1235 Pearl St.* ☎ *303/449– 5847 or 800/447–6905).* Gardeners will find treasures at the **West End Gardener** (⊠ *777 Pearl St.* ☎ *303/938–0607),* purveyors of vintage garden tools and accessories.

OUTDOOR GEAR

Boulder Army Store (⊠ *1545 Pearl St.* ☎ *303/442–7616)* packs the racks and shelves tightly with genuine, name-brand, surplus outdoor clothing and camping gear marked a few dollars less than regular retail. **McGuckin Hardware** (⊠ *Village Shopping Center, 2525 Arapahoe St.* ☎ *303/443–1822)* is a Boulder institution that stocks home appliances and gadgets, hardware, and a mind-boggling array of outdoor merchandise. The omniscient salespeople know where everything is. **REI** (⊠ *1789 28th St.* ☎ *303/583–9970)* carries outdoor equipment for all sports and has some rental gear.

EN ROUTE   Scenic Sunshine Canyon Road/Gold Hill Road links Boulder to the Peak-to-Peak Highway (Route 72) near Ward. Drive west from Broadway on Mapleton Avenue, which becomes Sunshine Canyon Road at the mouth of Sunshine Canyon and then Gold Hill Road farther up the canyon. This largely untraveled shortcut to Estes Park is only partially paved, but suitable for all vehicles. You'll wind through Sunshine Canyon up to the ridge with views of the Indian Peaks and the Continental Divide. The road drops down into the former mining town of Gold Hill with a current population of 118.

SIDE TRIP TO NEDERLAND

16 mi west of Boulder via Canyon Blvd. (Rte. 119).

A former mining and mill town at the top of Boulder Canyon and on the scenic Peak-to-Peak Highway, "Ned" embodies that small, mountain-town spirit in look and attitude: laid-back, independent, and friendly. All the legends of its gold-mining past notwithstanding (the now-extinct town of Caribou was the locus of the gold mining), Nederland was well known for its tungsten mining during World War I. Around town you'll see references to "wolf's tongue," a word play on wolframite, the ore from which tungsten is extracted. The downtown retains the character of its gold-milling days and has several good bars, cafés, and restaurants. Shops sell used books, antiques, organic groceries, fabrics, and gemstones. Nederland is the gateway to skiing at Eldora Mountain Resort and high-altitude hiking in the Indian Peaks Wilderness.

★   The **Peak-to-Peak Highway,** which winds from Central City through Nederland to Estes Park, is not the quickest route to the eastern gateway to Rocky Mountain National Park, but is certainly the most scenic. You'll pass through the old mining towns of Ward and Allenspark and enjoy spectacular mountain vistas. Mount Meeker and Longs Peak rise magnificently behind every bend in the road. The descent into Estes Park provides grand vistas of snow-covered alpine peaks and green valleys.

An afternoon drive along this route is a rite of autumn, when the sky is deeper blue and stands of aspens distinguish themselves from the evergreen pine forests with golden leaves. A stop at Boulder Falls is de rigueur; the route can take a couple of directions after Nederland. You could continue on to Estes Park via Routes 72 and 7 for a relaxing dinner as the sun sets behind the peaks of Rocky Mountain National Park. Or, turn off just before Ward to the former mining town of Gold Hill for dinner. Then wind down Sunshine Canyon as the lights of nighttime Boulder flicker before you. ✧ *From Nederland drive north on Hwy. 72. Turn left at intersection with Hwy. 7 and continue to Estes Park.*

FESTIVALS   The Nederland Music & Arts Festival, a weekend of bluegrass, world beat, and jazz music known as the **NedFest** (⊕ *www.nedfest.com*), takes place in late August on the west shore of Barker Reservoir. A couple of thousand people come to relax in the sun, dance, or stroll by the art stands. Entrance ($22–$90) is steep, but children under 12 get in for free.

SPORTS & THE OUTDOORS

HIKING   If you aren't used to it, high altitude can catch you off guard. Drink plenty of water to help stave off the effects of altitude sickness—dizziness, shortness of breath, headache, and nausea. Slather on the sunscreen—it's easy to get sunburned up here. And, in summer, an early morning start is best, as afternoon thunderstorms are frequent and potentially dangerous above the tree line.

★   The **Indian Peaks Wilderness** has some of the most popular hiking in the area, and you'll always have company on the trails in summer. Wildflowers are prolific and peak in late July and early August. Cinquefoil, harebell, stonecrop, flax, wild geranium, yarrow, larkspur, lupine, and columbine, the state flower, all mix in a mosaic of colors on the slopes and in the meadows. Parking at trailheads in the wilderness area is limited, so plan to start out early in the day. "No Parking" signs are posted, and, if the designated parking lot is full, the etiquette is to park your car on the outbound side of the road at a spot where there's still room for vehicles to pass. There's no central access point to the area; contact the U.S. Forest Service or check its Web site for trail information and driving directions. Permits are not required for day visitors.

The easy, 2.5-mi (round-trip) hike to **Lost Lake** has enough altitude to give you views of the high peaks under the brilliant blue sky. You'll gain a mere 777 feet on this two-hour walk. The well-traveled trail to **Diamond Lake** starts out as the Arapaho Pass Trail at the Fourth of July trailhead. It's steep as you climb through the pines, but the elevation gain between the trailhead and the lake is only 1,191 feet. The trail levels off and follows along the side of the valley at 10,400 feet with endless views of Jasper Peak and the Arapaho Peaks. In late July when the snowfields are gone, the wildflowers cover the slopes and meadows with bursts of color. At the junction with the Diamond Lake trailhead to the left, the trail passes a waterfall and crosses a stream (with a bridge) before it descends to Diamond Lake. Relax at the lake and enjoy the views before returning. Allow three hours to hike the 4-mi round-trip. ⊠*Boulder Ranger District Office, Arapaho National Forest, 2140 Yarmouth Ave.* ☎*303/541–2500 or 303/541–2519* ⊕*www. fs.fed.us/arnf/recreation/wilderness/indianpeaks/index.shtml.*

The **DeLonde Trail/Blue Bird Loop** at the Caribou Ranch Open Space is an easy 4.5-mi walk through forests and meadows with wildflowers. An elk herd resides on the open space, so listen for the bulls bugling in fall. The 1.2-mi DeLonde Trail starts to the left of the trailhead information kiosk and connects to the Blue Bird Loop just above the former DeLonde homestead site. You can take a break at the picnic table overlooking the pond near the ranch house before continuing on the loop to the former Blue Bird Mine complex. Allow about one to two hours to complete the hike. ⊹*Trailhead: From Nederland, drive north on CO Hwy. 72 to County Rd. 126, turn left, and go 1 mi to trailhead.*

Indian Peaks Ace Hardware (⊠*74 Hwy. 119* ☎*303/258–3132*) is a good place to get information, maps, and gear. You can get water and food for your hike at the **B&F Mountain Market** (⊠*60 E. Lakeview Dr.* ☎*303/258–3105*) in town.

SKIING & SNOW-BOARDING   With a 1,600-foot vertical drop (the longest run is 3 mi), **Eldora Mountain Resort** has 53 trails, 12 lifts, and 680 acres; 25 mi (40 km) of groomed Nordic track; and four terrain parks accommodating different ability levels for snowboarders and skiers. Tucked away in the mountains at 9,200 feet (summit elevation is 10,800 feet), Eldora's annual snowfall is more than 300 inches. The Indian Peaks Lodge rents skis, runs a ski school, and has a cafeteria-style restaurant. ⊹*5 mi west of Nederland off Hwy. 119* ☎*303/440–8700* ⊕*www.eldora.com* ☜*$53* ⊙*Mid-Nov.–mid-Apr., weekdays 9–4; weekends and holidays 8:30–4.*

WHERE TO STAY & EAT

$–$$ ✕**Savory Café.** The menu ranges from Cajun-blackened rib-eye steak to chicken marsala to Korean beef BBQ in this bright and striking café. The lunch menu is mostly hot sandwiches and includes a Kobe beef burger. Join the locals and other day-trippers for a casual Sunday brunch that includes cinnamon-apple fritters, seven-grain French toast with strawberries, and flavorful omelets. If you're passing through on a Friday evening, stop in for the fish fry. ⊠ *20 E. Lakeview Dr., north side of Caribou Shopping Center, ground level* ☎ *303/258–7329* ⊟*AE, D, DC, MC, V*

$–$$ ✕**Backcountry Pizza & Subs.** Although the decor is not much to get excited about, the pizza at this locals hangout is. Select a pie from the menu or create your own combo. The toppings include all the usual candidates as well as sun-dried tomatoes, pine nuts, banana peppers, and broccoli. Pizza by the slice is also available. ⊠ *20 E. Lakeview Dr., south side of Caribou Shopping Center, 2nd level* ☎ *303/258–0176* ⊟*MC, V*

$ 🏨 **Best Western Lodge at Nederland.** Built in 1994 with rough-hewn timber, this lodge is ultramodern within. Upstairs rooms have cathedral ceilings, and those downstairs have gas fireplaces; all are spacious and have coffeemakers and hair dryers. The enthusiastic staff will help to arrange any outdoor activity you desire—and the possibilities are just about endless. An excellent choice for those who want to be central, the property is within a half-hour's drive of Boulder, the Eldora ski area, and Central City. **Pros:** property has mountain style, in spite of being a franchise; quiet; good value for location. **Cons:** Nederland can feel remote unless you're spending a lot of time hiking and skiing, hotel is on a heavily traveled road. ✉*55 Lakeview Dr., Nederland 80466* ☎*303/258–9463 or 800/279–9463* ⇨*23 rooms, 1 suite* ⚒*In-room: no a/c, refrigerator, Wi-Fi. In-hotel: parking (no fee), no-smoking rooms* ▤*AE, D, DC, MC, V* ⏐◎⏐*CP.*

SIDE TRIP TO NIWOT

10 mi northeast of downtown Boulder via the Diagonal Hwy. (Rte. 119).

Niwot is the Arapaho Indian word for "left hand," and this is where Chief Niwot (born circa 1820) and his tribe lived along the banks of Left Hand Creek until the early 1860s. European settlers arrived in the latter half of the 1800s to take up farming after gold mining in the mountains became less lucrative. The town's importance grew once the railroad came in the 1870s. Antiques aficionados have made Niwot their mecca in Boulder County. The historic district, full of brick buildings decorated with flower boxes, runs along 2nd Avenue and the cross streets Franklin and Murray.

EN ROUTE

On the way to Niwot from Boulder, you pass by the Celestial Seasonings tea factory and the Leanin' Tree Museum of Western Art. Both are worth a visit, so plan an extra hour or two if you stop.

Celestial Seasonings, North America's largest herbal-tea producer (sealing 8 million tea bags every 24 hours), offers free tours of its factory. Before the tour, you can sample from more than 60 varieties of tea. The famous "Mint Room" will clear your tear ducts and sinuses. ✉*4600 Sleepytime Dr.,* ✛ *8 mi northeast of downtown Boulder* ☎*303/581–1202* ⊕*www.celestialseasonings.com* ▨*Free* ◎*Tours hourly; Mon.–Sat. 10–3, Sun. 11–3.*

The **Leanin' Tree Museum of Western Art** is one of the country's largest privately owned collections of post-1950 cowboy and Western art. More than 200 paintings of Western landscapes, wildlife, and the pioneers' ranch life, and 85 bronze sculptures by renowned, contemporary artists including Bill Hughes and Frank McCarthy, recall an era in the Boulder Valley before lattes. ✉*6055 Longbow Dr.* ☎*303/530–1442* ⊕*www.leanintreemuseum.com* ▨*Free* ◎ *Weekdays 8–5, weekends 10–5.*

WHERE TO STAY & EAT

$$ ✕**Treppeda's.** For lunch try a tasty panini made from authentic ingredients and fresh focaccia at this casual and elegant Italian café with shaded outdoor seating. Enjoy a crunchy house-made cannoli or cookie and an espresso for dessert at the bar. Dinner in the cozy terra-cotta-painted dining room with classy paintings features traditional dishes like primavera gnocchi, lemon and garlic shrimp bucatini, and lamb

Siciliana along with some delicious daily specials like roasted white sea bass. Desserts include *tres leches* cake, berry napoleon, and chocolate truffles with fresh strawberries. ✉*300 2nd Ave.* ☎*303/652–1607* ▤*AE, MC, V* ⊘*Closed Sun.*

¢ ✕**Eye Opener.** This small coffeehouse serves delicious coffee drinks, breakfast burritos, and bagels plus gourmet sandwiches and fresh pastries, muffins, and Danishes. ✉*136 2nd Ave.* ☎*303/652–8137* ▤*MC, V* ⊘*No dinner.*

$$ ⌂**Niwot Inn.** A wood-trim, two-story, vaulted atrium gives the feel of a grand Colorado lodge, but with a more-contemporary and understated elegance. The inviting sitting room with a grand fireplace, hardwood floors with carpets, and leather couches is where the complimentary breakfast buffet is served. Colorado mountain scenery is rendered in photographs and chalk drawings found throughout the inn. Spacious, handsome rooms, all named for Colorado "Fourteeners," are done in light tones and are outfitted with such luxuries as custom-made duvet covers and writing desks. Some rooms have gas fireplaces and sitting chairs. **Pros:** off the beaten path and in a nice area, quiet neighborhood, close to excellent restaurants. **Con:** drive to Boulder can be horribly congested. ✉*342 2nd Ave.* ⌖*Box 1044, Niwot 80544* ☎*303/652–8452* ⊕*www.niwotinn.com* ⇱*14 rooms* ᏟᏂ*In-room: Wi-Fi. In-hotel: no elevator, public Wi-Fi, parking (no fee), no-smoking rooms* ▤*AE, D, DC, MC, V* ⍾*CP.*

SHOPPING

Antiques dealers and a few notable shops selling vintage women's clothing and quilts are in the Niwot historic district along 2nd Avenue. Just 0.25 mi east of old-town Niwot is Cottonwood Square, with a grocer, a gas station, a handful of gift shops, and a few eateries, including a Chinese restaurant.

Niwot Antiques (✉*135 2nd Ave.* ☎*303/652–2587*) has a large selection of antiques and antique furniture. **Wise Buys Antiques** (✉*190 2nd Ave.* ☎*303/652–2888*) restores fireplace mantels—some with mirrors—and usually has more than a hundred in stock.

SIDE TRIP TO LYONS

14 mi north of Boulder on U.S. 36.

Lyons is the Front Range's ideal feng shui town according to resident Timothy Oakes, professor and expert in the geography of China—a quirky yet appropriate description for this peaceful, down-to-earth community just inside the red-sandstone foothills at the confluence of the North St. Vrain and South St. Vrain creeks. The cafés, restaurants, art galleries, and antiques stores serve more than just the small population of 1,600. Visitors also come for the recreation opportunities and top-notch music festivals.

FESTIVALS The many professional musicians and instrument makers who live in Lyons are behind its vibrant music scene. The summer outdoor music season kicks off with **Lyons Good Old Days** at the end of June, and goes into September with midweek concerts in Sandstone Park (at 4th and Railroad avenues). Cafés and restaurants host bands regularly, and some residents even invite performers to use their living rooms as stages. For information about current events, check the Web site ⊕*www.musicinlyons.com.*

Planet Bluegrass (☎*303/823–0848 or 800/624–2422 ⊕www.bluegrass. com*) presents artists such as the Indigo Girls, Patty Griffin, and Warren Haynes at the three bluegrass festivals it holds in Lyons: RockyGrass, at the end of July, the Folks Festival in August, and the Festival of the Mabon in September.

SPORTS & THE OUTDOORS

BIRD-WATCHING Ornithologists gather at **Bohn Park** at sunrise and sunset to spot some of the many species of songbirds that reside along St. Vrain Creek. Golden eagles have been sighted in the red cliffs on the southwest side of town. Lazuli Buntings inhabit the foliage along both the **Old St. Vrain Road** southwest of town and **Apple Valley Road** northwest of town. ⌖*From northbound U.S. 36, turn left onto Park St. and then left onto 2nd St.*

HIKING & MOUNTAIN BIKING ★ More than 12 mi of trails at **Hall Ranch** are open to hikers, mountain bikers, and equestrians. The **Bitterbrush Trail/Nelson Loop** follows the Bitterbrush Trail for 3.7 mi and has a 680-foot elevation gain, crossing meadows and ascending and descending through stands of pine trees and rock outcroppings. It connects to the 2.2-mi Nelson Loop, which leads to the original Nelson Ranch House. The slight 400-foot elevation gain of the Nelson Loop brings you up onto a plateau that provides great views of the mountains to the north. Allow five to six hours to hike the trail and get back to the trailhead, less for cycling it. ⊠*Boulder County Parks and Open Space,* ⌖*0.75 mi west of Lyons on Hwy. 7 ⊕www.co.boulder.co.us/openspace.*

Rabbit Mountain has several lengthy but easy trails that afford views of the High Rockies and the plains. Be sure to pick up the interpretive pamphlet at the trailhead that explains the history of the area, including the dramatic metamorphosis of Rabbit Mountain from a lush, tropical swamp inhabited by dinosaurs to the present-day, mile-high desert that's home to raptors, prairie dogs, coyotes, and the occasional rattlesnake. The 2-mi round-trip **Little Thompson Overlook Trail** forks off to the left before you come to the gravel road and climbs a mere 500 feet to the point where you can see Longs Peak, the plains to the east, and Boulder Valley to the south. The 5-mi **Eagle Wind Trail** loop has short spurs to viewpoints. From the parking area head out on the trail to the gravel road and then right onto the single-track loop. ⊠*Boulder County Parks and Open Space,* ⌖*2 mi east of Lyons ⊕www. co.boulder.co.us/openspace.*

WHERE TO EAT

$$$ ✕**Gateway Café.** Locals head here to enjoy an upscale fusion of Japanese and Western cuisines in a casual atmosphere. Start with some vegetarian or shrimp *gyozas* (dumplings) and move on to tempura soft-shell crabs with wasabi sauce. Grass-fed lamb chops and chokecherry braised buffalo short ribs are just two of the succulent organic meat dishes that are smoked and then grilled. Produce is grown locally and organically. Enjoy a slice of award-winning pie with flaky, buttery crust for dessert. The cozy dining room is filled with paintings, stained glass, and a huge wood-frame mirror. ✉*432 Main St.* ☎*303/823–5144* ▭*AE, MC, V* ⊘*Closed Mon. and Tues. No lunch.*

$$ ✕**Oskar Blues Brewery.** Try Dale's Pale Ale; it's not as hoppy as most American ales and took first place in an exclusive ale tasting by the *New York Times*. Cajun specialties, gourmet burgers, and pizza are on the menu at this lively brewpub, decorated with blues instruments and covers of blues CDs. Tours are available by appointment. ✉*303 Main St.* ☎*303/823–6685* ▭*AE, D, MC, V.*

ESTES PARK

40 mi northwest of Boulder via U.S. 36 (28th St. in Boulder) and U.S. 34.

The scenery on the U.S. 36 approach to Estes Park gives little hint of the grandeur to come. If ever there was a classic picture-postcard Rockies view, Estes Park has it. The town is at an altitude of more than 7,500 feet before a stunning backdrop of 14,255-foot Longs Peak and surrounding mountains. The town itself is very family-oriented, albeit somewhat kitschy: many of the small hotels lining the roads are mom-and-pop outfits that have been passed down through several generations.

As a resort town, Estes attracted the attention of genius entrepreneur F. O. Stanley, inventor of the Stanley Steamer automobile and several photographic processes. In 1905, having been told by his doctors he would soon die of tuberculosis, he constructed the regal **Stanley Hotel** on a promontory overlooking the town. Stanley went on to live another 30-odd years, an extension that he attributed to the area's fresh air. The hotel soon became one of the most glamorous resorts in the Rockies, a reputation it holds to this day. The hotel was the inspiration for Stephen King's horror novel, *The Shining,* part of which he wrote while staying here.

Archaeological evidence displayed at the **Estes Park Area Historical Museum** makes an eloquent case that Native Americans used the area as a summer resort. The museum also has an assortment of pioneer artifacts, displays on the founding of Rocky Mountain National Park, and changing exhibits. The museum publishes a self-guided walking tour of historic sites, mostly along Elkhorn Avenue downtown. ✉*200 4th St.* ☎*970/586–6256* ▭*Free* ⊘*May–Oct., Mon.–Sat. 10–5, Sun. 1–5; Nov.–Apr., Fri. and Sat. 10–5, Sun. 1–5.*

The **MacGregor Ranch Museum,** on the National Register of Historic Places and a working ranch, offers views of the Twin Owls and Longs Peak (towering more than 14,000 feet). Although the ranch was homesteaded in 1873, the present house was built in 1896; it provides a well-preserved record of typical ranch life. ⊠*MacGregor Ave. off U.S. 34* ☎*970/586–3749* ⊠*$3* ⊙*June–Aug., Tues.–Fri. 10–4.*

WORD OF MOUTH

"Estes Park is kinda kitschy, but it's a great gateway to the truly spectacular Rocky Mountain National Park. It's true that it can snow in May, so be prepared for cold weather in the higher altitudes (it snowed several inches in Boulder on my graduation on May 9)."

—katks

OFF THE BEATEN PATH

Trail Ridge Winery. Colorado may not show up on oenologists' maps with California and France, but grapes once grew wild in the state, and today they are cultivated for wines. This inconspicuous winery produces a spicy gewürztraminer, buttery chardonnays, oakey merlots, creamy Rieslings, and smooth cabernet sauvignons, all with grapes from Colorado's famous fruit-growing regions near Grand Junction. ⊠*4113 W. Eisenhower Blvd., U.S. 34, Loveland* ✛*drive east on U.S. 34 from Estes Park. The winery is on the left side of U.S. 34 before the city. Watch for the sign on the left as you leave the canyon* ☎*970/635–0949* ⊕*www.trailridgewinery. com* ⊙*Daily 10–5:30.*

SPORTS & THE OUTDOORS

Rocky Mountain National Park, 4 mi from Estes Park, is ideal for hiking, fishing, wildlife viewing, rock climbing, snowshoeing, and cross-country skiing. *See the Rocky Mountain National Park chapter in this book.*

FISHING The Big Thompson River, east of Estes Park along U.S. 34, is popular for its good stock of rainbow and brown trout. Anyone older than 16 needs a Colorado fishing license, which you can obtain at local sporting-goods stores. See *www.wildlife.state.co.us/fishing* for more information. **Rocky Mountain Adventures** (☎970/586–6191 or 800/858–6808) offers guided fly- and float-fishing trips on the Cache la Poudre River.

HORSEBACK RIDING **Sombrero Ranch** (☎970/586–4577) leads one- to two-hour trail rides through the Estes Park region, including Rocky Mountain National Park. They also offer breakfast rides and steak dinner rides.

RAFTING & KAYAKING White-water rafting trips fill up fast, so it's a good idea to book with an outfitter a couple of weeks in advance.

Rapid Transit Rafting (☎970/586–8852 or 800/367–8523) arranges guided rafting trips on the Colorado and Cache la Poudre rivers.

Rocky Mountain Adventures (☎970/493–4005 or 800/858–6808 ⊕*www. shoprma.com*) provides half- and full-day kayaking-instruction trips on Lake Estes. All gear is included.

WHERE TO STAY & EAT

$$$ ✕**Hunter's Chophouse.** This popular steak house fills quickly in the evening, and for good reason. The locals head here for the savory and spicy barbecue: steaks, venison, buffalo, chicken, and seafood. If you're not hungry enough for a 20-ounce porterhouse steak, Hunter's has gourmet burgers like the avocado bacon burger and a list of sandwiches that spans a traditional French dip and salmon pancetta on focaccia. There's a good kids' menu, too, with fish-and-chips, a junior sirloin, and a mini chophouse burger. ✉*1690 Big Thompson Ave.* ☎*970/586–6962* ⚑*Reservations essential* ⊟*MC, V.*

★ $$ ✕**Bighorn Restaurant.** An Estes Park staple since 1972, this family-run outfit is where the locals go for breakfast. Opening as early as 6 AM, you can get a double-cheese omelet, huevos rancheros, or grits before heading into the park. Owners Laura and Sid Brown are happy to pack up a lunch for you—just place your order with breakfast, and your sandwich, chips, homemade cookie, and drink will be ready to go when you leave. This homey spot also serves lunch and dinner. ✉*401 W. Elkhorn Ave.* ☎*970/586–2792* ⊟*D, MC, V.*

$$ ✕**Estes Park Brewery.** If you're not sure which beer suits you or would go with your meal, head downstairs to the tasting area to sample a couple of brews. There are eight beers and four seasonals on tap. The Staggering Elk, a crisp lager, and the Estes Park Gold ale come highly recommended. The beer chili is the specialty here. The menu otherwise includes pizza, burgers, sandwiches, and chicken or steak dinners. ✉*470 Prospect Village Dr.* ☎*970/586–5421* ⊟*AE, D, MC, V.*

$$ ✕**Mama Rose's.** If you've worked up an appetite hiking or rock climbing, a $14 four-course meal is for you: all the salad or soup, bread, and spaghetti you can eat, with a good portion of spumoni to top it off. The lasagna with sliced meatballs and sausage and the tricolor baked pasta are popular entrées, and the wine cellar has a good selection. The spacious Victorian dining room with plenty of fine art harkens to earlier eras in Estes Park, minus the formal dress code. ✉*338 E. Elkhorn Ave.* ☎*970/586–3330* ⚑*Reservations essential* ⊟*AE, D, DC, MC, V* ⊘*Closed Jan. No lunch.*

🕑 ★ $$ ✕**Sweet Basilico Café.** This family-owned and family-friendly restaurant is the locals' favorite for basic Italian classics like lasagna, manicotti, and eggplant parmesan as well as the great service. The calamari fritti is crisp and spicy, sandwiches made with homemade focaccia are delicious, and the minestrone satisfies wonderfully. All meals, including home-style entrées like the savory and spicy chicken scarpelli, are prepared fresh. Enjoy dinner alfresco on the large covered patio or in the well-lighted, brick-wall dining room accented with photos of Italian scenery. Don't forget the spumoni cheesecake with mascarpone frosting for dessert. ✉*430 Prospect Village Dr.* ☎*970/586–3899* ⚑*Reservations essential* ⊟*AE, D, MC, V.*

$ ✕**Ed's Cantina and Grill.** The Cantina Special burrito and the tasty burgers are what make this hangout with the well-stocked bar so popular. The decor is bright with light woods and large windows. Try to get patio seating by the river. ✉*390 E. Elkhorn Ave.* ☎*970/586–2919* ⊟*AE, D, MC, V.*

$ ✗**Poppy's Pizza & Grill.** The spinach, artichoke, and feta pie made with sun-dried tomato sauce at this family-friendly pizzeria is excellent. Try a pizza with Rocky Mountain smoked trout, capers, and cream cheese, or create your own specialty from the five sauces and 40 toppings on the menu. The Straziante (pepperoni, salami, capicola, sausage, and smoked mozzarella) is one of five pizzas from which part of the profits go to local charities. Poppy's has patio seating at the river and an extensive selection of beers. ⌧*342 E. Elkhorn Ave.* ☎*970/586–8282* ▭*AE, D, DC, MC, V* ⊘*Closed Jan.*

¢ ✗**Malt Shop.** Enjoy a handmade ice-cream malt or shake in a traditional parfait glass at this retro-style parlor with antique red-and-white chairs. Go with an eternal favorite like Chocolate Suicide, Very Berry, or the Grasshopper, or opt for the house specialty malt: Apple Pie. You can also get a traditional egg cream or sundae. ⌧*125 Moraine Ave.* ☎*970/586–3542* ▭*MC, V* ⊘*Closed except in summer.*

$$ ✗▥**Marys Lake Lodge.** This 1913 chalet-style lodge with brown siding, white trim, and a green roof overlooks peaceful Mary's Lake a couple of miles south of town. Original woodwork and some of the original antiques adorn the rooms; look for the Victorian floral lamps in the hallways. Some rooms still have claw-foot tubs, and others have Jacuzzi tubs. The elegant Grandmaison's Chalet Room ($$$–$$$$) serves such entrées as cioppino, bouillabaise, and provimi veal chops and has an excellent wine list. Reservations are essential. The Tavern ($$) is more casual and has seating on the porch with expansive views. Popular dishes are the shepherd's pie and the lamb chops. The lodge also rents fully modern luxury condominiums. **Pros:** two excellent on-site restaurants, beautiful views. **Cons:** not within walking distance of attractions or other dining; large, older hotel. ⌧*2625 Mary's Lake Rd., 80517* ☎*970/586–5958 or 877/442–6279* ⊕*www.maryslakelodge.com* ⬐*16 rooms, 1 cabin, 40 condos* ♿*In-room: Wi–Fi. In-hotel: 2 restaurants, pool, spa, no elevator, parking (no fee), no-smoking rooms* ▭*AE, D, MC, V* ⦿*CP.*

$$$ ▥**Boulder Brook.** Luxury suites at this secluded spot on the river are tucked in the pines, yet close to town and 1.5 mi from Rocky Mountain National Park. Sleep regally on linens with at least 300-thread count. Three themed suites are furnished and appointed individually—stylishly and elegantly—and given fitting names like Cowboys & Indians or Shabby Chic. Suites have either a full kitchen or kitchenette, a private deck, a gas fireplace, and all but two have a jetted tub. **Pros:** scenic location, quiet area, attractive grounds. **Cons:** not within walking distance of attractions, no nearby dining. ⌧*1900 Fall River Rd., 80517* ☎*970/586–0910 or 800/238–0910* ⊕*www.boulderbrook.com* ⬐*19 suites* ♿*In-room: kitchen, DVD, VCR. In-hotel: parking (no fee), no-smoking rooms* ▭*D, MC, V.*

★ $$$ ▥**Stanley Hotel.** Perched regally on a hill commanding the town, the Stanley is one of Colorado's great old hotels, impeccably maintained in its historic state, yet with all the modern conveniences. F. O. Stanley (the inventor of the Stanley Steamer) began construction in 1907, and when it opened in 1909 it was the first hotel in the world with electricity and the first in the United States with in-room telephones. The hotel that inspired Stephen King's novel *The Shining* conducts historical and ghost tours daily. Many of the sunny rooms have mountain views and are decorated with antiques and period reproductions. **Pros:** many rooms have been updated recently, good restaurant, some rooms have mountain views. **Cons:** some rooms are small and tight, building is old, no air-conditioning. ⊠*333 Wonderview Ave., 80517* ☎*970/586–3371 or 800/976–1377* ⊕*www.stanleyhotel.com* ⬅*156 rooms* ⬥*In-room: no a/c, Wi-Fi. In-hotel: restaurant, bar, pool, spa, public Wi-Fi, parking (no fee), no-smoking rooms* ⊟*AE, D, DC, MC, V.*

$$$ 🖫**Taharaa Mountain Lodge.** Every room at this luxury B&B accesses the wraparound deck and its views of the High Rockies and Estes Valley. Rooms are decorated with individual themes, from Ute Indian to Southwestern, and all have a fireplace. Enjoy happy hour in the Great Room. The full breakfast hints at the owners' Southern heritage. Note that there is no smoking on the property. **Pros:** beautiful mountain views, friendly hosts. **Cons:** not within walking distance of attractions, not on bus route, no young children. ⊠*3110 S. St. Vrain, 80517* ⊹*4 mi south of downtown Estes Park* ☎*970/577–0098 or 800/597–0098* ⊕*www.taharaa.com* ⬅*18 rooms* ⬥*In-room: DVD, VCR, Wi-Fi. In-hotel: gym, parking (no fee), no kids under 13, no-smoking rooms* ⊟*AE, D, MC, V* ⬅*2-night minimum* 🍽*BP.*

☕ $$ 🖫**Glacier Lodge.** Families are the specialty at this secluded, 19-acre guest resort on the banks of the Big Thompson River. The kids will take home plenty of fun memories from the twice-weekly "soda saloons," nature walks, arts-and-crafts workshops, Tuesday evening campfire stories, and Thursday campfire sing-along. The whole family will enjoy the once-weekly "mountain breakfast" with omelets and flap-jacks before a guided trail ride, some into Rocky Mountain National Park. You can stay in former Colorado governor James Peabody's (in office 1902–04) summer residence. There's a minimum stay of four nights. All bed and bath linens and kitchen utensils and dinnerware are provided. **Pros:** great place for families, attractive grounds on the river, on bus route. **Cons:** not within walking distance of attractions, along rather busy road. ⊠*2166 CO Hwy. 66* ⬧*Box 2656, Estes Park 80517* ☎*970/586–4401 or 800/523–3920* ⊕*www.glacierlodge.com* ⬅*24 single-family cabins, 4 cabins for 12–30* ⬥*In-room: no a/c, kitchen, DVD. In-hotel: pool, children's programs (ages 4–10), parking (no fee), no-smoking rooms* ⊟*AE, D, MC, V.*

☕ $ 🖫**Estes Park Center/YMCA of the Rockies.** This 890-acre, family-friendly property has a wealth of attractive and clean lodging options among its four lodges and many cabins. Sign up for a class and learn a skill like calligraphy, fly-fishing, or compass reading. A couple can rent a simple, rustic pine cabin, and newer cabins which have modern kitchen appliances and televisions accommodate 10–40 people. An extended family can reserve the Reunion Cabin that houses 40 people. Lodge rooms can be outfitted with queen beds or bunk beds for the kids. A meal plan is available for the all-you-can-eat buffet. There's a Frisbee-golf course, and a climbing wall to hone your rock-climbing skills. **Pros:** good value for large groups and for longer stays, lots of family-oriented activities and amenities, stunningly scenic setting. **Cons:** very large, busy, and crowded property; fills fast; location requires vehicle to visit town or the national park. ✉ *2515 Tunnel Rd., 80511* ☎ *970/586–3341, 303/448–1616, or 800/777–9622* ⊕ *www.ymcarockies.org* ↘ *688 rooms, 220 cabins* ☂ *In-room: no a/c, no TV. In-hotel: restaurant, tennis court, pool, no elevator, children's programs (ages 3–18), parking (no fee), no-smoking rooms* ☰ *MC, V* ◐ *MAP.*

$ 🏚 **Riverview Pines.** Fish in the Fall River or just sit and read on the expansive lawn at this peaceful motel. It's the least expensive along the beautiful Fall River Road to Rocky Mountain National Park. The simple, recently updated rooms have coffeemakers. The luxury, log-style, duplex cabins ($$$–$$$$) accommodate up to six persons, have full kitchens, fireplaces, DVD/VCRs, and decks that face the river. A two-night stay is required for rooms; cabins are a four-night minimum. **Pros:** friendly and helpful owner-managers, quiet and scenic location on river, low rates for the area. **Cons:** very basic rooms without much decoration, on a busy road. ✉ *1150 W. Elkhorn Ave.* ⌂ *Box 690, Estes Park 80517* ☎ *970/586–3627 or 800/340–5764* ⊕ *www.riverviewpines.com* ↘ *18 rooms, 8 cabins* ☂ *In-room: no a/c, kitchen (some), refrigerator. In-hotel: no elevator, laundry facilities, parking (no fee), no-smoking rooms* ☰ *D, MC, V.*

$ 🏚 **Saddle & Surrey Motel.** Friendly owners manage this comfortable and quiet 1950s-style motel that is close to town and outdoor activities. The pristine rooms are all ground level and have all been updated with new bathrooms, plumbing, and carpet. Some have fireplaces. Note that there is no smoking on-site. **Pros:** good value, on shuttle-bus route, quiet area at night. **Con:** not within walking distance of attractions or downtown dining. ✉ *1341 S. St. Vrain* ⌂ *Box 591, Estes Park 80517* ☎ *970/586–3326* ⊕ *www.saddleandsurrey.com* ↘ *26 rooms* ☂ *In-room: kitchen (some), refrigerator, Wi-Fi. In-hotel: pool, parking (no fee), no-smoking rooms* ☰ *D, MC, V* ◐ *CP.*

CABIN & **Range Property Management** (⌂ *Box 316, Estes Park 80517* ☎ *970/586–* CONDO *7626 or 888/433–5211* 🖶 *970/577–8881* ⊕ *www.rangeprop.com* RENTALS ☰ *No credit cards*) rents fully equipped houses, condos, and cabins in the Estes Park area. Pets are not allowed.

NIGHTLIFE & THE ARTS

THE ARTS Visit 20 galleries and artists' studios on the self-guided **Summer Art Walk** daily from mid-June through Labor Day. Maps and information are available at **Cultural Arts Council of Estes Park** (✉ *304 E. Elkhorn Ave.* ☎ *970/586–9203* ⊕ *www.estesarts.com*). The Council also hosts three other art walks during the year: mid-May through mid-June, mid-September through October, and Thanksgiving through December.

The **Estes Park Music Festival** (☎ *970/586–9519 or 800/443–7837* ⊕ *www.estesparkmusicalfestival.org*) stages concerts at 2 PM on Sunday afternoons from November through April at the Stanley Hotel.

Relax with some chamber music while taking in views of the mountains at the **Rocky Ridge Music Center** (✉ *465 Longs Peak Rd.,* ⊹ *9 mi south of Estes Park off CO Hwy. 7 at the turnoff to Longs Peak Campground*

☏ *970/586–4031* ⊕ *www.rockyridge.org*). The faculty hold their own classical chamber music concerts June through August.

NIGHTLIFE Blues and rock bands play Friday and Saturday at **Lonigans** (✉ *110 W. Elkhorn Ave.* ☏ *970/586–4346*), and there's karaoke on Wednesday.

The Tavern (✉ *Mary's Lake Lodge, 2625 Mary's Lake Rd.* ☏ *970/586–5958*) has live entertainment nightly in summer and on Friday and Saturday in winter. The venerable **Wheel Bar** (✉ *132 E. Elkhorn Ave.* ☏ *970/586–9381*) is among the choice watering holes.

SHOPPING

Shopping in Estes Park includes far fewer run-of-the-mill trinket, T-shirt, and souvenir shops than is typical of resort towns, and the number of proper galleries is increasing as Estes Park becomes a more-upscale destination.

CRAFTS & ART The cooperative **Earthwood Artisans** (✉ *145 E. Elkhorn Ave.* ☏ *970/586–*
GALLERIES *2151*) features the work of jewelers, sculptors, wood-carvers, and potters. **Earthwood Collectibles** (✉ *145 E. Elkhorn Ave.* ☏ *970/586–2151*) is a cooperative that sells the work of stained-glass artists and photographers. **Glassworks** (✉ *323 Elkhorn Ave.* ☏ *970/586–8619*) offers glass-blowing demonstrations and sells a rainbow of glass creations. **Images of Rocky Mountain National Park** (✉ *205A Park La.* ☏ *970/372–5212*) is Erik Stenslands' gallery of his stunning photography of park motivs. **Spectrum** (✉ *No. 8 Park Theatre Mall, Elkhorn Ave.* ☏ *970/586–2497*) sells fine arts and crafts exclusively by Colorado studio artists, including spectacular nature photography, hand-thrown and signed pottery, and hand-turned woodcrafts made from mesquite, aspen, or cedar.

Wild Spirits, Ltd. (✉ *148 W. Elkhorn Ave.* ☏ *970/586–4392*) carries large-format photos and paintings of both the Southwest and Rocky Mountain National Park.

GIFTS There are no knockoffs or cheap imitations at **Thirty Below Leather** (✉ *356 E. Elkhorn Ave.* ☏ *970/586–2211* ⊘ *Closed Sun.*). High-quality travel gear, handbags, wallets, and accessories are all priced at less than $30.

WESTERN **Rustic Mountain Charm** (✉ *135 E. Elkhorn Ave.* ☏ *970/586–4344*) sells clothing, local foodstuffs, and home accessories with the lodge look, including furniture, quilts, baskets, and throws. **Twisted Pine** (✉ *450 Moraine Ave.* ☏ *970/586–4539* ✉ *157 E. Elkhorn Ave.* ☏ *970/586–3280*) carries certified Native American–made weavings and traditional leather or fur western clothing with an elegant flair as well as alpaca rugs and jewelry.

GRAND COUNTY

Grand County is the high country and rolling ranchlands at once. Vistas of the Rockies to the east and south and of the Gore Range to the west seem out of place for these grasslands that the early French explorers named Middle Park. By the time the Moffat Railroad came to Grand County in 1905, ranchers were already living on the flat, open meadows.

Although Grand County is ranching country, the word "range" today evokes more the excellent golf courses instead of the plain where a cowboy herds cattle. The town of Granby has two golf courses, and Grand County hosts several annual tournaments. Summer brings droves of anglers and cyclists, and large-game hunters replace them in the late fall. The area west of Granby along U.S. 40 is marked by a number of small towns with resorts and guest ranches.

GRAND LAKE

1.5 mi west of Rocky Mountain National Park via Hwy. 34.

Grand Lake village is doubly blessed by its surroundings. It's the western gateway to Rocky Mountain National Park and also sits on the shores of the state's largest natural lake, the highest-altitude yacht anchorage in America. With views of snowy peaks and verdant mountains from any vantage point, Grand Lake Village is favored by Coloradans for sailing, canoeing, waterskiing, and fishing. In winter it's *the* snowmobiling capital and ice-fishing destination. Even with its wooden boardwalks, Old West–style storefronts, and usual assortment of souvenir shops and motels, the town seems less spoiled than many other resort communities.

> **WORD OF MOUTH**
>
> "Grand Lake is beautiful. It's a blast to rent motorboats at Lake Granby and tool around on both lakes for a half day or so. (Just watch for afternoon thunderstorms.)" —MaureenB

★ According to Ute legend, the fine mists that shroud **Grand Lake** at dawn are the risen spirits of women and children whose raft capsized as they were fleeing a marauding party of Cheyennes and Arapahoes. Grand Lake feeds into two much larger man-made reservoirs, Lake Granby and Shadow Mountain lake, forming the "Great Lakes of Colorado."

SPORTS & THE OUTDOORS

Rocky Mountain National Park, 2 mi from Grand Lake village, is ideal for hiking, fishing, wildlife viewing, rock climbing, snowshoeing, and cross-country skiing. *See the Rocky Mountain National Park chapter in this book.*

Grand Lake Sports (⊠ *900 Grand Ave.* ☎ *970/627–8124* ⊕ *www.grandlakeoutdoorsports.com*) is an all-purpose outfitter that rents snowshoes, cross-country skis, kayaks, canoes, and pet gear. When they're not at work, staff members are out hiking and bicycling the region, and therefore give excellent advice about fun outdoor experiences for thrill-seeking adventurers as well as families.

BICYCLING   Car traffic can be heavy on U.S. 34, whose shoulders are broad south of Grand Lake village but narrow in spots to the north of it. The route from Grand Lake south to U.S. 40 west and then north on Route 125 to **Willow Creek Pass** is over rolling terrain and climbs 1,770 feet to the summit through quiet aspen and pine forests. You'll encounter little traffic, and moose and deer are often just off the road.

BIRD-
WATCHING

The islands in Shadow Mountain Reservoir and Lake Granby are wildlife refuges. The best way to get close to the osprey that nest on the islands as well as other migrating birds is by canoe or foot trail. Be sure to take binoculars, because you're not permitted to land on the islands. **East Shore Trail** and **Knight Ridge Trail** will take you along the shores of Shadow Mountain Reservoir and Lake Granby for spotting opportunities. ⊹*Access trails either from Grand Lake Village between Grand Lake and Shadow Mountain Reservoir, or from Green Ridge Campground at south end of Shadow Mountain Reservoir.*

BOATING &
FISHING

There's plenty of water to share here. Anglers enjoy plentiful catches of trout, mackinaw, and kokanee salmon; recreational sailors and waterskiers ply acres of water; and paddlers still get to canoe in peace. Ice fishers will not want to miss the big contest held the first weekend in January on Lake Granby. Contestants must catch five different species of fish, and winners collect from the booty of $20,000 in cash and prizes. Anyone older than 16 needs a Colorado fishing license, which you can obtain at local sporting-goods stores. See ⊕*www.wildlife. state.co.us/fishing* for more information.

Beacon Landing rents 20-, 24-, and 29-foot pontoon boats and fishing equipment, including ice augers and ice rods. ⊹*1 mi off Hwy. 34 on County Rd. 64. Drive south 5 mi on U.S. 34 to County Rd. 64, turn left and go 1 mi* ☎*970/627–3671.*

Call the **Trail Ridge Marina** (⊠*Shadow Mountain Lake,* ⊹*2 mi south of Grand Lake on U.S. 34* ☎*970/627–3586*) for information on renting pontoon boats for two to eight hours.

HIKING

Although a hike in and of itself can be the destination, know that the trails on this side of the Continental Divide are generally longer, and you'll trek farther and higher into the high peaks of the park to your destination. Many trails take you 5 mi one-way before you reach a lake or peak. Of course, a peaceful walk of any length in the forest or through riparian meadows is wonderful relaxation, especially since the trails here tend to have fewer hikers on them than on the east side of the national park. Nonetheless, a couple of trails are relatively short walks to a lake or a waterfall and still afford you gorgeous scenery. If you hike in the backcountry, be sure you're outfitted for adverse weather. The *National Geographic Trails Illustrated Map* No. 503 (Winter Park/ Grand Lake) has excellent coverage of hiking and biking trails in the area with information about regulations.

� At the southeast end of Lake Granby, the **Indian Peaks Wilderness Area** is great for hiking. You can access the wilderness area by driving south from Grand Lake village on U.S. 34 to County Road 6. Follow the lakeshore road about 10 mi to the parking area. The area around the Monarch Lake is popular with families for the selection of trails and the views of the Indian Peaks and the Continental Divide. Trails range in distance from 1.5 to 10.8 mi one-way. The easy **Monarch Lake Loop** is 3.8 mi and a mere 110 feet in elevation gain. You can get a day pass ($5) from the staff or at the self-serve pay station. ⊠*Sulphur Ranger District, Arapaho National Forest* ☎*970/887–4100* ⊕*www.fs.fed. us/r2/arnf.*

HORSEBACK RIDING
Sombrero Ranches, Inc. Sombrero offers guided rides into the wilderness and national park, including scenic and relaxing early-morning breakfast rides and pack trips. The Boulder-based company also arranges private camping trips. Guided horseback-riding trips last two to five hours. ⊠*Grand Lake Stables, 304 W. Portal Rd., 80447* ☎*970/627–3514* ⊕*www.sombrero.com* ⊠*$30–$80* ☺*Mid-May–mid-Sept.*

NORDIC SKIING & SNOWBOARDING
When crystalline snow glitters under the clear blue sky, it's time to strap on skis or snowshoes and traverse the hiking trails in Rocky Mountain National Park, the Arapaho National Recreation Area, and the Indian Peaks Wilderness Area. The **Grand Lake Metropolitan Recreation District** (☎*970/627–8872*) has 18 mi (29 km) of cross-country ski trails with vistas of the Never Summer Range and the Continental Divide. **Never Summer Mountain Sports** (⊠*919 Grand Ave.* ☎*970/627–3642*) rents tents, packs, and camping equipment as well as cross-country skis.

Many consider Grand Lake to be Colorado's snowmobiling capital, with more than 300 mi of trails (150 mi groomed), many winding through virgin forest. There are several rental and guide companies in the area. If you're visiting during the winter holidays, it's wise to make reservations about three weeks ahead. **Grand Adventures LLC** (⊠*143 County Rd. 48* ☎*970/627–3098 or 800/726–9247* ⊕*www. grandadventures.com*) offers guided tours and arranges unguided rentals. **On The Trail** (⊠*902 Grand Ave.* ☎*970/627–0171 or 888/627–2429* ⊕*www.onthetrailrentals.com*) rents snowmobiles.

WHERE TO STAY & EAT

$$ ✕**Bear's Den.** The real standouts at this casual family restaurant are the nightly specials, especially the T-bone steaks, fried chicken, and chicken-fried steak, cooked in cast-iron skillets for homemade flavor. The regular menu at this rustic, vertical-log restaurant includes Rocky Mountain oysters, New York strip steak, seafood, and homemade desserts. ⊠*612 Grand Ave.* ☎*970/627–3385* ⊟*D, MC, V.*

$$ ✕**Sagebrush BBQ & Grill.** Barbecue ribs, chicken, and catfish draw local and out-of-town attention to this homey café. Meals can be sized appropriately for larger or smaller appetites. Comforting sides such as baked beans, corn bread, coleslaw, and potatoes top off the large plates. The breakfast menu includes omelets, pancakes, and biscuits as well as chicken-fried steak and *huevos rancheros* platters for heartier appetites. ⊠*1101 Grand Ave.* ☎*970/627–1404* ⊟*AE, D, DC, MC, V.*

¢ ✕**Grand Lake Brewery.** A handcrafted beer and a bratwurst with the works or a pulled pork or chicken sandwich will hit the spot at this brewpub with a wooden bar with brass rails. Eat at the bar or at a table in the small but sunny dining area. The crisp and light White Rabbit Wheat took the gold medal at the 2003 Colorado State Fair; the brewery's 2004 gold medal winner is the Plaid Bastard, a rich Scotch ale served in a brandy snifter to highlight its deep aromas and flavors. ⊠*915 Grand Ave.* ☎*970/627–1711* ▤*AE, D, MC, V.*

$–$$ ✕▥ **Historic Rapids Lodge & Restaurant.** This handsome lodgepole-pine
Fodor's Choice structure on the Tonahutu River dates to 1915. The seven lodge
★ rooms—each with ceiling fan—are done in the Rocky Mountain rustic style with a mix of antique furnishings such as claw-foot tubs and carved-hardwood beds. The innkeepers also rent condos for large groups or families. The delightful Rapids Restaurant ($$$$) is Grand Lake's most romantic for fine dining, with stained glass and timber beams. Select a cocktail from the excellent wine list and enjoy it creekside before dinner. The specialty is Rapids' tournedo—an 8-ounce filet mignon with artichokes and béarnaise sauce. **Pros:** in-house restaurant, condos are great for longer stays, quiet area of town. **Cons:** unpaved parking area, hotel rooms are above restaurant. ⊠*209 Rapids La., 80447* ☎*970/627–3707* ⊕*www.rapidslodge.com* ⇘*7 rooms, 8 suites, 5 cabins, 10 condos* ⚭*In-room: no a/c, kitchen (some). In-hotel: restaurant, bar, no elevator, parking (no fee), some pets allowed, no-smoking rooms* ▤*AE, MC, V* ☉*Closed Apr. and Nov.*

$$ ▥ **Mountain Lakes Lodge.** The scent of the pine forest welcomes you to the Parkers' charming and comfortable log cabins whimsically decorated with animal and sports themes—down to the curtains and drawer pulls. The Little Log House has three bedrooms and can house nine people. Some cabins have private decks and gas stoves. Dogs are enthusiastically welcomed with treats in the cabins as well as given their own private fenced yards. Cabins accommodate two to six humans. **Pros:** dog friendly, close to fishing, good value. **Cons:** dogs are the only pets allowed; two-day minimum year-round, three-day minimum for holidays and special events. ⊠*10480 U.S. 34, 80447* ☎*970/627–8448* ⊕*www.mountainlakeslodge.com* ⇘*10 cabins, 1 house* ⚭*In-room: no a/c, no phone, kitchen, Wi-Fi. In-hotel: parking (no fee), some pets allowed, no-smoking rooms* ▤*MC, V.*

$$ ▥ **Western Riviera.** All rooms in this friendly motel face the lake. It books up far in advance due to its low prices, affable owners, and comfortable accommodations. Even the cheapest units—although small—are pleasant, done in mauve and earth tones. The motel also rents cabins with fully equipped kitchens in Grand Lake, some lakeside, for up to six persons. **Pros:** helpful and friendly staff, views of the lake, clean rooms. **Cons:** rooms and bathrooms can be a little cramped, lobby is a bit small. ⊠*419 Garfield Ave., 80447* ☎*970/627–3580* ⊕*www.westernriv.com* ⇘*16 rooms, 22 cabins* ⚭*In-room: no a/c. In-hotel: no elevator, no-smoking rooms* ▤*MC, V.*

CABIN & **Grand Mountain Rentals** (⚷*Box 808, Grand Lake 80447* ☎*970/627–*
CONDO *1131 or 877/982–2155* ⊕*www.grandmountainrentals.com*) arranges
RENTALS rentals—some pet friendly—around Grand Lake for three days to six months.

NIGHTLIFE & THE ARTS

The popular **Lariat Saloon** (⊠*1121 Grand Ave., on Boardwalk* ☎*970/627–9965*) is the local hot spot with live rock music almost every night.

Look for the talking buffalo in the honest, eclectic Western decor. The bar also has pinball, pool, and darts.

The professional **Rocky Mountain Repertory Theatre** (☎970/627–3421 ⊕www.rockymountainrep.com) stages performances of popular Broadway shows like *Annie Get Your Gun* and musicals such as *Footloose* and *Seussical* in a cabin-style theater.

SHOPPING

Shopping in Grand Lake tends toward the usual resort-town souvenir shops, although a handful stand out.

Grand Lake Art Gallery (✉1117 *Grand Ave.* ☎970/627–3104) purveys superlative photography, original oil paintings, wood carvings, weavings, pottery, stained glass, and paintings done by more than 180 Colorado artists.

Humphrey's Cabin Fever (✉1100 *Grand Ave.* ☎970/627–8939), the log building with the green roof, sells upscale cabin collectibles, rustic home furnishings, clothes, bedding, and ceramics in all price ranges.

For outdoor gear and clothing, head for **Never Summer Mountain Products** (✉919 *Grand Ave.* ☎970/627–3642).

GRANBY

20 mi south of Grand Lake via U.S. 34.

The small, utilitarian town of Granby (elevation 7,935 feet) serves the working ranches in Grand County, and you'll see plenty of cowboys, especially if you go to one of the weekly rodeos in summer. What the town lacks in attractions, it makes up for with the views of Middle Park and the surrounding mountains of the Front and Gore ranges and with its proximity to outdoor activities, particularly its top-class golf courses just south of town. Granby is 20 minutes from Rocky Mountain National Park and 15 minutes from the ski resorts Winter Park and Mary Jane and the mountain-biking trails of the Fraser Valley.

RODEO Watch cowboys demonstrate their rodeo skills at the **Flying Heels Rodeo Arena** (☎970/887–2311) in Granby every Saturday night beginning Memorial Day weekend. The rodeo finale and fireworks show is on the Saturday nearest the July 4 holiday. Contact the Greater Granby Area Chamber of Commerce for information. *See the Sports & the Outdoors section in this chapter.*

SPORTS & THE OUTDOORS

The **Greater Granby Area Chamber of Commerce** (✉365 *E. Agate, Suite B* ☎970/887–2311) has a free *Grand County Trail Map* that shows trails for hiking, biking, horseback riding, snowmobiling, and snowshoeing as well as information about regulations.

BIRD-WATCHING The reservoir at **Windy Gap Wildlife Viewing Area** is on the waterfowl migration route for geese, pelicans, swans, eagles, and osprey. The park has information kiosks, viewing scopes, viewing blinds, a picnic area, and a nature trail that's also wheelchair accessible. ✛ *2 mi west of Granby on U.S. 40 where it meets Rte. 125* ☎ *970/725–6200* ☉ *May–Sept., daily dawn–dusk.*

FISHING   Although Shadow Mountain Reservoir, Lake Granby, and Grand Lake yield big catches, including kokanee salmon and mackinaws, serious fly fishers head to the rivers and streams of Grand County for relaxing solitude with excellent fishing in riparian areas. Angling on the **Fraser River** begins downstream from Tabernash and is not appropriate for families or dogs. At **Willow Creek** you'll bag plenty of rainbow trout and brookies. The **Colorado River** between Shadow Mountain Dam and Lake Granby and downstream from Hot Sulphur Springs is open to anglers. Anyone older than 16 needs a Colorado fishing license, which you can obtain at local sporting-goods stores. See ⊕ *www.wildlife.state.co.us/ fishing* for more information.

GOLF   The scenery and wildlife-viewing opportunities at Grand County's four golf courses make good excuses for being distracted during a critical putt or drive. You can expect secluded greens, expansive vistas, and a deer or grouse interrupting the game at these courses.

★   **Grand Elk Ranch & Club.** You might share a tee with an elk. Designed by PGA great Craig Stadler, the challenging course is reminiscent of traditional heathland greens in Britain. ✉ *1321 Tenmile Dr.* ☎ *970/887–9122 or 877/389–9333* ⊕ *www.grandelk.com* ⚲ *Reservations essential* ⛳ *18 holes. Yards: 7,144/5,095. Par: 71/71. Green Fee: $60/$125.*

Headwaters Golf Course at Granby Ranch. Tucked back in a valley at the end of a gravel road, entirely within the mountains and meadows, this club has roomy practice facilities as well as a large deck at the clubhouse. Drive 2 mi south on U.S. 40 from Granby to the Inn at Silver Creek. Turn left and drive past the lodge to the gravel road marked by the sign. Follow the road about 3 mi into the valley. ✉ *1000 Village Rd.* ☎ *970/887–2709 or 888/850–4615* ⊕ *www.granbyranch.com* ⚲ *Reservations essential* ⛳ *18 holes. Yards: 7,206/5,095. Par: 72/72. Green Fee: $60/$80.*

MOUNTAIN   Indian Peaks Wilderness Area is not open to mountain biking, but there
BIKING   are moderate and difficult trails in the Arapaho National Forest. Grand County has several hundred miles of easy-to-expert–level bike trails, many of which are former railroad rights-of-way and logging roads. The **Doe Creek Trail, Strawberry Trail, and West Strawberry Trail** (ending at Strawberry Lake) network is a good workout of steep uphill climbs (and descents) with deadfall and plenty of forest scenery. ✛ *From Tabernash take County Rd. 84 (Meadow Creek Rd.) to gate at trailhead.*

WHERE TO STAY & EAT

$$ ✕ **Longbranch Restaurant.** This smoke-free Western-style family restaurant has a warming fireplace, rustic wood interior, and wagon-wheel chandeliers and is popular for its delicious German food: bratwurst, goulash, schnitzel, sauerbraten, and heavenly homemade spaetzle. The traditional German desserts are authentic, and the strudel gets particu-

larly high marks. The bar serves many domestic and foreign beers as well as a few microbrews. ⊠*185 E. Agate Ave., U.S. 40* ☎*970/887–2209* ⊟*D, MC, V Closed Sun. No lunch.*

GUEST RANCH

☼ $$$$

🖼**C Lazy U Guest Ranch.** Secluded in a broad, verdant valley, this deluxe guest ranch attracts an international clientele, including both Hollywood royalty and the real thing. You enjoy your own personal horse, luxurious Western-style accommodations (with humidifiers), fine meals, live entertainment, and any outdoor activity you can dream up—it's the ultimate in hedonism without ostentation. The instructors are top-notch, the ratio of guests to staff is nearly one to one, and the children's programs are unbeatable. The minimum stay is seven days in summer and five days during the December holiday season. All meals are included. **Pros:** kid and family friendly, helpful staff. **Con:** rather distant from other area attractions. ⌂*Box 379, Granby 80446* ✚*3.5 mi north on CO Rte. 125 from U.S. Hwy. 40 junction* ☎*970/887–3344* ⊕*www.clazyu.com* ➲*19 rooms, 20 cabins* ⌂*In-room: no a/c, no phone, no TV. In-hotel: restaurant, bar, tennis courts, pool, gym, children's programs (ages 3–17), parking (no fee), no-smoking rooms* ⊟*AE, MC, V* ☺*Late May–early Sept. and mid-Dec.–early Jan.*

6

HOT SULPHUR SPRINGS

10 mi west of Granby via U.S. 40.

The county seat, Hot Sulphur Springs (population 512), is a faded resort town whose hot springs were once the destination for trains packed with people, including plenty of Hollywood types in the 1950s.

Soak or pamper yourself with a massage, wrap, facial, or salt glow at the newly renovated **Hot Sulphur Springs Resort & Spa.** Temperatures range from 85° to 112°F in 20 open-air pools and four private, indoor pools. For views at 102°F, head for the slate pools uphill from the others. The seasonal swimming pool is just right for recreation at a comparatively frigid 80°F. ⊠*U.S. 40* ☎*970/725–3306 or 800/510–6235* ⊕*www.hotsulphursprings.com* 🎫*$17.50* ☺*Daily 8 AM–10 PM.*

The old Hot Sulphur School is now the **Grand County Museum.** Artifacts depict Grand County history, including the original settlers 9,000 years ago, the role of pioneer women, and the archaeology of Windy Gap. Photographs show life in the early European settlements, and the original county courthouse and jail are on the site. ⊠*110 Byers Ave., U.S. 40* ☎*970/725–3939* 🎫*$4* ☺*Wed.–Sat. 10–5.*

WHERE TO STAY

$ 🖼**Hot Sulphur Springs Resort & Spa.** The 1940s rooms are newly refurnished and have comfortable lodgepole beds, desks, and en-suite showers, although the trains passing nearby can be noisy. Room rates include unlimited use of the pools during your stay. You can soak or pamper yourself with a massage, wrap, facial, or salt glow. The premises have no restaurant, but a diner in town serves breakfast, and the Riverside Hotel occasionally serves dinner. Restaurants in Granby and Grand Lake are about 15 minutes and 30 minutes away respectively. **Pros:**

clean lodging, quick access to hot pools and spa, close enough that a visit can be tacked onto an outdoor activity. **Cons:** trains passing through during the night are noisy, dining establishments can be 30 minutes away. ⊠*U.S. 40, 80451* ☎*970/725–3306 or 800/510–6235* ⊕*www.hotsulphursprings. com* ⤴*17 rooms, 1 cabin* ⚿*In-room: no a/c, no phone, no TV. In-hotel: pool, parking (no fee), no-smoking rooms* ▤*MC, V.*

GUEST RANCH

$$$$

⚏**Latigo Ranch.** Considerably more down-to-earth than many other Colorado guest ranches, Latigo has a caring staff that helps create an authentic ranch experience. You can test your skills as a cowboy on a cattle drive or an overnight pack trip. The ranch also organizes white-water rafting excursions. Children's programs are tailored by age group, and the "Ute Scouts" overnight camping trip is a popular outing geared specifically to 6- to 10-year-olds. Accommodations are in comfortable, carpeted, one- to three-bedroom contemporary log cabins fitted with wood-burning stoves. Although providing fewer amenities than comparable properties, the ranch offers views of the Indian Peaks range, complete seclusion, and superb cross-country trails. Remember to bring your own beer. **Pros:** stunning scenery, quiet and secluded area. **Cons:** somewhat long drive from Denver, no nearby restaurants or other attractions. ⊠*County Rd. 1911,* ⌂*Box 237, Kremmling 80459* ☎*970/724–9008 or 800/227–9655* ⊕*www.latigotrails.com* ⤴*10 cabins* ⚿*In-room: no a/c, no phone, no TV. In-hotel: restaurant, pool, children's programs (ages 3–13), laundry facilities, public Wi-Fi, parking (no fee), no-smoking rooms* ▤*MC, V* ☻*Closed Apr., May, and mid-Oct.–mid-Dec.*

> ## THE GRAND DAYS OF THE SPA
>
> Colorado's scenery has long attracted high-profile personalities like Teddy Roosevelt and Walt Whitman, but many early travelers were asthma, tuberculosis, and arthritis sufferers who came to the dry climate to convalesce. From the early to the mid-20th century, healing spas and resorts like Hot Sulphur Springs and Eldorado Springs were destinations for long-term visitors. The list of the rich or famous who visited is long and it includes Robert Frost and Dwight and Mamie Eisenhower. The therapeutic tradition continues today.

FORT COLLINS

Fort Collins received the prestigious Preserve America Award for its efforts in historic preservation. A walk through Old Town Square and the neighborhoods to its south and west validates the designation. The city sits on the cusp of the high plains of eastern Colorado but is sheltered on the west by the lower foothills of the Rockies, giving residents plenty of nearby hiking and mountain-biking opportunities. By plugging a couple of gaps in the foothills with dams, the city created Horsetooth Reservoir, which you won't be able to see from town. To view the high mountains, you'll need to head up into Lory State Park or Horsetooth Mountain Park, which are just west of town.

The city was established in 1868 to protect traders from the natives, while the former negotiated the treacherous Overland Trail. After the flood of 1864 swept away Camp Collins—a cavalry post near today's town of LaPorte—Colonel Will Collins established a new camp on 6,000 acres where Fort

WORD OF MOUTH

"[M]ake sure to try the local Colorado microbrews (you should really try the New Belgium brews from Fort Collins—particularly Fat Tire amber ale)."   —travman

Collins stands today. The town grew on two industries: education (CSU was founded here in 1879) and agriculture (rich crops of alfalfa and sugar beets). Today, there are plenty of shops and art galleries worth visiting in this relaxed university city. With the Budweiser brewery and six microbreweries—the most microbreweries per capita in the state—crafting ales, lagers, and stouts, it's the perfect venue for the two-day Colorado Brewers' Festival every June.

1 The Fort Collins Convention & Visitors Bureau has designated a historic walking tour of more than 20 buildings, including the original university structures and the stately sandstone **Avery House**, named for Franklin Avery, who planned the old town's broad streets when he surveyed the city in 1873. ⊠ *328 W. Mountain Ave.* ☎ *970/221–0533* ⧉ *Free* ⊘ *Wed. and Sun. 1–3.*

2 **Old Town Square** (⊠ *Mountain and College Aves.*), a National Historic District, is a pedestrian zone with sculptures and fountains. Restored buildings house shops, galleries, jewelers, boutiques, and bars. The square's several restaurants and cafés have plenty of shaded outdoor seating that fills quickly. In summer, musicians and theater groups entertain Tuesday at noon and Thursday and Friday evenings.

3 The **Fort Collins Museum** has an 1860s cabin from the original military camp and a 1905 vintage schoolhouse on its grounds. The collection contains artifacts representing Fort Collins history, from Native Americans through fur trappers to CSU professor Donald Sutherland, held hostage by terrorists in Beirut during the 1980s. ⊠ *200 Matthews St.* ☎ *970/221–6738* ⊕ *www.fcgov.com/museum* ⧉ *Free* ⊘ *Tues.–Sat. 10–5, Sun. noon–5.*

4 CSU's **Environmental Learning Center** is a 1.2-mi trail loop within a 200-acre nature preserve. The raptor cages and the walk-through wetland animal habitat are an excellent educational family activity, and fun for anyone curious about animal habitats. Staff conduct special walks like the full-moon hike. The learning center loop is 1 mi east of the Timberline and Drake Road intersection, on Drake Road. ⊠ *Colorado Welcome Center, 3745 E. Prospect Rd.* ☎ *970/491–1661* ⊕ *www.cnr. colostate.edu/elc* ⧉ *Free* ⊘ *Information center mid-May–Aug., daily 10–5; Sept.–Apr., weekends 10–5. Learning Center year-round, daily dawn–dusk.*

5 **Swetsville Zoo** is the unique creation of an insomniac dairy farmer, who stayed up nights fashioning more than 150 dinosaurs, birds, insects, and other fantastic creatures from old farm equipment. ⊠ *4801 E.*

Harmony Rd., 0.25 mi east of I–25 ☎*970/484–9509* ☜*Free* ⊙*Daily dawn–dusk.*

❻ Famous for its **Fat Tire** brand, the **New Belgium Brewing Company** also crafts a few brews available only on-site at the "mother ship" (the employees' term of endearment for their brewery). Tours of the first 100% wind-powered brewery in the United States are first-come, first-served. ✉*500 Linden St.* ☎*970/221–0524* ⊕*www.newbelgium.com* ☜*Free* ⊙*Tours weekdays. Call ahead for times.*

❼ Take in the brewing process up close and personally in a nearly interactive tour at the **Odell Brewing Company,** one of the first microbreweries to open shop in town in 1989—out of a pickup-truck bed. Eternally favorite 90 Shilling, Easy Street Wheat, and 5 Barrel Pale Ale are not to be missed. In winter try the seasonal Isolation Ale. ✉*800 E. Lincoln Ave.* ☎*970/498–9070* ☜*Free* ⊙*Tours weekdays 11, 2, and 4; Sat. 1, 2, and 3.*

❽ Learn lots of facts about the large-scale brewing process at **Anheuser-Busch** during a free tour. Tours start every 30 minutes and last one hour and 15 minutes. ✉*2351 Busch Dr.* ☎*970/490–4691* ⊕*www.budweisertours.com* ☜*Free* ⊙*June–Aug., daily 9:30–4:30; Sept., daily 10–4; Oct.–May, Thurs.–Mon. 10–4.*

> ### NORTHERN FRONT RANGE BREWERIES
>
> The Front Range boasts several brewing firsts. In 1959 Coors of Golden introduced the first beer in an aluminum can. Boulder Beer is Colorado's first microbrewery, founded in 1979. The Great American Beer Festival started in 1981 in Boulder (now in Denver), was the nation's first beer festival. A tour of northern Front Range breweries could take you through Boulder, Nederland, Lyons, Longmont, Loveland, Greeley, and finally Fort Collins, where you can visit the legendary Clydesdales at Anheuser-Busch.

OFF THE BEATEN PATH

Colorado State Forest State Park. Rugged peaks, thick forests, and burbling streams make up this 70,768-acre park. Here you can fish for trout, boat the azure alpine lakes, ride horseback, hike or bicycle 130 mi of trails, and explore a few four-wheel-drive roads with views of the 12,000-foot Medicine Bow and Never Summer mountain ranges. Yurts and camping are available in winter so you can explore the 70 mi of groomed snowmobiling trails or the 50 mi of groomed and signed cross-country skiing and snowshoeing trails. Outfitters in Walden, 21 mi west of the park, arrange guided fly-fishing and horseback-riding trips. **Never Summer Nordic** (✉*4401 County Rd. 41* ☎*970/723–4070* ⊕*www.neversummernordic.com*) rents the yurts in the state park to cross-country skiers for hut-to-hut ski trips. ✉*56750 Hwy. 14, Walden* ✛*Drive 75 mi west on Rte. 14 from Fort Collins or 53 mi north of Granby on U.S. 40 and Rte. 125 to Walden and 21 mi east on Rte. 14 to park* ☎*970/723–8366* ⊕*www.parks.state.co.us* ☜*$5 a day per vehicle.*

FESTIVALS Colorado is ranked third in the United States in the number of brewpubs and small breweries, and during the last full weekend of June more

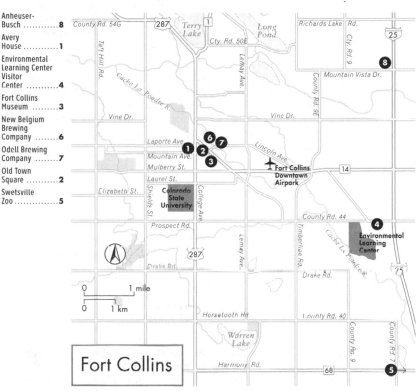

than 40 Colorado brewers show off their finest with 300 kegs of beer in Old Town Fort Collins at the **Colorado Brewers' Festival** (⊠ *Old Town Sq.* ☎ *970/484–6500* ⊕ *www.downtownfortcollins.com*). There's live music by regional talent for the two-day, Colorado-brews-only festival that Fort Collins brewers started in 1989.

SPORTS & THE OUTDOORS

BICYCLING

Both paved-trail cycling and single-track mountain biking are within easy access of town.

The **Poudre River Trail** (17 mi round-trip) is an easy riparian jaunt within Fort Collins. ⊠ *Trailhead: Lions Park on North Overland Trail; Trailhead: Environmental Learning Center on East Drake Rd.*

For short, single-track rides, Pineridge and Maxwell trails do not disappoint and connect to other trails for longer adventures: Head west on Drake Road to where it bends right and becomes South Overland Trail; turn left on County Road 42C and drive almost 1 mi to the posted fence opening. Serious gearheads crank at **Horsetooth Mountain Park** on the southwest side of Horsetooth Reservoir. Several single tracks and jeep trails provide any level of challenge.

Recycled Cycles (⊠*4031 S. Mason St.* ☎*970/223–1969* ⊕*www.recy-cled-cycles.com*) rents city bikes, mountain bikes, road bikes, kid trailers, and tandem cycles for $25–$50 per day.

FISHING

The North Platte, Laramie, and Cache la Poudre rivers are locally renowned for excellent fishing. Anyone older than 16 needs a Colorado fishing license, which you can obtain at local sporting-goods stores. See ⊕*www.wildlife.state.co.us/fishing* for more information.

★ The knowledgeable chaps at **St. Peter's Fly Shop** (⊠*202 Remington St.* ☎*970/498–8968* ⊕*www.stpetes.com*) arrange half-day to full-day guided or instructional wade and float trips in northern Colorado and southern Wyoming that can include permits for waters not open to the public. The store also sells gear, and the staff gladly provides information on conditions to independent fishermen.

GOLF

Mariana Butte Golf Course. This hilly course in Loveland has 30-mi views of the mountains. The course, designed by Dick Phelps, along the Big Thompson River skirts rock outcroppings and plenty of ponds. Don't forget your camera. ⊠*701 Clubhouse Dr., Loveland* ✛*Go west on 1st St. to Rossum Dr. and turn right on Clubhouse Dr.* ☎*970/667–8308* ⊕*www.golfloveland.com* ⌧*Reservations essential* ⅂.*18 holes. Yards: 6,572/5,420. Par: 36/72. Green Fee: $30/$55.*

HIKING

Twenty-nine miles of trails in **Horsetooth Mountain Park** offer easy to difficult hikes, some with views of the mountains to the west and the plains to the east. An easy 2.25-mi round-trip walk to **Horsetooth Falls** is a good hike that takes you into the foothills for a couple of hours. From the trailhead at the parking area, head up the Horsetooth Falls Trail and keep right at the junction with the Soderberg Trail. Go left at the next junction to get to the falls. *Drive west on Harmony Rd., which becomes County Rd. 38E at Taft Hill Rd. Follow 38E to park entrance* ☎*970/679–4570* ⊕*www.larimer.org/parks* ⌧*$6 per vehicle.*

Wildlife, songbirds, and springtime wildflowers abound along the trails in **Lory State Park.** For unbelievable views of the Front Range and the city from 7,000-foot Arthur's Rock, take **Arthur's Rock Trail** (⊠*Trailhead: Parking area at end of service road*). You climb fast on the switchbacks in the sparse woods before the trail levels off to cross the meadow, a breather before the final steep approach to the summit. Allow about two to three hours to hike the trail (3.4 mi round-trip and about 1,300 feet gain in elevation). Watch for poison ivy; be mindful of the occasional rattlesnake, and tap your walking stick on stones to shoo them off. ⊠*708 Lodgepole Dr., Bellvue* ✛*Drive north on Overland Trail and turn left on Bingham Hill Rd. Turn left at County Rd. 23 north and go 1.3 mi to County. Rd. 25G and turn right. It's 1.5 mi to park entrance* ⌧*$5 per vehicle.*

RAFTING & KAYAKING

The Cache la Poudre River is famous for its rapids, and river trips fill fast. It's wise to book with an outfitter at least two weeks in advance. The state-certified guides of **A-1 Wildwater** (✉ *2801 N. Shields St., 80524* ☎ *970/224–3379 or 800/369–4165* ⊕ *www.a1wildwater.com*) arrange guided tours as well as daylong and half-day trips for groups. A-1 also rents "duckies" (inflatable rafts for one to two people).

WHERE TO STAY & EAT

Lodging in Fort Collins is mainly national chain franchises. However, the city has a couple of enchanting inns that are close to downtown and outdoor activities. Dining establishments cover most cuisines and range from coffee shops with tasty sandwiches and soups to elegant restaurants serving continental classics.

$$$$ ✕ **Nico's Catacombs.** The chefs here excel in traditional Continental cuisine—including table-side cooking. Diners savor the house specialties (Dover sole, bouillabaisse, chateaubriand, and rack of lamb) in subterranean brick caverns outfitted with wood tables and dark upholstery—the appropriate old-world ambience for a restaurant that offers more than 500 wines. Daily specials may be fresh sea bass, elk loin, or veal. ✉ *115 S. College Ave.* ☎ *970/482–6426* ⚞ *Reservations essential* ▤ *AE, D, DC, MC, V* ⊘ *No lunch.*

★ $$ ✕ **Canino's.** Hearty Italian specialties are served in this historic, four-square house that still has a few stained-glass windows. Tables are set in wood-trim rooms that have hardwood floors with carpets. Appetizers like bruschetta and entrées such as cioppino, pollo alla cacciatora, and veal marsala are made in classic Italian style. Homemade cheesecake, tiramisu, or gelato—paired with a robust espresso—finish dinner on a sweet note. ✉ *613 S. College Ave.* ☎ *970/493–7205* ⚞ *Reservations essential* ▤ *AE, D, MC, V.*

$$ ✕ **Rio Grande Mexican Restaurant.** The Rio Grande always satisfies with old favorites such as tacos, quesadillas, burritos, flame-broiled Yucatan shrimp, and fajita steak dishes, as well as more-fiery Tex-Mex fare such as *camarones diabla* (shrimp in chilé de árbol). This spacious restaurant with old storefront windows draws mostly casual diners out for a wonderful, relaxed dinner. ✉ *143 W. Mountain Ave.* ☎ *970/224–5428* ▤ *AE, D, MC, V.*

$$ ✕ **Suehiro.** Sit at the high bar overlooking Linden Street in this light and open restaurant or, for more intimacy, ask for a table in the tearoom. The sushi is made fresh at the bar, and seafood entreés like salmon teriyaki or tempura always satisfy. Choose from more than 10 hot and cold sakes and specialty drinks to accompany your meal. The green-tea ice cream will refresh your palate at dessert. ✉ *223 Linden St., Suite 103* ☎ *970/482–3734* ▤ *AE, D, MC, V* ⊘ *No lunch Sun.*

$ ✕ **Cozzola's.** Base your pizza on thin "New York"–style crust, thick herb crust, or whole-wheat and poppy-seed crust, and then select a sauce: basil-tomato, fresh garlic, pesto, or spinach ricotta. Finally, select from the seemingly endless list of toppings that includes everything from banana peppers to feta cheese to sliced almonds. The roomy restaurant is done in rough-hewn wood and is bright and airy. You can get a couple of slices as a snack—made to order with your choices of toppings. ⊠*241 Linden St.* ☎*970/482–3557* ▤*AE, MC, V.*

$ ✗**Silver Grill Cafe.** This cool café, sleek with hardwood floors, red soda-fountain stools, and boxy booths serves up delicious breakfasts and lunchtime specials. The cinnamon rolls are legendary, and the cinnamon-roll French toast is also popular. The café's coffee is custom roasted, and the espresso drinks are good, too. The breakfast menu ranges from omelets to biscuits and gravy to hotcakes and homemade granola. Lunch is burgers and platters of chicken-fried steak, pot roast, meat loaf, and a few other traditional, homey comfort foods. There are also sandwiches or salads if you want a lighter lunch. ⊠*218 Walnut St.* ☎*970/484–4656* ▤*D, MC, V* ⊙*No dinner.*

¢ ✗**Starry Night.** Espresso drinkers sip their sustenance, including espresso smoothies, on leather couches or at tables under the night-blue ceiling while reading, chatting, or mulling over the sunflowers and the mural *Starry Night over Fort Collins* inspired by van Gogh. Beyond breakfast, there are soups, salads, and sandwiches at lunch and dinnertime. The café serves wine and sangria by the glass. For dessert there are pastries and tiramisu. ⊠*112 S. College Ave.* ☎*970/493–3039* ▤*MC, V.*

★ $$ ⊡**Edwards House B&B.** This quiet Victorian inn with hardwood floors and light, birchwood trim is four blocks from downtown. Guests enjoy gourmet breakfasts and dishes such as gingerbread pancakes or eggs Florentine. The video library is well stocked for those who forego relaxing on the large front porch or reading in the parlor. Unfussy, old-fashioned rooms are elegantly appointed with sleigh or canopy beds, gas stoves, Jacuzzis or claw-foot tubs, writing desks, and slate fireplaces. **Pros:** on a busy but quiet street near downtown, helpful and professional staff, pleasant grounds. **Cons:** small inn, fills up quickly. ⊠*402 W. Mountain Ave., 80521* ☎*970/493–9191 or 800/281–9190* ⊕*www.edwardshouse.com* ↝*8 rooms* ⌂*In-room: VCR, Wi-Fi. In-hotel: gym, no elevator, public Wi-Fi, parking (no fee), no kids under 10, no-smoking rooms* ▤*AE, D, MC, V* ⦿*BP.*

$ ⊡**Armstrong Hotel.** Walk into this refurbished 1923 downtown hotel's lobby with the original terrazo floor and pressed-tin ceiling and go back in time to the art deco 1920s. Take the sweeping staircase to a vintage room with hardwood floors and antique or reproduction furnishings and a claw-foot tub. Even the modern rooms have a retro look and feel at the Armstrong, which is on the National Register of Historic Places. The beds are made up with cotton sheets and feather duvets and pillows, and each room has a writing desk and coffeemaker. For a longer stay, two studio rooms and three apartment suites all with full kitchens provide more-personal space. Note that this is a no-smoking hotel. **Pros:** helpful staff; downtown location; low rates for a classy, historic lodging. **Con:** on a rather noisy street, particularly on weekend nights. ⊠*259 S. College Ave., 80524* ☎*970/484–3883 or 866/384–3883* ↝*32 rooms, 3 apartments, 2 studios* ⌂*In-room: kitchen (some), Wi-Fi. In-hotel: parking (no fee, no smoking rooms)* ▤*AE, D, MC, V.*

¢ ⊡**Fort Collins Plaza Inn.** This locally owned establishment is clean, bright, well maintained, and a better buy than the nearby franchise competitors. Rooms are simple and standard: beige walls, veneered furniture, and queen- or king-size beds. **Pros:** good value, near interstate for easy access. **Cons:** rather distant from dining and attractions, along busy and noisy thoroughfare. ✉ *3709 E. Mulberry St., 80524* ☎ *970/493–7800 or 800/434–5548* ⊕ *www.plaza-inn.com* 🛏 *135 rooms* ⟍ *In-hotel: restaurant, bar, pool, no elevator, laundry service, parking (no fee), no-smoking rooms* 🖃*AE, D, DC, MC, V* ⦿*CP.*

GUEST RANCH   🏨 **Colorado Cattle Company & Guest Ranch.** A real-deal working cattle
$$$$ ranch, the adults-only Cattle Company has 750 head of cattle and 10,000 acres of land in the plains of northeast Colorado. Saddle up with the ranch hands and help with the daily chores, drive cattle for days, and eat meals around the campfire while learning the basics of roping, tying, branding, and cutting. You can participate in a weeklong "cowboy adventure," where guests stay in rustic cabins with private baths and porches. Prices include lodging, meals, and activities. **Pros:** truly authentic experience, ability to mix cattle work with relaxation. **Cons:** no kids allowed, authentic experience includes chores. ✉*70008 Weld County Rd. 132, New Raymer 80742* ☎*970/437–5345* ⊕*www. coloradocattlecompany.com* 🛏*13 cabins* ⟍*In-hotel: bar, pool, laundry service, parking (no fee), some pets allowed, no kids under 21, no-smoking rooms* 🖃*AE, D, MC, V* ⊘*Closed Nov.–mid-Apr.*

NIGHTLIFE

BARS & CLUBS

College students line the bar at **Lucky Joe's Sidewalk Saloon** (✉*25 Old Town Sq.* ☎*970/493–2213*)for live music Wednesday–Sunday nights.

Mishawaka Inn (✉*13714 Poudre Canyon,* ⊹*25 mi north of Fort Collins on Rte. 14* ☎*970/482–4420*), an outdoor amphitheater on the banks of the Poudre River, corrals bands on the weekends. Most shows are evenings, and some are afternoons. Call for times.

BREWPUBS & MICROBREWERIES

The sports bar **C, B & Potts/Big Horn Brewery** (✉*1415 W. Elizabeth St.* ☎*970/221–1139*) is known for its burgers, barbecue, and international selection of beers. The establishment has a game room and a pool hall with a full bar. The brewery always has six house beers and two seasonals on tap. Favorites include the Vanilla Porter and the Big Horn Light. Try a seasonal like the Apricot Ale or the Big Red. All brews are crafted and bottled on-site in a 15-barrel, direct-fire brewing system. Tours are available by appointment. After taking a tour of the brewery at **Coopersmith's Pub & Brewery** (✉*5 Old Town Sq.* ☎*970/498–0483*), you can enjoy lunch on the patio with a crisp Punjabi Pale Ale or one of the other seven house-made beers on tap. The brewery always has three to five seasonal specialties to offer. Tours are offered by appointment. Coopersmith's own pool hall just outside the front door at 7 Old Town Square has 12 tables and serves pizza.

SHOPPING

Old Town Square (⊠*College and Mountain Aves. and Jefferson St.*) and adjacent Linden Street have historic buildings that house galleries, bookshops, cafés, brewpubs, and shops. Fifteen Old Town art galleries host the **First Friday Gallery Walk** on the first Friday of each month—no matter the weather—with appetizers and music from 6 PM to 9 PM. **Alpine Arts** (⊠*112 N. College Ave.* ☎*970/493–1941*)has some real standouts, particularly the photography and watercolors, among the more-usual pottery, carved wooden boxes, and jewelry. Everything is made by Colorado artists. Peruse the sculptures and the Colorado landscapes rendered in paintings and photography at **Art On Mountain** (⊠*102 W. Mountain Ave.,* ☎*970/223–6450*). The shopkeepers at the **Clothes Pony** (⊠*111 N. College Ave.* ☎*970/224–2866*) enjoy playing with the toys as much as the young customers do. The shop carries books, CDs, imported toys like Lego and Rokenbok, and classics like marbles, dolls, and stuffed animals. **Green Logic** (⊠*261 Linden St.* ☎*970/484–1740*) purveys boxes made from books, notepads with old floppy disks as covers, clocks made from 45-rpm vinyl records, and dishes made from recycled glass. There are also biodegradable bags for leaves, and clothing made from organic cotton. Western furniture is handcrafted and signed at **Mountain Woods Furniture** (⊠*11 Old Town Sq.* ☎*970/416–0701 or 877/686–9663*). Throws, pillows, blankets, and other accessories—all handmade by artisans—complement the aspen and pine lodge-style pieces. Shipping is available. **Repeat Boutique** (⊠*239 Linden St.* ☎*970/493–1039*) carries classy castoffs: silverware, antique furniture, paintings, and suits, vintage wedding dresses, casual outfits, and furs—mostly for women. **Right Card** (⊠*17 Old Town Square* ☎*970/482–8127*)carries a huge selection of greeting cards—everything from tasteful to tacky and classy to quirky, hip handbags, gorgeous handmade leather journals, and gifts that are a step above "trinket." **Trimble Court Artisans** (⊠*118 Trimble Ct.* ☎*970/221–0051*), a co-op with more than 40 members, sells paintings, jewelry, clothing, weavings, stained glass, and pottery. **Wagz** (⊠*132 N. College Ave.* ☎*970/482–9249*) has just the perfect treat or toy to take home to your favorite pooch.

BOULDER & NORTH CENTRAL COLORADO ESSENTIALS

TRANSPORTATION

BY AIR

Denver International Airport (DEN), 23 mi northeast of downtown Denver, is the primary commercial passenger airport serving north central Colorado. Allegiant Air connects Fort Collins and Las Vegas with scheduled service to the Fort Collins/Loveland Airport. Boulder and Granby have municipal airports but no commercial service.

Information **Denver International Airport (DEN)** (⊠ *8500 Peña Blvd., Denver* ☎ *800/247-2336 or 303/342-2000* ⊕ *www.flydenver.com).*

TRANSFERS The Denver Airport's Ground Transportation Information Center assists visitors with car rentals, door-to-door shuttles, public transportation, wheelchair services, charter buses, and limousine services. Boulder is approximately 45 mi (45 minutes–1 hour) from DIA; Granby approximately 110 mi (a little more than 2 hours); Fort Collins approximately 80 mi (1.25–1.5 hours); and Estes Park approximately 80 mi (about two hours).

Estes Park Shuttle (reservations essential) serves Estes Park and Rocky Mountain National Park from Denver, Denver International Airport, and Boulder. Super Shuttle serves Boulder, and Shamrock Airport Shuttle serves Fort Collins. Home James serves Granby, Grand Lake, and the guest ranches.

Contacts **Estes Park Shuttle** (☎ *970/586-5151).* **Ground Transportation Information Center** (☎ *800/247-2336 or 303/342-4059).* **Home James** (☎ *970/726-5060 or 800/359-7536).* **Shamrock Airport Express** (☎ *970/482-0505)* **Super Shuttle** (☎ *303/227 0000 Boulder).*

BY BUS

Greyhound Lines serves Boulder and Fort Collins. The expansive network of the Regional Transportation District (RTD) includes service from Denver and Denver International Airport to and within Boulder, Lyons, Niwot, Nederland, and the Eldora Ski Resort. The Hop bus (part of the RTD network) is a circulator that makes for easy carless travel within Boulder between the university, the Hill, the Twenty-Ninth Street shopping area, and downtown. Buses run in both directions every 6–10 minutes weekdays, and 15–20 minutes on weekends. Transfort serves Fort Collins's main thoroughfares.

Contacts **Greyhound Lines** (☎ *800/229-9424* ⊕ *www.greyhound.com).* **Regional Transportation District** *(RTD* ☎ *303/299-6000 or 800/366-7433* ⊕ *www.rtd-denver. com).* **Transfort** (☎ *970/221-6620* ⊕ *fcgov.com/transfort).*

BY CAR

Interstate 25, the most direct route from Denver to Fort Collins, is the north–south artery that connects the cities in the urban corridor along the Front Range. From Denver, U.S. 36 runs through Boulder, Lyons, and Estes Park to Rocky Mountain National Park. The direct route from Denver to Grand County is I–70 west to U.S. 40 (Empire Exit) and to U.S. 34. If you're driving directly to Fort Collins or Estes Park and Rocky Mountain National Park from Denver International Airport, the E–470 tollway connects Denver International Airport's Peña Boulevard to Interstate 25. U.S. 36 between Boulder and Estes Park is heavily traveled. Colorado Routes 119, 72, and 7 have much less traffic.

Information **AAA Colorado** (☎ *303/753-8800).* **CDOT Road Information** (☎ *303/639-1111 or 877/315-7623* ⊕ *www.dot.state.co.us).* **Colorado State Patrol** (☎ *303/239-4501, *277 from cellular phone).* **Rocky Mountain National Park Road Information** (☎ *970/586-1333).*

BY TAXI

Contacts **Yellow Cab** (✉ *Boulder* ☎ *303/777-7777*).

BY TRAIN

Amtrak provides all passenger rail service to and within north central Colorado. The Chicago–San Francisco *California Zephyr* stops in downtown Denver, in Winter Park/Fraser, and in Granby, once each day in both directions.

Contact **Amtrak** (☎ *800/872-7245, 303/534-2812* ⊕ *www.amtrak.com*).

CONTACTS & RESOURCES

EMERGENCIES

Ambulance or Police (☎ *911*).

24-Hour Medical Care Boulder Community Hospital (✉ *1100 Balsam Ave.* ☎ *303/440-2186* ⊕ *www.bch.org*). **Estes Park Medical Center** (✉ *555 Prospect Ave.* ☎ *970/586-2317* ⊕ *www.epmedcenter.com*). **Poudre Valley Hospital** (✉ *1024 S. Lemay Ave., Fort Collins* ☎ *970/495-7000* ⊕ *www.pvhs.org*). **St. Anthony Granby Medical Center** (✉ *480 E. Agate [U.S. 40], Granby* ☎ *970/887-2117* ⊕ *www.stanthonyhosp.org*).

VISITOR INFORMATION

Contacts **Boulder Convention & Visitors Bureau** (✉ *2440 Pearl St., 80302* ☎ *303/442-2911 or 800/444-0447* ⊕ *www.bouldercoloradousa.com*). **Lyons Chamber of Commerce** (✉ *Box 426, Lyons 80540* ☎ *303/823-5215 or 877/596-6726* ⊕ *www.lyons-colorado.com*). **Estes Park Convention and Visitors Bureau** (✉ *Box 1200]* ✉ *500 Big Thompson Ave., 80517* ☎ *970/577-9900 or 800/443-7837* 🖷 *970/586-1677* ⊕ *www.estesparkcvb.com*). **Fort Collins Convention & Visitors Bureau** (✉ *19 Old Town Square, Suite 137, 80524* ☎ *970/232-3840 or 800/274-3678* ⊕ *www.ftcollins.com*). **Granby Chamber of Commerce** (✉ *Box 35* ✉ *365 E. Agate, Suite B, 80446* ☎ *970/887-2311 or 800/325-1661* 🖷 *970/887-3895* ⊕ *www.granbychamber.com*). **Grand Lake Chamber of Commerce** (✉ *Box 429, Grand Lake 80447* ☎ *970/627-3402 or 800/531-1019* 🖷 *970/627-8007* ⊕ *www.grandlakechamber.com*). **Nederland Area Chamber of Commerce** (✉ *Box 85, Nederland 80466* ☎ *303/258-3936* ⊕ *www.nederlandchamber.org*).

Rocky Mountain National Park

WORD OF MOUTH

"I've seen it rainin' fire in the sky,
Yours truly, can talk to God
and listen to the casual reply,
Rocky Mountain high ..."
—John Denver, "Rocky Mountain High"

WELCOME TO ROCKY MOUNTAIN

TOP REASONS TO GO

★ **Gorgeous scenery:** Peer out over dozens of lakes, gaze up at majestic mountain peaks, and look around at pine-scented woods that are perfect for whiling away an afternoon.

★ **350 mi of trails:** Hike to your heart's content on mostly moderate trails crisscrossing the park.

★ **Continental Divide:** Straddle this great divide, which cuts through the western part of the park, separating water's flow to either the Pacific or Atlantic Ocean.

★ **Awesome ascents:** Trek to the summit of Longs Peak or go rock climbing on Lumpy Ridge. In winter, you can even ice climb.

★ **Wildlife viewing:** Spot elk and bighorn sheep; there are more than 3,000 and 800 of them, respectively.

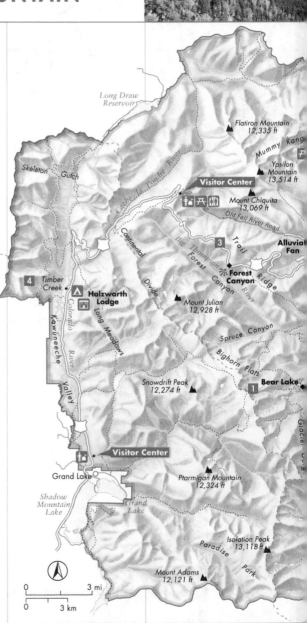

1 **Bear Lake.** One of the most photographed places in the park, Bear Lake is the hub for many trailheads. It gets crowded in summer.

2 **Longs Peak.** The highest peak in the park and the toughest to climb, this Fourteener pops up in many park vistas. If you want to reach the summit on a day-long trek, it's recommended you begin at 3 AM.

3 **Trail Ridge Road.** The alpine tundra of the park is the highlight here as the road climbs beyond the timberline.

4 **Timber Creek.** The park's western area is much less crowded, though it has its share of amenities and attractions, including a campground, historic sites, and a visitor center.

5 **Wild Basin Area.** Far from the crowds, the park's southeast quadrant consists of lovely expanses of sub-alpine forest punctuated by streams and lakes.

COLORADO

GETTING ORIENTED

Rocky Mountain National Park's 416-square-mi wilderness of meadows, mountains, and mirror-like lakes lie just 65 mi from Denver. The park is nine times smaller than Yellowstone, yet it receives almost as many visitors—3 million a year.

7

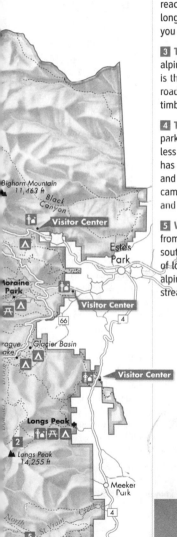

KEY	
🏠	Ranger Station
⛺	Campground
🪵	Picnic Area
🍴	Restaurant
🏨	Lodge
🚶	Trailhead
🚻	Restrooms
🔭	Scenic Viewpoint
·····	Walking/Hiking Trails
······	Bicycle Path

ROCKY MOUNTAIN NATIONAL PARK PLANNER

When to Go

Visiting Rocky Mountain is pleasurable any season, though **more than two-thirds of the park's annual 3 million visitors come in summer and fall.** But there is a good reason to put up with summer crowds: Only from Memorial Day to mid-October can you make the unforgettable drive over Trail Ridge Road. (It also closes occasionally in summer due to weather.) **For thinner high-season crowds, come in early June or September,** when many students are in school.

Spring is capricious—75°F one day and a blizzard the next (snowfall is the highest in March). June conditions can range from hot to cool and rainy. July typically ushers in high summer, which can last through September. Up on Trail Ridge Road and the Continental Divide, temperatures can be 15°–20° cooler. Spring and summer are the best times for wildlife viewing and fishing. In early fall, the trees blaze with brilliant foliage. Winter, when backcountry snow can be 4 feet deep and the wind brutal at high elevations, is the time for skiing, snowshoeing, and ice fishing.

Flora & Fauna

Volcanic uplifts and the savage clawing of receding glaciers have brought about Rocky Mountain's majestic landscape. You'll find three distinct ecosystems here—verdant mountain valleys towering with proud ponderosa pines and Douglas firs; higher and colder subalpine mountains with wind-whipped trees (krummholz) that grow at right angles; and harsh, unforgiving alpine tundra with dollhouse-size versions of familiar plants and wildflowers. The high, wind-whipped ecosystem of alpine tundra is seldom found outside the Arctic, yet it makes up one-third of the park's terrain. Few plants can survive at the tundra's elevation, but many beautiful wildflowers—including alpine forget-me-nots—bloom briefly in late June or early July.

The park has so much wildlife that you can often enjoy prime viewing from the seat of your car. Fall, when many animals begin moving down from higher elevations, is an excellent time to spot the park's animal residents. This is also when you'll hear the male elk bugle mating calls (popular "listening" spots are Horseshoe Park, Moraine Park, and Upper Beaver Meadows).

May through mid-October is the best time to see the bighorn sheep that congregate in the Horseshoe Park–Sheep Lakes area, just past the Fall River entrance. If you want to glimpse a moose, try Kawuneeche Valley, on the park's western side. Other animals in the park include mule deer, squirrels, chipmunks, pikas, beavers, and marmot. Common birds are broad-tailed and rufous hummingbirds, peregrine falcons, woodpeckers, mountain bluebirds, and Clark's nutcracker, as well as the white-tailed ptarmigan, spotted year-round on the alpine tundra.

Mountain lions, black bears, and bobcats also inhabit the park but are rarely spotted by visitors. Altogether, the park is home to 63 species of mammals and 280 bird species.

Getting There & Around

Estes Park and Grand Lake are the Rocky Mountain's gateway communities; from these you can enter the park via U.S. 34 or 36. The closest commercial airport is **Denver International Airport** (DEN). Its **Ground Transportation Information Center** (☎ 800/247–2336 or 303/342–4059) assists visitors with car rentals, door-to-door shuttles, and limousine services. From the airport, the eastern entrance of the park is 80 mi (about two hours). **Estes Park Shuttle** (☎ 970/586–5151; reservations essential) serves Estes Park and Rocky Mountain from Denver, the airport, and Boulder. Greyhound Lines serve Denver, Boulder, and Fort Collins, and Amtrak's California Zephyr stops in downtown Denver, Winter Park/Fraser, and Granby.

U.S. 36 runs from Denver through Boulder, Lyons, and Estes Park to the park; the portion between Boulder and Estes Park is heavily traveled—especially on summer weekends. Colorado Routes 119, 72, and 7 have much less traffic. If you're driving directly to Rocky Mountain from the airport, the E–470 tollway connects Peña Boulevard to Interstate 25.

The Colorado Department of Transportation plows roads efficiently, but winter snowstorms can slow traffic and create wet or icy conditions. For road conditions, call **CDOT Road Information** (P 303/639–1111).

The main thoroughfare in the park is Trail Ridge Road; in winter, it's plowed up to Many Parks Curve on the east side and the Colorado River trailhead on the west side. Gravel-surfaced, extremely curvy Old Fall River Road is open from July to September. Pulled trailers and vehicles longer than 25 feet are prohibited.

Two free park shuttle-bus routes operate along the park's popular Bear Lake Road from mid-June to mid-October. Unless you arrive early enough to get one of the few parking spaces beyond the park-and-ride, you must take the shuttle to access this area of the park. One bus line runs every 30 minutes between 7:30 AM and 7:30 PM from near the Fern Lake Trailhead to the Moraine Park Museum and on to Glacier Basin Campground. The other runs every 15 minutes between 7 AM and 7 PM from the campground to the Bear Lake Trailhead. There is also a shuttle bus running from the Estes Park Visitor Center to the park during the peak summer season. The bus passes most lodging and shopping areas, and many visitors like to use it as a free sightseeing tour, too. The Estes Park shuttle is free, but you must have a park pass if you transfer to the buses that enter the national park.

Festivals & Events

MID-MAY. Jazz Fest. Pack a picnic and bring the kids for a weekend afternoon of jazz performances and an art walk at the outdoor amphitheater downtown. ☎ 800/443–7837 ⊠ Estes Park ☎ Free.

JUNE. The Wool Market. Watch shearing, spinning, and herding contests, and see animal shows where angora goats, sheep, llamas, and alpacas are judged for their wool. . ☎ 800/443–7837 ⊠ Estes Park ☎ Free.

JULY. Rooftop Rodeo. A tradition for more than 00 years, this six-day event features a parade and nightly rodeos. ☎ 800/443–7837 ⊠ Estes Park.

SEPT. Longs Peak Scottish/ Irish Highland Festival. A traditional tattoo kicks off this three-day fair of athletic competitions, Celtic music, dancing, a parade, and seminars on topics such as heraldry and Scotch whisky. ☎ 970/586–6308 or 800/903–7837 ⊕ www.scotfest. com ⊠ Estes Park.

NOV.–APR. The **Estes Park Music Festival** stages concerts at 2 PM on Sunday afternoons from November through April at the Stanley Hotel. ☎ 970/586–9519 or 800/443–7837 ⊕ www. estesparkmusicalfestival.org.

7

By Debbie
Harmsen &
Molly Moker

Updated by
Gregory Robl

ANYONE WHO DELIGHTS IN ALPINE lakes, mountain peaks, and an abundance of wildlife—not to mention dizzying heights—should consider Rocky Mountain National Park. Here, a single hour's drive leads from a 7,800-foot elevation at park headquarters to the 12,183-foot apex of the twisting and turning Trail Ridge Road. More than 350 mi of hiking trails take you to the park's many treasures: meadows flushed with wildflowers, cool dense forests of lodgepole pine and Engelmann spruce, and the noticeable presence of wildlife, including elk and bighorn sheep.

SCENIC DRIVE

Bear Lake Road. This 9-mi drive offers superlative views of Longs Peak (14,255-foot summit) and the glaciers surrounding Bear Lake, winding past shimmering waterfalls perpetually shrouded with rainbows. ⊠ *Runs from the Beaver Meadow Entrance Station to Bear Lake.*

Old Fall River Road. A one-way 11-mi loop up to the Alpine Visitor Center and back down along Trail Ridge Road is a scenic alternative to driving Trail Ridge Road twice. Start at West Horseshoe Park, which has the park's largest concentrations of sheep and elk, and head up the paved and gravel Old Fall River Road, passing Chasm Falls. Early visitors to the park traveled Old Fall River Road before Trail Ridge Road was built.

Fodor's Choice
★

Trail Ridge Road. This is the park's star attraction and the world's highest continuous paved highway, topping out at 12,183 feet. The 48-mi road connects the park's gateways of Estes Park and Grand Lake. The views around each bend—of moraines and glaciers, and craggy hills framing emerald meadows carpeted with columbine and Indian paintbrush—are truly awesome. As it passes through three ecosystems—montane, subalpine, and arctic tundra—the road climbs 4,300 feet in elevation. As you drive the road, take your time at the numerous turnouts to gaze over verdant valleys, brushed with yellowing aspen in fall, that slope between the glacier-etched granite peaks. **Many Parks Curve** affords views of the crest of the Continental Divide and of the **Alluvial Fan,** a huge gash a vicious flood created after an earthen dam broke in 1982. ■ TIP→ Pick up a copy of the *Trail Ridge Road Guide,* available at visitor centers, for an overview of what you will be seeing as you drive the road. In normal traffic, it's a two-hour drive across the park, but it's best to give yourself three to four hours to allow for leisurely breaks at the overlooks. Note that the middle part of the road closes down again by mid-October, though you can still drive up about 10 mi from the west and 8 mi from the east. ⊠ *Trail Ridge Rd. (U.S. 34)* ☉ *June–mid-Oct.*

WHAT TO SEE

HISTORIC SITES

Rocky Mountain has more than 100 sites of historic significance. In order to be nominated for the National Register of Historic Places, a park building must tie in strongly to the park's history in terms of architecture, archaeology, engineering, or culture. Most buildings at Rocky Mountain are done in the rustic style, a design preferred by the National Park Service's first director, Stephen Mather. The rustic style is a way to incorporate nature within man-made structures.

Eugenia Mine. A moderate, 1.4-mi hike takes you to this abandoned mine. ⊠*Longs Peak* 🔋*Free.*

🕒 **Holzwarth Historic Site.** A scenic 0.5-mi interpretive trail leads you over the Colorado River to the original "dude ranch" that the Holzwarth family ran between the 1920s and 1950s. Allow about an hour to explore the buildings and chat with a ranger. It's a great place for families to learn about homesteading. ⊠*Trail Ridge Rd., ⊹about 13 mi west of the Alpine Visitor Center* 🔋*Free* 🕙*Daily 10–4.*

Lulu City. A few remnants of cabins and mining equipment are all that's left of this onetime silver mining town, established in 1880. Reach it by hiking the 3.6-mi Colorado River Trail. Look for wagon ruts from the old Stewart Toll Road and the ruins of cabins in Shipler Park. The Colorado River is a mere stream at this point, flowing south from its headwaters at nearby La Poudre Pass. ⊠*Off Trail Ridge Rd., ⊹10.5 mi north of Grand Lake.*

Moraine Park Museum. Lectures, slide shows, and displays explain the park's geology, botany, and history. ⊠*Bear Lake Rd., ⊹off U.S. 36* 🔋*Free* 🕙*May–Sept., daily 9–5.*

SCENIC STOPS

Alluvial Fan. On July 15, 1982, the 79-year-old dam at Lawn Lake burst, and water roared into Estes Park, killing three people and causing major flooding. The flood created the alluvial fan, a pile of glacial and streambed debris up to 44 feet deep on the north side of Horseshoe Park. A 0.5-mi trail allows you to explore it up close. You also can view it from the Rainbow Curve lookout on Trail Ridge Road. ⊠*Fall River Rd., ⊹3 mi from the Fall River entrance station.*

★ **Bear Lake.** Thanks to its picturesque location, easy accessibility, and the good hiking trails nearby, this small alpine lake below Flattop Mountain and Hallett Peak is one of the most popular destinations in the park. Free park shuttle buses can take you here. ⊠*Bear Lake Rd., ⊹ 10 mi southwest of Beaver Meadows Visitor Center.*

Farview Curve Overlook. At an elevation of 10,120 feet, this lookout affords a panoramic view of the Colorado River near its origin and the Grand Ditch, a water diversion project dating from 1890 that's still in use today. You can also see the once-volcanic peaks of Never Summer Range along the park's western boundary. ⊠*Trail Ridge Rd., ⊹ about 18 mi west of Alpine Visitor Center.*

Forest Canyon Overlook. Beyond the classic U-shape glacial valley lies a high-alpine circle of ice-blue pools (the Gorge Lakes) framed by ragged peaks. ⊠*Trail Ridge Rd., ⊹ 14 mi east of Alpine Visitor Center.*

VISITOR CENTERS

Alpine Visitor Center. At the top of Trail Ridge Road, this visitor center is open only when that road is navigable. There's a snack bar inside. ⊠*Trail Ridge Rd., ⊹ at Fall River Pass 22 mi from the Beaver Meadows entrance* ☎*970/586–1206* ⊙*Memorial Day–mid-Oct., daily 9–5.*

★ **Beaver Meadows Visitor Center.** Housing park headquarters, this visitor center was designed by students of the Frank Lloyd Wright School of Architecture at Taliesen West using the park's popular rustic style, which integrates buildings into their natural surroundings. Completed in 1966, it was named a National Historic Landmark in 2001. The surrounding utility buildings are also on the National Register and are noteworthy examples of the rustic-style buildings that the Civilian Conservation Corps constructed during the Depression. The visitor center has a terrific orientation film and a large relief map of the park. ⊠*U.S. 36, before the Beaver Meadows entrance* ☎*970/586–1206* ⊙*Mid-June–Labor Day, Mon.–Wed. 8–8 and Thurs.–Sat. 8–9; early Sept.–mid-June, daily 8–4:30.*

Fall River Visitor Center. The Discovery Room, which houses everything from old ranger outfits to elk antlers, coyote pelts, and bighorn sheep skulls for hands-on exploration, is a favorite with kids (and adults) at this northeast center. ⊠*U.S. 34 at the Fall River entrance station* ☎*970/586–1206* ⊙*Mid-June–Labor Day, daily 9–5; winter hrs vary.*

Kawuneeche Visitor Center. The park's only west-side source of visitor information has exhibits on the plant and animal life of the area, as well as a large three-dimensional map of the park and an orientation film. ⊠*U.S. 34, before the Grand Lake entrance station* ☎*970/586–1206* ⊙*Mid-June–mid-Aug., daily 8–6; mid-Aug.–mid-June, daily 8–4:30.*

SPORTS & THE OUTDOORS

BIRD-WATCHING

Spring and summer, early in the morning, are the best times for bird-watching in the park. **Lumpy Ridge** is a nesting ground for raptors such as golden eagles, red-tailed hawks, and peregrine falcons. Migratory songbirds from South America have summer breeding grounds near the **Endovalley Picnic Area.** The **alpine tundra** is habitat for white-tailed ptarmigan. The **alluvial fan** is the place for viewing broad-tailed hummingbirds, hairy woodpeckers, ouzels, and the occasional raptor.

FISHING

Rocky Mountain is a wonderful place to fish, especially for trout—German brown, brook, rainbow, cutthroat, and greenback cutthroat—but check at a visitor center about regulations and information on specific closures, catch-and-release areas, and limits on size and possession. No fishing is allowed at Bear Lake. Rangers recommend the more-remote backcountry lakes, since they are less crowded. Anyone older than 16 needs a Colorado fishing license, which you can obtain at local sporting-goods stores. See ⊕*www.wildlife.state.co.us/fishing* for details.

OUTFITTERS & EXPEDITIONS

Estes Angler arranges four-, six-, and eight-hour fly-fishing trips—including on horseback—into the park's quieter regions. ⊠*338 W. Riverside Dr., Estes Park* ☎*970/586-2110 or 800/586-2110* ⊕*www.estesangler.com.*

Scot's Sporting Goods. Scot's provides four-, six-, and eight-hour fishing instruction trips daily from May through September. Clinics, geared toward first-timers, focus on casting, reading the water, identifying insects for flies, and properly presenting natural and artificial flies to the fish. Half-day excursions into the park are available for three or more people. You can also rent and buy gear here. ☎*2325 Spruce Ave.* ⊠*870 Moraine Ave., Estes Park* ☎*970/586-2877* ⌑*$80–$190* ⊗*May–Sept., daily 8–8.*

ACCESSIBLE HIKES

Alluvial Fan—0.2-mi interpretive trail.

Bear Lake—0.6-mi loop nature trail.

Coyote Valley—1-mi loop on gravel; look for elk and moose.

Lily Lake—0.7-mi loop on gravel; view wildflowers.

Sprague Lake—0.5 mi loop walk; view the Continental Divide.

HIKING

Fodor's Choice ★

Rocky Mountain National Park contains 350 mi of hiking trails, so you could theoretically wander the park for weeks. Most visitors explore just a small portion of these trails, so some of the park's most accessible and scenic paths can resemble a backcountry highway on busy summer days. The high-alpine terrain around Bear Lake is the park's most popular hiking area, and it's well worth exploring. However, for a truly remote experience, hike one of the trails in the far northern end of the park or in the Wild Basin area to the south. Keep in mind that trails at higher elevations may have some snow on them even in July. And because of afternoon thunderstorms on most summer afternoons, an early morning start is highly recommended; the last place you want to be when a storm approaches is on a peak or anywhere above the tree line. All trails are round-trip unless stated otherwise.

EASY ★

Bear Lake. The virtually flat nature trail around Bear Lake is an easy, 1-mi walk that's wheelchair accessible. Sharing the route with you will likely be plenty of other hikers as well as songbirds and chipmunks. ⊠*Trailhead: Bear Lake, Bear Lake Rd.*

☺ **Copeland Falls.** The 0.6-mi hike to these Wild Basin area falls is a good option for families, as the terrain is relatively flat (only a 15-foot elevation gain). ⊠*Trailhead: Wild Basin.*

Cub Lake. This 4.6-mi, three-hour hike takes you through meadows and stands of aspen trees and up 540 feet in elevation to a lake with water lilies. ⊠*Trailhead: Cub Lake.* ✛ *Take Bear Lake Rd. to Moraine Park Campground, turn right, then left at road to trailhead.*

East Inlet Trail. You can get to **Adams Falls** in about 15 minutes on this 0.3-mi route with an 80-foot climb in elevation. The trail to the falls will likely be packed with visitors, so if you have time, continue east on the trail past the falls to enjoy more solitude, see wildlife, and catch views of Mount Craig from near the East Meadow campground. Note, however, that beyond the falls the elevation climbs between 1,500 and 1,900 feet, making it a challenging hike. ✉ *Trailhead: East Inlet, end of W. Portal Rd., ✛ W. Portal Rd. spurs off Trail Ridge Rd. by entrance to Grand Lake Village. Stay left at junction with Grand Ave.*

Glacier Gorge Trail. The 5-mi hike to **Mills Lake** can be crowded, but the reward is one of the park's prettiest lakes, set against the breathtaking backdrop of Longs Peak, Pagoda Mountain, and the Keyboard of the Winds. There's a modest elevation gain of 700 feet. About 1 mi in, you pass **Alberta Falls,** a popular destination in and of itself. The hike travels along Glacier Creek, under the shade of a subalpine forest. Give yourself at least four hours for hiking and lingering time. ✛ *Off Bear Lake Rd., 9 mi south of the Beaver Meadows entrance station.*

★ **Sprague Lake.** With virtually no elevation gain, this 1-mi, pine-lined path is wheelchair accessible and provides views of Hallet Peak and Flattop Mountain. ✉ *Trailhead: Sprague Lake, Bear Lake Rd.*

MODERATE **Bear Lake to Emerald Lake.** This scenic, calorie-burning hike begins at Bear Lake and takes you first on a moderately level, 0.5-mi journey to

Fodor's Choice ★ **Nymph Lake.** From here, the trail gets steeper, with a 425-foot elevation gain, as it winds around for 0.6 mi to **Dream Lake.** The last stretch is the most arduous part of the hike, an almost all-uphill 0.7-mi trek to lovely **Emerald Lake,** where you can perch on a boulder and enjoy the view. Round-trip, the hike is 3.6 mi, with an elevation gain of 605 feet. Allow two hours or more, depending on stops. ✉ *Trailhead: Bear Lake, off Bear Lake Rd.*

Colorado River Trail This walk to the ghost town of Lulu City on the west side of the park is excellent for looking for the bighorn sheep, elk, and moose that reside in the area. Part of the former stagecoach route that went from Granby to Walden, the 7.4-mi trail parallels the infant Colorado River to the meadow where Lulu City once stood. Elevation gain is 350 feet. ✉ *Trailhead: Colorado River, Trail Ridge Rd.*

Fern Lake Trail. Heading to Odessa Lake from the north involves a steep hike, but usually you'll encounter fewer fellow hikers than if you begin at Bear Lake. Along the way, you'll come to the Arch Rocks; The Pool, an eroded formation in the Big Thompson River; two waterfalls; and

---

SHUTTLE TO THE TRAILS

The many trails in the Bear Lake area of the park are so popular that parking areas at the trailheads usually cannot accommodate all of the hikers' cars. Shuttle buses connect a large park-and-ride facility at the Glacier Basin Campground with the Cub Lake, Fern Lake, Glacier Gorge Junction, Sprague Lake, and Bear Lake trailheads. Buses run daily between mid-June and mid-September. The Bear Lake shuttle runs approximately every 15 minutes between 7 AM and 7 PM; the Moraine Park shuttle runs approximately every 30 minutes between 7:30 AM and 7:30 PM.

Fern Lake (4 mi from your starting point). Odessa Lake itself lies at the foot of Tourmaline Gorge, below the craggy summits of Gabletop Mountain, Little Matterhorn, Knobtop Mountain, and Notchtop Mountain. For a full day of spectacular scenery, continue past Odessa to Bear Lake (8.5 mi total), where you can pick up the shuttle back to the Fern Lake Trailhead. Total elevation gain is 1,375 feet. ⊠ *Off Bear Lake Rd., ✛ about 1.5 mi south of the Beaver Meadows entrance station.*

Mills Lake. From this popular lake you can admire the high peaks and the ever-imposing Longs Peak. The 5.6-mi hike gains 750 feet in elevation as it takes you past Alberta Falls and Glacier Falls en route to the shimmering lake at the mouth of Glacier Gorge. Give yourself four hours for the hiking and lingering time. ⊠ *Trailhead: Glacier Gorge Junction.*

Sun Valley Trail System. The Continental Divide Trail is comprised of two loops—2.6 mi to 4.5 mi—that will take you through pine forests to the Colorado River, where there are excellent views of the high mountains in the Never Summer Wilderness. The elevation gain is minimal, and except for equestrian traffic, the loops are peaceful compared to other hikes in the area. ⊠ *Trailhead: Harbison Meadows Picnic Area, Trail Ridge Rd., ✛ about 1 mi inside park from Grand Lake Entrance.*

DIFFICULT   **Bluebird Lake Trail.** The 4.8-mi climb from the Wild Basin trailhead to Ouzel Lake (1,510-feet elevation gain) is especially scenic. You pass Copeland Falls, Calypso Cascades, and Ouzel Falls, plus an area that was burned in a lightning-instigated fire in 1978—today a mix of bright pink fireweed and charred tree trunks. ✛ *Off Rte. 7, 12.7 mi south of Estes Park.*

Chasm Lake Trail. Nestled in the shadow of Longs Peak and Mount Meeker, Chasm Lake offers one of Colorado's most impressive backdrops, so en route to it, expect to encounter plenty of other hikers. The 4.2-mi Chasm Lake Trail, reached via the Longs Peak Trail, has a 2,360-foot elevation gain. Just before the lake, you'll need to climb a small rock ledge, which can be a bit of a challenge for the less surefooted; follow the cairns for the most straightforward route. Once atop the ledge, you'll catch your first memorable view of the lake. ✛ *Off Rte. 7, 9 mi south of Estes Park.*

Deer Mountain Trail. This 6-mi round-trip trek to the top of 10,083-foot Deer Mountain is a great way for hikers who don't mind a bit of a climb to enjoy the views from the summit of a lesser peak. You'll gain more than 1,000 feet in elevation as you follow the switchbacking trail through ponderosa pine, aspen, and fir trees. The reward at the top is a panoramic view of the park's east-side mountains. ⊠ *Deer Ridge Junction, U.S. 34 at U.S. 36, ✛ 3 mi north of the Beaver Meadows entrance station.*

★   **Longs Peak Trail.** Climbing this 14,255-foot mountain (one of 54 "Fourteeners" in Colorado) is an ambitious goal for many people—but only those who are very fit and acclimated to the altitude should attempt it. The 16-mi round-trip hike up Longs requires a predawn start (3 AM is

Longs Peak: The Northernmost Fourteener

At 14,255 feet above sea level, **Longs Peak** has long fascinated explorers to the region. Isabella L. Bird wrote of it, "It is one of the noblest of mountains, but in one's imagination it grows to be much more than a mountain. It becomes invested with a personality."

It was named after Major Stephen H. Long, who led an expedition in 1820 up the Platte River to the base of the Rockies. Long never ascended the mountain—in fact, he didn't even get within 40 mi of it—but a few decades later, in 1868, the one-armed Civil War veteran John Wesley Powell climbed to its summit.

In the park's southeast quadrant, Longs Peak is northernmost of the 54 mountains in Colorado that reach above the 14,000-foot mark, and one of more than 114 named mountains in the park higher than 10,000 feet. You can see its distinctive flat-top, rectangular-shape summit from many spots on the park's east side and Trail Ridge Road.

If you want to make the ambitious climb to Longs summit—and it's only recommended for those who are strong climbers and well acclimated to the altitude—you should begin by 3 AM so that you're down from the summit when the typical afternoon thunderstorm hits.

ideal) so that you're off the summit before the typical summer afternoon thunderstorm hits. Also, the last 2 mi or so of the trail are very exposed—you have to traverse narrow ledges with vertigo-inducing drop-offs. That said, summiting Longs can be one of the most rewarding hikes you'll ever attempt. The Keyhole route is the traditional means of ascent, and the number of people going up it on a summer day can be astounding given the rigors of the hike. Though just as scenic, the Loft route, between Longs and Mount Meeker from Chasm Lake, is not clearly marked and is therefore difficult to navigate. ✛ *Off Rte. 7, 9 mi south of Estes Park.*

HORSEBACK RIDING

Horses and riders can access 260 mi of trails in Rocky Mountain.

OUTFITTERS & EXPEDITIONS
Allenspark Livery. The stable offers one- to four-hour rides into Roosevelt National Forest and all-day pack and fishing trips into the Wild Basin area in the park's southeast corner. ⊠ *211 Main St., Allenspark* ☎ *303/747–2551* ⊠ *$30–$65* ☉ *June–mid Sept.*

National Park Gateway Stables and Cowpoke Corner Corrals. Guided trips into the national park range from two-hour rides to Little Horseshoe Park to full-day rides along the Roaring River to Lawn or Ypsilon Lake. ⊠ *46000 Fall River Rd., Estes Park 80517* ☎ *970/586–5269 or 970/586–5890* ⊕ *www.nationalparkgatewaystables.com* ⊠ *$45–$125* ▭ *D, MC, V* ☉ *Mid May–early Oct.*

Sombrero Ranches, Inc. Sombrero offers guided rides into the wilderness and national park, including scenic and relaxing early-morning breakfast rides and pack trips. The Boulder-based company also arranges private camping trips. Guided horseback riding trips last two to five hours.

✉*Grand Lake Stables, 304 W. Portal Rd., Grand Lake* ☎*970/627–3514* ⊕*www.sombrero.com* ✍*$30–$80* ☉*Mid-May–mid-Sept.*

ROCK CLIMBING

Expert rock climbers as well as novices can try hundreds of classic climbs here. The burgeoning sport of ice climbing also thrives in the park. The Diamond, Lumpy Ridge, and Petit Grepons are the places for rock climbing, while well-known ice-climbing spots include Hidden Falls, Loch Vale, and Emerald and Black lakes.

The Diamond. Named for its distinctive shape, this sheer cliff on the east face of Longs Peak is the site of more than 30 routes. The "easiest," the Casual Route, is rated 5.10. ✉*Rte. 7,* ⊕*9 mi south of Estes Park.*

Lumpy Ridge. These granite crags 1 mi north of Estes Park draw climbers from along Colorado's Front Range. Some of the routes are closed from March to July, due to nesting raptors. Its rock outcroppings, including the distinctive Twin Owls, rise behind the Stanley Hotel and can be seen from town. Mainliner, a 5.9-rated, six-pitch route on Lumpy's Sundance Buttress, is one of the classics. ✉*MacGregor Ave.,* ⊕*off Rte. 34.*

★ **Petit Grepon.** If you're interested in a spectacular setting, try this internationally famous spire, southwest of Bear Lake, above Sky Pond. It attracts rock climbers from all over the world. Hike south from the Glacier Gorge Trailhead. ✉*End of Bear Lake Rd.*

OUTFITTER **Colorado Mountain School** is the oldest continuously operating U.S. guide service and an invaluable resource. You can take introductory half-day and one- to seven-day courses on climbing and rappelling technique, or sign up for guided introductory trips, full-day climbs, and longer expeditions. Make reservations as far as six weeks in advance for summer climbs. The school also runs a 16-bed hostel. ✉*341 Moraine Ave., Estes Park* ☎*800/836–4008 Ext. 3* ⊕*www.totalclimbing.com* ✍*$75–$245.*

WINTER SPORTS

Each winter, the popularity of snowshoeing in the park increases. It's a wonderful way to experience Rocky Mountain's majestic winter side, when the jagged peaks are softened with a blanket of snow and the summer hordes are nonexistent. You can snowshoe any of the summer hiking trails that are accessible by road; many of them also become well-traveled cross-country ski trails.

Backcountry skiing within the park ranges from gentle cross-country outings to full on telemarking down steep chutes and glaciers. Come spring, when avalanche danger decreases, the park has some classic ski descents for those on telemark or alpine touring equipment. Ask a ranger about conditions and gear up as if you were spending the night. If you plan on venturing off trail, take a shovel, probe pole, and avalanche transceiver. Two trails to try are Tonahutu Creek Trail (near Kawuneeche Visitor Center) and the Colorado River Trail to Lulu City (start at the Timber Creek Campground).

7

FODOR'S FIRST PERSON

Barbara Colligan
Colorado Resident

In September and October, there are traffic jams at the park as people drive up to listen to the elk bugling. It's a lot of fun. The rangers and park volunteers keep track of where the elk are and direct visitors to the mating spots. The bugling is high-pitched, and if it's light enough, you can see the elk put his head in the air. He really puts his whole head and shoulders into it, and his throat puffs out. It's fascinating to listen to. It echoes across the forest.

The call is to let the other bulls know "These are my females. You other males stay away." They sometimes have clashes. I've seen a big elk chase a smaller one off. The females are grouped around the bulls. Once I saw a female start to move away and the bull pushed her back into line.

Having binoculars really makes a difference, too. With those I could see the elk even when it got dark.

Only on the west side of the park are you permitted to snowmobile, but you must register at Kawuneeche Visitor Center before traveling up the unplowed section of Trail Ridge Road up to Milner Pass. Check the park newspaper, *High Country Headlines*, for ranger-guided tours.

OUTFITTERS & EXPEDITIONS   **Estes Park Mountain Shop.** Rent snowshoes and skis here, as well as fishing, hiking, and climbing equipment. The store gives half- and full-day guided fly-fishing trips into the park year-round for all levels as well as four- and eight-hour climbing trips to areas near Rocky Mountain National Park. ✉*2050 Big Thompson Ave., Estes Park* ☎*970/586–6548 or 866/303–6548* ⊕*www.estesparkmountainshop.com.*

Never Summer Mountain Sports (✉*919 Grand Ave., Grand Lake* ☎*970/627–3642*) rents cross-country skis, boots, and poles, and sells hiking and some climbing gear.

Outdoor World (✉*156 E. Elkhorn Ave., Estes Park* ☎*970/586–2114*) has daily snowshoe rentals, which include gaiters and poles.

EDUCATIONAL OFFERINGS

ART PROGRAM

Artist-in-Residence. Professional writers, sculptors, composers, and visual and performing artists can stay in a rustic cabin for two weeks in summer while working on their art. During their stay, they must do two park presentations, and donate a piece of original work to Rocky Mountain that relates to their stay. Applications must be received by December for requests for the following summer. ☎*970/586–1206.*

CLASSES & SEMINARS

★ **Rocky Mountain Field Seminars.** The Rocky Mountain Nature Association sponsors some 100 hands-on seminars for adults and children on such topics as natural history, geology, bird-watching, wildflower identification, wildlife biology, photography, and sketching. Children's classes run three hours, and adult classes last one to five days. All are taught by expert instructors. College students often receive academic credit, and teachers can receive recertification credit. ⊠*1895 Fall River Rd., Estes Park* ☎*970/586–3262* ⊕*www.rmna.org* ⊠*$20–$75 per day* ☉*Jan.–Oct.*

RANGER PROGRAMS

☾ **Junior Ranger Program.** Pick up a Junior Ranger activity book (in English or Spanish) at any visitor center. Program content has been developed for children ages 6–12 and focuses on environmental education, identifying birds and wildlife, and outdoor safety skills. Once a child has completed all of the activities, a ranger will look over the book and award a Junior Ranger badge. ☎*970/586–1206* ⊠*Free.*

☾ ★ **Ranger-Led Programs.** With more than 150 programs each summer, there are many opportunities to join in on free hikes, talks, and activities conducted by those who know the park best. Topics may include the wildlife, geology, vegetation, or park history. At night, storytelling, slide shows, and talks may be part of the evening campfire program, held in summer at park campgrounds and at Beaver Meadows Visitor Center. There are also evening hikes and stargazing sessions. On Friday, stories, songs, and marshmallow roasts take place at Holzwarth Historic Site. In winter, rangers lead snowshoeing and cross-country ski tours. Special programs for kids include "Ranger for a Day," "Skins and Skulls," and "Tales for Tots" (for preschool-age kids with an accompanying adult). Look for the extensive program schedule in the park's newspaper. ☎*970/586–1206* ⊠*Free.*

NEARBY TOWNS

Estes Park, 5 mi east of Rocky Mountain, is the park's most popular gateway. The town sits at an altitude of more than 7,500 feet, with 14,255-feet Longs Peak and a chorus of surrounding mountains as its stunning backdrop. Many of the small hotels lining the roads are mom-and-pop outfits that have been passed down through several generations. Estes Park's quieter cousin, **Grand Lake,** 1.5 mi outside the park's west entrance, gets busy in summer, but overall has a low-key, Western graciousness. In winter, it's *the* snowmobiling capital and ice-fishing destination for Coloradans. At the park's southwestern entrance are Arapaho National/Roosevelt Forest, Arapaho National Recreational Area, and the small town of **Granby,** the place to go for big-game hunting, mountain biking, and skiing at nearby SolVista resort, Winter Park, and Mary Jane. *For more information about Estes Park, Grand Lake, and Granby, see the Boulder & North Central Colorado chapter in this book.*

WHERE TO STAY & EAT

ABOUT THE RESTAURANTS

In the park itself, there are no real dining establishments, though you can get snacks and light fare at the top of the Trail Ridge Road. The park also has a handful of scenic picnic areas, all with tables and pit or flush toilets. *For restaurants near the park, see the Estes Park, Grand Lake, and Granby sections in the Boulder & North Central Colorado chapter in this book.*

ABOUT THE CAMPGROUNDS

Five top-notch campgrounds in the park meet the needs of campers, whether you're staying in a tent, trailer, or RV (only two campgrounds accept reservations; the others fill up on a first-come, first-served basis). Backcountry camping requires advance reservations or a day-of-trip permit; contact **Backcountry Permits, Rocky Mountain National Park** (⊠ *Beaver Meadows Visitor Center, U.S. 36 southwest of Estes Park* ☎ *970/586–1242* ⊙ *May–Sept., daily 7–7; Oct.–Apr., daily 8–4:30*) before starting out.

The park has no hotels or lodges. *For accommodations near the park, see the Estes Park, Grand Lake, and Granby sections in the Boulder & North Central Colorado chapter in this book.*

WHAT IT COSTS					
	¢	$	$$	$$$	$$$$
RESTAURANTS	under $8	$8–$12	$13–$18	$19–$25	over $25
CAMPING	under $10	$10–$17	$18–$35	$36–$49	over $50

Restaurant prices are for a main course at dinner, excluding 3.7% sales tax. Camping prices are for a standard (no hookups, pit toilets, fire grates, picnic tables) campsite per night.

WHERE TO EAT

¢ ✕ **Trail Ridge Store Snack Bar.** Pick up snacks and sandwiches, burgers, salads, and soups at the Alpine Visitor Center. ⊠ *Trail Ridge Rd.* ▤ *AE, D, MC, V* ⊙ *Closed mid-Oct.–May.*

PICNIC AREAS **Endovalley** (⊠ *U.S. 34, at the beginning of Old Fall River Rd.*), with 32 tables and 30 fire grates, is the largest picnic area in the park. The views here are of aspen groves, Fall River Pass, and a beautiful lake.

Hollowell Park (✛ *Off Bear Lake Rd., between the Moraine Park Museum and Glacier Basin campground*), in a meadow near Mill Creek, is a lovely spot for a picnic. The Mill Creek Basin trailhead is nearby. There are nine tables, no running water, and no fire grates.

⟲ **Sprague Lake** (✛ *0.6-mi from the intersection of Bear Lake Rd. and U.S. 36*) has 23 tables, all wheelchair accessible, and restrooms.

WHERE TO STAY

$$ ⚠ **Aspenglen Campground.** This quiet, east-side spot near the north entrance is set in open pine woodland along Fall River. It doesn't have the views of Moraine Park or Glacier Basin, but it is small and peace-

ful. There are a few excellent walk-in sites for those who want to pitch a tent away from the crowds but still close to the car. All sites accommodate RVs, tents, trailers, or campers. Firewood and ice are for sale. ⊕*Drive past Fall River Visitor Center on U.S. 34 and turn left at the campground road.* ⌒*54 sites* ⌂*Flush toilets, drinking water, fire grates, public telephone* ⌀*Reservations not accepted* ☰*AE, D, MC, V* ☺*Late May–mid-Sept.*

$$ ⌂**Glacier Basin Campground.** Rest in the shade of lodgepole pines on the banks of Glacier Creek and take in views of the Continental Divide. There's easy access to a network of many popular trails, and rangers come here for campfire programs. All sites accommodate RVs, tents, trailers, or campers. Firewood and ice are for sale. ⊕*Drive 5 mi south from U.S. 36 along Bear Lake Rd.* ☎*877/444–6777* ⌒*150 sites* ⌂*Flush toilets, dump station, drinking water, fire grates, public telephone* ⌀*Reservations essential* ☰*AE, D, MC, V* ☺*Late May–mid-Sept.*

$$ ⌂**Longs Peak Campground.** Hikers going up Longs Peak can stay at this year-round, tent-only campground. Sites are limited to eight people; ice and firewood are sold in summer. ⊕*9 mi south of Estes Park on Rte. 7* ⌒*26 tent sites* ⌂*Flush toilets, pit toilets, drinking water (mid-May–mid-Sept.), fire grates, ranger station* ⌀*Reservations not accepted* ☰*AE, D, MC, V* ☺*Open year-round.*

★ $$ ⌂**Moraine Park Campground.** This popular campground hosts ranger-led campfire programs and is near hiking trails. You'll hear elk bugling if you camp here in September or October. Sites accommodate RVs, tents, trailers, and campers, but are limited to eight people (except at group sites). Reservations are essential from mid-May to late September. ⊕*Drive south on Bear Lake Rd. from U.S. 36, 0.75 mi to campground entrance* ☎*877/444–6777* ⌒*245 sites* ⌂*Flush toilets, pit toilets, dump station, drinking water (mid-May–mid-Sept.), fire grates, public telephone* ☰*AE, D, MC, V* ☺*Open year-round.*

$$ ⌂**Timber Creek Campground.** Anglers love this spot on the Colorado River, 10 mi from Grand Lake village. In the evening you can sit in on ranger-led campfire programs. All sites accommodate RVs, tents, trailers, or campers, and are limited to eight people. Firewood is sold here. ✉*Trail Ridge Rd. 1,* ⊕*2 mi west of Alpine Visitor Center* ⌒*98 sites* ⌂*Flush toilets, pit toilets, dump station, drinking water (mid-May to mid-Sept.), fire grates, public telephone* ⌀*Reservations not accepted* ☰*AE, D, MC, V* ☺*Open year-round.*

ROCKY MOUNTAIN ESSENTIALS

ACCESSIBILITY

All visitor centers are fully accessible to mobility-impaired people. The Sprague Lake, Coyote Valley, and Lily Lake trails are hard-packed gravel, 0.5 to 1 mi, fairly easily accessible loops. Bear Lake is moderately accessible with some inclines. A backcountry campsite at Sprague Lake accommodates up to 12 campers, including 6 in wheelchairs. Bear Lake shuttles are wheelchair accessible.

ADMISSION FEES

Entrance fees are $20. If you enter on bicycle, motorcycle, horseback, or on foot, you pay $10 for a weekly pass. An annual pass costs $35.

ADMISSION HOURS

The park is open 24/7, year-round; some roads close in winter.

Contacts **Country Supermarket** (✉ *900 Moraine Ave., U.S. 36, next to the Conoco, Estes Park* ☎ *970/586-2702*). **Lone Eagle gas station** (✉ *720 Grand Ave., Grand Lake* ☎ *970/627-3281*). **US Bank** (✉ *363 E. Elkhorn Ave., Estes Park* ☎ *970/586-4412*).

AUTOMOBILE SERVICE STATIONS

Contacts **Conoco-National Park Village** (✉ *900 Moraine Ave., U.S. 36, Estes Park* ☎ *970/586-2139*). **Lakeview Conoco** (✉ *14626 U.S. 34, Grand Lake* ☎ *970/627-3479*). **Schrader's Country Store** (✉ *561 Big Thompson Ave., Estes Park* ☎ *970/586-0235*).

EMERGENCIES

Call 911. You can also call the park's dispatch office at 970/586–1203. There are emergency phones at Cow Creek, Lawn Lake, Longs Peak, and Wild Basin trailheads. Medical assistance is available at visitor centers and ranger stations at Longs Peak and Wild Basin (daily in summer, weekends only in winter). Estes Park and Granby have medical centers.

LOST AND FOUND

It's at the backcountry office next to Beaver Meadows Visitor Center (970/586–1206), or on the west side of the park at Kawuneeche Visitor Center (970/586–1206).

PERMITS

From May through October, the backcountry camping cost is $15 per party (it's free the rest of the year, but you'll still need the permit). You can pick up the permit at the backcountry office, east of Beaver Meadows Visitor Center, or at Kawuneeche Visitor Center. Phone reservations for backcountry campsites can be made between March 1 and May 15 and after October 1 by calling the backcountry office at 970/586–1206. To fish in the park, you must have a valid Colorado fishing license if you're more than 16 years old. Licenses are available from sporting goods stores.

PUBLIC TELEPHONES

These may be found at the Beaver Meadows, Kawuneeche, and Fall River visitor centers and at most park campgrounds. Cell phone reception is good in much of the park.

VISITOR INFORMATION

Contact **Rocky Mountain National Park** (✉ *1000 U.S. 36, Estes Park 80517-8397* ☎ *970/586–1206* ⊕ *www.nps.gov/romo*)

Northwest Colorado & Steamboat Springs

WORD OF MOUTH

"We really enjoyed Steamboat, found the people particularly friendly and liked the politeness of the snow boarders who were thin on the ground on the main slopes (good!!)."

—schnauzer

"[W]e went to Colorado National Monument and did a 23-mile rim drive. It was excellent with many opportunities to hike a variety of trails. The formations were quite spectacular and unique. . . . I was [also] really impressed with Grand Junction. There are lots of activities (art galleries, museum, theatre, symphony, raft, etc.) to do there and it is a really nice area."

—DebitNM

Updated by
Kyle Wagner

AEONS OF EROSION HAVE SCULPTED the northwest's varied terrain that, millions of years ago, was submerged under a roiling sea. These days, the water flows in mighty rivers coursing through spectacular canyons, carrying nature lovers and thrill seekers to a place that still feels largely undiscovered.

Adventures in these far-western and northern regions of the state might range from a bone-jarring mountain-bike ride on the Kokopelli Trail—a 142-mi route through remote desert sandstone and shale canyon from Grand Junction to Moab—to a heart-pounding raft trip down the Green River, where Major John Wesley Powell took his epic exploration of this continent's last uncharted wilderness in 1869. Colorado National Monument and Dinosaur National Monument offer endless opportunities for hiking. For the less adventurous, a visit to the wine country makes for a relaxing afternoon, or try your hand at excavating prehistoric bones from a dinosaur quarry. Rich in more-recent history as well, the area is home to the Museum of Western Colorado and Escalante Canyon, named after Spanish missionary explorer Francisco Silvestre Velez de Escalante, who with father Francisco Atanasio Dominguez led an expedition through the area in 1776.

Farther east, flanked by mountains that boast some of the softest snow in the world, even the cowboys don skis. Steamboat Springs is Colorado at its most authentic, where hay bales and cattle crowd pastures, McMansions are regarded with disdain, high schoolers compete in local rodeos, deer hang from front porches during hunting season, and high-fashion means clean jeans. Steamboat Ski Resort has none of the pretensions of the glitzier Colorado resorts. Ask a local about the last celebrity he saw in town and he's liable to tell you the name of the kid who won the steer-roping competition.

Even the less-visited corners of the region have plenty of cultural opportunities for those willing to seek them out. Dotting the area are art galleries, antiques shops, and many quaint eateries with alfresco seating. People are friendly and offer plenty of tourist tips just for the asking. As for quirky festivals, you might have a hard time choosing between the Olathe Sweet Corn Festival, Country Jam, or the Mike the Headless Chicken Festival. The laid-back lifestyle here is the perfect example to follow—chill out and explore the region at your own pace.

EXPLORING NORTHWESTERN COLORADO & STEAMBOAT SPRINGS

So much distance, so little time. A little planning goes a long way when deciding what attractions to visit in this region. Grand Junction, the largest city between Denver and Salt Lake City, makes the ideal hub for exploring the region. Many of the sights, with the notable exception of Steamboat Springs, are less than a two-hour drive from Grand Junction. You can make the loop from Delta to Cedaredge and Grand Mesa to Palisade easily in a day. If you want to break up the trip, stop at one of the clusters of cabins atop the mesa, or in the lovely town of Cedaredge overnight. The loop in the opposite direction—including

TOP REASONS TO GO

Colorado National Monument: The sandstone canyons yield a sense of solitude and peace that the more-frequented parks of Utah and Arizona simply can't provide. Gaze out over Grand Junction toward the Bookcliffs from the comfort of your car along the 23-mi Rim Rock Drive or hike one of the many trails.

Wine tasting in Grand Junction and Palisade: More than a dozen wineries call the area home; they have garnered national attention for their wines made from grapes grown in the unique high-altitude soil. At harvest time, folks bike from vineyard to vineyard for the tasting celebrations.

Strawberry Park Hot Springs: This is one of the best natural hot springs

in the state. Though it takes some work to get here, it's well worth the effort to soak away what ails you in the rustic, rock-lined setting.

Horseback riding in Steamboat Springs: From an authentic dude ranch experience to a pack trip into the Mount Zirkel Wilderness to simply whiling away a few hours along a gentle alpine trail, horses are serious business in Steamboat.

Dinosaur National Monument: The surrounding area is rugged and barely inhabited, which makes a visit to the famous fossilized bones all the more poetic. Wander among thousands of skulls and other skeletons that remain embedded in the hillsides, an incomparable connection to the past.

Rifle, Meeker, Craig, Dinosaur National Monument, and Rangely—is quite a bit longer, but there's decent lodging in any of the stops along the way, with the exception of Dinosaur National Monument (unless you're prepared to camp).

If you're headed to Steamboat Springs from Denver in winter, exercise caution on Highway 40. It sees less traffic than I–70, but it can be treacherous in the Berthoud Pass stretch during snowstorms.

ABOUT THE PARKS & RECREATION AREAS

The blushing red-rock cliffs of the **Colorado National Monument** are easily accessible by winding roads that open to miles of hiking trails. **Dinosaur National Monument** holds a stunning cache of fossils as well as spectacular scenery aboveground for family-friendly hiking.

Grand Mesa National Forest (⊕ *www.fs.fed.us/r2/gmug*) shimmers with peaceful alpine lakes and great fishing and hiking in summer, along with trails for snowmobiling in winter. A bird-watcher's paradise (from ducks to bald eagles), the remote **Browns Park Wildlife Refuge** (⊕ *www. fws.gov/brownspark*) northwest of Maybell can be navigated by car, horseback, or on foot. The **Flat Tops Wilderness** (⊕ *www.fs.fed.us/r2/ whiteriver*) is an alpine mesa with good stream and lake fishing and excellent deer and elk hunting. It's southwest of Steamboat Springs. Steamboat Springs is surrounded by the **Medicine Bow/Routt National Forests** (⊕ *www.fs.fed.us/r2/mbr*), which stretch across northern Colorado and into southern Wyoming, embracing more than half a dozen

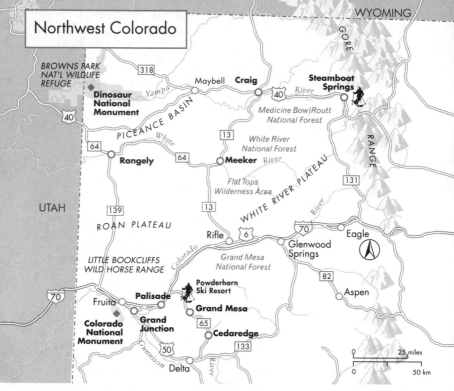

Northwest Colorado

mountain ranges, including the Gore, Flat Tops, Park, Medicine Bow, Sierra Madre, and Laramie.

ABOUT THE RESTAURANTS

Once restricted to chicken-fried steak and burgers, the region's dining scene has expanded far past the Old West. The usual chain restaurants (Olive Garden, Chili's, Outback Steakhouse) ring Grand Junction, but they're joined by eclectic gourmet pizza joints and authentic Mexican restaurants. Look for made-from-scratch delicacies at mom-and-pop bakeries—especially worth seeking out during summer fruit harvests. In season, Palisade peaches, Olathe sweet corn, and Cedaredge apples find their way onto menus, paired with the multitude of increasingly mature local wines. Still, there's nothing wrong with a great hand-battered chicken-fried steak smothered in creamy gravy—which you can still find in just about any town in the area.

The town of Steamboat Springs, in the heart of cattle country, has far more-carnivorous delights—including elk, deer, and bison—than you're likely to find in the trendier resorts of Aspen, Telluride, and Vail. The Steamboat ski resort, separated geographically from town, works toward a more-cosmopolitan mix with small sushi bars and Mediterranean cafés hidden among the boutiques.

ABOUT THE HOTELS

The region is growing and that means more lodging choices. In Grand Junction, Horizon Drive has the largest concentration of hotels and motels, conveniently located near Walker Field Airport and within walking distance of a handful of restaurants. For the budget conscious, there are many clean, no-frills motels as well as most of the well-known chains. History buffs might enjoy a stay at a dude ranch, one of the many rustic cabin rentals, or the famed Meeker Hotel, once frequented by Teddy Roosevelt. For those looking for the comforts of home, the area has a nice selection of bed-and-breakfasts, including one that has a llama herd and others set in fruit orchards and vineyards. Be sure to ask for off-season lodging rates, which could save you a bundle.

Steamboat Springs is unique in the state because it has high-end dude ranches and ranch resorts, which are absent in resort areas like Aspen, Summit County, and Vail.

WHAT IT COSTS					
	¢	$	$$	$$$	$$$$
RESTAURANTS	under $8	$8–$12	$13–$18	$19–$25	over $25
HOTELS	under $80	$80–$120	$121–$170	$171–$230	over $230

Restaurant prices are for a main course at dinner, excluding 6.5%–8.4% tax. Hotel prices are for two people in a standard double room in high season, excluding service charges and 9.4%–10.65% tax.

TIMING

The region has four distinct seasons. The heaviest concentration of tourists is in summer, when school is out and families hit the road for a little together time. Temperatures in summer frequently reach into the high 80s and 90s, although the mercury has been known to top triple digits on occasion. You might have a hard time finding a hotel room during late May and late June due to the National Junior College World Series (baseball) and Country Jam music festival, both in Grand Junction. Hotels fill quickly in fall, which brings an explosion of colors. Days are warm, but nights are crisp and cool. There's still time to enjoy activities like fishing, hiking, and backpacking before the snow flies. Grand Mesa is a winter favorite among locals who are looking for a quick fix for cabin fever. Powder hounds can't wait to strap on their newly waxed skis and hit the slopes at Steamboat and Powderhorn ski resorts.

8

GRAND JUNCTION

255 mi west of Denver via I–70.

Grand Junction is where the mountains and desert meet at the confluence of the mighty Colorado and Gunnison rivers (a grand junction indeed). No matter which direction you look, there's an adventure waiting to happen. The city, with a population of approximately 42,000, is nestled between the picturesque Grand Mesa to the south and the towering Bookcliffs to the north. Surprisingly sophisticated, with a small-town flair, this city is a great base camp for a vacation—whether you're into art galleries, boutiques, hiking, horseback riding, rafting, mountain biking, or winery tours.

The Art on the Corner exhibit showcases leading regional sculptors, whose latest works are installed on the Main Street Mall. Passersby may find their faces reflected in an enormous chrome buffalo (titled, "Chrome on the Range") or, a few streets down, encounter an enormous cactus made entirely of rusted (but still prickly) chainsaw chains.

Art Center rotates a fine permanent collection of Native American tapestries and Western contemporary art, including the only complete series of lithographs by noted printmaker Paul Pletka. The fantastically carved doors—done by a WPA artist in the 1930s—alone are worth the visit. Take time to view the elegant historic homes along North 7th Street afterward. ⌧ *1803 N. 7th St.* ☎ *970/243–7337* ⊕ *www.gjart center.org* ⌧ *$3* ⊙ *Tues.–Sat. 9–4.*

The **Museum of Western Colorado/Museum of the West** relates the history of the area since the 1880s, with a time line, a firearms display, and a Southwest pottery collection. The area's rich mining heritage is perfectly captured in the uranium mine that educates with interactive sound and exhibit stations. The museum also runs the Cross Orchards Living History Farm and the Dinosaur Journey Museum, and oversees paleontological excavations. ⌧ *462 Ute Ave.* ☎ *970/242–0971* ⊕ *www.wcmuseum.org* ⌧ *$5.50* ⊙ *May–Sept., Mon.–Sat. 9–5, Sun. noon–4; Oct.–Apr., Tues.–Sat. 10–3.*

The **Cross Orchards Living History Farm** re-creates a historic agricultural community of the early 20th century on its 24½-acre site, listed on the National Register of Historic Places. A workers' bunkhouse, blacksmith shop, country store, and an extensive collection of vintage farming and road-building equipment are among the exhibits. Tours lasting 1½–2 hours, or tailored to visitors' interests, are available upon request. ⌧ *3073 F Rd.* ☎ *970/434–9814* ⊕ *www.wcmuseum.org* ⌧ *$4* ⊙ *Apr.–Oct., Tues.–Sat. 9–4.*

OFF THE BEATEN PATH

Little Bookcliffs Wild Horse Range. One of just three ranges in the United States set aside for wild horses, it encompasses 30,261 acres of rugged canyons and plateaus in the Bookcliffs. Eighty to 120 wild horses roam the sagebrush-covered hills. Most years, new foals can be spotted with their mothers in spring and early summer on the hillsides just off the main trails. Local favorites for riding include the Coal Canyon Trail and Main Canyon Trail, where the herd often goes in winter. Vehicles are permitted on designated trails. ⌧ *2815 H Rd.,* ⌖ *about 8 mi northeast of Grand Junction* ☎ *970/244–3000* ⊕ *www.co.blm.gov* ⌧ *Free* ⊙ *Daily dawn–dusk.*

FESTIVALS   **Country Jam and Rock Jam** (⌧ *Country Jam USA Ranch, Mack* ☎ *800/ 530–3020* ⊕ *countryjam.com; www.rockjam.com/rock*). Country Jam is held every June and draws the biggest names in country music, such as Faith Hill and Toby Keith, while Rock Jam is held in September with headliners such as Def Leppard.

SPORTS & OUTDOOR ACTIVITIES

GOLF **The Golf Club at Redlands Mesa.** The
★ 18-hole championship course is set
at an elevation of 4,600 feet in the
shadows of the Colorado National
Monument, just minutes from
downtown. ⊠*2325 W. Ridges
Blvd.* ☎*970/263–9270* ⊕*www.
redlandsgolf.com* ⛳*Reservations essential* ⛳*18 holes. Yards:
7,007/4,916. Par: 72/72. Green
Fee: $59/$84.*

MOUNTAIN **Kokopelli Trail** links Grand Junc-
BIKING tion with the famed Slickrock Trail
★ outside Moab, Utah. The 142-mi
stretch winds through high desert and the Colorado River valley
before climbing the La Sal Mountains. Those interested in bike tours
should contact the **Colorado Plateau Mountain Bike Trail Association**
(☎*970/244–8877* ⊕*www.copmoba.org*). **Over the Edge Sports** (⊠*202
E. Aspen Ave., Fruita* ☎*970/858–7220* ⊕*www.otesports.com*) offers
mountain-biking lessons and half- or full-day customized bike tours.

WHERE TO STAY & EAT

$$$–$$$$ ✗**The Winery.** This is *the* place for the big night out and special occa-
sions. It's very pretty, awash in stained glass, wood beams, exposed
brick, and hanging plants. The menu isn't terribly adventuresome,
but the kitchen does turn out fresh-fish specials and top-notch steak,
chicken, prime rib, and shrimp in simple, flavorful sauces. ⊠*642 Main
St.* ☎*970/242–4100* ⊟*AE, D, DC, MC, V* ⊗*No lunch.*

★ $$–$$$ ✗**Il Bistro Italiano.** With a chef hailing from the birthplace of Parmi-
giano-Reggiano, this restaurant's authenticity is assured, down to that
perfectly delivered final shredded topping. Diners are greeted by a case
of pasta made fresh daily and pampered by a staff who knows the
origins of each home-style dish. Entrées include seafood lasagna and
wood-fired pizzas along with veal, pork, and chicken dishes finished
with innovative sauces. ⊠*400 Main St.* ☎*970/243–8622* ⊟*AE, D,
MC, V* ⊗*Closed Sun. and Mon.*

¢–$ ✗**Crystal Cafe & Bake Shop.** Locals flock to this European-style café
for made-from-scratch pastries and filling breakfasts, such as apple
pancakes and a decadent French toast cinnamon roll. The lunch menu
includes innovative sandwiches, salads, and vegetarian items. Dinner's
equally fresh fare is accompanied by a list of local wines. ⊠*314 Main
St.* ☎*970/242–8843* ⊟*MC, V.*

⟳ ¢–$ ✗**Pablo's Pizza.** Drawing inspiration from Pablo Picasso's artwork, the
pizzas at this funky joint make for a diverse palette of flavors and
fun. Specialties include creations such as Popeye's Passion (featuring

---

HIP BONE'S CONNECTED TO THE THIGH BONE

Ever wonder what it's like to
be on a dinosaur expedition?
Here's your chance. The Museum
of Western Colorado sponsors
one- to five-day Dino Digs all
over northwestern Colorado, and
folks find fresh fossils all the time.
The area includes some rich Late
Jurassic soil, Morrison Formation
sites, and other well-preserved
zones that make for impressive
discoveries, and you never know
what might be unearthed. Check
out ⊕*www.dinodigs.org* or call
888/488–DINO to see what's hap-
pening during your visit.

8

spinach and "olive oyl") or Dracula's Nemesis (studded with roasted garlic). For kids, they even offer (we're not making this up) a peanut butter and jelly pizza. With brick walls covered only by eclectic local paintings, Pablo's can get loud when busy. They offer local wines by the glass and Palisade Brewery beer (and root beer) by the bottle. ⊠*319 Main St.* ☎*970/255–8879* ⊟*AE, D, MC, V.*

$–$$ ⊡ **Los Altos Bed & Breakfast.** This luxurious, panoramic hilltop is a peaceful, centralized home base for exploring the area. Only a few minutes from downtown Grand Junction, the modern-yet-cozy home opens to views stretching from Colorado National Monument to the Bookcliffs and Grand Mesa. Set on 3.5 acres perched above a quiet residential neighborhood, the B&B boasts seven large rooms (including one sprawling executive suite) furnished with elegant hardwood beds. Breakfast includes cream cheese–filled French toast and fresh fruit. Call for directions; it's easy to get lost in the nearby neighborhood. **Pros:** close to downtown but quiet, stunning views, private baths. **Con:** thin walls mean sometimes you can hear your neighbors. ⊠*375 Hillview Dr., 81503* ☎*970/256–0964 or 888/774–0982* ⊕*losaltosgrandjunction.com* ➽*4 rooms, 3 suites* ♿*In-hotel: no elevator, public Wi-Fi, no-smoking rooms* ⊟*MC, V* ⊚*BP.*

★ $–$$ ⊡ **Two Rivers Winery & Chateau.** Open a bottle of wine inside the vineyard where it was created at this country French–styled inn set among acres of vines. Roses and lavender bloom at the entrance, and there are views of the Colorado National Monument as well as an expansive balcony. Large, elegant rooms are furnished with beautiful hardwood beds and heavy, comfortable couches. The inn adjoins the Two Rivers Winery, which offers tastings and tours throughout the day and bottles for purchase in every room. **Pros:** idyllic locale for weddings or other special occasions, tasty wines always at hand, expanded continental breakfast. **Cons:** winery and other guests' special occasions mean noisier than the usual B&B, rooms are chilly in winter, kitchen is inconsistent. ⊠*2087 Broadway, 81503* ☎*970/241–3155 or 866/312–9463* ⊕*www.tworiverswinery.com* ➽*10 rooms* ♿*In-room: VCR, Wi-Fi. In-hotel: no elevator, some pets allowed, no-smoking rooms* ⊟*AE, D, DC, MC, V* ⊚*BP.*

$ ⊡ **Grand Vista Hotel.** Plush, high-back chairs invite visitors to relax in the spacious lobby of this hotel that lives up to its name. A private-club look dominates the hotel's main restaurant, and an old-fashioned charm characterizes the rooms, although recent updates, including new artwork, furniture and re-tiled bathrooms, have given the rooms a fresher, more-modern feel. There is also a recently completed cardio-oriented fitness center on-site. **Pros:** you can't beat the views, they will store your bike for you, the price is right. **Cons:** the breakfast buffet is terrible, service is hit or miss, children are allowed to run rampant. ⊠*2790 Crossroads Blvd., 81506* ☎*970/241–8411* 🖷*970/241–1077* ⊕*www.grandvistahotel.com* ➽*158 rooms* ♿*In-room: Wi-Fi. In-hotel: restaurant, bar, pool, gym, public Wi-Fi, airport shuttle, no-smoking rooms* ⊟*AE, D, DC, MC, V.*

¢   ⊡ **Super 8.** Extensive remodeling has put the building into a classier category than many in the chain. Clean, spacious rooms, a complimentary continental breakfast, and a small pool add to the appeal. **Pros:** close to the highway but not too noisy; top value for families and groups, especially the family suites with two queens and sleeper sofas. **Con:** chain hotel. ⊠*728 Horizon Dr., 81506* ☎*970/248–8080* ⊕*www.super8. com* ⤶*130 rooms* ⌂*In room: refrigerator (some), ethernet (some), Wi-Fi (some). In hotel: pool, gym, some pets allowed, no-smoking rooms* ⊟*AE, D, DC, MC, V.*

NIGHTLIFE & THE ARTS

THE ARTS The 65-piece **Grand Junction Symphony** (☎*970/243–6787* ⊕*www. gjsymphony.org*) is highly regarded and performs in venues throughout the city.

NIGHTLIFE **Bistro 743 Lounge** (⊠*743 Horizon Dr.* ☎*970/241–8888 Ext. 121*) inside the Doubletree Hotel serves beverages, appetizers, and light snacks. Occasionally entertainers perform outside on the beer garden stage. The **Blue Moon** (⊠*120 N. 7th St.* ☎*970/242–4506*) is a favorite neighborhood bar; a Cheers-like atmosphere encourages patrons to nurse their favorite brew while catching up with colleagues or friends. The **Rockslide Brewery** (⊠*401 Main St.* ☎*970/245–2111*) has won awards for its ales, porters, and stouts. The patio is open in summer.

SHOPPING

The best place in the area for Tony Lama boots and Minnetonka moccasins is **Champion Boots & Saddlery** (⊠*545 Main St.* ☎*970/242–2465*), in business since 1936. The sweetest deal in town, **Enstrom's** (⊠*200 S. 7th St.* ☎*970/242–1655*) is known for its scrumptious candy and world-renowned toffee. The Main Street boutique **Girlfriends** (⊠*316 Main St.* ☎*970/242–3234*) offers a line of comfy clothes, pottery, benches, candles, and one-of-a-kind gifts. The cute but upscale boutique **Heirlooms for Hospice** (⊠*635 Main St.* ☎*970/254–8556*) offers great secondhand designer clothing and shabby-chic furniture. **Working Artists Studio and Gallery** (⊠*520 Main St.* ☎*970/256–9952*) carries prints, pottery, stained glass, and unique gifts.

SIDE TRIP TO PALISADE

12 mi east of Grand Junction via I–70.

Palisade is Colorado's version of Napa Valley, with the highest concentration of wineries in the state. It's an easy day trip from Grand Junction; meander through the vineyards and surrounding peach orchards, and stop for lunch in the tiny, slow-paced town framed by stately Victorian homes and sweetened by homespun festivals.

Fodor's Choice ★ One of Colorado's best-kept secrets is its **winery tours.** It's a great way to see how your favorite wine goes from vineyard to glass. You can learn about the grape-growing process and what varieties of grapes grow best in Western Colorado's mild climate. Depending on the time of the year, you may also see the grape harvesting and crushing process. For a self-guided tour, visit ⊕*www.visitgrandjunction.com* and print out its maps and directions to the wineries. If you're taking the self-guided route, call to reserve tours that take you beyond the tasting room and into the winemaking process. Of course the best part of the tour is sampling the wines.

American Spirit Shuttle operates scheduled tours in 14-passenger vans. The tours visit at least four wineries and last approximately four hours. Wine lovers get to sample a variety of Colorado wines in the tasting rooms with the added benefit of having someone else do the driving. ⊠ *204 4th St., Clifton* ☎ *970/523–7662* ⊕ *www.americanspiritshuttle.net* 🖅 *$30* ⊘ *May–Oct., Sat. 1–5.*

FESTIVALS In summer **Grande River Vineyards** (⊠ *787 Elberta Ave.* ☎ *970/464– 5867* ⊕ *www.granderiverwines.com*) hosts a concert series of between four and nine shows featuring classical, country, blues, and rock music. The natural landscape contributes to the good acoustics, not to mention the spectacular sunsets. Concertgoers lounge in lawn chairs, enjoying picnics and dancing barefoot on the grass, and sometimes the concerts are held in the cellars.

> **DOWN ON THE FARM**
>
> Considering the plethora of produce in the Grand Junction and Palisade area, you would think that great restaurants would be easy to come by, but not so. Better to eat the ingredients in their most unadulterated form straight from the source; spend some time stopping by the dozens of farm stands that dot the landscape. A favorite is Talbott Farms and its store, the Mountain Gold Market, where two dozen kinds of peaches can be had, as well as other local products. Look for local jams, honey, fruits and vegetables, cider and freshly baked items, all perfect for an impromptu picnic.

Palisade celebrates the harvest for four days every August during the **Palisade Peach Festival** (☎ *970/464–7458* ⊕ *www.palisadepeach fest.com*). September brings the annual **Colorado Mountain Winefest** (☎ *800/704–3667* ⊕ *www.coloradowinefest.com*).

WHERE TO STAY & EAT

¢ ✕ **Palisade Café.** Changing artwork decorates this light and airy café with a nice selection of breakfast and lunch items, including soups, salads, burgers, French dips, Reuben sandwiches, and vegetarian dishes. Breads are from the Slice O' Life Bakery, and local beer and wine are served. ⊠ *113 W. 3rd St.* ☎ *970/464–0657* ⊟ *D, MC, V* ⊘ *No dinner.*

¢ ✕ **Slice O' Life Bakery.** Aromatic goodies are baked with whole grains
Fodor'sChoice and fresh local fruits at this down-home–style bakery known around
★ the region for its melt-in-your-mouth pastries, sweet rolls, Jamocha brownies, and fresh fruit cobblers. Owners Tim and Mary Lincoln have even made the lowly fruitcake into a craveable commodity, studding them with fresh Palisade peaches and mailing them around the country (in fact, they do some of the best things with peaches in town, including pie). Cold sandwiches and fresh-baked bread are also available. ⊠ *105 W. 3rd St.* ☎ *970/464–0577* ⊟ *No credit cards* ⊘ *Closed Sun. and Mon. No dinner.*

$ 🏠 **Orchard House Bed & Breakfast.** Set in a peaceful peach orchard a few miles from downtown, this home lives up to its name. During harvest season in August, it's possible to pick your own sweet snack from the grove. A large porch spanning two sides of the house beckons you to sit a spell and enjoy views of Grand Mesa and the Bookcliffs. **Pros:** homey, elaborate breakfasts with fresh peaches in season. **Con:** pet policy is not popular with everyone. ✉*3573 E½ Rd., 81526* ☎*970/464–0529* ⊕*www.theorchardhouse.com* ➪*4 rooms, 3 with bath* ⚬*In-room: no a/c (some), no TV. In-hotel: no elevator, some pets allowed, no-smoking rooms* ▤*AE, D, MC, V* ⦾|*BP.*

SHOPPING

Harold and Nola Voorhees (✉*3702 G 7/10 Rd.* ☎*970/464–7220*) sell a range of dried fruits, including cherries, pears, apricots, and peaches. **Talbott Farms Mountain Gold Market** (✉*3782 F½ Rd.* ☎*877/834–6686*) puts out nearly two dozen kinds of peaches, as well as apples and pears and the juices of all three. The huge, fourth generation–run operation also offers local products and will take you on a tour of the place if you ask.

COLORADO NATIONAL MONUMENT

23 mi west of Grand Junction via Rte. 340.

Sheer red-rock cliffs open to 23 mi of steep canyons and thin monoliths that sprout as high as 450 feet from the floor of the **Colorado National Monument.** This vast tract of rugged, ragged terrain was declared a national monument in 1911 at the urging of an eccentric visionary named John Otto. Cold Shivers Point is just one of the many dramatic overlooks along **Rim Rock Drive,** a 23-mi scenic route with breathtaking views.

The town of Fruita, at the base of the Colorado National Monument, is a haven for mountain bikers and hikers. It makes a great center to explore the area's canyons—whether from the seat of a bike or the middle of a raft, heading for a leisurely float trip.

Scheduled programs, such as guided walks and campfire talks, are posted at the **visitor center** (☎*970/858–3617* ⊙*Memorial Day–Labor Day, daily 8–6; Labor Day–Memorial Day, daily 9–5. Closed Dec. 25*). Maps and trail information are also available. Rock climbing is popular at the Monument, as are horseback riding, cross-country skiing, biking, and camping. ✉*Fruita 81521* ☎*970/858–3617* ⊕*www. nps.gov/colm* ⛟*$7 per wk per vehicle. Visitors entering on bicycle, motorcycle, or foot pay $4 for weekly pass* ⊙*Daily.*

Roaring robotic stegosaurs and meat-shredding animatronic Allosaurs prowl **Dinosaur Journey,** a fun, informative attraction just off I–70 a few minutes from the western entrance to the Colorado National Monument. Unlike many museums, kids are encouraged to touch everything (friendly paleontologists may even allow kids to hold a chunk of fossilized dino dung). In addition to the amazing lifelike replicas, there are more than 20 interactive displays. Children can stand in an earthquake simulator, dig up "fossils" in a mock quarry, or make dino prints in dirt (along with reptile and bird tracks for comparison). The museum also sponsors daily

8

digs nearby, where many of the fossils were found. Local volunteers are at work cleaning and preparing fossils for study. ⊠*550 Jurassic Ct., Fruita* ☎*970/858–7282 or 888/488–3466* ⊕*www.dinosaurjourney.com* ☜*$7* ⊙*May–Sept., daily 9–5; Oct.–Apr., Mon.–Sat. 10–4, Sun. noon–4.*

Fodor's Choice ★ Ten miles west of Grand Junction, stretching from Fruita to just across the Utah border, the **McInnis Canyons National Conservation Area** (formerly Colorado Canyons National Conservation Area) is rife with natural arches, along with numerous rock canyons, caves, coves, and spires. **Rattlesnake Canyon** has nine arches, making it the second-largest concentration of natural arches in the country. The canyon can be reached in summer from the upper end of Rim Rock Drive with four-wheel-drive vehicles or via a 7-mi hike by the intrepid.

Though much of the territory complements the red-dirt canyons of Colorado National Monument, McInnis Canyons is more accessible to horseback riding, mountain biking, all-terrain vehicle and motorcycle trails, and for trips with dogs (most of these activities aren't allowed at the Monument). Designated in 2000 by a Congressional act, the conservation area was created from a desire of nearby communities to preserve the area's unique scenery while allowing multiple-use recreation. Be prepared for biting gnats from late May to late July. Contact the Bureau of Land Management for a map before venturing out. ⊠*2815 H Rd.* ☎*970/244–3000* ⊕*www.blm.gov/co/st/en/fo/mcnca. html* ☜*Free* ⊙*Year-round.*

FESTIVALS Fruita celebrates **Mike the Headless Chicken Days** (☎*970/858–3894* ⊕*www.miketheheadlesschicken.org*) every May with the Chicken Dance and the Run Like A Headless Chicken 5K Race.

SPORTS & THE OUTDOORS

HIKING A good way to explore the **Colorado National Monument** is by trail. There are more than a dozen short and backcountry trails that range in distance from 0.25 mi to 8.5 mi. An easy 30-minute stroll with sweeping canyon views, **Otto's Trail** (⊕*Trailhead: Rim Rock Dr., 1 mi from western gate visitor center*) greets hikers with breezes scented by sagebrush and juniper, which stand out from the dull red rock and sand. The trail leads to stunning, sheer drop-offs and endless views. At the end of the half-mile trail at Otto's Overlook, you can hear the wind in the feathers of birds as they soar out of the canyon. **Serpents Trail** (⊕*Trailhead: Serpents Trail parking lot, 0.25 mi from east gate*) has been called the "Crookedest Road in the World" because of its more than 50 switchbacks. The fairly steep but rewarding trail, which ascends several hundred feet, takes about two hours to complete, depending on your ability (and the heat). ☎*970/858–3617* ⊕*www.nps.gov/colm.*

HORSEBACK RIDING **Rimrock Adventures** (⊠*927 Hwy. 340, Fruita* ☎*970/858–9555 or 888/712–9555* ⊕*www.rradventures.com*) offers horseback rides near Colorado National Monument as well as through Little Bookcliffs Wild Horse Preserve.

The Legacy of Mike the Headless Chicken

Mike the Headless Chicken was a freak bound for fame. It all started with a run-in with a Fruita farmer who had bad aim, or so the tale goes. The year was 1945. Mike, a young Wyandotte rooster, was minding his own business in the barnyard when farmer Lloyd Olsen snatched him from the chicken coop. It seems Clara, the farmer's wife, wanted chicken for dinner that night. Mike was put on death row. Well, faster than you can say pinfeathers, farmer Olsen stretched Mike's neck across the chopping block and whacked off his head. Apparently undaunted by the ordeal, Mike promptly got up, dusted off his feathers and went about his daily business pecking for food, fluffing his feathers and crowing, except Mike's crow was now reduced to a gurgle. Scientists surmised that Mike's brain stem was largely untouched, leaving his reflex actions intact. A blood clot prevented him from bleeding to death. The headless chicken dubbed "Miracle Mike" toured the freak-show circuit, where the morbidly curious could sneak a peek at his nogginless nub for a quarter. Mike's incredible story of survival (he lived for 18 months without a head!) soon hit the pages of two national magazines, *Time* and *Life*. The headless wonder, who was fed with an eyedropper, eventually met his demise in an Arizona motel room, where he choked to death. His legacy lives on in Fruita, where the tiny town throws a gigantic party every May to celebrate Mike's life. Even in death, Mike is still making headlines.

RAFTING **Adventure Bound River Expeditions** (⊠ *2392 H Rd.* ☎ *970/245–5428 or 800/423–4668* ⊕ *www.raft-colorado.com*) runs trips on the Colorado, Green, and Yampa rivers (the latter through the canyons of Dinosaur National Monument). **Rimrock Adventures** (⊠ *927 Hwy. 340, Fruita* ☎ *970/858–9555 or 888/712–9555* ⊕ *www.rradventures.com*) also has a variety of rafting excursions and easygoing float trips.

ROCK CLIMBING The stunning stark sandstone and shale formations of Colorado National Monument are a rock climber's paradise. Independence Monument is a favorite climb. Experienced desert-rock guide Kris Hjelle owns and operates **Desert Crags & Cracks** (⊠ *Box 2803, Fruita 81502* ☎ *970/245–8513* ⊕ *www.desertcrags.com*), specializing in guiding and instruction on the desert rocks of western Colorado and eastern Utah.

WHERE TO EAT

$–$$ ✕ **Fiesta Guadalajara Restaurant.** Authentic and family friendly, this Mexican restaurant serves up good food. Try the chiles rellenos, super nachos, and especially the chili Colorado: fork-tender beef simmered in a savory red-pepper sauce. The appetizer combo plate is a meal in itself, and to feed an army, order Fiesta Fajitas. ⊠ *103 Hwy. 6 and 50, Fruita* ☎ *970/858–1228* ☰ *AE, D, MC, V.*

$–$$ ✕ **Hot Tomato Café and Pizzeria.** This tiny storefront spot is big on flavor with thin-crust pizzas, oversize salads, and fat sandwiches. Run by mountain bikers Jen Zeuner and Anne Keller, who worked around town before taking over an established eatery, the place has an inviting small-town feel. They bake the bread themselves (try the homemade breadsticks slathered with molten cheese and marinara sauce for dipping), there's beer on tap, and they make a mean espresso. The Granny's Pesto Pie is the one to try: a base of pesto topped with mozzarella and feta cheese and plenty of garlic. ⊠ *201 E. Aspen St., Fruita* ☎*970/858–1117* ⊕*www.hottomatocafe.com* ☰*MC, V.*

GRAND MESA

47 mi southeast of Grand Junction via I–70 and Hwy. 65.

The world's largest flattop mountain towers nearly 11,000 feet above the surrounding terrain and sprawls an astounding 50 square mi. **Grand Mesa National Forest** attracts the outdoor enthusiast who craves the simple life: fresh air, biting fish, spectacular sunsets, a roaring campfire under the stars, and a little elbow room to take it all in. The landscape is filled with more than 300 sparkling lakes—a fisherman's paradise in summer. The mesa, as it's referred to by locals, offers excellent hiking and camping (try Island Lake Campground) opportunities. There are also a handful of lodges that rent modern cabins. You can also downhill ski at Powderhorn Resort, cross-country ski, snowshoe, snowmobile, or ice fish. ⊠ *2250 Hwy. 50, Delta* ☎*970/874–6600* ⊕*www.fs.fed. us/r2/gmug.*

SPORTS & OUTDOOR ACTIVITIES

DOWNHILL SKIING
Powderhorn Resort has 36 trails, 4 lifts, 600 acres, and a 1,650-foot vertical drop. The slopes intriguingly follow the fall line of the mesa, carving out natural bowls. Those bowls on the western side are steeper than they first appear. Lift tickets are reasonable, and the skiing is surprisingly good. Powderhorn averages 250 inches of snowfall per year. ⊠*Rte. 65, Mesa* ☎*970/268–5700* ⊕*www.powderhorn.com* ▱*Lift ticket $38–$48* ☉*Dec.–Apr., daily 9–4.*

FISHING
The lakes and reservoirs provide some of the best angling opportunities in Colorado for rainbow, cutthroat, and brook trout.

☾ **Battlement Mesa Outfitters** (⊠*20781 Kimball Creek Rd.* ☎*970/487– 9918* ⊕*www.bmoutfitters.com*) sits about 40 minutes north of Grand Mesa and will take you fishing in just about any of its 200 lakes, custom-fitting the trip to your interests.

HIKING
☾ **Grand Mesa Discovery Trail** (⊕*Trailhead: Grand Mesa Visitor Center, near intersection of Hwy. 65 and Trickel Park Rd.*) is a great beginning hike for kids and adults attempting to acclimate themselves to the altitude—and the slow-paced attitude—of the mesa. Pick up a brochure at the visitor center for information on the landscape. The gently sloping 20-minute trail gives a fascinating glimpse of what to expect on longer hikes.

WHERE TO STAY & EAT

★ $$ ✕▥ **Spruce Lodge Resort.** French doors on each of the spacious cabins open into pure, thin air perfumed by the pine forest of the mesa. The decor inside the lodge, built in 1956, changes with the season, but remains comfy. The restaurant ($$–$$$) has a diverse menu. The modern cabins, heated by propane fireplaces, have kitchenettes, microwaves, coffeemakers, and hair dryers. Each cabin's deck has a table, chairs, and an umbrella, as well as an outside grill with picnic table and fire pit. Pros: pay cash and save $20–$35, cabins have secluded feel, hot tubs are delightful in cooler temps. Con: it might be too remote for some. ⊠*20658 Baron Lake Dr., ⊹16 mi north of Cedaredge; 1 mi from Grand Mesa Visitor Center on Hwy. 65 and Forest Rd. 121, 81413* ☎*970/856–6240 or 800/850-7221* ⊕*www.sprucelodgecolorado.com* ⇨*11 cabins* ⌂*In-room: no a/c, no phone, kitchen, no TV (some). In-hotel: restaurant, bar, no elevator. no-smoking rooms* ⊟*AE, D, DC, MC, V.*

$ ✕⊡ **Alexander Lake Cabins.** The mirror-calm Alexander Lake reflects towering pine trees that also overlook the vast majority of this resort's cozy cabins, which are designed for tranquillity. Still, there's plenty of room for fishing, horseback riding, boating, or snowmobiling. Many cabins—which hold as many as seven people—were renovated in 2005 with modern, comfortable beds and kitchens of varying sizes. Pros: pay cash and save $20–$35, fishing and snowmobiling right on the property, quiet and peaceful. Cons: rather remote, no restaurant. ⊠*21221 Baron Lake Dr., ⊹17 mi north of Cedaredge, 2 mi from Grand Mesa Visitor Center on Forest Rd. 121, 81413* ☎*970/856–6240 or 800/850-7221* ⊕*www.alexanderlakelodge.com* ⇨*7 cabins* ⌂*In-room: no phone, kitchen, no TV. In-hotel: no elevator, no-smoking rooms* ⊟*AE, D, MC, V.*

EN ROUTE The **Grand Mesa Scenic Byway** (☎970/856–3100) is 63 mi long and winds its way along Highway 65 through meadows sprinkled with wildflowers, shimmering aspen groves, aromatic pine forests, and endless lakes. Scenic overlooks (Land-O-Lakes is a standout), rest areas, and picnic areas are clearly marked. There are two visitor centers on the Byway, which has endpoints at I-70 near Palisade and in Cedaredge.

CEDAREDGE

15 mi south of Grand Mesa via Hwy. 65.

Cedaredge is called the gateway to the Grand Mesa, the world's largest flat-topped mountain. An elevation of 6,100 feet makes for a mild climate that is perfect for ranching, as well as for growing apples, peaches, and cherries. The town is charming with its abundance of galleries, gift shops, antiques stores, and wineries.

The town site was originally the headquarters of a cattle spread, the Bar-I Ranch. **Pioneer Town,** a cluster of 23 authentic buildings that re-create turn-of-the-20th-century life, includes a country chapel, the Lizard Head Saloon, original silos from the Bar-I Ranch, and a working blacksmith shop. ⊠*Rte. 65* ☎*970/856–7554* ⊕*www.pioneertown. org* ⊡*$5* ⊗*Memorial Day–Labor Day, Mon.–Sat. 9–4, Sun. 1–4.*

WHERE TO STAY & EAT

$–$$ ✕**Grill at Deer Creek Village.** With dishes ranging from crab-and-artichoke dip to Thai chicken satay, this casual but elegant restaurant satisfies golfers from the adjoining Deer Creek Golf Club, as well as tourists looking to fill up after a long day on the mesa or antiques-shopping. Steaks and seafood dishes are the mainstay, accompanied by an extensive local wine list. Call for directions. ⊠*500 S. E. Jay Ave.* ☎*970/856–7782* ⊕*deercreekvillage-golf.com* ⊟*D, MC, V.*

¢ ✕**Highway 65 Burgers.** The good old-fashioned hamburgers here are cooked just the way you like them; all meat is fresh, and the burgers are hand pressed. Favorites include the bacon cheeseburger (get it with a side and a drink for two bucks more) and hickory cheeseburger, topped off with a thick, frosty malt filled with local fruits in season. ⊠*1260 S. Grand Mesa Dr.* ☎*970/856–4465* ⊟*MC, V.*

🖐 **$** ▦**Cedars' Edge Llamas B&B.** A herd of curious llamas greets visitors to the quaint but modern cedar house and guest cottage and its four neatly furnished rooms, each with its own theme, overlooking 100-mi views of the Grand Valley. The innkeepers, Ray and Gail Record, are more than happy to share their encyclopedic knowledge of llamas; after guests enjoy their breakfast in the breakfast room or on their own private deck, they are welcome to help feed hay to the herd. **Pros:** breakfast on your private deck is a nice option, close proximity to national forest, who doesn't love a llama? **Cons:** dated decor, maybe everyone doesn't love a llama. ⊠*2169 Hwy. 65, 81413* ☎*970/856–6836* ⊕*www.llamabandb.com* ➯*4 rooms, 1 cottage* ⚒*In-room: no phone, refrigerator (some), no TV. In-hotel: no elevator, no-smoking rooms* ⊟*AE, MC, V* ⎟⊚⎟*BP.*

SHOPPING

Once an apple packing shed, the **Apple Shed** (⊠*250 S. Grand Mesa Dr.* ☎*970/856–7007*) has been restored and remodeled into a series of unique gift shops and arts and crafts galleries. The attached deli ($) serves fresh peach milk shakes (when in season), sure to fuel your drive up the next pass.

MEEKER

43 mi north of Rifle via Rte. 13.

Once an outpost of the U.S. Army, Meeker is still a place where anyone in camouflage dress always remains in fashion. Famous for its annual sheepdog championships (a sheepdog statue keeps watch over the sleepy town), it remains a favorite spot for hunting, fishing, and snowmobiling. Interesting historical buildings include the Meeker Hotel on Main Street, where Teddy Roosevelt stayed.

The **White River Museum** is housed in a long building that served as a barracks for U.S. Army officers. Inside are exhibits such as a collection of guns dating to the Civil War and the plow used by Nathan Meeker to dig up the Ute's pony racetrack. ⊠*565 Park Ave.* ☎*970/878–9982* ⊕*www.meekercolorado.com/museum.htm* ✉*Free* ⊙*May–mid-Nov., weekdays 9–5, weekends 10–5; mid-Nov.—Apr., Fri. and Sat. 11–4.*

EVENTS ⓒ You can watch professional sheepdogs in action at the annual **Meeker Classic Sheepdog Trials,** a prestigious five-day international competition and one of the town's biggest draws. Sheepdogs and their handlers perform sheepherding maneuvers on a closed course while competing for a $10,000 purse. The event takes place the weekend after Labor Day. ☏*970/878–5510 or 970/878–0080* ⊕*www.meekersheepdog. com* ✆*$10.*

SPORTS & THE OUTDOORS

FISHING The White River valley is home to some of the best fishing holes in Colorado, including Meeker Town Park, Sleepy Cat Access, and Trappers Lake. Some of the best fishing is on private land, so you need to ask permission and you might have to pay. Your best bet—if you don't want to go it alone—is to hire a guide familiar with the area, such as **JML Outfitters** (⊠*300 Country Rd. 75* ☏*970/878–4749* ⊕*www.jmloutfitters.com*), which has been in the outfitting business for three generations, offering photography and wildlife-viewing trips, kids' camps, and trail rides.

SNOW-MOBILING One of Meeker's best-kept secrets is the fantastic snowmobiling through pristine powder in the backcountry, which some say rivals Yellowstone—without the crowds. Trail maps for self-guided rides are available through the Chamber of Commerce or the U.S. Forest Service, or from **Welder Outfitting Services** (☏*970/878–9869* ⊕www.flattops. com), which guides snowmobiling in the White River National Forest and Flat Tops Wilderness.

WHERE TO STAY & EAT

$$ ✕🖾 **Sleepy Cat Lodge and Restaurant.** Beneath the massive exposed beam ceiling of this lodge, a cozy fireplace is flanked by the requisite trophies and bearskins mounted on the walls. Soup and salad bar accompany the filling dinners ($$—$$$) of ribs, huge cuts of steak, teriyaki chicken, and panfried trout. Rustic cabins are heated and have full kitchens and showers; some have fireplaces. There's a TV-viewing area in the lodge. **Pros:** nice rustic setting, fishing right out the front door. **Con:** 17-mi away from Meeker. ⊠*16064 County Rd. 8, 81641* ✛*17 mi east of Meeker* ☏*970/878–4413* ⊕*www.sleepycatguestranch.com* ✆*14 cabins, 6 motel rooms* ⚲*In-room: no phone, kitchen (some), refrigerator, no TV. In-hotel: restaurant, bar, no elevator, some pets allowed. no-smoking rooms* ▭*D, MC, V* ☾*Call for restaurant hrs.*

$ ✕🖾 **Meeker Hotel and Cafe.** At this Old West–style restaurant ($$–$$$) you'll feel like you're being watched—dozens of massive trophy elk and deer peer down from every wall. Peruse the menu with lively stories of Meeker's past, then try the homemade soup, chicken-fried steak, and mashed potatoes with cream gravy. The hotel, listed on the National Register of Historic Places, is filled with a veritable forest of rustic furniture. The lobby is lined with framed broadsheet biographies of famous figures—such as Teddy Roosevelt and, more recently, Dick Cheney—who stayed here. Rooms have claw-foot tubs and heavy beds; the bargain-price bunk wing has rooms with shared baths. **Pros:** delightful decor, delicious food in the café, bargain-hunters can go the communal-bathroom route. **Cons:** the café can get crowded and noisy,

8

the walls are paper thin. ✉*560 Main St., 81641* ☎*970/878–5062 or 970/878–5255* ⊕*www.themeekerhotel.com* ⌁*24 rooms* ⌂*In-room: no phone. In-hotel: restaurant, bar, no elevator, no-smoking rooms* ▤*AE, D, MC, V.*

SHOPPING

Featuring original watercolor paintings and limited edition prints by Colorado artist John T. Myers, **Fawn Creek Gallery** (✉*574 Main St.* ☎*970/878–0955* ⊕*www.fawncreek.com*) also sells Fremont and Ute rock-art replicas and duck carvings made from 100-year-old cedar fence posts.

An old-fashioned mercantile building with original display cases, tin ceilings, and wood floors, **Wendll's Wondrous Things** (✉*594 Main St.* ☎*970/878–3688*) sells an eclectic mix of clothing, housewares, body-care products, greeting cards, Brighton jewelry, and Native American turquoise and sterling silver from Arizona.

CRAIG

48 mi north of Meeker via Rte. 13.

Craig is home to some of the best fishing in the area. Guided trips to some of the hottest fishing spots are available, as are horseback pack trips into the wilderness. Depending on the season, you might spot bighorn sheep, antelope, or nesting waterfowl, including the Great Basin Canada goose.

One of Craig's most prized historical possessions, the **Marcia Car** in City Park was the private Pullman car of Colorado magnate David Moffat, who at one time was full or partial owner of more than 100 gold and silver mines. Moffat was also instrumental in bringing railroad transportation to northwest Colorado. He used his private car to inspect construction work on the Moffat Railroad line. Named after his only child, the car has been restored and makes for an interesting tour. ✉*U.S. 40* ☎*970/824–5689* ▤*Free* ☉*Mid-Apr.–mid-Oct., weekdays 8–5.*

The **Museum of Northwest Colorado** elegantly displays an eclectic collection of everything from arrowheads to a fire truck. The upstairs of this restored county courthouse holds the largest privately owned collection of working cowboy artifacts in the world. Bill Mackin, one of the leading traders in cowboy collectibles, has spent a lifetime gathering guns, bits, saddles, bootjacks, holsters, and spurs of all descriptions. ✉*590 Yampa Ave.* ☎*970/824–6360* ⊕*www.museumnwco.org* ▤*Free, donations accepted* ☉*Mon.–Sat. 9–5.*

SPORTS & THE OUTDOORS

FISHING Around Craig and Meeker, the Yampa and Green rivers, Trappers Lake, Lake Avery, and Elkhead Reservoir are known for pike and trout. Contact the **Sportsman's Center at the Craig Chamber of Commerce** (✉*360 E. Victory Way* ☎*970/824–3046*) for information. Get the scoop on hot fishing spots from **Craig Sports** (⌗*124 W. Victory Way* ☎*970/824–4044*) while loading up on tackle and other supplies.

WHERE TO EAT

$$–$$$ ✗**Bad to the Bone BBQ & Grill.** Kids get a kick out of throwing their peanut shells on the floor at this no-frills barbecue joint. Fresh-cut steaks, prime rib, Cajun dishes, and homemade side dishes are some of the other draws. There's a large deck outside. ⌗*572 Breeze St.* ☎*970/824–8588* ▤*D, MC, V.*

$$–$$$ ✗**Golden Cavvy.** A cavvy is the pick of a team of horses, and this restaurant is a favorite in town, for the price. Its coffee shop atmosphere is enlivened by mirrors, hanging plants, faux-antique chandeliers, and masonry of the 1900s fireplace of the Baker Hotel (which burned down on this spot). Hearty breakfasts, homemade pies and ice cream, burgers, pork chops, and anything deep-fried (try the mesquite-fried chicken) are your best bets. ⌗*538 Yampa Ave.* ☎*970/824–6038* ▤*MC, V.*

STEAMBOAT SPRINGS

42 mi east of Craig via U.S. 40; 160 mi west of Denver via I–70, Rte. 9, and U.S. 40.

Steamboat got its name from French trappers who, after hearing the bubbling and churning hot springs, mistakenly thought a steamboat was chugging up the Yampa River. The town is a place where Stetson hats are sold for shade and not for souvenirs, and the Victorian-era buildings, most of them fronting the main drag of Lincoln Avenue, were built to be functional, not ornamental. It was founded in the 1800s as a ranching and farming community, setting it apart from the mining towns of Breckenridge and Aspen. These early settlers were responsible for the advent of skiing in the area; they strapped wooden boards to their feet so they could get around town in winter. The entrance to town is roughly marked by the amusingly garish 1950s neon sign from the Rabbit Ears Motel, a designated historic landmark.

Steamboat Springs is aptly nicknamed Ski Town, U.S.A., since it has sent more athletes to the Winter Olympics than any other ski town in the nation. The most famous alumnus is probably 1964 slalom silver medalist Billy Kidd, whose irrepressible grin and 10-gallon hat are instantly recognizable. When he's around in his position as director of skiing at the resort, Kidd takes visitors for a run down the mountain and gives free pointers.

When sizing up the mountain, keep in mind that the part that's visible from below is only the tip of the iceberg—much more terrain lies concealed in back. Steamboat is famed for its eiderdown-soft snow; in fact, the term "champagne powder" was coined (and amusingly enough registered as a trademark) here to describe the area's unique feathery drifts, the result of Steamboat's fortuitous position between the arid desert to the west and the moisture-magnet of the Continental Divide to the east, where storm fronts duke it out.

8

If you're looking for hellacious steeps and menacing couloirs, you won't find them in Steamboat, but you will discover what is perhaps the finest tree skiing in America. Beginning and intermediate skiers rave about the wide-open spaces of Sunshine Bowl and Storm Peak. Steamboat also earns high marks for its comprehensive children's programs and the Billy Kidd Center for Performance Skiing, where you can learn demanding disciplines such as powder, mogul, and tree skiing.

The mountain village, with its maze of upscale condos, boutiques, and nightclubs, is certainly attractive. It's a bit too spread out—and too new—to have developed much character. To its credit, though, this increasingly trendy destination has retained much of its down-home friendliness, providing the trappings while avoiding the trap of other resorts.

> **BROKEN SPRING**
>
> Don't waste time looking for Steamboat Spring, the one for which the town was named—it is dry now. It sits next to the Yampa River along the 13th Street Bridge, and once was so feisty people miles away thought the 15-foot-high spewer sounded like a steamboat churning down the river. When the railroad came to Steamboat in 1909, the spring mysteriously became nothing but a burble; some believe the railroad company somehow had something to do with that.

The **Tread of Pioneers Museum,** in a beautifully restored Queen Anne Victorian home, is an excellent spot to bone up on local history. It includes ski memorabilia dating to the turn of the 20th century, when Carl Howelsen opened Howelsen Hill, still the country's preeminent ski-jumping facility. ⊠*8th and Oak Sts.* ☎*970/879–2214* ⊕*www. treadofpioneers.org* ⊠*$5* ⊙*Tues.–Sat. 10–5.*

There are more than 150 mineral springs of varying temperatures in the Steamboat Springs area. In the middle of town, **Old Town Hot Springs,** formerly called Steamboat Springs Health and Recreation Hot Springs, gets its waters from the all-natural Heart Spring. The modern facility has a lap pool, relaxation pool, waterslide, and health club. It was renovated in the summer of 2007, adding two new waterslides and a climbing wall as well as revamping the lobby. ⊠*136 Lincoln Ave.* ☎*970/879–1828* ⊠*$7.50* ⊙ *Weekdays 5:30 AM–9:45 PM, Sat. 7 AM– 8:45 PM, Sun. 8 AM–8:45 PM.*

Fodor's Choice
★ About 7 mi west of town, the **Strawberry Park Hot Springs** is a bit remote and rustic. If you're not sure of the way, go with a guide. After dark, clothing is optional and no one under 18 is admitted, but the way the pool is set up to offer semi-privacy at this extremely popular, family-oriented spot makes for an intimate setting and relaxation. ⊠*Strawberry Park Rd.* ☎*970/879–0342* ⊕*www.strawberryhotsprings.com* ⊠*$10* ⊙*Sun.–Thurs. 10 AM–10:30 PM; Fri. and Sat. 10 AM–midnight* ⊟*No credit cards.*

In summer, Steamboat serves as the gateway to the magnificent **Medicine Bow/Routt National Forests,** with a wealth of activities from hiking to mountain biking to fishing. Among the nearby attractions are the

283-foot **Fish Creek Falls** and the splendidly rugged **Mount Zirkel Wilderness Area**. To the north, two sparkling man-made lakes, **Steamboat** and **Pearl,** each in its own state park, are a draw for those into fishing and sailing. In winter the area is just as popular. Snowshoers and backcountry skiers are permitted to use the west side of Rabbit Ears Pass, whereas snowmobilers are confined to the east side. ⊠ *Hahns Peak-Bears Ears Ranger District Office* ☎*970/879–1870* ⊕*www. fs.fed.us/r2/mbr.*

DOWNHILL SKIING & SNOWBOARDING

The **Steamboat Springs Ski Area** is perhaps best known for its tree skiing and "cruising" terrain—the latter term referring to wide, groomed runs perfect for intermediate-level skiers. The abundance of cruising terrain has made Steamboat immensely popular with those who ski once or twice a year and who aren't looking to tax their abilities. On a predominantly western exposure—most ski areas sit on north-facing exposures—the resort benefits from intense sun, which contributes to the mellow atmosphere. In addition, one of the most extensive lift systems in the region allows skiers to take many runs without having to spend much time waiting in line. The Storm Peak and Sundown high-speed quads, for example, each send you about 2,000 vertical feet in less than seven minutes. Do the math: A day of more than 60,000 vertical feet is entirely within the realm of possibility.

All this is not to suggest, however, that Steamboat is a piece of cake for more-experienced skiers. Pioneer Ridge encompasses advanced and intermediate terrain. Steamboat is renowned as a breeding ground for top mogul skiers, and for good reason. There are numerous mogul runs, but most are not particularly steep. The few with a vertical challenge, such as Chute One, are not especially long. If you're looking for challenging skiing at Steamboat, take on the trees. The ski area has done an admirable job of clearing many gladed areas of such nuisances as saplings, underbrush, and fallen timber, making Steamboat tree skiing much less hazardous than at other areas. The trees are also where advanced skiers—as well as, in some places, confident intermediates—can find the best of Steamboat's much-ballyhooed powder. Statistically, Steamboat doesn't report significantly more snowfall than other Colorado resorts, but somehow snow piles up here better than at the others. Ask well-traveled Colorado skiers, and they'll confirm that when it comes to consistently good, deep snow, Steamboat is hard to beat. ⊠*2305 Mount Werner Circle* ☎*970/879–6111* ⊕*www.steamboat.com* ⊙*Late-Nov.–mid-Apr., daily 8:30–3:30.*

The tiny **Howelsen Hill Ski Area,** in the heart of Steamboat Springs, is the oldest ski area still open in Colorado. Howelsen, with three lifts, 15 trails, one terrain park and a 440-foot vertical drop, is home of the Steamboat Springs Winter Sports Club, which boast more than 700 members. The ski area not only has an awesome terrain park, but has night skiing as well. It's the largest ski-jumping complex in America, and a major Olympic training ground. ⊠*845 Howelsen Pkwy.* ☎*970/879–8499* ⊙*Nov.–Mar., Mon. 11–6:30, Tues.–Fri. 11–8, Sat. 9–8, Sun. 9–4:30.*

FACILITIES
3,668-foot vertical drop; 2,965 skiable acres; 13% beginner, 56% intermediate, 31% advanced; 1 8-passenger gondola, 4 high-speed quad chairs, 1 quad chair, 6 triple chairs, 6 double chairs, and 7 surface lifts.

LESSONS & PROGRAMS
Half-day group lessons begin at $34; all-day lessons are $39. Clinics in moguls, powder, snowboarding, and "hyper-carving"—made possible by the design of shaped skis—are available. General information about the ski areas is available through the **Steamboat Ski and Resort Corporation** (☎970/879–6111). Intensive two- and three-day training camps in racing and advanced skiing are scheduled through the **Billy Kidd Center for Performance Skiing** (☎800/299–5017). Programs for kids from 6 months to 15 years of age are given through the **Kids' Vacation Center** (☎970/871–5375). Day care is also available.

Snowcat skiing—where a vehicle delivers you to hard-to-reach slopes—has been called the poor man's version of helicopter skiing, although at $200 to $300 a day, it's not exactly skiing for the lunch-pail crowd. But snowcat users don't have to worry about landing and can get to places that would be inaccessible by helicopter. Buffalo Pass, northeast of Steamboat, is reputed to be one of the snowiest spots in Colorado, and that's why it's the base for **Steamboat Powder Cats** (☎970/879–5188 or 800/288–0543). There's a maximum of 24 skiers per group, so the open-meadow skiing is never crowded.

LIFT TICKETS
$74. Savings of 5% or less on multiday tickets. Children 12 and under ski free when adults purchase a five-day ski ticket.

RENTALS
Equipment packages are available at the gondola base as well as at ski shops in town. Packages (skis, boots, and poles) average about $41 a day, less for multiday rentals. Call **Steamboat Central Reservations** (☎970/879–0740 or 800/922–2722) for rental information.

NORDIC SKIING

BACKCOUNTRY SKIING
The most popular area for backcountry skiing around Steamboat Springs is Rabbit Ears Pass, southeast of town. It's the last pass you cross if you're driving from Denver to Steamboat. Much of the appeal is its easy access to high-country trails from U.S. 40. There are plenty of routes you can take. Arrangements for backcountry tours can be made through **Steamboat Ski Touring Center** (✐Box 775401, Steamboat Springs 80477 ☎970/879–8180).

A popular backcountry spot is Seedhouse Road, about 25 mi north of Steamboat near the town of Clark. A marked network of trails across the rolling hills has good views of distant peaks. For maps and information on snow conditions, contact the **Hahns Peak Ranger Office** (✉925 Weiss Dr., 80487 ☎970/879–1870).

Touring and telemarking rentals are available at ski shops in the Steamboat area. One of the best is the **Ski Haus** (✉*1457 Pine Grove Rd.* ☎*970/879–0385*).

TRACK SKIING Laid out on and along the Sheraton Steamboat Golf Club, **Steamboat Ski Touring Center** has a relatively gentle 18.5-mi trail network. A good option for a relaxed afternoon of skiing is to pick up some vittles at the Picnic Basket in the main building and enjoy a picnic along Fish Creek Trail, a 3-mi-long loop that winds through pine and aspen groves. Rental packages (skis, boots, and poles) are available. ✐*Box 775401, Steamboat Springs 80477* ☎*970/879–8180* ⊕*nordicski.net* ⊠*Trail fee $15.*

★ **Vista Verde Guest Ranch** (✐*Box 465, Steamboat Springs 80477* ☎*970/ 879–3858 or 800/526–7433*) has a well-groomed network of tracks, as well as access to the adjacent national forest.

OTHER SPORTS & THE OUTDOORS

Dogsledding, hot-air ballooning, and snowmobiling can be arranged by calling the activities department at **Steamboat Central Reservations** (☎*970/879–4070 or 800/922–2722*).

GOLF **Haymaker Golf Course.** Three miles south of Steamboat Springs, this public-access 18-hole Keith Foster course has a pro shop and café. The rolling course has been voted among the top 20 by *Golf Digest* and has hills, streams, and native grasses. ✉*34855 U.S 40* ☎*970/870– 1846* ⊕*www.haymakergolf.com* ⚑*Reservations essential* ⚐*18 holes. Yards: 7,308/6,728. Par: 72/72. Green Fee: $83/$99.*

Sheraton Steamboat Resort & Golf Club. Expect to see plenty of wildlife; a bear was once spotted on the 18-hole championship course designed by the legendary Robert Trent Jones Jr. ✉*2000 Clubhouse Dr.* ☎*970/879–1391* ⊕*www.sheratonsteamboatgolf.com* ⚑*Reservations essential* ⚐*18 holes. Yards: 6,902/5,462. Par: 72/72. Green Fee: $65/$110.*

HIKING In the **Medicine Bow/Routt National Forests,** a mellow half-mile trail leads
★ to a 280-foot waterfall at **Fish Creek Falls.** You can extend your hike another 2 mi to the Upper Falls and then another 5 mi to 9,850-foot-high Long Lake. ✉*Hahns Peak-Bears Ears Ranger District Office* ☎*970/879–1870* ⊕*www.fs.fed.us/r2/mbr.*

HORSEBACK Because of the ranches surrounding the Yampa and Elk rivers, Steamboat is full of real cowboys as well as visitors trying to act the part.
RIDING
★ **Horseback riding** is one of the most popular pastimes here, with good reason: Seeing the area on horseback is not only easier on the legs, but it also allows riders to get deeper into the backcountry—which is crisscrossed by a web of deer and elk trails—and sometimes closer to wildlife than is possible on foot. Riding, however, isn't for everyone. There's usually a personal weight limit of 250 pounds, and children need to be able to handle their own mount. If you've never ridden a horse before, book a short test ride first. Allergies and sore muscles can turn a dream ride into an epic journey. Riding, instruction, and extended pack trips are offered at a number of ranches in the area, although some may require a minimum stay of a week.

One facility that has the full gamut of activities, from hour-long tours to journeys lasting several days, is **Del's Triangle 3 Ranch** (🖂 *Box 893, Clark 80428* ☎*970/879–3495* ⊕*www.steamboathorses.com*). It's about 20 mi north of Steamboat via Highway 129. **Sombrero Ranch** (🖂*835 River Rd.* ☎*970/879–2306* ⊕*www.sombrero.com/steam boatsprings*) is right in town and has one-hour guided tours perfect for novices. Every Friday and Saturday evening in summer, rodeos are held at the **Howelsen Rodeo Grounds** (🖂*5th St. and Howelsen Pkwy.* ☎*970/879–1818*).

MOUNTAIN BIKING
Fodor'sChoice
★

Steamboat Springs' rolling mountains, endless aspen glades, mellow valleys, and miles and miles of jeep trails and single-track make for great **mountain biking.** In summer, when Front Range trails are baking in the harsh summer sun and cluttered with mountain bikers, horse riders, and hikers, you can pedal some of the cool backcountry trails in Steamboat without passing a single cyclist.

RAFTING
High Adventures/Bucking Rainbow Outfitters (🖂*730 Lincoln Ave.* ☎*970/879–8747* ⊕*www.buckingrainbow.com*) runs rafting excursions to the Yampa, Elk, and Eagle rivers. Half-day to two-day trips are available for all levels.

SNOW-MOBILING
Steamboat Snowmobile Tours (☎*970/879–6500* ⊕*www.steamboatsnow mobile.com*) has guided tours. A shuttle serves most hotels.

WHERE TO EAT

$$$-$$$$ ✕**Antares.** The owners of this hot spot cut their culinary teeth at some of Steamboat's finest restaurants, including Harwig's/L'Apogée. With fieldstone walls, pressed-tin ceilings, and beautiful stained-glass windows, the splendid Victorian building attracts all the attention at first. Then Paul LeBrun's exciting, eclectic dishes arrive. You might feast on elk medallions with a Bing cherry–merlot sauce, or Maine lobster over chili pepper linguine. 🖂*57½ 8th St.* ☎*970/879–9939* ⚖*Reservations essential* ⊟*AE, MC, V* ⊗*No lunch.*

★ $$$-$$$$ ✕**Harwig's/L'Apogée.** Steamboat's most intimate restaurant, Harwig's/L'Apogée is in a building that once housed Harwig's Saddlery and Western Wear. There are two dining rooms, one that is more formal, the other casual. The classic French cuisine, with subtle Asian influences, is well crafted. Especially fine are the half crispy duck over oven-roasted yams, the Alaskan King–crab cakes, and pan-seared foie gras topped with warm chèvre. Still, the menu takes a backseat to the admirable wine list. Oenophile alert: Owner Jamie Jenny is a collector whose magnificent wine cellar—cited by *Wine Spectator* as one of America's best—contains more than 10,000 bottles; you can order more than 40 wines by the glass. 🖂*911 Lincoln Ave.* ☎*970/879–1919* ⊕*www.lapogee.com* ⚖*Reservations essential* ⊟*AE, DC, MC, V* ⊗*No lunch.*

$$$-$$$$ ✕**La Montaña.** This Tex-Mex establishment is among Steamboat's most popular restaurants, and with good reason. The kitchen incorporates indigenous specialties into the traditional menu. Among the standouts are sunflower seed–crusted tuna with a margarita beurre blanc, enchiladas layered with Monterey Jack and goat cheese and roasted peppers, and elk loin crusted with pecan nuts and bourbon cream sauce.

⊠*Après Ski Way and Village Dr.* ☎*970/879–5800* ⊕*www.la-montana.com* ⊟*AE, D, MC, V* ⊘*No lunch.*

$$–$$$ ✗**Riggio's.** In a dramatic industrial space, this Italian eatery evokes the old country with tapestries, murals, and landscape photos. The menu includes tasty pizzas (with toppings such as goat cheese and clams) and pasta dishes (*sciocca*, with rock shrimp, eggplant, tomatoes, and basil, is superb). Standards such as manicotti, chicken cacciatore, and saltimbocca are also well prepared. Try the house salad with Gorgonzola vinaigrette. ⊠*1106 Lincoln Ave.* ☎*970/879–9010* ⊕*www.riggiosfineitalian.com* ⊟*AE, D, DC, MC, V* ⊘*No lunch.*

$–$$ ✗**Cugino's Pizzeria & Italian Restaurant.** The south Philly sensibility of this pizzeria lends authenticity to its filling strombolis, stuffed pizzas that purportedly originated just outside Philadelphia. Food comes in big portions, there are two patios for people-watching and views of the Yampa River, and the staff here will take good care of you. Try the crispy New York–style pizza and the authentic-tasting spaghetti. ⊠*41 8th St.* ☎*970/879–5805* ⊟*MC, V.*

☾ ¢–$ ✗**Creekside Café & Grill.** This café offers hearty breakfasts and lunches crafted to get folks through a day of skiing or biking, served in a casual atmosphere that's family—and group—friendly. The most popular item on the menu, and for good reason, is the roster of a dozen eggs Benedicts, including "the Arnold," with smoked bacon, ham, and chorizo. On nice days, ask to sit on the patio next to pretty Soda Creek. In season, the place is usually jam-packed. ⊠*131 11th St.* ☎*970/879-4925* ⌂*Reservations essential* ⊟*D, MC, V* ⊘*No dinner.*

☾ ¢–$ ✗**Johnny B. Good's Diner.** Between the appealing kids' menu and the memorabilia that suggests Elvis has not left the building, Johnny's is all about fun and family. Breakfast (until 2 PM), lunch, and dinner are served daily, and they are all budget minded and large portioned. The menu is mostly what you'd expect—meat loaf and mashed potatoes, burgers, milk shakes, biscuits and gravy—but they also do an above-average rib eye and some better-than-gringo Mexican, as well as a popular roster of hot "dawgs." ⊠*738 Lincoln Ave.* ☎*970/870–8400* ⊕*www.johnnybgoodsdiner.com* ⊟*D, MC, V.*

WHERE TO STAY

$$$$ ▦**Sheraton Steamboat Resort & Conference Center.** This bustling high-rise is Steamboat's only true ski-in ski-out property. The amenities are classic resort-town, with a ski shop, golf course, and four rooftop hot tubs with sweeping views of the surrounding ski slopes. The large rooms in the main building are standard issue, with muted color schemes and comforts like refrigerators. **Pros:** convenient location, with the slopes, restaurants, and town right there; great for the business traveler, with plenty of computer-oriented amenities; enough rooms for very large groups. **Cons:** all the charm of a big chain, on-site food is not great, service can be indifferent. ⊠*2200 Village End Ct., 80477* ☎*970/879–2220 or 800/848–8877* ⊕*www.starwood.com* ⇌*315 rooms* ⌂*In-room: safe, refrigerator. In-hotel: 2 restaurants, room service, bar, golf course, pool, gym, concierge, laundry service, no-smoking rooms* ⊟*AE, D, DC, MC, V.*

8

$$$ ▦**Inn at Steamboat.** Rustic, knotty pine, leather furniture, quilts on the beds, and panoramic views of the Yampa Valley make the inn a good choice for folks looking to stay somewhere that feels like a mountain lodge at slightly lower-than-ski-resort prices. Each room has sliding doors that let you step out into the mountain air and onto a common balcony. It's located near the shuttle and bus services to the ski area and town. Continental breakfast, including make-your-own waffles, is included. **Pros:** magnificent views, even from the pool and particularly in fall; reasonable rates. **Con:** pool not always heated. ⊠*3070 Columbine Dr., 80487* ☎*800/872–2601 or 970/879–2600* ⊕*www.innatsteamboatonline.com* ➥*34 rooms* ♿*In room: refrigerator, VCR, dial-up. In hotel: pool, laundry facilities, public Internet, public Wi-Fi, no-smoking rooms* ⊟*AE, D, MC, V.*

$$$ ▦**Ptarmigan Inn.** Situated on the slopes, this laid-back lodging, once part of the Best Western chain but now independently owned, couldn't have a more-convenient location. The modest rooms, decorated in pastels, have balconies with views of the surrounding mountains. **Pros:** great location, mountain views. **Con:** chain hotel feel. ⊠*2304 Après Ski Way* ⟐*Box 773240, Steamboat Springs 80477* ☎*970/879–1730 or 800/538–7519* ⊕*www.steamboat-lodging.com* ➥*77 rooms* ♿*In-room: refrigerator, VCR, ethernet, Wi-Fi. In-hotel: restaurant, bar, pool, no-smoking rooms* ⊟*AE, D, DC, MC, V.*

$$ ▦**Alpine Rose Bed and Breakfast.** Views of Strawberry Park and an easy walk into town make the Alpine Rose a wonderful alternative to pricey hotels, especially during ski season. The owners offer simple breakfasts, such as fruit with omelets or waffles, and the rooms are homey. One room offers an adjoining room with a bunk bed for kids. The efficiency apartment, with its own entrance and Jacuzzi tub, is ideal for longer stays. **Pros:** close to town, relatively close to ski area (five-minute drive), reasonably priced. **Con:** nothing fancy. ⊠*724 Grand St., 80477* ☎*970/879–1528 or 888/879–1528* ⊕*www.alpinerosesteamboat.com* ➥*5 rooms* ♿*In room: no a/c, no phone, kitchen (some), VCR (some). In hotel: no elevator, public Wi-Fi, no kids under 6, no-smoking rooms* ⊟*MC, V.*

⟳ **$$**   ▦**Hotel Bristol.** A charming, small hotel nestled in a 1948 building, the Bristol not only has location working for it, but also old-fashioned personalized service. Situated right downtown, it is surrounded by shops and eateries and it has an immediately inviting lobby, with a fireplace and bookshelf. The staff goes out of its way to recommend local sights and dining, and although the Western-style decor is a bit faded, the cramped but serviceable rooms are well kept and tidy. Families and groups will appreciate their special family-style rooms, which offer four people the ability to stay in two rooms connected by a bathroom, for about $40–$50 more per night. **Pros:** families and groups can stay comfortably for a small extra fee, convenient location, ski lockers, computer in lobby. **Cons:** rooms may seem uncomfortably small, bathrooms even more so. ⊠*917 Lincoln Ave., 80477* ☎*970/879–3083 or 800/851–0872* ⊕*www.steamboathotelbristol.com* ➥*24 rooms* ♿*In room: DVD (some), Wi-Fi. In hotel: restaurant, no-smoking rooms* ⊟*AE, D, MC, V.*

$–$$ 🏠**Rabbit Ears Motel.** The playful, pink-neon bunny sign outside this motel has been a local landmark since 1952, making it an unofficial gateway to Steamboat Springs. The location is ideal if you're visiting the springs (across the street); the ski area (the bus stops outside); and the downtown shops, bars, and restaurants. All the rooms are clean and attractive, and most have balconies with views of the Yampa River. Continental breakfast is included. **Pros:** great location, family and pet friendly. **Cons:** kitschy, nothing fancy. ⊠*201 Lincoln Ave., 80477* ☎*970/879–1150 or 800/828–7702* ⊕*www.rabbitearsmotel. com* ↩*65 rooms* ♿*In-room: refrigerator, Wi-Fi. In-hotel: laundry facilities, some pets allowed, no-smoking rooms* ▭*AE, D, DC, MC, V* ⧖*CP.*

¢   🏠**Bunkhouse Lodge.** River or mountain views await you at the budget-minded Bunkhouse, which counts a river-rock fireplace surrounded by cozy couches and a Jacuzzi on the deck among its charms. Continental breakfast is included and served in the cheery great room, and the free bus leaves from the end of the driveway to take you to the mountain or downtown. Rooms are sparse but adequate. **Pros:** great views, bargain prices. **Con:** linens are not exactly luxury. ⊠*3155 S. Lincoln St., 80487* ☎*877/245–6343 or 970/871–9121* ⊕*www.thebunkhouselodge.com* ↩*38 rooms* ♿*In-room: refrigerator, Wi-Fi. In hotel: no elevator, laundry facilities, no-smoking rooms* ▭*AE, D, MC, V.*

GUEST RANCHES
★ $$$$ 🏠**Home Ranch.** You won't be roughing it at this all-inclusive retreat, a Relais & Chateaux property nestled among towering stands of aspen north of Steamboat near Clark. With a magnificent fieldstone fireplace surrounded by plush leather armchairs and sofa, the main room couldn't be cozier. The dining room, where the chef turns out gourmet Southwestern fare, has soaring ceilings and wonderful views. Accommodations are in the main lodge or in individual cabins with terraces and private hot tubs. The decor leans toward Native American rugs and prints, lace curtains, terra-cotta tile or hardwood floors, and stenciled walls. A seven-night minimum stay is required. **Pros:** luxury experience, gourmet food, family friendly. **Cons:** pricey, seven-day stay can be prohibitive, less authentic. ⊠*54880 County Rd. 129, Clark 80428* ☎*970/879–1780* ⊕*www.homeranch.com* ↩*6 rooms, 8 cabins* ♿*In-hotel: bar, pool, no-smoking rooms* ▭*AE, D, MC, V* ⧖*Closed late Mar.–May and early Oct.–late Dec.* ⧖*FAP.*

$$$$
Fodor's Choice
★   🏠**Vista Verde Guest Ranch.** On a working ranch, the luxurious Vista Verde provides city slickers with an authentic Western experience. Lodge rooms are huge and beautifully appointed, with lace curtains, Western art, and lodgepole furniture. Cabins are more rustic, with pine paneling and old-fashioned wood-burning stoves, plus refrigerators, coffeemakers, and porches. Three-, five- and seven-night packages are available. Two weeks a year, you can participate in a cattle drive; there are also weeks for adults only. **Pros:** authentic experience, variable stays, family friendly. **Con:** pricey. ⊠*3100 County Rd. 64, Clark 80428* ☎*970/879–3858 or 800/526–7433* ⊕*www.vistaverde. com* ↩*3 rooms, 9 cabins* ♿*In-room: no a/c, no TV. In-hotel: gym, no-smoking rooms* ▭*No credit cards* ⧖*Closed mid-Mar.–late May and Oct.–mid-Dec.* ⧖*FAP.*

8

CONDOS   **Mountain Resorts** (✉*2145 Resort Dr., Suite 100, 80487* ☎*800/525–2622* ⊕*www.mtn-resorts.com*) manages condominiums at more than 15 locations. Torian Plum, one of the properties managed by **Resort Quest Steamboat** (✉*1855 Ski Time Sq., 80487* ☎*970/879–8811 or 800/228–2458* 🖷*970/879–8485*), has elegant one- to five-bedroom units in a ski-in ski-out location. Hot tubs are available. **Steamboat Resorts** (✉*Box 772995, Steamboat Springs 80477* ☎*800/525–5502* ⊕*www.steamboatresorts.com*) rents plenty of properties near the slopes.

NIGHTLIFE

FESTIVALS   **Strings in the Mountains Music Festival.** The focus is on chamber music and chamber orchestra music presented by more than 150 musicians, including Grammy winners and other internationally renowned talents, throughout summer, primarily in the tent on the weekends. But Strings also offers big names in jazz, country, big band, bluegrass, and world music, as well as free concerts during its "Music on the Green" lunchtime series at Yampa River Botanic Park on Thursday in summer. ✉*Steamboat Springs Music Festival Tent at the corner of Mt. Werner and Pine Grove Rds.* ☎*970/879–5056* ⊕*stringsinthemountains.com.*

Mahogany Ridge Brewery & Grill (✉*5th St. and Lincoln Ave.* ☎*970/879–3773*) serves superior pub grub and pours an assortment of homemade ales, lagers, porters, and stouts. The **Old Town Pub** (✉*600 Lincoln Ave.* ☎*970/879–2101*) has juicy burgers and music from some great bands. On the mountain, the **Tugboat** (✉*Ski Time Sq.* ☎*970/879–7070*) is the place for loud rock and roll. You can also challenge locals to a game of pool.

SHOPPING

At the base of the ski area are three expansive shopping centers—Ski Time Square, Torian Plum Plaza, and Gondola Square.

Downtown Steamboat's **Old Town Square** (✉*7th St. and Lincoln Ave.*) is a collection of upscale boutiques and retailers. There are also plenty of places to get a good cup of coffee.

BOOKS   **Off the Beaten Path** (✉*56 7th St.* ☎*970/879–6830*) is a throwback to the Beat Generation, with poetry readings, lectures, and concerts. It has an excellent selection of New Age works, in addition to the usual best sellers and travel guides.

BOUTIQUES &   In Torian Plum Plaza, the **Silver Lining** (✉*1855 Ski Time Square Dr.*
GALLERIES   ☎*970/879–7474*) displays art, crafts, and clothing from around the world, including Balinese cradle watchers, carved wooden figures

believed to keep evil spirits away from sleeping children. You can make your own earrings at the bead counter.**White Hart Gallery** (⊠ *843 Lincoln Ave.* ☎ *970/879–1015*) is a magnificent clutter of Western-theme paintings and objets d'art.Native American images adorn the walls of the **Wild Horse Gallery** (⊠ *2200 Village End Ct.* ☎ *970/879–7660*). This shop inside the Sheraton Steamboat is the place to buy artwork, jewelry, and blown glass.

SPORTING **Ski Haus** (⊠ *1457 Pine Grove Rd.* ☎ *970/879–0385*) can outfit you for
GOODS the slopes.**Straightline Sports** (⊠ *744 Lincoln Ave.* ☎ *970/879–7568*) is a good bet for downhill necessities.

WESTERN Owned by the same family for four generations, **F.M. Light and Sons** (⊠ *830 Lincoln Ave.* ☎ *970/879–1822*) caters to the Marlboro man in us all. If you're lucky you'll find a bargain—how about cowboy hats for $4.98?**Into the West** (⊠ *807 Lincoln Ave.* ☎ *970/879–8377*) is owned by Jace Romick, a former member of the U.S. Ski Team and a veteran of the rodeo circuit. He crafts splendid, beautifully textured lodgepole furniture. There are also antiques (even ornate potbellied stoves), cowhide mirrors, and handicrafts such as Native American–drum tables and fanciful candleholders fashioned from branding irons. **Two Rivers Gallery** (⊠ *56 9th St.* ☎ *970/879–0044*) sells such cowboy collectibles as antler chandeliers and cow-skull lamps, as well as vintage photographs, prints, sculpture, and paintings.

DINOSAUR NATIONAL MONUMENT

8

90 mi west of Craig via U.S. 40.

Fodor's Choice ★

☺ Straddling the Colorado–Utah border, **Dinosaur National Monument** is a must for any dinosaur enthusiast. A two-story hill teeming with fossils—many still in the complete skeletal shapes of the dinosaurs—greets visitors at one of the few places in the world where you can touch a dinosaur bone still embedded in the earth. The **Dinosaur Quarry** (⚐ *Visitor center: 7 mi north of Jensen, Utah, on Rte. 139* ☎ *970/374–3000*), is closed because of damage to the structural integrity of the building. There is a temporary visitor center set up, and although the main exhibit wall of dinosaur fossils is also closed, some of them can still be seen by hiking about a half mile from the temporary site. A shuttle bus carries visitors from the temporary visitor center to the quarry. The Colorado side of the park offers some of the best hiking in the West, along the Harpers Corner and Echo Park Drive routes, and the ominous-sounding Canyon of Lodore (where the Green River rapids buffet rafts). The drive is only accessible in summer—even then, four-wheel drive is preferable—and some of the most breathtaking overlooks are well off the beaten path. ⊠ *4545 E. Hwy. 40, Dinosaur* ☎ *435/781–7700* ⊕ *www.nps.gov/dino* ☺ *Daily.*

SPORTS & THE OUTDOORS

HIKING The **Desert Voices Nature Trail** (⊠ *Split Mountain area, across from boat*
☺ *ramp*) is near the quarry. The 1.5-mi loop is moderate in difficulty and features a series of trail signs produced for kids by kids.

WHITE-WATER
RAFTING

One of the best ways to experience the rugged beauty of the park is on a white-water raft trip. **Adventure Bound River Expeditions** (✉2392 H Rd., Grand Junction ☎800/423–4668 ⊕www.raft-colorado.com) offers two- to five-day white-water raft excursions on the Colorado, Yampa, and Green rivers.

WHERE TO EAT

🕲 ¢–$ ✕**Miner's Cafe.** Adorned with homey embroidered patterns on the wall and a community jigsaw puzzle table, this small café is friendly and simple. The food includes Mexican and American dishes at breakfast, lunch, and dinner. ✉420 E. Brontosaurus Blvd., Dinosaur ☎970/374–2020 ⊟AE, D, MC, V ⊘Closed Sun.

🕲 ★ ¢ ✕**Bed Rock Depot.** Co-owners and longtime residents Leona Hemmerich and Bill Mitchem understand both the cravings of the area's visitors and the spectacular vistas they come to see. New batches of homemade ice cream show up almost every day at their roadside shop where the walls are a gallery for their photography and artwork. The shop sells fresh sandwiches and gourmet coffees (with names like "Mochasaurus") and bottled root beer, cream soda, and ginger ale. The Depot's immaculate restroom makes for one of the most pleasant pit stops on the long drive ahead. Call for winter hours. ✉214 Brontosaurus W. Blvd., Dinosaur ☎970/374–2336 ⊟AE, D, MC, V ⊘Closed Wed.

RANGELY

20 mi southeast of Dinosaur National Monument, 96 mi northwest of Grand Junction via Rte. 139 and 1–70.

The center of one of the last areas in the state to be explored by European settlers, Rangely was dubbed an "isolated empire" by early pioneers. You can search out the petroglyphs left by Native American civilizations or just stroll the farmers' market in Town Square. If you enjoy backroad mountain biking, the Raven Rims have an abundance of trails. A good starting point is at the corrals in Chase Draw. You may even spot elk, mule, deer, coyotes, and other wildlife as you spin your wheels through the multihued sandstone rims and mesas north of town. Kenney Reservoir 5 mi north of town offers fishing and swimming, and a trip to the Cathedral Bluffs gives new definition to "isolated empire."

★   One of Rangely's most compelling sights is the superb Fremont petroglyphs—carved between 600 and 1300—in Douglas Creek canyon, south of town along Route 139. This stretch is known as the **Canyon Pintado National Historic District** and the examples of rock art are among the best preserved in the West; half the fun is clambering up the rocks to find them. A brochure listing the sights is available at the Rangely Chamber of Commerce. ✉209 E. Main St. ☎970/675–5290 ⊕www. co.blm.gov ⊠Free ⊘Daily.

SPORTS & THE OUTDOORS

FISHING Just below Taylor Draw Dam, **Kenney Reservoir** draws anglers in search of black crappie, channel catfish, and rainbow trout. The best fishing is right below the dam. If you hook one of Colorado's endangered pike-minnow, you'll have to throw it back. You can also go camping, boating, waterskiing, wildlife-watching, and picnicking. Locals come to the reservoir to watch the sun's last rays color the bluffs behind the lake.

MOUNTAIN The best mountain-biking trails north of town are in the Raven Rims,
BIKING named in honor of the abundant population of the large, noisy birds that live in the area. Contact the **Town of Rangely** (⊠ *209 E. Main St.* ☎ *970/675–8476*) for trail information. **Rangely Chamber of Commerce** (⊠ *209 E. Main St.* ☎ *970/675–5290*) is another good source of information.

WHERE TO STAY & EAT

$-$$ ✕**Cowboy Corral.** One of the oldest restaurants in town, this laid-back eatery serves burgers, sandwiches, pork chops, steaks, and some Mexican food. The super burrito, buckaroo burger, and chicken-fried steak are popular. Separate dining areas with tables and booths are designated for smoking and nonsmoking patrons ⊠ *202 W. Main St.* ☎ *970/675–8986* ▤ *AE, D, MC, V.*

¢-$ ✕**Los Tres Potrillos.** This casual Mexican restaurant has the usual selection of burritos and tacos and the only patio in town. Try the fajitas, enchiladas, and carne asada. Mexican pottery, serapes, and sombreros in green, orange, and black make up the colorful backdrop. ⊠ *302 W. Main St.* ☎ *970/675–8870* ▤ *AE, D, MC, V* ☽ *Closed Sun.*

¢ ▥**Adora Inn.** A room at this motel in the heart of Rangely, which had been the Four Queens Motel, comes with a queen- or king-size bed, a table, two chairs, and a coffeemaker. A microwave, refrigerator, and coin laundry are available in the common area. **Pros:** in an area with few choices, it's reasonably priced and clean; centrally located. **Con:** the loss of the rec center when it was sold is a blow. ⊠ *206 E. Main St., 81648* ☎ *970/675–5035* ▤ *970/675–5037* ⊳ *32 rooms* ⌂ *In-room: refrigerator, Wi-Fi. In-hotel: no elevator, laundry facilities, no-smoking rooms* ▤ *AE, D, MC, V.*

SHOPPING

Fresh produce, baked goods, and live entertainment can be found at the **Main Street Farmers' Market** (⊠ *Town Sq.* ☎ *970/675–5290*), held Saturday from 8:30 to 12:30. One of the more-popular items is the elk jerky. A wood-burning stove graces the front of charming **Sweetbriar** (⊠ *781 W. Hwy. 64* ☎ *970/675–5353*), a little store that sells a variety of gifts and home decor. It carries everything from candles to clocks and angels to dragons.

8

NORTHWEST COLORADO & STEAMBOAT SPRINGS ESSENTIALS

TRANSPORTATION

BY AIR

Walker Field Airport (GJT) is in Grand Junction. It's served by America West Express, Sky West, Great Lakes (Frontier), and United Express.

Yampa Valley Airport (HDN) is in Hayden, 22 mi from Steamboat Springs. American, Continental, Delta, Northwest, and United fly non-stop from various gateways during ski season.

Information Walker Field Airport (GJT) (⊠ *Grand Junction* ☎ *970/244–9100* ⊕ *www.walkerfield.com*). **Yampa Valley Airport (HDN)** (⊠ *Hayden* ☎ *970/276–3669*).

TRANSFERS A Touch With Class has regular limo service into Grand Junction and outlying communities. Sunshine Taxi serves Grand Junction.

To and from Steamboat Springs, take Alpine Taxi.

Contacts A Touch With Class (☎ *970/245–5466*). **Alpine Taxi** (☎ *970/879–2800*). **Sunshine Taxi** (☎ *970/245–8294*).

BY BIKE

Several routes through Grand Junction are well suited to bicycle use. The city also has designated bike lanes in some areas. You can bike along the Colorado Riverfront Trails, a network that winds along the Colorado River, stretching from the Redlands Parkway to Palisade. Bike travel between towns in this region is discouraged due to the prevalence of narrow, shoulderless two-lane highways—due as well to the sheer distance between the towns. Several shops rent state-of-the-art bikes by the day or longer.

Contacts Brown Cycles (☎ *970/245–7939* ⊕ *www.browncycles.com*). **Ruby Canyon Cycles** (☎ *970/241–0141* ⊕ *www.rubycanyoncycles.com*).

BY BUS

Greyhound Lines stops in Grand Junction and Delta.

Steamboat Springs Transit provides free shuttle service between the ski area and downtown Steamboat year-round. Most of the major properties also provide shuttles between the two areas for their guests.

Contacts Greyhound Bus Service (☎ *800/231–2222* ⊕ *www.greyhound.com*). **Steamboat Springs Transit** (☎ *970/879–3717*).

BY CAR

In northwestern Colorado, I–70 (U.S. 6) is the major thoroughfare, accessing Grand Junction, Rifle, and Grand Mesa (via Route 65, which runs to Delta). Meeker is reached from Rifle via Route 13 and Rangely and Dinosaur via Route 64. U.S. 40 east from Utah is the best way to reach Dinosaur National Monument and Craig.

From Denver, Steamboat Springs is about a three-hour drive northwest via I–70 and U.S. 40. The route traverses some high-mountain passes, so it's a good idea to check road conditions before you travel.

Grand Junction has gas stations that are open 24 hours. Most gas stations in the smaller towns are open until 10 PM in summer, and even some automated credit-card pumps shut down at that hour.

Most roads are paved and in fairly good condition. Summer is peak road construction season, so expect some delays. Be prepared for winter driving conditions at all times. Enterprise is in downtown Grand Junction, with free pickup. Avis and Hertz are in the Walker Field Airport terminal. Depending on where you're traveling, you might want a four-wheel drive.

Avis has car rentals in Steamboat Springs.

Information AAA Colorado (☎ *970/245–2236* ⊕ *www.aaa.com*).**Colorado State Patrol** (☎ *970/249–4392* ⊕ *www.csp.state.co.us*). **Road Report** (☎ *877/315–7623* ⊕ *www.cotrip.org*).

BY TRAIN
Amtrak provides daily service to the east and west coasts through downtown Grand Junction.

Contact Amtrak (☎ *800/872–7245* ⊕ *www.amtrak.com*).

CONTACTS & RESOURCES

EMERGENCIES
Ambulance or Police (☎ *911*).

24-Hour Medical Care Craig Memorial Hospital (✉ *785 Russell Ave.* ☎ *970/824–9411*). **Delta County Memorial Hospital** (✉ *100 Stafford La.* ☎ *970/874–7681*). **Pioneers Hospital** (✉ *345 Cleveland St., Meeker* ☎ *970/878–5047*). **Routt Memorial Hospital** (✉ *1024 Central Dr., Steamboat Springs* ☎ *970/879–1322*). **St. Mary's Hospital** (✉ *2635 N. 7th St., Grand Junction* ☎ *970/244–2273*).

TOURS
Steamboat's Sweet Pea Tours visits nearby hot springs. American Spirit Shuttle offers scheduled and customized tours of Colorado National Monument, Grand Mesa, and area wineries. Dinosaur Journey leads one- and three-day paleontological treks that include work in a dinosaur quarry. Eagle Tree Tours runs tours of Colorado National Monument and the Grand Junction area, including some with four-wheel-drive vehicles, hiking, or biking.

Contacts American Spirit Shuttle (✉ *204 4th St., Clifton* ☎ *970/523–7662* ⊕ *www.americanspiritshuttle.net*). **Dinosaur Journey** (✉ *550 Jurassic Ct., Fruita* ☎ *970/858–7282* ⊕ *www.dinosaurjourney.org*). **Eagle Tree Tours** (✉ *538 Teller, Grand Junction* ☎ *970/241–4792*). **Sweet Pea Tours** (✉ *Steamboat Springs* ☎ *970/879–5820*).

VISITOR INFORMATION

Snow reports **Steamboat Springs** (☏ *970/879-7300*).

Contacts **Battlement Mesa Chamber of Commerce** (⌂ *Box 93, Parachute 81635* ☏ *970/285-7934* ⊕ *www.parachutechamber.org*). **Cedaredge Chamber of Commerce** (⌂ *Box 278, Cedaredge 81413* ☏ *970/856-6961* ⊕ *www.cedar edgecolorado.com*). **Greater Craig Chamber of Commerce** (✉ *360 E. Victory Way, 81625* ☏ *970/824-5689* ⊕ *www.colorado-go-west.com*). **Grand Junction Visitor & Convention Bureau** (✉ *740 Horizon Dr., 81506* ☏ *800/962-2547* ⊕ *www.visit grandjunction.com*). **Meeker Chamber of Commerce** (⌂ *Box 869, Meeker 81641* ☏ *970/878-5510* ⊕ *www.meekerchamber.com*). **Palisade Chamber of Commerce** (✉ *319 Main St., 81526* ☏ *970/464-7458* ⊕ *www.palisadecoc.com*). **Plateau Valley Chamber of Commerce** (✉ *103 Main St., Collbran 81624* ☏ *970/487-3833* ⊕ *www.coloradodirectory.com/plateauvalleycc*). **Rangely Chamber of Commerce** (✉ *209 E. Main St., 81648* ☏ *970/675-5290* ⊕ *www.rangely.com*).

Steamboat Ski & Resort Corporation (✉ *2305 Mount Werner Circle, Steamboat Springs 80487* ☏ *970/879-6111* ⊕ *steamboat.com*). **Steamboat Springs Chamber Resort Association** (✉ *1255 S. Lincoln Ave., 80477* ☏ *970/879-0880 or 800/922-2722* ⊕ *steamboatchamber.com*).

Southwest Colorado

THE SAN JUAN MOUNTAINS & BLACK CANYON OF THE GUNNISON

WORD OF MOUTH

"I wish you could see Crested Butte in December when it is full of snow, as I did for the first time. I remember driving up from the Gunnison area, the mountains surrounded us as we made our way up the road. It is just beautiful."

—valeriesgallery

"The scenery on the drive back to Durango was one of the most spectacular views we have ever seen—had to make several stops."

—LvSun

Revised &
Updated by
Ann Miller &
Kyle Wagner

THE RUDDY OR RED-HUE ROCKS found in much of the state, particularly in the southwest, give Colorado its name. The region's terrain varies widely—from yawning black canyons and desolate monochrome moonscapes to pastel deserts and mesas, glistening sapphire lakes, and wide expanses of those stunning red rocks. It's so rugged in the southwest that a four-wheel-drive vehicle or hiker's sturdiness is necessary to explore much of the wild and beautiful backcountry.

The region's history and people are as colorful as the landscape. Southwestern Colorado, as well as the "Four Corners" neighbors of northwestern New Mexico, northeastern Arizona, and southeastern Utah, was home to the Ancestral Puebloan peoples formerly known as Anasazi, meaning "ancient ones." They constructed impressive cliff dwellings in what are now Mesa Verde National Park, Ute Mountain Tribal Park, and other nearby sites. This wild and woolly region, dotted with rowdy mining camps and boomtowns, also witnessed the antics of such notorious outlaws as Butch Cassidy, who embarked on his storied career by robbing the Telluride Bank in 1889, and Robert "Bobby" Clark, who hid out in Creede from the James Gang after he shot Jesse in the back. Even today, the more-ornery, independent locals, disgusted with the political system, periodically talk of seceding from the union. They can be as rough as the country they inhabit.

Southwest Colorado offers such diversity that, depending on where you go, you can have radically different vacations. You can spiral from the towering peaks of the San Juan range to the plunging Black Canyon of the Gunnison, taking in alpine scenery along the way, as well as the eerie remains of old mining camps, before winding through striking desert landscapes, the superlative Ancestral Puebloan ruins, and the Old West railroad town of Durango. If you're not here to ski or golf in the resorts of Crested Butte, Purgatory, or Telluride, there's still much to experience in this part of the state.

EXPLORING SOUTHWEST COLORADO

Southwest Colorado is the land beyond the interstates. It's a landscape of towering mountains, arid mesa-and-canyon country, and roiling rivers. Old mining roads, legacies of the late 19th and early 20th centuries when gold and silver mining was ascendant, lead through drop-dead gorgeous mountain valleys to the rugged high country. However, much of this part of the state is designated as wilderness area—including the nearly 1-million-acre Weminuche Wilderness, the state's largest protected area—which means that no roads may be built and no wheeled or motorized vehicles are permitted. This is a region where some state highways are unpaved, a federal highway known as U.S. 550 corkscrews over a high mountain pass known for heavy snows and a lack of guardrails, and snowmobiles regularly replace other motor vehicles as winter transportation. High-clearance, four-wheel-drive vehicles in summer and snowmobiles in winter are required for backcountry exploration, but regular passenger cars can travel most roads.

TOP REASONS TO GO

The Colorado Trail: Bike, hike, or photograph the more than 500 mi of volunteer-maintained trail traversing six wilderness areas and eight mountain ranges from Durango to Denver, with breathtaking views of old-growth forests alternating with wildflower-covered meadows, lakes, and creeks.

Mountain Biking Crested Butte: There's a reason the Mountain Bike Hall of Fame resides here—the town is one of the birthplaces of fat-tire biking, and the up-close mountain scenery, sweet single-track, and the sheer variety of trails and terrain are a testament to the reason of it's location.

Durango & Silverton Narrow Gauge Railroad: This year-round, nine-hour journey along the Animas River from Durango to Silverton will take you back in time. The train is powered by coal and steam and the railroad line has been in continuous operation since 1882. The views include dramatic canyons and the sweeping panoramas of the San Juan National Forest.

Downhill Skiing and Snowboarding at Telluride Ski Resort: There's rarely a wait to get at the sweeping, groomed trails and seemingly endless tree runs and moguls available at this, the largest collection of 14,000-foot mountains in the country. Expansive views, varied terrain, and remote slopes that hold powder add to the experience.

ABOUT THE PARKS & RECREATION AREAS

Southwest Colorado includes a wealth of national and state parks and recreational areas. Of the 13 rivers designated as "gold medal" waters by the Colorado Wildlife Commission, the Animas, Gunnison, and Rio Grande are all here. Blue Mesa Reservoir, the state's largest lake, is a destination for boaters, kayakers, water-skiers, windsurfers, anglers, and scuba divers. Up in rustic Almont, a small community near the Gunnison headwaters, they *live* fly-fishing.

The precipitous **Black Canyon of the Gunnison National Park** is a mysterious and powerful attraction, while nearby **Blue Mesa Reservoir** has some of the best fishing in the state. Some of the most intact of what remains of the ancient, little-known Puebloan culture is inside Mesa Verde National Park and **Canyon of the Ancients National Monument.** Both are testaments to the area's long history, to remind us that others found this area a habitable and desirous place before us. *For information about Mesa Verde National Park, see the Mesa Verde National Park chapter in this book.*

The San Juan Mountains stretch through 12,000 square mi of southwest Colorado, encompassing the **Weminuche Wilderness Area,** half a million acres along the Continental Divide administered by three federal agencies. The **San Juan National Forest,** which ranges from east of Pagosa Springs to the western border of the state, is a virtual paradise for all kinds of adventuring, with mountains, rivers, and trails for any level of outdoor activity. The **Colorado Trail,** the premier backpacking experience in the state, goes north near Durango 500 mi to Denver.

9

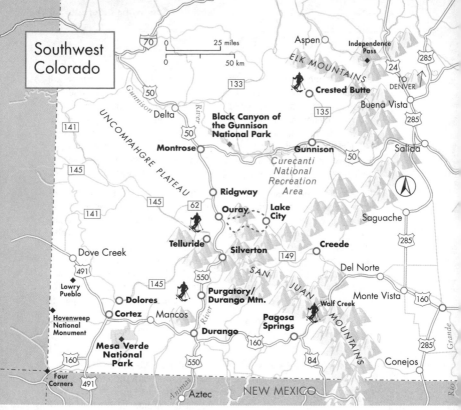

The **Rio Grande National Forest** stretches from the magisterial Sangre de Cristo Mountains across the San Luis Valley—at 7,600-feet elevation, the world's largest alpine valley—to the eastern San Juan Mountains on its western borders. It is less well known, but no less spectacular, than the rest of the area.

Anglers love **Ridgway State Park** with access to rainbow trout and other prize fish, and camping and hiking areas.

ABOUT THE RESTAURANTS

With dining options ranging from creative contemporary cuisine in the posh ski resorts of Telluride (and to a lesser extent in Crested Butte and Durango) to no-frills American fare in down-home ranching communities, no one has any excuse to visit a chain restaurant here. The leading chefs are tapping into the region's local bounty, so you can find innovative recipes for ranch-raised game, lamb, and trout. Many serve only locally raised, grass-fed meats. Olathe sweet corn is a delicacy enjoyed across the state in restaurants and grocery stores. Seasonal produce is always highlighted on the best menus.

ABOUT THE HOTELS

No matter what you're looking for in vacation lodging—luxurious slope-side condominium, landmark inn in a historic town, riverside cabin, quaint bed-and-breakfast inn, budget motel, or chock-full-of RVs campground—southwest Colorado has it in abundance. In ski resorts, especially, the rates vary from season to season. Some properties close in fall once the aspens have shed their golden leaves, open in winter when the lifts begin running, close in spring after the snow melts, and open again in mid-June.

WHAT IT COSTS					
	¢	$	$$	$$$	$$$$
RESTAURANTS	under $8	$8–$12	$13–$18	$19–$25	over $25
HOTELS	under $80	$80–$120	$121–$170	$171–$230	over $230

Restaurant prices are for a main course at dinner, excluding 5.9%–8.1% tax. Hotel prices are for two people in a standard double room in high season, excluding service charges and 7.6%–9.9% tax.

TIMING

Southwest Colorado, like the rest of the state, is intensely seasonal. Snow begins falling in the high country in late September or early October, and by Halloween seasonal closures turn most unpaved roads into routes for snowmobiles. The San Juan Mountains are the snowiest region of the Colorado Rockies, with average annual snowfalls approaching 400 inches in some spots. Winter lingers well into the season that is called spring on the calendar—the greatest snowfalls generally occur in March and April. Skiing winds down in early to mid-April, and ski towns virtually shut down until summer. Gunnison and Durango, being college towns, keep rolling throughout the year.

In mid-April the snow in the higher elevations begins to melt. Cresting streams offer thrilling, if chilling, white-water rafting and kayaking. Hiking trails become accessible, and wildflowers begin their short, intense season of show. Summer is glorious in the mountains, with brilliant sunshine in cobalt blue skies. Late summer brings brief and often intense showers on many an August afternoon, sometimes accompanied by dramatic thunder and lightning. Summer tourism winds down after Labor Day and shuts down completely in October and the cycle begins again. Spring and fall are the best times to visit the harsh dry climate of the mesa-and-canyon country around the Four Corners.

9

CRESTED BUTTE & GUNNISON

THE ELK MOUNTAINS & BLUE MESA RESERVOIR

The area is dominated and shaped by the Gunnison River basin, which gathers water from the Continental Divide and finally hooks up with the Colorado River near Grand Junction. Near Cimarron the river has cut the Black Canyon of the Gunnison, a forbidding, 48-mi abyss often deeper than it is wide. Farther upriver is the Blue Mesa Reservoir, the state's largest lake with boating, sporting, and backpacking opportunities. The Elk Mountains stretch from the north edge of the Black Canyon through Crested Butte. Almont, off Highway 135 between Crested Butte and Gunnison, is a still-rustic fly-fishing hideaway.

CRESTED BUTTE

30 mi north of Gunnison via Rte. 135, 90 mi northeast of Montrose.

Like Aspen, the town of Crested Butte was once a quaint mining village. The Victorian gingerbread-trim houses remain—albeit painted in whimsical shades of hot pink, magenta, and chartreuse. Unlike Aspen, however, Crested Butte never became chic. A controversial ad campaign for the ski area touted it as "Aspen like it used to be, and Vail like it never was."

A more-lovely setting could not be imagined. The town sits at the top of a long, broad valley that stretches 17 mi all the way south to Gunnison. Mount Crested Butte, which looms over the town, is the most visible landmark in the entire valley. The Elk Mountains, north of Crested Butte, stretch to the Maroon Bells and Aspen, and the West Elk Mountains extend southwest to the Black Canyon.

Crested Butte has always been cutting edge when it comes to embracing new ways to take advantage of the powdery snow. It was an early hotbed of telemark skiing, a graceful, free-heel way of cruising downhill; and was popular with snowboarders back when few people had heard of the sport. But it's as an extreme-skiing mecca that Crested Butte earned its reputation with some of the best skiers in the land. Although many resorts are limiting their "out-of-bounds" terrain owing to increasing insurance costs and lawsuits, Crested Butte has steadily increased its extreme-skiing terrain to 550 ungroomed acres. The Extreme Limits and the North Face should only be attempted by advanced or expert skiers, but there are plenty of cruise-worthy trails for skiers of all levels.

Crested Butte is just as popular in summer. Blanketed with columbine and Indian paintbrush, the landscape is mesmerizing. It has grown into one of the country's major mountain-biking centers. Once the snow melts, mountain bikers challenge the hundreds of miles of trails surrounding the town.

Crested Butte is just over the mountain from Aspen, but a short drive in summer turns into a four-hour trek by car in winter, when Kebler Pass (on Route 135) is closed and it's necessary to drive a circuitous route. Both Aspen and Crested Butte are surrounded by designated wilderness areas, which means that few roads pass through this region.

The ski resort, at the base of the lifts a couple of miles uphill from the old town, is properly called Mount Crested Butte. When people talk about Crested Butte, they might be referring to the old town, the ski resort, or both. You'll have to figure it out from the context. There's reliable shuttle-bus service between the town and the resort, which are about 3 mi apart. Although a car is unnecessary and even unnerving for those not comfortable with driving on snow and ice, having one makes the going much easier. The town more or less shuts down between mid-April and Memorial Day, and again between October and the start of ski season in mid-December. Businesses may stay shuttered for a month or more.

Crested Butte Mountain Heritage Museum & Mountain Bike Hall of Fame. Housed in a turn-of-the-20th-century hardware store, the museum uses its front room to produce an exact replica of the essentials marketed for survival in a rugged mining town. There's an exquisite diorama of the town in the 1920s, complete with a moving train; information on the Utes who used to roam the area, skiing, sledding, Flauschink (a traditional ceremony for the welcoming of Spring), and biking exhibits; and the Mountain Bike Hall of Fame. ⊠ *331 Elk Ave.* ☎ *970/349–1880* ⊕ *www.mtnbikehalloffame. com.* 🖼 *$3* ⊙ *Summer, daily 10–8, winter, daily noon–6.*

> ## WILDFLOWERS
>
> Take a four-wheel-drive tour any time in summer and picnic in a galaxy of wildflowers. Look for the blue-and-white columbine, Colorado's state flower. But remember to bring your friend to the flower, not the flower to your friend—it is illegal to pick a blue columbine within state borders. After lunch take a short hike, or drive to the old ghost town sites of Gothic or Irwin.

FESTIVALS   The surrounding mountains are carpeted with such abundant growth that Crested Butte has been nicknamed the "Wildflower Capital of Colorado." For one glorious week in mid-July, the town celebrates this beautiful bounty with the **Crested Butte Wildflower Festival**. (☎ *970/349–2571* ⊕ *www.crestedbuttewildflowerfestival.com*). There are guided wildflower walks, wildflower identification workshops, wildflower photography classes, hayrides, and four-wheel-drive wildflower tours. Augment this visual feast with an audible one by attending a concert

★   offered by the **Crested Butte Music Festival** (☎ *970/349–0619* ⊕ *www. crestedbuttemusicfestival.com*). Running from early July through early August, the festival offers concerts in a variety of venues including jazz, bluegrass, opera, chamber, dance, and symphony. About a month later, in August, you might pop up at the **Wild Mushroom Festival** (☎ *970/596–4841* ⊕ *www.crested-butte-wild-mushroom-festival.com*), with workshops, talks, seminars, cooking, and the thrill of the hunt for the finest fungi.

For information about Fat Tire Bike Week, see Mountain Biking below.

DOWNHILL SKIING & SNOWBOARDING

Crested Butte skiing has a split personality, which is plain to see when you check out the skiers who come here year after year. Its traditional side is the trail network, characterized by long lower-intermediate and intermediate runs. There's a wonderful expanse of easy terrain from the Keystone lift—not just a trail network but rolling, tree-dotted meadows with plenty of opportunities to poke around off the beaten track. Families flock to Crested Butte for the excellent slope-side child care and children's ski school facilities, as well as the resort's laid-back and friendly ambience.

The wilder side of Crested Butte's personality is the Extreme Limits, several hundred acres of steep bowls, gnarly chutes, and tight tree skiing. It's no surprise that Crested Butte has hosted the U.S. Extreme Freeskiing Championship and the U.S. Extreme Borderfest, both nationally televised events full of thrills and spills. That's not to say you have to be a hotshot to enjoy some of Crested Butte's more-challenging terrain. You do, however, need to be able to handle snow that hasn't been groomed.

> ## BABY, IT'S COLD OUTSIDE
>
> The Ice Bar is here today, gone tomorrow, but that's only because its existence relies on the temperatures being in the freezing range. Made from garbage cans filled and covered with water and then smothered in snow, the bar is set up in November near Twister Lift midway on Mount Crested Butte, next to what is now known as the Ice Bar Restaurant. When the sun starts to warm things up, the Ice Bar goes away, as do the fur-clad servers and bartenders who wait on the 15–20 stools set up around this chilly, but very cool, après-ski spot.

The best skiing on the main trail network is on the front side of the mountain. The Silver Queen high-speed quad shoots you up 2,000 vertical feet in one quick ride. From there you have a choice of lifts and runs, roughly segmented by degree of challenge, with the steep twisters off to the right, the easier cruisers concentrated on the left, and the gnarly steeps above. The Paradise Chair Lift brings you directly to Crested Butte's half-pipe, and the best intermediate terrain.

The Extreme Limits is backcountry-style skiing and riding that's not for the faint of heart. If you're lucky enough to have good snow, skiing in this steep and rocky region will be the thrilling highlight of your visit. Strong, confident skiers and riders ready to tackle this terrain should sign up for a group tour. ✉ *12 Snowmass Rd., Mount Crested Butte, 81225* ☎ *970/349–2222 or 800/544–8448* ⊕ *www.skicb.com* ⊗ *Open mid-Nov. or mid-Dec.–mid-Apr., daily 9–4.*

FACILITIES 2,775-foot vertical drop; 1,167 skiable acres; 23% beginner, 51% intermediate, and 20% advanced; 4 detachable high-speed quad chairs, 2 fixed-grip quad chairs, 2 triple chairs, 3 double chairs, 3 surface lifts, and 2 magic carpets (beginners' lifts).

LESSONS & The Beginner's Shortcut offers a choice of a half-day group lesson and
PROGRAMS lift ticket that costs $107 or a full-day group lesson and lift ticket that costs $127. The full-day lesson practically guarantees you'll be skiing or snowboarding green runs by the end of the day. For kids ages 3 through 16, Kid's World all-day lessons are $120 and half-day lessons are $110. Teen workshops are $140 for the day. Intermediate, advanced, and private lessons are also available. For more informa-

tion, contact **CB Mountain School** (☎970/349–2252, 800/444–9236, 800/600–7349 *Kid's World* ⊕*www.skicb.com*).

LIFT TICKETS The walk-up rates for lift tickets range from $79 for one day to $504 for a week; prices are less in early and late season. Discounts are available online at ⊕*www.skicb.com*. There are also some days when everybody skis free, check the Web site for these dates.

RENTALS Full rental packages (including skis, boots, and poles), as well as telemark, snowshoe, and snowboard equipment, are available through **Crested Butte Sports** (✉35 *Emmons Loop Rd.* ☎970/349–7516 *or* 800/301–9169 ⊕*www.crestedbuttesports.com*). Rates start at $16 per day. They also have a full repair shop.

NORDIC SKIING

BACKCOUNTRY SKIING Crested Butte abounds with backcountry possibilities. Skiing or snowshoeing on the old mining roads that radiate from town are among the most popular pastimes. Washington Gulch, Slate River Road, and Gothic Road are among the most accessible routes. Dogs are permitted, and you'll have to contend with snowmobiles on some trails. Hardy locals hike up the slopes for above-tree-line telemarking, but this requires strong legs, strong lungs, and real avalanche awareness. You'll need the right equipment, including a functioning beacon and a shovel. Make sure you ski with a group—this is territory where going it alone is asking for trouble. Keep in mind that this is the high country (the town itself is around 9,000 feet, and things go up from there). Weather conditions can change with little or no warning.

To play it safe, arrange a tour into the backcountry with the **Crested Butte Nordic Center** (✉620 *2nd St.* ☎970/349–1707 ⊕*www.cbnordic. org*). The center offers half- and full-day packages that include transportation, guides, and equipment. For those wishing to extend their experience, staff can make arrangements for the rental of a ski hut located in the old town site of Gothic. The center also hosts the Annual Alley Loop Marathon, held in early February. This is an American Birkebeiner qualifying race, but townsfolk, as well as visitors, join the experts in their cross-country race through the town's snow-covered streets and alleys, past snow-corniced homes, and down the scenic trails along the edge of town.

RENTALS The **Alpineer** (✉419 *6th St.* ☎970/349–5210 *or* 800/847–0244 ⊕*www. alpineer.com*) rents top-notch backcountry and telemark equipment and provides information on routes and snow conditions.

TRACK SKIING The **Crested Butte Nordic Center** (✉620 *2nd St.* ☎970/349–1707 ⊕*www.cbnordic.org*) maintains an extensive network of Nordic trail systems. There are 50 km (31 mi) of trails which are roughly divided into the northwest, south, and east sides of Crested Butte. The trails cover flat and moderately rolling terrain across meadows and through aspen groves near the valley floor. The views of some of the distant peaks are stunning. Snowshoers are allowed on all tracks and dogs are permitted on some. One activity of note is the Moonlight Tour—on

9

full-moon nights, participants are guided down a moon-washed trail to a cozy yurt for snacks and hot chocolate; the cost is $15 per person.

LESSONS &
PROGRAMS The **Crested Butte Nordic Center** (⊠ *620 2nd St.* ☎ *970/349–1707* ⊕ *www. cbnordic.org*) offers snowshoeing, skate skiing, and classic track skiing lessons. Learn to Ski adult packages run $48 for classic track and $50 for skate skiing. The package includes a trail pass, rentals, and a 75-minute group lesson. An annual **Thanksgiving Training Camp** is held every November. Former Olympians and collegiate coaches present clinics for expert, advanced, intermediate, and beginning students. Clinic fees are $40. Waxing clinics are free.

TRAIL PASSES An adult day pass costs $15. The center also offers a variety of season passes, ranging from $55 for a child's season pass to $130 for one adult and $325 for a family.

RENTALS The **Crested Butte Nordic Center** (⊠ *620 2nd St.* ☎ *970/349–1707* ⊕ *www. cbnordic.org*) rents classic track skis, skate skis, backcountry touring skis, snowshoes, skates, and sleds.

OTHER SPORTS & THE OUTDOORS

Alpine Express. Take an open-top four-wheel-drive tour on the old mining roads that crisscross the Elk Mountain range. Visit meadows of wildflowers and sit by pristine mountain lakes (four-person minimum). ☎ *970/641–5074* ⊕ *www.alpineexpressshuttle.com.*

Adventures to the Edge (⊠ *308 3rd St.* ☎ *970/209–3980* ⊕ *www.atedge. com*) creates customized high-country treks, cross-country skiing expeditions, and alpine ascents in the Crested Butte area.

Crested Butte Mountain Guides. These outfitters offer packages tailored to your needs in rock climbing, ice climbing, mountain biking, cross-country and backcountry skiing, backpacking, hiking, snowshoeing, and sea kayaking. They also offer four-wheel-drive tours in summer. Expect a small guide-to-client ratio. ⟟ *Box 1061, Crested Butte 81224* ☎ *970/349–5430* ⊕ *www.crestedbutteguides.com.*

Three Rivers Resort & Outfitting (⊠ *130 County Rd. 742, Almont* ☎ *970/ 641–1303 or 888/761–3474* ⊕ *www.3riversresort.com*) offers guided fly-fishing excursions, kayaking lessons, and white-water rafting trips.

FISHING At Almont, south of Crested Butte, the East and Taylor rivers join to form the Gunnison River, making this tiny angler-oriented hamlet one of Colorado's top **fly-fishing** centers. It's also one of the most crowded with tourists, however. Local fishing outfitters rent equipment, teach fly-fishing, and lead guided wading or float trips both to public and private waters. Anyone older than 16 needs a Colorado fishing license, which you can obtain at local sporting-goods stores. See ⊕ *www.wild-life.state.co.us/fishing* for more information.

Almont Anglers (⊠ *10209 Hwy. 135, Almont* ☎ *970/641–7404* ⊕ *www. almontanglers.com*) has a solid fly and tackle shop with an enormous selection of flies. They offer clinics for beginners and guided wading and float-fishing trips on the East, Taylor, and Gunnison rivers.

Dragonfly Anglers (⊠ *307 Elk Ave.* ☎ *970/349–1228 or 800/491–3079* ⊕ *www.dragonflyanglers.com*) is Crested Butte's oldest year-round guide service and fly-fishing outfitter. They guide half- and full-day trips to choice fly-fishing spots including the famed Gunnison Gorge (full-day only) in the Black Canyon. Their shop concentrates on high-tech rods, and offers a selection of reels, flies, and outdoor gear.

At Three Rivers Resort & Outfitting, **Willowfly Anglers** (⊠ *130 County Rd. 742, Almont* ☎ *970/641–1303 or 888/761–3474* ⊕ *www.3riversresort. com*) provides gear for anglers of all skill levels.

GOLF   **The Club at Crested Butte.** Golf legend Robert Trent Jones Jr. designed this ravishing 18-hole course. The course belongs to the country club, but it's open to the public. The dress code bars denim and mandates stand-up collars for all. ⊠ *385 Country Club Dr.* ☎ *970/349–6127* ⊕ *www. theclubatcrestedbutte.com* ⚑ *Reservations essential* ⚑ *18 holes. Yards: 7,208/5,702. Par: 72/72. Green Fee: $165/$95.*

HIKING   Near three designated wilderness areas (Maroon Bells–Snowmass to the north, Raggeds to the west, and Collegiate Peaks to the east), as well as other areas with equally stunning scenery, Crested Butte offers an extensive system of trails. In wilderness areas, you can find splendid trails for off the beaten path. Outside of these protected areas, you may have to share routes with mountain bikers and even four-wheel-drive vehicles.

One of the easiest hiking trails is a 2-mi round-trip to **Judd Falls.** The path climbs about 100 feet and slices through groves of aspen and, in spring, a crop of glacier lilies and more than 70 local wildflower varieties. At the end, look over Judd Falls from a bench named after Garwood Judd, "the man who stayed" in the mining town of Gothic. ⊠ *Gunnison Ranger District, Gunnison National Forest* ☎ *970/641– 0471* ⊕ *www.fs.fed.us/r2/gmug.*

The maintenance roads at the **Crested Butte Mountain Resort** make nice hiking trails in summer for moderate to serious hikers. Start at the resort's Gothic Building and create your own path up, following well-signed roads and paths to the summit at 12,162 feet, where you can take in the entire Crested Butte valley. Those who prefer a more-aerial view may buy a lift ticket to the top and walk back downhill.

HORSEBACK RIDING   One of the best ways to see Crested Butte is from atop a horse. **Fantasy Ranch** (⊠ *Gothic Rd.* ☎ *970/349–5425 or 888/688–3488* ⊕ *www. fantasyranchoutfitters.com*) gives guided horseback tours into the Elk Mountains, Maroon Bells, and Gunnison National Forest.

HOT-AIR BALLOONING   The conditions must be just right, but on a clear, windless morning, this wide-open basin, surrounded by mountain ranges, must surely be one of the country's best places to be aloft in a balloon. For information on these flights of fancy, contact **Big Horn Balloon Company** (☎ *970/596– 1008* ⊕ *www.balloon-adventures.com*). Trips are $245; group and family discounts are available.

9

ICE SKATING   If you're eager to practice a figure eight, the **Crested Butte Nordic Center** (⊠*620 2nd St.* ☎*970/349–1707* ⊕*www.cbnordic.org*) operates the adjacent outdoor skating rink. The lodge rents skates for $8.

KAYAKING &   The rivers around Crested Butte are at their best from May through
RAFTING   September. **Three Rivers Resort & Outfitting** (⊠*130 Country Rd. 742, Almont* ☎*970/641–1303 or 888/761–3474* ⊕*www.3riversresort. com*) takes you on rafting trips and gives kayaking lessons on the Gunnison River.

MOUNTAIN   Crested Butte is probably the **mountain-biking** center of Colorado. This
BIKING   is a place where there are more bikes than cars, and probably more
★   bikes than residents. Many people own two mountain bikes: a town bike for hacking around and a performance bike for *serious* hacking around. Mountain-bike chroniclers say that Pearl Pass is the route that got the mountain-biking craze started in the mid-1970s. After a group of Aspen motorcylists rode the rough old road over Pearl Pass to Crested Butte, that town's mountain bikers decided to retaliate and ride to Aspen. They hopped on board their clunky two-wheelers—a far cry from the sophisticated machinery of today—and with that, a sport was born. The 40-mi trip over Pearl Pass can be done in a day, but you must be in excellent condition and acclimatized to the elevation to have a chance of finishing. Altitude is your main foe; the pass crests at 12,700 feet. The trip is daunting and not to be undertaken lightly. One option for your return journey to Crested Butte is a scenic two-day ride along the road—better than retracing your route over the pass. Otherwise you'll need to make arrangements to travel by car or even by plane.

The **Lower Loop** (⊹*Trailhead: Near the 4-way stop at the corner of Elk Ave. and Hwy. 135*) is a popular 8- to 9-mi trail that will help orient you to the area. It's a 1½-hour ride mostly on pavement with a couple of miles of single-track, and it hooks up to several longer, easy rides with views of mountain peaks, the Paradise Divide, and the Slate River valley. Along the Lower Loop, watch for **Tony's Trail,** a moderate climb for the more-serious biker. The trail gains 1,200 feet on a 9-mi loop, and it rewards your efforts by winding through aspen forests and alpine meadows bursting (in season) with wildflowers to a final elevation of about 10,000 feet.

The **Alpineer** (⊠*419 6th St.* ☎*970/349–5210* ⊕*www.alpineer.com*) prides itself on having the latest gear and a staff knowledgeable enough to get you on the right bike and trail as quickly as possible. If you're going to spend time here, find local rider Holly Annala's *Crested Butte Singletrack,* a fascinating guide to the local biking landscape. Guided tours of nearby trails are available through **Crested Butte Mountain Guides** (⌂*Box 1061, Crested Butte 81224* ☎*970/349–5430* ⊕*www.crested butteguides.com*).

Each summer, mountain-biking enthusiasts roll in for the **Fat Tire Bike Week** (⌂*Crested Butte Chamber of Commerce, Box 1288, Crested Butte 81224* ☎*800/545–4505 or 970/349–6438* ⊕*www.ftbw.com*), the country's longest-running mountain-bike festival. The event, held in late June, is a solid week of racing, touring, silly competitions, and mountain-biker bonding.

RENTALS **Crested Butte Sports** (⊠*35 Emmons Loop Rd.* ☎*970/349–7516 or 800/301–9169* ⊕*www.crestedbuttesports.com*) rents mountain bikes, gear, and helmets. Discounts are offered for multiday rates. They also have a full bike repair shop.

WHERE TO STAY & EAT

★ $$$$ ✕ **Soupçon.** Soupçon ("soup's on," get it?) occupies two intimate rooms in the historic Kochevar cabin and dishes up nouveau American cuisine with a strong French accent. Local produce is accented with organic herbs grown on the premises. Try the chef's signature almond-crusted rack of lamb, or the seared Hudson Valley foie gras with roasted pear, complemented by a glass of wine from the comprehensive wine cellar. ⊠*127A Elk Ave. (behind Kochevar's)* ☎*970/349–5448* ⌖*Reservations essential* ▭*AE, MC, V* ⊗*Closed Sun. and Nov.–early Dec. No lunch.*

$$$$ ✕ **Timberline.** This elegant, two-story restaurant changes its menu monthly but always has a selection of wild game. The upper floor has a formal European feel to it, while the downstairs area, with its huge windows, is a great place to watch the snow falling while discussing your triumphs on the slopes. Elk medallions, smoked scallops with saffron, and coriander Hawaiian ahi are among the many delicacies served on a seasonal basis. There is a handsome bar and a respectable wine list. Top off your epicurean experience by indulging in an after-dinner liqueur or the award-winning Belgian chocolate soufflé. ⊠*201 Elk Ave.* ☎*970/349–9831* ⊕*www.timberlinerestaurant.com* ⌖*Reservations essential* ▭*AE, D, MC, V* ⊗*No lunch.*

$$ ✕ **Ginger Café.** The small, sun-color dining room provides a cheerful backdrop for the superb East–West fusion and pan-Asian food. There is also a full bar and inventive cocktail menu including ginger-infused martinis and mango ginger mojitos. Try the pad thai with a delicious homemade tamarind sauce. ⊠ *425 Elk Ave.* ☎*970/349–7291* ▭*MC, V* ⊗*Closed daily 3–4* PM.

$$ ✕ **Slogar.** Set in a lovingly renovated Victorian tavern awash in handmade lace and stained glass, this restaurant is just plain cozy. Slogar turns out some of the juiciest fried chicken west of the Mississippi. The fixings are sensational: flaky biscuits fresh from the oven, creamy mashed potatoes swimming in chicken gravy, and sweet-and-sour coleslaw from a Pennsylvania Dutch recipe. Served family style, dinner, including ice cream, is only $14.95 (or $24.95 for steak). ⊠*2nd and Whiterock Sts.* ☎*970/349–5765* ▭*MC, V* ⊗*Closed late Sept.–mid-Dec. and mid-Apr.–mid-June. No lunch.*

$ ✕ **Donita's Cantina.** This down-home, adobe-washed Mexican restaurant is housed in an 1880s hotel and still has the original tin pressed ceilings. The food is simply good, with solid standards such as fajitas and enchiladas served with homemade red and green chile. The specialty at the bar is predictably the margarita—concocted in all flavors and colors with 100% Agave tequila. The cantina is popular with local families as well as with extreme skiers. ⊠*330 Elk Ave.* ☎*970/349–*

9

6674 ⚠Reservations not accepted ☐AE, D, MC, V ⊘Closed Apr. and Nov. No lunch.

¢ ✕Teocalli Tamale. A small, historic building is the venue for tasty, inexpensive Mexican takeout (or a claustrophobic eat-in experience). For breakfast which lasts until 11-ish, order the *huevos paperos,* eggs over-easy topped with chilies and salsa over potatoes instead of the usual corn tortillas, or *huevos tamaleros,* eggs with mild and spicy homemade tamales. Bacon or chorizo can be added to any dish. Locals know this place for its generous proportions and strong French press coffee. ⊠311½ Elk Ave. ☎970/349–2005 ☐MC, V.

WORD OF MOUTH

"The Grand Lodge is one of the nicest places in Crested Butte. It is a two-minute walk from the lifts. We stayed in a suite and everything was great. They have a nice inside/outside pool, a hot tub, and a huge fireplace in the lobby. Every time we came back from skiing they had hot apple cider and fresh chocolate chip cookies sitting out. The shuttle stop to downtown is right next to the Grand Lodge."   —rlmrlm

$$$$ 🏨Crested Butte Club. Quaint and stylish, this inn in the town of Crested Butte is a Victorian dream. Each sumptuous, individually furnished room contains a gas fireplace, brass or mahogany bed, and cherrywood antiques or quality reproductions. Some rooms have wet bars and all have jet aromatherapy baths. The downstairs bar, with its marble fireplace and hand-carved woodwork, creates a richly quiet ambience. Best of all is the full-service spa and health club. The complimentary continental breakfast always includes a few extras. **Pros:** definitely the place to go for that pampered experience, in the center of old-town Crested Butte, full-service gym. **Cons:** 3 mi from the ski area, not for the fragrance-sensitive, no pets. ⊠512 2nd St., 81224 ☎970/349–6655 or 800/815–2582 ⊕www.crestedbutteclub.com ⇗9 rooms ⌂In-room: no a/c, refrigerator (some), Wi-Fi. In-hotel: bar, pool, gym, spa, public Wi-Fi, no-smoking rooms. ☐D, MC, V ⎮⊙⎮CP.

$$$ 🏨Grand Lodge Crested Butte. This luxurious ski-in ski-out lodge is popular with upscale skiers and business travelers. A warm, stone-log lobby with a huge fireplace welcomes you. Spacious rooms are decorated in muted earth and pastel tones with copper accents. Both bar and grill have fireplaces and the pool is indoor-outdoor to accommodate seasonal changes. **Pros:** next to ski area, luxurious with numerous amenities, nice touches such as cookies left out for guests. **Cons:** windows don't open, 3 mi from old town of Crested Butte, can feel impersonal. ⊠6 Emmons Loop, Mount Crested Butte, 81225 ☎888/823–4446 ⊕www.grandlodgecrestedbutte.com ⇗226 rooms, 106 suites ⌂In-room: no a/c, safe, refrigerator, dial-up, Wi-Fi. In-hotel: restaurant, bar, pool, gym, spa, laundry service, public Wi-Fi, some pets allowed, no-smoking rooms ☐AE, MC, V.

$$ 🏨Elk Mountain Lodge. Step into the lobby of the Elk Mountain Lodge and encounter a slower pace of life and unsurpassed attention to detail. Originally a boardinghouse built for miners in 1919, this historic hotel has been painstakingly renovated. The rooms are full of light and the full-service bar is a deep, rich walnut. There's a library and a mini-

grand piano on which jazz is played every Friday night. An enhanced continental breakfast is served in a cheerfully trimmed breakfast nook. **Pros:** historic building; warm, intimate atmosphere; located in the middle of old-town Crested Butte. **Cons:** 3 mi from ski area, stairs are a bit steep. ⊠*129 Gothic Ave., 81224* ☎*970/349–7533 or 800/374–6521* ⊕*www.elkmountainlodge.net* ⤏*19 rooms* ♨*In-room: no a/c, Wi-Fi (some). In-hotel: bar, no elevator, public Wi-Fi, no-smoking rooms* ▤*AE, D, MC, V.*

$$ ⊡**Nordic Inn.** This slope-side inn with alpine-style trim is one of the last old-style ski lodges in a sea of cookie-cutter condominiums. Simply decorated rooms, a cozy lobby perfect for lounging, and an inviting breakfast room are reminders of the way mountain vacations used to be. An outdoor hot tub graces a modest deck with a stupendous view of the mountains. **Pros:** 1 block from ski lifts; small, informal setting; continental breakfast included. **Cons:** old and starting to fray, 3 mi from the old town of Crested Butte. ⊠*14 Treasury Rd., Mount Crested Butte, 81224* ☎*800/542–7669* ⊕*www.nordicinncb.com* ⤏*27 rooms* ♨*In-room: no a/c, safe, kitchen (some), refrigerator (some), dial-up. In hotel: no elevator, public Wi-Fi, no-smoking rooms* ▤*AE, MC, V* ¶⊙*CP.*

$$ ⊡**Pioneer Guest Cabins** Situated on a riverside meadow in the Gunnison National Forest, this getaway is about 8 mi from town. You can hike, bike, cross-country ski, or snowshoe from trails that start right at their door. The East River, 2 mi away, is a world-class fishing stream. Or, you can simply watch hummingbirds while lounging in Adirondack chairs. Rustic log cabins from the 1930s have been appointed with down comforters and antique furnishings. Each cabin has hardwood floors, a fully equipped kitchen, and a fireplace. Cabins are open year-round and are dog friendly. **Pros:** beautiful, secluded setting; close to trails and fishing. **Cons:** 8 mi from town, no restaurant. ⊠*Cement Creek Rd., 81224* ☎*970/349–5517* ⊕*www.pioneerguestcabins.com* ⤏*8 cabins* ♨*In-room: no a/c, kitchen, no TV. In-hotel: some pets allowed, no-smoking rooms* ▤*MC, V.*

$ ⊡**Cristiana Guesthaus.** This alpine-style ski lodge with a huge stone fireplace in a high-beam lobby provides a cozy, unpretentious haven. Wood-panel rooms are decorated in neutrals with traditional country pine furnishings. The hot tub is located on a redwood deck facing a breathtaking view of the mountains. Historic downtown is within walking distance, and hiking, biking, and Nordic ski trails are only minutes away. The innkeepers are avid sports people and happily give winter and summer trail advice. Homemade muesli and pastries are included in the generous continental breakfast. **Pros:** friendly, comfortable atmosphere; knowledgeable hosts; great value. **Cons:** children under five discouraged, TV only in common area. ⊠*621 Maroon Ave., 81224* ☎*970/349–5326 or 800/824–7899* ⊕*www.cristianaguesthaus. com* ⤏*21 rooms* ♨*In-room: no a/c, no TV, Wi-Fi. In-hotel: no elevator, public Wi-Fi, no kids under 5, no-smoking rooms* ▤*AE, D, MC, V* ⊙*Closed mid-Apr.–early May* ¶⊙*CP.*

9

CONDOS **Crested Butte Property Management Vacation Rentals.** Historic homes to condos are offered for your vacation needs. ✉ *107 Elk Ave., Crested Butte 81224* ☎ *970/349–5780 or 800/945–0184* ⊕ *www. cbprop.com.*

NIGHTLIFE & THE ARTS

THE ARTS The **Crested Butte Center for the Arts** (✉*606 6th St.* ☎*970/349–7487* ⊕*www.crestedbuttearts.org*) is a 215-seat theater that hosts local and touring concerts, theater, dance, movies, and more. Upstairs, the Piper Gallery is a multimedia art space where local artists display their work.

NIGHTLIFE **Kochevar's** (✉*127 Elk Ave.* ☎*970/349–6745*), a hand-hewn 1896 log cabin, is a classic saloon where locals play pool. The popular **Wooden Nickel** (✉*222 Elk Ave.* ☎*970/349–6350*) is packed for happy hour each day from 4 to 6. Stay for a fine steak dinner.

SHOPPING

Cookworks (✉ *321 Elk Ave.* ☎ *970/349–7398* ⊕ *www.cookworks. com*) is a delightful cookware and tableware shop housed in a quaint Victorian home. **Creekside Pottery** (✉ *311 5th St.* ☎ *970/349–6459* ⊕ *www.crestedbuttepottery.com*) showcases local artist Mary Jursinovic's imaginative pottery and lamps.

GUNNISON

60 mi east of Montrose, 28 mi south of Crested Butte via Rte. 135.

At the confluence of the Gunnison River and Tomichi Creek, Gunnison is a traditional ranching community that has been adopted by nature lovers because of the excellent fishing and hunting nearby. In fact, long before these types arrived, the Utes used the area as summer hunting grounds. Gunnison provides economical lodging and easy access to Crested Butte and Blue Mesa Reservoir. Gunnison's other claim to fame is that it has recorded some of the coldest temperatures ever reported in the continental United States.

Nine miles west of Gunnison is the **Curecanti National Recreation Area,** set amid a striking eroded volcanic landscape and stretching for more than 60 mi. Dams built along the Gunnison River during the 1960s created three reservoirs, including **Blue Mesa Reservoir,** the state's largest body of water. Here you can fish, swim, or even windsurf. The reservoirs provide a wealth of recreational opportunities, including fine camping and hiking. Rangers lead education programs, including twice-daily boat tours of the Upper Black Canyon of the Gunnison. The tour-head is 232 stairs up the Pine Creek Trail and reservations are required. At the western entrance to the Curecanti National Recreation Area, the **Cimarron Visitor Center** (✉*U.S. Hwy. 50* ☎*970/249–4074* ☉*June–Sept., hrs vary*) displays vintage locomotives, a reconstructed stockyard, and an 1882 trestle that's listed on the National Register of Historic Places. The **Elk Creek Campground** (✉*102 Elk Creek, off U.S. Hwy. 50* ☎*970/641–2337* ⊕*www.nps.gov/cure*) has a small bookstore and information center where boat permits for the Blue Mesa

Reservoir may be purchased and reservations for the boat tours can be made. The center also has information about the various camping sites around the Blue Mesa and is open Memorial Day to Labor Day.

☾ Those interested in the region's history shouldn't miss the **Pioneer Museum.** The complex spreads out over 6 acres and includes an extensive collection of vehicles from Model As & Ts to 1960s sedans. There's a great train complete with coal tender, caboose, and boxcar; a red barn with wagons and displays of ranch life; and an old schoolhouse. ✉ *U. S. 50 and S. Adams St.* ☎970/641–4530 💲$7 ⊙*Memorial Day–Sept. 30, Mon.–Sat. 9–5, Sun. 11–5.*

RODEO Get a feel for the life of the cowboy at Gunnison's **Cattlemen's Days** held at the Fred R. Field Western Heritage Center, July 4–13 (✉*275 S. Spruce St.* ⊕*www.cattlemensdays.com*). Thrill to the sight of bare bronc and bull riding, barrel racing, and calf roping, or listen to the dulcet strains of cowboy poetry. For an amazing display of marksmanship combined with horsemanship, attend **Gunsmoke-n-Gunnison,** (☎970/641–4787) held at the Fred R. Field Western Heritage Center during the last weekend in July.

SPORTS & THE OUTDOORS

FISHING **High Mountain Drifters** (✉*201 W. Tomichi Ave.* ☎970/641–1532) offers guided lake and river fishing tours. The lake tours are on the Blue Mesa Lake and fly-fishing tours will take you to one of four sections of private water along the Gunnison or one of its tributaries. All equipment is provided.

For information about fly-fishing near Almont, see the Crested Butte section in this chapter.

HORSEBACK **Lazy F Bar Outfitters** (✉*2991 County Rd. 738* ☎970/349–1755 ⊕*www.*
RIDING *lazyfbarranch.com*) rents horses for rides in the high country from June to early September and sleigh rides in the valleys from December to early April.

Tenderfoot Outfitters (✉*501 Tomichi [Hwy. 50]* ☎970/641–0504 *or 800/641–0504* ⊕*www.tenderfootoutfitters.com*) specializes in guided wilderness rides.

WATER At 26 mi long, Blue Mesa Reservoir ranks as Colorado's largest body of
SPORTS water. Created in the mid-1960s when the state dammed the Gunnison River in three places, the lake is some 7,500 feet above sea level. It has become a mecca for water-sports enthusiasts. Anglers are drawn by the 3 million stocked rainbow, lake, brown, and brook trout and kokanee salmon. Anyone older than 16 needs a Colorado fishing license, which you can obtain at local sporting-goods stores. See ⊕*www.wildlife. state.co.us/fishing* for more information.

In addition to the Cimarron Visitor Center at Curecanti National Recreation Area, there are smaller seasonal ranger stations at Lake Fork, Cimarron, and East Portal. If you have your own boat, you can use the ramps at Ponderosa (northern end at Soap Creek Arm), Stevens Creek (eastern end of the north shore), and Lola (eastern end on the south shore). A two-day boat permit is $4, and a two-week permit is $10. Annual boat permits run $30.

Elk Creek Marina (✛ *East side of lake* ☎970/641–0707 ⊕*www.bluemesalake.com*), about 15 mi from Gunnison on U.S. 50, rents pontoon boats, rowboats, and aluminum fishing boats from May 1 to October 1, 7 AM to 7 PM. The marina also runs guided fishing trips to Blue Mesa and Morrow Point reservoirs. A convenient restaurant is located above the dock where you can sit and enjoy a light repast while watching other fishermen try their luck.

WHERE TO STAY & EAT

$$$ ✕**Garlic Mike's.** The menu at this unpretentious Italian spot is surprisingly rich and complex. Don't miss the fried green tomatoes, homemade pizza, and eggplant Parmesan. The marinated strip-steak carbonara wins hands down as the house favorite. Be prepared for a leisurely dinner, the service can be slow. ⊠*2674 Hwy. 135* ☎*970/641–2493* ⊕*www.garlicmikes.com* ▤*AE, MC, V* ⊗*No lunch.*

$$ ✕**Ol' Miner Steakhouse.** A meat-lover's dream—choose T-bone, strip, kabob, rib eye, or prime rib cooked the way you like it. Rocky Mountain oysters (bull testicles) are available for culinary risk-takers. There's also an unlimited soup-and-salad bar starting at $6.99, a respectable array of sandwiches for lunch, and a traditional, as well as steak-enhanced, breakfast. ⊠*139 N. Main St.* ☎*970/641–5153* ▤*AE, D, MC, V.*

$ ✕**Gunnison Brewery.** A revolving list of home-crafted brews are on tap at this busy old downtown bar. They're known for a fine Dunkel Weisen, a strong-flavored, dark, wheat beer; the menu offers the usual brewery fare. There is live music on Tuesday, Wednesday, and Friday nights from 10 PM to 2 AM. ⊠*138 N. Main St.* ☎*970/641–2739* ▤*MC, V* ⊗*No lunch Sun.–Thurs.*

¢ ✕**The Bean.** This brightly hued coffee shop is a great place for a morning or afternoon break. The walls are decorated a revolving art exhibit and there are plenty of papers and magazines available. Hook up your laptop to their Wi-Fi or use one of the two computers provided. An impressive selection of espresso drinks is served, plus smoothies, bagels, crepes, fresh-baked pastries, and sandwiches. Ask about the crepe of the day; it's always delicious. ⊠*120 N. Main St.* ☎*970/641–2408* ▤*MC, V.*

$$ ▦**Holiday Inn Express Hotel.** Opulence is the byword for this recently opened hotel. The lobby is high-ceilinged, with a large gray stone fireplace and leather couches. The muted earth tones of the lobby are carried over throughout the rooms which are all equipped with a flat-screen TV, refrigerator, microwave, and Wi-Fi. There's a splendid indoor pool, indoor and outdoor hot tubs, and gym. Continental breakfast is included. **Pros:** numerous amenities, business facilities, reasonably priced. **Cons:** 1 mi from town, no restaurant, large and impersonal, chain hotel. ⊠*910 E. Tomichi Ave., Gunnison 81230* ☎*970/641–1288* ⊕*www.hiexpress.com* ⊷*107 rooms, 23 suites* ⌂*In-room: refrigerator, Wi-Fi. In-hotel: pool, gym, concierge, laun-*

dry facilities, laundry service, public Wi-Fi, no-smoking rooms ⊟*AE, D, DC, MC, V* ⦿*CP.*

$ ⊡**Rockey River Resort.** A tetherball on the turf, an old ford pickup parked in the shadow of the milk house, sheets hung on the line, and the smell of cowboy coffee perking: These are just a few of the touches that make this old homestead a uniquely pleasant place to stay. There are 15 modernized cabins with fully equipped kitchens on the Gunnison River. You can fish right outside your door, or drive to the Blue Mesa Reservoir, just 18 mi away. The resort is dog friendly and the proprietors are knowledgeable about fishing, trails, and local history. **Pros:** close to fishing, historical setting, very pet friendly. **Cons:** 6 mi from Gunnison; some RVs on grounds; TV only in common area, not in cabins. ⊠*4359 CR 10, off CO 135, 81230* ☎*970/641–0174* ⊕*www. coloradodirectory.com/rockeyriverresort* ⇌*15 cabins* ⬧*In-room: no a/c, no phone, no TV. In-hotel: public Internet, some pets allowed, no-smoking rooms* ⊟*MC, V.*

SHOPPING

Hope and Glory and Misty Mountain Floral (⊠ *234 N. Main St.* ☎*970/641–1638 or 970/641–5102*) has a nifty selection of specialty food items, kitchen aids, flower arrangements, and gift items. **Buckhorn Trading Company** (⊠*125 N. Main St.* ☎*970/641–0927* ⊕*www.buckhorntradingco. com*) has an impressive inventory of Native American and regional Western art. They sell pottery, silver and gold jewelry, kachinas and Navajo dolls, fetishes, flutes, dream catchers, paintings, and prints. Many of their items are one-of-a-kind. **Western World** (⊠ *200 W. Tomichi Ave.* ☎*970/641–6566*) is the place to go for all things cowboy. They have a large selection of cowboy hats, boots, belts, jeans, and shirts for adults and kids. They also sell saddles, bridles, bits, and lassos. It's fun just to go in and look around.

BLACK CANYON OF THE GUNNISON NATIONAL PARK & MONTROSE

By John
Blodgett

South Rim: 15 mi east of Montrose, via U.S. 50 and Rte. 347. North Rim: 11 mi south of Crawford, via Rte. 92 and N. Rim Rd.

Black Canyon of the Gunnison River is one of Colorado's, and indeed the West's, most awe-inspiring wonders. A vivid testament to the powers of erosion, the 2,722-foot-deep gash in the Earth's crust is 1,000 feet across at its rim but then narrows to only 40 feet across at the bottom. The steep angles of the cliffs make it difficult for sunlight to fully break through during much of the day, and ever-present shadows bounce off the canyon walls, leaving some places in almost perpetual darkness—nearly pitch-black at night and a sort of dusk with tunnel vision during the day. No wonder it's called the "Black Canyon."

The primary gateway to Black Canyon is **Montrose,** 15 mi northeast of the park. The legendary Ute chief, Ouray, and his wife, Chipeta, lived near here in the mid-19th century. Today, Montrose straddles

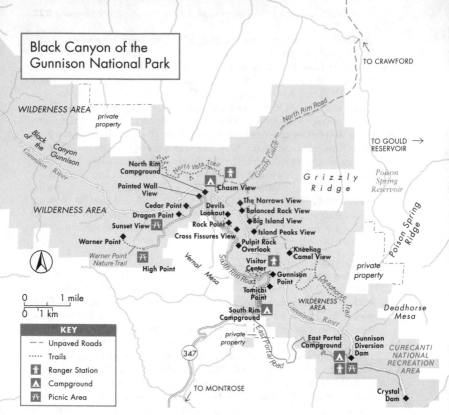

Black Canyon of the
Gunnison National Park

the important agricultural and mining regions along the Uncompahgre River, and its traditional downtown is a shopping hub.

EXPLORING BLACK CANYON OF THE GUNNISON NATIONAL PARK

The vast depths that draw thousands of visitors each year to Black Canyon have also historically prevented any extensive human habitation from taking root, so cultural attractions are lacking here. But what the park lacks in historic sites, it more than makes up for in scenic attractions.

The park itself has no restaurants, but it does have several picnic areas; *see the* Black Canyon of the Gunnison National Park *map for their locations. Stock up on fixings in nearby Montrose and Crawford.*

TIMING Summer is the busiest season in the park, with July experiencing the greatest crowds. A spring or fall visit gives you two advantages: fewer people and cooler temperatures—in summer, especially in years with little rainfall, daytime temperatures often reach into the 90s. A winter visit to the park brings even more solitude, as campgrounds are shut down and only about 2 mi of South Rim Road are plowed.

November through February is when the snow hits, with 9 to 24 inches of the white stuff each month on average. The months of April and May, and September through November are the rainiest, June is generally the driest. Temperatures at the bottom of the canyon tend to be 8° warmer than at the rim.

GETTING
THERE &
AROUND

In southwest Colorado, Black Canyon of the Gunnison is sandwiched between Gunnison and Montrose. Both have small regional airports.

The park has three roads. South Rim Road, reached by Route 347, is the primary thoroughfare and winds along the canyon's South Rim. From about late November to early April, depending on snow conditions, the road is not plowed past the visitor center at Gunnison Point. North Rim Road, reached by Route 92, is usually open from May through Thanksgiving; in winter the road is unplowed. The serpentine East Portal Road descends abruptly to the Gunnison River on the park's south side. The road is usually open from the beginning of May through the end of November, again depending upon snowfall. Because of the grade, vehicles or vehicle–trailer combinations longer than 22 feet are not permitted.

A bridge that would span the canyon's two rims was proposed in the 1930s. Unfortunately, it was never built, so it'll take you two to three hours to drive from one rim around to the other—it might be a long drive, but it's filled with unforgettable scenery.

SCENIC
DRIVES

Two scenic rim roads offer deep and distant views into the canyon. The various hikes into the canyon are steep and strenuous, not to mention relatively unmarked. They are not for the faint of heart.

East Portal Road. The only way to access the Gunnison River from the park by car is via this paved route, which drops approximately 2,000 feet down to the water in only 5 mi, giving it a steep, 16% grade. (Vehicles longer than 22 feet are not allowed on the road; if you're towing a trailer, you can unhitch it at a parking area near the entrance to South Rim Campground.) The bottom is actually in the adjacent Curecanti National Recreation Area. A tour of East Portal Road, with a brief stop at the bottom, takes about 45 minutes.

North Rim Road. Black Canyon's North Rim is much less frequented, but no less spectacular—the walls here are near vertical. To reach the 15.5-mi North Rim Road, take the signed turnoff from Route 92 in Crawford. The road is paved for about the first 4 mi; the rest is gravel. After 11 mi, turn left at the intersection (North Rim Campground is to the right). There are six overlooks as the road snakes along the rim's edge. Kneeling Camel, 4.5 mi out at road's end, provides the broadest view of the canyon. Set aside about two hours for a tour of the North Rim.

South Rim Road. This paved 7-mi stretch from Tomichi Point to High Point is the park's main road. The drive follows the canyon's level South Rim; 12 overlooks are accessible from the road, most via short gravel trails. Several short hikes onto the rim also begin roadside. Allow between two and three hours round-trip.

WHAT TO SEE

SCENIC STOPS   **Chasm View.** From this heart-in-your-throat viewpoint, the canyon walls plummet 1,820 feet to the river, but are only 1,100 feet apart at the top. As you peer down into the depths, keep in mind that this section is where the Gunnison River descends at its steepest rate, dropping 240 feet within the span of a mile. ⊹ *3.5 mi from South Rim Visitor Center on South Rim Rd.*

★ **Narrows View.** Look upriver from this North Rim overlook and you'll be able to see into the canyon's narrowest section, just a slot really, with only 40 feet between the walls. The canyon is also taller (1,725 feet) here than it is wide at the rim (1,150 feet). ⊠ *North Rim Rd.,* ⊹ *1st overlook past the ranger station.*

★ **Painted Wall.** Best seen from Painted Wall View along South Rim Road, this is Colorado's tallest cliff, 2,250 feet high. Pinkish swaths of pegmatite (a crystalline, granitelike rock) give the cliff a colorful, marbled appearance. ⊹ *3.7 mi from South Rim Visitor Center off South Rim Rd.*

VISITOR   **North Rim Ranger Station.** This small facility on the park's North Rim
CENTERS   provides information and assistance when North Rim Road is open. ⊠ *North Rim Rd.,* ⊹ *11 mi from Rte. 92 turnoff* ⊙ *Memorial Day– Labor Day, daily 8–6.*

South Rim Visitor Center. The park's only visitor center offers interactive exhibits as well as two orientation videos: One details the geology and history of the canyon, the other includes the history of the Gunnison Water Diversion Tunnel and descriptions of the flora and fauna in the park. ⊹ *1.5 mi from the entrance station on South Rim Rd.* ☎ *970/249–1914 Ext. 423* ⊙ *Memorial Day–Labor Day, daily 8–6; Labor Day–Memorial Day, daily 8:30–4.*

SPORTS & THE OUTDOORS

Recreational activities in Black Canyon run the gamut, from short and easy nature trails to world-class rock climbing and kayaking. The cold waters of the Gunnison River are well known to trout anglers, and though horseback riding is limited to one trail in the park, you can at least get right up to the canyon rim and gaze far below.

BICYCLING

Bikes are not permitted on any of the trails, but cycling along South Rim Road or mountain biking on the unpaved North Rim Road is a great way to view the park. No shops rent bikes in the immediate vicinity.

BIRD-WATCHING

The sheer cliffs of Black Canyon, though prohibitive for human habitation, provide diverse habitat for birds. Naturally, cliff dwellers such as peregrine falcons and white-throated swifts revel in the dizzying heights, while at river level the American dipper is a common sight as it forages for food in the rushing waters. Canyon wrens, which nest in

CLOSE UP

Black Canyon Flora & Fauna

Spring and early summer are the best times for bird-watching: You may spot peregrine falcons nesting in May and June, especially in the vicinity of Painted Wall, or other birds of prey such as red-tailed hawks, Cooper's hawks, and golden eagles circling overhead at any time of year. In summer, turkey vultures join the flying corps, and in winter, bald eagles. Also keep an eye out for blue grouse, which frequent the trails and roadsides.

Mule deer, elk (most commonly seen in winter), and the very shy bobcat (occasionally glimpsed in fall, winter,

and spring) also call the park home. In spring and fall you may see a porcupine among pinyon pines on the rims. Listen for the distinctive, high-pitched chirp of the yellow-bellied marmot, which hangs out on sunny, rocky outcrops near South Rim Visitor Center, Oak Flat Trail, and Chasm View Lookout. From the campgrounds at night, you're likely to hear the spine-tingling yips of coyotes, as they gather on the rim. Though rarely seen, mountain lions also live in the park, as do black bears, which are sometimes spotted in dry years, when they have to forage more widely for food.

the cliffs, are more often heard than seen, but for many its hauntingly beautiful song is the epitome of canyon country. Great horned owls and Steller's jays frequent the canyon rims. Best times for birding: spring and early summer.

BOATING & RAFTING

The spectacular 14-mi stretch of the Gunnison River that passes through the park is so narrow in some sections that the rim seems to be closing up above your head. The river is one of the premier kayak challenges in North America, with Class IV and Class V rapids, and portages required around bigger drops. Early visitors to the canyon declared this section unnavigable, and the fact that a few intrepid kayakers make the journey today is somewhat amazing. Once you're downstream from the rapids, the canyon opens up into what is called the Gunnison Gorge. The rapids ease considerably, and the trip becomes more of a quiet float on Class I to Class III water. The Gunnison Gorge National Conservation Area is under the jurisdiction of the Bureau of Land Management. Rafting is not allowed on the Gunnison River through the national park. However, several outfitters offer guided raft trips in the Gunnison Gorge National Conservation Area to the west.

FISHING

★ The three dams built upriver in Curecanti National Recreation Area have created prime trout fishing. In fact, the section of Gunnison River that goes through the park is designated "gold medal" water, with abundant rainbows, browns, and lakes. Certain restrictions apply: Only artificial flies and lures are permitted, and a Colorado fishing license is required for people ages 16 and older. Rainbow trout are catch-and-release only, and there are size and possession limits on brown trout (check at the visitor center). Most anglers access the river

9

from the bottom of East Portal Road; an undeveloped trail goes along the riverbank for about 0.75 mi.

HIKING

All trails can be hot in summer and most don't receive much shade, so bring water and wear a hat. Dogs are permitted on leash, on Rim Rock, Cedar Point Nature, and Chasm View Nature trails. Hiking into the inner canyon, while doable, is not for the faint of heart—or step. Six named routes lead down to the river, but they are not maintained or marked. In fact, the park staff won't even call them trails; they refer to them as "controlled slides." These super-steep, rocky routes vary in one-way distance from 1 to 2.75 mi, and the descent can be anywhere from 1,800 to 2,702 feet. Your reward, of course, is a rare look at the bottom of the canyon and the fast-flowing Gunnison. ■TIP➔ Don't attempt an inner-canyon hike without plenty of water (the park's recommendation is 4 quarts per person). For descriptions of the routes, and the necessary permit to hike them, stop at the visitor center or North Rim ranger station. Dogs are not permitted in the inner canyon.

EASY **Cedar Point Nature Trail.** This short (0.7 mi round-trip) interpretive trail leads out from South Rim Road to two overlooks. It's an easy stroll, and signs along the way detail the surrounding plants. ⊠ *South Rim Rd.,* ⊹ *4.2 mi from South Rim Visitor Center.*

↺ **Chasm View Nature Trail.** The park's shortest trail (0.3 mi round-trip) starts at North Rim Campground and offers an impressive 50-yard walk right along the canyon rim as well as an eye-popping view downstream of Painted Wall and Chasm View, 1,100 feet across on the South Rim. ⊠ *North Rim Campground,* ⊹ *11.25 mi from Rte. 92.*

Rim Rock Trail. The terrain on this 1-mi round-trip nature trail is primarily flat and exposed to the sun, with a bird's-eye view into the canyon. An interpretative pamphlet, which corresponds to markers along the route, is available at the visitor center and the campground trailhead. ⊹ *Begin hiking at either the Tomichi Point overlook or at the trailhead near Loop C in South Rim Campground.*

MODERATE **Deadhorse Trail.** Despite its somewhat sinister name, Deadhorse Trail (5 to 6 mi round-trip) is actually an easy-to-moderate hike, starting on an old service road from the Kneeling Camel Overlook. The trail's farthest point provides the park's easternmost viewpoint. From this overlook, the canyon is much more open, with pinnacles and spires rising along its sides. If you want to give yourself a bit of a scare, take the mile-long loop detour, about halfway through the hike. (The detour isn't marked—just look for the only other visible trail.) At the two informal overlooks, you'll be perched—without guardrails—atop the highest cliff in this part of the canyon. Make sure to keep your children by your side at all times. ⊹ *Trailhead at the end of North Rim Rd.*

North Vista Trail. The trail begins at North Rim ranger station. The moderate round-trip hike to and from Exclamation Point is 3 mi; a more-difficult foray to the top of 8,563-foot Green Mountain (a mesa, really), with about 800 feet of elevation gain, is 7 mi round-trip. You'll hike along the North Rim; keep an eye out for especially gnarled pinyon pines—the North Rim is the site of some of the oldest groves of pinyons in North America, between 400 and 700 years old. ⊠ *North Rim Rd.,* ⚓ *11 mi from Rte. 92 turnoff.*

Fodor'sChoice **Warner Point Nature Trail.** The 1.5-mi round-trip hike starts from High
★ Point. You'll enjoy fabulous vistas of the San Juan and West Elk mountains and Uncompahgre Valley. Warner Point, at trail's end, has the steepest drop-off from rim to river: a dizzying 2,702 feet. ⚓ *At the end of South Rim Rd.*

DIFFICULT **Oak Flat Trail.** This 2-mi loop trail is the most demanding of the South Rim hikes, as it brings you about 300 feet below the canyon rim. In places, the trail is narrow and crosses some steep slopes, but you won't have to navigate any steep drop-offs. Oak Flat is the shadiest of all the South Rim trails; small groves of aspen and thick stands of Douglas fir along the loop offer some respite from the sun. ⚓ *Begins and ends just west of the South Rim Visitor Center.*

HORSEBACK RIDING

Don't take the name "Deadhorse Trail" literally, because horses are permitted *only* on this easy-to-moderate .5-mi loop that begins east of North Rim Road. Horses are not allowed on the South Rim. They are allowed only in the North Rim Campground or on the North Rim Road during transport in a trailer.

Black Canyon of the Gunnison has no facilities geared toward horses, and only one outfitter runs trips into the park. If you bring your own horse, go to the end of North Rim Road and park your trailer at Kneeling Camel Overlook. No permit is required.

OUTFITTERS & **Elk Ridge Trail Rides.** The only outfitter allowed to guide rides in Black
EXPEDITIONS Canyon, Elk Ridge offers a four-hour ride to the canyon rim. Riders must be at least eight years old and can weigh no more than 230 pounds. Be sure to make advance reservations as they have a tendency to get booked up. ⊠ *10203 Bostwick Park Rd., Montrose* ☎ *970/240–6007* ⊕ *www.elkridgetrailrides.com* ⊗ *May–Sept., weather permitting.*

ROCK CLIMBING

Fodor'sChoice Climbing Black Canyon's sheer cliffs is one of Colorado's premier big-
★ wall challenges for advanced rock climbers, and some routes can take several days to complete, with climbers sleeping on narrow ledges or "portaledges." Closures due to nesting birds of prey apply at certain times of the year. Though there's no official guide to climbing in the park, reports from other climbers are kept on file at the South Rim Visitor Center.

If you want to get in some easier climbing, head for the Marmot Rocks bouldering area, about 100 feet south of South Rim Road between Painted Wall and Cedar Point overlooks (park at Painted Wall). Four boulder groupings offer a variety of routes rated from easy to very difficult; a pamphlet with a diagrammed map of the area is available at the South Rim Visitor Center.

9

OUTFITTERS & **Crested Butte Mountain Guides.** Advanced climbers can take a full-day guided
EXPEDITIONS   tour for $250. ✉ *218 Maroon Ave., Crested Butte* ☎ *970/349–5430 or
877/455–2307* ⊕ *www.crestedbutteguides.com* ⊘ *Year-round.*

Skyward Mountaineering. Intermediate to advanced climbers can take
a one-, three-, or five-day guided tour. ✆ *Box 323, Ridgway 81432*
☎ *970/209–2985* ⊕ *www.skywardmountaineering.com* ⊘ *Mar.–Nov.*

WINTER SPORTS

From late November to early April, South Rim Road is not plowed past
the visitor center, offering park guests a unique opportunity to cross-
country ski or snowshoe on the road. It's possible to ski or snowshoe
on the unplowed North Rim Road, too, but it's about 4 mi from where
the road closes, through sagebrush flats to the canyon rim.

OUTFITTERS & **Guided Snowshoe Walks.** In winter, the park offers ranger-led snowshoe
EXPEDITIONS   walks, usually once a day on weekends. Tours leave from the South
Rim Visitor Center and go along the rim for about 2 mi, often on Rim
Rock Trail. A limited supply of snowshoe gear is available for use at
no charge. Call ahead to reserve equipment and a space on a tour.
☎ *970/249–1914 Ext. 423.*

WHERE TO STAY

There are two campgrounds in the national park. The smaller North
Rim Campground is first-come, first served, and is closed in winter.
South Rim Campground is considerably larger, and has a loop that's
open year-round. Reservations are accepted in South Rim Loops A
and B. Power hookups only exist in Loop B, and vehicles more than
35 feet long are discouraged from either campground. At both of the
park's drive-to campgrounds there's a limit of eight people per site, and
camping is limited to 14 days. Water has to be trucked up to the campgrounds, so use it in moderation; it's shut off in mid- to late September.
Generators are not allowed at South Rim and are highly discouraged
at North Rim. Nearby communities such as Montrose have RV parks
with more amenities, and Crawford State Park has options that include
a boat ramp.

CAMPGROUNDS & RV PARKS

$–$$ ⛺ **South Rim Campground.** Stay on the canyon rim at this main camp-
Fodor'sChoice   ground right inside the park entrance. The RV hookups are in Loop B
★   and those sites are priced higher. It's possible to camp here year-round,
but the loops are not plowed, so you'll have to hike in with your tent.
✉ *South Rim Rd.,* ⊹ *1 mi from the visitor center* ⇋ *65 tent sites, 23
camper sites* ♿ *Pit toilets, partial hookups (electric), drinking water,
fire grates, picnic tables, public telephone* ⊟ *No credit cards.*

$ ⛺ **North Rim Campground.** This small campground, nestled amid pinyon
and juniper, offers the basics along the quiet North Rim. ✉ *North Rim
Rd., 11.25 mi from Rte. 92* ⇋ *13 sites* ♿ *Pit toilets, drinking water, fire
grates, picnic tables, ranger station* ⊟ *No credit cards* ⊘ *May–Oct.*

MONTROSE

15 mi southwest of Black Canyon of the Gunnison; 65 mi west of Gunnison via U.S. 50.

The self-described "Home of the Black Canyon" sits amid glorious surroundings, but it's an otherwise nondescript town with little more than a collection of truck stops, trailer parks, strip malls, and big-box stores frequented by area residents. Montrose also has a small airport that's a good gateway for skiers heading to Telluride, whose airport is often closed due to weather, and to Crested Butte. Montrose is perfectly placed for exploring the Black Canyon of the Gunnison and Curecanti National Recreation Area to the east; the San Juan Mountains to the south; the world's largest flattop mountain, Grand Mesa, to the north; and the fertile Uncompahgre Plateau to the west.

If you're interested in the lives of the region's original residents, stop by the excellent **Ute Indian Museum,** 3 mi south of town on U.S. 550. The museum contains several dioramas and the most comprehensive collection of Ute materials and artifacts in Colorado. ⊠ *17253 Chipeta Rd.* ☎ *970/249–3098* ⊕ *www.coloradohistory.org* ▨ *$3* ⊙ *Tues.–Sat. 9–4:30.*

SPORTS & THE OUTDOORS

BOATING The **Lake Fork Marina** (⊠ *West side of lake* ☎ *970/641–3048* ⊕ *www. whresorts.com*) rents all types of boats on Blue Mesa Reservoir. If you have your own boat, there's a ramp at the marina. A two-day boat permit is $5; a two-week permit is $10.

HIKING For information on backcountry hiking in the Uncompahgre Plateau and other nearby wilderness areas, contact the district office of the **Grand Mesa, Uncompahgre, and Gunnison national forests** (⊠ *2250 U.S. 50, Delta 81416* ☎ *970/641–6600* ⊕ *www.fs.fed.us/r2/gmug*).

WHERE TO STAY & EAT

$$–$$$ ✕ **Camp Robber.** The name refers to a native Colorado bird called the Canada jay, famous for stealing food from campsites; you'll want to steal the recipes for hearty Southwestern dishes such as spicy chimayo shrimp and the signature green chile potato soup. Generous portions for reasonable prices make it popular with families and groups, and the servers are friendly, accommodating, and knowledgeable. ⊠ *1515 Ogden Rd.* ☎ *970/252–1590* ⊕ *www.restaurant.com/camprobbercafe* ▤ *AE, DC, MC, V* ⊙ *No dinner Sun.*

¢–$ ✕ **Cazwellas.** Consistently voted the best in the valley by the locals, the comfortably upscale, internationally themed eatery sports exposed-brick walls and a laid-back attitude. The menu, mostly organically and seasonally focused, contains complicated dishes and simple preparations. The bison cocktail meatballs and seared sea scallops with roasted grapes are favorite starters, and you can't go wrong with the double-cut pork chop or any of the Angus steaks, especially the rib eye rubbed with ancho chilies. ⊠ *320 E. Main St.* ☎ *970/252–9200* ⊕ *www.cazwellas.com* ▤ *AE, DC, MC, V* ⊙ *Closed Sun. No lunch.*

9

$ ⚏**Best Western Red Arrow Motor Inn.** This low-key establishment is one of the nicest lodgings in the area, mainly because of the large, prettily appointed rooms filled with handsome mahogany furnishings. The full baths include soothing whirlpool tubs. **Pros:** reasonably priced, convenient downtown location, good-size rooms. **Con:** Main Street can be noisy. ⊠*1702 E. Main St., 81401* ☎*970/249–9641 or 800/468–9323* ⊕*www.bestwestern.com* ⤢*60 rooms* ⟐*In-room: dial-up. In-hotel: pool, gym, laundry service, no-smoking rooms* ☰*AE, D, DC, MC, V* ⦿*CP.*

¢   ⚏**Black Canyon Motel.** Spacious, well-maintained rooms with refrigerators and microwaves, friendly staff, and reasonable prices make this motel a good option for families. A small swimming pool and above-average complimentary breakfast (make-your-own waffles, bagels, muffins, and juices) add to the appeal. **Pros:** excellent value, pets allowed. **Cons:** nothing fancy, Main Street can be noisy. ⊠*1605 E. Main St., 81401* ☎*800/348–3495* ⊕*www.blackcanyonmotel.com* ⤢*49 rooms* ⟐*In room: refrigerator, ethernet. In hotel: pool, some pets allowed, no-smoking rooms* ☰*AE, D, DC, MC, V.*

SHOPPING

Got a sweet tooth? The **Russell Stover Factory Outlet** (⊠*2185 Stover Ave.* ☎*970/249–5372* ⊙*May 6–Sept. 8, Mon. –Thurs. 9–8 and Fri.–Sat. 9–9, Sun. 11–8; Sept. 9–May 5, Mon.–Sat. 9–8, Sun. 11–7*) sells fresh chocolates made in the factory across the street. The store is easy to find—it's south of downtown off U.S. 550. Local artist Lynne Anderson displays her finely crafted pottery at **Shekinah Gallery** (☎*970/240–8724 for appointment* ⊕*www.shekinahclay.com*). Pack a picnic lunch for the Black Canyon with local bounty at the **Uncompahgre Farmers' Market** (⊠*Centennial Plaza, intersection of Main and Uncompahgre Sts.* ⊙*Late spring–early fall, Wed. and Sat. 8:30–1*). In late summer, keep your eyes peeled for locally grown and locally beloved sweet corn.

TELLURIDE

66 mi south of Montrose, 125 mi north of Durango.

Tucked like a jewel in a tiny valley caught between azure sky and gunmetal mountains is Telluride, once so inaccessible that it was a favorite hideout for desperadoes such as Butch Cassidy, who robbed his first bank here in 1889. The savage but beautiful terrain of the San Juan Mountains, with peaks like 14,157-foot Mount Sneffels, and rivers, like the San Miguel, now attracts mountain people of a different sort—alpinists, snowboarders, freestylers, mountain bikers, and free-wheeling four-wheelers—who attack any incline, up or down, and do so with abandon.

The town's independent spirit is shaped not only by its mining legacy, but by the social ferment of the 1960s and early '70s. Before the ski area opened in 1971, Telluride had been as remote as it was back in Cassidy's day. It was even briefly included on the "Ghost Town Club of Colorado" itinerary, but that was before countercultural types moved in, seeking to lose themselves in the wilderness. By 1974 the town's orientation had changed so radically that the entire council was composed of hippies. An enduring Telluride tradition called the Freebox (Pine Street and Colorado Avenue), where residents can sort through and take whatever used clothing and appliances they need, remains as a memento of those times. (One memorable day, just after a fur shop had the temerity to open in town, surprised residents found a wide selection of minks, sables, and chinchillas at the box. After the mysterious break-in, the furriers got the point and moved on.)

Despite such efforts at keeping visible signs of wealth away, more and more locals are finding they can no longer afford to live here. And thanks to the construction of the Telluride Regional Airport in the mid-1980s, it has drawn ever more people. Today Telluride is an upscale alternative to Vail and Aspen, and celebrities who need only be identified by their first names (Arnold and Oprah, for example) have been spotted here.

Although the resort and the town are distinct areas, you can travel between them via a 2.5-mi, over-the-mountain gondola, one of the most beautiful commutes in Colorado. The gondola makes a car unnecessary for local transportation; both the village and the town are pedestrian friendly. This innovative form of public transportation operates summer and winter from early morning until late at night, and unless you have skis or a snowboard, the ride is free.

Telluride magazine prints an excellent historic walking tour in its "Visitors' Guide" section. The town offers one pastel Victorian residence or frontier trading post after another. It's hard to believe that the lovingly restored shops and restaurants once housed gaming parlors and saloons known for the quality of their "waitressing." That party-hearty spirit lives on, evidenced by numerous annual summer celebrations.

Telluride has two off-seasons, when most restaurants and many lodgings are closed. Nearly everyone flees town after the ski area shuts down in mid-April, to return in early or mid-June. The town closes up from late September or early October until ski season gets going in late November to early December.

The 1887 brick **San Miguel County Courthouse** (⊠*301 Colorado Ave.*) was the county's first courthouse, and it still operates as one today.

William Jennings Bryan spoke at the **New Sheridan Hotel & Opera House** (⊠*231 W. Colorado Ave.* ☎970/728–4351) during his 1896 presidential campaign. The opera house, added in 1914 and completely redone in 1996, is now home to the thriving Sheridan Arts Foundation.

In the old Miner's Hospital, **Telluride Historical Museum** was constructed in 1888 and carefully restored in 2000. Exhibits on the town's past, including work in the nearby mines and techniques practiced by doctors who once practiced here, are on display. ⊠*201 W. Gregory Ave.* ☎*970/728–3344* ⊕*www.telluridemuseum.org* ☞*$5* ⊙*Tues., Wed., Fri., and Sat. 11–5; Thurs. 11–7; Sun. 1–5.*

Operated by local thespian Ashley Boling, **Historic Tours of Telluride** (☎*970/728–6639*) provides humorous walking tours around the downtown streets, adding anecdotes about infamous figures such as Butch Cassidy and Jack Dempsey.

> ## NOTHING FEST
>
> Telluride is famous for its seemingly endless stream of festivals—so much so that its nickname is "Festival City." In 1991, a resident wrote a tongue-in-cheek letter to the city requesting that a Nothing Festival be implemented to give the citizens a break. Much to everyone's surprise, it was. During the festival, as listed on the Web site ⊕*www.nothingfestival.com*, "Sunrises and sunsets as normal." T-shirts with a special logo are for sale each year and festivalgoers are encouraged to tie a piece of string on their wrists to indicate nonparticipation.

★ U.S. 550 and Route 62 fan out from Ridgway to form one of the country's most stupendously scenic drives, the **San Juan Skyway.** The roadway weaves through a series of Fourteeners (a Rockies term for peaks reaching more than 14,000 feet) and picturesque mining towns. U.S. 550 continues south to historic Ouray and over Red Mountain Pass to Silverton and Durango. Take Route 62 west and Route 145 south to see the extraordinary cliff dwellings of Mesa Verde National Park. U.S. 160 completes the San Juan Skyway circuit to Durango. In late September and early October this route offers some of the most spectacular aspen viewing in the state.

FESTIVALS Highly regarded wine and wild-mushroom festivals alternate with musical performances celebrating everything from bluegrass to jazz to chamber music. Displaying a keen sense of humor, the town even promotes the Nothing Festival, when nothing whatsoever is on the calendar.

★ The **Telluride Film Festival** (☎*510/665–9494* ⊕*www.telluridefilm festival.com*) in early September is considered one of the world's leading showcases for foreign and domestic films. The **Telluride Bluegrass Festival** (⊕*www.bluegrass.com/planet*) in June has gone far beyond its bluegrass roots and is now one of the premier acoustic folk–rock gatherings. *For information about Bluegrass in Colorado, see the Woodstock of the West box in this chapter.*

Fodor'sChoice **DOWNHILL SKIING & SNOWBOARDING**

★ **Telluride** is really two ski areas in one. For many years, Telluride had a reputation as being an experts-only ski area. Indeed, the north-facing trails are impressively steep and long, and by spring the moguls are massive. The terrain accessed by Chairlift 9, including the famed Spiral Staircase and the Plunge, is for experts only (although one side of the Plunge is groomed so advanced skiers can have their turn).

Woodstock of the West

Bluegrass may have evolved from country's "mountain music," with bands like Bill Monroe's Blue Grass Boys, but Colorado's Telluride Bluegrass Festival added another layer to the genre beginning in 1973.

Traditional bluegrass bands from across the nation played the festival from the start, but when contemporary Colorado bands that had never previously played bluegrass started adding the quintessential instruments—mandolin, fiddle, guitar, upright bass, and banjo—to their lineups, their adoption of the "high lonesome sound" garnered national attention. It forced bluegrass to undergo several transformations, sometimes right before audience's eyes in Telluride, as the bands' enthusiasm prompted more and more experimentation.

As the festival gained in popularity, it brought more artists to Colorado, who came for the music and stayed for the agreeable climate and focus on nature that tie in so well with bluegrass's folksy sensibilities. Crossover between rock and bluegrass and other musical styles became more common, and the festival began to earn the moniker "Woodstock of the West." Colorado bands such as String Cheese Incident, Leftover Salmon, and Yonder Mountain String Band performed regularly at the event, appealing to a younger audience and encouraging more experimentation.

Now the Telluride Bluegrass Festival in June draws such popular acts as Emmylou Harris, Alison Krauss, Los Lobos, and Counting Crows. It has also spawned other popular and successful gatherings, including its sister festival held each July at Planet Bluegrass Ranch in Lyons, a town of about 1,600 that has become a bluegrass artists colony of sorts. In fact, most evenings throughout summer, you can wander the streets and hear impromptu porch jams, and the planned picking jams happen almost nightly at places such as Oskar Blues, where sometimes dozens of pickers will show up to play. The towns of Greeley and Pagosa Springs have gotten in on the act, too, both hosting bluegrass festivals in August.

But then there is the other side—literally—of the ski area, the gently sloping valley called Goronno Basin, with long runs excellent for intermediates and beginners. On the ridge that wraps around the ski area's core is the aptly named See Forever, a long cruiser that starts at 12,255 feet and seems to go on and on. Below that are numerous intermediate runs and a phenomenal terrain park called Sprite Air Garden, designed for snowboarders. Near Goronno Basin is another section that includes super-steep, double-diamond tree runs on one side and glorious cruisers on the other.

Slide through a Western-style gate and you come to Prospect Bowl, a 733-acre expansion that includes three chairlifts and a network of runs subtly cut around islands of trees. One cluster of intermediate runs is served by a swift high-speed quad. The terrain runs the gamut from almost-flat, beginner terrain to double-diamond fall-away chutes, cliff bands, and open glades. ⊠ *565 Mountain Village Blvd., 81435*

9

☎970/728–6900 or 800/778–8581 ⊕*www.tellurideskiresort.com* ⊙*Late Nov.–early Apr., daily 9–4.*

FACILITIES 3,530-foot vertical drop; 1,700 skiable acres; 24% beginner, 38% intermediate, 38% advanced/expert; 2 gondolas, 7 high-speed quad chairs, 2 triple chairs, 2 double chairs, 2 surface lifts, 1 moving carpet. (☎*970/728–7425*).

LESSONS & PROGRAMS The **Telluride Ski & Snowboard School** (✉*565 Mountain Village Blvd.* ☎*800/801–4832* ⊕*www.tellurideskiresort.com*) offers half-day group clinics beginning at $55. Lessons for first-timers are available for alpine and telemark skiers, as well as snowboarders. A five-hour clinic with rentals and restricted lift tickets costs $115. Children's programs for ages 3 to12 are $120 a day for lifts, lessons, and lunch. Telluride was a pioneer in creating Women's Week programs, five days of skills-building classes with female instructors. Sessions are scheduled for February and March.

LIFT TICKETS The one-day walk-up rate is $85. On multiday, advance-purchase tickets the daily rate can drop as low as $59.

RENTALS Equipment rentals are available at **Paragon Ski and Sport** (✉*236 S. Oak St.* ☎*970/728–4581* ⊕*www.paragontelluride.com*). Beginner packages (skis, boots, and poles) are $22 a day, and top-of-the-line packages are $42 a day. Paragon also rents telemark and cross-country gear, as well as snowshoes and snowblades.

Ski rentals are available from the ubiquitous **Telluride Sports** (✉*150 W. Colorado Ave.* ☎*970/728–4477 or 800/828–7547* ⊕*www.telluridesports. com*). Complete packages (skis, boots, and poles) start at around $28. There are 10 other locations in the area.

NORDIC SKIING

BACKCOUNTRY SKIING Among the better backcountry skiing routes is the **San Juan Hut System** (✉*224 E. Colorado Ave., 81435* ☎*970/626–3033* ⊕*www.san juanhuts.com*). It leads toward Ridgway along the Sneffels Range. The five huts in the system are about 7 mi apart and are well equipped with beds, blankets, wood-burning stoves, and cooking stoves. Previous backcountry experience is not essential to ski here, though it's highly recommended. Rental equipment is available, and reservations are recommended at least two weeks in advance. The San Juan Hut System also offers a guide service as an introduction to the backcountry tracks.

TRACK SKIING **Telluride Nordic Center** (✉*Town park* ☎*970/728–1144* ⊕*www.telluridetrails.org*) gives you access to 10 mi of cross-country trails. The areas around Molas Divide and Mesa Verde National Park are extremely popular. The center also rents equipment for both adults and children.

The **Topaten Touring Center** (☎*970/728–7517*), near the Chair 10 unload, offers 6.25 mi of trails groomed for cross-country skiing and snowshoeing in a high-mountain setting.

OTHER SPORTS & THE OUTDOORS

Telluride Outside (⊠*121 W. Colorado Ave.* ☎*970/728–3895 or 800/ 831–6230* ⊕*www.tellurideoutside.com*) organizes a variety of summer and winter activities in the Telluride area, including hot-air ballooning, sleigh rides, snowmobile tours, mountain-biking trips, and even winter fly-fishing excursions.

FISHING For an afternoon in some of the finest backcountry wilderness around, as well as a plethora of rainbow, cutthroat, brown, and brook trout, head for the beautiful San Miguel and Delores rivers. Anyone older than 16 needs a Colorado fishing license, which you can obtain at local sporting-goods stores. See ⊕*www.wildlife.state.co.us/fishing* for more information.

Telluride Outside (⊠*121 W. Colorado Ave.* ☎*970/728–3895 or 800/ 831–6230* ⊕*www.tellurideoutside.com*), Colorado's second-largest fishing-guide service, offers guided fly-fishing trips from its fly-fishing store, the Telluride Angler.

FOUR-WHEELING The Tomboy Road, accessed directly from North Fir Street at the edge of town, leads to one of the country's most interesting mining districts. It went down in history in 1901 when the Western Federation of Miners organized a strike at Tomboy Mine. The state militia was eventually called in to put an end to the strike. The ruins of Tomboy Mine, Tomboy Mill, and parts of the town of Tomboy are all that remain of those turbulent times. The road offers fabulous views of Bridal Veil Falls and passes through the Social Tunnel on its way to the high country. After 7.5 mi, the road crests over 13,114-foot-high Imogene Pass, the highest pass road in the San Juan Mountains. If you continue down the other side, you will end up near Yankee Boy Basin near Ouray.

Dave's Mountain Tours (ⓓ*Box 2736, Telluride 81435* ☎*970/728–9749* ⊕*www.telluridetours.com*) conducts summer jeep tours over Imogene Pass and other historic areas. If you want an in-town adventure, go on the Segway historical tour. Dave's offers snowmobile tours in season.

GLIDER RIDES Offering an unusual look at the San Juans, **Telluride Soaring** (☎*970/209– 3497*) operates out of the Telluride Regional Airport. Rates are about $110 per half hour, $160 per hour; rides are offered daily, weather permitting.

HIKING The peaks of the rugged San Juan Mountains around Telluride require some scrambling, occasionally bordering on real climbing, to get to the top. A local favorite is Mount Wilson, a roughly 4,000-vertical-foot climb for which only the last 400 vertical feet call for a scramble across steep, shale slopes. July and August are the most likely snow-free months on this 8-mi round-trip hike.

Sound a bit too grueling? An immensely popular 2-mi trail leads to **Bear Creek Falls.** The route is also used by mountain bikers. On the opposite side of the valley, the 3-mi **Jud Wiebe Trail** begins as an excellent hike that is often passable from spring until well into fall. From here you have amazing views of Utah's LaSal Mountains. For more-ambitious hikers, the Jud Wiebe Trail links with the 13-mi Sneffels Highline Trail.

This route leads through wildflower-covered meadows. Another trail leads to 425-foot **Bridal Veil Falls,** the state's highest cascade. It tumbles lavishly from the head of a box canyon. A beautifully restored powerhouse sits beside the falls.

HORSEBACK RIDING
Roudy Roudebush rode through America's living rooms courtesy of a memorable television commercial in which he and his horse, Cindy, trotted right up to the bar at the New Sheridan Hotel. Roudy is now riding Cindy's son, Golly, and you can join them. His slogan has long been "Gentle horses for gentle people, fast horses for fast people, and for people who don't like to ride, horses that don't like to be rode." **Ride with Roudy** (☎970/728–9611 ⊕*www.ridewithroudy.com*) is in a barn on an old ranch 6 mi from Telluride. Trail rides pass through aspen groves and across open meadows with views of the Wilson Range. Winter rides leave from Roudy's other ranch, in Norwood. Hour-long rides cost about $35.

MOUNTAIN BIKING
Having a fully equipped hut awaiting at the end of a tough day of mountain biking 35 mi makes the **San Juan Hut System** (⊠*224 E. Colorado Ave., 81435* ☎970/626–3033 ⊕*www.sanjuanhuts.com*) the backcountry biker's choice. The system operates two 215-mi routes, one from Telluride to Moab, Utah, the other from Durango to Moab. Dirt roads, desert slick rock, and canyon country—the areas along the way where there are canyons to explore, such as in Moab and Grand Junction—are all part of the experience, and the huts supply the beds, blankets, wood-burning stoves, and cooking stoves, which cuts down on what you need to haul on your bike.

RAFTING
There are plenty of rapids around Telluride. **Telluride Outside** (⊠*121 W. Colorado Ave.* ☎970/728–3895 or 800/831–6230 ⊕*www.tellurideoutside.com*) explores the Gunnison, Dolores, Colorado, and Animas rivers.

ROCK CLIMBING
Many people would consider being suspended from a wall of ice or a sheer cliff to be a bizarre form of torture. For those who think it might be fun, **Fantasy Ridge Mountain Guides** (⊠*28 Village Ct.,* ☐*Box 405, Placerville 81430* ☎970/728–3546 ⊕*www.fantasyridge.com*) offers introductory ice-climbing and rock-climbing courses. A three-day ice-climbing course costs about $900 (lodging included). Rock-climbing classes range from hourly instruction costing $25 to five-day programs that start at $1,120. Many use the famous Ophir Wall. Fantasy Ridge also guides Fourteener climbs and other expeditions in the San Juan Mountains.

WHERE TO EAT

$$$$ ✕**Allred's.** After riding up in the gondola, diners are still astounded by the views from this mountainside eatery. Try the free-range Canadian veal chop with potato-chanterelle hash, or the seared yellowfin tuna with vegetable risotto, fried oyster mushrooms, and red pepper au jus. The bittersweet chocolate cake and the passion-fruit sorbet will send you home smiling. ⊠*Top of San Sophia gondola* ☎970/728–7474 ☐*AE, D, MC, V* ☉*Closed early Apr.–early June and Oct.–late Nov. No lunch.*

★ **$$$$** ✕**Cosmopolitan.** Hotel Columbia, a sleek lodge at the base of the gondola, is home to this elegant restaurant specializing in dishes such as salmon with a spicy dipping sauce and seared tuna with coconut-vanilla rice. Try the New Orleans–style beignets with a cappuccino for dessert, cheekily listed as "coffee and donuts" on the menu. For a romantic evening, book a table for two in the cozy wine cellar. ✉*300 W. San Juan Ave.* ☎*970/728–1292* ⚭*Reservations essential* ▤*AE, MC, V* ☽*Call for seasonal closings. No lunch.*

$$$$ ✕**La Marmotte.** With its rough brick walls, lacy curtains, and baskets
Fodor'sChoice overflowing with flowers or strings of garlic bulbs, this romantic bis-
★ tro would be right at home in Provence. Fish dishes, such as seared Alaska salmon in a red wine sauce, are particularly splendid. ✉*150 W. San Juan Ave.* ☎*970/728–6232* ⚭*Reservations essential* ▤*AE, D, MC, V* ☽*Closed mid-Apr.–early June, Oct.–late Nov., and Tues. mid-June–Sept. No lunch.*

$$$$ ✕**221 South Oak Bistro.** In a pretty Victorian cottage, this elegant bistro entices you to linger. Chef-owner Eliza Gavin, who trained in Paris, New Orleans, and the Napa Valley, creates such dishes as Muscovy duck breast paired with duck confit, spinach, shiitakes, and pine nuts; rack of lamb with zucchini and potato-chèvre ravioli; and potato-crusted halibut with asparagus and fennel. Regulars come on Wednesday evenings to sample special martinis. ✉*221 S. Oak St.* ☎*970/728–9507* ▤*AE, MC, V* ☽*Closed Sun., early Apr.–mid-June, and early Oct.– early Dec. No lunch.*

$$$ ✕**Honga's Lotus Petal & Tea Room.** A local favorite, this tearoom serves up Japanese-, Thai-, and Balinese-influenced fare in a restored Victorian. The sushi bar is one of the best in town. Though the place caters mostly to vegetarians, it also puts free-range chicken and organic beef on the menu. Blackened tofu is the signature dish, and the crowds go wild for the crunchy shrimp roll and pineapple-coconut curry. Don't leave town without sampling the addictive pot stickers. ✉*135 E. Colorado Ave.* ☎*970/728–5134* ▤*AE, MC, V* ☽*Closed early Apr.–late May and mid-Oct.–late Nov.*

$$ ✕**Fat Alley BBQ.** Messy, mouthwatering ribs and Carolina-style pulled-pork sandwiches are complemented by delectable side dishes such as red beans and rice, baked sweet potatoes, and snap-pea and feta salad. More than a dozen beers, 30 bourbons, and a few wines are available, in addition to homemade iced tea and pink lemonade. A few long tables flanked by benches let you dine family-style and old skis adorn the walls at this no-frills joint. ✉*122 S. Oak St.* ☎*970/728–3985* ⚭*Reservations not accepted* ▤*AE, MC, V.*

$ ✕**Baked in Telluride.** Racks of fresh-baked breads, rolls, bagels, donuts, and other pastries are on display everywhere in this bakery, which also makes heavenly pasta sauces (check out the Alfredo), pizzas, and huge, inexpensive salads. Get it to go or sit in one of the tables in the back. ✉*127 S. Fir St.* ☎*970/728–4705* ▤*AE, MC, V.*

¢ ✕**Maggie's Bakery & Café.** A little spot with a blue awning and a couple of tables set up outside, Maggie's often has the front door propped open and the smell of fresh-baked fruit pies and oatmeal cookies lures customers in. You can grab breakfast and lunch here as well as a sweet

9

treat (the sticky buns are the best), including piled-high sandwiches, pizza, and soup. They also make their own jams. ✉*217 E. Colorado Ave.* ☎970/728–3334 ▭*No credit cards* ⊘*No dinner.*

WHERE TO STAY

$$$$ ⌂**Camel's Garden.** In a curious contradiction, this ultramodern lodging that is all gleaming glass and sleek surfaces bears the name of one of the town's oldest mines. Fireplaces keep the rooms toasty on winter evenings. There are plenty of nice touches, including CD players. The continental breakfast is loaded with fresh-baked pastries from the bakery next door. The hotel is steps away from the Oak Street chairlift. **Pros:** convenient to lift, tasty breakfast, romantic atmosphere. **Cons:** very modern, not especially kid friendly. ✉*250 W. San Juan Ave., 81435* ☎*970/728–9300 or 888/772–2635* ⊕*www.camelsgarden.com* ⬭*30 rooms, 7 condos* ⌂*In-room: no a/c, VCR. In-hotel: restaurant, spa, no-smoking rooms* ▭*AE, D, DC, MC, V* ⦿*CP* ⊘*Closed Oct.–Nov.*

★ **$$$$** ⌂**Hotel Columbia Telluride.** It's hard to go wrong with views of the mountains, the gondola, and the San Miguel River. Play oversize checkers in your charmingly decorated rustic-chic room with a fireplace or walk out the front door and wander around town. They will store your mountain bike or your skis, and with the gondola right there, it's easy to access just about anything. The Cosmopolitan restaurant (*see* Where to Eat *above*) housed in this hotel is one of the best in town and the complimentary breakfast there is above average. **Pros:** stunning views; charming, spacious rooms; convenient to gondola. **Cons:** some street noise, must keep your shutters closed or gondola riders can see right in. ✉*300 W. San Juan Ave., 81435* ☎*800/201–9505* ⊕*www. columbiatelluride.com* ⬭*21 rooms* ⌂*In room: no a/c, VCR, Wi-Fi. In hotel: restaurant, concierge, parking (no fee), no-smoking rooms* ▭*AE, D, MC, V.*

$$$$ ⌂**Hotel Telluride.** The rooms are far more upscale than the pricing would suggest, and the building itself looks like an old stone mansion nestled against the mountain. All of the rooms have San Juan views from a patio or balcony, and a complimentary breakfast buffet is offered at the Bistro, a lodge-style eatery on-premises. The fitness center has been nicely updated, massages are offered in the spa, and the hot tubs on the roof are delightful when it's snowing. **Pros:** terrific value, abundant breakfast, romantic hot tubs. **Cons:** hot tubs often taken, hotel fills up in season. ✉*199 N. Cornet St., 81435* ☎*866/468–3504* ⊕*www. thehoteltelluride.com* ⬭*59 rooms, 2 suites* ⌂*In room: safe, refrigerator, Wi-Fi. In hotel: restaurant, bar, gym, spa, concierge, public Wi-Fi, no-smoking rooms* ▭*AE, D, MC, V.*

$$$$ ⌂**Ice House Lodge.** An appealing blend of Scandinavian and Southwestern decor makes this lodging unique. Native American tapestries and polished wood ceilings are complemented by rich fabrics. Spacious rooms have balconies that let you enjoy the view, while the baths have oversize tubs. The hotel provides a free continental breakfast and a place to store your skis. Best of all, the Oak Street chairlift is little more than a block away. **Pros:** gorgeous views, lovely decor, comfortable rooms, near restaurants. **Con:** pricey. ✉*310 S. Fir St., 81435* ☎*970/728–6300 or 800/544–3436* ⊕*www.icehouselodge.com*

⌐ª42 rooms, 16 condos ⌂In-room: no a/c, DVD, Wi-Fi. In-hotel: pool, spa, no-smoking rooms ▭AE, D, DC, MC, V ⓉⓄⒾCP ⊗Closed mid-Apr.–early June.

$$$$ 🏨**Inn at Lost Creek.** A grand stone-and-wood structure with the architecture of a European alpine lodge, this rambling five-story, luxury lodge is next to the Mountain Village Gondola (which carries you to downtown Telluride) and just two blocks from the conference center. You can literally ski out the front door. Most of the rooms are suites with balconies, ideal for a romantic getaway, and the rooftop spa is a nice extra. **Pros:** ski in ski out, romantic, convenient location. **Cons:** pricey, rooftop spa usually crowded. ✉*119 Lost Creek La., Mountain Village 81435* ☎*970/728–5678 or 888/601–5678* ⊕*www.innatlost creek.com* ⌐ª*29 suites, 3 studios* ⌂*In-room: kitchen (some), DVD, VCR, Wi-Fi. In-hotel: restaurant, bar, gym, spa, laundry facilities, airport shuttle, no-smoking rooms* ▭*AE, D, DC, MC, V.*

$$$ 🏨**New Sheridan Hotel.** William Jennings Bryan delivered his rousing "Cross of Gold" speech here in 1896, garnering a presidential nomination in the process. Antiques fill the space, from old tintypes to fringed lamps, marble-top dressing tables to red velour love seats. The four Aspen rooms are a great value; each has a queen-size bed and shares a single-sex bathroom with multiple sinks and showers. The gorgeous Victorian-era bar, a favorite among locals, is the original. A complimentary breakfast and afternoon tea complete the picture of gracious fin de siècle living. **Pros:** charming atmosphere, accommodating staff. **Cons:** when it's full, the shared baths can be annoying. ✉*231 W. Colorado Ave., 81435* ☎*970/728–4351* ⊕*www.newsheridan.com* ⌐ª*26 rooms, 18 with bath; 6 suites* ⌂*In-room: no a/c, dial-up. In-hotel: restaurant, bar, gym, public Wi-Fi, no-smoking rooms* ▭*AE, MC, V* ⊗*Closed mid-Apr.–mid-May and mid-Oct.–mid-Nov.* ⓉⓄⒾBP.

$$$ 🏨**The Peaks Resort & Golden Door Spa.** The somewhat forbidding exterior at this luxury resort no longer seems worth mentioning when you first catch sight of Mount Wilson, the peak pictured on every can of Coors. Make sure to ask for a room with a balcony. The rooms are sizable, decorated in Norwegian wood and muted shades of green. The range of activities here is vast, from an indoor pool to tennis courts—there's even an indoor climbing wall. And then there are the invigorating, revitalizing treatments at the five-story Golden Door Spa. More than 55 treatments are offered in the 44 private rooms, from skin-tightening wraps to muscle-taming massages. **Pros:** spacious rooms, great views, something for everyone. **Cons:** easy to feel overwhelmed, popular activities are often booked well in advance. ✉*136 Country Club Dr., 81435* ☎*970/728–6800 or 800/789–2220* ⊕*www.thepeaksresort.com* ⌐ª*174 rooms, 32 suites* ⌂*In-room: no a/c, VCR, ethernet, Wi-Fi. In-hotel: 2 restaurants, room service, bar, tennis courts, pools, gym, spa, no-smoking rooms* ▭*AE, DC, MC, V* ⊗*Closed early Apr.– mid-May and mid-Oct.–mid-Nov.*

$$$ 🏨**San Sophia B&B.** Gingerbread trim gives this turreted Victorian-style inn a fanciful feeling. Pristine mountain light streams into the rooms, which are warmly accented with whitewashed-oak woodwork. Rooms have brass beds covered with handmade quilts and tables and chairs

9

crafted by local artisans. The stained-glass windows over the over-size tubs are a nice touch. Owners Alicia Bixby and Keith Hampton are overachievers; they also run a marketing firm in town, sponsor the annual wine festival, and raise two young children, but they still find time to mingle with the guests. Condo rentals are also available. **Pros:** romantic, centrally located but not on the busiest street, beautiful decor. **Con:** not much soundproofing between rooms. ⊠*330 W. Pacific St., 81435* ☎*970/728–3001 or 800/537–4781* ⊕*www.sansophia.com* ⤴*16 rooms* ♿*In-room: no a/c, VCR. In hotel: no elevator, no-smoking rooms* ▤*AE, MC, V* ⊗*Closed early Apr.–early May and 2 wks in Nov.* ⦿*BP.*

CONDOS **Telluride Central Reservations** (☎*800/525–3455* ⊕*www.visittelluride. com*) handles all the properties at Telluride Mountain Village, and several more in town. **Telluride Rentals** (☎*800/970–7541* ⊕*www.telluriderentals.com*) rents several top-notch accommodations.

NIGHTLIFE & THE ARTS

THE ARTS The **Lizard Head Theatre Company** (☎*970/728–3133*) brings big-name actors to perform a summer repertory season at the Sheridan Opera House. The **Sheridan Arts Foundation** (⊠*110 N. Oak St.* ☎*970/728–6363* ⊕*www.sheridanoperahouse.com*) is a mentoring program that brings top actors and singers to town to perform alongside budding young artists in the Sheridan Opera House. The **Telluride Repertory Theatre Company** (☎*970/728–4539* ⊕*www.telluridetheatre.org*) gives free performances in the town park each summer.

NIGHTLIFE **Allred's** (⊠*Top of San Sophia gondola* ☎*970/728–7474*) is a divine après-ski location. Take in eye-popping views of the mountains and the lights twinkling in the town below as you enjoy an excellent selection of wines by the glass. Appetizers can make for an early dinner. **Excelsior Café** (⊠*200 W. Colorado Ave.* ☎*970/728–4250*) is the spot to hear the best folk–rock. The **Fly Me to the Moon Saloon** (⊠*132 E. Colorado Ave.* ☎*970/728–6666* ⊕*www.flymetothemoonsaloon.com*) has live music—jazz, blues, funk, ska, rock, you name it—most nights. The action gets wild on the spring-loaded dance floor. The **Last Dollar Saloon** (⊠*100 E. Colorado Ave.* ☎*970/728–4800*) has a jukebox filled with old favorites.The century-old bar at the **New Sheridan Hotel** (⊠*231 W. Colorado Ave.* ☎*970/728–4351*) is a favorite hangout for skiers returning from the slopes. Prime time is between 4 PM and 8 PM. In summer, folks gather to socialize and watch the world go by. On July 4, a cowboy named Roudy is known to ride into the bar and enjoy his drink while astride his horse.

SHOPPING

BOOKS **Between the Covers Bookstore & Coffee House** (⊠*224 W. Colorado Ave.* ☎*970/728–4504*) has the perfect ambience for browsing through the latest releases while sipping a foam-capped cappuccino.

BOUTIQUES The **Bounty Hunter** (⊠*226 W. Colorado Ave.* ☎*970/728–0256*) is the spot for leather items, especially boots and vests. It also has an astonishing selection of hats, among them Panama straw, beaver felt, Australian Outback, and just plain outrageous.

CRAFT & ART
GALLERIES

Hell Bent Leather & Silver (⊠ *209 E. Colorado Ave.* ☎ *970/728–6246* ⊕ *www.hellbentleather.com*) is a fine source for Native American arts and crafts.

SPORTING
GOODS

Telluride Sports (⊠ *150 W. Colorado Ave.* ☎ *970/728–4477 or 800/828– 7547* ⊕ *www.telluridesports.com*) has equipment and clothing for all seasons.

RIDGWAY

45 mi from Telluride via Rtes. 62 and 145; 26 mi south of Montrose via U.S. 550.

The 19th-century railroad town of Ridgway has been the setting for some classic Westerns, including *True Grit* and *How the West Was Won.* Though you'd never know it from the rustic town center, the area is also home to many swank ranches, including one belonging to fashion designer Ralph Lauren.

The **Ridgway Railroad Museum** (⊠ *Junction U.S. 550 and CO 62* ☎ *970/ 626-5158* ⊕ *www.ridgwayrailroadmuseum.org* ✉ *Free*) celebrates the town's importance during the heyday of the railroad. The first exhibits were rolling stock, including a wooden boxcar built for the filming of *Butch Cassidy and the Sundance Kid.*

SPORTS & THE OUTDOORS

GOLF

Fairway Pines Golf Club. This 18-hole, Byron Coker–designed course twists through a maze of mountain forest and offers mountain views and wildlife. It's long and often demanding, but at 8,000 feet, your drives might go a little farther and higher than at sea level. Course and driving range are open from April to October. Cart rental is $15. ⊠ *105 Badger Trail* ☎ *970/626–5284* 🏌 *18 holes. Yards: 6,841/5,291. Par: 72/72. Green Fee: $75/$85.*

WATER
SPORTS

At the **Ridgway State Park & Recreation Area** (⌂ *2855 U.S. 550, 81432* ☎ *970/626–5822* ⊕ *www.parks.state.co.us*), 12 mi north of Ridgway, the reservoir is stocked with plenty of rainbow trout, as well as the larger and tougher German brown. Anglers also pull up kokanee, yellow perch, and the occasional large-mouth bass. Anyone older than 16 needs a Colorado fishing license, which you can obtain at local sporting-goods stores. See ⊕ *www.wildlife.state.co.us/fishing* for more information.

WHERE TO STAY & EAT

$$ ✕ **True Grit Café.** Scenes from *True Grit* were filmed here, and the local hangout is a shrine to the film and its star, John Wayne. This neighborhood pub serves standard fare—burgers, nachos, and delicious chicken-fried steak. ⊠ *123 N. Lena Ave.* ☎ *970/626–5739* ▭ *D, MC, V.*

$$ ⊡ **Chipeta Sun Lodge & Spa.** The dramatic Southwestern-style adobe's rooms have rough-hewn log beds, hand-painted Mexican tiles, and stunning views from the decks. The inn is a stone's throw from the year-round outdoor activities in this stretch of the San Juan Mountains. When you're finished hiking or biking, return to the spa for a little

9

pampering. The hearty complimentary breakfast is served in a sunny solarium. **Pros:** unique rooms, hearty breakfasts, ideal location for outdoor activities in the area. **Cons:** none. ✉ *304 S. Lena St., 81432* ☎ *970/626–3737 or 800/633–5868* ⊕ *www.chipeta.com* ⇩ *23 rooms* ⚷ *In-room: kitchen (some), refrigerator, VCR, no TV (some). In-hotel: pool, spa, no-smoking rooms* ☰ *MC, V* ⦿ *BP.*

OURAY

10 mi south of Ridgway via U.S. 50; 23 mi from Silverton via U.S. 550 north.

The town of Ouray (pronounced *you-ray*) nestles in a narrow, steep-wall valley in the shadows cast by rugged peaks of the San Juan Mountains. It was named for the great Southern Ute chief Ouray, labeled a visionary by the U.S. Army and branded a traitor by his people because he attempted to assimilate the Utes into white society. The former mining town is the proud owner of a National Historic District, with lavish old hotels, commercial buildings, and residences. The town's ultimate glory lies in its surroundings, and it has become an increasingly popular destination for climbers (both the mountain and ice varieties), mountain-bike fanatics, and hikers.

More than 25 classic edifices are included in the walking-tour brochure issued by the Ouray County Historical Society. Among the points of interest are the grandiose Wright's Opera House, the Western Hotel, and the St. Elmo Hotel.

One of the loveliest buildings in town is the **Beaumont Hotel** (✉ *505 Main St.* ☎ *970/325–7000*). This 1887 landmark, a confection of French, Italian, and Romanesque Revival design, stood vacant for years before Dan and Mary King set about restoring it. The project cost millions of dollars—the owners strove for perfection at every step. The building was added to the National Register of Historic Places in 1973.

The **Ouray County Museum** preserves the history of ranching and mining in the San Juan Mountains and Ouray. Mining equipment, railroad paraphernalia, and commercial artifacts are carefully arranged in the former St. Joseph's Hospital, built in 1887. ✉ *420 6th Ave.* ☎ *970/325–4576* ⊕ *www.ourayhistoricalsociety.org* ▤ *$5* ⊙ *Call for hrs.*

Fodor's Choice ★ Ouray is also the northern end of the Million Dollar Highway, the awesome stretch of U.S. 550 that climbs over **Red Mountain Pass.** As it ascends steeply from Ouray, the road clings to the cliffs hanging over the Uncompahgre River far below. This two-laner bears little resemblance to the image one usually has of U.S. highways. Guardrails are few, hairpin turns are many, and behemoth RVs often seem to take more than their share of road. It earned its nickname either because the crushed ore used for the roadbed was rumored to contain gold and silver, or because of the fortune that 19th-century road builder Otto Mears spent to create it. This priceless road is kept open all winter by heroic plow crews. The Ouray side, on the whole, is steeper and narrower than the Silverton side. It is the most spectacular part of the 236-mi **San Juan Skyway,** designated as an All-American Road for its scenic splendor and historic significance.

One particularly gorgeous jaunt is to **Box Canyon Falls.** The turbulent waters of Clear Creek thunder 285 feet down a narrow gorge. A steel suspension bridge and well-marked trails afford breathtaking vistas. Birders flock to the park, and a visitor center has interpretive displays. ⊠ *West end of 3rd Ave. off U.S. 550* ☎*970/325–4464* ☜*$3* ⊘*Mid-Oct.–mid-May, daily 10–10; mid-May–mid-Oct., daily 8* AM*–dusk.*

Another option is to immerse yourself in nature at the area's various hot springs. At **Ouray Hot Springs Pool** it's hard to tell which is more refreshing, the pools brimming over with 96°F to 106°F water or the views of surrounding peaks. There's a fitness center in the bathhouse. ⊠*1220 Main St.* ☎*970/325–7073* ☜*$10* ⊙*Summer, daily 10–10; winter, weekdays noon–8:45* PM*, weekends 11* AM*–8:45* PM.

Historic Wiesbaden Hot Springs Spa & Lodge is at the source of the springs. In an underground chamber, you can soak in the steamy pools and inhale the pungent vapors. There's also an outdoor pool. Massage and mud wraps are offered at the spa. Note that they request that anyone who has smoked in the last three months not use their facilities because of guests' allergy issues. ⊠*625 5th St.* ☎*970/325–4347 or 888/846–5191* ⊕*www.wiesbadenhotsprings.com* ☜*$15 for the public, guests use pool and caves free* ⊙*Daily 8* AM*–9:45* PM.

On the **Bachelor-Syracuse Mine Tour,** a mine train hauls visitors down 3,500 feet into one of the region's great mines. Explanations of mining techniques, a visit to a blacksmith shop, and panning for gold are part of the experience. Tours depart every half hour. ⊠*1222 County Rd. 14* ☎*970/325–0220* ⊕*www.bachelorsyracusemine.com* ☜*$17.95* ⊙ *May 20–June 15, 9–4; June 16–Aug. 19, 9–5; Aug.20–Sept 15, 9–4.*

SPORTS & THE OUTDOORS

FOUR-WHEELING Off-roaders delight in the more than 500 mi of four-wheel-drive roads around Ouray. Popular routes include the Alpine Loop Scenic Byway to the Silverton and Lake City areas, and Imogene Pass or Black Bear Pass to Telluride. Figure on the four-wheeling season running from May to September, but you'll have to keep an eye on the weather.

About the first 7 mi of the road to **Yankee Boy Basin** are accessible by regular cars, but it takes a four-wheel drive to reach the heart of this awesome alpine landscape. The route, designated County Road 361, veers off U.S. 550 just south of Ouray and climbs west into a vast basin ringed with soaring summits and carpeted with one of Colorado's most lavish displays of wildflowers. This is one of the region's pre-

9

mier day-trip destinations. Contact the **Ouray Ranger District** (✉ *County Rd. 361* ☎ *970/240–5300* ⊕ *www. fs.fed.us/r2/gmug*).

If you have the skill and confidence but not the right vehicle, you can rent one from **Switzerland of America Tours** (✉ *226 7th Ave.* ☎ *970/325– 4484 or 800/432–5337* ⊕ *www. soajeep.com*). The company also offers guided tours in open-air six-passenger jeeps. Full-day tours cost $60–$125.

> ## WORD OF MOUTH
>
> "I love Ouray and recommend: Yankee Boy jeep tour (but may be too late for wildflowers in Sept); hot springs pool; Ouray Historical Museum (small but interesting) and one side trip to either Telluride or Mesa Verde." —karens

ICE CLIMBING

★ Ouray is known in ice-climbing circles for its abundance of frozen waterfalls. The Ouray Ice Festival, held each January, helped to cement its reputation. The **Ouray Ice Park** (⬓ *Box 1058, Ouray 81427* ☎ *970/325–4288* ⊕ *www.ourayicepark.com*) is the world's first facility dedicated to ice climbing. Located in the Uncompahgre Gorge south of town, the Ice Park has three main climbing areas with more than 40 routes. **Ouray Mountain Sports** (✉ *722 Main St.* ☎ *970/325–4284* ⊕ *www.ouraysports.com*) arranges lessons and guided climbs.

NORDIC SKIING

About 9 mi south of Ouray, Ironton Park is a marked trail system for Nordic skiers and snowshoers. Several interconnecting loops let you spend a day on the trails. Local merchants stock trail maps. For information, contact **Ouray County Nordic Council** (⬓ *Box 469, Ouray 81427* ☎ *970/325–4932*).

WHERE TO STAY & EAT

$$$

Fodor's Choice

★ ╳⌂ **Beaumont Hotel.** No detail has been overlooked in the restoration of this 1887 hotel, a gold-rush era landmark that stood vacant for 34 years. Soundproof, individually decorated rooms, deep soaking tubs, and a spa are among the thoroughly modern features that make this such a relaxing place to stay. The outdoor patio area has heated floors so you can enjoy the stunning views of the Amphitheater Range on chilly mornings. Tundra Restaurant ($$$–$$$$) is grand, with a cathedral ceiling and a balcony (where a classical guitarist plays in the evenings). Local ingredients, wild game, and fresh fish are well matched by the stellar wine list. Don't miss the to-die-for risotto. **Pros:** soundproofing means a quiet stay, heated outdoor patio is a nice touch, other updates make this a bargain and a delightful spot. **Con:** restaurant is expensive. ✉ *505 Main St., 81427* ☎ *970/325–7000 or 888/447–3255* ⊕ *www.beaumonthotel.com* ⬐ *10 rooms, 2 suites* ⌂ *In-room: DVD, VCR, dial-up, Wi-Fi. In-hotel: 2 restaurants, bar, spa, public Wi-Fi, no-smoking rooms* ▭ *MC, V.*

$$$

⌂ **China Clipper Inn.** In a departure from the typical Western- and Victorian-style inns in this area, the China Clipper is tastefully decorated with Asian antiques. Most rooms open onto a charming flower-filled patio with hot tub. The inn was built almost entirely—with great attention to detail—by a retired Navy commander from Louisville, Kentucky. Full breakfast and afternoon tea are included in the rate. **Pros:** small, romantic. **Con:** can be noisy between rooms. ✉ *525 2nd St.,*

81427 ☎970/325–0565 or 800/315–0565 ⊕www.chinaclipperinn.com ⇨12 rooms ♿In-room: DVD (some), VCR (some), dial-up. In hotel: no elevator, public Wi-Fi, no-smoking rooms ▤AE, D, MC, V ⚭BP.

$$ 🏨**Black Bear Manor Bed & Breakfast.** Hosts Phil and Lucie Mims (and their little Scottish terrier) make you feel right at home in their modern space, which offers a terrific view of the surrounding San Juan Mountains from its observatory. Ten of the twelve suites have private baths, and all but one have interior and exterior entrances, so you can walk through the house or not. Some rooms offer fireplaces and jetted tubs, and all feature a bottle of wine, chocolates, and robes upon arrival. Breakfast includes fresh-baked pastries made by Lucie and served in a sunny, cheerful room that looks out onto the mountains. **Pro:** very welcoming hosts, setup means you don't have to see other guests if you don't want to, generous amenities. **Con:** not a typical antiques-filled B&B. ✉118½ 6th Ave., 81427 ☎970/325–4219 or 800/845–/512 ⊕www.blackbearmanor.com ⇨12 rooms ♿In-room: no a/c, no TV (some). In-hotel: no elevator, no-smoking rooms ▤D, MC, V ⚭BP.

$$ 🏨**Box Canyon Lodge & Hot Springs.** If soaking with the masses at the local hot springs is not your cup of tea, opt for a private plunge at this friendly lodge. This mineral spring was used first by the Utes and later by the Cogar Sanitarium. Soak away your cares in four redwood tubs full of steaming 103°F to 107°F water, with mountain views. The lodge has a great location off the main drag and near the stream. The rooms are nondescript, but modern and comfortable and there is a continental breakfast included. A charming collection of more than 145 Big Ben alarm clocks tick away the minutes in the lobby. **Pros:** proximity to hot springs, welcoming staff, off-the-beaten-path feel. **Con:** no-frills rooms. ✉45 3rd Ave., 81427 ☎970/325–4981 or 800/327–5080 ⊕www.boxcanyonouray.com ⇨33 rooms, 5 suites ♿In-room: no a/c, refrigerator, DVD, Wi-Fi. In-hotel: no elevator, no-smoking rooms ▤AE, D, DC, MC, V.

$$ 🏨**St. Elmo Hotel.** This tiny 1898 hostelry was originally a haven for "miners down on their luck," or so the story goes. Its original owner was Kitty Heit, who couldn't resist a sob story. Family ghosts reputedly hover about protectively. The rooms are graced with stained-glass windows, marble-top armoires, brass or mahogany beds, and other antiques. A complimentary breakfast buffet is served in a sunny parlor. The Bon Ton ($$) restaurant serves Continental cuisine with an Italian flair. **Pro:** reasonable rates. **Con:** can feel a bit cramped. ✉426 Main St., 81427 ☎970/325–4951 or 866/243–1502 ⊕www.stelmohotel. com ⇨7 rooms, 2 suites ♿In-room: no a/c, no TV. In-hotel: restaurant, no elevator, no-smoking rooms ▤AE, D, DC, MC, V ⚭BP.

SHOPPING

In the restored Beaumont Hotel, **Buckskin Booksellers** (✉505 Main St. ☎970/325–4044 has books about such topics as mining, railroading, and ranching, as well as collectibles and Native American items. Also in the Beaumont, **North Moon** (✉505 Main St. ☎970/325–4885) carries irresistible pieces of jewelry. **Ouray Glassworks & Pottery** (✉619 Main St. ☎800/748–9421) sells exquisite handblown glass created by Sam Rushing and pottery by Diane Rushing.

SILVERTON

23 mi south of Ouray via U.S. 550, 20 mi north of Purgatory via U.S. 550.

Glorious peaks surround Silverton, an isolated, unspoiled old mining community. It reputedly got its name when a miner exclaimed, "We ain't got much gold but we got a ton of silver!" Silverton is the county seat, as well as the only remaining town, in San Juan County. The last mine went bust in 1991 (which is recent as such things go), leaving Silverton to boom only in summer when the Durango & Silverton Narrow Gauge Railroad *(see the Durango section in this chapter)* deposits four trainloads of tourists a day. The Silverton Mountain ski area has also helped the town to shake off its long slumber, and more businesses are finding it worthwhile to stay open year-round.

The downtown area has been designated a National Historic Landmark District. Be sure to pick up the walking-tour brochure that describes—among other things—the most impressive buildings lining Greene Street: **Miners' Union Hall, Teller House,** the **Town Hall,** the **San Juan County Courthouse** (home of the county historical museum), and the **Grand Imperial Hotel.** These structures have historical significance, but more history was probably made in the raucous red-light district along Blair Street.

The **San Juan County Historical Museum** is in the old San Juan County Jail. It was erected in 1902 from prefabricated parts that were shipped by train from St. Louis. The museum houses a mineral collection, mining memorabilia, and local artifacts. ⊠*1559 Greene St.* ☎*970/387–5838* ⊑*$4* ⊗*Daily 9–5.*

Ask at the **Chamber of Commerce** about a Heritage Pass, good for savings on admission to the Silverton Jail and Museum, Old Hundred Gold Mine, and Mayflower Mill. ⊠*414 Greene St.* ☎*970/387–5654 or 800/752–4494* ⊕*www.silvertoncolorado.org* ⊗*May, June, and Oct., daily 9–5; July–Sept., daily 9–6; Nov.–Apr., daily 10–4.*

A tram takes visitors 1,500 feet into the **Old Hundred Gold Mine** for a tour of one of the town's oldest mining facilities. Old Hundred operated for about a century, from the first strike in 1872 until the last haul in the early 1970s. ⊹*5 mi north of Silverton on Hwy. 110, then County Rd. 4* ☎*970/387–5444 or 800/872–3009* ⊕*www.minetour. com* ⊑*$17* ⊗*May 10–Oct. 15, daily 10–4.*

The nearby **Mayflower Mill** has been designated a National Historic Landmark. Tours explain how precious metals are extracted from the earth. ⊹*5 mi north of Silverton on Hwy. 110* ☎*970/387–0294* ⊑*$7* ⊗*Memorial Day–late Sept.*

If you look north toward Anvil Mountain, you'll see the community's touching tribute to miners, the **Christ of the Mines Shrine.** It was built in the 1950s out of Carrara marble. A moderately strenuous 1-mi hike leads to the shrine, which has memorable views of the surrounding San Juan Mountains.

SPORTS & THE OUTDOORS

DOWNHILL
SKIING &

Run by the town, **Kendall Mountain** (☎970/387–5522 ☒$7) is a single-tow ski center open weekends during ski season, weather permitting. It's not a challenging slope, so it's perfect for beginners. Sledding and tubing are also permitted.

About 6 mi north of town, **Silverton Mountain** is one of the country's simplest yet most innovative ski areas. With a single lift accessing the never-groomed backcountry steeps and a maximum of 475 people per day allowed on the vast and challenging terrain on unguided days and 80 on guided days (which kind of day it is depends on conditions and time of year), Silverton Mountain gained instant cult status with some of the country's best skiers. Fans say the experience is like heli-skiing without a chopper. From the 10,400-foot base, the lift ascends to 12,300 feet, and you can hike up to 13,300 feet if you want an extra-long run. This is for advanced and expert skiers only and reservations are mandatory for guided skiing and strongly suggested for unguided. ☒ *Rte. 110A* ☎ *970/387–5706* ⊕ *www.silvertonmountain. com* ☒*$49–$119.*

FOUR-
WHEELING

Silverton provides easy access to such popular four-wheel-drive routes as Ophir Pass to the Telluride side of the San Juans, Stony Pass to the Rio Grande Valley, and Engineer and Cinnamon passes, components of the Alpine Loop. With an all-terrain vehicle you can see some of Colorado's most famous ghost towns, remnants of mining communities, and jaw-dropping scenery. The four-wheeling season is May to mid-October, weather permitting. In winter these unplowed trails are transformed into fabulous snowmobile routes.

Silver Summit RV Park (☒ *640 Mineral St.* ☎*970/387–0240 or 800/352–1637* ⊕*www.silversummitrvpark.com*) rents four-wheelers for about $145–$175 per day. Full-day tours with a guide cost about $110 per person. **Triangle Jeep Rental** (☒*864 Greene St.* ☎*970/387–9990 or 877/522–2354* ⊕*www.trianglejeeprental.com*) rents four-wheel-drive vehicles for about $145 a day.

ICE SKATING

At the Kendall Mountain Recreation Area, the **Silverton Town Rink** (☒*14th St.* ☎*970/387–5522*) lets you skate for free, weather permitting. You can rent skates at the visitor center.

NORDIC
SKIING

The local snowmobile club grooms a cross-country skiing and snow-shoeing loop completely around Silverton, so the route is flat, easy, and safe. Molas Pass, 6 mi south of Silverton on U.S. 550, offers a variety of Nordic routes, from easy half-milers in broad valleys to longer, more-demanding ascents.

St. Paul Lodge (✉*Box 463, Silverton 81433* ☎*970/387–5494*) is an incredible find for anyone enchanted by remote high country. Above 11,000 feet and about a half-hour ski-in from the summit of Red Mountain Pass between Ouray and Silverton, the lodge (a converted mining camp) provides access to a series of above–tree line bowls and basins. Included in the lodge rates are guide service (essential in this area), ski equipment, and telemark lessons, along with meals and lodging. Be prepared for rather primitive facilities.

9

WHERE TO STAY & EAT

$$ ✕**Handlebars.** As much a museum as an eatery, the restaurant is crammed with mining artifacts, odd antiques, and mounted animals— including a full-grown elk. Don't pass up the huge platter of baby back ribs basted with the restaurant's own barbecue sauce (bottles of sauce are also for sale). The hearty menu also includes steaks, hamburgers, chicken, pasta, mashed potatoes, and more. On weekends the action heats up on the dance floor with rock and country bands. ⊠*117 13th St.* ☎*970/387–5395* ▭*D, MC, V* ☉*Closed Nov.–Apr.*

$ ✕**Avalanche Coffee House.** This warm and cozy hangout is the place for delicious coffees, freshly made baked goods, and a chance to mingle with the locals. House-made deli sandwiches, soups, and quiches make for filling lunches. More-substantial fare is served Friday and Saturday evenings. Happy hour starts at 5:30, so be sure to grab your seat at the bar. ⊠*1067 Blair St.* ☎*970/387–5282* ▭*No credit cards* ☉*Closed Mon. No dinner Sun.–Thurs.*

$$ ▦**Animas B&B at Wingate House.** Owner Judy Graham, a landscape artist, adorns the walls of this 1886 inn with her own work and family photos dating from the Civil War. The library of books on hand are souvenirs of her travels. The effect is both sophisticated and homey. The breezy front porch overlooks Kendall Mountain, a majestic "Thirteener" (a mountain higher than 13,000 feet). Large, sunny rooms are filled with antiques and beds piled with down pillows and comforters. A well-set dining room table is the scene of breakfast, with home-baked treats. **Pros:** terrific views, comfortable rooms. **Con:** two rooms have a shared bath. ⊠*1045 Snowden St., 81433* ☎*970/387–5520* ⊕*www. wingatehouse.com* ⤺*5 rooms, 3 with bath* ⌂*In-room: no a/c, no TV. In hotel: no elevator, some pets allowed, no-smoking rooms* ▭*MC, V* ❖*CP.*

$$ ▦**Wyman Hotel & Inn.** Listed on the National Register of Historic Places, this wonderful red-sandstone building dates from 1902. It has 24-inch-thick walls, so the builders obviously expected it to last a while. The attractive rooms, many with beautiful arched windows, are filled with period antiques. Five have whirlpool tubs, where you can soak after a morning on the slopes. In summer you can opt to stay in a romantically refurbished caboose with private hot tub. Full breakfast and afternoon tea are included. **Pros:** quiet, centrally located, updated amenities. **Con:** the walls are so thick, sometimes it's too quiet. ⊠*1371 Greene St., 81433* ☎*970/387–5372 or 800/609–7845* ⊕*www.thewyman.com* ⤺*13 rooms, 4 suites* ⌂*In-room: no a/c, DVD (some), VCR, Wi-Fi. In-hotel: no elevator, no-smoking rooms* ▭*AE, D, MC, V* ❖*BP.*

THE ARTS

In the Miners Union Theatre, **A Theatre Group** (⊠*1069 Greene St.* ☎*970/387–5337 or 800/752–4494*) stages a summer repertory season running from May to October and a winter season lasting from December to April.

SHOPPING

Remember that the majority of Silverton's retail establishments only operate in the months when the Durango & Silverton Narrow Gauge Railroad is operating, May to October.

Blair Street Emporium (⊠ *1147 Blair St.* ☎*970/387–5323*) specializes in all manner of Christmas ornaments, lights, and decorations.The gift shop **My Favorite Things** (⊠*1145 Greene St.* ☎*970/387–5643*) stocks porcelain dolls, antique jewelry, and romantic, lacy wearables.

EN ROUTE The tortuous route between Silverton and Purgatory includes a dizzying series of switchbacks as it climbs over Coal Bank Pass and Molas Pass and past splendid views of the Grand Turks, the Needles Range, and Crater Lake. This is prime mountain-biking and four-wheeling territory.

PURGATORY

20 mi south of Silverton via U.S. 550; 25 mi north of Durango via U.S. 550.

North of the U.S. 160 and U.S. 550 junction are two well-known recreational playgrounds: the ravishing golf course and development at the Lodge at Tamarron, and Purgatory at Durango Mountain Resort. Purgatory, as everyone still calls this ski area despite its recent name change, is about as down-home as a ski resort can get. The clientele includes cowboys, families, and college students on break.

DOWNHILL SKIING & SNOWBOARDING

★ **Purgatory at Durango Mountain Resort** (formerly known simply as Purgatory) has plenty of intermediate runs and glade and tree skiing. What's unique about Purgatory is its stepped terrain: lots of humps and dips and steep pitches followed by virtual flats. This trail profile makes it easier for skiers and snowboarders to stay in control (or simply get their legs back under them after they've conquered a section a little steeper than they might be accustomed to). A great powder day on the mountain's backside will convince anyone that Purgatory isn't just "Pleasant Ridge," as it's somewhat condescendingly known in Crested Butte and Telluride.

FACILITIES 2,029-foot vertical drop; 1,200 skiable acres; 23% beginner, 51% intermediate, 26% advanced; 1 high-speed 6-passenger chair, 1 high-speed quad chair, 4 triple chairs, 3 double chairs, 1 surface lift, and 1 moving carpet (beginners' lift).

LESSONS & PROGRAMS Durango Mountain Resort's **Adult Adventure School** (☎*970/385–2149*) offers 2½-hour group lessons for everyone from newcomers to experts at 9:45 AM and 1:15 PM each day during the season. The cost is $49. There are also daily lessons in snow biking and twice-monthly lessons in telemark skiing.

Teaching children to ski or snowboard is a cinch at **Kids Mountain Adventure** (☎970/385–2149). There are three age-appropriate classes for kids 3 to 12 years old. There's also child care for those between two months and three years. A full day costs $87.

LIFT TICKETS　The at-the-window rates are $60 to $65 for a one-day lift ticket. A Guaranteed to Green ski package, which means that they promise you will be able to ski from top to bottom on a green run by the end of it, is a good deal for beginner skiers, as it combines a half-day morning lesson with an all-day lift ticket. The cost is $165.

RENTALS　**Bubba's Boards** (✉ *Village Plaza* ☎970/259–7377 or 866/860–7377) is Durango Mountain Resort's full-service snowboard shop. Rentals begin at $29 per day.

Performance Peak (☎970/247–9000) rents top-of-the-line demo and retail skis and boots from K2, Salomon, Dynastar, Volkl, Nordica, Dolomite, and Rossignol; full packages (skis, boots, and poles) begin at $39. Snowshoe rentals are $12. The shop also offers custom boot fitting, ski tuning, and equipment repair.

Purgatory Rentals (✉ *Village Center* ☎970/385–2182) offers skis, boots, and poles, as well as other equipment. Rates begin at $21 per day for the basic package, rising to $29 for the high-performance package.

OTHER SPORTS & THE OUTDOORS

GOLF　**Glacier Club at Tamarron.** Near the spectacular Hermosa Cliffs, this splendid course has 27 holes of scenic masters-level golf. This club, part of the Lodge at Tamarron, is considered one of the country's top resort courses. ✉40290 U.S. 550 ☎970/375–8300 or 866/375–8300 ⊕ *www.theglacierclub.com* ✍ *Reservations essential* ⛳ *18 holes. Yards: 6,885/5,330. Par: 72/72. Green Fee: $69/$125.*

Snowmobile Adventures (✉ *Village Center* ☎970/247–9000 or 970/385–2110) offers guided snowmobile tours on more than 60 mi of nearby trails.

WHERE TO STAY & EAT

★ $$$　✕ **Sow's Ear.** It's a toss-up between the Ore House in downtown Durango and this watering hole in the Silverpick Lodge for the area's "best steak house" award. The Sow's Ear has the edge, though, for its great views of the mountain. If you prefer more action, there's also an open kitchen in the dining area where you can view your meal being prepared. The mouthwatering, fresh-baked jalapeño-cheese rolls and honey-wheat rolls, and creative entrées such as blackened filet mignon are a few more reasons Sow's Ear leads the pack. Complement your meal with a selection from their extensive domestic wine list. ✉48475 U.S. 550 ☎970/247–3527 ✍ *Reservations essential* ▤ AE, D, MC, V ⊘ *Closed mid-Mar.–Memorial Day and Labor Day–mid-Dec.*

$　✕ **Olde Schoolhouse Cafe & Saloon.** The pizza and calzones are made with homemade dough and fresh ingredients, and the local SKA brew is on tap in this funky building, now far astray from its scholarly roots. There are darts, a pool table, even an old shuffleboard, and later in the evening this becomes the local hangout for conversation and relaxation. ✉46778 Hwy. 550, Durango ☎970/259–2257 ▤MC, V ⦵No lunch weekdays.

$$$ ⊞**Lodge at Tamarron.** This handsome lodge, on 750 acres surrounded by the San Juan National Forest, fits in beautifully with the natural environment. The sprawling main lodge seems to be an extension of the nearby Hermosa Cliffs. The well-appointed rooms are a blend of frontier architecture and Southwestern decor, and nearly all feature a fireplace, a full kitchen, and a private terrace. The lodge is famed for the Glacier Club at Tamarron, and tennis and horseback riding are also popular pastimes. **Pros:** ability to cook your own food, stunning setting, multiple activities make it a great family spot. **Con:** pricey. ✛ 18 mi north of Durango on U.S. 550 ✍Drawer 3131, 81302 ☎970/259–2000, 800/982–6103, or 800/525–0892 ⊕www.lodgeattamarron.com ⟿412 rooms ⚷In-hotel: 2 restaurants, bar, golf course, tennis courts, pool, spa, no-smoking rooms ▤AE, D, DC, MC, V.

$$ ⊞**Purgatory Village Hotel at Durango Mountain Resort.** This comfortable slope-side lodging has generously proportioned rooms decorated with contemporary furnishings. If you want a bit of pampering, the one-and two-bedroom condos have wood-burning fireplaces and whirlpool baths. **Pros:** slope-side location, good restaurants, reasonable price considering locale. **Con:** in season, the hotel is very chaotic. ✉1 Skier Pl., 81302 ☎970/385–2100 or 800/982–6103 ⊕www.durangomountain-resort.com ⟿133 rooms ⚷In-room: no a/c, kitchen (some). In-hotel: 2 restaurants, bar, pool, public Wi-Fi, no-smoking rooms ▤AE, D, MC, V.

CONDOS There are 110 apartments at **Cascade Village** (✉50827 U.S. 550, Purgatory 81301 ☎970/259–3500 or 800/982–6103), about 1.5 mi north of the ski area.

NIGHTLIFE

Check out **Purgy's Pub** (✉Village Center ☎970/247–9000), which attracts a lively, youthful crowd and hosts bands on weekends.

SHOPPING

Honeyville (✉33633 U.S. 550, Hermosa ☎800/676–7690) south of Durango Mountain Resort, sells jams, jellies (try the chokecherry), condiments, and, of course, honey. You can watch how the bees go about their work in glass hives and listen to a lecture by a fully garbed beekeeper.

EN ROUTE U.S. 550 toward Durango parallels the Animas River and the tracks of Durango & Silverton Narrow Gauge Railroad. Scenes from *Butch Cassidy and the Sundance Kid* were filmed in this canyon.

DURANGO

25 mi south of Purgatory via U.S. 550; 45 mi east of Cortez via U.S. 160; 62 mi west of Pagosa Springs via U.S. 160.

Wisecracking Will Rogers had this to say about Durango: "It's out of the way and glad of it." His statement is a bit unfair, considering that as a railroad town Durango has always been a cultural crossroads and melting pot (as well as a place to raise hell). Laid out at 6,500 feet along the winding Animas River, with the San Juan Mountains as backdrop, the town was founded in 1879 by General William Palmer, president of the all-powerful Denver & Rio Grande Railroad, when nearby Animas City haughtily refused to donate land for a depot. Within a decade Durango had completely absorbed its rival. The booming town quickly became the region's main metropolis and a gateway to the Southwest. A walking tour of the historic downtown bears eloquent witness to Durango's prosperity during the late 19th century. The northern end of Main Avenue offers the usual assortment of cheap motels and fast-food outlets, all evidence of Durango's present status as the major hub for tourism in the area.

The intersection of 13th Avenue and Main Avenue (locals also refer to it as Main Street) marks the northern edge of Durango's **National Historic District**. Old-fashioned streetlights line the streets, casting a warm glow on the elegant Victorians now filled with upscale galleries, restaurants, and the occasional factory outlet store. The three-story sandstone **Newman Building** (⊠ *8th St. and Main Ave.*) is one of the elegant edifices restored to their original grandeur. Dating from 1887, the **Strater Hotel** (⊠ *7th St. and Main Ave.*) is a reminder of when this town was a stop for many people headed west. Awash in flocked wallpaper and lace, the hotel's Diamond Belle Saloon is dominated by a gilt-and-mahogany bar. A player piano and scantily clad waitresses call to mind an old-time honky-tonk. The **Durango Depot** (⊠ *4th St. and Main Ave.*), dating from 1882, is a must for those who dream of riding the rails.

The **3rd Avenue National Historic District** (known simply as "The Boulevard"), two blocks east of Main Avenue, contains several Victorian residences, ranging from the imposing mansions built by railroad barons to more-modest variations erected by well-to-do merchants. The hodgepodge of styles veers from Greek revival to Gothic Revival to Queen Anne to Spanish Colonial and Mission designs.

The most entertaining way to relive the halcyon days of the Old West is to take a ride on the **Durango & Silverton Narrow Gauge Railroad,** a nine-hour, round-trip journey along the 45-mi railway to Silverton. You'll travel in comfort in lovingly restored coaches or in the open-air cars called gondolas as you listen to the train's shrill whistle as it chugs along. You get a good look at the Animas Valley, which in some parts is broad and green and in others is narrow and rimmed with rock. The train runs from mid-May to late October, with four departures daily between June and August and one daily at other times. A shorter excursion—to Cascade Canyon—is available in winter. ⊠ *479 Main Ave.* ☎ *970/247–2733 or 888/872–4607* ⊕ *www.durangotrain.com* 🎫 *$65.*

FodorsChoice ★

About 7 mi north of Durango, **Trimble Hot Springs** is a great place to soak your aching bones, especially if you've been doing some hiking. The complex includes an Olympic-size swimming pool and three natural mineral pools ranging from 83°F to 107°F. Massage and spa treatments are also available. ✉ *County Rd. 203 off U.S. 550* ☎ *970/247–0212* ⊕ *www.trimblehotsprings.com* 🎫 *$15* ⏱ *June–Aug., daily 8 AM–11 PM; Sept.–May, daily 10–10.*

High on a mesa southeast of Durango, **Fort Lewis College** brings a bit of culture to the Four Corners area. The Center for Southwest Studies gallery has rotating exhibitions of contemporary artists, Native American treasures, and Western cultural collections. **Art Gallery** (⏱ *Weekdays 10–4*) is a beautifully lighted contemporary space showcasing the creations of a creative and diverse student body. ✉ *1000 Rim Dr.* ☎ *970/247-7184* ⊕ *www.fortlewis.edu.*

> ## LEAP OF FAKE
>
> The famous scene in the 1969 movie *Butch Cassidy and the Sundance Kid,* where Paul Newman and Robert Redford—playing Cassidy and the Kid, respectively—jump off a 30-foot cliff, was shot 13 mi north of Durango at Baker's Bridge. It draws visitors to the site to see the dramatic drop, but some are disappointed to find that the camera angle and much manipulation of the rapids conspired to make it seem more dangerous. In reality, the actors were shot jumping onto a platform 6 feet down, and the real jump into the Animas River was done by stuntmen. The river shot was taken later in California.

SPORTS & THE OUTDOORS

Contact the rangers of the **San Juan National Forest** (✉ *15 Burnett Ct., 80301* ☎ *970/247-4874* ⊕ *www.fs.fed.us/r2/sanjuan*) for information about rock climbing and other outdoor activities in the San Juan Mountains.

The **San Juan Public Lands Center** (✉ *15 Burnett Ct., 80301* ☎ *970/247-4874* ⏱ *Weekdays 8–5*) gives out information on hiking, fishing, and camping, as well as cross-country skiing, snowshoeing, and snowmobile routes. This office also stocks maps and guidebooks.

BICYCLING With a healthy college population and a generally mild climate, Durango is extremely bike friendly and a destination for single-track enthusiasts. Many locals consider bikes to be their main form of transportation. The bike lobby is active, the trail system is well developed, and mountain biking is a particularly popular recreational activity.

Get an overview of the scene at ⊕ *www.trails2000.org*, home of the very active local advocacy trail group. Although everybody in town seems to be an expert, a good place to go for advice and maps before you head off is **Mountain Bike Specialists** (✉ *949 Main Ave.* ☎ *970/247-4066* ⊕ *www.mountainbikespecialists.com*), where you can also rent a bike, arrange a tour, or get hooked up with the trail of your dreams.

9

To get around town, start with the **Animas River Trail,** which parallels the river from North City Park to the south part of town along a 5-mi route. It is the main artery linking up with other trail systems. With its many access points, you might consider it rather than driving around town, especially on a busy weekend.

Everybody likes the **Hermosa Creek Trail,** an intermediate-to-difficult 20-mi jaunt. It has a couple of steep spots and switchbacks, but it rolls through open meadows, towering aspen and pine forests, and along the sides of mountains before dumping out in a parking lot in Hermosa, 9 mi north of Durango. Don't try it too early in the season while the snow is melting because there are two creek crossings. Starting at the same spot as the Hermosa Creek Trail is the Lime Creek Trail, which will test you as it mostly follows the old stage road; it covers 11 mi from Purgatory to Silverton. ✛ *Trailhead: Take Hwy. 550 north 28 mi from Durango. Look for parking lot on right, north of Cascade Village near Purgatory..*

CLIMBING **SouthWest Adventure Guides** (⊠ *1205 Camino del Rio* ☎ *970/259–0370 or 800/642–5389* ⊕ *www.mtnguide.net*) is a climbing school that takes you to some of the area's most beautiful peaks. Other programs include rock climbing, ice climbing, Nordic skiing, snowshoeing, and mountaineering.

FISHING In business since 1983, **Duranglers** (⊠ *923 Main Ave.* ☎ *970/385–4081 or 888/347–4346* ⊕ *www.duranglers.com*) sells rods and reels, gives fly-fishing lessons, and runs custom trips to top fishing spots in the area, including the San Juan River in nearby northern New Mexico.

GOLF **Dalton Ranch Golf Club.** About 6 mi north of Durango, Dalton Ranch is a Ken Dye–designed 18-hole championship course with inspiring panoramas of red-rock cliffs. Dalton's Grill has become a popular hangout for locals who like watching the resident elk herd take its afternoon stroll, especially in late fall and winter. The golf season here is early April to late October, weather permitting. ⊠ *589 County Rd. 252, off U.S. 550* ☎ *970/247–8774* ⊕ *www.daltonranch.com* ⚐ *Reservations essential* 🏌 *18 holes. Yards: 6,934/5,539. Par: 72/72. Green Fee: $59–$89.*

Hillcrest Golf Course. Hillcrest is an 18-hole public course perched on a mesa near the campus of Fort Lewis College. The course is open from February to December, weather permitting. ⊠ *2300 Rim Dr.* ☎ *970/247–1499* ⚐ *Reservations essential* 🏌 *18 holes. Yards: 6,838/5,252. Par: 71/71. Green Fee: $30.*

HIKING Hiking trails are ubiquitous around Durango. Many trailheads around the edges of town lead to backcountry settings, and the San Juan Forest has plenty of mind-boggling walks and trails for those who want to backpack into wilderness. Before you go, check the local hiking organization, **Trails2000** (⊕ *www.trails2000.org*) for directions, information, and news about hiking in and around Durango.

If you're cramped for time, try the 0.66-mi **Animas View Overlook Trail** for spectacular views. It passes interpretive signs on geology, history, and flora before bringing you to a precipice with an unparalled view of the valley in which Durango sits and the Needle Mountains. It's the only wheelchair-accessible trail in the area, and you can picnic there, too.

The **Lion's Den Trail** hooks up with the **Chapman Hill Trail** west of Fort Lewis College for a nice moderate hike, climbing switchbacks that take you away from city bustle and hook up with the **Rim Trail.**

Fodor'sChoice ★ The **Colorado Trail** starts not far north of Durango and goes all the way to Denver. Though you're not obliged to go that far, just a few miles in and out will give you a taste of this epic trail, which winds through mountain ranges and high passes and some of the most amazing scenery in any mountains. ⊕ *www.coloradotrail.org.*

HORSEBACK RIDING **Southfork Stables & Outfitters** (⊠ *28481 U.S. 160* ☎ *970/259–4871*) offers guided trail rides in summer and one-hour trips to view an elk herd in winter. You can also take part in cattle drives.

RAFTING **Durango Rivertrippers** (⊠ *720 Main Ave.* ☎ *970/259–0289 or 800/292–2885* ⊕ *www.durangorivertrippers.com*) runs two- and four-hour trips down the Animas River, as well as 2- to 10-day wilderness expeditions on the Dolores River.

WHERE TO EAT

$$$$ ✕ **Chez Grand-mère.** It's hard to decide whether to work your way through the à la carte menu or go with a prix-fixe dinner. Either way, the French and Belgian dishes served in the sweet dining room made to look, yes, just like Grandma's, are as comforting as you'd expect; try the succulent crab cakes, grilled squab, roast lamb, or lobster and shrimp sausages. The chef makes some of the ingredients himself, like the vinegar for the vinaigrettes, forages for local mushrooms, and makes a point of tracking down top-quality produce and meats. ⊠ *3 Depot Pl.* ☎ *970/247–7979* ⚏ *Reservations essential* ⊟ *AE, D, MC, V* ⊘ *Closed Sun. and Mon. No lunch.*

$$$$ ✕ **Ore House.** Durango is a meat-and-potatoes kind of town, and this is Durango's idea of a steak house. The aroma of beef smacks you in the face as you walk past. This local favorite serves enormous slabs of aged Angus that are hand cut daily. If you're watching your cholesterol, better "steer" clear. ⊠ *147 E. College Dr.* ☎ *970/247–5707* ⊟ *D, MC, V.*

$$$$ ✕ **Red Snapper.** If you're in the mood for fresh fish, head to this congenial spot, which is full of saltwater aquariums. Try the oysters Durango, with jack cheese and salsa; salmon Wellington; or snapper Monterey, with jack cheese and tarragon. Delicious steaks and prime rib are also available. The salad bar is enormous. ⊠ *144 E. 9th St.* ☎ *970/259–3417* ⊟ *AE, MC, V* ⊘ *No lunch weekends.*

$$$ ✕ **Ariano's Northern Italian Restaurant.** In a dimly lighted room plastered with local art, this northern Italian restaurant offers a selection of pastas that are made fresh daily. Try the veal scaloppine with fresh sage and garlic or the fettuccine Alfredo. ⊠ *150 E. College Dr.* ☎ *970/247–8146* ⊟ *AE, D, DC, MC, V* ⊘ *No lunch.*

$$$ ✕ **East by Southwest.** Pan-Asian food with a strong Japanese bent gets a bit of a Latin treatment in this snazzy but comfortable space. Steaks (using Kobe beef), sushi and sashimi, tempura, and other traditional

9

dishes are attractively presented and layered with complementary flavors; the seven-course tasting menu is a smart way to try it all. The sake, beer, and wine selections are well varied, and the tea and tonic bar is fun, too. ✉ *160 E. College Dr.* ☎ *970/247–5533* ⏱ *No lunch Sun.*

$$ ✕ **Carver's Bakery & Brew Pub.** The "Brews Brothers," Bill and Jim Carver, have about eight beers on tap at any given time, including such flavors as Raspberry Wheat Ale, Jackrabbit Pale Ale, and Colorado Trail Nut Brown Ale. If you're feeling peckish, try one of the bread bowls filled with soup or salad. There's a patio out back where you can soak up the sun. From breakfast to the wee hours, the place is always hopping. ✉ *1022 Main Ave.* ☎ *970/259–2545* ⚑ *Reservations not accepted* ▤ *AE, D, MC, V.*

$$ ✕ **Cyprus Café.** In warm weather, sit on the patio to listen to live jazz, and the rest of the time cozy up to your fellow diners in this tiny space. Mediterranean food receives upscale treatment here, from chicken breasts stuffed with artichokes, feta, and mint to rigatoni layered with shrimp, spinach, and ricotta to a salt-roasted duck that makes your mouth water when it hits the table. The wine list is small, eclectic, and reasonably priced. Lunch is also interesting; try the wild salmon with caramelized onions or chicken sausage with fresh mozzarella sandwiches. ✉ *725 E. 2nd Ave.* ☎ *970/385–6884* ▤ *AE, D, MC, V.*

$$ ✕ **Ken & Sue's Place.** This might well be Durango's favorite restaurant. Locals are wild for the artfully prepared contemporary cuisine enlivened with a light touch of Asian and Southwestern accents. Try the pistachio nut–crusted grouper with vanilla-rum butter, or lemon-pepper linguine. ✉ *636 Main Ave.* ☎ *970/385–1810* ▤ *AE, D, DC, MC, V* ⏱ *No lunch weekends.*

$ ✕ **Brickhouse Cafe & Coffee Bar.** Great lattes await at this popular little place set in a restored historic house with wonderful landscaping. Don't miss the malted buttermilk waffles, pigs in a blanket, or big burgers. Breakfast and lunch are served all day. ✉ *1849 Main Ave.* ☎ *970/247–3760* ▤ *AE, D, MC.*

$ ✕ **Olde Tymer's Café.** If you're longing to meet a local, look no farther than the bustling Olde Tymer's, located in a beautiful old building with an inviting patio in the back. The hamburger is a huge specimen on a fat, fresh bun, and folks swear by the piled-high salads and sandwiches. ✉ *100 Main Ave.* ☎ *970/259–2990* ▤ *AE, D, MC, V.*

WHERE TO STAY

$$$

Fodor'sChoice

★

▥ **Strater Hotel.** The grand dame of Durango's hotels opened for business in 1887, and a loving restoration has returned her luster. Inside, the Diamond Belle Saloon glitters with crystal chandeliers, rustic oak beams, and plush velvety curtains. The individually decorated rooms are exquisite: after all, the hotel owns the country's largest collection of Victorian walnut antiques and has its own wood-carving shop to create exact period reproductions. Your room might have entertained Butch Cassidy, Louis L'Amour (he wrote *The Sacketts* here), Francis Ford Coppola, John Kennedy, or Marilyn Monroe (the latter two stayed here at separate times). **Pros:** location right in the thick of things, space has Old West feel, they will safely store your mountain bike for you. **Con:** when the bar downstairs gets going, rooms right above it get no peace. ✉*699 Main Ave., 81301* ☎*970/247–4431 or 800/247–4431* ⊕*www.strater.com* ☞*93 rooms* ⏾*In-room: dial-up, Wi-Fi (some). In-hotel: restaurant, room service, bar, no-smoking rooms* ⊟*AE, D, DC, MC, V* ⦿*CP.*

$$ ⚏**Apple Orchard Inn.** About 8 mi from downtown Durango, this little gem sits on 5 acres in the lush Animas Valley. The main house and six cottages surround a flower-bedecked pond, complete with geese. Cherrywood antiques, fluffy feather beds, and handcrafted armoires add a graceful touch to the handsome rooms. In the evening, relax on your cottage swing, enjoying views of the surrounding cliffs. The owners' experience at European cooking schools is evident in the breakfasts— and in the "train cookies" sometimes sent along with guests who make the journey to Silverton. **Pros:** inspiring views, off the beaten path, cottages are intimate and romantic. **Con:** not right in town. ✉*7758 County Rd. 203, 81301* ☎*970/247–0751 or 800/426–0751* ⊕*www.appleorchardinn.com* ☞*4 rooms, 6 cottages* ⏾*In-room: no a/c, VCR (some). In-hotel: no elevator, no-smoking rooms* ⊟*D, MC, V* ⦿*BP.*

$$ ⚏**General Palmer Hotel.** Named after William Jackson Palmer, the owner of the Denver & Rio Grande Railroad and the founder of Durango, the 1898 building has been faithfully restored, giving it a clean, bright look. Period furniture and Victorian touches reinforce the historical feel, and the library and "teddy bear room" are quiet areas for relaxing. The beds are poster, brass, or pewter, and the rooms are quaint without being cutesy. Cookies, coffee, and tea are always available in the lobby, and continental breakfast with homemade muffins is included. **Pros:** nicely restored lodging, rooms are quiet, top-notch service. **Con:** pricey in season. ✉*567 Main Ave., 81301* ☎*970/247–4747 or 800/523–3358* ⊕*generalpalmerhotel.com* ☞*39 rooms, 4 suites* ⏾*In-room: safe, dial-up. In-hotel: concierge, no-smoking rooms* ⊟*AE, D, DC, MC, V.*

★ **$$** ⚏**New Rochester Hotel.** This one-time flophouse is funky yet chic, thanks to the mother-and-son team of Diane and Kirk Komick, who rescued some of the original furnishings. Marquee-lighted movie posters from Hollywood Westerns line the airy hallways, and steamer trunks, hand-painted settees, wagon-wheel chandeliers, and fluffy quilts in the rooms contribute to a laid-back retro vibe. Windows from Denver & Rio Grande Railroad carriages convert the back porch into a parlor car, and gas lamps add a warm glow to the courtyard. A full gourmet breakfast, with plenty of coffee and several varieties of tempting mini-muffins and scones is included. The owners also run the nearby Leland House B&B. **Pros:** inviting atmosphere, large rooms. **Con:** can be noisy. ✉*726 E. 2nd Ave., 81301* ☎*970/385–1920 or 800/664–1920* ⊕*www.rochesterhotel.com* ☞*13 rooms, 1 suite* ⏾*In-hotel: restaurant, no elevator, some pets allowed, no-smoking rooms* ⊟*MC, V* ⦿*BP.*

$ ⚏**Comfort Inn.** This is one of the nicer budget properties along Durango's strip, because it's clean, comfortable, and has sizable rooms. The hot tubs are nice after a day on the trails. **Pros:** spacious rooms, reasonable rates. **Con:** typical chain feel. ✉*2930 N. Main Ave., 81301* ☎*970/259–5373 or 800/532–7112* ☞*48 rooms* ⏾*In room: Internet, Wi-Fi. In-hotel: pool, some pets allowed, no-smoking rooms* ⊟*AE, D, DC, MC, V* ⦿*CP.*

9

GUEST RANCH ⚏**Wilderness Trails Ranch.** It's only an hour's drive to Durango, but this
$$$$ family-owned and -operated guest ranch, nestled in the Upper Pine
River valley, on the borders of the Piedra and Weminuche wilderness
areas, might as well be a lifetime away. The riding programs are the
main attraction here; guests are individually matched with horses to
fit their experience and comfort level. Other activities include hiking,
rafting, waterskiing, and fishing. Cozy log cabins, complete with gas
stoves, modern baths, and terry robes, are arranged in a semicircle
around the main lodge, campfire ring, and pool; Cordon Bleu–trained
chefs are at the helm in the dining room, which has views of the mountains and busy hummingbird feeders through large picture windows.
Pros: very friendly owners, family friendly, gorgeous setting. **Con:**
minimum stay required. ⊠*23486 County Rd. 501, Bayfield 81122*
☎*970/247–0722 or 800/527–2624* ⊕*www.wildernesstrails.com*
⤳*10 cabins* ♻*In-room: no phone, refrigerator, no TV. In-hotel: bar,
pool, no elevator, children's programs (ages 3–17), no-smoking rooms*
⊟*D, MC, V* ⊗*Closed Oct.–May* ¶⃝*FAP.*

NIGHTLIFE & THE ARTS

THE ARTS The **Diamond Circle Theater** (⊠*699 Main Ave.* ☎*970/247–3400*) stages
rip-roaring melodramas all summer long. The **Durango Lively Arts Co.**
(⊠*802 2nd Ave.* ☎*970/259–2606*) presents fine community theater
productions. The **Fort Lewis College Community Concert Hall** is a modern
600-seat auditorium that hosts local, regional, and touring performers.
The college's outdoor amphitheater is the setting for the **Durango Shakespeare Festival** (☎*970/247–7657* ⊕*www.durangoconcerts.com*).

BARS & CLUBS Even though it opened more than a century ago, the hottest spot in
town is still the **Diamond Belle Saloon** (⊠*699 Main Ave.* ☎*970/247–
4431*). The honky-tonk player piano and waitresses dressed as 1880s
saloon girls pack them in to this spot in the Strater Hotel. **Lady Fal-
conburgh's Barley Exchange** (⊠*640 Main Ave.* ☎*970/382–9664*) is a
favorite with locals. The pub serves more than 140 types of beer.Taste
many fine brews, including True Blonde Ale, Mexican Logger Octo-
berfest, and Pinstripe Red Ale, at **Ska Brewery & Tasting Room** (⊠*545
Turner Dr.* ☎*970/247–5792* ⊕*www.skabrewing.com*). The Bodo Park
brewery is open from noon to 7 PM weekdays and from noon to 3 PM
on Saturday.

CASINOS About 25 mi southeast of Durango, the **Sky Ute Casino & Lodge** (⊠*14826
Hwy. 172, Ignacio* ☎*970/563–3000 or 800/876–7017* ⊕*www.sky-
utecasino.com*), offers limited-stakes gambling. There are 400 slot
machines and tables for blackjack, poker, and bingo. Call for free
shuttle service from Durango.

DINNER The **Bar D Chuckwagon** (⊠*8080 County Rd. 250, E. Animas Valley*
SHOWS ☎*970/247–5753 or 888/800–5753* ⊕*www.bardchuckwagon.com*)
serves up mouthwatering barbecued beef, beans, and biscuits. Many
people head to this spot 9 mi from Durango to hear the Bar D Wran-
glers sing.

SHOPPING

BOOKS **Maria's Bookshop** (✉*960 Main Ave.* ☎*970/247–1438* ⊕*www.marias-bookshop.com*) specializes in regional literature and nonfiction.

BOUTIQUES **Appaloosa Trading Co.** (✉*501 Main Ave.* ☎*970/259–1994* ⊕*www.appaloosadurango.com*) is one of the best venues for all things leather, from purses to saddles, hats to boots. The exotic belts are especially nice when paired with sterling silver buckles. The shop also sells locally produced weavings and other handicrafts.

GALLERIES The selection of arts and crafts from Mexico and elsewhere is remarkable at **Artesanos** (✉*700 E. 2nd Ave.* ☎*970/259–5755* ⊕*www.artesanosdesign.com*) **Dietz Market** (✉*26345 U.S. 160* ☎*970/259–5811 or 800/321–6069* ⊕*www.dietzmarket.com*) carries pottery, metalwork, candles, weavings, and foodstuffs, all celebrating the region. **Lime Berry** (✉ *925 Main Ave.* ☎*970/375–9199* ⊕*www.limeberryonline.com*) has an eclectic, fantastical mix of rugs, fine art, and home furnishings. **Toh-Atin Gallery** (✉ *145 W. 9th St.* ☎*970/247–8277 or 800/525–0384* ⊕*www.toh-atin.com*) is one of the best Native American galleries in Colorado, specializing in Navajo rugs and weavings. There's also a wide range of paintings, pottery, and prints.

PAGOSA SPRINGS

62 mi east of Durango via U.S. 160.

Although not a large town, Pagosa Springs has become a major center for outdoor sports. Hiking, biking, and cross-country skiing opportunities abound not far from the excellent ski area of Wolf Creek. It has no lodging facilities, so Pagosa Springs is a logical place to stay.

With water ranging in temperature from 84°F to 114°F, the **Springs Resort** is a great place to relax. There are 17 outdoor tubs, a Mediterranean-style bathhouse, private rooms for massage therapy and spa treatments, a mountain sports shop, and an organic café. ✉*165 Hot Springs Blvd.* ☎*800/225–0934* ⊕*pagosahotsprings.com* 🖭*$17* ⊙*June 12–Sept. 6, daily 7 AM–1 AM; Sept. 7–June 11, Sun.–Thurs. 7 AM–11 PM, Fri. and Sat. 7 AM–1 AM* 🖃*AE, D, DC, MC, V.*

DOWNHILL SKIING & SNOWBOARDING

With more than 450 average inches of snow annually, **Wolf Creek Ski Area** is Colorado's best-kept white-powder secret. It's set in 1,600 acres of Forest Service land in the San Juan Wilderness. The trails are designed to accommodate any level of ability and traverse every kind of ski terrain in ever-changing conditions, from wide-open bowls to steep glades, with a commanding view of remote valleys and towering peaks.

Because there are no overnight accommodations and it's a family-owned business, Wolf Creek has a reputation as a laid-back place for those with an aversion to lift lines and the faster-paced, better-known ski areas.

Arguably the best area stretches back to Horseshoe Bowl from the Waterfall area, serviced by the Alberta Lift. The more intrepid will want to climb the Knife Ridge Staircase to the more-demanding Knife Ridge Chutes. Just below is the groomed Sympatico, which runs down a gentler ridge and through dense forest below the Alberta Lift. The 50 trails run the gamut from wide-open bowls to steep glades.

Lodging options from rustic log cabins, bed-and-breakfasts, and motels in all price ranges are nearby along or off Highway 160: Creede, South Fork, and Monte Vista on the east and Pagosa Springs on the west. ⊠ *U.S. 160 at top of Wolf Creek Pass* ☎ *970/264–5629* ⊕ *www.wolf-creekski.com* ⊙ *Early Nov.–mid-Apr., daily 8:30–4.*

FACILITIES 1,604-foot vertical drop; 1,600 skiable acres; 20% beginner, 35% intermediate, 25% advanced, 20% expert; 1 quad, 2 triples, 2 doubles, 2 surface lifts.

LESSONS & **Wolf Creek Ski School** holds group lessons—$55 for four hours and
PROGRAMS $40 for two-hour sessions. First-day beginner packages (ages nine and up) are $47 ($57 snowboard). Private, one-hour lessons are $65 ($95 for two). Children over four can join the Wolf Pups program, which includes lift tickets and lunch. It's $45 for a half day, $55 for a full day.

LIFT TICKETS The walk-up rate is $48 for adults, $36 for half day, with three-day lift passes for $141.

RENTALS **Wolf Creek Ski Rental,** in the Sports Center Building across from the ticket office, rents skis and boards. Adult sets (skis, boots, poles) are $14–$31 and $18 for telemark. Boards are $26 with or without boots; boot rentals are $10.

OTHER SPORTS & THE OUTDOORS

GOLF **Pagosa Springs Golf Club.** The 27 championship holes here can be played in three combinations, essentially creating three 18-hole courses. A bonus is the gorgeous mountain scenery. The regular season runs from May 15 to October 15. Cart rental is $15 for 18 holes. Reservations are recommended during peak season. ⊠ *1 Pine Club Pl.* ☎ *970/731–4755* ⊕ *www.golfpagosa.com* ⅄ *27 holes. Yards: 5,074/7,228. Par: 71/72. Green Fee: $49–$79.*

HIKING Pagosa Springs sits in a wondrous landscape, and there's no better way to enjoy its isolated natural beauty than to experience it from a trail. Around here, trails pass through green forests and along cold mountain streams or mountain plateaus. Don't forget comfortable shoes, water, a map, and warm, wet-weather clothing—conditions can deteriorate quickly any month of the year.

If you aren't used to it, high altitude can catch you off guard. Drink plenty of water to help stave off the effects of altitude sickness—dizziness, shortness of breath, headache, and nausea. Slather on the sunscreen—it's easy to get sunburned up here. And, in summer, an early morning start is best, as afternoon thunderstorms are frequent and a danger above the tree line.

The **Piedra Falls Trail** is a leisurely half-hour, 1.2-mi stroll through the scenic landscape of the San Juan Mountains to the falls, which tumble down a narrow wedge cut through volcanic rocks and boulders. Up close, the falls are quite wet and from anywhere they are quite noisy. ⊠*Pagosa Ranger District, San Juan National Forest* ☎*970/264–2268* ⊕*www.fs.fed.us/r2/sanjuan.*

For serious hikers and backpackers, the **Continental Divide Trail** (⊕*www. cdtrail.org*) passes through 80 mi of the Weminuche Wilderness near the Wolf Creek summit.

WHERE TO STAY & EAT

¢ ✕**Elkhorn Café.** Filling and fiery Mexican fare (try the stuffed sopaipillas), as well as the usual burgers and chili fries, makes this a popular drop-in spot for locals. Fill up on a breakfast burrito before attacking the Wolf Creek bowls. ⊠*438 Main St.* ☎*970/264–2146* ▭*AE, D, MC, V.*

★ $-$$ ☷**Springs Resort.** Wrap yourself in a big white spa robe and head directly for the pools. Multiple soaking pools are terraced on several levels overlooking the San Juan River, and hotel guests have 24-hour access. Pick your temperature (from Tranquility to Lobster Pot), and relax. Rooms are standard but comfortable, and the larger configurations have lots of space and kitchenettes. Pros: proximity to hot springs, can cook your own meals. Con: service can be indifferent. ⊠*165 Hot Springs Blvd., 81147* ☎*800/225–0934* ⊕*www.pagosahotsprings.com* ⌂*46 rooms, 4 suites* ⚒*In-room: kitchen (some). In-hotel: pool, spa, some pets allowed, no-smoking rooms* ▭*D, MC, V.*

$ ☷**Davidson's Country Inn B&B.** This three-story log cabin is on a 32-acre working ranch in the middle of Colorado's San Juan Mountains. It's just north of Pagosa Springs, meaning you can stay here and still enjoy the slopes at the Wolf Creek Ski Area. Rooms are comfortable and crammed with family heirlooms and antiques. A full breakfast is included, although not for cabin guests. Pros: beautiful setting, family friendly, feels like a getaway. Con: a bit off the beaten path. ⊠*2763 U.S. 160, 81147* ☎*970/264–5863* ⊕*www.davidsonsinn.com* ⌂*1 cabin; 8 rooms, 4 with bath* ⚒*In-room: no a/c, no TV. In hotel: no elevator, no-smoking rooms* ▭*AE, D, MC, V* ⧆*BP.*

LAKE CITY & CREEDE

Lake City and Creede are in one of the most beautiful areas of Colorado. Both have colorful histories, and both offer excellent access to the many hiking and mountain-biking trails in the Gunnison National Forest and the Rio Grande National Forest. If you're driving through here, especially on the Silver Thread Scenic Byway or the Alpine Loop Scenic Byway, allow plenty of time because you'll want to keep stopping to take pictures of the surrounding mountains.

LAKE CITY

45 mi from Ouray via Alpine Loop Scenic Byway (summer only); 55 mi southwest of Gunnison via U.S. 50 and Rte. 149; 49 mi northwest of Creede via Rte. 149.

Lake City—with its collection of lacy gingerbread-trim houses and false-front Victorians—claims to have the largest National Historic District in Colorado. But the history the town is perhaps best known for is the lurid story of a notorious rogue named Alfred Packer. Packer led a party of six prospectors who camped near Lake San Cristobal during the winter of 1874. That spring, only Packer emerged from the mountains, claiming that after he had been deserted by the rest he subsisted on roots and rabbits. Soon after, a Ute traveling near Lake San Cristobal came across a grisly pile of human flesh and crushed skulls. Packer protested his innocence and fled, but a manhunt ensued. He was caught nine years later and sentenced to life in prison.

Lake City is the point of departure for superb hiking and fishing in the Gunnison National Forest. A geological phenomenon known as the Slumgullion Earthflow occurred some 800 years ago, when a mountainside sloughed off into the valley, blocking the Lake Fork of the Gunnison River and creating Lake San Cristobal, the state's second-largest natural lake. There's a scenic overlook along Highway 149, just south of town, with a sign explaining how this happened.

Lake City is the northern tip of the **Silver Thread Scenic Byway,** whose tail is 75 mi south in Southfork. The route, also called Highway 149, climbs over Slumgullion Pass from Lake City, overlooks the headwaters of the Rio Grande, and then drops down into the lush Rio Grande Valley. It's paved, so passenger cars have no problem getting through.

The inspiring **Alpine Loop Scenic Byway** joins Lake City with Ouray and Silverton. This part of the route is only open in summer and is not paved over Cinnamon Pass and Engineer Pass. However, this is heaven for four-wheelers, dizzily spiraling from 12,800-foot-high passes to gaping valleys.

SPORTS & THE OUTDOORS

FISHING Numerous high-alpine lakes and mountain streams make Lake City a fisherman's heaven. Lake San Cristobal is known around the region for its rainbow and brown trout. The Lake Fork of the Gunnison offers anglers rainbow and brook trout. Anyone older than 16 needs a Colorado fishing license, which you can obtain at local sporting-goods stores. See ⊕*www.wildlife.state.co.us/fishing* for more information. For information about guided trips, fishing licenses, or renting gear, check with **Dan's Fly Shop** (⊠*723 Gunnison Ave.* ☎*970/944–2281* ⊕*www.dansflyshop.com*).

HIKING There are lots of trails in this region, for varying abilities. Inquire locally for directions to the trailheads. Many are located on logging roads, so it's best to get the latest scoop on conditions from a resident. Ambitious hikers often overnight in Lake City to depart for three of Colorado's easier Fourteeners. Sunshine and Redcloud are generally climbed together, and Handies is across the valley. This means it is fairly easy for fit hikers to bag three Fourteeners in just two days.

WHERE TO STAY

$–$$ **Old Carson Inn.** This peaceful A-frame log cabin is nestled among stands of towering aspen and spruce. The seven rooms are brimming with rustic charm and are nicely appointed with down comforters. The country breakfast, served family style, should get you off to a good start. **Pros:** beautiful setting, excellent food, comfortable rooms. **Con:** not centrally located. *Box 144, County Rd. 30, 81235 ☎970/944–2511 or 800/294–0608 ⊕www.oldcarsoninn.com ⇨7 rooms ⌂In-room: no a/c, no TV. In-hotel: no elevator, no-smoking rooms ⊟AE, D, MC, V ⧾BP.*

CREEDE

105 mi south of Gunnison via U.S. 50 and Rte. 149; 52 mi southeast of Lake City via Rte. 149.

Creede once earned a reputation as Colorado's rowdiest mining camp and was immortalized in an evocative poem by the local newspaper editor, Cy Warman. "It's day all day in daytime," he wrote, "and there is no night in Creede." Every other building back then seems to have been a saloon or bordello. Bob Ford, who killed Jesse James, was himself gunned down here; other notorious residents included Calamity Jane and Bat Masterson. As delightful as the town is today, its location is even more glorious. About 96% of Mineral County is public land, including the nearby Weminuche Wilderness to the south and west, and the Wheeler Geological Area to the west, where the unusual rock formations resemble playful abstract sculptures or M. C. Escher creations. The Colorado Trail and the Continental Divide Trail, two of the country's most significant long-distance recreational paths, pass through Mineral County.

The **Underground Mining Museum** is housed in rooms that local miners blasted out of solid rock to commemorate the life of the hard-rock miner. Exhibits tracing the history of mining from 1892 to the 1960s teach you the difference between a *winze* (reinforced shaft leading straight down) and a *windlass* (hand-operated hoist). There are guided tours (at 10 and 2:30 daily), but you can also poke about on your own. After you've toured the mine, ask if you can look into the world's only underground firehouse, directly next door. If a volunteer firefighter is around, he'll gladly show you. Donations are welcome. ⊠*5034 Service Rd.* ☎*719/658–0811* ⊙*Memorial Day–Labor Day, daily 10–4; Labor Day–mid-Oct., Mon.–Sat. 10–3; mid Oct.–Memorial Day, weekdays 10–3* 🎫*$10 guided tour; $5 self-guided tour.*

The **Creede Museum,** occupying the original Denver & Rio Grande Railroad Depot, paints a vivid portrait of those rough-and-tumble days. ⊠*Main St. behind Basham Park* ☎*719/658–2374* 🎫*$1* ⊙*Memorial Day–Labor Day, Mon.–Sat. 10–5.*

9

WHERE TO STAY & EAT

¢–$ ✕ # 1 **Old Firehouse.** The decor in this casual Italian restaurant, ice-cream parlor, and Internet café reflects the building's heritage, with old-fashioned fire equipment, red ladders, and patches from fire departments around the country left by customers. Step up to the marble bar with its antique stained-glass back for a variety of ice-cream flavors. ⊠*123 N. Main St.* ☎*719/658–0212* ▤*D, MC, V* ⊗*Closed Mon. and Tues. in winter. No dinner.*

$ ⌂ **Antler's Rio Grande Lodge.** Dating to the late 1800s, this cozy lodge has rooms in the main building as well as rustic, secluded cabins along the river that are rented on a weekly basis. RV campsites are also available. The restaurant offers cuisine with a flamboyant flair—European dishes, island fare, and up to five nightly specials. The deck offers fine mountain views. **Pros:** rustic setting, solid restaurant, ability to cook your own meals in some of the cabins. **Con:** off the beaten path. ⊠*26222 Hwy. 149, Creede 81130* ☎*719/658–2423* ⊕*www.antlerslodge.com* ⤸*9 rooms, 14 cabins* ⌂*In-room: no a/c, kitchen (some), no TV. In-hotel: pool, no elevator, no-smoking rooms* ⊗*Closed Sept.–May* ▤*MC, V.*

$ ⌂ **Creede Hotel.** A relic of silver-mining days, this charming 1890s structure with a street-front balcony has been fully restored. Comfortable rooms offer the usual Victoriana. Excellent lunch and dinner, as well as complimentary breakfast, are served in the gracious dining room. **Pro:** in-town location. **Con:** town can be noisy at night. ⊠*120 Main St., 81130* ☎*719/658–2608* ⊕*www.creedehotel.com* ⤸*4 rooms* ⌂*In-room: no a/c, no TV. In-hotel: restaurant, no elevator, no-smoking rooms* ▤*AE, D, MC, V* ⎮⊚⎮*BP.*

$ ⌂ **Wason Ranch.** Enjoy tranquillity in a spacious riverside cottage or cozy cabin, both with kitchens. The original ranch house, dating from the 1870s, is a local landmark. Set on the Rio Grande, this sprawling spread affords miles of great fly-fishing. **Pros:** can cook your own food, beautiful river setting, great location. **Con:** off the beaten path. ⊠*19082 Hwy. 149, 81130* ☎*719/658–2413 or 877/927–6626* ⊕*www.wason-ranch.com* ⤸*9 cottages* ⌂*In-room: no a/c, kitchen (some), no TV (some). In-hotel: no elevator, no-smoking rooms* ▤*D, MC, V.*

THE ARTS

★ **Creede Repertory Theatre** (✉*Box 269, Creede 81130* ☎*866/658–2540* ⊕*www.creederep.org*), housed in the beautifully restored 1892 Creede Opera House, (⊠*124 N. Main St., 81130*) has a summer season of up to five shows a week. The fall season is known for productions of works by new playwrights. The theater adjoins the Creede Hotel on Main Street.

SHOPPING

San Juan Sports (⊠*102 S. Main St.* ☎*719/658–2359 or 888/658–0851*) specializes in sales and rentals of outdoor gear for hiking, biking, backpacking, camping, and winter backcountry expeditions. There are also good selections of maps, books, and the ubiquitous Colorado T-shirts.

EN ROUTE Continue along Route 149—the Silver Thread National Scenic Byway—on its beautiful journey east through South Fork. The road flirts with the Rio Grande and passes near the majestic North Clear Creek Falls.

You need a four-wheel-drive vehicle to navigate the 24 mi from Creede to the **Wheeler Geological Area,** distinguished by dramatically eroded pinnacles of volcanic tuff, but it's worth the drive through subalpine terrain and open parks until you reach the magical-looking spires, pinnacles, and domes. Once there, exploring is by foot or horseback only.

CORTEZ

45 mi west of Durango via U.S. 160.

The northern escarpment of Mesa Verde and the volcanic blisters of the La Plata Mountains to the west dominate sprawling Cortez. A series of Days Inns, Dairy Queens, and Best Westerns, the town has a layout that seems to have been determined by neon-sign and aluminum-siding salesmen of the 1950s. Hidden among these eyesores, however, are fine galleries and a host of secondhand shops that can yield surprising finds.

The exterior of the excellent **Cortez Cultural Center** has been painted to resemble the cliff dwellings of Mesa Verde. Exhibits focus on regional artists and artisans, the Ute Mountain branch of the Ute tribe, and various periods of Ancestral Puebloan culture. The Cultural Park at the Cortez Cultural Center contains an authentic Navajo hogan and a Ute tepee. The park itself is open 9 to 5; admission is free. Summer evenings there are Native American dances; sandpainting, rug weaving, and pottery-making demonstrations; theatrical events; and storytelling. ⌂*25 N. Market St.* ☎*970/565–1151* ⊕*www.cortezculturalcenter.org* ⌂*Free* ☉*June–Aug., Mon.–Sat. 10–10; Sept.–May, Mon.–Sat. 10–5.*

Visitor information is available at the **Colorado Welcome Center** (⌂*Cortez City Park, 928 E. Main St.* ☎*970/565–3414 or 800/253–1616* ⊕*www.mesaverdecountry.com*).

9

Native American guides at **Ute Mountain Tribal Park** lead grueling hikes into this dazzling repository of Ancestral Puebloan ruins, including the majestic Tree House cliff dwelling and enchanting Eagle's Nest petroglyphs. Tours usually start at the Ute Mountain Pottery Plant, 15 mi south of Cortez, on U.S. 491. Overnight camping can also be arranged. ⌂*Box 109, Towaoc 81334* ☎*970/565–3751* ⊕*www.utemountainute.com.*

Crow Canyon Archaeological Center promotes understanding and appreciation of Ancestral Puebloan culture by guiding visitors through excavations and botanical studies in the region. Also included in the weeklong programs are day trips to isolated canyon sites and hands-on lessons in weaving and pottery-making with Native American artisans. ⌂*23390 County Rd. K, 81321* ☎*970/565–8975 or 800/422–8975* ⊕*www.crowcanyon.org.*

A brass plaque set on a granite platform surrounded by four state flags marks the only spot where four states—Colorado, Arizona, Utah, and

New Mexico—meet at a single point. **Four Corners Monument** (✉*U.S. 160* ☎*No phone* ⊕*www.navajonationparks.org* 💲*$3 per vehicle* ☽*Sept.–May, daily 8–5; May–Sept., daily 7–8*) is photo-op country. Snacks and souvenirs are sold by Native Americans from rickety wood booths. To get here, travel south from Cortez on U.S. 160 for about 40 mi. You can't miss the signs.

OFF THE BEATEN PATH

Mud Creek Hogan. This endearing bit of classic American kitsch features more than a dozen enormous arrows stuck in the ground to mark the spot of a hokey trading post and museum, where you get the feeling that everything is for sale. The grounds are adorned with tepees and a giant plastic horse. Beside the shop is a re-creation of a frontier town, complete with saloon, hotel, bank, jail, and livery station. Don't breathe too hard or you'll blow the town over: The paper-thin buildings don't exist past the facades. ✉*East U.S. 160 from Mesa Verde National Park* ☎*970/533–7117.*

WHERE TO STAY & EAT

$$ ✕**Nero's.** Chef Richard Gurd's menu features a spicy "Cowboy" steak, and exotic lasagna and shrimp dishes, the most popular being shrimp with artichoke hearts in lemon sauce. The decor is Southwestern accented with regional art. ✉*303 W. Main St.* ☎*970/565–7366* ▭*AE, D, DC, MC, V.*

¢ ▣**Anasazi Motor Inn.** This is definitely the nicest motel on the strip, mostly because its air-conditioned rooms are spacious and pleasantly decorated in desert colors. The pool is a godsend after a long drive. **Pros:** clean, reasonably priced. **Con:** nothing fancy. ✉*640 S. Broadway, 81312* ☎*970/565–3773 or 800/972–6232* ☎*970/565–1027* ⊕*www.anasazimotorinn.com* ⇨*86 rooms* ♿*In-room: refrigerator (some). In-hotel: restaurant, bar, pool, no elevator, airport shuttle, no-smoking rooms* ▭*AE, D, DC, MC, V.*

NIGHTLIFE

At the base of the legendary Sleeping Ute Mountain, the state's largest casino rings with the sound of more than 500 slot machines. **Ute Mountain Casino** (✉*3 Weminuche Dr., Towaoc* ☎*970/565–8800* ⊕*www.utemountainute.com*) also draws the crowds for bingo, blackjack, and poker (both the live and the video versions). Near Four Corners, the casino is 11 mi south of Cortez on U.S. 160. If you're planning on staying awhile, Kuchu's restaurant and a full-service RV park are next door.

SHOPPING

Mesa Indian Trading Company (✉*27601 U.S. Hwy. 160* ☎*970/565–4492* ⊕*www.mesaverdepottery.com*) sells ceramics from most Southwestern tribes. **Clay Mesa Art Gallery and Studio** (✉*29 E. Main St.* ☎*970/565–1902*) showcases original works by local artists Richard St. John and Lesli Diane. **Notah Dineh Trading Company and Museum** (✉*345 W. Main St.* ☎*800/444–2024* ⊕*www.notahdineh.com*) specializes in rugs, hand-carved kachinas, cradleboards, baskets, beadwork, and silver jewelry. Be sure to stop in the free museum to see relics of the Old West, as well as a noteworthy rug in the Two Grey Hills pattern. **Ute Mountain**

Pottery Plant (⊠ *U.S.160 at U.S. 491, Towaoc* ☎ *970/565–8548*) invites you to watch the painstaking processes of molding, trimming, cleaning, painting, and glazing pottery before adjourning to the showroom so that you can buy pieces straight from the source.

DOLORES

10 mi northeast of Cortez via U.S. 160 and Rte. 145.

In 1968, state officials approved the construction of an irrigation dam across the Dolores River, forming the **McPhee Reservoir**, the second largest in the state. It draws fishermen looking to bag a variety of warm- and cold-water fish along its 50 mi of shoreline, which is surrounded by spectacular specimens of juniper and sage, as well as large stands of pinyon pine. Camping, a boat ramp, and a generous fish-cleaning station add to the appeal. A relatively easy mountain-bike trail and hiking in the area, as well as a small marina and panoramic views off the mesa of the San Juan National Forest make this a popular recreation area.

★ ☾ The **Anasazi Heritage Center** houses the finest artifacts culled from more than 1,500 excavations in the region. A full-scale replica of an Ancestral Puebloan pit-house dwelling illustrates how the people lived around AD 850. The first explorers to stumble upon Ancestral Puebloan ruins were the Spanish friars Dominguez and Escalante, who set out in 1776 from Santa Fe to find a safe route west to Monterey. The two major ruins at the Anasazi Heritage Center are named for the pair. The Dominguez site is the less impressive of the two, although it's of great archaeological interest because here scientists uncovered extremely rare evidence of a "high-status burial." The Escalante site is a 20-room masonry pueblo standing guard over the McPhee Reservoir. ⊠ *27501 Rte. 184,* ⊹ *3 mi west of Dolores* ☎ *970/882–4811* ⊕ *www.co.blm.gov/ahc* ⊠ *$3* ⊙ *Mar.–Oct., daily 9–5; Nov.–Feb., daily 0–4.*

The gentle rising hump to the southwest of town is **Sleeping Ute Mountain**, which resembles the reclining silhouette of a Native American replete with headdress. The site is revered by the Ute Mountain tribe as a great warrior god who, mortally wounded in a titanic battle with the evil ones, lapsed into eternal sleep, his flowing blood turning into the life-giving Dolores and Animas rivers.

In town, the enchanting **Galloping Goose Museum** (⊠ *5th St. at Rte. 145* ☎ *970/882–7082*) is a replica of an 1881 train station that contains an original narrow-gauge railcar. This distinctive vehicle connected Telluride with the rest of the world in the declining years of rail travel.

Spread across 164,000 acres of arid mesa-and-canyon country, the **Canyons of the Ancients National Monument** holds more than 20,000 known archaeological sites, the greatest concentration anywhere in the United States. There are 40, 60, or sometimes even 100 sites per square mile. Some, like apartment-style cliff dwellings and hewn-rock towers, are impossible to miss. Others are as subtle as evidence of agricultural fields, springs, and water systems. They are powerful evidence of the complex and mystical civilization of the Ancestral Puebloan people

9

(also known as the Anasazi, "the ancient ones") who inhabited the area between AD 450 and 1300 and are believed to have been the ancestors of today's Pueblo peoples.

The national monument includes several sites previously under federal protection: **Hovenweep National Monument,** straddling the Colorado–Utah border, is known for distinctive square, oval, round, and D-shape towers that were engineering marvels when they were built around AD 1200. **Lowry Pueblo,** in the northern part of the monument, is a 40-room pueblo. It features eight kivas (round chambers thought to have been used for sacred rituals). Its Great Kiva is one of the largest yet discovered in the Southwest. Also look for the Painted Kiva, which provides insight into Ancestral Puebloan decorative techniques.

Located in the vast and rugged backcountry area west of Mesa Verde National Park, the monument is a must if you're fascinated by the culture of the Ancestral Puebloans. The going may be rough, however. Roads are few, hiking trails are sparse, and visitor services are all but nonexistent. The Anasazi Heritage Center at Lowry Pueblo serves as the visitor center for the Canyon of the Ancients National Monument. A brochure, which details the self-guided tour, is available at the entrance to the site. ✛ *From Dolores, take Hwy. 184 west to U.S. 491, then head west onto County Rd. CC for 9 mi* ☎970/562–4282 ⊕*www.co.blm.gov/canm* ✑*$3* ⊘*Daily 8–4.*

SPORTS & THE OUTDOORS

FISHING &
BOATING

McPhee Reservoir, filled in 1987, is popular with boaters and anglers. The Colorado Division of Wildlife stocks this large artificial lake with plenty of trout. Other species found here include bass, bluegills, crappies, and kokanee salmon. The most easily reached fishing access spot is at the end of Highway 145, west of downtown Dolores. Anyone older than 16 needs a Colorado fishing license, which you can obtain at local sporting-goods stores. See ⊕*www.wildlife.state.co.us/fishing* for more information.

McPhee Marina (✉*25021 Hwy. 184* ☎*970/882–2257*) has boat ramps, boat slips, and other amenities. You can also sign up for fishing licenses here.

RAFTING
★

Beginning in the San Juan Mountains of southwestern Colorado, the Dolores River runs north for more than 150 mi before joining the Colorado River near Moab, Utah. This is one of those rivers that tend to flow madly in spring and diminish considerably by midsummer, and for that reason rafting trips are usually run between April and June. Sandstone canyons, Ancestral Puebloan ruins, and the spring bloom of wildflowers and cacti are trip highlights. The current's strength depends mostly on how much water is released from McPhee Reservoir, but for the most part this trip is a float interrupted by rapids that—depending on the flow level—can rate a Class IV.

WHERE TO EAT

$ ╳**Dolores River Brewery.** This brewpub, which gleefully advertises itself as "Dolores' Oldest Operating Brewery," is also the only one in town. Order an ale and a stout to wash down good pub grub in this fun spot. The usual pizzas, calzones, and sandwiches are matched on the menu with such lighter fare as salmon Caesar or yellowfin tuna salad. ✉ *100 S. 4th St.* ☎*970/882–4677* ☰*AE, D, MC* ☽*Closed Tues. No lunch*

SOUTHWEST COLORADO ESSENTIALS

TRANSPORTATION

BY AIR

The Gunnison–Crested Butte Regional Airport (GUC) serves the nearby resort area. GUC is served by American Airlines, United, and United Express.

The closest regional airport to the Black Canyon of the Gunnison National Park is Montrose Airport (MTJ). It's served by American, Continental, United, Skywest, and Delta.

Telluride is notorious for being one of the hardest ski resorts in the country to fly into, mainly because the elevation of Telluride Regional Airport (TEX) is well above 9,000 feet. A little turbulence, a few clouds, and the next thing you know you're landing at Montrose Airport, 67 mi away, and taking a shuttle to Telluride. Telluride Airport welcomes flights from America West, Frontier, Great Lakes Aviation, and United.

The Durango–La Plata Airport (DRO) is your closest option for Silverton, Durango, Pagosa Springs, Mesa Verde National Park, and the Four Corners region. It's served by America West Express, Delta, US Airways, and United Express.

Something to consider for travel to the Four Corners region, given your location and airline schedules, is to at least check into flying to Albuquerque instead of Denver. The Albuquerque International Sunport (ABQ) is host to many of the major airlines and is closer than Denver.

Information **Albuquerque International Sunport (ABQ)** (☎*505/244–7700* ⊕*www.cabq.gov/airport*). **Durango–La Plata Airport (DRO)** (☎*970/247–8143* ⊕*www.durangoairport.com*). **Gunnison–Crested Butte Regional Airport (GUC)** (☎*970/641–2304*). **Montrose Airport (MTJ)** (☎*970/249–3203* ⊕*airport. co.montrose.co.us*). **Telluride Regional Airport (TEX)** (☎*970/728–5313* ⊕*www. tellurideairport.com*).

TRANSFERS Several companies offer transportation between the airports and the resorts. Shuttles average $15–$30 per person. In Crested Butte, Gunnison, and Montrose try Alpine Express. Advance reservations may be required. Telluride Express serves Telluride Regional Airport. In Durango, the best service is Durango Transportation.

Contacts **Alpine Express** (☎970/641–5074 or 800/822–4844 ⊕alpine expressshuttle.com). **Durango Transportation** (☎970/247–4161 or 800/626–2066). **Telluride Express** (☎970/728–6000 or 888/212–8294 ⊕www.telluride express.com).

BY BUS

If you're traveling between the major towns, Greyhound is your best bet. In Crested Butte, Mountain Express shuttles regularly between the town and the ski area every 15 minutes during ski season. The Galloping Goose loops around Telluride every 15 minutes in summer and winter, less often in the off-season. Durango Lift has regular bus service up and down Main Street, as well as to Purgatory during ski season.

Contacts **Durango Lift** (☎970/259–5438). **Galloping Goose** (☎970/728–5700). **Greyhound** (☎800/231–2222)**Mountain Express** (☎970/349–5616).

BY CAR

Dollar, Thrifty, Hertz, and National car rental agencies have counters at the Montrose Airport. Avis, Budget, Dollar, Hertz, and National all have counters at Gunnison–Crested Butte Regional Airport, Telluride Regional Airport, and Durango–La Plata Airport.

Crested Butte is 230 mi southwest of Denver. Take U.S. 285 south (it briefly becomes U.S. 24 and then reverts to U.S. 285) to U.S. 50 west to Gunnison. From Gunnison take Route 135 north to Crested Butte. Telluride is 330 mi southwest of Denver. There is no such thing as a direct route, but the fastest is probably U.S. 285 south to U.S. 50 west to Montrose. Take U.S. 550 south to Ridgway. From Ridgway, take Route 62 west to Placerville and Route 145 south to Telluride. In winter, the only way out of Crested Butte is to head toward Gunnison, because the alternate route to Aspen, Kebler Pass over Route 133, is closed.

Getting to the remote Four Corners region is a bit simpler. If you're entering Colorado from the south, U.S. 550, U.S. 160, and U.S. 491 lead to the Four Corners region. From the east or west, I–70 (U.S. 6) intersects U.S. 50 in Grand Junction; U.S. 550 runs south to the San Juan Mountains and Four Corners from Montrose. From the Denver area, take Interstate 25 to Interstate 70 west for a long drive to U.S. 50.

The main roads in the region are Route 135 between Crested Butte and Gunnison; U.S. 50 linking Poncha Springs, Gunnison, Montrose, and Delta; Route 149 between Gunnison, Lake City, and Creede; U.S. 550 from Montrose to Ridgway to Silverton to Durango; Route 62 and Route 145 linking Ridgway with Telluride, Dolores, and Cortez; and U.S. 160, which passes from Cortez to Durango to Pagosa Springs via the Mesa Verde National Park north entrance. With the exception of Kebler Pass, none of these roads officially closes for winter, but be prepared at any time during snowy months for portions of the roads to be closed or down to one lane for avalanche control or to clear ice or snowdrifts.

Information **American Automobile Association of Colorado** (☎866/625–3601 ⊕www.aaacolo.com). **Colorado Road Report** (☎877/315–7623). **Colorado State Patrol** (☎970/249–4392 ⊕www.csp.state.co.us).

BY TAXI

In most resort towns you'll need to call for a cab. The wait is seldom more than 15 minutes.

Contacts **Durango Transportation** (☎ *970/259–4818*). **Telluride Shuttle & Taxi** (☎ *970/728–6668*). **Telluride Transit** (☎ *970/728–6000*).

BY TRAIN

The Durango & Silverton Narrow Gauge Railroad can take you from Durango to Silverton in lovingly restored coaches. The train runs from mid-May to late-October, with four departures daily from June to August and only one in the other months.

Contact **Durango & Silverton Narrow Gauge Railroad** (✉ *479 Main Ave.* ☎ *970/247–2733 or 888/872–4607* ⊕ *www.durangotrain.com* 💲 *$65*).

CONTACTS & RESOURCES

EMERGENCIES

Ambulance or Police (☎ *911*).

24-Hour Medical Care Gunnison Valley Hospital (✉ *711 N. Taylor* ☎ *970/641–1456* ⊕ *www.gvh-colorado.org*). **Mercy Medical Center** (✉ *375 E. Park Ave., Durango* ☎ *970/247–4311* ⊕ *www.mercydurango.org*). **Montrose Memorial Hospital** (✉ *800 S. 3rd St.* ☎ *970/249–2211* ⊕ *www.montrosehospital.com*). **Southwest Memorial Hospital** (✉ *1311 N. Mildred St., Cortez* ☎ *970/565–6666* ⊕ *www.swhealth.org*). **Telluride Medical Center** (✉ *500 W. Pacific Ave.* ☎ *970/728–3848* ⊕ *www.telluridemedicalcenter.org*).

VISITOR INFORMATION

Contact **Southwest Colorado Travel Region** (☎ *800/933–4340* ⊕ *www.swcolotravel.org*).

Crested Butte & Gunnison Crested Butte–Mount Crested Butte Chamber of Commerce (✉ *601 Elk Ave., Crested Butte 81224* ☎ *970/349–6438 or 800/545–4505* ⊕ *www.cb.chamber.com*). **Crested Butte Snow Report** (☎ *888/442–8883*). **Crested Butte Vacations** (✉ *Box 5700, Mount Crested Butte, 81225* ☎ *970/349–2222 or 888/223–3530* ⊕ *www.skicb.com*). **Gunnison County Chamber of Commerce** (✉ *500 E. Tomichi Ave., Gunnison 81230* ☎ *970/641–1501 or 800/274–7580* ⊕ *www.gunnisonchamber.com*).

Durango, Silverton & Pagosa Springs Durango Chamber Resort Association (✉ *111 S. Camino del Rio, Durango 81302* ☎ *970/247–0312 or 800/525–8855* ⊕ *www.durango.org*). **Pagosa Springs Chamber of Commerce** (✉ *402 San Juan St., 81147* ☎ *970/264–2360 or 800/252–2204* ⊕ *www.pagosaspringschamber.com*). **Silverton Chamber of Commerce** (✉ *414 Greene St., 81433* ☎ *970/387–5654 or 800/752–4494* ⊕ *www.silvertoncolorado.com*). **Wolf Creek Snow Report** (☎ *800/754–9653*).

Four Corners Cortez Area Chamber of Commerce (✉ *928 E. Main St., Cortez 81321* ☎ *970/565–3414* ⊕ *www.mesaverdecountry.com*). **Mesa Verde Country** (✉ *Box HH, Cortez 81321* ☎ *800/253–1616* ⊕ *www.mesaverdecountry.com*).

9

Ouray & Montrose **Montrose Chamber of Commerce** (✉ *1519 E. Main St., Montrose 81401* ☎ *970/249–5000* ✉ *17253 Chipeta Rd., 81401* ☎ *970/249–1726* ⊕ *www.montrosechamber.com*). **Ouray County Chamber** (✉ *1230 Main St., 81427* ☎ *970/325–4746 or 800/228–1876* ⊕ *www.ouraycolorado.com*).

Telluride **Telluride and Mountain Village Visitor Services** (✉ *630 W. Colorado Ave., Box 653, Telluride 81435* ☎ *970/728–3041 or 800/525–3455* ⊕ *www.visittelluride.com*). **Telluride Ski Resort** (✉ *565 Mountain Village Blvd., 81435* ☎ *970/728–6900 or 866/287–5015* ⊕ *www.tellurideskiresort.com*). **Telluride Snow Report** (☎ *970/728–7425*).

Mesa Verde National Park

WORD OF MOUTH

"Mesa Verde National Park is America's first cultural park. . . . it celebrates a culture that slipped silently into history centuries earlier, and it is separated from today by an abyss of time."

—Author Duane A. Smith

WELCOME TO MESA VERDE

TOP REASONS TO GO

★ **Ancestral Mansions:** Explore Cliff Palace and the Long House, each with 150 rooms. They're among the 600 cliff dwellings tucked into Mesa Verde.

★ **Pueblo Places:** View kivas, petroglyphs, wall paintings, and more. More than 4,000 archaeological sites and 3 million objects of the ancestral Puebloans have been unearthed at Mesa Verde.

★ **Geological Goodies:** Get low and look close; the desert landscape has a story to tell. Ripple marks suggest the area was once covered with water, turtleback weathering notes the effects of erosion, and flower-patterned solution rills reveal the power of acidic rain on the sandstone's structure.

★ **Bright Nights:** Gaze into the sky's starry depths. With no major cities nearby to reflect light at night, the Four Corners area is an ideal place to be an amateur astronomer.

1 Morefield Campground. Near the entrance, this large campground is a natural center of operations for any visitor to Mesa Verde. It includes a village area with a gas station and grocery store. The park's best-known sites are farther in, but there are a few hiking trails close-by.

2 Far View Visitor Center. Almost an hour's drive from Mesa Verde's entrance, the main visitor center is near the park's only overnight lodge (seasonal), and from where you can access 12-mi Wetherill Mesa Road (seasonal) to the east and 12-mi Mesa Top Loop Road to the south.

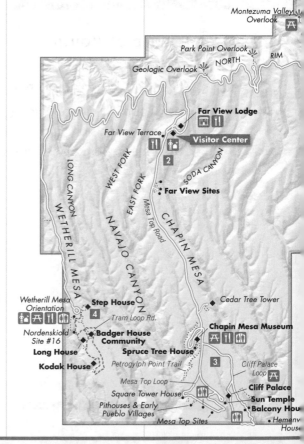

3 Chapin Mesa. In many ways the heart of Mesa Verde, this southern swath is where the famous 150-room Cliff House dwelling is located.

COLORADO

Hopi eagle dancers at Spruce Tree House.

4 Wetherill Mesa. This western area of the park includes sites accessible, if you so choose, by tram: the Long House, Kodak House, and Badger House Community. Also here is Step House, reached by a steep staircase.

GETTING ORIENTED

Perhaps no area offers as much evidence into the ancestral Pueblo's existence as Mesa Verde National Park does. Several thousand archaeological sites have been found, and research is ongoing to discover more. The carved-out homes and assorted artifacts, displayed at the park's Chapin Mesa Archeological Museum, belonged to ancestors of today's Hopi, Zuni, and Pueblo tribes, among others. Due to the sensitive nature of these remants, hiking in the park is restricted to designated trails, and certain cliff dwellings may only be accessed under accompaniment of a ranger during the peak summer season.

10

Petroglyphs

KEY	
🏠	Ranger Station
⛺	Campground
🎪	Picnic Area
🍴	Restaurant
🏨	Lodge
🚶	Trailhead
🚻	Restrooms
⛰	Scenic Viewpoint
⋯⋯	Walking/Hiking Trails
⋯⋯	Bicycle Path

MESA VERDE NATIONAL PARK PLANNER

When to Go

The best times to visit the park are late May, early June, and most of September, when the weather is fine but the summer crowds have thinned. Mid-June through August are Mesa Verde's most crowded months. In July and August you must stop at the Far View Visitor Center to purchase tickets for the Balcony House, Cliff House and Long House tours. At times, the lines at the museum and visitor center may last for 15 to 20 minutes. Afternoon thunder showers are common in July and August.

The mesa gets as many as 100 inches of snow in winter. Snow may fall as late as May and as early as October, but there's rarely enough to hamper travel. In winter, the Wetherill Mesa Road and Far View Lodge are closed, but the sight of the sandstone dwellings sheltered from the snow in their cliff coves is spectacular.

AVG. HIGH/LOW TEMPS

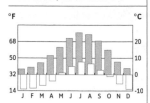

Flora & Fauna

Since 2000, wildfires have claimed thousands of Mesa Verde's acres. Visitors will see the scars for a long time, as it can take 300 years for an evergreen woodland to restore itself. In spring and summer, however, you'll still see brightly colored blossoms, like the yellow Perky Sue, sage, yucca, and mountain mahogany. Sand-loving blue lupines are seen along the roadways in the higher elevations, and bright-red Indian paintbrushes are scattered throughout the rocky cliffs.

Mule deer are the park's most frequently sighted larger animals. About 200 species of birds, including red-tailed hawks and golden eagles, live in Mesa Verde, as does the poisonous prairie rattler (give it plenty of space and it'll likely just mosey along on its way). The animals seek shade in trees and under brush, so the best times to spot them are in the early morning and just before dusk.

Getting There & Around

The park is located off U.S. 160, between Cortez and Durango in what's known as the Four Corners. The nearest bus station and regional airport are 35 mi away in Durango, Colorado, a small city worth exploring.

Most of the scenic drives at Mesa Verde involve steep grades and hairpin turns, particularly on Wetherill Mesa. Vehicles over 8,000 pounds or 25 feet are prohibited on this road. Towed vehicles are prohibited past Morefield Campground. Check the condition of your vehicle's brakes before driving the road to Wetherill Mesa. For the latest road information, tune your radio to Traveler's Information Station at 1610 AM, or call the ranger station at ☏970/529–4461. Off-road vehicles are prohibited in the park.

By John
Blodgett

Updated by
Lois Friedland

UNLIKE MOST NATIONAL PARKS OF the west, Mesa Verde earned its status from its rich cultural history rather than its geological treasures. President Theodore Roosevelt established it in 1906 as the first national park to "preserve the works of man." The Ancestral Puebloan people, who lived in the region from roughly 600 to 1300, left behind more than 4,800 archaeological sites spread out over 80 square mi. Their ancient dwellings, set high into the sandstone cliffs, are the heart of the park.

Mesa Verde, "Green Table" in Spanish, is much more than an archaeologist's dreamland, however. It's one of those windswept places where man's footprints and nature's paintbrush—some would say chisel—meet. Rising dramatically from the San Juan Basin, the jutting cliffs are cut by a series of complex canyons and covered with green, from pines in the higher elevations down to sage and other mountain brush on the desert floor. From the tops of the smaller mesas, you can look across to the cliff dwellings in the rock faces of other mesas. Dwarfed by the towering cliffs, the sand-color dwellings look almost like a natural occurrence in the midst of the desert's harsh beauty.

SCENIC DRIVES

Mesa Top Loop Road. This 6-mi drive skirts the scenic rim of Chapin Mesa, reaching several of Mesa Verde's most important archaeological sites. Two of the parks' most impressive viewpoints are also on this road: Navajo Canyon Overlook and Sun Point Overlook, from which you can see Cliff Palace, Sunset House, and other dwellings. ☉*Daily* 8 AM–*sunset.*

Park Entrance Road. The main park road leads you from the entrance to Far View Visitor Center, on 15 mi of switchbacks, which reveal far-ranging vistas of the surrounding areas. You can stop at a couple of pretty overlooks along the way, but hold out for Park Point, which, at the mesa's highest elevation (8,572 feet), affords unobstructed 360-degree views.

10

WHAT TO SEE

HISTORIC SITES

Many of the historic sites are clustered along specific drive loops. **Step House, Long House, Badger House Community,** and **Kodak House** are all on the **Wetherill Mesa** loop. There are three driving loops on **Chapin Mesa.** The shortest one goes to the **Chapin Mesa Archeological Museum** and **Spruce House.** A second loop goes to the **Sun Temple, Square Tower House,** and **Mesa Top** sites. The third loop includes the **Cliff Palace** and the **Balcony House.**

Badger House Community. A self-guided walk takes you through a group of subterranean dwellings, called pit houses, and aboveground storage rooms. The community dates to 650, the Basket Maker period, and covers 7 acres of land. Most of the pit houses and kivas—religious or ceremonial rooms—were connected by an intricate system of tunnels, some up to 41 feet long. Allow about an hour to see all the sites. ⊠ *On Wetherill Mesa Rd.,* ⊹ *12 mi from the Far View Visitor Center* ⊘ *Memorial Day–Labor Day, daily 8–4:30.*

ⵙ ★ **Balcony House.** The stonework of this 40-room cliff dwelling, which once housed about 40 or 50 people, is impressive, but you're likely to be even more awed by the skill it took to reach this place. Perched in a sandstone alcove 600 feet above the floor of Soda Canyon, Balcony House seems almost suspended in space. Even with the aid of modern steps and a partially paved trail, today's visitors must climb two wooden ladders (the first one 32 feet high) to enter. Surrounding the house are a courtyard with a parapet wall and the intact balcony for which the house is named. A favorite with kids, the dwelling is only accessible on a ranger-led tour. Youngsters love climbing the ladders, crawling through the tunnels, and clambering around its nooks and crannies. Purchase your ticket at the Far View Visitor Center. ⊠ *On Cliff Palace Loop Rd.,* ⊹ *8.5 mi southeast of the Far View Visitor Center* ⊠ *$3* ⊘ *Late May–mid-Oct., daily 9–5.*

Fodor's Choice
★ **Cliff Palace.** This was the first major Mesa Verde dwelling seen by cowboys Charlie Mason and Richard Wetherill in 1888. It is also the largest, containing about 150 rooms and 23 kivas on three levels. The tour involves a steep downhill hike and four ladders. Purchase tickets at the Far View Visitor Center for the one-hour, ranger-led tour through this dwelling. ⊠ *On Cliff Palace Loop Rd.,* ⊹ *7 mi south of the Far View Visitor Center* ⊠ *$3* ⊘ *Mid-May–mid-Oct., daily 9–5.*

Far View Sites Complex. This is believed to have been one of the most densely populated areas in Mesa Verde, comprising as many as 50 villages in a 0.5-square-mi area at the top of Chapin Mesa. Most of the sites here were built between 900 and 1300. Begin the self-guided tour at the interpretive panels in the parking lot, then proceed down a 0.5-mi, level trail. ⊠ *On the park entrance road,* ⊹ *1.5 mi south of the Far View Visitor Center* ⊘ *Mid-May–mid-Oct., daily 8–6:30.*

Long House. Excavated in 1959 through 1961, this Wetherill Mesa cliff dwelling is the second largest in Mesa Verde. It is believed that about 150 people lived in Long House, so named because of the size of its cliff alcove. The spring at the back of the alcove is still active today. The ranger-led tour begins a short distance from the parking lot and takes about 1½ hours; purchase tickets for the tour at the Far View Visitor Center. ⊠ *On Wetherill Mesa Rd.,* ⊹ *12 mi from the Far View Visitor Center* ⊠ *$3* ⊘ *Memorial Day–Labor Day, daily 10–4.*

GOOD READS

Mesa Verde National Park: The First 100 Years by Rose Houk, Faith Marcovecchio, and Duane A. Smith captures the park as it celebrated its centennial.

Fire on the Mesa, by Tracey Chavis discusses the wildfires that have been scarring Mesa Verde.

Mesa Verde: Ancient Architecture by Jesse Walter Fewkes tells the stories behind the park's dwellings.

Spruce Tree House. The best-preserved site in the park, this dwelling contains 130 living rooms and eight kivas. It's the only dwelling where you can actually enter a kiva, via a short ladder, just as the original inhabitants did. Tours are self-guided, but a park ranger is on-site to answer questions. The short trail starts behind the Chapin Mesa Archeological Museum and descends 170 feet—you'll find yourself puffing on the way back up, but it's worth the effort. The site is open year-round, with guided tours from mid-November to early March. ☒ *On the park entrance road,* ✚ *5 mi south of the Far View Visitor Center* ⊗ *Mar.–Nov., daily 9–5.*

Step House. So named because of a crumbling prehistoric stairway leading up from the dwelling, Step House on Wetherill Mesa is reached via a paved, though steep, trail. The house is one of the least-visited dwellings in the park. ☒ *On Wetherill Mesa Rd.,* ✚ *12 mi from the Far View Visitor Center* ⊗ *Memorial Day–Labor Day, daily 8–4:30.*

Sun Temple. Although researchers assume the Sun Temple on the Cliff Palace Loop was probably a ceremonial structure, they are unsure of the purpose of this complex, which has no doors or windows in most of its chambers. ☒ *On Cliff Palace Loop Rd.,* ✚ *8 mi south of the Far View Visitor Center* ⊗ *Daily 8–sunset.*

Triple Village Pueblo Sites. Three dwellings built atop each other from 750 to 1150 at first look like a mass of jumbled walls, but an interpretive panel helps identify them. The 325-foot trail from the walking area is paved and wheelchair accessible. ☒ *On Mesa Top Loop Rd.,* ✚ *8 mi south of the Far View Visitor Center* ⊗ *Daily.*

SCENIC STOPS

Cedar Tree Tower. A self-guided tour takes you to, but not through, a tower and kiva built between 1100 and 1300 and connected by a tunnel. The tower-and-kiva combinations in the park are thought to have been either religious structures or signal towers. ☒ *On the park entrance road,* ✚ *4 mi south of the Far View Visitor Center* ⊗ *Daily.*

Kodak House Overlook. Get an impressive view into Kodak House and its several small kivas from here. The house, closed to the public, was named for a Swedish researcher who stored his Kodak camera here in 1891. ☒ *On Wetherill Mesa Rd. 1,* ✚ *2 mi from the Far View Visitor Center* ⊟ *$3 at Far View Visitor Center* ⊗ *Memorial Day–Labor Day, daily.*

Soda Canyon Overlook. Get your best view of Balcony House here and read interpretive panels about the house and canyon geology. ☒ *On Mesa Top Loop Rd.,* ✚ *9 mi south of the Far View Visitor Center* ⊗ *Daily.*

VISITOR CENTERS

There are two visitor centers at Mesa Verde, though one is called a museum (but in fact, it serves as the official visitor center when the other closes for the season in the middle of October).

10

★ **Chapin Mesa Archeological Museum.** The museum tells the entire story of the cliff-dwelling people and gives as complete an understanding as possible of the Basket Maker and Ancestral Puebloan cultures through detailed dioramas and exhibits, including original textiles, sandals, and kiva jars. ⊠ *On the park entrance road,* ⚓ *5 mi south of the Far View Visitor Center* ☎ *970/529–4465* ⊠ *Free* ⊙ *Apr.–mid-Oct., daily 8–6:30; mid-Oct.–Mar., daily 8–5.*

★ **Far View Visitor Center.** Buy tickets for the Cliff Palace, Balcony House, and Long House ranger-led tours here. An extensive selection of books and videos on the history of the park are also for sale. Rangers are on hand to answer questions and explain the history of the Ancestral Puebloans. ⚓ *15 mi south of the park entrance* ☎ *970/529–5036* ⊙ *Mid-Apr.–mid-Oct., daily 8–5.*

SPORTS & THE OUTDOORS

Outdoor activities are restricted on account of the fragile nature of the archeological treasures contained here. Hiking is the best option, especially as a way to view some of the Ancestral Puebloan dwellings.

BIRD-WATCHING

Turkey vultures soar between April and October, large flocks of ravens hang around all summer, and ducks and waterfowl fly through Mesa Verde from mid-September through mid-October. Among the park's other large birds are red-tailed hawks, great horned owls, and a few golden eagles. The dark-blue Steller's jay frequently pierces the pinyon pine–juniper forest with its cries, and hummingbirds dart from flower to flower.

HIKING

No backcountry hiking is permitted in Mesa Verde due to the fragile nature of the ancient dwellings and artifacts. However, several trails lead beyond the park's most-visited sites. Most trails are easily navigable, with length being what separates the most difficult from the easiest, though a few have some elevation changes and switchbacks. Certain trails are seasonal only, so check with a ranger before heading out.

EASY **Knife Edge Trail.** Take this trail for an easy 2-mi (round-trip) walk around the north rim of the park. If you stop at all the flora identification points that the trail guide pamphlet suggests, the hike should take about 1½ to 2 hours. The patches of asphalt you're likely to spot along the way are leftovers from Knife Edge Road, built in 1914 as the main entryway into the park.

☾ **Soda Canyon Overlook Trail.** One of the easiest and most rewarding strolls in the park, this little trail travels 1.5 mi round-trip through the forest on almost completely level ground. The overlook is an excellent point from which to photograph the cliff dwellings. The trailhead is about 0.25 mi past the Balcony House parking area.

MODERATE **Farming Terrace Trail.** This 30-minute, 0.5-mi loop beginning and ending on the spur road to Cedar Tree Tower, meanders through a series of check dams the Ancestral Puebloans built in order to create farming terraces.

Fodor'sChoice ★ **Petroglyph Point Trail.** The highlight of this 2.8-mi loop is the largest and best-known group of petroglyphs in Mesa Verde. Since the trail offshoots from Spruce Tree House Trail, it is only accessible when Spruce Tree House is open, March through November, daily 9–5.

Spruce Canyon Trail. If you want to venture down into the canyon, this is your trail. It's only 2 mi long, but you can go down about 300 feet in elevation. It is only accessible when Spruce Tree House is open, from March through November, daily 9–5, and registration is required.

DIFFICULT **Prater Ridge Trail.** This loop, which starts and finishes at Morefield Campground, is the longest hike (7.8-mi round-trip) you can take inside the park and affords fine views of Morefield Canyon to the south and the San Juan Mountains to the north.

STARGAZING
Since there are no large cities in the Four Corners area, there is very little artificial light to detract from the stars in the night sky. Some ideal locations in the park for stargazing are Far View Lodge, Morefield Campground, and the Montezuma and Mancos scenic overlooks.

> ### ANTSY POTS
>
> Anthills contribute an important ingredient to the pottery that vastly improved the Basket Maker standard of living. Pueblo potters, as did their ancestors, collect the small pebbles from the ants' nests to grind up and use as temper, the material added to clay to prevent the vessels from cracking as they dry.

EDUCATIONAL OFFERINGS

RANGER PROGRAMS
ARAMARK. The park concessionaire provides half-day ranger-guided tours of the Mesa Top Loop Road sites from mid-April through mid-October. The tours depart in vans or buses from Far View Terrace. Tours cover the history, geology, and excavation process in Mesa Verde. *ARAMARK Mesa Verde, Box 277, Mancos 81328 ☎970/564–4300 or 800/449–2288 ⊕www.visitmesaverde.com ☞$49 ☉Mid-Apr.–mid-Oct., daily.*

Evening Ranger Campfire Program. A park ranger presents a different 45-minute program or slide presentation each night of the week. ⊠*Morefield Campground Amphitheater,* ✛*4 mi south of the park entrance* ☎*970/529–4465* ☉*Memorial Day–Labor Day, daily 9 PM–9:45 PM.*

Junior Ranger Program. Children ages 4–12 can earn a certificate and badge for successfully completing a two-page questionnaire about the park. ⊠*Far View Visitor Center or Chapin Mesa Museum* ☎*970/529–4465.*

Ranger-Led Tours. Balcony House, Cliff Palace, and Long House can only be explored on a ranger-led tour; each lasts about an hour. Buy tickets for these at Far View Visitor Center the day of the tour, or at the More-

10

field Campground Ranger Station the evening before the tour, 5 PM to 8:30 PM. ☎970/529–4465 ✆$3 per tour ☉Mid-Apr.–mid-Oct.

SHOPPING

Chapin Mesa Archeological Museum Shop. Books and videos are the primary offering here with more than 400 titles on Ancestral Puebloan and Southwestern topics. ✛21 mi southwest of the park entrance on Mesa Top Loop Rd. ☎970/529–4465 ☉Daily 8–5.

Far View Terrace Store. This is the largest gift shop in the park and has a wide selection of gifts and toys for children, Native American art, a Christmas section, and T-shirts galore. ✛15 mi south of the park entrance on Mesa Top Loop Rd. ☎970/529–4421 or 800/449–2288 ☉Daily 8–5.

NEARBY TOWNS

A onetime market center for sheep and cattle ranchers 30 mi from the park, **Cortez** is the gateway town to Mesa Verde, and some tourists use this small town or Mancos as a base for visiting the Four Corners region of Colorado. You can still see a rodeo and cattle drive here at least once a year. Tiny **Dolores**, steeped in a rich railroad history, is set on the Dolores River, 20 mi north of the entrance to Mesa Verde. Neighboring both the San Juan National Forest and McPhee Reservoir, the second-largest lake in the state, Dolores is a favorite of outdoor enthusiasts. East of Mesa Verde by 56 mi, **Durango**, the region's main hub, is about a one-hour drive from the park. It became a town in 1881 when the Denver and Rio Grande Railroad pushed its tracks across the neighboring San Juan Mountains. *For more information about Cortez, Dolores, and Durango, see the Southwest Colorado chapter in this book.*

SPORTS & THE OUTDOORS

FISHING **McPhee Reservoir.** The second-largest lake in Colorado provides some of the state's best boating, waterskiing, and fishing—minus the crowds. To date, McPhee Reservoir has been stocked with 4.5 million fish, including trout, bass, bluegills, crappies, and kokanee salmon. The marina, where you can sign up for a fishing license, is 8 mi north of Dolores. ⊠Rte. 184, Dolores ☎970/882–7296 ✆Free ☉Daily.

WHERE TO STAY & EAT

ABOUT THE RESTAURANTS

Dining options in Mesa Verde are comparatively plentiful and varied, ranging from cafeterias with standard American fare to fine-dining options with a Southwestern influence. *For restaurants near Mesa Verde, see the Cortez, Dolores, and Durango sections in the Southwest Colorado chapter in this book.*

ABOUT THE HOTELS

All 150 rooms of the park's Far View Lodge, open April through October, have private balconies, are nonsmoking, and fill up quickly—so reservations are recommended, especially if you plan to visit on a weekend in summer. *For accommodations near Mesa Verde, see the Cortez, Dolores, and Durango sections in the Southwest Colorado chapter in this book.*

ABOUT THE CAMPGROUNDS

Morefield Campground is the only option within the park and is an excellent one. Reservations are accepted; it's open April through October.

WHAT IT COSTS					
	¢	$	$$	$$$	$$$$
RESTAURANTS	under $8	$8–$12	$13–$18	$19–$25	over $25
HOTELS	under $80	$80–$120	$121–$170	$171–$230	over $230
CAMPING	under $10	$10–$17	$18–$35	$36–$49	over $50

Restaurant prices are per person for a main course at dinner, excluding 3.35% tax. Hotel prices are per night for two people in a standard double room in high season, excluding service charges and 5.25% tax. Camping prices are for a standard (no hookups, pit toilets, fire grates, picnic tables) campsite per night.

WHERE TO EAT

$$$ ✕**Metate Room.** Tables in this Southwestern-style dining room are can-
★ dlelit and cloth covered, but the atmosphere remains casual. A wall of windows affords wonderful Mesa Verde vistas. The menu includes American staples like steak and seafood, but game meats such as quail, venison, and rabbit occasionally appear as well. Try Anasazi beans and mesa bread to start. ⊠*Far View Lodge, ✛across from the Far View Visitor Center* ☎*970/529–4421* ⊟*AE, D, DC, MC, V* ⊗*Closed late Oct.–early Apr. No lunch.*

¢ ✕**Far View Terrace.** This full-service cafeteria offers great views, plentiful choices, and reasonable prices. Fluffy blueberry pancakes are often on the breakfast menu. Dinner options might include a Navajo taco piled high with all the fixings. Don't miss the creamy malts and homemade fudge; a shot at the espresso bar will keep you going all day. ⊠*On Mesa Top Loop Rd., ✛across from the Far View Visitor Center* ☎*970/529–4444* ⊟*D, MC, V* ⊗*Closed late Oct.–early Apr.*

¢ ✕**Knife Edge Café.** An all-you-can-eat pancake breakfast is served every morning from 7:30 to 10 at this café in Morefield Campground. ✛*4 mi south of the park entrance* ☎*970/565–2133* ⊟*AE, D, MC, V* ⊗*Closed Labor Day–Memorial Day. No lunch or dinner.*

¢ ✕**Spruce Tree Terrace.** A limited selection of hot food and sandwiches is all you'll find at this cafeteria, but the patio is pleasant, and since it's across the street from the Chapin Mesa Archeological Museum, it's convenient. The Terrace is also the only food concession open year-round. ⊠*On the park entrance road, ✛4 mi from the Far View*

10

Visitor Center ☎*970/529–4521* ▤*AE, D, DC, MC, V* ☉*No dinner Dec.–Feb.*

♻ **Park Headquarters Loop Picnic Area.** This is the nicest and largest picnic area in the park. It has 40 tables under shade trees and a great view into Spruce Canyon, as well as flush toilets and running water. ⊕*6 mi south of the Far View Visitor Center.*

Wetherill Mesa Picnic Area. Ten tables placed under lush shade trees, along with drinking water and restrooms, make this a very pleasant spot for lunch. ⊕*12 mi southwest of the Far View Visitor Center.*

WHERE TO STAY

★ $$ ▦**Far View Lodge.** Talk about a view—many rooms in the older buildings have private balconies, from which you can admire the neighboring states of Arizona, Utah, and New Mexico up to 100 mi in the distance. The Kiva rooms in the newer buildings have handcrafted furniture and are more comfortable but do not have the views. In either building, quarters are motel-style and basic, with a Southwestern touch. Talks by guest speakers on various park topics and multimedia shows on the Ancestral Puebloans are held occasionally. The hotel also offers enthusiastically guided tours of the park. The Metate Room, the lodge's main dining room, is acclaimed for its fine steaks and excellent Southwestern fare. ⊕*15 mi southwest of the park entrance, across from the Far View Visitor Center* ✉*Reservations: ARAMARK Mesa Verde, Box 277, Mancos 81328* ☎*970/564–4300 or 800/449–2288* ⊕*www.visitmesaverde.com* ⇆*150 rooms* ⚷*In-room: refrigerator (some). In-hotel: restaurant, bar, laundry facilities, some pets allowed, no-smoking rooms* ▤*AE, D, DC, MC, V* ☉*Closed mid-Oct–mid-Apr.*

⛺**Morefield Campground.** With about 400 shaded campsites, access to trailheads, and plenty of amenities, the only campground in the park is an appealing mini-city for campers. Reservations are accepted for all sites. ⊕*4 mi from the park entrance* ✉*Box 277, Mancos 81328* ☎*970/564–4300 or 800/449–2288* ⊕*www.visitmesaverde.com* ⇆*380 sites, 15 with hookups* ⚷*Flush toilets, full hookups for RVs, drive campsites for cars, dump station, drinking water, guest laundry, showers, fire grates, grills, picnic tables, food service, electricity, public telephone, general store, ranger station, service station* ▤*AE, D, DC, MC, V* ☉*Late-Apr.–mid-Oct.*

$$$
FodorśChoice
★

★ $$–$$$ ⛺**A & A Mesa Verde RV Park and Campground.** This 30-acre lot, directly across the highway from the park, has all the facilities of a hotel. There's a modern bathhouse, recreation room, miniature golf course, sports field, a pool and hot tub, and a kennel. You can even camp in a log cabin. ✉*34979 U.S. 160, Mancos 81328* ☎*800/972–6620* ⊕*www.mesaverdecamping.com* ⇆*73 sites, 45 with hookups; 4 cabins* ⚷*Grills, flush toilets, full hookups, dump station, drinking water, guest laundry, showers, fire grates, picnic tables, electricity, public telephone, general store, play area, swimming (pool)* ▤*D, MC, V* ☉*Apr.–Sept.*

$ ⛺**McPhee Campground.** The largest and best-equipped campground in the San Juan National Forest, McPhee is surrounded by paved roads and has several wheelchair-accessible sites. It's at an altitude of about

7,400 feet, and many of the sites overlook McPhee Reservoir. Reach it by taking Route 184 south 7 mi from Dolores to Country Road 25, then turn north to onto Forest Road 271. ⊠*Forest Rd. 271, 15 Burnett Ct., Durango 81301* ☎ *970/247–4874 or 877/444–6777* ⊕*www.fs.fed.us/ r2/sanjuan* ⟿*76 sites, 16 with hookups* ♿*Grills, flush toilets, partial hookups (electric and water), dump station, drinking water, showers, fire pits, picnic tables, electricity, public telephone* ⊙*May–Sept.*

MESA VERDE ESSENTIALS

ACCESSIBILITY
Steep cliffs, deep canyons, narrow trails, and hard-to-reach archaeological sites mean accessibility is limited within Mesa Verde. Service dogs cannot be taken into Balcony House, Cliff Palace, or Long House because of ladders in those sites. None of these sites is accessible to those with mobility impairments. If you have heart or respiratory ailments, you may have trouble breathing in the thin air at 7,000 to 8,000 feet. Wheelchairs with wide-rim wheels are recommended on trails, some of which do not meet legal grade requirements. For the hearing impaired, park videos are open captioned. Mesa Top Loop Road provides the most comprehensive and accessible view of all the archaeological sites.

ADMISSION FEES
At this writing, a seven-day vehicle permit costs $15 between Memorial Day and Labor Day; this summer fee is scheduled to increase to $20 in 2009. The rest of the year, the permit is $10. An annual permit for Mesa Verde is $30. Ranger-led tours of Cliff Palace, Long House, and Balcony House are $3 per person.

ADMISSION HOURS
The facilities open each day at 8 AM and close at sunset from Memorial Day through Labor Day. The rest of the year, the facilities close at 5. Wetherill Mesa, all the major cliff dwellings, and Morefield ranger station are open only from Memorial Day through Labor Day, Far View Visitor Center, Far View Lodge, and Morefield Campground are open mid-April through mid-October.

ATM/BANKS
There are no ATMs in the park. The closest bank is in Cortez.

Citizens State Bank (⊠*77 W. Main, Cortez* ☎*970/565–8421* ⊙*Weekdays 9–5*).

AUTOMOBILE SERVICE STATION
Sinclair Service Station offers the basics: gas and oil changes. (⊠*Morefield Campground, ✛ 4 mi from the park entrance* ☎*970/565–2407*).

EMERGENCIES
To report a fire or call for aid, dial 911 or 970/529–4465. First-aid stations are located at Morefield Campground, Far View Visitor Center, and Wetherill Mesa.

10

LOST & FOUND

The park's lost and found is at the **Chief Ranger's office** at park headquarters, 5 mi south of Far View Visitor Center (☎ *970/529–4469*).

PERMITS

Backcountry hiking and fishing are not permitted at Mesa Verde.

POST OFFICE

Mesa Verde National Park Post Office ✉ *Near park headquarters, Chapin Mesa 81330* ☎ *970/529–4554* ⊙ *Weekdays 8:30–4:30).*

PUBLIC TELEPHONES

Public telephones can be found at Morefield Campground and Morefield Village, Far View Visitor Center, Far View Lodge, Far View Terrace, Spruce Tree Terrace, park headquarters (5 mi from the Far View Visitor Center), and the Wetherill Mesa snack bar. Cell-phone reception in the park varies in quality.

RESTROOMS

Public restrooms may be found at Morefield Campground and Morefield Village, Far View Visitor Center, Far View Lodge, Far View Terrace, Spruce Tree Terrace, park headquarters, the Wetherill Mesa snack bar, Montezuma Valley Overlook, Cliff Palace, and Balcony House.

SHOPS & GROCERS

Morefield Campground has a nicely stocked grocery store that is open 7 AM to 9 PM, mid-May to early Oct.

VISITOR INFORMATION

Mesa Verde National Park (✆ *Box 8, Mesa Verde, 81330-0008* ☎ *970/529–4465* ⊕ *www.nps.gov/meve).*

South Central Colorado

COLORADO SPRINGS, ROYAL GORGE & GREAT SAND DUNES

WORD OF MOUTH

"From Manitou you can easily do Pikes Peak, Garden of the Gods, day trips to Florissant [Fossil Beds] . . . the Olympic Training Center, the Air Force Academy, Seven Falls, and Cave of the Winds (a little campy but still cool looking)."

—Toucan2

"Early May is my favorite time to visit the Sand Dunes. If there has been sufficient snowpack during the winter months there is a creek that flows across the base of the dunes. You have to cross it to climb the dunes, but you will see adults and kids playing Frisbee and football in the creek and just having a good time."

—wtm003

Revised and
Updated by
Lois Friedland

RUNNING FROM MAJESTIC MOUNTAINS INTO rugged high desert plains, south central Colorado has a collection of 14,000-foot peaks, striking red-rock outcroppings, rivers that boil with white-water rapids in spring, and even the incongruous sight of towering sand dunes dwarfed by a mountain range at their back. It's worth a few days of exploration—embarking on a white-water rafting trip, shopping in stores set in historic downtowns, and hiking in the backcountry. Although Colorado Springs is bustling, much of south central Colorado has a barely discovered feel. If it's peace and quiet you're after, staying put in a cabin in the woods, perhaps with a fishing stream close by, can make for an utterly relaxed week.

At the foot of looming Pikes Peak, Colorado Springs is the region's population center and, bucking the mining-nostalgia trend, a hub for the military and the high-tech industry. The city has been a destination for out-of-towners since its founding in 1870, due to the alleged healing power of the local springwater and clean air. The gold rush fueled the city's boom through the early 20th century, as the military boom did following World War II—the missile defense complex inside Cheyenne Mountain—and the Air Force Academy are products of the latter.) Now more than 500,000 residents strong, the city offers a mix of history and modernity, as well as incredible access to the trails and red-rock scenery in this section of the Rockies.

Surrounding Colorado Springs is a ring of smaller cities and alluring natural attractions. To the west, between alpine and desert scenery, are the Florissant Fossil Beds and the Royal Gorge, both worth a short visit if not an entire day. Cripple Creek offers low-stakes gambling, Cañon City rafting, and Pueblo a nice dash of public art and history museums. Outdoorsy types love the entire area: Camping and hiking are especially superb in the San Isabel and Pike national forests. Climbers head to the Collegiate Peaks around Buena Vista and Salida (west of Colorado Springs) and the Cañon City area for a variety of ascents, from moderate to difficult.

South central Colorado was first explored by the United States in 1806, three years after it made the Louisiana Purchase. Zebulon Pike took up the assignment of scout, but he never did climb the peak that is now named for him, nor did he have the scientific background of his contemporaries, the famous explorers Lewis and Clark. Weaving through the southeastern section of the state are the haunting remains of the Santa Fe Trail, which guided pioneers westward beginning in the 1820s.

EXPLORING SOUTH CENTRAL COLORADO

Pikes Peak, one of the most famous of Colorado's Fourteeners, forms the backdrop for Colorado Springs. Farther west, the Arkansas River towns of Buena Vista and Salida are within view of the Fourteeners of the Collegiate Peaks. Farther south, the Rio Grande runs through the flat San Luis Valley which is lined by the Sangre de Cristo range. Cuchara Valley, just north of New Mexico, is framed by the Spanish Peaks.

TOP REASONS TO GO

Pikes Peak: Katharine Bates wrote "America the Beautiful" after taking a wagon and then a mule ride to the top of Pikes Peak. Today you can ride in a train on a cog railway to the top for the same see-forever views of Colorado Springs to the Kansas border.

Sporting on the Arkansas: The Arkansas River is one of the most popular rivers for rafting and kayaking in the United States. Several companies offer a variety of rafting trips from gentle floats to Class V rapids.

The U.S. Air Force Academy: Visitors from all over the country come to this mountainside campus to see the cadets marching on the parade ground and learn more about the Academy that trains the future leaders of the Air Force. Many also attend services in the stunning, non-denominational Cadet Chapel, whose sleek towers framed by mountains

make it the second-most-visited site in the state, after Rocky Mountain National Park.

Hiking a Fourteener: Coloradans collect hikes to the summit of Four-teeners—mountains that top 14,000 feet above sea level—like trophies. Choose your mountain wisely, because some climbs are much tougher than others, but if you're a hiker in good shape and have the proper equipment, you might want to tackle a route on one of the region's Fourteeners, such at Mount Princeton, Mount Yale, or Mount of the Holy Cross.

Playing on the Sand Dunes: Great Sand Dunes National Park and Preserve, one of nature's most spectacular sandboxes, will allow you to feel like a kid again as you hike up a 750-foot dune—sinking in every step of the way—and then roll down the other side.

The meeting of Interstate 25 and U.S. 24 is vital to the life and commerce of Colorado Springs. This crossroads was also significant to the Ute Indians who followed roughly the same trails when they ruled the land for centuries. (That's why the road to the city of Woodland Park is called "Ute Pass.") Today the intersection is vacation junction for travelers headed for high altitude and high adventure, using the Springs as a comfortable base camp. With the Front Range always outlining the West, it's hard to get lost.

The most direct route from Colorado Springs to the state's southern border is Interstate 25, but it's certainly not the most interesting. Instead of wedding yourself to the interstate, consider making one of the following loops. If you want to explore these regions, plan on a couple of days for each loop. In a two- or three-day trip you could start in Cripple Creek and Victor, on the far side of the massive Pikes Peak from Colorado Springs, then visit the Florissant Fossil Beds. Next, head to Buena Vista or Salida and, perhaps, go rafting, hiking, or mountain biking before heading back to Interstate 25 via Pueblo. Another option would be to drive to Cañon City and the Royal Gorge (an easy day trip from Colorado Springs); then, if you're heading south from there, go directly to Pueblo on U.S. 50 before rejoining Interstate 25.

If you want an off-the-beaten-path trip, head eastward from Pueblo to visit Bents Fort or the parks near La Junta, and then rejoin Interstate 25 in Trinidad. Another beautiful drive is the Highway of Legends, which travels westward through the lovely Cuchara Valley. Instead of following the route right back to Interstate 25, you could keep going west over La Veta pass and down into the Alamosa area. Overnight in the Alamosa area to visit the Great Sand Dunes National Park and Preserve. Any of these routes will let you experience a variety of south central Colorado's charms.

ABOUT THE PARKS & RECREATION AREAS

South central Colorado is chock-full of parks and recreational areas, from the mountains in Pike and the San Isabel national forests to the rolling parks owned by the city of Colorado Springs. Strolling on the more-gentle trails, hiking or mountain biking up and down the mountainsides on old logging trails, or driving to the top of peaks provides a nonending series of incredible settings. Almost every chamber of commerce will have a list of local trails in the near vicinity, so when you're asking for general information about the city, ask for a list of trails, too. The Arkansas River flows through this region, so every spring and summer people come here to raft through a mix of challenging whitewater rapids interspersed with smoothly flowing sections. Pike, bass, and trout are plentiful in this region: Popular fishing spots include Spinney Mountain Reservoir (between Florissant and Buena Vista), the Arkansas and South Platte rivers, and Trinidad Lake.

Arkansas Headwaters Recreation Area (☏719/539–7289) is unique because it follows a linear 150-mi stretch of the Arkansas River, from the mountains near Leadville to Lake Pueblo. The Arkansas River is popular for rafting and kayaking, and fisherman love it for the brown trout. There are six campgrounds along the river.

The **Collegiate Peaks Wilderness Area** (☏719/486–0749), northwest of Buena Vista, includes 14 mountains above 14,000 feet and is known for superb hiking, mountain biking, and climbing.

Great Sand Dunes National Park and Preserve (☏719/378–6300 ⊕www.nps.gov/grsa) in the San Luis Valley is perfect for walking up (and sliding down) the dunes, hiking on mountain trails, kite flying, and wildlife viewing.

Pike National Forest (☏719/636–1602) encompasses millions of acres of public land that stretch along the Front Range and go deep into the Rockies. Pikes Peak is the best-known 14,000-footer in Pike.

In Colorado Springs alone there are numerous types of parks, including Bear Creek Canyon, Fountain Creek, Garden of the Gods, and Monument Valley Park. **El Paso County Parks and Leisure Services** (☏719/520–6375 ⊕http://adm.elpasoco.com/parks_and_leisure_services) can provide information about facilities in the Colorado Springs/Pikes Peak area. The **Colorado Springs Parks, Recreation and Cultural Services Department** (☏719/385–5940) is also handy with outdoors information.

Ring of the Peak (⊕ *www.ringthepeak.com*) is a collection of trails, four-wheel-drive roads, and a few roads that circle Pikes Peak. This is a work in progress, and only a portion of the trail system is complete. Altitudes range between 6,400 and 11,400. Check the Web site for trail access.

Monarch, west of Salida, is the nearest ski area.

ABOUT THE RESTAURANTS

Many restaurants serve regional trout and game, as well as locally grown fruits and vegetables. In summer look for cantaloupe from the town of Rocky Ford, dubbed the "Melon Capital of the World." Other than top-notch Mexican eateries, there's not much variety in terms of ethnic foods outside Colorado Springs. Colorado Springs offers unique Colorado cuisine that zings taste buds without zapping budgets (plus the ubiquitous chain restaurants).

ABOUT THE HOTELS

The lodging star is the Broadmoor resort in Colorado Springs, built from the booty of the late-19th-century gold-rush days, but there are also predictable boxy-bed motel rooms awaiting travelers at the junctions of major highways throughout the region. Interspersed are quaint mom-and-pop motels, as well as bed-and-breakfasts and small luxury hotels in tourist districts.

WHAT IT COSTS					
	¢	$	$$	$$$	$$$$
RESTAURANTS	under $8	$8–$12	$13–$18	$19–$25	over $25
HOTELS	under $80	$80–$120	$121–$170	$171–$230	over $230

Restaurant prices are for a main course at dinner, excluding 7.4% tax. Hotel prices are for two people in a standard double room in high season, excluding service charges and 9.4%–11.7% tax.

TIMING

Colorado Springs is a good year-round choice, because winters are relatively mild. The early summer is best if you want adrenaline-rush rafting, because the snowmelt is feeding the rivers. Summer is tourist season everywhere in south central Colorado. Early fall is another good time to visit, especially when the aspen leaves are turning gold. Many of the lodging properties in the smaller towns are closed in winter, although there are always some open for the cross-country skiers who enjoy staying in the small high-mountain towns.

COLORADO SPRINGS

The contented residents of the Colorado Springs area believe they live in an ideal location, and it's hard to argue with them. To the west, the Rockies form a majestic backdrop. To the east, the plains stretch for miles. Taken together, the setting ensures a mild, sunny climate year-round, and makes skiing and golfing on the same day feasible with no more than a two- or three-hour drive. You don't have to choose between adventures here: you can climb the Collegiate Peaks one day, and go white-water rafting on the Arkansas River the next.

The region abounds in natural and man-made wonders, from the red sandstone monoliths of the Garden of the Gods to the space-age architecture of the U.S. Air Force Academy's Cadet Chapel. The most indelible landmark is unquestionably Pikes Peak (14,110 feet); after seeing the view from the peak, Katharine Lee Bates penned "America the Beautiful." Pikes Peak is a constant reminder that this very contemporary city is still close to nature. Purple in the early morning, snow-packed after winter storms, capped with clouds on windy days, the mountain is a landmark for directions and, when needed, a focus of contemplation.

General William Jackson Palmer, president of the Denver & Rio Grande Railroad, founded Colorado Springs in the 1870s and shaped it as a utopian vision of fine living. Original broad, tree-lined boulevards still grace sections of the city. With the discovery of hot springs in the area, the well-to-do descended on the bustling resort town to take the waters and to enjoy the mild climate and fresh air. It became known as "Saratoga of the West" and "Little London," the latter for the snob appeal of its considerable resident and visiting English population. Folks who had tuberculosis also came here, and spent days sitting on the wide porches in the more-historic sections of the city, believing that the clean, clear air would help heal them. The discovery of gold at nearby Cripple Creek toward the end of the 19th century signaled another boom for the Springs. In the early part of the 1900s, until the mines petered out just before World War I, the residents' per-capita wealth was the highest in the nation.

After World War II, city leaders invited the military to move in, and the Colorado Springs personality changed drastically. Today, the military is the largest employer in the city; the local economy is dependent on Department of Defense contracts related to the army's Fort Carson (Colorado's largest military base, just south of downtown Colorado Springs), NORAD, Shreiver Air Force Base, and the Peterson Air Force Base complex.

If Colorado Springs is anything, it's organized, and it manages all the utilities, one of the hospitals, and the airport. The state's second-largest city, it is known as a politically and socially conservative bastion, and the reputation is somewhat deserved (the evangelical group Focus on the Family has its headquarters here). Yet, though tax-raising school bond issues have a hard time at the polls, the Springs voted to fund new open-space initiatives by a two-to-one margin. This is the West, but a West that understands the value of stewardship when it comes to its natural resources.

FESTIVALS   The **Colorado Festival of World Theatre** (☎719/473–1737 ⊕*www.cfwt. org*) is a two-week Pandora's box of exciting theater for all ages. The early fall festival ranges from Broadway-style evenings to comedians and serious drama. Check the Web site or call for information on the current festival.

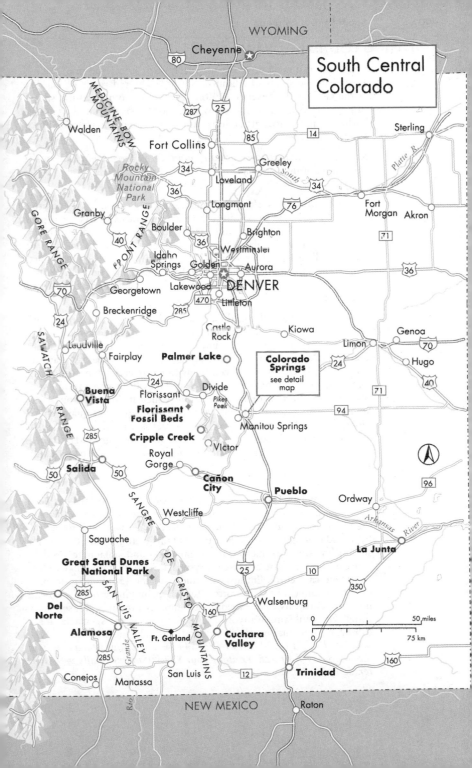

EXPLORING COLORADO SPRINGS

Pikes Peak is a must-do and pairs nicely with an afternoon of poking around in the shops of Manitou Springs. The red rocks of Garden of the Gods and Cheyenne Cañon Park are the other natural show-stoppers—mix and match them with exploring the surrounding neighborhoods and tourist attractions. And don't forget the U.S. Air Force Academy, just north of town.

Numbers in the text correspond to numbers in the margin and on the Colorado Springs Vicinity map.

PIKES PEAK & MANITOU SPRINGS

Access points for scaling the mighty Pikes Peak are in Manitou Springs. The home of Manitou Springs mineral water is set in this quaint National Historic Landmark District, which exudes an informal charm. The chamber of commerce offers free walking tours of the naturally effervescent springs. (You can also do self-guided tours. Stop at the chamber for a map.) Stop by Soda Springs or Twin Springs during the day, or for an after-dinner spritz (it tastes and acts just like Alka-Seltzer).

TIMING
This is not a "been there, done that, and got a T-shirt to prove it" type of area. Allow yourself enough time here to explore some of the region's most interesting sites and experiences. It takes a full day to visit Pikes Peak, explore Manitou Springs, and visit some of the attractions along Highway 24, if you want to enjoy each without doing a marathon sprint. Whether you head up Pikes Peak in a car and stop for lunch at the top, or take the train (which includes a stop at the summit), plan at least three hours. Visiting the variety of quaint shops along historic Manitou Springs' main street is a good way to stretch your legs after the journey to the Peak. Heading underground into Cave of the Winds, or visiting the Cliff Dwellings Museum will easily fill up the rest of the day.

WHAT TO SEE

★ ❷ **Cave of the Winds.** Discovered by two boys in 1880, the cave has been exploited as a tourist sensation ever since. The entrance is through the requisite "trading post," but once inside the cave you'll forget the hype and commercialism. The cave contains examples of every major sort of limestone formation, from stalactites and stalagmites to delicate cave flowers, rare anthracite crystals, flowstone (rather like candle wax), and cave coral. Enthusiastic guides for the 45-minute tour, most of them members of the Grotto Club (a spelunking group), also run more-adventurous cave expeditions. Summer evenings, a laser show transforms Williams Canyon, the backdrop for the spectacle. It's a campy, yet undeniably effective, sound-and-light show. ⊠ *Cave of the Winds Rd. off Hwy. 24* ☎ *719/685–5444* ⊕ *www.caveofthewinds.com* ☞ *Discovery Tour $18, Lantern Tour $22* ☉ *Summer, daily 9–9; winter, daily 10–5.*

★ ❺ **Manitou Cliff Dwellings Museum.** Some Ancestral Puebloan cliff dwellings that date from the 1100s have been moved from other sites in southern Colorado to the museum. Two rooms of artifacts in the museum offer information on the history of the dwellings. Native American dance demonstrations take place several times a day in summer. ⊠ *U. S. 24* ☎ *719/685–5242* ⊕ *www.cliffdwellingsmuseum.com* ☞ *$8.50* ☽ *May–Sept., daily 9–6; Oct. and Nov., Mar. and Apr., daily 9–5; Dec.–Feb. 1, 9–4.*

❹ **Manitou Springs.** The town grew around the springs, so all 10 of them are smack in the middle of downtown. Competitions to design the fountains that bring the springwater to the public ensured that each fountain design is unique. It's a bring-your-own-cup affair; the water (frequently tested) is potable and free. The chamber of commerce publishes a free guide to the springs. ☎ *719/685–5089* ☞ *Free.*

❸ **Miramont Castle Museum.** This Byzantine extravaganza was commissioned in 1895 as the private home of French priest Jean-Baptiste Francolon. The museum is a mad medley of exhibits, with more than 40 rooms offering a wide variety of displays, from original furnishings to antique doll and railroad collections. ⊠ *9 Capitol Hill Ave.* ☎ *719/685–1011* ⊕ *www.pikes-peak.com* ☞ *$6* ☽ *Summer, Mon.–Sat. 9–5; fall and spring, Mon.–Sat. 1–4; winter, Mon.–Sat. noon–3.*

★ **Pikes Peak.** If you want to see the view from the top of Pikes Peak, the view that Katharine Bates described in "America the Beautiful," head up this 14,110-foot-high mountain on a train, in a car, or in a pair of hiking boots, if you've got the stamina. Summit House is a pit-stop café and trading post at the very top of the mountain. Whichever route you choose to take, do take time to visit the top of this spectacular peak, so prominent that pioneers heading West via wagon train used to say: "Pikes Peak or Bust."

You can drive the 19-mi **Pikes Peak Highway** (☞ *$10; $35 maximum per carload*), which rises nearly 7,000 feet in its precipitous, dizzying climb; stop at the top for lunch and to enjoy the view; then be at the base again in approximately three hours. This is the same route that leading race-car drivers follow every year in the famed Pikes Peak Hill Climb, at speeds that have reached 123 mi per hour. The 12.6-mi hike up **Barr Trail** gains 7,510 feet in elevation before you reach the summit. Halfway up the trail is Barr Camp, where many hikers spend the night. ✛ *U. S. 24 west to Cascade, 4 mi from Manitou Springs* ☎ *719/684–9383* ☽ *Summit House May–Oct., daily 7–7; Nov.–Apr., daily 9–3, weather permitting.*

❶ **Pikes Peak Cog Railway.** The world's highest cog railway departs from Manitou and follows a frolicking stream up a steep canyon, through stands of quaking aspen and towering lodgepole pines, before reaching the timberline and the 14,110-foot summit of Pikes Peak. ⊠ *Depot, 515 Ruxton Ave.* ☎ *719/685–5401* ⊕ *www.cograilway.com* ☞ *$30* ☽ *Open year-around; check Web site or call for schedule.*

THE BROADMOOR & CHEYENNE CAÑON

Up in the Cheyenne Cañon section of town there are some terrific natural sites. Along the way you can view some of the city's exclusive neighborhoods and stop for lunch at the Broadmoor.

TIMING This is a good drive if there are kids in your group, because you can include stops at the Cheyenne Mountain Zoo and the Will Rogers Shrine of the Sun. Young ones can also blow off any extra energy racing up and down the paths at Seven Falls. Depending upon where you decide to stop, this could take a half to a full day.

WHAT TO SEE

6 | Fodor's Choice ★

The Broadmoor. This pink-stucco Italianate complex, which was built in 1918, is truly one of the world's great luxury resorts. Even if you don't stay here, stop by for lunch on one of the restaurant patios in summer and to take a paddleboat ride on Lake Cheyenne, which anchors several of the resort's buildings. ⊠*1 Lake Circle* ☎*719/634–7711 or 800/634–7711* ⊕*www.broadmoor.com.*

☪ ★ **7**

Cheyenne Mountain Zoo. America's highest zoo, at 6,800 feet, has more than 500 animals amid mossy boulders and ponderosa pines. You can hand-feed the giraffe herd in the zoo's African Rift Valley, and check out the animals living in Primate World, Wolves Alley, or the Asian Highlands. ⊠*4250 Cheyenne Mountain Zoo Rd.* ☎*719/633–9925* ⊕*www.cmzoo.org* ☎*$12, includes admission to Will Rogers Shrine* ☾*Memorial Day–Labor Day, daily 9–6; Labor Day–Memorial Day, daily 9–5. Gate closes at 4.*

☪ **10**

North Cheyenne Cañon Park. This is Colorado Springs at its best. Nearby Seven Falls has the hand of man all over its natural wonders, but the 1,600 acres of this city park manifest nature and natural history without a hint of commercialism—or charge. Start at **Starsmore Discovery Center** (☾*Apr.–Oct., daily. Call for hrs; vary by season*) at the mouth of the canyon off Cheyenne Boulevard. The center is chock-full of nature exhibits and a climbing wall where kids can try their hands and feet against gravity. The canyon's moderate hikes include lower Columbine and Mount Cutler trails, each less than a 3-mi round-trip. Both afford a view of the city and a sense of accomplishment. ⊠*2120 S. Cheyenne Cañon Rd.* ☎*719/385–6086* ☎*Free* ☾*Summer, daily 9–5; fall and spring, Wed.–Sun. 9–5.*

★ **9**

Seven Falls. The road up to this transcendent series of cascades is touted as the "grandest mile of scenery in Colorado." That's an exaggeration, but the red-rock canyon *is* amazing—though no more so than the falls themselves, plummeting into a tiny emerald pool. A set of 224 steep steps leads to the top, but there's an elevator, too. Hours vary seasonally so it may be wise to call ahead. ⊠*2850 Cheyenne Canyon Rd.*

☎719/632–0765 🖹$8.75 before 5 PM; $10.25 after 5 PM ⊙May–Sept., daily 8:30 AM–10:30 PM; Oct.–Apr., daily 9–4.

⑧ Will Rogers Shrine of the Sun. This five-story tower was dedicated in 1937 after the tragic plane crash that claimed Rogers's life. Its interior is painted with all manner of Western murals (in which Rogers and Colorado Springs benefactor Spencer Penrose figure prominently) and is plastered with photos and homespun sayings of America's favorite cowboy. In the chapel are 15th- and 16th-century European artworks. ⊠*Cheyenne Mountain Zoo Rd.* ☎719/578–5367 🖹$12, includes admission to Cheyenne Mountain Zoo ⊙Memorial Day–Labor Day, daily 9–5:30; Labor Day–Memorial Day, daily 9–4:30. Last entrance time in summer is 4; in winter, 3.

GARDEN OF THE GODS & URBAN COLORADO SPRINGS

This tour combines a chance to see some outstanding artworks, visit some unique museums, and stroll through one of the most beautiful city parks in the country.

TIMING Depending on which museums you decide to visit, a tour of Garden of the Gods and urban Colorado Springs could take from two-thirds of a day to a full day to take everything in, from learning how the pioneers struggled to survive and thrive, to strolling through the stunning red-rock cliffs and visiting the Trading Post at Garden of the Gods.

WHAT TO SEE

🖑 **⑭ ANA Money museum.** The American Numismatic Association's Money Museum has a collection of old gold coins, mistakes made at the U.S. Mint, and currency from around the world. ⊠*818 N. Cascade Ave.* ☎800/367–9723 ⊕*www.money.org* 🖹Free ⊙Tues.–Fri. 9–5, Sat. 10–5, Sun. noon–5. Tours are available weekdays

⑬ Colorado Springs Fine Arts Center. This regional museum has just added to the existing building, doubling its exhibition space, and is being lauded by architects and locals. The museum has a fine permanent collection of modern art, and rotating exhibits. Some highlight the cultural contributions of regional artists; others focus on famous artists, such as the glassmaker Dale Chihuly. ⊠*30 W. Dale St.* ☎719/634–5581 ⊕*www.csfineartscenter.org* 🖹$7.50 ⊙Mon. and Tues. 9–5, Thurs.–Sat. 10 AM–8 PM, Sun. 10–5.

⑰ Garden of the Gods. These magnificent, eroded red-sandstone formations—from gnarled jutting spires to sensuously abstract monoliths—were sculpted more than 300 million years ago. Follow the road as it loops through the Garden of the Gods, past such oddities as the Three Graces, the Siamese Twins, and the Kissing Camels. High Point, near the south entrance, provides camera hounds with the ultimate photo op: a formation known as Balanced Rock, and jagged formations that frame Pikes Peak. The visitor center has several geologic, historic, and hands-on displays, as well as a café. ⊠*Visitor and Nature Center, 1805 N. 30th St., at Gateway Rd.* ☎719/634–6666 ⊕*www.gardenofgods.com* 🖹Free ⊙May–Oct., daily 5 AM–11 PM; Nov.–May, 5 AM–9 PM.

Fodor'sChoice
★

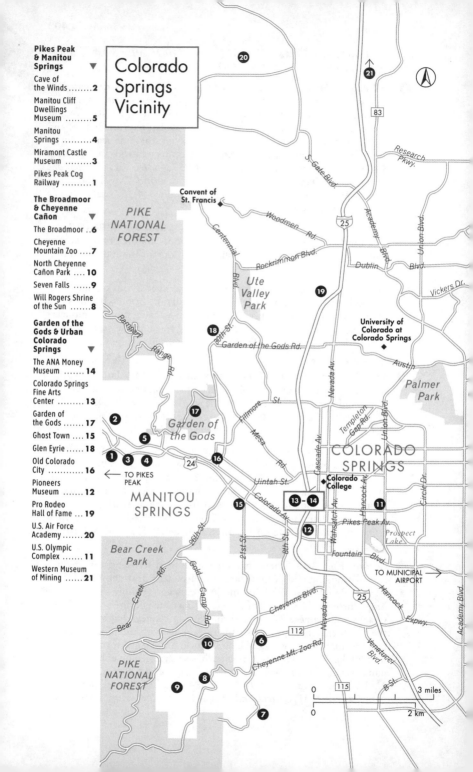

Colorado Springs Vicinity

PIKE NATIONAL FOREST

Convent of St. Francis

Ute Valley Park

University of Colorado at Colorado Springs

Palmer Park

Garden of the Gods

COLORADO SPRINGS

Colorado College

MANITOU SPRINGS

TO PIKES PEAK

Bear Creek Park

PIKE NATIONAL FOREST

Prospect Lake

TO MUNICIPAL AIRPORT

Research Pkwy.

Woodmen Rd.

Rockrimmon Blvd.

Dublin Blvd.

Vickers Dr.

Austin

S. Gate Blvd.

Centennial Blvd.

Garden of the Gods Rd.

Fillmore St.

Mesa Rd.

Uintah St.

Colorado Av.

Pikes Peak Av.

Fountain Blvd.

Cheyenne Blvd.

Cheyenne Mt. Zoo Rd.

Bear Creek Rd.

Gold Camp Rd.

26th St.

21st St.

8th St.

Nevada Av.

Cascade Av.

Wahsatch Av.

Hancock Av.

Circle Dr.

Templeton Gap Rd.

Union Blvd.

Academy Blvd.

Hancock Expwy.

Nevada Av.

Venetucci Blvd.

B St.

Range Rd.

Beaver Rd.

31st St.

0 ____ 3 miles

0 ____ 2 km

CLOSE UP

A Walk in the Founder's Footsteps

11

General William Jackson Palmer was the city founder of Colorado Springs and an obsessed Europhile. He built the Springs in his image of "Little London" and gave his personal estate, Glen Eyrie, a Scottish name. Though he built his castlelike home for his wife, whom he adoringly called Queenie, you could say he was the homemaker in the relationship. Gathering treasures from the four corners of the old country, he was responsible for furnishing and decorating their expansive abode. Despite his preference for all things European, Palmer was as American as any other Andrew Carnegie-era philanthropist. He carefully planned Colorado Springs, donated a fortune in land for parks, and brought cottonwood trees from the Arkansas River valley to shade the streets. Take a day to trace the good general's steps, spending a night at the castle, just north of the Garden of the Gods. Awaken to the same sight he did: early-morning sun lighting the red-rock formations beneath a blue Colorado sky. Then hike a bit on the local trails (you can get permission for this from the present caretakers, the Navigators Christian ministry). Palmer was known to survey the grounds daily, by foot or horseback. Breathe the mountain air and listen to babbling brooks before returning to the landscaped green lawns. When done with your day at Glen Eyrie, drive to the intersection of Platte and Nevada in downtown Colorado Springs, where a statue of the general seems to direct traffic adjacent to Acacia Park, one of many parks that came to be because of his generous land donations. In the cool of the shade, offer the old boy a salute.

---

⑮ Ghost Town. You can play a real player piano and a nickelodeon at this Western town with a sheriff's office, general store, saloon, and blacksmith. ⊠ *400 S. 21st St.* ☎ *719/634–0696* 🖻 *$6.50* ☉ *June–Aug., Mon.–Sat. 9–6, Sun. 11–6; Sept.–May, Mon.–Sat. 10–5, Sun. 11–5.*

⑱ Glen Eyrie. General William Jackson Palmer, the founder of Colorado Springs, was greatly influenced by European architecture and lifestyle and lived in this evolving mansion-turned-castle from its beginnings in the 1870s until his death in 1909. Original gas lamps and sandstone structures remain. Many of its rocks were hewn with the moss still clinging, to give them an aged look. There's an extravagant drive-through nativity scene at Christmastime. The grandiose estate is maintained by a nondenominational fundamentalist Christian ministry called the Navigators, which runs programs and seminars, and publishes religious literary works. An afternoon English tea is offered daily in summer. ⊠ *3820 30th St.* ☎ *719/634–0808* ⊕ *www.gleneyrie. org* 🖻 *$5* ☉ *Tours: June–Aug., Tues.–Fri. at 11; Sept.–May, Fri.–Sun. at 1. Tea at 2:30. Reservations required for tours and tea.*

⑯ Old Colorado City. Once a separate, rowdier town where miners caroused, today the stretch of Colorado Avenue between 24th Street and 28th Street, west of downtown, is a National Historic Landmark District whose restored buildings house choice galleries and boutiques as well as tourist shops with inexpensive souvenirs. ⊠ *Colorado Ave. between 24th and 28th St.,* ⊕ *west of downtown.*

⑫ **Pioneers Museum.** Once the Old El Paso County Courthouse, this repository has artifacts relating to the entire Pikes Peak area. The historic courtroom is absolutely elegant, and so perfectly appointed that it looks as if a judge will walk in any minute to start a trial. It's most notable for the special exhibits the museum puts together or receives on loan from institutions like the Smithsonian, such as the quilt competition that commemorated the 100th anniversary of the song "America the Beautiful." ⊠ *215 S. Tejon St.* ☎ *719/385–5990* ⊕ *www.cspm.org* ✉ *Free* ⊙ *Summer, Tues.–Sat. 10–5, Sun. 1–5; call for winter hrs.*

⑲ **Pro Rodeo Hall of Fame and Museum of the American Cowboy.** Even a tenderfoot would get a kick out of this museum, which includes changing displays of Western art; permanent photo exhibits that capture both the excitement of bronco-bustin' and the lonely life of the cowpoke; gorgeous saddles and belt buckles; and multimedia tributes to rodeo's greatest competitors. ⊠ *101 Pro Rodeo Dr., Exit 147 off I–25* ☎ *719/528–4764* ⊕ *www.prorodeo.com* ✉ *$6* ⊙ *Daily 9–5.*

⑳ **U.S. Air Force Academy.** The academy, which set up camp in 1954, is one
Fodor's Choice of the most popular attractions in Colorado. Highlights include the
★ futuristic design, 18,000 beautiful acres of land, and antique and historic aircraft displays. At the visitor center you'll find photo exhibits, a model of a cadet's room, a gift shop, a snack bar, and a 14-minute film designed to make you want to enlist on the spot. Other stops on the tour include a B-52 display, sports facilities, a parade ground (the impressive cadet review takes place on Monday, Wednesday, and Friday at noon; at other times of day, watch the freshmen square off their corners), and the chapel. The Air Force chapel, which can accommodate simultaneous Catholic, Jewish, and Protestant services, is easily recognized by its unconventional design, which features 17 spires that resemble sharks' teeth or billowing sails. ⊠ *Visitors can enter through North Gate, from Exit 156B, off I–25, or the South Gate, from Exit 150, off I–25* ☎ *719/333–2025* ⊕ *www.usafa.af.mil/* ✉ *Free* ⊙ *Daily 9–5.*

★ ⑪ **U.S. Olympic Complex.** America's hopefuls come to train and be tested here, and depending on which teams are in residence at the time, you might catch a glimpse of some future Wheaties-box material. The hourly guided tours begin with an 8-minute video, followed by a 30-minute walk around the facilities. ⊠ *1750 E. Boulder St.* ☎ *719/866–4618* ✉ *Free* ⊙ *Mon.–Sat. 9–5.*

㉑ **Western Museum of Mining and Industry.** The rich history of mining is represented through comprehensive exhibits of equipment and techniques and hands-on demonstrations, including gold panning. The 27-acre mountain site has several outdoor exhibits, and is a great spot for a picnic. ⊠ *Exit 156A, off I–25* ☎ *719/488–0880* ⊕ *www.wmmi.org* ✉ *$8* ⊙ *Mon.–Sat. 9–4.*

SPORTS & THE OUTDOORS

ADVENTURE TOURS

A number of activities are available within an hour or two of Colorado Springs, including hot-air ballooning, white-water rafting, and access jeep tours. Riding in a jeep is one way to view the backcountry; a horseback ride on trails through meadows and along mountainsides is another.

THE EAST COURSE

The Broadmoor's East Course has been toughened up for the U.S. Senior Open in summer 2008, and will remain a challenge long after the pros leave. See how your skills compare with the pros when hitting out of the tougher rough and putting on the slick greens.

Adventures Out West (⊠*1680 S. 21st St.* ⊕*www.adventuresoutwest. com* ☎ *719/578–0935 or 800/755–0935*) offers high-adventure trips through the Royal Gorge and gentler trips through Bighorn Sheep Canyon. They can also arrange other activities, such as ballooning, horseback riding, and jeep tours. **Echo Canyon River Expeditions** (⊠*45000 U.S. Hwy. 50, Cañon City* ☎*800/755–3246* ⊕*www.raftecho.com*) offers rafting on the Arkansas and Colorado rivers. They have a Raft and Rail trip, which includes a morning on the Arkansas River and a ride on the Royal Gorge Railroad in the afternoon. They will also customize trips.

GOLF

★ **The Broadmoor Golf Club.** The three courses here offer distinctly diverse challenges, in part because they travel over a variety of terrain on the resort's 3,000 acres in the Rocky Mountain foothills. Donald Ross designed the original resort course in 1918, but today the East Course is a mix including nine of the original holes and nine more designed by Robert Trent Jones Sr. in 1965. Since the Broadmoor arranged to host the 2008 U.S. Senior Open, the course has been toughened dramatically to fit PGA tournament standards. Some of the fairways were narrowed—one now has a landing area just 22 feet wide—grass on the greens was tweaked so balls look like they're sliding over ice, and balls hit in the rough are now hard to find. The West Course is also a combination of holes designed by each golf-course architect, but it's at a higher elevation (6,800 feet above sea level), and has more-vicious doglegs, rolling fairways, and multilevel greens. The Mountain Course, which reopened in July 2006 after an extensive redesign by Nicklaus Design, has some wide forgiving fairways and large greens but there are major elevation changes that add special challenges, while providing outstanding mountain views. ⊠*1 Lake Circle* ☎*719/577–5790* ⊕*www.broadmoor.com* ⌕*Reservations essential* ⚲*East Course: 18 holes. Yards: 7,310. Par: 72. Mountain Course: 18 holes. Yards: 7,637. Par: 72. West Course: 18 holes. Yards: 7,016. Par: 72. Green Fee: $95/$190, depending on season and course.*

HIKING

Some of the best choices for hiking in the Pikes Peak area are the Barr Trail, which heads up the mountain, and trails in North Cheyenne Cañon Park.

Red Rock Canyon (✛ *Trailhead: Just south of U.S. 24 near 31st St.*), is a Colorado Springs city park. The are a few formal trails—many more are in the works. You can ramble among the red sandstone monoliths and spires, balanced by white limestone and yellow-brown sandstone hogbacks.

Red Rock Loop Trail, on Manitou Section 16, is a 5.5-mi, moderately difficult loop with an elevation gain up to 1,100 feet. The topography varies from steep, mountainous terrain to moderate slopes, mesas, and canyons. There are views of sandstone formations and old quarries, as well as a terrific perspective of Colorado Springs and of Pikes Peak. ✛ *Trailhead: From I–25, Exit 141, west on U.S. 24 (Cimarron) to 21st St., south on 21st St. to Lower Gold Camp Rd.; west on Lower Gold Camp Rd. to Upper Gold Camp Rd.; south on Upper Gold Camp Rd. to trailhead on west side of road.*

> **WORD OF MOUTH**
>
> "The absolutely biggest hit of the trip was the white-water rafting in the Arkansas River close to the Royal Gorge. We went as a family and we all loved it. It was one of the most exhilarating things I have ever done. The boys liked it so much that they took an all-day, more-intense ride the next day. We also went on a helicopter ride in the Gorge, that was pretty exciting too."   —BellaD

Santa Fe Trail and Pikes Peak Greenway Trails. The two combined offer about 26 mi of multi-surface trails for hiking and biking. The trails run from Tejon Street through Colorado Springs into the Air Force Academy and north to Palmer Lake. A 6.9-mi section goes through the Air Force Academy, but you are expected to stay on the 6-foot-wide trail. (Helmets and ID are required on the Academy grounds, which may be closed at times.) Past the Academy, the trail then flows over gently rolling hills and finally follows a straight line and level course over an abandoned railroad track for the last 6.5 mi into Palmer. ⊠*El Paso County Parks* ☎*719/520–6375* ⊕*http://adm.elpasoco. com/parks_and_leisure_services.*

HORSEBACK RIDING
Academy Riding Stables (⊠*4 El Paso Blvd.* ☎*719/633–5667*) offers trail rides.

MOUNTAIN BIKING
Challenge Unlimited (☎*800/798–5954*) offers bike tours throughout Colorado, including the twice-daily 20-mi bike tour down Pikes Peak May through mid-October. The tours include helmets and bikes. **Pikes Peak Mountain Bike Tours** (☎*888/593–3062*) will take you to the top of Pikes Peak, then let you ride all the way down on one of their lightweight mountain bikes. An alternative tour is the 20-mi bike tour on Upper Gold Camp Road, which is a self-paced downhill ride along an old railroad tract converted to a hiking–bicycling trail that cuts through the mountains.

WHERE TO EAT

$$$$ ✕**Charles Court at the Broadmoor.** Charles Court's contemporary country-manor decor lends warmth to a fine-dining setting. Many of the tables in the large open space have a wonderful view of Cheyenne Lake. Table-top items such as napkin rings and centerpieces made from hand-blown glass add a lovely touch. The menu is American-oriented, with a Rocky Mountain flair. Try the Colorado rack of lamb, the tenderloin of buffalo, or the halibut during a leisurely dinner. The restaurant, which faces the hotel's interior grounds and lake, has a wine cellar with more than 3,000 bottles. ✉ *The Broadmoor West, 1 Lake Circle* ☎ *719/577–5733* ▤ *AE, D, MC, V.*

★ $$$$ ✕**Penrose Room at the Broadmoor.** Whatever number of courses you order, you're guaranteed a memorable culinary and visual experience here. Executive Chef Bertrand Bouquin varies the menu seasonally, offering fine dining without the constraints of Continental, American, or any other single cuisine. Appetizers such as sautéed fois gras with caramelized apple butter, and entrées such as monkfish and lobster tail wrapped in country bacon with black truffle risotto and baby fennel, are plated to look like edible works of art. The best choice is the seven-course meal with wine pairings ($130). Request a table in the small glassed-in area and you can watch the sun set behind Cheyenne Mountain, or if you're with a group of friends, ask about sitting at the 16-seat Chef's Table in the demonstration kitchen. ✉ *The Broadmoor South, 1 Lake Circle* ☎ *719/577–5733* ⌂ *Reservations essential* ▤ *AE, D, MC, V.*

$$$–$$$$ ✕**Briarhurst Manor.** One of the most exquisitely romantic restaurants in Colorado, Briarhurst Manor has several dining rooms, each with its own look and mood. The rich decor includes cherrywood wainscoting, balustrades, and furnishings; Van Briggle wood-and-ceramic fireplaces, tapestries, chinoiserie, and hand-painted glass. Dine in the Garden Room, which has massive bow windows, or in the book-lined Library. In the Drawing Room, with its ornate chandelier and fireplace, the tables are nicely spaced for conversation. The restaurant offers small plates, such as Red Deer Diane (venison tenderloin with mushrooms, shallots, brandy, and demi-glace) and Maroon Bells trout, plus entrées including lemon pesto wild salmon and Manitou Beef Wellington. ✉ *404 Manitou Ave.* ☎ *719/685–1864* ▤ *AE, MC, V.*

$$$–$$$$ ✕**Craftwood Inn.** This intimate restaurant, more than 50 years old, regularly hosted such luminaries as Cary Grant, Bing Crosby, and Liberace. A delightful Old English feel is achieved through wrought-iron chandeliers, stained-glass partitions, heavy wood beams, and a majestic stone-and-copper fireplace. Craftwood focuses on game, so try the Wild Grill, an elk, antelope, and venison sausage combo; the roasted loin of antelope, served with a porcini mushroom cream sauce; or stuffed boneless breast of pheasant baked in phyllo pastry and served with roasted garlic linguine. Accompany your dinner with a selection from the well-considered wine list. ✉ *404 El Paso Blvd., Manitou Springs* ☎ *719/685–9000* ▤ *AE, D, DC, MC, V* ☉ *No lunch.*

$$$–$$$$ ✕ **La Petite Maison.** Pale pink walls, floral tracery, Parisian gallery posters, and pots overflowing with flowers create the cozy atmosphere of a French country home in this pretty Victorian house. Chef–owner Henri Chaperont prepares imaginative dishes such as grilled magret de canard with ginger and coriander sauce, and lobster napoleon with vanilla sauce. Reservations are recommended for the two romantic dining rooms. ⊠ *1015 W. Colorado Ave.* ☎ *719/632–4887* ▭ *AE, D, DC, MC, V* ⊘ *Closed Mon. No lunch weekends.*

$$$–$$$$ ✕ **Pepper Tree.** From its hilltop position, the Pepper Tree enjoys stellar views of the city that enhance the restaurant's aura of quiet sophistication. It's one of those old-fashioned places where table-side preparations (including the inevitable and delectable pepper steak) are the stock-in-trade, and flambé is considered the height of both elegance and decadence. There are several fish selections, as well as entrées such as the Veil Neill—sautéed veal slices topped with king crab and hollandaise sauce. Reservations are recommended. ⊠ *888 W. Moreno Ave.* ☎ *719/471–4888* ▭ *AE, MC, V* ⊘ *Closed Sun. No lunch.*

★ $$$ ✕ **Blue Star.** Perch on a high stool in the bar while enjoying a glass of wine and tapas such as flash-fried calamari with sweet Thai chili sauce or rosemary pesto chicken pita pizza, or head to the simple and elegant dining room for a leisurely dinner. Influences drift around the globe, from pan-Asian to Mediterranean, and the kitchen at this hip restaurant works miracles regularly, whether you're in the mood for a half-pound Angus burger, sautéed crab cakes, or a spinach and artichoke salad. It's a place frequented by everyone from blue-haired ladies to college students, so it's best to make a reservation. Blue Star offers half-price wine on Sunday and the ever-popular Martini Monday. ⊠ *1645 S. Tejon St.* ☎ *719/632–1086* ▭ *AE, MC, V.*

$$$ ✕ **Carlos Bistro.** Although this chic spot, with its copper-and-black decor, is located a ways from the main tourist areas, it's a local favorite because of both its casual ambience and the quality of its food. Here you'll find patrons—some wearing jeans, others in suits—dining in the dim light on what appear to be pieces of art framed by triangular white plates. Start with fresh oysters or a blue-lump crab cake. Then move on to seared filet mignon with a black-peppercorn brandy sauce or Filet à la Oscar—lump blue-crab meat on filet mignon, topped with a béarnaise sauce. If you're not full, try the New Orleans chocolate bread pudding, or the white-chocolate bread pudding with macadamia nuts. ⊠ *1025 S. 21st St.* ☎ *719/471–2905* ▭ *AE, MC, V* ⊘ *Closed Sun. No lunch Sat.*

$$$ ✕ **Summit.** The ambience in the Broadmoor's "American Brasserie," along with the innovative contemporary American cuisine, is a successful blend of big-city elegance and Western casualness. The 14-foot wine tower revolving slowly behind the bar immediately grabs your eye; next you may take in Summit's curved room, with windows interspersed with wood columns. The menu includes year-round favorites and a seasonal section; you may enjoy the subtle blending in the chestnut-and-apple soup; the Maine lobster and persimmon salad; or the pan-seared wild striped bass with roasted salsify, black trumpet mushrooms, and veal jus. Thirty wines are served by the glass, and half the fun of din-

FodorśChoice
★

ing here is the conversation with the sommelier or the knowledgeable waitstaff about pairing the wine to food. Reservations are strongly recommended. ⊠*19 Lake Circle.* ☎*719/577–5775 or 800/634–7711* ⊟*AE, D, MC, V* ☉*Closed Mon.*

$–$$ ✗**Adam's Mountain Café.** In August 2007 this homey café moved to a new location in the historic Manitou Spa Building, taking along with it mismatched tables, drawings by a local artist, and the community table where you can sit to meet other diners. The new long dining room has tall windows overlooking the patio. The food still has an organic bent, with many vegetarian options. Smashing breakfasts include orange-almond French toast and huevos rancheros; dinners such as peanut-crusted salmon or orzo with sautéed broccoli and sun-dried tomatoes are hits as well. ⊠*634 Manitou Ave.* ☎*719/685–4370* ⊟*AE, D, MC, V* ☉*No dinner Sun. and Mon.*

$ ✗**El Tesoro Restaurant and Gallery.** At the turn of the 20th century this building served as a brothel, and then for many years it was an artists' atelier. Today, it's a restaurant that doubles as an art gallery. The adobe and exposed-brick walls and the tile work are original; rugs, textiles, and the ubiquitous garlands of chili add color. The sterling northern New Mexican food is the real thing—a savvy, savory blend of Native American, Spanish, and Anglo American influences. The *posole* (hominy with pork and red chili) is magical, the green chile heavenly, and innovative originals such as mango quesadillas (a brilliant pairing of sweet and spicy elements) are simply genius. ⊠*10 N. Sierra Madre St.* ☎*719/471–0106* ⊟*AE, D, MC, V* ☉*Closed Sun.*

☉ ¢ ✗**Poor Richards.** This is a four-in-one store loved by locals of all ages. On one side there's a pizza parlor, where you stand in line to order hand-tossed pizza, salads, and sandwiches. Step through a doorway and you're in a toy store. Step through another door and you'll find yourself in Rico's Coffee, Chocolate, & Wine Bar, where the ambience is more upscale, with wood floors and simple tables, and the menu veers toward organic. Order a sandwich or a cheese plate, or try a wine and chocolate pairing. Step though another doorway and you've entered a used-book store. You can enter each store from outside or through inside doors. ⊠*320–324½ N. Tejon St.* ☎*719/632–7721 for restaurant, 719/630–7723 for wine bar* ⊕*www.poorrichardswebsite. com* ⊟*MC, V.*

WHERE TO STAY

$$$$ ▦**The Broadmoor.** After a more than $200-million renovation, the B, as
Fodor'sChoice   frequent guests call this hostelry, truly shines. The Old World ambience
★   in Broadmoor Main—the signature pink building with the Mediterranean-style towers—was gussied up; small rooms were made larger, bathrooms were remodeled, and craftsmen restored the frescoes, walls, and ceilings in public areas. The spacious rooms in the cozier Lakeside building, most with fireplaces and either patios or balconies, are standouts. The South Tower's newly renovated rooms vary in size from snug to immense—request one with a lake-view balcony. In summer, families gather around the large infinity pool, which appears to flow into

Cheyenne Lake. The award-winning spa offers innovative treatments such as a pearl glow body therapy, which uses pearl powder combined with a body lotion to hydrate and exfoliate the skin, and a range of massages including Thai, Swedish, hot stone, and Ashiatsu. The tennis center and its instructors are excellent. **Pros:** you'll be thoroughly pampered at this world-class resort, choosing where to eat may be difficult because there are so many good options. **Cons:** very expensive, rooms in the original West building are the least desirable. ⊠*1 Lake Circle, 80906* ☎*719/634–7711 or 800/634–7711* ⊕*www.broadmoor. com* ⤴*993 rooms, 107 suites* ⟐*In-room: safe (some), DVD (some), VCR (some), ethernet. In-hotel: 11 restaurants, bars, golf courses, tennis courts, pools, gym, spa, concierge, children's programs (ages 4–12), laundry service, public Wi–Fi, airport shuttle, parking (fee), some pets allowed, no-smoking rooms* ▭*AE, DC, MC, V.*

$$–$$$ ⚏**Antlers Hilton Colorado Springs.** The marble-and-granite lobby strikes an immediate note of class, but the rooms are basic Hilton in style and size at this downtown hotel, whose location provides easy access to restaurants, shopping, and offices. The atrium off the lobby holds a day spa, which is not part of the hotel. **Pros:** good service, convenient location. **Con:** not enough ambience or amenities for a romantic getaway or a family trip. ⊠*4 S. Cascade Ave., 80903* ☎*719/955–5600 or 866/299–4602* ⊕*www.antlerscoloradosprings.hilton.com* ⤴*285 rooms, 7 suites* ⟐*In-room: ethernet. In-hotel: 2 restaurants, room service, bar, pool, gym, public Wi-Fi, laundry service, parking (fee), no-smoking rooms* ▭*AE, D, DC, MC, V.*

$$–$$$ ⚏**Cliff House.** This Victorian-era jewel was built in 1874 as a Manitou Springs stagecoach stop between Colorado Springs and Leadville. Crown princes, U.S. presidents, and famous entertainers have been past guests, and their names live on as monikers for several distinctly different and extremely attractive suites: the Katharine Bates, the Teddy Roosevelt, and the Clark Gable are a few. The Cliff House is a special occasion getaway plump with accoutrements that pamper: bathtubs for two, steam showers, and even heated towel racks and toilet seats. It's right off the main street, a two-minute walk from Manitou's shops and restaurants. **Pros:** convenient location, old-fashioned charm. **Con:** not a good choice for those who prefer contemporary ambience. ⊠*306 Cañon Ave., Manitou Springs 80829* ☎*719/685–3000 or 888/212–7000* ⊕*www.thecliffhouse.com* ⤴*38 rooms, 17 suites* ⟐*In-room: safe, refrigerator, VCR, ethernet. In-hotel: restaurant, room service, bar, gym, laundry service, public Wi-Fi, airport shuttle, parking (fee), no-smoking rooms* ▭*AE, D, MC, V.*

★ $$ ⚏**Cheyenne Mountain Resort.** At this 217-acre resort on the slopes of Cheyenne Mountain, superb swimming facilities (including an Olympic-size pool), a variety of tennis courts, and a Pete Dye championship golf course tempt you to remain on property, despite the easy access to the high country. The main lodge is an attractive setting for relaxing and dining, with a massive stone fireplace and thick wooden beams supporting the soaring ceiling. The elaborate Sunday brunch is delicious. The guest rooms, in eight separate buildings on the hillside, are simply but attractively decorated, with private balconies. Most have white walls and wood furniture with colorful spreads on the beds.

The views of nearby mountains are outstanding. **Pro:** despite the many business meetings here, the property has a resort ambience, especially if you stay in a room that overlooks the golf course. **Con:** you must walk outside to get to the main building. *✉3225 Broadmoor Valley Rd., 80906 ☎719/538–4000 or 800/428–8886 🌐www.cheyennemountain.com ⇨311 rooms, 5 suites ♨In-room: refrigerator, Wi-Fi. In-hotel: 2 restaurants, room service, bar, golf course, tennis courts, pools, gym, bicycles, concierge, children's programs (ages 5–12), laundry service, public Internet, airport shuttle, parking (no fee), no-smoking rooms ▭AE, D, DC, MC, V.*

$$ **Embassy Suites.** Situated at the northern end of the Springs, this hotel is one of the original properties in the chain. It was recently renovated; the airy atrium lobby is filled with plants and has two waterfalls. Suites, which are actually two rooms, unlike the suites at many hotels, are comfortable. The pool deck offers a view of Pikes Peak. **Pros:** two-room suites allow for privacy, free breakfast includes cooked-to-order options. **Cons:** right off the highway, to get to some of the downtown tourist attractions a few miles away, you may have to fight rush hour traffic on Interstate 25. *✉7290 Commerce Center Dr., 80919 ☎719/599–9100 or 800/362–2779 🌐www.embassysuites.com ⇨207 suites ♨In-room: refrigerator, ethernet. In-hotel: restaurant, bar, pool, gym, public Wi-Fi, no-smoking rooms ▭AE, D, DC, MC, V ⓘBP.*

$$ Fodor's Choice ★ **Holden House.** Innkeepers Sallie and Welling Clark realized their dream when they lovingly restored this 1902 Victorian home and transformed it into a B&B. Two rooms in the main house, two in the adjacent carriage house, and one in the Victorian next door are filled with family heirlooms and antiques. Guest rooms are cozy with fireplaces and down pillows and quilts; turn-down service and triple sheeting are some of the amenities that will make you feel well taken care of. The staff knows the region well and can be helpful to guests trying to decide what to do in Colorado Springs. A full breakfast is served in a dining room that looks like it's ready for Victorian ladies to walk in and have tea. **Pro:** good choice for travelers who want something a touch—but not overly—homey. **Con:** in a residential neighborhood, so you'll have to drive to attractions and restaurants. *✉1102 W. Pikes Peak Ave., 80904 ☎719/471–3980 🌐www.holdenhouse.com ⇨5 rooms ♨In-room: refrigerator, DVD, Wi-Fi. In-hotel: no elevator, no kids under 12, no-smoking rooms ▭AE, D, DC, MC, V ⓘBP.*

$–$$ **Victoria's Keep.** This turreted 1892 Queen Anne B&B has been restored: It is furnished with antiques and collectibles, but happily updated with modern bathrooms and amenities. Some of the six rooms have whirlpool tubs big enough for two and fireplaces. The only TV and VCR are in the parlor but are available for movie watching. The B&B is within walking distance of downtown Manitou Springs. Full breakfasts are served. **Pros:** charming period decor in rooms, a five-minute walk to Manitou's Main Street. **Cons:** one side of the B&B edges up to the intersection of a fairly busy street, no TVs in rooms. *✉202 Ruxton Ave., Manitou Springs 80829 ☎719/685–5354 or 800/905–5337 🌐www.victoriaskeep.com ⇨6 rooms ♨In-rooms: no phone, no TV, Wi-Fi. In-hotel: no elevator, public Internet, some pets allowed, no-smoking rooms ▭AE, D, MC, V ⓘBP.*

NIGHTLIFE & THE ARTS

THE ARTS

Colorado Springs' **Pikes Peak Center** (✉*190 S. Cascade Ave.* ☎*719/520–7469*) presents a wide range of musical events as well as touring theater and dance companies.

NIGHTLIFE

BARS & CLUBS **Cowboys** (✉*3910 Palmer Park Blvd.* ☎*719/596–1212*) is for hard-core two-steppers. The **Golden Bee** (✉*International Center at the Broadmoor, 1 Lake Circle* ☎*719/634–7711*) is an institution. The gloriously old-fashioned bar, with pressed-tin ceilings and magnificent woodwork, features a piano player leading sing-alongs. Watch out for the bees—as part of a long-standing tradition, they flick bee stickers into the audience during the show. You might be covered before the night is over. The **Ritz** (✉*15 S. Tejon* ☎*719/635–8484*), located downtown, fills up at cocktail hour and has a bistro-style menu for dining, but the action is on Wednesday, Friday, and Saturday when the live music starts. Locals say to get there before 7 PM if you want to eat. There are bands playing rock from the '50s, '60s, and other decades several nights a week at the Broadmoor **Tavern** (✉*1 Lake Circle* ☎*719/634–7711*).

BREWPUBS At **Bristol Brewing** (✉*1647 S. Tejon St.* ☎*719/633–2555* ☉*Weekdays 10–9, Sat. 9–9*) you can get fresh brews, like Laughing Lab, Red Rocket, and Beehive, in the tasting bar. **Judge Baldwin's** (✉*Antlers Hilton, 4 S. Cascade Ave.* ☎*719/473–5600*) is a brewpub in the Antlers Hilton Colorado Springs hotel. **Phantom Canyon Brewing Co.** (✉*2 E. Pikes Peak Ave.* ☎*719/635–2800*), in a turn-of-the-20th-century warehouse, has billiards in an upstairs hall. There's great pub grub, plus sinful black-and-tan brownies.

COMEDY & **Loonees Comedy Corner** (✉*1305 N. Academy Blvd.* ☎*719/591–0707*) SHOWS showcases live stand-up comedy Wednesday–Sunday evenings; some of the performers here are nationally known.

★ The **Flying W Ranch** (✉*3330 Chuckwagon Rd.* ☎ *719/598–4000 or 800/232–3599*), open mid-May–September, ropes them in for the sensational Western stage show and chuck-wagon dinner. The **Iron Springs Chateau** (✉*444 Ruxton Ave.,* ✢*across from Pikes Peak Cog Railway* ☎*719/685–5104*) stages comedy melodramas along with dinner, mid-May–October and December.

SHOPPING

COLORADO SPRINGS

Colorado Springs has a mix of upscale shopping in boutiques and major chain stores. Many boutiques and galleries cluster in Old Colorado City and the posh Broadmoor One Lake Avenue Shopping Arcade.

SHOPPING **Chapel Hills Mall** (✉*1710 Briargate Blvd.*), at the north end of town, has DISTRICTS & a Sears Roebuck, a Macy's, and a Dick's Sporting Goods, plus many MALLS other stores. **Citadel** (✉*750 Citadel Dr. E*) counts Macy's, Dillard's, JCPenney, and American Eagle Outfitters among its more than 175 stores. Among the tenants at the **Shops at Briargate** (✉*1885 Briargate Pkwy.*, ✛*Exit 151 on I-25* ☎*719/265–6264*) are clothiers Ann Taylor and Coldwater Creek, plus other retailers such as Pottery Barn and Williams-Sonoma.

CRAFT & ART GALLERIES **Flute Player Gallery** (✉*2511 W. Colorado Ave.* ☎*719/632–7702*) carries southwest Native American art. **Michael Garman Gallery** (✉*2418 W. Colorado Ave.* ☎*719/471–1600*) offers Western-style paintings and contemporary sculpture.

FOOD **Patsy's Candies** (✉*1540 S. 21st St.* ☎*719/633–7215*) is renowned for its saltwater taffy and chocolate. Tours weekdays June through September. **Rocky Mountain Chocolates** (✉*2431 W. Colorado Ave.* ☎*719/635–4131*) tempts with chocolates of every variety, in delightful seasonal and holiday arrangements.

MANITOU SPRINGS

This small town, tucked between Garden of the Gods and Pikes Peak, is a historic district where the chamber of commerce offers free walking tours of the naturally effervescent springs in summer. There's a large artists' population; walk along Manitou Avenue and Ruxton Avenue, where you'll find a mix of galleries, quaint shops, and stores selling souvenirs.

Commonwheel Artists Co-Op (✉*102 Cañon Ave.* ☎*719/685–1008*) exhibits jewelry and fiber, clay, and glass art. Like the sweet sounds of a dulcimer? At the **Dulcimer Shop** (✉*740 Manitou Ave.* ☎*719/685–9655*) you can buy one, buy a kit to make one, or even get some lessons to start you off. **Kinfolks Mountain Outfitters** (✉*950 Manitou Ave.* ☎*719/685–4433*) is a unique operation. It's chock-full of gear and information for hikers, bikers, and mountain climbers, but in the back they serve beer, wine, and coffee, so you can relax and swap stories while sitting creek side. There's live music on Friday and Saturday evenings. The **Ruxton Trading Post** (✉*22 Ruxton Ave.* ☎*719/685–9024*) has cowboy-and-Indian antiques and collectibles, Native American art, and nostalgia items from old TV programs and movies.

SIDE TRIP TO CRIPPLE CREEK

46 mi west of Colorado Springs via U.S. 24 and Rte. 67.

Colorado's third legalized gambling town, Cripple Creek once had the most lucrative mines in the state—and 10,000 boozing, brawling, bawdy citizens. Today, its old mining structures and the stupendous curtain of the Collegiate Peaks are marred by slag heaps and parking lots. Although the town isn't as picturesque as Central City or Black Hawk, the other gambling hot spots, Cripple Creek—a little rougher and dustier—feels more authentic.

The **Cripple Creek District Museum** provides a glimpse into mining life at the turn of the 20th century. ✉*5th and Bennett Ave.* ☎*719/689–2634* 🖙*$5* ⊙*June 1–Sept. 30, daily 10–5; Oct. 7–May 31, Fri.–Sun. noon–4.*

The **Cripple Creek and Victor Narrow Gauge Railroad** weaves over reconstructed trestles and past abandoned mines to the Anaconda ghost town, then back up to Cripple Creek during the 45-minute ride. In the boom days of the 1870s through the silver crash of 1893, more than 50 ore-laden trains made this run daily. For years, Victor has been a sad town, virtually a ghost of its former self. Walking the streets—past abandoned or partially restored buildings—has been an eerie experience that does far more to evoke the mining (and post-mining) days than tarted-up Cripple Creek. But there's a partial renewal of the town, because Victor is again home to a gold mine, the Cripple Creek & Victor Mining Company, which is the largest gold mine in the state. ⊠ *520 E. Carr St., at Bennett Ave.* ☎ *719/689–2640* ⊡ *$11* ☉ *Mid-June–Aug., daily 10–5; trains depart every 40 mins. Runs in spring and fall but less frequently; call for hrs.*

The **Mollie Kathleen Gold Mine Tour** descends 1,000 feet into the bowels of the earth in a mine that operated continuously from 1892 to 1961. The tours are wonderful, occasionally led by a former miner, but definitely not for the claustrophobic. ⊠ *Rte. 67, north of town* ☎ *719/689–2466* ⊡ *$15* ☉ *Apr.–Oct., daily 9–4; tours every 20 mins.*

CASINOS

Miners gathered around card games in most of the 100 saloons in town, which opened during the wild years after Bob Womack discovered gold in 1890. Today, there's a lineup of casinos set into storefronts and buildings, with outsides meticulously maintained to retain the aura they had a century ago. But inside the 18 casinos and gambling parlors here today there's no question that these are gambling halls, chock-full of slot machines, video and live poker tables, and blackjack tables. Today, there are even a few casinos in modern buildings, too. Limited stakes gambling is allowed up to $5 per bet.

Peek into the mining era's high life at the **Imperial Hotel and Casino** where you'll see antiques, chandeliers, and hand-painted wallpaper from France, as you play the latest slot machines. ⊠ *123 N. 3rd St.* ☎ *719/689–7777.*

The Rocky Mountain Victorian look of the **Gold Rush Hotel & Casino** is fairly typical of the establishments that line historic East Bennett Avenue. ⊠ *209 E. Bennett Ave.* ☎ *719/689–2646 or 800/235–8239.*

WHERE TO STAY & EAT

Most of the casinos on East Bennett Avenue house predictable (albeit inexpensive) restaurants. Beef is the common denominator across all of the menus. The price goes up, along with the quality, at restaurants like the Steakhouse at Bronco Billy's Casino and Winfield's, located below Gold Creek Casino.

¢ ⬚ **Victor Hotel.** The public spaces of this hotel, which is listed on the National Register of Historic Places, evoke Victorian splendor. Unfortunately, aside from the original open brickwork and a few old-fashioned tubs and radiators—as well as the oldest operating birdcage elevator west of the Mississippi—decor and furnishings in rooms are prosaically modern, and bathrooms are tiny. **Pros:** inexpensive, mountain views. **Con:** you'll get a fairly unvarnished taste of the Old West. ✉*4th and Victor Sts., Victor 80860* ✛*6 mi southeast of Cripple Creek* ☎*719/689–3553 or 800/713–4595* 📠*719/689–4197* ⊕*www. victorhotelcolorado.com* �’*20 rooms* ⌂*In-room: no a/c, Wi-Fi. In-hotel: public Wi-Fi, parking (no fee), some pets allowed, no-smoking rooms* ▭*AE, D, MC, V.*

SIDE TRIP TO FLORISSANT FOSSIL BEDS

35 mi west of Colorado Springs via U.S. 24.

Fodor'sChoice
★
Florissant Fossil Beds National Monument is a primeval rain forest that was perfectly preserved by volcanic ash 35–40 million years ago. This little-known site is a treasure trove for paleontologists. The visitor center offers guided walks into the monument, or you can follow the well-marked hiking trails and lose yourself in the Eocene epoch, among 300-foot petrified redwoods. From Cripple Creek, take Teller County Road 1, which goes right through the monument. It's about 17 mi from town. ✉*15807 Teller County 1, Florissant* ☎*719/748–3253* ⊕*www. nps.gov/flfo* ▭*$3* ☉*Daily 9–5; closed Thanksgiving, Christmas, and New Year's Day.*

SIDE TRIP TO PALMER LAKE

25 mi north of Colorado Springs via I–25 and Hwy. 105.

Photogenic, artsy, and very sleepy, Palmer Lake is a magnet for hikers who set out for the evergreen-clad peaks at several in-town trailheads. The town is also home to more good restaurants and working artists than one would expect from a population of 1,500. The town developed around the railroad tracks that were laid here in 1871—the lake itself was used as a refueling point for steam engines.

In a landmark Kaiser-Frazer building on the north fringe of town, the **Tri-Lakes Center for the Arts** hangs rotating exhibits in its auditorium-gallery that also serves as a venue for music and theater. Classes and workshops are offered and several resident artists work from studios on-site. ✉*30 Hwy. 105* ☎*719/481–0475* ⊕*www.trilakesarts.org* ▭*Free* ☉*Wed.–Sat. noon–5.*

Larkspur (7 mi north of Palmer Lake) is home to just a few hundred residents, but it knows how to throw a heck of a party—and a medieval
★ ☺
one at that. The **Colorado Renaissance Festival** annually throws open its gates to throngs of families, chain mail–clad fantasy enthusiasts, tattooed bikers, and fun lovers of every other kind. Within the wooded, 350-acre "kingdom," there are performers who deliver everything from juggling stunts and fire-eating to hypnotism and comedy. The big event happens three times a day, when knights square off in the arena for a theatrical joust. There are also more than 200 artisans selling their wares (from hammocks to stained-glass "Sunsifters"), games, rides, and myriad food and drink booths. It's a great way to while away

a summer day, though it can be a bit much to handle in the hottest weather. To reach Larkspur from Denver, take Interstate 25 south to Exit 173; if you're coming from Colorado Springs, take Interstate 25 north to Exit 172. ☎303/688–6010 ⊕*www.coloradorenaissance.com* ✉*$17.95* ☉*Early June–early Aug., weekends 10–6:30.*

SPORTS & THE OUTDOORS

FISHING Palmer Lake is stocked with trout. A more-secluded angling spot, the **Upper Palmer Lake Reservoir** (☎*719/481–3282*) offers a mix of trout and bottom-feeders in a peaceful mountain setting. Anyone older than 16 needs a Colorado fishing license, which you can obtain at local sporting-goods stores. See ⊕*www.wildlife.state.co.us/fishing.* for more information.

HIKING The **New Santa Fe Regional Trail** now goes both north and south out of town. Heading south, it goes along the shore of Palmer Lake and continues for 14 mi, following an abandoned railroad right-of-way; heading north, it goes through the town up to Greenland Ranch. The trail is also popular with equestrians and bikers, as well as cross-country skiers and snowshoers. ✉*El Paso County Parks* ☎*719/520–6375* ⊕*http://adm.elpasoco.com/parks_and_leisure_services.*

One of the most popular hiking trails between Denver and Colorado Springs, the **Palmer Lake Reservoirs Trail** (⚓*Trailhead: At bottom of Old Palmer Rd.* ☎*719/481–3282*) begins near Glen Park. After a fairly steep incline, the 3-mi trail levels out and follows the shoreline of upper and lower Palmer Lake Reservoir, tucked between forested mountains. Bikes and leashed dogs are permitted.

WHERE TO EAT

$$ ✕**B & E Filling Station.** Though it doesn't look like much from outside, casually elegant dining is the name of the game at this eatery. With stained-glass windows, mountain views, and local art on the walls, the place is easy on the eyes—and the food is easy on the palate. The best dishes are the crab cakes, bacon-wrapped beef tenderloin, and the daily fresh fish special. Reservations are recommended. ✉*25 Hwy. 105* ☎*719/481–4780* ▬*D, MC, V* ☉ *Closed Sun. and Mon. No lunch.*

¢ ✕**Rock House Ice Cream.** This is a popular stop for hikers on their way home. Choose from among 24 different types, including cake batter, cookie dough, or rainbow sherbert, for your cone or milk shake. ✉*24 Hwy. 105* ☎*719/488–6917* ▬*MC, V.*

NIGHTLIFE

A roadhouse eatery where you get to play chef (patrons can cook steaks to their liking on a communal grill), **O'Malley's Steak Pub** (✉*104 Hwy. 105* ☎*719/488–0321*) is the most reliable nightlife in the area, with an upstairs poolroom, occasional bands, and plenty of local color. The outdoor deck has a great view of the nearby mountainside.

SHOPPING

The fun and eclectic **Finders Keepers** (✉*91 Hwy. 105* ☎*719/487–8020*) sells jewelry, antiques, homemade jams and jellies, and local arts and crafts.

BUENA VISTA & SALIDA

11

Buena Vista and Salida are comfortable base towns for vacationers who love hiking and mountain biking the trails that zigzag up and down the 14,000 footers called the Collegiate Peaks. These towns are also favorites for folks who want to stay in rustic cabins or small mom-and-pop motels, perhaps take a rafting trip on the Arkansas River, and come home with a wallet still intact.

BUENA VISTA

94 mi west of Colorado Springs on U.S. 24 and U.S. 285.

Sky scraping mountains, the most impressive being the Collegiate Peaks, ring Buena Vista (pronounced *byoo*-na *vis*-ta by locals). The 14,000-foot, often snowcapped peaks were first summited by alumni from Yale, Princeton, Harvard, and Columbia, who named them for their respective alma maters. A small mining town–turned–resort community, Buena Vista's main street is lined with Wild West–style historic buildings. On U.S. 24, which bisects the town, there are inexpensive roadside motels. The town is also a hub for the white-water rafting industry that plies its trade on the popular Arkansas River, and a great central location for hiking, fishing, rafting, and horseback riding.

> WORD OF MOUTH
>
> "One of my favorite sights after going over Kenosha Pass on CR 285 from Denver is seeing South Park spread out for miles in front of you. BEAUTIFUL mountains on both sides with grazing lands dotted with ranches and buffalo, cattle, also, elk, deer, etc. Also, real cowboys! The sun may be shinning brightly in one place and the skies in another spot look like the earth may come to an end! And it all may change within moments. The sight can take your breath away." —polaris

FodorsChoice
★ Taking its own name from the many peaks named after famous universities, the 167,714-acre **Collegiate Peaks Wilderness Area** includes more 14,000-foot-high mountains (14) than any other wilderness area in the lower 48 states, and 6 more peaks with summits above 13,800 feet. Forty miles of the Continental Divide snake through the area as well. The most compelling reason to visit Buena Vista is for the almost unequaled variety of hikes, climbs, and biking trails here. Two ranger offices, one in Leadville and one in Salida, handle inquiries about this region. ⌧*Leadville Ranger District, 810 Front St., Leadville* ☎*719/486–0749.* ⌧*Salida Ranger District, 325 W. Rainbow Blvd., Salida* ☎*719/539–3591.*

★ To relax sore muscles visit **Mount Princeton Hot Springs Resort,** 8 mi from Buena Vista, for a restorative soak. The springs have three swimming pools and several "hot spots in the creek"—the water temperature ranges between 85°F and 105°F. The resort here also has 9 rooms in the lodge, 40 others in two different buildings, and 10 cabins ($$), which are quietly upscale in style and are underpriced for what they offer. The restaurant has a large stone fireplace and a dramatic view of the

Chalk Cliffs. ⊠*15870 County Rd. 162,* ✛*4.5 mi west of Nathrop on County Rd. 162* ☎*719/395–2447* ⊕*www.mtprinceton.com* ☞*$6* ⊙*Lower pools: daily 9–9 ; upper pool with waterslide: Memorial Day–Labor Day, daily 11–6 .*

Before leaving downtown, meander through the four rooms of the **Buena Vista Heritage Museum.** The falling-down miner's cabin and pretty carriage outside give a hint of what's in the building. Each room is devoted to an aspect of regional history: one to mining equipment and minerals, another to fashions and household utensils, a third to working models of the three railroads that serviced the area in its heyday, and the last to historical photos. ⊠*506 E. Main St.* ☎*719/395–8458* ☞*$3* ⊙*Memorial Day weekend–Sept., Mon.–Sat. 10–5, Sun. noon–5.*

> ### RAFTING THE ARKANSAS
>
> Adrenaline-charging rapids range from Class II to Class V on Colorado's Arkansas River, one of the most commercially rafted rivers in the world. Among the most-fabled stretches of the Arkansas are the Narrows, the Numbers, and Browns Canyon, but extreme paddlers tend to jump on trips through the Royal Gorge, which the river has carved out over aeons. Plan your trip for the early summer snowmelt for the biggest thrills.

SPORTS & THE OUTDOORS

HIKING   **Trailhead** (⊠*707 Hwy. 24* ☎*719/395–8001*) is an outdoor specialty shop where you can get maps, guidebooks, gear, and clothing to hike or climb in the region.

WHITE-WATER   The rafting and kayaking on the **Arkansas River** can be the most chal-
RAFTING   lenging in the state, ranging from Class II to Class V, depending on the season.

Independent Whitewater (☎*800/428–1479 or 719/539–7737* ⊕*www. independentrafting.com*) is a family-owned company that's been running the Arkansas River for nearly 20 years. Trip sizes are small, and leave from a private take-out area to run Seidel's Suckhole and Twin
Fodor'sChoice   Falls on regular half-day trips. **River Runners** (☎*800/723–8987* ⊕*www.*
★   *whitewater.net*) has been offering rafting trips on the Arkansas for more than 30 years. This group also runs the Royal Gorge stretch, which is classed expert, but there are choices for families who want a gentler experience.

WHERE TO STAY & EAT

There are many cabins and some B&Bs in this region. For information about rental units in the Buena Vista area contact the **Buena Vista Chamber of Commerce** ☎*719/395–6612* ⊕*www.buenavistacolorado.org).*

$–$$ ✕ **Casa del Sol.** Inhabiting an old blacksmith's shop (1890), this stucco-clad restaurant has a quasi–tiki-hut feel inside and a nice outdoor seating area. The smothered burritos are tasty and hearty, the homemade salsa is hot, and the service is quick and friendly. Among the most popular entrées are the spicy Santa Fe, which has stacked corn enchiladas with meat sauce and cheddar cheese, and the Pechuga Suiza, a chicken breast rolled in a tortilla with Monterey Jack cheese and sour cream. The full-service bar here specializes in tart but potent margaritas. ⊠*333 U.S. 24* ☏*719/395–8810* ▤*MC, V.*

¢–$ ✗**mothers bistro.** A surprising find in this small town, this eatery offers
Fodor's Choice   midday meals such as a whole-wheat wrap stuffed with smoked tur-
★   key, fresh cilantro, curried mayo, cucumbers, and mango; or a fig and Brie panini on fresh ciabatta. Small plates in the evening range from gourmet mac and cheese made with tortiglioni, shallots, white wine, vintage sharp cheddar, and romano; or smoked salmon with crème fraîche, capers, and freshly baked bread. Set in a historic former hotel, the tiny restaurant, which focuses on organic and regional foods, has a lovely outdoor patio. Wine and beer are available. ⊠*413 E. Main St.* ☏*719/395–4443* ⊙*Summer, daily; call for winter hrs* ▤*MC, V.*

★ $$ ▥ **Liar's Lodge.** Right on the banks of the Arkansas River, this rugged, rustic B&B is surrounded by 23 acres of woodland. The Great Room, under 25-foot-high ceilings, is centered around a huge river-rock fireplace, and the uniquely decorated rooms are named after landmarks in the river: the Pinball Room has a king bed, a sleeping loft, and a two-person hot tub (but alas, no pinball machine); the Frog Rock Room has a queen and a twin and opens onto a river deck. Larger groups might opt for the 1,200-square-foot house that overlooks the river. You'll hear the river gurgling from your room if you leave a window open. **Pro:** gorgeous setting. **Con:** you'll have to go into Buena Vista for dinner. ⊠*30000 County Rd. 371, 81211* ☏*719/395–3444 or 888/542–7756* ⊕*www.liarslodge.com* ⇲*5 rooms, 1 house* ⚒*In-room: no a/c, no phone, Wi-Fi. In-hotel: no elevator, parking (no fee), no-smoking rooms* ▤*MC, V* ⦿*BP.*

$–$$ ▥ **Adobe Inn Bed & Breakfast.** The sister property of the restaurant Casa del Sol, this adobe hacienda has three charming rooms and two suites, each named for its predominant decorative motif: antique, Mexican, Indian, and wicker. Some rooms have a fireplace. The airy solarium is dominated by a magnificent kiva. Breakfast is included in the room rate. **Pro:** right behind the Casa del Sol, so you're only a few steps from a great place to eat and drink. **Con:** adobe-style means there may not be a lot of natural light in some rooms. ⊠*303 U.S. 24, 81211* ☏*719/395–6340 or 888/343–6340* ⊕*www.bbonline.com/co/adobe* ⇲*3 rooms, 2 suites* ⚒*In-room: no a/c. In-hotel: no elevator, no-smoking rooms* ▤*MC, V* ⦿*BP.*

NIGHTLIFE

Head to the **Green Parrot** (⊠*304 E. Main St.* ☏*719/395–9046*), a long-standing Buena Vista watering hole with live music some weekends. The **Lariat** (⊠*206 E. Main* ☏*719/395–9494*) is another locals' hangout, where pool, video games, and darts are the main diversions. There's music some Friday nights.

SHOPPING

There are a few antique shops right across the highway from the Buena Vista Visitors Center. **Rustic Woods** (⊠*310 U.S. 24* ☏*719/395–2561*) has attractive decorative items to heavy furniture, all centered around various wood, of course.

SALIDA

25 mi south of Buena Vista via U.S. 24 and 285 and Rte. 291; 102 mi southwest of Colorado Springs.

Imposing peaks, including 14,000-plus-foot Mount Shavano, dominate the town of Salida, which is on the Arkansas River. Salida draws some of the musicians who appear at the Aspen Music Festival—classical pianists, brass ensembles, and the like—for its Salida–Aspen Concerts in July and August. The town's other big event is the annual kayak and rafting white-water rodeo in June, on a section of river that cuts right through downtown. It's been taking place for more than 50 years.

SPORTS & THE OUTDOORS

BICYCLING **Absolute Bikes** (⊠*330 W. Sackett Ave.* ☎*719/539–9295*) rents cruisers and mountain bikes for $10 to $50 a day, and provides repair service, maps, advice, and equipment for sale. The **Banana Belt Bicycle Weekend** (☎*719/539–2068 or 877/772–5432*) is a two-day mountain-bike race held every September at Riverside Park in downtown Salida.

DOWNHILL **Monarch** is a small ski resort that tops out on the Continental Divide.
SKIING The ski area has five chairlifts, 54 trails, 800 acres, and a 1,170-foot vertical drop. It's a family-friendly place, with moderate pricing. The resort also offers snowcat skiing on steep runs off the Divide, plus the 130 acres of extreme terrain (accessible by hiking) in Mirkwood Basin. ⊠*U.S. 50* ✛*18 mi west of Salida* ☎*719/530–5000 or 888/996–7669* ☞*$52* ☉*Mid-Nov.–mid-Apr., daily 9–4.*

FISHING The Arkansas River, as it spills out of the central Colorado Rockies on its course through the south central part of the state, reputedly supports a brown-trout population exceeding 3,000 fish per mile. Some of the river's canyons are deep and some of the best fishing locations are difficult to access, making a guide or outfitter a near necessity. See ⊕*www.wildlife.state.co.us/fishing* for more information. **ArkAnglers** (⊠*7500 W. Hwy. 50* ☎*719/539–4223* ⊕*www.arkanglers.com*) is a good fly shop with an experienced staff of guides, offering guided float and wade trips, fly-fishing lessons, and equipment rentals.

HORSEBACK **High Country Trail Rides** offers scenic guided trail rides near Monarch ski
RIDING area. It's $25 per hour or $110 per day. ⊠*22763 W. U.S. 50* ✛*18 mi west of Salida* ☎*719/539–9819.*

JEEP TOURS **High Country Jeep Tours** (⊠*410 U.S. Hwy. 24, Buena Vista* ☎*719/395–6111 or 866/45–TOURS*) takes customers on four-wheel-drive trips to old mines, ghost towns, and mountain vistas.

SNOW- **Monarch Snowmobile Tours** takes customers on winter excursions around
MOBILING Monarch Park. Rentals start at $60 for a one-hour single rental and go up to $165 for six hours. Two-hour guided tours are $60 for a single and go up to $160 for a six-hour tour. ⊠*Garfield,* ✛*18 mi west of Salida* ☎*719/539–2572 or 800/539–2573.*

WHITE-WATER The Salida area is a magnet for rafting aficionados, and there are doz-
RAFTING ens of outfitters. Salida is constantly jockeying with Buena Vista for the

title of "Colorado's White-Water Capital." *For outfitters, see the Buena Vista section in this chapter.*

WHERE TO STAY & EAT

$$$

Fodor's Choice

★

✕**Laughing Ladies.** When you want fine food in a relaxed atmosphere, head to Laughing Ladies, where you'll dine at a linen-covered table set on a century-old oak floor surrounded by exposed brick walls. Colorful oils, watercolors, and ceramics by local artists adorn the walls. The menu changes seasonally, but some of the more-popular dishes include whiskey BBQ duck with corn-bread pudding and a sweet corn salsa; the double-thick honey-grilled pork chop with yams and ancho chili glacé; and the house-smoked salmon with basil corn cakes. Laughing Ladies has the largest wine selection in the area. Reservations, suggested year-round, are essential on summer weekends. ✉*128 W. 1st St.* 🕾*719/539–6209* ▤*MC, V* 🕓*Closed Tues. and Wed.*

$

⌂**River Run Inn.** On the Arkansas River, this gracious Victorian home has breathtaking mountain prospects. Rooms are filled with antiques and family memorabilia. **Pros:** convenient for fishing, very quiet, terrific river and mountain views. **Con:** 3 mi from restaurants, shopping, and nightlife in downtown Salida. ✉*8495 County Rd. 160, 81201* 🕾*719/539–3818 or 800/385–6925* ⊕*www.riverruninn.com* ⇶*6 rooms, 1 dorm* ⌂*In-room: no a/c, no TV. In-hotel: no elevator, parking (no fee), no-smoking rooms* ▤*AE, D, MC, V* ⍏*BP.*

$

⌂**Tudor Rose.** Isolated, beautifully furnished, and idyllic—if you like a Victorian feel—this B&B sits on a 37-acre spread of pine forest and mountain ridges. The proprietors, John and Terré Terrell, redid the original private residence as a luxury mountain inn. An oak staircase with a two-story waterfall cascading down the adjacent wall to the foyer is the centerpiece, but the deck overlooking the nearby Mosquito Range is a close second. The rooms are tastefully Victorian, without an overload of frill and lace. There are also three chalets near the house. **Pro:** excellent choice for those traveling with horses, because owners will stable horses in their barn. **Cons:** dirt road leading to house can be treacherous for low-slung cars, not an option for those with young children. ✉*6720 County Rd. 104, 81201* 🕾*719/539–2002 or 800/379–0889* ⊕*www.thetudorrose.com* ⇶*64 rooms, 2 suites* ⌂*In-room: no a/c, refrigerator (some), VCR (some), no TV (some). In-hotel: no elevator, public Wi-Fi, parking (no fee), no kids under 10, no-smoking rooms* ▤*D, MC, V* ⍏*BP.*

$

⌂**Woodland Motel.** Since 1975, Steve and Viva Borbas have run this impeccable mom-and-pop motel on the outskirts of downtown Salida. Standard rooms are smallish but very clean and have nice furnishings and amenities for the price. The more-expensive rooms—condominium units and efficiency studios—are larger and have kitchenettes. Dogs receive royal treatment here: Treats and freshly laundered doggie beds are included in the rate. **Pro:** nothing fancy but the rooms are inexpensive. **Con:** it's a 12-minute walk to the downtown area. ✉*903 W. 1st St., 81201* 🕾*719/539–4980 or 800/488–0456* ⊕*www.woodlandmotel.com* ⇶*16 rooms, 2 condos* ⌂*In-room: kitchen (some), ethernet. In-hotel: no elevator, some pets allowed, parking (no fee), no-smoking rooms* ▤*AE, D, MC, V.*

THE ARTS

Salida Steam Plant Theater (⊠*Sackett and G Sts.* ☎*719/530–0933* ⊕*www.steamplant.org*) puts on several productions each summer, ranging from drama to comedy to music to cabaret, on a stage in Salida's former steam plant.

SHOPPING

First Street is home to many antiques shops and art galleries, including specialists in contemporary art, photography, and jewelry. The annual Salida ArtWalk takes place in late June. Ask the chamber of commerce for the *Art in Salida* or *Antique Dealers* brochures for information about the ArtWalk. **All Booked Up** (⊠*134 E. 1st St.* ☎*719/539–2344*) has Native American art and jewelry, mixed media artwork and more. **cultureclash** (⊠*101 N. F St.* ☎*719/539–3118*) has original artwork, glass, and intricately handcrafted jewelry. **Gallery 150** (⊠*150 W. 1st St.* ☎*719/539–2971*) has jewelry and wearable art, plus blown glass and fiber art. The **Rock Doc at Prospectors Village** (⊠*17897 U.S. 285* ☎*719/539–2019* ⊕*www.therocdoc.net*), midway between Salida and Buena Vista, is an enormous rock shop with gold-panning equipment, metal detectors, and rock art. The shop also gives gold-panning lessons. **Spirit Mountain, Antler & Design** (⊠*223 E. 1st St.* ☎*719/539–1500*) has stunning handcrafted tables inlaid with turquoise and other handmade furniture.

CAÑON CITY

59 mi east of Salida via U.S. 50; 45 mi southwest of Colorado Springs.

Cañon City is an undeniably quirky town. From its easy access to the nearby Royal Gorge, a dramatic slash in the earth, to its aggressive strip-mall veneer (softened, fortunately, by some handsome old buildings), you'd think Cañon City existed solely for tourism. Nothing could be further from the truth: Cañon City's livelihood stems from its lordly position as "Colorado's Prison Capital"—there are nine prisons here and four more in nearby Florence. Fremont County citizens actually lobbied to get these 13 prisons, which may seem like a perverse source of income to court but have pumped nearly $200 million into the local economy.

☾ Cañon City is the gateway to the 1,053-foot-deep **Royal Gorge,** which

Fodor'sChoice was carved by the Arkansas River more than 3 million years ago. The

★ famed Royal Gorge War between the Denver & Rio Grande and Santa Fe railroads occurred here in 1877. The battle was over the right-of-way through the canyon, which could only accommodate one rail line. Rival crews would lay tracks during the day and dynamite each other's work at night. The dispute was finally settled in court—the Denver & Rio Grande won. Today, along one part of the gorge there's a commercially run site, the **Royal Gorge Bridge and Park.** ✛ *12 mi west of Cañon City.*

11

The **Royal Gorge Bridge and Park** has the world's highest **suspension bridge.** Never intended for traffic, it was constructed in 1929 as a tourist attraction. The 1,053-foot-high bridge sways on gusty afternoons, adding to the thrill of a crossing. You can also ride the astonishing **aerial tram** (2,200 feet long and 1,178 feet above the canyon floor) or descend the steepest **incline rail line** in the world to stare at the bridge from 1,000 feet below. A ride on the **Royal Rush Skycoaster** ensures an adrenaline rush—you'll swing from a free-fall tower and momentarily hang over the gorge. Also on hand is a theater that presents a 25-minute multimedia show, outdoor musical entertainment in summer, and the usual assortment of food and gift shops. ✉ *4218 Fremont County Rd. 3A* ☎ *719/275–7507* ⊕ *www.royalgorgebridge.com* ✎ *$23* ⊙ *Hrs vary seasonally; call ahead or check Web site.*

A ride on the **Royal Gorge Route Railroad** takes you under the bridge and through one of the most dramatic parts of the canyon. The train leaves several times a day for the two-hour ride. The lunch ride is pleasant and the food is good, although not exactly "gourmet" as advertised. For an extra fee, you can ride in the cab with the engineer driving the train. The train leaves from the Santa Fe depot in Cañon City. ☎ *888/724– 5748* ⊕ *www.royalgorgeroute.com* ✎ *$29.95 and up.*

☺ Not only is **Buckskin Joe Frontier Town** the largest Western-style theme park in the region, but it's also an authentic ghost town that was moved here from 100 mi away. Such famous films as *True Grit* and *Cat Ballou* were shot in this place, which vividly evokes the Old West, especially during the re-created gunfights and hangings that occur daily. Children love the horse-drawn trolley rides, horseback rides, and gold panning, while adults appreciate live entertainment in the Crystal Palace and Saloon. ✉ *Cañon City off U.S. 50* ☎ *719/275–5149* ⊕ *www.buckskin-joe.com* ✎ *$17* ⊙ *May and Sept 10–5; mid-June–Aug., daily 9–6.*

Morbid curiosity seekers and sensationalists will revel in the **Museum of Colorado Prisons,** which formerly housed the Women's State Correctional Facility. Now it exhaustively documents prison life in Colorado, through old photos and newspaper accounts, as well as with inmates' confiscated weapons and contraband, and one warden's china set. There's also a video room where you can view titles such as *Prisons Ain't What They Used to Be* and *Drug Avengers*. The gas chamber sits in the courtyard. This museum is grim, grisly, gruesome, and fascinating. ✉ *201 N. 1st St.* ☎ *719/269–3015* ⊕ *www.prisonmuseum.org* ✎ *$7* ⊙ *May–Oct., daily 8:30–6; mid-Oct.–Apr., Wed.–Sun. 10–5.*

OFF THE BEATEN PATH

Winery at Holy Cross Abbey. The Benedictine monks once cloistered in the Holy Cross Abbey came to Cañon City for spiritual repose. But for the faithful who frequent the winery on the eastern edge of the monastery's property, redemption is more easily found in a nice bottle of merlot or a two-year-old Riesling. Although the monastery has been sold and will no longer be home to monks, tours of the winery's production facility, now owned by Larry Oddo and Sally Cookson, are possible by advance reservation in spring and summer. The Tasting Room, in a historic building, is open year-round. ✉ *3011 E. Hwy. 50* ☎ *719/276–*

5191 or 877/422-9463 ⊕www.
abbeywinery.com ✉Free ☉Spring
and summer, Mon.–Sat. 10–6, Sun.
noon–5; Jan.–Mar., Mon.–Sat. 10–
5, Sun. noon–5.

SPORTS & THE OUTDOORS

HIKING For a pleasant stroll, try the **Arkansas River Walk** (✛ *Trailhead: Go south on 9th St., and turn east immediately south of bridge over river. It's about two blocks to trailhead*). The 4-mi trail is virtually flat, and the elevation is only 5,320 feet. It follows the Arkansas River for 3 mi through woods, wetlands, and the riparian river environment. Cañon City–owned **Red Canyon Park**, 12 mi north of town, offers splendid easy to moderate hiking, although no formal trails, among the rose-color sandstone spires.

FLORENCE PRISONS

The tiny, main-street town of Florence has just about one of everything: one coffee shop, one diner, one bookstore, although there are several antiques stores. When it comes to prisons, however, they have more than their share, with four correctional facilities, including the infamous ADX Supermax where an unruly population passes time in 23-hour lockdown. The ADX is home to scores of men with sinister claims to fame: Ted Kazinski and Timothy McVeigh are former residents, and Ramsey Yusef, the alleged architect of the 1993 bombing of the World Trade Center, and Richard Reid, aka "The Shoebomber," are current inmates.

WHITE-WATER RAFTING Rafting through the Royal Gorge is not an experience for the faint of heart; you'll pass between narrow canyon walls through rolling Class IV and V waves, with hordes of tourists watching from the suspension bridge above.

With dozens of outfitters working from Salida, Buena Vista, and Cañon City, south central Colorado is one of the top places in the country to go rafting. The **Colorado River Outfitters Association** (☎303/280–2554 ⊕www.croa.org) is an organization of more than 50 licensed outfitters who run rafting trips on Colorado's 13 river systems. **Echo Canyon River Expeditions** (☎719/275–3154 or 800/748–2953) offers float trips with gentle rapids on the Arkansas for first-time rafters in Bighorn Sheep Canyon, family trips through Brown Canyon, and adrenaline-inducing rides through the Royal Gorge.

WHERE TO STAY & EAT

$$$ ✕**Merlino's Belvedere.** This Italian standby has ritzy coffee-shop decor, with floral banquettes, centerpieces, and a rock grotto. Locals swear by the top-notch steaks, seafood, and pasta choices, which range from penne *vegetali* (with grilled vegetables) and manicotti to Angelas' Combo, which has cavatelli and spaghetti with garlic and Romano cheese. There are half-price martinis on Wednesday and music some weekend nights. ✉1330 Elm Ave. ☎719/275–5558 ▭AE, D, DC, MC, V.

$ ✕**El Caporal.** With colorful booths indoors and a comfortable outdoor patio, this is a fun and casual spot for an inexpensive lunch or dinner. Mexican combination plates dominate the menu, but there are plenty of meat and seafood entrées, plus a standout dessert selection, including flan and fried ice cream. The bar makes more than seven flavors of succulent margaritas and the proprietor, Miguel Lopez, is constantly coming up with new tequila-based concoctions. ⊠*1028 Main St.* ☎*719/276–2001* ▤*AE, D, MC, V.*

11

$ ⛛**Quality Inn and Suites.** Some of the famous people who have stayed here—John Belushi, Tom Selleck, Jane Fonda, John Wayne, Glenn Ford, and Goldie Hawn among them—now have their names emblazoned on the door of a hotel room. Spacious and ultracomfortable, basic accommodations are offered in the two wings. **Pro:** close to the Royal Gorge Bridge and Park. **Con:** day trips to Pikes Peak and Colorado Springs require a solid hour of driving each way. ⊠*U.S. 50 and Dozier St., 81212* ☎*719/275–8676 or 800/525–7727* ⊕*www.choice hotels.com* ⇆*150 rooms* ♿*In-room: ethernet (some), Wi-Fi (some). In-hotel: restaurant, bar, pool, no elevator, public Wi-Fi, no-smoking rooms* ▤*AE, D, DC, MC, V.*

PUEBLO

40 mi east of Cañon City via U.S. 50; 42 mi south of Colorado Springs via I–25.

In 1842 El Pueblo trading post, on the bank of the Arkansas River, was a gathering place for trappers and traders. Today, the trading post is an archaeological dig set in a pavilion next to the new El Pueblo History Museum. The thriving city of Pueblo surrounds the museum, and the Arkansas River runs through the city in a concrete channel, tamed by the Pueblo Dam. To get a sense of the city and its offerings, start at the museum, stroll through the Union Avenue Historic District, and then take a ride on one of the tour boats leaving from the Historic Arkansas Riverwalk, an urban waterfront area that restored the Arkansas River channel to its original location.

The **Union Avenue Historic District** is a repository of century-old stores and warehouses that make for a commercial district filled with a mix of stores ranging from kitschy to good. Among the landmarks are the glorious 1889 sandstone-and-brick Union Avenue Depot; and Mesa Junction, at the point where two trolleys met, which celebrates Pueblo as a crossroads. Pitkin Avenue, lined with fabulous gabled and turreted mansions, attests to the town's more-prosperous times. Walking-tour brochures of various districts are available at the **chamber of commerce** (⊠*302 N. Santa Fe Ave.* ☎*719/542–1704*).

Historic Arkansas Riverwalk of Pueblo is a 26-acre urban waterfront, where the Arkansas River channel has been restored to its original location. Stroll on the paths or take to the water on a boat tour or in a paddleboat (available at 101 South Union). The Riverwalk extends across several blocks, including Union and Victoria. ☎*719/595–0242, 719/595–1589 boat reservations* ⊕*www.puebloharp.com.*

El Pueblo History Museum is a nicely designed holding place for the city's history, but it extends its scope to chronicle life on the plains since the prehistoric era, as well as Pueblo's role as a cultural and geographic crossroads, beginning when it was a trading post in the 1840s.

Remnants of the original trading post are now an archaeological dig enclosed in a pavilion next to the museum. ⊠ *301 N. Union Ave.* ☎ *719/583–0453* ⊠*$4* ⊙ *Tues.–Sat. 10–4.*

Rosemount Victorian Museum is one of Colorado's finest historical institutions. This splendid 24,000-square-foot, 37-room mansion, showplace of the wealthy Thatcher family, gleams with exquisite maple, oak, and mahogany woodwork throughout, with ivory glaze and gold-leaf trim. Italian marble fireplaces, Tiffany-glass fixtures, and fresco ceilings complete the opulent look, and rooms seem virtually unchanged. The top floor—originally servants' quarters—features the odd Andrew McClelland Collection: objects of curiosity this eccentric philanthropist garnered on his worldwide travels, including an Egyptian mummy. ⊠ *419 W. 14th St.* ☎ *719/545–5290* ⊕ *www.rosemount.org* ⊠*$6* ⊙ *Tues.–Sat. 10–4; tours every half hr.*

⟳ Rotating exhibits at the **Sangre de Cristo Arts Center** celebrate regional arts and crafts. The center also houses the superb Western art collection donated by Francis King; a performing arts theater; and the **Buell Children's Museum,** which provides fun, interactive audiovisual experiences. ⊠ *210 N. Santa Fe Ave.* ☎ *719/295–7200 or 719/543–0130* ⊠*$4* ⊙ *Tues.–Sat. 11–4.*

⟳ The uncommonly fine **City Park** (⊠ *Pueblo Blvd. and Goodnight Ave.*) has fishing lakes, playgrounds, kiddie rides, tennis courts, a swimming pool, and the excellent **Pueblo Zoo** (☎ *719/561–9664* ⊕ *www. pueblozoo.org* ⊠*$6* ⊙ *June–Aug., daily 10–5; call for winter hrs*)—a biopark that includes an ecocenter with a tropical rain forest, black-footed penguins, ringtail lemurs, and green-tree pythons.

At the airport, the **Pueblo-Weisbrod Aircraft Museum** traces the development of American military aviation with more than two dozen aircraft in mint condition, ranging from a Lockheed F-80 fighter plane to a Boeing B-29 Super Fortress of atomic-bomb fame. ⊠ *31001 Magnuson, Pueblo Memorial Airport* ☎ *719/948–9219* ⊕ *www.pwam.org* ⊠*$6* ⊙ *Weekdays 10–4, Sat. 10–2, Sun. 1–4.*

OFF THE BEATEN PATH

Bishop Castle. This elaborate creation, which resembles a medieval castle replete with turrets, buttresses, and ornamental iron, is the prodigious (some might say monomaniacal) one-man undertaking of Jim Bishop, a self-taught architect who began work in 1969. Once considered a blight on pastoral Highway 165, which winds through the San Isabel Forest, the castle is now a popular attraction; not yet complete, it is three stories high with a nearly 165-foot tower. Those who endeavor to climb into the structure must sign the guest book–cum–liability waiver. Bishop finances this enormous endeavor through donations and a gift shop. If you're lucky he'll be there himself, perhaps railing against the Establishment. ⊠ *12705 Hwy. 165* ☎ *719/564–4366* ⊕ ⊠*Free* ⊙ *Daily, hrs vary.*

The Pueblo Levee

11

In 1978, a group of University of Southern Colorado art students headed out in the cover of night, set up lookouts, and lowered themselves over the wall of the Pueblo Levee. Outfitted with makeshift rope-suspension devices and armed with buckets of paint, the students spent the wee hours crafting a large blue cod on the levee's concrete wall, watching for police as they mixed up their acrylics. Overnight, the waterway—which directs the Arkansas River through the center of town—became home to a public art project that would eventually capture the imagination of the Pueblo community, as well as the attention of the art world and the *Guinness Book of World Records*. Pueblo Levee is a fantastic, colorful vision field that sprawls over 175,000 square feet, stretches for a mile, and is recognized as the largest mural in the world.

Organizers estimate that more than 1,000 painters have contributed to the mural—everyone from self-taught father-and-son teams who come to paint on weekends, to the entire members of fire precincts, to classically trained muralists and art students from New York and Chicago. Witty graffiti, comic illustrations, narrative scenes, and cartoons line the levee, which is visible to passengers zooming along Interstate 25. Today, you can take the walking or biking path along the levee to look at the murals, or even take a kayak lesson below it.

SPORTS & THE OUTDOORS

BICYCLING Pueblo has an extensive **bike trail system,** which loops the city, following the Arkansas River partway, and then goes out to the reservoir. There are popular in-line skating routes along these trails, too. The **Pueblo Parks and Recreation Department** (☎719/553–7790) can provide information.

BOATING, KAYAKING & FISHING Along the stretch of the Arkansas River near the Pueblo Levee, there's a kayak course. The **Edge Ski, Paddle and Pack** (⊠*107 N. Union Ave.* ☎*719/583–2021* ⊕*www.edgeskiandpaddle.com*) rents kayaks and gives lessons. There's excellent camping and fishing at **Lake Pueblo State Park** (⊕*Off U.S. 50* ☎*719/561–9320*), as well as many other outdoor activities. The **south shore marina** (☎*719/564–1043*) rents pontoon boats. See ⊕*www.wildlife.state.co.us/fishing* for more information.

GOLF **Walking Stick Golf Course.** This challenging links-style course is named after the native cholla, the cacti in the rugged terrain and arroyos that surround the rolling green fairways. ⊠*4301 Walking Stick Blvd.* ☎*719/584–3400* ⅃*18 holes. Yards: 7,147/5,181. Par: 72/72. Green Fee: $28–$30, plus $10 per person for cart.*

HIKING More than 110 parks, in addition to hiking and bicycling trails, help to define Pueblo as a sports and recreation center. You can bicycle, hike, and canoe along the 35 mi in the river trail system that follows the Arkansas River. For more information call the **Greenway and Nature Center** (⊠*Off 11th St.* ☎*719/549–2414*). A small interpretive center describes the flora and fauna unique to the area, and a **Raptor Rehabili-**

tation Center, part of the nature center, cares for injured birds of prey. You can hike in relative solitude on many trails threading the **San Isabel National Forest** (☎*719/545–8737*), 20 mi southwest of Pueblo.

WHERE TO STAY & EAT

$$$ ✕**La Renaissance.** This converted church and parsonage is the most imposing and elegant space in town, and the impeccably attired, unfailingly courteous waitstaff completes the picture. Guests order five-course dinners (including sinful desserts), which are served with style. Standbys are filet mignon in mushroom sauce, superb baby back ribs, and Norwegian salmon. ⊠*217 E. Routt Ave.* ☎*719/543–6367* ▤*AE, D, DC, MC, V* ⊗*Closed Sun.*

$$–$$$ ✕**dc's on b street.** There are two dining areas in this restaurant, which is housed in the historic redbrick Coors building across from the Union Depot. At lunchtime you can get sandwiches, Greek salads, and other light fare in a room with simple tables, brick walls, and a tin ceiling. For dinner in the more-elegant dining room, try the steak au poivre; the mahi served with a fruity Caribbean salsa; or the Pine Island shrimp with sautéed mushrooms, garlic, white wine, and sour cream served over angel-hair pasta. ⊠*115 B St.* ☎*719/584–3410* ▤*AE, MC, V.*

$$ ✕**Shamrock Brewing Company.** This consistently jam-packed hot spot is a bar and grill with a good kitchen. With dishes like corned beef and cabbage and Irish bangers, this is the place for authentic Irish pub grub. And of course, they brew their own beer—there are usually six or seven varieties on tap. ⊠*108 W. 3rd St.* ☎*719/542–9974* ▤*AE, D, MC, V.*

★ $$–$$$ ▥**Abriendo Inn.** This exquisite 1906 home, which is listed on the National Register of Historic Places, overflows with character. The house has original, restored parquet floors, stained glass, Minnequa oak wainscoting, and guest rooms that are richly appointed with antiques, oak armoires, quilts, crocheted bedspreads, and either brass or four-poster beds. Although all rooms have private bathrooms, one has a shower down the hall rather than en suite. Fresh fruit and cookies are left out for nibbling, and gourmet breakfasts are included in the rate. **Pro:** a classy place to stay with a primarily upscale, adult clientele. **Con:** some rooms have only showers, not bathtubs. ⊠*300 W. Abriendo Ave., 81004* ☎*719/544–2703* ⊕*www.abriendoinn.com* ⤶*10 rooms* ♿*In-room: refrigerator (some). In-hotel: no elevator, public Wi-Fi, no-smoking rooms* ▤*AE, MC, V* ⥮*BP.*

$$ ▥**Pueblo Convention Center Marriott.** A comfortable brand-name hotel, which was recently remodeled, the Marriott is geared for the convention crowd and offers comfortable rooms for the money. **Pros:** located in the downtown area, connected to the Pueblo Convention Center. **Con:** not much nearby for tourists. ⊠*110 W. 1st St., 81003* ☎*719/542–3200 or 888/238–6507* ⊕*www.marriott.com* ⤶*163 rooms* ♿*In-room: refrigerator (some), ethernet. In-hotel: restaurant, pool, gym, laundry service, public Wi-Fi, parking (no fee), no-smoking rooms* ▤*AE, D, MC, V.*

NIGHTLIFE & THE ARTS

THE ARTS **Broadway Theatre League** (✉ *210 N. Santa Fe Ave.* ☎ *719/295–7222*) presents three touring shows a year, such as *Evita* and *The Producers*. The **Pueblo Symphony** (✉ *301 N. Main St., Suite 106* ☎ *719/545–7967*) performs music, from pop to classical. **Sangre de Cristo Arts and Conference Center** (✉ *210 N. Santa Fe Ave.* ☎ *719/295–7200*) presents local and touring acts.

NIGHTLIFE The **Shamrock Brewing Company** (✉ *108 W. 3rd St.* ☎ *719/542–9974*) is always hopping after the workday.

SHOPPING

Pueblo's beautifully restored and renovated **Union Avenue Historic District** has a mixture of shops that range from places to buy interesting gifts to inexpensive clothing stores. Around the Union Avenue Depot—an elegantly restored building worth walking to—along Union Avenue and B Street, there are some art galleries, clothing stores, boutiques, and restaurants.

SIDE TRIP TO LA JUNTA

60 mi east of Pueblo via U.S. 50; 105 mi southeast of Colorado Springs.

For an easy day trip from Pueblo into Colorado's past, head east to La Junta. The Koshare Indian Museum is in town, and Bent's Old Fort National Historic Site and the dinosaur tracks and ancient rock art of the canyonlands are nearby. ⊕ *www.lajuntachamber.com.*

EN ROUTE Heading east on U.S. 50 from Pueblo, leaving the Rockies far behind, you travel toward the eastern plains, where rolling prairies of the northeast give way to hardier desert blooms and the land is stubbled with sage and stunted pinyon pines. One fertile spot—50 mi along the highway—is the town of **Rocky Ford**, dubbed the "Melon Capital of the World" for the famously succulent cantaloupes grown here.

La Junta (which roughly translated from Spanish means "the meeting place") was founded as a trading post in the mid-19th century. It was a stop for the Santa Fe and Kansas Pacific railroads, and today is home to 7,600 residents.

The **Koshare Indian Museum** contains extensive holdings of Native American artifacts and crafts (Navajo silver, Zuni pottery, Shoshone buckskin clothing), as well as pieces from Anglo artists, such as Remington, known for their depictions of Native Americans. The Koshare Indian Dancers (actually a local Boy Scout troop) perform regularly. ✉ *115 W. 18th St.* ☎ *719/384–4411* ⊕ *www.koshare.org* 🎟 *$4* ⊘ *Daily noon–5, call for extended summer hrs.*

NEED A BREAK? **For a food stop, try the watering hole with a quirky personality, the Hog's Breath Saloon** (✉ *808 E. 3rd St.* ☎ *719/384–7879*), **a local institution.**

★ **Bent's Old Fort National Historic Site,**
8 mi east of La Junta, is a per-
fect example of a living museum,
with its painstaking re-creation of
the original adobe fort. Founded
in 1833 by savvy trader William
Bent, one of the region's historical giants, the fort anchored the
commercially vital Santa Fe Trail,
providing both protection and a
meeting place for the soldiers, trappers, and traders of the era. The
museum's interior reveals daily life
at a trading post, with recreations
of a smithy, soldiers' and trappers' barracks, and more. ⊠*35110
Hwy. 194* ☎*719/383–5010* ⊠*$3*
⊙*June–Aug., daily 8–5:30; Sept.–
May, daily 9–4.*

> ### SANTA FE TRAIL
>
> Southern Colorado played a major
> role in opening up the West,
> through the Mountain Branch of
> the Santa Fe Trail. Bent's Fort was
> the most important stop between
> the route's origin in Independence,
> Missouri, and its terminus in Santa
> Fe, New Mexico. U.S. 50 roughly
> follows its faded tracks from the
> Kansas border to La Junta, where
> U.S. 350 picks up the trail, travel-
> ing southwest to Trinidad. If you
> detour onto the quiet county
> roads, you can still discern its faint
> outline over the dip of arroyos,
> and with a little imagination, con-
> jure up visions of the pioneers.

SPORTS & THE OUTDOORS

HIKING **Comanche National Grassland**
(⊠*1420 E. 3rd St.* ☎*719/384–2181*) has a pair of canyon loops where
there's a fair amount of rock art. Some of the largest documented sets
of fossilized dinosaur tracks in the United States are in **Picketwire Canyonlands,** a part of the grassland. There are picnic tables but camping is
prohibited. In addition to touring here by car, hiking, mountain biking,
and horseback riding are popular.

TRINIDAD

*80 mi south of Pueblo via I–25, Trinidad is just across the border from
New Mexico; 127 mi south of Colorado Springs.*

If you're traveling on Interstate 25 and want to stop for a night in a historic town with character, instead of a motel on the outskirts of a bigger
city, check out Trinidad. Trinidad's central historic section, Corazon de
Trinidad, is on the cusp of renovation and the surrounding areas are
growing, too. The town has four superb museums, a remarkably large
number for a town of about 11,000 residents. Trinidad was founded
in 1861 as a rest-and-repair station along the Santa Fe Trail. Starting
in 1878 with the construction of the railroad and the development of
the coal industry, the town grew and expanded during the period from
1880 to 1910. But the advent of natural gas, coupled with the Depression, ushered in a gradual decline in population. During the 1990s
there was a modest increase in the population and a major interest in
the upkeep of the city's rich cultural heritage. Although newcomers
are moving in, and Trinidad is coming to life again, with restaurants,
cafés, and galleries, the streets in the heart of town are still paved with
brick, keeping a sense of the town's history alive. From Memorial Day
to Labor Day you can take the free Trinidad Trolley and the driver

will give you an informal history of Trinidad between the stops at the Colorado Welcome Center (✉ *309 Nevada Ave.* ◷ *10–3*) and all of the museums.

For more information and a walking tour map, check with the **Trinidad and Las Animas County Chamber of Commerce** (☎ *866/480–4750* ⊕ *www. historictrinidad.com*).

Downtown, called the **Corazon de Trinidad** *(Heart of Trinidad)*, is a National Historic Landmark District with original brick-paved streets, several Victorian mansions, churches, and the bright-red domes and turrets of Temple Aaron, Colorado's oldest continuously used Reform synagogue.

The **Trinidad History Museum,** a complex that includes three separate museums and a garden, represents the most significant aspects of Trinidad's history. Felipe Baca was a prominent Hispanic farmer and businessman whose 1870s residence, **Baca House,** has period furnishings. Displays convey a mix of Anglo (clothes, furniture) and local Hispanic (santos, textiles) influences. Next door, **Bloom Mansion** is an interesting contrast to the Baca House. Frank Bloom made his money through ranching and banking, and although he was no wealthier than Baca, his mansion (built in 1882) reveals a very different lifestyle. Using rail transportation, he was able to fill his ornate Second Empire–style Victorian (with mansard roof and elaborate wrought ironwork) with fine furnishings and fabrics brought from the East Coast and abroad. The adjacent **Santa Fe Trail Museum** is dedicated to the effect of the trail and railroad on the community. Inside are exhibits covering the heyday of Trinidad as a commercial and cultural center, up through the 1920s. Finish up with a stop in the **Kitchen Garden,** filled with native plants and century-old grapevines similar to those tended by the pioneers. The museum is a property of the Colorado Historical Society. ✉ *312 E. Main St.* ☎ *719/846–7217* ⊕ *www.coloradohistory.org* 🎟 *$6* ◷ *May–Sept., daily 10–4. Call for winter hrs.*

The **A.R. Mitchell Memorial Museum and Gallery** celebrates the life and work of the famous Western illustrator, whose distinctive oils, charcoal drawings, and watercolors graced the pages of pulp magazines and ranch romances. The museum is in an old historic building with the original tin ceiling. Also on display are photos by the Aultman family; dating from 1889, they offer a unique visual record of Trinidad. ✉ *150 E. Main St.* ☎ *719/846–4224* 🎟 *$3, free on Sun.* ◷ *May–Sept., Tues.–Sat. 10–4; call for off season hrs.*

On the other side of the Purgatoire River, the **Louden-Henritze Archaeology Museum** takes viewers back millions of years to examine the true origins of the region, including early geologic formations, plant and marine-animal fossils, and prehistoric artifacts. ✉ *Trinidad State Junior College* ☎ *719/846–5508* ⊕ *historictrinidad.com/tour/arc.html* 🎟 *Free* ◷ *Jan.–Nov., weekdays 10–3.*

☾ The **Old Firehouse No. 1 Children's Museum** is in the delightful Old Firehouse Number 1, with displays of fire-fighting memorabilia, such as a

1936 American LaFrance fire truck (children love clanging the bell) and the city's original fire alarm system. Upstairs is a fine re-creation of an early 1900s schoolroom. ⊠*314 N. Commercial St.* ☎*719/846–8220* *Free* ⊗*June–Sept., weekdays 11–3.*

There's hiking, fishing in the 800-acre lake, horseback riding (allowed on one trail), and camping in the Purgatoire River valley at the **Trinidad Lake State Park** (☎*719/846–6951*), 3 mi west of Trinidad on Route 12.

WHERE TO STAY & EAT

¢–$ ✕ **The Café.** Set in a downtown historic building, the café serves imaginative and delicious sandwiches, such as the Stonewall Gap, which has honey-smoked ham and melted Brie slathered with chutney in a ciabatta roll. This spot is usually crowded at breakfast and lunch, but you order at the counter so things move quickly. Drop in for a muffin or pecan sticky bun and a cup of strong coffee or chai tea if you don't want a full meal. The café is inside Danielson Dry Goods, and the other half of the building, which you can explore while waiting for your food, is an upscale-lifestyle store, with an eclectic array of humorous signs. ⊠*135 E. Main St.* ☎*719/846–7119* 🖃*AE, MC, V* ⊗*No dinner.*

¢–$ ✕ **Nana and Nano's Pasta House.** The aroma of garlic and tomato sauce saturates this tiny, unpretentious eatery. Pastas, including standards like homemade ravioli, gnocchi Bolognese, and rigatoni with luscious meatballs, are consistently excellent. If you don't have time for a sit-down lunch, stop at the deli counter for smashing heroes and gourmet sandwiches or takeouts of imported cheeses and olives. ⊠*418 E. Main St.* ☎*719/846–2696* 🖃*MC, V* ⊗*Closed Sun. and Mon.*

$–$$ ✕🖫 **Black Jack's Saloon, Steak House & Inn.** Step inside this 1890s downtown building, where you can toss your peanut shells on the floor from your perch at the full-service antique bar. Between this bar and the leafy-salad kind of bar is an open grill where the most succulent steaks on the Santa Fe Trail are prepared. Those avoiding red meat can go for salmon, swordfish, or chicken. The owners have also restored five rooms overhead, each named after some of the "ladies" who lived upstairs. The rooms are decorated in bordello style, as if the ladies just slipped outside for a break. The bathrooms are similarly tricked up but have been modernized. The rooms have robes and Wi-Fi, are air conditioned, and come with a light continental breakfast. **Pro:** these rooms take you back to another era when bordellos were acceptable. **Con:** it's over a colorful and popular saloon. ⊠*225 W. Main St., 81082* ☎*719/846–9501* ⊕*www.blackjackssaloon.com* ◁*5 rooms* ⌂*In-room: no phone, Wi-Fi. In-hotel: no elevator, no-smoking rooms* 🖃*AE, MC, V* ⟊*CP* ⊗*Restaurant closed Sun.*

$ 🖫 **Tarabino Inn.** This turn-of-the-20th-century Italianate–Victorian brick B&B in the Corazon de Trinidad National Historic District is the former abode of the Tarabino brothers, the proprietors of one of Trinidad's first department stores. The rooms are frilly, immaculate, and comfortable, with a dose of modern convenience. **Pro:** inn is filled with work by local artists, which is for sale. **Con:** feels like staying in someone's private home. ⊠*310 E. 2nd St., 81082* ☎*719/846–2115*

or 866/846–8808 ⊕www.tarabinoinn.com ⟐2 suites, 2 rooms with-
out bath ⌂In-room: refrigerator, VCR, dial-up. In-hotel: no-smoking
rooms ▤AE, D, MC, V ⦿BP.

SHOPPING

In the heart of the historic district there's a growing number of interesting shops selling handmade candles, colorful Mexican home ware, and
Western artworks by such painters as Frank LaLumia, Lois Petersen,
and Tom Scarborough. **Purgatoire River Trading Company** (✉*113 E.*
Main St. ☎*719/845–0202*) is the place to find authentic old Navajo
rugs, Native American pottery, Pima baskets, and old-pawn jewelry.
Fragrant smells fill the air in **Sweet Senses** (✉*115 N. Commercial St.*
☎*719/845–8880*), where the shelves are stocked with homemade
soaps, essential oils, and teas and spices from around the world. **Cora-**
zon Gallery (✉*149 E. Main St.* ☎*719/846–0207*) is a local artists' co-
op, with oils, handwoven clothing, and mixed-media artwork.

NIGHTLIFE

Lucky Monkey (✉*137 Cedar St.* ☎*719/846–2449*) is a combination
nightclub—with a small bar called Little Monkey inside—and venue
in a historic building, where special events, such as the annual PreFest
to the Blues Fest are held. Choose from a variety of lagers and ales,
depending upon what's being traditionally brewed, at the **Trinidad Brew-**
ing Company (✉*516 Elm St.* ☎*719/846–7069*). There's an open micro-
phone most Wednesdays and a band on Friday. The **Other Place** (✉*466*
W. Main St. ☎*719/846–9012*) hires DJs and top local rock bands on
weekends to play its intimate classy space.

CUCHARA VALLEY

55 mi from Trinidad (to town of Cuchara) via Rte. 12; 117 mi south
of Colorado Springs.

★ From Trinidad, Route 12—the scenic **Highway of Legends**—curls north
through the Cuchara Valley. As it starts its climb, you'll pass a series of
company towns built to house coal miners.

Cokedale is nestled in Reilly Canyon. The entire town is a National
Historic Landmark District, and it's the most significant example of
a turn-of-the-20th-century coal–coke camp in Colorado. As you drive
through the area, note the telltale streaks of black in the sandstone
and granite bluffs fronting the Purgatoire River and its tributaries, the
unsightly slag heaps, and the spooky abandoned mining camps dotting
the hillsides.

The impressive **Stonewall Gap,** a monumental gate of rock, roughly
marks the end of the mining district.

As you approach Cuchara Pass, several switchbacks snake through
rolling grasslands and dance in and out of spruce stands whose clear-
ings afford views of Monument Lake. You can camp, fish, and hike
throughout this tranquil part of the **San Isabel National Forest,** which in
spring and summer is emblazoned with a color wheel of wildflowers.

Four corkscrewing miles later, you'll reach a dirt road that leads to the twin sapphires of **Bear and Blue lakes.** The resort town of **Cuchara** is about 4 mi from the Highway 12 turnoff to the lakes. Nestled in a spoon valley (*cuchara* means "spoon"), the area became popular as a turn-of-the-20th-century camping getaway for Texans and Oklahomans because of its cool temperatures and stunning scenery.

In the Cuchara Valley you'll begin to see fantastic rock formations with equally fanciful names, such as Profile Rock, Devil's Staircase, and Giant's Spoon. With a little imagination you can devise your own legends about the names' origins. There are more than 400 of these upthrusts, which radiate like the spokes of a wheel from the valley's dominating landmark, the **Spanish Peaks.** In Spanish they are known as *Dos Hermanos,* or "Two Brothers"; in Ute, their name *Huajatolla* means "breasts of the world." The haunting formations are considered to be a unique geologic phenomenon for their sheer abundance and variety of rock types.

The Highway of Legends passes through the tiny, laid-back resort town of **La Veta** before intersecting with Highway 160 and going on to Walsenburg, another city built on coal and the largest town between Pueblo and Trinidad.

SPORTS & THE OUTDOORS

GOLF **Grandote Peaks Golf Club.** This Weiskopf Morrish–designed course is an underutilized gem that sits close to the base of the Spanish Peaks. Weekends you need reservations to play the classic 18-hole mountain course, but it might be easy to get on at the last minute weekdays. ⊠ *5540 Hwy. 12, La Veta* ☎ *719/742–3391 or 800/457–9986* ⊕ *www. grandotepeaks.com* 🏌 *18 holes. Yards: 7,085/5,608. Par: 72/73. Green Fee: $58/$78.*

HIKING The **San Isabel National Forest** (⊠ *3170 E. Main St., Cañon City, 81212* ☎ *719/269–8500*) has myriad hiking trails, not to mention campgrounds, fishing streams, and mountain-biking terrain. In winter, it's a cross-country skiing destination.

WHERE TO STAY

The rental of condominiums, homes, and cabins is handled by **Cuchara Cabins and Condos** (☎ *719/742–3340* ⊕ *www.coloradodirectory. com/cucharavacation*).

★ $ 🏨 **Inn at the Spanish Peaks Bed & Breakfast.** This Southwestern-style B&B is set in an adobe-style home, with open beams and high ceilings. The attractive great room has a fireplace. The three themed guest suites all have decks with views of the surrounding mountains; the nicely done St. Andrews suite focuses on golf, and the Colorado suite has a handmade log bed. **Pro:** mountain views. **Con:** you are really in the outback of Colorado. ⊠ *310 E. Francisco St., La Veta 81055* ☎ *719/742–5313* ⊕ *www.innatthespanishpeaks.com* 🛏 *3 suites* ⚴ *In-room: no a/c, no TV, Wi-Fi. In-hotel: no elevator, public Wi-Fi, no-smoking rooms* ▭ *MC, V* ⊺◯⊺ *BP.*

11

$ ⚞**La Veta Inn.** The shady courtyard, with its fireplace, is a selling point at this inn in the historic district of La Veta. There are some antiques in the guest rooms, but it's not a fancy place. The restaurant serves three meals a day. **Pros:** next to galleries, a few blocks from Tom Weiskopf's Grandote Peaks Golf Course. **Con:** La Veta is in Colorado's outback, so it's not ideal for travelers who want a more-urban atmosphere. ✉*103 W. Ryus Ave.* ✆*Box 300, La Veta 81055* ☎*719/742–3700, 888/806–4875 reservations* ⊕*www.lavetainn.com* ⬅*18 rooms* ⌂*In-room: kitchen (some), VCR (some), Wi-Fi. In-hotel: restaurant, bar, no elevator, some pets allowed, no-smoking rooms* ▭*AE, MC, V.*

THE SAN LUIS VALLEY

At 8,000 square mi, the San Luis Valley is the world's largest alpine valley, sprawling on a broad, flat, dry plain between the San Juan and La Garita mountains to the west and the Sangre de Cristo range to the east. But equally important is that the valley, like the Southwest, remains culturally rooted in the early Hispanic tradition rather than the northern European one that early prospectors and settlers brought to central and northern Colorado.

Despite its average elevation of 7,500 feet, the San Luis Valley's sheltering peaks help to create a relatively mild climate. The area is one of the state's major agricultural producers, with huge annual crops of potatoes, carrots, canola, barley, and lettuce. In many ways, it's self-sufficient; in the 1950s, local business owners threatened to secede to prove that the state couldn't get along without the valley and its valuable products. Half a century later, however, the reality is that the region is economically disadvantaged and contains two of the state's poorer counties. The large and sparsely populated valley contains some real oddities, including an alligator farm, a UFO-viewing tower, and the New Age town of Crestone, with its spiritual centers.

Watered by the Rio Grande and its tributaries, the San Luis Valley also supports a magnificent array of wildlife, including flocks of birds, such as migrating sandhill cranes. The range of terrain is equally impressive, from soaring Fourteeners, to the stark moonscape of the Wheeler Geologic Area, to the undulating landscape of the Great Sand Dunes National Park.

Great Sand Dunes National Park & Preserve is a draw for hikers. World-class climbing can be found outside Del Norte in the Penitente Canyon. The Rio Grande National Forest west of the valley and the San Isabel National Forest to the east offer millions of acres of back-country pleasures.

This area was settled first by the Ute, then by the Spanish, who left their indelible imprint in the town names and architecture. The oldest town (San Luis), the oldest military post (Fort Garland), and the oldest church (Our Lady of Guadalupe in Conejos) in the state are in this valley.

GREAT SAND DUNES NATIONAL PARK & PRESERVE

Fodor's Choice
★ *35 mi northeast of Alamosa via U.S. 160 and Rte. 150; 198 mi southwest of Colorado Springs.*

Created by winds that sweep the San Luis Valley floor, the up-to-750-foot-high sand dunes that form the heart of Great Sand Dunes National Park and Preserve are an improbable, unforgettable sight. The dunes, as curvaceous as Rubens's nudes, stretch for more than 30 square mi. The sand is fine and feathery, making the dunes' very existence seem tenuous, as if they might blow away before your eyes, yet they're solid enough to withstand the stress of hikers and saucer-riding thrill-seekers.

TIMING   Even though only about 300,000 visitors come to the park each year, they tend to come in summer and congregate in one area, making the park crowded June through August. In fact, in peak season, the section of the dunes closest to the parking lots sounds a lot like a playground; if you visit in summer, hike away from the main area up to the High Dune. Fall and spring are the prettiest times to visit. In late May, the mountains are still capped with snow, ensuring a vivid contrast to the golden dunes. In September and early October, leaves on aspen trees are turning gold. In winter the park is a place for contemplation and repose, the silence broken only by passing birds and the faint rush of water from the Medano or Sand creeks.

GETTING   Great Sand Dunes National Park and Preserve is about 230 mi from
THERE &   both Denver and Albuquerque, and about 170 mi from Colorado
AROUND   Springs and Santa Fe. The fastest route from the north is Interstate 25 south to U.S. 160, heading west to just past Blanca, to Highway 150 north. When traveling from Albuquerque, go north on Interstate 25, then merge with U.S. 285 at Santa Fe, going north to U.S. 160 to Highway 150. From the west, Highway 17 and County Lane 6 take you to the park.

The closest Amtrak train stop is in Trinidad, near the New Mexico border. Greyhound buses go to Alamosa and Blanca. Colorado Springs Airport is the largest in the south central Colorado area.

The park itself only has one road. It's about a mile from the tollbooth at the entrance to the visitor center and the Dunes Parking Lot is about a mile farther. There are no shuttle services.

SCENIC DRIVE   **Medano Pass Primitive Road.** This 22-mi road connects Great Sand Dunes with the Wet Mountain valley and Highway 69 on the east side of the Sangre de Cristo Mountains as well as the Great Sand Dunes National Preserve via a climb to Medano Pass (10,040 feet above sea level). It is a four-wheel-drive-only road that is best driven by someone who already has good four-wheel-drive skills. (Your four-wheel-drive vehicle must have high clearance and be engineered to go over rough roads.) The road has sections of deep, loose sand, and it crosses Medano Creek nine times. Before you go, stop at the visitor center for a map and ask about current road conditions. Drive time pavement to pavement is 2½ to 3 hours.

FLORA & FAUNA

The park is spread over several ecological zones, so visitors see an amazing array of animals and plant life. The wetlands are filled with broad-leaved cattail and colorful Rocky Mountain iris. The sand sheet and grasslands are dotted with prickly pear, rabbit brush, and yucca. The dune field looks barren from afar, but up close you see various grasses have rooted in swales among the dunes. Montane, pine, and pinyon pine trees grow on the lower portions of the mountain, stunted trees survive in the subalpine forest zone, and tiny flowers cling to rock at the top.

You may see beavers and pelicans in the wetlands; short-horn lizards, elk, and mule deer in the sand sheet and grassland; and Great Sand Dunes tiger beetles and Ord's kangaroo rats in the dune field. On the mountainsides, falcons fly overhead, while black bears, bobcats, and Rocky Mountain bighorn sheep graze.

WHAT TO SEE

★ **Dunefield.** The more than 30 square mi of big dunes in the heart of the park is the main attraction, although the surrounding grasslands do have some smaller dunes. You can start putting your feet in the sand 3 mi past the main park entrance.

High Dune. This isn't the highest dune in the park, but it is a dune that's high enough in the dunefield so visitors can get a view of all the dunes. It's on the first ridge of dunes that you see from the main parking area.

Visitor Center. At the sole park visitor center you can view exhibits, browse in the bookstore, and watch a 20-minute film with an overview of the dunes. Rangers are on hand to answer questions. Facilities include restrooms and a vending machine stocked with soft drinks spring, summer, and fall. Coffee is available November through February. The Great Sand Dunes Oasis, just outside the park boundary, has a café that is open year-round. ⊠ *Near the park entrance* ☎ *719/378–6399.*

SPORTS & THE OUTDOORS

The park is a good choice for hikers and overnight campers. It's not for mountain bikers or other cyclists, because there aren't any mountain-bike trails and the conditions are too sandy.

BIRD-WATCHING In the wetlands there are migratory birds such as the American white pelican and American avocet. On the forested sections of the mountains there are goshawks, northern harriers, gray jays, and Steller's jays. In the alpine tundra there are golden eagles, hawks, horned larks, and white-tailed ptarmigan.

FISHING Fly fishermen can angle for Rio Grande cutthroat trout in Medano Creek, but it's catch and release. See ⊕ *www.wildlife.state.co.us/fishing* for more information. There's also fishing in Upper and Lower Sand Creek lake, but it's a very long hike.

HIKING

Visitors can walk just about anywhere on the sand dunes in the heart of the park. The best view of all the dunes is from the top of High Dune. There are no formal trails because the sand keeps shifting; however, the majority of visitors trek up it, and all of those feet can create a sort of rough path in the sand.

Before taking any of the trails in the preserve, rangers recommend stopping at the visitor center and picking up the handout that lists the trails, including their degree of difficulty. The dunes can get very hot in summer, reaching up to 140°F in the afternoon. If you're hiking, carry plenty of water: if you're going into the backcountry to camp overnight, carry even more water or a water filtration system. A free permit is needed to backpack in the park. Also, watch for weather changes. If there's a thunderstorm and lightning, get off the dunes or trails immediately, and seek shelter. Before hiking, leave word with someone of where you're planning to hike and when you expect to be back. Tell that contact to call the area-wide dispatcher at ☎719/589–5807 if you don't show up when expected.

Hike to High Dune. Get a panoramic view of all the surrounding dunes. Since there's no formal path, the smartest approach is to zigzag up the dune ridgelines. High Dune is 650 feet high, and to get there and back takes about 1½ to 2 hours. It's 1.2 mi each way. If you add on the walk to Star Dune, which is a few more miles, plan on another two hours and a strenuous workout up and down the dunes to get there. ✛ *Start from main dune field.*

DID YOU KNOW?

Native Americans used to peel ponderosa pines in order to eat the inner bark (which is rich in calcium) and use the pine gum for medicinal purposes. You can view many of these "culturally modified" trees at Great Sand Dunes National Park.

Fodor'sChoice
★

Mosca Pass Trail. This moderately easy trail follows the route laid out centuries ago by Native Americans and then the Mosca Pass toll road used in the late 1800s and early 1900s. This is a good afternoon hike, because the trail rises through the trees and subalpine meadows, often following Mosca Creek. It is 3.5 mi one way, with a 1,480-foot gain in elevation. Hiking time is two to three hours each way. ✛ *The lower end of the trail begins at the Montville Trailhead, just north of the visitor center.*

Music Pass Trail. This steep, difficult trail offers superb views of the glacially carved Upper Sand Creek basin, ringed by many 13,000-foot peaks and the Wet Mountain valley to the east. At the top of the pass you are at about 11,000 feet and surrounded by yet higher mountain peaks. The trail also accesses the Sand Creek Lakes Trail and the Little Sand Creek Lakes Trail, with terrain ranging from moderately difficult to very rough and requiring good route-finding ability. It's 3.5 mi and a 2,000-foot elevation gain one way from the lower parking lot, and 1 mi from the upper parking lot (only reachable in a four-wheel-drive vehicle). Depending on how fit you are and how often you stop, it could take six hours round-trip. ✛*The trailhead is reached via Hwy. 69, 4.5* *mi south of Westcliffe. Turn off Hwy. 69 to the west at the sign for Music Pass and South Colony Lakes trails. At the "T" junction turn left onto South Colony Rd. At the end of the ranch fence on the right you'll see another sign for Music Pass.*

HORSEBACK RIDING Riding is allowed throughout the preserve and in much of the park. There are certain restrictions. For example, riding is not allowed in areas with high pedestrian traffic, such as the Pinyon Flats Campground. Camping with horses is permitted in certain areas; stop at the visitor center to pick up a horseback-riding and camping map and a free permit for camping with a horse and parking your horse trailer.

JEEP TOURS **Great Sand Dunes Oasis.** In warmer months, you can book a Medano Pass Primitive Road Tour in an open-air, four-wheel-drive vehicle. The tours follow a sandy road along the eastern edge of the dunes and go partway up the road, then turn around. ✉*5400 Hwy. 150 (just outside the park), Mosca* ☎*719/378–2222* 🎟*$21* 🕓*Memorial Day–Labor Day, at 10 and 2 roughly; minimum 6 people.*

EDUCATIONAL OFFERINGS

CLASSES & SEMINARS **Nature Conservancy.** June through August, guest speakers are on hand to lecture on all kinds of topics, from birds in the park to the region's history, and there are conservation seminars in spring, summer, and fall. ✉*Medano-Zapata Ranch* ☎*719/378–6399, 719/378–2356 for the Nature Conservancy workshops* 🎟*Cost varies according to program.*

PROGRAMS & TOURS ☺ **Bison Tour and Hayride.** On these Saturday-morning tours, visitors see the "Wild West" section of the park, where more than 1,000 bison roam in the grasslands and wetlands. ✉*Tours begin at the Nature Conservancy's Medano-Zapata Ranch* ☎*719/580–0136* 🎟*$20.*

RANGER PROGRAMS **Interpretive Programs.** Terrace talks and nature walks designed to help visitors learn more about the park are scheduled most days from late May through September. (Contact the park in advance about winter schedule.) ✉*Visitor center* ☎*719/378–6399* 🎟*Free.*

Junior Ranger Programs. During summer months, children ages 3–12 can join age-appropriate activities to learn about plants, animals, and the park's ecology, and they can become Junior Rangers by working successfully through an activity booklet. Ask for schedules and activity booklets at the visitor center. Youngsters can learn about the park prior to their trip via an interactive online program for kids at 🌐*www.nps.gov/archive/grsa/pphtml/forkids.html.* ☎*719/378–6399* 🎟*Free.*

WHERE TO STAY & EAT

There are no hotels or restaurants inside the park. *For information about where to stay and eat nearby, see the Alamosa section in this chapter.*

PICNIC AREA **Mosca Creek.** The park's only picnic area is shaded by cottonwood trees. It has a dozen places where visitors can park a car or RV near a picnic table and a grill. ✥*South of the Dunes Parking Lot.*

CAMPGROUND   ⚠️**Pinyon Flats Campground.** Set in a pinyon pine forest about a mile past
¢   the visitor center, this campground has a trail leading to the dunes.
Sites are available on a first-come, first-served basis, although groups
of 10 or more might be able to reserve in advance. RVs are allowed,
but there are no hookups. The campground fills up rapidly on summer
weekends, and tends to have lots of families when school is out. Quiet
hours start at 10 PM. Register at the kiosk. **Pro:** wandering among the
dunes in the early morning or after the day crowds leave brings you
closer to nature. **Con:** you must show up early to get a space, because
it's first-come, first served. ✉️*On the main park road, near the visitor
center* ☎️*719/378–6399* 🛏️*88 sites* ⚕️*Flush toilets, fire grates, picnic
tables* ▭*No credit cards.*

ALAMOSA

*35 mi southwest of Great Sand Dunes via U.S. 160 and Rte. 150; 163
mi southwest of Colorado Springs.*

The San Luis Valley's major city is a casual, central base from which to
explore the region and visit the Great Sand Dunes.

Just 3 mi outside town is the **Alamosa National Wildlife Refuge.** These
natural and man-made wetlands bordering the Rio Grande River—
an anomaly amid the arid surroundings—are an important sanctuary
for myriad migrating birds. ✉️*9383 El Rancho La.* ☎️*719/589–4021*
🎫*Free* 🕐*Daily sunrise–sunset.*

From late February to mid-March, birders flock to nearby Monte Vista
to view the migration of the sandhill cranes at the **Monte Vista National
Wildlife Refuge.** Nicknamed the Valley of the Cranes, the park is one
place where you can see these interesting creatures at close range. Every
morning during the Festival of the Cranes, buses shuttle visitors to the
refuge from Alamosa. ✉️*6140 Hwy. 15, Monte Vista* 🎫*Free* 🕐*Daily
sunrise–sunset.*

The **San Luis Valley Museum** showcases Indian artifacts, photographs, military regalia, and collectibles of early railroading, farming, and ranch
life. Exhibits feature the multicultural influence of Hispanic, Japanese-
American, Mormon, and Dutch settlers. ✉️*401 Hunt* ☎️*719/587–0667*
🎫*$2* 🕐*Tues.–Sat. 10–4.*

WHERE TO STAY & EAT

$$ ✕ **True Grits.** At this steak house the cuts of beef are good, as are the
burgers, but that's not the real draw. As the name implies, this locals'
hangout is really just a shrine to John Wayne. It's worth a stop to see
his portraits, which hang everywhere: the Duke in action; the Duke in
repose; the Duke lost in thought. Reservations are suggested. ✉️*Junc-
tion U.S. 160 and Rte. 17* ☎️*719/589–9954* ▭*AE, D, MC, V* 🕐*No
lunch.*

¢   ✕ **East West Grill.** Noodles and teriyaki are on the menu at this casual,
fast-food-style place, where you order and get your food at the counter.
Offerings include rice bowls, noodle bowls, salads, and bento boxes
filled with wild salmon, sesame chicken, or soba noodles and steamed

fresh veggies. The pad thai is tasty and the sesame chop salad is nicely dressed. Dine in or carry out. ⊠*4th and Denver Sts.* ☎*719/589–4600* ▤*MC, V.*

★ ¢ ✕**Milagro's Coffeehouse.** The coffee is full-bodied at this combination coffeehouse, Internet café, and used-book store, where all profits go to help local charities. The decor is secondhand basic, but the tuna salad sub and the Reuben are especially tasty. Free Wi-Fi makes this a popular spot for locals. The used-book selection is very eclectic and includes some obscure titles. Dine in or carry out. ⊠*Main and State Sts.* ☎*719/589–9299* ▤*MC, V.*

$ ▦**Conejos River Guest Ranch.** On the Conejos River, this peaceful, family-friendly retreat is in Antonito, about 42 mi southwest of Alamosa. The seven cabins and eight guest rooms are pleasantly outfitted with ranch-style decor, including lodgepole pine furnishings. Breakfast is complimentary in the lodge only. **Pro:** great fishing on the area rivers. **Con:** city lovers will find this ranch too isolated. ⊠*25390 Hwy. 17, Antonito 81120* ☎*719/376–2464* ⊕*www.conejosranch.com* ➪*8 rooms, 7 cabins* ♿*In-room: no a/c, kitchen (some), no TV. In-hotel: restaurant, no elevator, no-smoking rooms* ▤*D, MC, V* ☽*Closed Dec.–Apr.* ⏐◎⏐*DP.*

$ ▦**Inn of the Rio Grande.** The city's largest hotel is a dog-friendly property, with comfortable rooms and suites. It's a full-service hotel, and kids will love the indoor pool and 150-foot waterslide, but it's also a good choice for businesspeople. **Pros:** indoor water park, pet friendly. **Con:** rooms are basic. ⊠*333 Santa Fe Dr., 81101* ☎*719/589–5833* ⊕*www. innoftherio.com* ➪*126 rooms* ♿*In-room: refrigerator (some), ethernet. In-hotel: restaurant, pool, gym, no elevator, public Wi-Fi, some pets allowed, parking (no fee), no-smoking rooms* ▤*AE, D, MC, V.*

SHOPPING

The San Luis Valley is noted for its produce. Mycophiles can take a tour of the **Rakhra Mushroom Farm.** Call ahead; mornings are preferred. (⊠*10719 Rd. 5 S* ☎*719/589–5882*). **Treasure Alley** (⊠*713 Main St.* ☎*719/587–0878*) offers an eclectic mix of gifts from jewelry and jewelry boxes to local artwork and clocks. **Vintage Garage Antiques Mall** (⊠*420 Main St.* ☎*719/587–5494*) is a renovated garage brimming with old stuff, jewelry, antiques, glassware, and much more.

MANASSA, SAN LUIS & FORT GARLAND LOOP

To get a real feel for this area, take an easy driving loop from Alamosa, which includes Manassa, San Luis, and Fort Garland. In summer take a few hours to ride one of the scenic railroads that take you into wilderness areas in this region.

The **Cumbres & Toltec Scenic Railroad** chugs through spectacular scenery in Colorado and New Mexico. The steam railroad is 64 mi long, and the depot is in Antonito. Several different itineraries are available. ☎*888/286–2737* ⊕*www.cumbrestoltec.com* ✉*Coach class $65–$129 in parlor car* ☽*Late May–mid-Oct., daily. Call or check Web site for times.*

The **Rio Grande Scenic Railroad** takes travelers from Alamosa up to La Veta pass. ☎*888/726–7245* ⊕*www.alamosatrainride.com* ✉*Coach class $48* ⊙*Late May–mid-Oct., daily. Call or check Web site for times.*

The town of **Manassa** is about 23 mi from Alamosa, south on U.S. 285 and 3 mi east on Route 142. Known as the Manassa Mauler, one of the greatest heavyweight boxing champions of all time is honored in his hometown at the **Jack Dempsey Museum** (⊠*401 Main St.* ☎*719/843–5207* ⊙*June–Aug., Tues.–Sat. 9–5; Sept.–May, town clerk will open it for visitors Mon.–Wed., other days by appointment*).

San Luis, founded in 1851, is the oldest incorporated town in Colorado. Murals depicting famous stories and legends of the area adorn several buildings in the town. A latter-day masterpiece is the **Stations of the Cross Shrine,** created by renowned local sculptor Huberto Maestas. The shrine is formally known as La Mesa de la Piedad y de la Misericordia (Hill of Piety and Mercy), and its 15 stations illustrate the last hours of Christ's life. The trail leads up to a chapel called Capilla de Todos Los Santos. San Luis's Hispanic heritage is celebrated in the **San Luis Museum & Cultural Center** (⊠*401 Church Pl.* ☎*719/672–3611* ✉*$2* ⊙*Summer, Mon.–Sat. 9–4, Sun. noon–4; winter, weekdays 9–4*). It has an extensive collection of artwork, *santos* (decorated figures of saints used for household devotions), *retablos* (religious paintings on wood), and *bultos* (carved religious figures).

Colorado's first military post, **Fort Garland,** was established in 1858 to protect settlers. It lies in the shadow of the Sangre de Cristo Mountains. They were named the Blood of Christ Mountains because of their ruddy color, especially at dawn. The legendary Kit Carson commanded the outfit, and the six original adobe structures are still standing. The **Fort Garland State Museum** features a re-creation of the commandant's quarters, period military displays, and a rotating local folk-art exhibit. The museum is 16 mi north of San Luis via Route 159 and 24 mi east of Alamosa via U.S. 160. ⊹*South of intersection U.S. 160 and Hwy. 159* ☎*719/379–3512* ✉*$4* ⊙*Apr.–Oct., daily 9–5; Nov.–Mar., Thurs.–Mon. 10–4.*

DEL NORTE

31 mi west of Alamosa via U.S. 160; 194 mi southwest of Colorado Springs.

In and around Del Norte are several historic sites, one of which is an original 1870s station belonging to the Barlow-Sanderson Stagecoach Line.

The **Rio Grande County Museum and Cultural Center** celebrates the region's multicultural heritage with displays of petroglyphs, mining artifacts, early Spanish relics, and rotating shows of contemporary art. ⊠*580 Oak St.* ☎*719/657–2847* ✉*$1* ⊙ *Tues.–Sat. 10–5.*

Just west of town is the gaping **Penitente Canyon.** Once a retreat and place of worship for a small, fervent sect of the Catholic Church known

11

as Los Hermanos Penitente, it is now a haven for rock climbers, hikers, and mountain bikers. Follow Route 112 about 3 mi from Del Norte, then follow the signs to the canyon.

In the nearby La Garita Wilderness is another marvel—the towering rock formation **La Ventana Natural Arch.**

FISHING **SPORTS & THE OUTDOORS**
The Rio Grande River—between Del Norte and South Fork—teems with rainbows, browns, and cutthroats. The area is full of "gold medal" waters, designated as great fishing spots by the Colorado Wildlife Commission. See ⊕*www.wildlife.state.co.us/fishing* for more information.

SHOPPING
Elk Ridge (⊠*610 Grand Ave.* ☎*719/657–2322*) is the place for antiques, gourmet products, and gift baskets overflowing with goodies. **Haefeli's Honey Farms** (⊠*425 Grand Ave.* ☎*719/657–2044*) sells delectable mountain-bloom honeys.

SOUTH CENTRAL COLORADO ESSENTIALS

TRANSPORTATION

BY AIR
Colorado Springs Airport (COS) is the major airport in the region, with more than a dozen nonstop destinations. Pueblo Memorial Airport (PUB) has commuter service to Denver twice daily weekdays and once a day weekends on Great Lakes Aviation, plus charter flights. Most South Central Colorado residents drive to Colorado Springs to fly out.

Alternatively, you can choose to fly to Denver International Airport (DEN). It's an 80-mi drive from Denver to the Springs, but during rush hour it might take a solid two hours, whether you're in your own car or in one of the Denver–Colorado Springs shuttles.

Information Colorado Springs Airport (COS) (☎*719/550–1972* ⊕*www. flycos.com*). **Denver International Airport (DEN)** (☎*303/342–2000* ⊕*www. flydenver.com*). **Pueblo Memorial Airport (PUB)** (☎*719/553–2760* ⊕*www. pueblo.us/airport*).

TRANSFERS **From Colorado Springs Airport** Colorado Springs Shuttle offers service from the Colorado Springs Airport (COS) and downtown. For taxi service, try Yellow Cab. From Pueblo Memorial Airport, take City Cab.

Contacts City Cab (☎*719/543–2525*).**Colorado Springs Shuttle** (☎*719/687–3456*). **Yellow Cab** (☎*719/634–5000*).

BY BUS
Greyhound Lines serves Colorado Springs and most of the major towns in south central Colorado. TNM & O Coaches serves Colorado Springs. Colorado Springs and Pueblo both have municipal bus services.

Contacts **Colorado Springs Transit** (☎ *719/385–7433*). **Greyhound Lines** (☎ *800/231–2222* ⊕ *www.greyhound.com*). **Pueblo Transit** (☎ *719/553–2727*).

BY CAR

In Colorado Springs (whose airport has the typical lineup of car-rental agencies), the main north–south roads are Interstate 25, Academy Boulevard, Nevada Avenue, and Powers Boulevard, and each will get you where you want to go in good time; east–west routes along Woodmen Road (far north), Austin Bluffs Parkway (north central), and Platte Boulevard (south central) can get backed up.

Running north–south from Wyoming to New Mexico, Interstate 25 bisects Colorado and is the major artery into the area. Colorado Springs and Pueblo (which also has a pair of car-rental counters at the airport) are on Interstate 25. Florissant and Buena Vista are reached via U.S. 24 off Interstate 25; Cañon City and the Royal Gorge via U.S. 50. Salida can be reached via Highway 291 from either U.S. 24 or U.S. 50. Palmer Lake and Larkspur are accessible via Interstate 25 and Highway 105. Most cities in south central Colorado besides Colorado Springs and Pueblo lack car-rental service.

Information **AAA Colorado** (☎ *719/591–2222, 719/632–8800 emergency road service*). **Colorado Department of Transportation Road Condition Hotline** (☎ *303/639–1111*). **Colorado State Patrol** (☎ *719/635–0385* ⊕ *www.csp.state. co.us*).

BY TRAIN

Amtrak stops in Trinidad and La Junta.

Contact **Amtrak** (☎ *800/872–7245* ⊕ *www.amtrak.com*).

CONTACTS & RESOURCES

CAMPING

The entire area is known for camping. The U.S. Forest Service operates many developed campgrounds, and there are numerous backcountry opportunities as well.

Information **Forest Service Office for the San Isabel National Forest** (✉ *3170 E. Main St., Cañon City, 81212* ☎ *719/269–8500*).

EMERGENCIES

Ambulance or Police (☎ *911*).

Colorado Springs Colorado Springs Memorial Hospital (✉ *1400 E. Boulder St.* ☎ *719/365–5000*). **Memorial Hospital Briargate Medical Campus** (✉ *8890 N. Union Blvd.* ☎ *719/365–2888*). **Penrose St. Francis Hospital** (✉ *2222 N. Nevada Ave.* ☎ *719/776–5000*). **Penrose Community Hospital** (✉ *3205 N. Academy Blvd.* ☎ *719/776–3000*).

South Central Colorado Cañon City: St. Thomas More Hospital (✉ *1338 Phay Ave.* ☎ *719/285–2000*). **La Junta: Arkansas Valley Regional Medical Center** (✉ *1100 Carson Ave.* ☎ *719/384–5412*). **Pueblo: Parkview Medical Center** (✉ *400 W. 16th St.* ☎ *719/584–4000*). **Salida: Heart of the Rockies Regional**

11

Medical Center (✉ *448 E. 1st St.* ☎ *719/539–6661*). **Trinidad: Mount San Rafael Hospital** (✉ *410 Benedicta Ave.* ☎ *719/846–9213*).

TOURS

Ramblin' Express offers shuttles to Cripple Creek. Gray Line offers tours of the Colorado Springs area, including Pikes Peak and Manitou Springs.

Contacts **Gray Line** (☎ *719/633–1181* ⊕ *grayline.com*). **Ramblin' Express** (☎ *719/590-8687* ⊕ *ramblinexpress.com*).

VISITOR INFORMATION

Colorado Springs Contacts **Colorado Springs Convention and Visitors Bureau** (✉ *515 S. Cascade Ave.* ☎ *719/635–7506 or 800/888–4748* ⊕ *www.experiencecoloradosprings.com*). **Manitou Springs Chamber of Commerce** (✉ *354 Manitou Ave.* ☎ *719/685–5089 or 800/642–2567* ⊕ *www.manitousprings.org*). **Tri-Lakes Chamber of Commerce (Palmer Lake)** (✉ *300 Hwy. 105, Monument* ☎ *719/481–3282* ⊕ *www.trilakes.net*).

South Central Colorado Contacts **Buena Vista Chamber of Commerce** (✉ *343 Hwy. 24* ☎ *719/395–6612* ⊕ *www.buenavistacolorado.org*). **Cañon City Chamber of Commerce** (✉ *403 Royal Gorge Blvd.* ☎ *719/275–2331 or 800/876–7922* ⊕ *www.canoncitycolorado.com*). **Heart of the Rockies Chamber of Commerce** (✉ *406 W. Hwy. 50* ☎ *719/539–2068 or 877/772–5432* ⊕ *www.salidachamber.org*). **Huerfano County Chamber of Commerce** (✉ *400 Main St., Walsenburg* ☎ *719/738–1065* ⊕ *www.huerfanocountychamberofcommerce.com*). **La Junta Chamber of Commerce** (✉ *110 Santa Fe Ave.* ☎ *719/384–7411* ⊕ *www.lajuntachamber.com*). **La Veta/Cuchara Chamber of Commerce** (☎ *719/742–3676* ⊕ *www.lavetacucharachamber.com*). **Pueblo Chamber of Commerce and Convention & Visitors Bureau** (✉ *302 N. Santa Fe Ave.* ☎ *719/542–1704 or 800/233–3446* ⊕ *www.pueblochamber.org*). **Trinidad/Las Animas Chamber of Commerce** (✉ *309 Nevada Ave., Trinidad* ☎ *719/846–9285* ⊕ *www.trinidadco.com*).

Colorado Essentials

PLANNING TOOLS, EXPERT INSIGHT, GREAT CONTACTS

There are planners and there are those who, excuse the pun, fly by the seat of their pants. We happily place ourselves among the planners. Our writers and editors try to anticipate all the issues you may face before and during any journey, and then they do their research. This section is the product of their efforts. Use it to get excited about your trip to Colorado, to inform your travel planning, or to guide you on the road should the seat of your pants start to feel threadbare.

www.fodors.com

GETTING STARTED

We're really proud of our Web site: Fodors.com is a great place to begin any journey. Scan Travel Wire for suggested itineraries, travel deals, restaurant and hotel openings, and other up-to-the-minute info. Check out Booking to research prices and book plane tickets, hotel rooms, rental cars, and vacation packages. Head to Talk for on-the-ground pointers from travelers who frequent our message boards. You can also link to loads of other travel-related resources.

▮ RESOURCES

ONLINE TRAVEL TOOLS
All About Colorado

Safety Transportation Security Administration (TSA; ⊕www.tsa.gov).

Time Zones Timeanddate.com (⊕www.timeanddate.com/worldclock) can help you figure out the correct time anywhere.

Weather Accuweather.com (⊕www.accuweather.com) is an independent weather-forecasting service with good coverage of hurricanes. **Weather.com** (⊕www.weather.com) is the Web site for the Weather Channel.

Other Resources CIA World Factbook (⊕www.odci.gov/cia/publications/factbook/index.html) has profiles of every country in the world. It's a good source if you need some quick facts and figures.

VISITOR INFORMATION
Almost every town, county, and resort area has its own tourist office. Contact information is provided in the Essentials section at the end of each regional chapter.

Contact Colorado Tourism Office (✉1625 Broadway, No. 2700, Denver ☎800/265–6723 ⊕www.colorado.com).

▮ THINGS TO CONSIDER

GEAR
For the most part, informality reigns in the Centennial State; jeans, sport shirts, and T-shirts fit in almost everywhere. If you plan to golf, a collared shirt may be required for men. No matter what your vacation plans are, don't forget to pack sunscreen, lip balm with SPF, sunglasses, and a cap or hat. No matter the season, the sunshine is intense at Colorado's altitude, and there are plenty of souvenirs available that you'll prefer over a sunburn.

If you plan to spend much time outdoors, and certainly if you go in winter, choose clothing appropriate for cold and wet weather. Cotton clothing, including denim, can be uncomfortable when it gets wet or when the weather's cold. Better choices are clothing made of wool or any of a number of new synthetics that provide warmth without bulk and maintain their insulating properties when wet. It's not a bad idea to save your shopping for Colorado, where you'll find a huge selection of suitable clothing and gear.

In summer you'll probably want to wear shorts during the day. Because early morning and night can be cold, particularly in the mountains, pack a sweater and a light jacket, and perhaps a wool cap and gloves. For walks and hikes, you'll need sturdy footwear. Boots should have thick soles and plenty of ankle support; if your shoes are new and you plan to do a lot of hiking, break them in at home. Bring a day pack for short hikes, along with a canteen or water bottle, and don't forget rain gear, a hat, sunscreen, and insect repellent.

In winter, prepare for subzero temperatures with good boots, warm socks and liners, long johns, a well-insulated jacket, and a warm hat and mittens. Layers are the best preparation for fluctuating temperatures.

SHIPPING LUGGAGE AHEAD

Imagine globe-trotting with only a carry-on in tow. Shipping your luggage in advance via an air-freight service is a great way to cut down on backaches, hassles, and stress—especially if your packing list includes strollers, car seats, etc. There are some things to be aware of, though.

First, research carry-on restrictions; if you absolutely need something that isn't practical to ship and isn't allowed in carry-ons, this strategy isn't for you. Second, plan to send your bags several days in advance to U.S. destinations. Third, plan to spend some money: It will cost at least $100 to send a small piece of luggage, a golf bag, or a pair of skis.

Some people use Federal Express to ship their bags, but this can cost even more than air-freight services. All these services insure your bag (for most, the limit is $1,000, but you should verify that amount); you can, however, purchase additional insurance for about $1 per $100 of value.

Contacts Luggage Concierge (☎800/288–9818 ⊕www.luggageconcierge.com). **Luggage Express** (☎866/744–7224 ⊕www. usxpluggageexpress.com). **Luggage Free** (☎800/361–6871 ⊕www.luggagefree.com). **Sports Express** (☎800/357–4174 ⊕www. sportsexpress.com) specializes in shipping golf clubs and other sports equipment. **Virtual Bellhop** (☎877/235–5467 ⊕www.virtualbell hop.com).

TRIP INSURANCE

We believe that comprehensive trip insurance is especially valuable if you're booking a very expensive or complicated trip or if you're booking far in advance. But whether you get insurance has more to do with how comfortable you are assuming all that risk yourself.

Comprehensive travel policies typically cover trip cancellation and interruption, letting you cancel or cut your trip short because of a personal emergency, illness, or, in some cases, acts of terrorism in your destination. Such policies also cover evacuation and medical care. Some also cover you for trip delays because of bad weather or mechanical problems as well as for lost or delayed baggage. Another type of coverage to look for is financial default—that is, when your trip is disrupted because a tour operator, airline, or cruise line goes out of business. Generally you must buy this when you book your trip or shortly thereafter, and it's only available to you if your operator isn't on a list of excluded companies.

Expect comprehensive travel insurance policies to cost about 4% to 7% or 8% of the total price of your trip (it's more like 8% to 12% if you're over age 70). A medical-only policy may or may not be cheaper than a comprehensive policy. Always read the fine print of your policy to make sure that you are covered for the risks that are of most concern to you. Compare several policies to make sure you're getting the best price and range of coverage available.

Trip Insurance Resources

INSURANCE COMPARISON SITES		
Insure My Trip.com	800/487–4722	www.insuremytrip.com
Square Mouth.com	800/240–0369	www.quotetravelinsurance.com
COMPREHENSIVE TRAVEL INSURERS		
Access America	866/807–3982	www.accessamerica.com
CSA Travel Protection	800/873–9855	www.csatravelprotection.com
HTH Worldwide	610/254–8700 or 888/243–2358	www.hthworldwide.com
Travelex Insurance	888/457–4602	www.travelex-insurance.com
Travel Guard International	715/345–0505 or 800/826–4919	www.travelguard.com
Travel Insured International	800/243–3174	www.travelinsured.com
MEDICAL-ONLY INSURERS		
International Medical Group	800/628–4664	www.imglobal.com
International SOS	215/942–8000 or 713/521–7611	www.internationalsos.com
Wallach & Company	800/237–6615 or 504/687–3166	www.wallach.com

BOOKING YOUR TRIP

Have you ever wondered just what the differences are between an online travel agent (a Web site through which you make reservations instead of going directly to the airline, hotel, or car-rental company), a discounter (a firm that does a high volume of business with a hotel chain or airline and accordingly gets good prices), a wholesaler (one that makes cheap reservations in bulk and then resells them to people like you), and an aggregator (a firm that compares all the offerings so you don't have to)?

Is it truly better to book directly on an airline or hotel Web site? And when does a real live travel agent come in handy?

▌ONLINE

You really have to shop around. A travel wholesaler such as Hotels.com or Hotel-Club.net can be a source of good rates, as can discounters such as Hotwire or Priceline, particularly if you can bid for your hotel room or airfare. Indeed, such sites sometimes have deals that are unavailable elsewhere. They do, however, tend to work only with hotel chains (which makes them just plain useless for getting hotel reservations outside major cities) or big airlines (so that often leaves out upstarts like jetBlue and some foreign carriers like Air India).

Also, with discounters and wholesalers you must generally prepay, and everything is nonrefundable. And before you fork over the dough, be sure to check the terms and conditions, so you know what a given company will do for you if there's a problem and what you'll have to deal with on your own.

▌**TIP→ To be absolutely sure everything was processed correctly, confirm reservations made through online travel agents, discounters, and wholesalers directly with your hotel before leaving home.**

Booking engines like Expedia, Travelocity, and Orbitz are actually travel agents, albeit high-volume, online ones. And airline travel packagers like American Airlines Vacations and Virgin Vacations—well, they're travel agents, too. But they may still not work with all the world's hotels.

An aggregator site will search many sites and pull the best prices for airfares, hotels, and rental cars from them. Most aggregators compare the major travel-booking sites such as Expedia, Travelocity, and Orbitz; some also look at airline Web sites, though rarely the sites of smaller budget airlines. Some aggregators also compare other travel products, including complex packages—a good thing, as you can sometimes get the best overall deal by booking an air-and-hotel package.

▌WITH A TRAVEL AGENT

If you use an agent—brick-and-mortar or virtual—you'll pay a fee for the service. And know that the service you get from some online agents isn't comprehensive. For example Expedia and Travelocity don't search for prices on budget airlines like jetBlue, Southwest, or small foreign carriers. That said, some agents (online or not) *do* have access to fares that are difficult to find otherwise, and the savings can more than make up for any surcharge.

A knowledgeable brick-and-mortar travel agent can be a godsend if you're booking a cruise, a package trip that's not available to you directly, an air pass, or a complicated itinerary including several overseas flights. What's more, travel agents that specialize in a destination may have exclusive access to certain deals and insider information on things such as charter flights. Agents who specialize in types of travelers (senior citizens, gays and lesbians, naturists) or types of trips

Online Booking Resources

AGGREGATORS

Kayak	www.kayak.com	also looks at cruises and vacation packages.
Mobissimo	www.mobissimo.com	also looks at car-rental rates and activities.
Qixo	www.qixo.com	also compares cruises, vacation packages, and even travel insurance.
Sidestep	www.sidestep.com	also compares vacation packages and lists travel deals.
Travelgrove	www.travelgrove.com	also compares cruises and packages.

BOOKING ENGINES

Cheap Tickets	www.cheaptickets.com	a discounter.
Expedia	www.expedia.com	a large online agency that charges a booking fee for airline tickets.
Hotwire	www.hotwire.com	a discounter.
lastminute.com	www.lastminute.com	specializes in last-minute travel; the main site is for the U.K., but it has a link to a U.S. site.
Luxury Link	www.luxurylink.com	has auctions (surprisingly good deals) as well as offers on the high-end side of travel.
Onetravel.com	www.onetravel.com	a discounter for hotels, car rentals, airfares, and packages.
Orbitz	www.orbitz.com	charges a booking fee for airline tickets, but gives a clear breakdown of fees and taxes before you book.
Priceline.com	www.priceline.com	a discounter that also allows bidding.
Travel.com	www.travel.com	allows you to compare its rates with those of other booking engines.
Travelocity	www.travelocity.com	charges a booking fee for airline tickets, but promises good problem resolution.

ONLINE ACCOMMODATIONS

Hotelbook.com	www.hotelbook.com	focuses on independent hotels worldwide.
Hotel Club	www.hotelclub.net	good for major cities worldwide.
Hotels.com	www.hotels.com	a big Expedia-owned wholesaler that offers rooms in hotels all over the world.
Quikbook	www.quikbook.com	offers "pay when you stay" reservations that let you settle your bill at checkout, not when you book.

OTHER RESOURCES

Bidding For Travel	www.biddingfortravel.com	a good place to figure out what you can get and for how much before you start bidding on, say, Priceline.

(cruises, luxury travel, safaris) can also be invaluable.

■**TIP**➔ Remember that Expedia, Travelocity, and Orbitz are travel agents, not just booking engines. To resolve any problems with a reservation made through these companies, contact them first.

Although it is by no means essential to book a vacation to Colorado through a travel agent, you may wish to consult one if you do not want to spend time on the phone or Internet researching flights and places to stay. For a fee, a travel agent can do that for you.

Agent Resources American Society of Travel Agents (☎703/739–2782 ⊕www.travelsense.org).

■ ACCOMMODATIONS

Accommodations in Colorado vary from the very posh ski resorts in Vail, Aspen, and Telluride to basic chain hotels and independent motels. Dude and guest ranches often require a one-week stay, and the cost is all-inclusive. Bed-and-breakfasts can be found throughout the state. Hotel rates peak during the height of the ski season, which generally runs from late November through March or April; although rates are high all season, they top out during Christmas week and in February and March. In summer months, a popular time for hiking and rafting, hotel rates are often half the winter price.

Properties are assigned price categories based on the cost of a standard double room during high season. Lodging taxes vary throughout the state. *For price category information, see the charts in the Where to Stay sections of each chapter.*

Most hotels and other lodgings require you to give your credit-card details before they will confirm your reservation. If you don't feel comfortable e-mailing this information, ask if you can fax it. However you book, get confirmation in writing and have a copy of it handy when you check in.

Be sure you understand the hotel's cancellation policy. Some places allow you to cancel without any kind of penalty—even if you prepaid to secure a discounted rate—if you cancel at least 24 hours in advance. Others require you to cancel a week in advance or penalize you the cost of one night. Small inns and B&Bs are most likely to require you to cancel far in advance. Most hotels allow children under a certain age to stay in their parents' room at no extra charge, but others charge for them as extra adults; find out the cutoff age for discounts.

General Information Colorado Hotel and Lodging Association (☎303/297–8335 ⊕www.coloradolodging.com).

BED & BREAKFASTS
Charm is the long suit of these establishments, which often occupy a restored older building with some historical or architectural significance. They're generally small, with fewer than 20 rooms. Breakfast is usually included in the rates. The owners often also manage the B&B, and you'll likely meet them and get to know them a bit. Breakfasts are usually substantial with hot beverages, cold fruit juices, and a hot entrée. Bed and Breakfast Innkeepers of Colorado prints a free annual directory of its members.

Reservation Services Bed & Breakfast.com (☎512/322–2710 or 800/462–2632 ⊕www.bedandbreakfast.com) also sends out an online newsletter.**Bed and Breakfast Innkeepers of Colorado** (☎800/265–7696 ⊕www.innsofcolorado.org). **Bed & Breakfast Inns Online** (☎615/868–1946 or 800/215–7365 ⊕www.bbonline.com). **BnB Finder.com** (☎212/432–7693 or 888/547–8226 ⊕www.bnbfinder.com).

CABIN, CONDO & HOUSE RENTALS
Rental accommodations are quite popular in Colorado's ski resorts and mountain towns. Condominiums and luxurious vacation homes dominate the Vail Valley and other ski-oriented areas, but there

Online Booking Resources

CONTACTS		
Interhomes	954/791–8282 or 800/882–6864	www.interhome.us
Vacation Home Rentals Worldwide	201/767–9393 or 800/633–3284	www.vhrww.com
Villas International	415/499–9490 or 800/221–2260	www.villasintl.com

are scads of cabins in smaller, summer-oriented towns in the Rockies and the Western Slope. Many towns and resort areas have rental agencies. *For contact information, see the Where to Stay sections in regional chapters.*

Local Agents Colorado Mountain Cabins & Vacation Home Rentals (☎719/636–5147 or 866/425–4974 ⊕www.coloradomountain-cabins.com).

GUEST RANCHES

If the thought of sitting around a campfire after a hard day on the range is your idea of a vacation, consider playing dude on a guest ranch. Wilderness-rimmed working ranches accept guests and encourage them to pitch in with chores and other ranch activities; you might even be able to participate in a cattle roundup. Most dude ranches don't require previous experience with horses, although a few working ranches reserve weeks in spring and fall—when the chore of moving cattle is more intensive than in summer—for experienced riders. Luxurious resorts on the fringes of small cities offer swimming pools, tennis courts, and a lively roster of horse-related activities such as breakfast rides, moonlight rides, and all-day trail rides. Rafting, fishing, tubing, and other activities are usually available at both types of ranches. In winter, cross-country skiing and snowshoeing keep you busy. Lodgings can run the gamut from charmingly rustic cabins to the kind of deluxe quarters you expect at a first-class hotel. Meals may be gourmet or plain but hearty. Many ranches offer packages and children's and off-season rates; ask when you book. No special equipment is necessary, although if you plan to do much fishing, you're best off bringing your own tackle (some ranches have tackle to loan or rent). Be sure to check with the ranch for a list of items you might be expected to bring. If you plan to do much riding, a couple of pairs of sturdy pants, boots, a wide-brim hat to shield you from the sun, and outerwear that protects from rain and cold should be packed. Nearly all dude ranches in Colorado offer all-inclusive packages: meals, lodging, and generally all activities. Weeklong stays cost between $1,300 and $3,600 per adult, depending on the ranch's amenities and activities.

Information Colorado Dude/Guest Ranch Association (☎970/641–4701 ⊕www.colo-radoranch.com).

HOME EXCHANGES

With a direct home exchange you stay in someone else's home while they stay in yours. Some outfits also deal with vacation homes, so you're not actually staying in someone's full-time residence, just their vacant weekend place.

Exchange Clubs Home Exchange.com (☎800/877–8723 ⊕www.homeexchange. com); $59.95 for a one-year online listing. **HomeLink International** (☎800/638–3841 ⊕www.homelink.org); $90 yearly for Web-only membership; $140 includes Web access and two catalogs. **Intervac U.S.** (☎800/756–4663 ⊕www.intervacus.com); $78.88 for Web-only membership; $126 includes Web access and a catalog.

HOTELS

Most hotels in Denver and Colorado Springs cater to business travelers, with facilities like restaurants, cocktail lounges, swimming pools, fitness centers, and meeting rooms. Many properties offer special weekend rates of up to 50% off regular prices. However, these deals are usually not extended during summer months, when city hotels are often full. In resort towns, hotels are decidedly more deluxe; rural areas generally offer simple, sometimes rustic accommodations.

RESORTS

Ski towns throughout Colorado are home to dozens of resorts in all price ranges; the activities lacking at any individual property can usually be found in the town itself in summer as well as winter. Off the slopes, there are both wonderful rustic and luxurious resorts, particularly in out-of-the-way spots near Rocky Mountain National Park and other alpine areas.

■ AIRLINE TICKETS

Most domestic airline tickets are electronic; international tickets may be either electronic or paper. With an e-ticket the only thing you receive is an e-mailed receipt citing your itinerary and reservation and ticket numbers.

The greatest advantage of an e-ticket is that if you lose your receipt, you can simply print out another copy or ask the airline to do it for you at check-in. You usually pay a surcharge (up to $50) to get a paper ticket, if you can get one at all.

The least-expensive airfares to Colorado are usually round-trip tickets and must generally be purchased in advance. Airlines typically allow you to change your return date for a fee; most low-fare tickets, however, are nonrefundable.

WORD OF MOUTH

Did the resort look as good in real life as it did in the photos? Did you sleep like a baby, or were the walls paper thin? Did you get your money's worth? Rate hotels and write your own reviews in Travel Ratings or start a discussion about your favorite places in Travel Talk on www.fodors.com. Your comments might even appear in our books. Yes, you, too, can be a correspondent!

■ RENTAL CARS

When you reserve a car, ask about cancellation penalties, taxes, drop-off charges (if you're planning to pick up the car in one city and leave it in another), and surcharges (for being under or over a certain age, for additional drivers, or for driving across state or country borders or beyond a specific distance from your point of rental). All these things can add substantially to your costs. Request car seats and extras such as GPS when you book.

Rates are sometimes—but not always—better if you book in advance or reserve through a rental agency's Web site. There are other reasons to book ahead, though: for popular destinations, during busy times of the year, or to ensure that you get certain types of cars (vans, SUVs, exotic sports cars).

■ TIP→ Make sure that a confirmed reservation guarantees you a car. Agencies sometimes overbook, particularly for busy weekends and holiday periods.

Rates in most major cities run about $58 a day and $230 a week for an economy car with air-conditioning, an automatic transmission, and unlimited mileage. This does not include tax on car rentals, which is 13.35% in the Denver metro area. Keep in mind if you're venturing into the Rockies that you'll need a little oomph in your engine to get over the passes. If you plan to explore any back roads, an SUV is the best bet because it will have higher

Car-Rental Resources

AUTOMOBILE ASSOCIATIONS		
American Automobile Association	315/797–5000	www.aaa.com; most contact with the organization is through state and regional members
National Automobile Club	650/294–7000	www.thenac.com; membership open to CA residents only
MAJOR AGENCIES		
Alamo	800/462–5266	www.alamo.com
Avis	800/331–1084	www.avis.com
Budget	800/472–3325	www.budget.com
Hertz	800/654–3131	www.hertz.com
National Car Rental	800/227–7368	www.nationalcar.com

clearance. Unless you plan to do much mountain exploring, a four-wheel drive is usually needed only in winter.

To rent a car in Colorado, you must be at least 25 years old and have a valid driver's license; most companies also require a major credit card. Some companies at certain locations set their minimum age at 21, and then add a daily surcharge. In Colorado, child-safety seats or booster seats are compulsory for children under five (with certain height and weight criteria).

You'll pay extra for child seats ($5–$12 a day), drivers under age 25 (at least $25 a day), and usually for additional drivers (about $10 per day). When returning your car to Denver International Airport, allow 15 minutes (30 minutes during busy weekends and around the holidays) to return the vehicle and to ride the shuttle bus to the terminal.

CAR-RENTAL INSURANCE

Everyone who rents a car wonders whether the insurance that the rental companies offer is worth the expense. No one—including us—has a simple answer. It all depends on how much regular insurance you have, how comfortable you are with risk, and whether money is an issue.

If you own a car and carry comprehensive car insurance for both collision and liability, your personal auto insurance will probably cover a rental, but read your policy's fine print to be sure. If you don't have auto insurance, then you should probably buy the collision- or loss-damage waiver (CDW or LDW) from the rental company. This eliminates your liability for damage to the car.

Some credit cards offer CDW coverage, but it's usually supplemental to your own insurance and rarely covers SUVs, minivans, luxury models, and the like. If your coverage is secondary, you may still be liable for loss-of-use costs from the car-rental company (again, read the fine print). But no credit-card insurance is valid unless you use that card for *all* transactions, from reserving to paying the final bill.

■TIP➜ Diners Club offers primary CDW coverage on all rentals reserved and paid for with the card. This means that Diners Club's company—not your own car insurance—pays in case of an accident. It *doesn't* mean that your car-insurance company won't raise your rates once it discovers you had an accident.

You may also be offered supplemental liability coverage; the car-rental company is required to carry a minimal level of liability coverage insuring all renters, but it's rarely enough to cover claims in a really serious accident if you're at fault. Your own auto-insurance policy will protect you if you own a car; if you don't, you have to decide whether you are willing to take the risk.

U.S. rental companies sell CDWs and LDWs for about $15 to $25 a day; supplemental liability is usually more than $10 a day. The car-rental company may offer you all sorts of other policies, but they're rarely worth the cost. Personal accident insurance, which is basic hospitalization coverage, is an especially egregious rip-off if you already have health insurance.

■TIP→ You can decline the insurance from the rental company and purchase it through a third-party provider such as Travel Guard (www.travelguard.com)—$9 per day for $35,000 of coverage. That's sometimes just under half the price of the CDW offered by some car-rental companies.

■ VACATION PACKAGES

Packages *are not* guided excursions. Packages combine airfare, accommodations, and perhaps a rental car or other extras (theater tickets, guided excursions, boat trips, reserved entry to popular museums, transit passes), but they let you do your own thing. During busy periods packages may be your only option, as flights and rooms may be sold out otherwise.

Packages will definitely save you time. They can also save you money, particularly in peak seasons, but—and this is a really big "but"—you should price each part of the package separately to be sure. And be aware that prices advertised on Web sites and in newspapers rarely include service charges or taxes, which can up your costs by hundreds of dollars.

■TIP→ Some packages and cruises are sold only through travel agents. Don't always assume that you can get the best deal by booking everything yourself.

Each year consumers are stranded or lose their money when packagers—even large ones with excellent reputations—go out of business. How can you protect yourself?

First, always pay with a credit card; if you have a problem, your credit-card company may help you resolve it. Second, buy trip insurance that covers default. Third, choose a company that belongs to the United States Tour Operators Association, whose members must set aside funds to cover defaults. Finally, choose a company that also participates in the Tour Operator Program of the American Society of Travel Agents (ASTA), which will act as mediator in any disputes.

You can also check on the tour operator's reputation among travelers by posting an inquiry on one of the Fodors.com forums.

Organizations American Society of Travel Agents (ASTA ☎703/739–2782 or 800/965–2782 ⊕www.astanet.com). **United States Tour Operators Association** (USTOA ☎212/599–6599 ⊕www.ustoa.com).

■TIP→ Local tourism boards can provide information about lesser-known and small-niche operators that sell packages to only a few destinations.

■ GUIDED TOURS

Guided tours are a good option when you don't want to do it all yourself. You travel along with a group, stay in prebooked hotels, eat with your fellow travelers (the cost of meals sometimes included in the price of your tour, sometimes not), and follow a schedule.

But not all guided tours are an if-it's-Tuesday-this-must-be-Belgium experience. A knowledgeable guide can take you places that you might never discover on your own. Tours aren't for everyone, but they can be just the thing for trips to places where making travel arrangements is difficult or time-consuming.

Whenever you book a guided tour, find out what's included and what isn't. A "land-only" tour includes all your travel (by bus, in most cases) in the destination, but not necessarily your flights to and from or even within it. Also, in most cases prices in tour brochures don't include fees and taxes. And remember that you'll be expected to tip your guide (in cash) at the end of the tour.

SPECIAL-INTEREST TOURS
Many trip organizers specialize in one type of activity. However, a few companies guide a variety of active trips. (In some cases, these larger companies also act as a clearinghouse or agent for smaller outfitters.) Be sure to sign on with a reliable outfitter; getting stuck with a shoddy operator can be disappointing, uncomfortable, and even dangerous. Some sports—white-water rafting and mountaineering, for example—have organizations that license or certify guides, and you should be sure that the guide you're with is properly accredited.

Outfitter Listings Colorado Outfitters Association (☎970/824–2468 ⊕www.coloradooutfitters.org).

BIKING
■TIP➔ Most airlines accommodate bikes as luggage, provided they're dismantled and boxed.

Contacts Adventure Cycling Association (☎406/721–1776 or 800/755–2453 ⊕www.adventurecycling.org) puts together all-inclusive cycling/camping tours of the canyons of western Colorado and eastern Utah. **Timberline Adventures** (☎303/759–3804 or 800/417–2453 ⊕www.timbertours.com) offers multiday, all-inclusive cycling trips in the mountains of Colorado.

HIKING
Contacts Off the Beaten Path (✉7 E. Beall St., Bozeman, MT59715 ☎406/586–1311 or 800/445–2995 🖷406/587–4147 ⊕www.offthebeatenpath.com) offers multiday camping/hiking excursions as well as customized

hiking trips in Colorado. **World Outdoors** (☎303/413–0938 or 800/488–8483 ⊕www.theworldoutdoors.com) organizes multiday backpacking/camping trips.

SKIING
Many ski resorts in Colorado offer lodging/lift ticket packages. Contact the resort for minimum-stay requirements, what packages include, and costs.

WHITE-WATER RAFTING
Unless you're an expert, pick a recognized outfitter if you're going into white water. Even then, you should be a good swimmer and in solid general health. Different companies are licensed to run different rivers, although there may be several companies working the same river. Some organizers combine river rafting with other activities, such as camping, pack trips, mountain-bike excursions, extended hikes, and fishing.

"Raft" can mean any of a number of things: an inflated raft in which passengers do the paddling; an inflated raft or wooden dory in which a licensed professional does the work; a motorized raft on which some oar work might be required. Be sure you know what kind of raft you'll be riding—or paddling—before booking a trip. Rafting adventures can be anything from a half-day float trip with a gourmet riverside lunch to overnight trips with wilderness camping where you help load and unload the gear.

Contacts OARS (☎800/346–6277 ⊕www.oars.com) offers multiday rafting/camping trips in Colorado. **Wilderness Aware Rafting** (☎719/395–2112 or 800/462–7238 ⊕www.inaraft.com) organizes all-inclusive river rafting/camping trips on five different rivers in Colorado.

TRANSPORTATION

Denver is Colorado's hub; all interstate highways intersect here, and most of the state's population lives within a one- or two-hour drive of the city. The high plains expand to the east from Denver, and the western edge of the metro area ends at the foothills of the Rocky Mountains. A corridor of cities along Interstate 25 parallels the foothills from Fort Collins to Pueblo, and most lonely stretches of highway are in the eastern portion of the state on the plains. Although scheduled air, rail, and bus service connects Denver to many smaller cities and towns, it is difficult to travel without a car.

▌ BY AIR

It takes about two hours to fly to Denver from Los Angeles, Chicago, or Dallas. From New York and Boston, the flight is about 3½ hours. If you're traveling during snow season, allow extra time for the drive to the airport. If you'll be checking skis, arrive even earlier.

Airline Security Issues Transportation Security Administration (⊕ www.tsa.gov) has answers for almost every question that might come up.

AIRPORTS

The major air gateway to the Colorado Rockies is Denver International Airport (DEN), 15 mi northeast of downtown Denver and 45 mi from Boulder. Flights to smaller, resort-town airports generally connect through it. During inclement weather, flights can be delayed or canceled. Although there are a few eateries in the airport, there are not any hotels on site. Most hotels are several miles away toward Denver.

Some of the major airlines and their subsidiaries serve communities around the state: Grand Junction (GJT), Durango (DRO), Steamboat Springs (HDN), Gunnison–Crested Butte (GUC), Telluride (TEX), Aspen (ASE), Vail (EGE). Some major airlines have scheduled service from points within the United States to Colorado Springs Airport (COS); the relatively mild weather in Colorado Springs means that its airport is sometimes still functional when bad weather farther north and west affect the state's other airports. During ski season, some of the major resort towns have increased service, and direct flights may be available.

You might want to consider the time saved—or not saved—by flying to your resort destination versus renting a car at Denver International Airport and driving the same distance. A car trip from Denver to Vail can take 90 minutes to two hours in smoothly flowing traffic. Aspen is about four hours by car from Denver. Steamboat Springs' airport is actually 22 mi away in Hayden, and Vail's airport is 34 mi away in Eagle, requiring some travel by car or shuttle. In winter, flights in and out of mountain towns are frequently diverted, delayed, or canceled in bad weather. Weigh the possible time savings gained by flying against the time spent driving and enjoying the scenery along the way to your destination.

Airport Information Colorado Springs Airport (COS) (☎719/550–1900 ⊕www.flycos. com).**Denver International Airport (DEN)** (☎303/342–2000, 800/247–2336, 303/342–2333 TTY, 800/688–1333 TTY ⊕www.flydenver. com).

GROUND TRANSPORTATION

If you are driving, the best way from Denver International Airport to Denver, the ski resorts, or the mountains is along Peña Boulevard to Interstate 70 and then south. If you are traveling south from Denver, take Interstate 25. You can bypass some traffic by using the E–470 tollway which intersects Peña a couple of miles west of the airport. It connects to Interstate 25 both south and north of Denver.

RTD has frequent bus service to Denver and Boulder; visit their booth in the main terminal for destinations, times, and tickets. There are taxis and various private airport shuttles to cities along the Front Range from the airport, and some offer door-to-door service. Many hotels and ski resorts have their own buses; check with your lodging or ski resort to see if they offer service. The Ground Transportation Information Center is on the fifth level of the main terminal and can direct travelers to companies' service counters. All services depart from and arrive on level five of the main terminal building.

FLIGHTS

Large airlines serve Denver International Airport (DEN) from many cities in the United States. A few international carriers serve Denver with nonstop flights from London, England; Frankfurt and Munich, Germany; as well as Vancouver, Calgary, Toronto, Winnipeg, and Montreal, Canada. Frontier Airlines and United Airlines are Denver's largest carriers with the most flights and the longest list of destinations. United Express and Great Lakes Airlines connect Denver with smaller cities and ski resorts within Colorado.

Airline Contacts **Air Canada** (☎888/247–2262 ⊕www.aircanada.com)flies nonstop to Denver from Vancouver, Winnipeg, Toronto, Montreal, and Calgary. **Alaska Airlines** (☎206/433–3100 or 800/252–7522 ⊕www.alaskaair.com). **American Airlines** (☎800/433–7300 ⊕www.aa.com). **British Airways** (☎800/247–9297 ⊕www.british airways.com) flies nonstop daily to Denver from London's Heathrow Airport. **Continental Airlines** (☎800/523–3273 for U.S. and Mexico reservations, 800/231–0856 for international reservations ⊕www.continental.com). **Delta Airlines** (☎800/221–1212 for U.S. reservations, 800/241–4141 for international reservations ⊕www.delta.com). **Frontier** (☎800/432–1359 ⊕www.frontierairlines. com) has its hub in Denver. **Great Lakes Airlines** (☎800/554–5111 ⊕www.greatlakesav.

com) connects Denver to several cities in the Midwest and to points within Colorado: Grand Junction, Pueblo, Telluride, Cortez, and Alamosa. **jetBlue** (☎800/538–2583 ⊕www. jetblue.com).**Lufthansa** (☎888/688–2345 ⊕www.lufthansa.com) has daily nonstop flights from both Frankfurt and Munich to Denver. **Mexicana** (☎800/531–7921 ⊕www. mexicana.com) serves Denver with flights connecting through Dallas. **Northwest Airlines** (☎800/225–2525 ⊕www.nwa.com). **Southwest Airlines** (☎800/435–9792 ⊕www. southwest.com). **United Airlines** (☎800/864–8331 for U.S. reservations, 800/538–2929 for international reservations ⊕www.united.com) **United Express** (☎800/864–8331 ⊕www. united.com) has flights to Steamboat Springs, Vail, Aspen, Grand Junction, Montrose, Telluride, Durango, Cortez, Pueblo, Colorado Springs, and Gunnison–Crested Butte. **USAirways** (☎800/428–4322 for U.S. and Canada reservations, 800/622–1015 for international reservations ⊕www.usairways.com).

❙ BY BICYCLE

Pedaling through Colorado is popular, especially in the Rocky Mountains. Many bicyclers travel from town to town (or between backcountry huts or campsites) in summer. Most streets in the larger cities have bike lanes and/or separated bike paths, and Denver, Boulder, Fort Collins, Durango, and Colorado Springs are especially bike friendly. Cities and tourism organizations often offer free bike maps.

High, rugged country puts a premium on fitness. Even if you can ride 40 mi at home without breaking a sweat, you might find yourself struggling terribly on steep climbs and in elevations exceeding 10,000 feet. If you have an extended tour in mind, acclimate yourself to the altitude and terrain by arriving a couple of days early. Pre-trip conditioning is likely to make your trip more enjoyable.

Bike Maps Many municipalities and cities in Colorado publish bicycle maps that show bike paths and streets with specially marked bike lanes. Some even include streets that are easy for cyclists to use because of low car traffic. Check with the particular city's visitor center to see if a map is available.

National Geographic/Trails Illustrated
(☎800/962–1643 ⊕maps.nationalgeographic. com).

BIKES IN FLIGHT

Most airlines accommodate bikes as luggage, provided they are dismantled and boxed; check with individual airlines about packing requirements. Some airlines sell bike boxes, which are often free at bike shops, for about $20 (bike bags can be considerably more expensive). International travelers often can substitute a bike for a piece of checked luggage at no charge; otherwise, the cost is about $100. Most U.S. and Canadian airlines charge $40 to $80 each way.

▌ BY BUS

Traveling by bus within the Denver–Boulder region is fairly easy with RTD since their coverage of the area is dense and most routes are not too circuitous. The free 16th Street MallRide and the lightrail routes within Denver make travel to and from downtown attractions easy.

Greyhound Lines has regular intercity routes throughout the region, with connections from Denver to Grand Junction. Smaller bus companies provide intrastate and local service.

Bus Information Colorado Mountain Express (☎800/525–6363). **Greyhound Lines** (☎800/231–2222 ⊕www.greyhound. com) serves cities and towns throughout Colorado, mostly along interstate highways. **RTD** (☎303/299–6000 or 800/366–7433 ⊕www. rtd-denver.com) serves the Denver metro area, Boulder, Nederland, Longmont, Golden, and Denver International Airport. Check their Web site or their kiosk at Denver International Airport for routes and fare information. **Mountain Metropolitan Transit** (☎719/385–7433)serves the Colorado Springs area.

▌ BY CAR

Colorado has the most mountainous terrain of the American Rockies and the scenery makes driving far from a tedious means to an end.

Before setting out on any driving trip, it's important to make sure your vehicle is in top condition. It's best to have a complete tune-up. At the least, you should check the following: lights, including brake lights, backup lights, and emergency lights; tires, including the spare; oil; engine coolant; windshield washer fluid; windshield-wiper blades; and brakes. For emergencies, take along flares or reflector triangles, jumper cables, an empty gas can, a fire extinguisher, a flashlight, a plastic tarp, blankets, water, and coins or a calling card for phone calls (cell phones don't always work in high mountain areas).

Car travel within the urban corridor north and south of Denver can be congested, particularly weekday mornings and afternoons. Congestion is not limited to the major highways; city arterials and smaller roads and streets can be slow during peak driving times. Weekends, too, can have quite a bit of traffic, particularly along I–70 between Denver and the high mountains. Heavy traffic is not limited to ski season or bad weather. It is nearly a matter of course now for eastbound I–70 to be heavily congested on Sunday afternoons. If you are returning to Denver International Airport for a Sunday-afternoon or evening flight, plan accordingly and allow plenty of time to reach the airport.

GASOLINE

At this writing, gasoline costs between $2.61 and $3.29 a gallon. In major cities throughout Colorado, gas prices are roughly similar to the rest of the continental United States; in rural and resort towns, prices are considerably higher. Although gas stations are plentiful in many areas, you can drive more than 100 mi on back roads without finding gas.

ROAD CONDITIONS

Colorado offers some of the most spectacular vistas and challenging driving in the world. Roads range from multilane blacktop to barely graveled backcountry trails; from twisting switchbacks considerately marked with guardrails to primitive campgrounds with a lane so narrow that you must back up to the edge of a steep cliff to make a turn. Scenic routes and lookout points are clearly marked, enabling you to slow down and pull over to take in the views.

One of the more-unpleasant sights along the highway is roadkill—animals struck by vehicles. Deer, elk, and even bears may try to get to the other side of a road just as you come along, so watch out for wildlife on the highways. Exercise caution both for the sake of the animal in danger and your car, which could be totaled in a collision.

FROM	TO	DISTANCE
Denver	Boulder	40–60 mins
Denver	Fort Collins	60 mins
Denver	Colorado Springs	60–75 mins
Denver	Estes Park	1½–2 hrs
Denver	Glenwood Springs	2½–3 hrs
Glenwood Springs	Aspen	1 hr
Glenwood Springs	Crested Butte	3 hrs
Denver	Grand Junction	4 hrs
Grand Junction	Telluride	2–3 hrs
Denver	Durango	6–7 hrs

Road Condition Information Colorado (☎303/639–1111 statewide ⊕www.cotrip.org).

ROADSIDE EMERGENCIES

Emergency Services AAA of Colorado (☎303/753–8800) Colorado State Patrol (☎303/239–4501 or * 277 from a cell phone) For police or ambulance, dial 911.

WINTER DRIVING

Modern highways make mountain driving safe and generally trouble free even in cold weather. Although winter driving can occasionally present real challenges, road maintenance is good and plowing is prompt. However, in mountain areas, tire chains, studs, or snow tires are essential. If you're planning to drive into high elevations, be sure to check the weather forecast and call for road conditions beforehand. Even main highways can close. It's a good idea to carry an emergency kit and a cell phone, but be aware that the mountains can disrupt service. If you do get stalled by deep snow, do not leave your car. Wait for help, running the engine only if needed, and remember that assistance is never far away. Winter weather isn't confined to winter months in the high country (it's been known to snow in July), so be prepared year-round.

▌ BY TRAIN

Amtrak connects nine stations in Colorado to both coasts and all major American cities. The *California Zephyr* and the *Southwest Chief* pass once per day with east- and west-bound trains that stop in Denver, Winter Park, Granby, Glenwood Springs, Grand Junction, and Trinidad. The Ski Train connects Denver's Union Station and the Winter Park ski resort during ski season and summer.

Information Amtrak (☎800/872-7245 ⊕www.amtrak.com). **Ski Train** (☎303/296-4754 ⊕www.skitrain.com).

ON THE GROUND

▮ COMMUNICATIONS

INTERNET

Internet access is available throughout Colorado. Most lodgings have wireless access for laptops, and many have computers available for guests. Many cafés, coffee shops, and restaurants have Wi-Fi though some charge a fee for access. Many municipal public libraries will allow patrons to use the Internet, either free or for a small fee

Contacts Cybercafes (⊕ www.cybercafes. com) lists more than 4,000 Internet cafés worldwide.

▮ EATING OUT

Dining in Colorado is generally casual. Dinner hours are typically from 6 PM to 10 PM, but many small-town and rural eateries close by 9 PM. Authentic ethnic food is hard to find outside the big cities and resort towns like Aspen.

MEALS & MEALTIMES

Although you can find all types of cuisine in Colorado's major cities and resort towns, don't forget to try native dishes like trout, elk, and buffalo (the latter two have less fat than beef and are just as tasty). Steak is a mainstay in the Rocky Mountains. Chile verde, also known as green chile, is a popular menu item at Mexican restaurants in Colorado. Many restaurants serve vegetarian items, and some are exclusively vegetarian. Organic fruits and vegetables are also readily available.

PAYING

For guidelines on tipping see Tipping in this chapter.

For information about our price categories, see the What It Costs charts in each chapter.

RESERVATIONS & DRESS

Regardless of where you are, it's a good idea to make a reservation if you can. We only mention them specifically when reservations are essential (there's no other way you'll ever get a table) or when they are not accepted. For popular restaurants, book as far ahead as you can, and reconfirm as soon as you arrive. We mention dress only when men are required to wear a jacket or a jacket and tie—which is almost never in the Rockies.

SMOKING

Smoking is prohibited in Colorado's public places, including restaurants and bars, as of 2006.

WINES, BEER & SPIRITS

The legal drinking age in Colorado is 21. Colorado liquor laws do not allow anyone to bring their own alcohol to restaurants. You'll find renowned breweries throughout Colorado, including, of course, the nation's third-largest brewer: Coors. There are dozens of microbreweries in Denver, Colorado Springs, Boulder, and the resort towns—if you're a beer drinker, be sure to try some local brews. Although the region is not known for its wines, the wineries in the Grand Junction area and along the Front Range have been highly touted recently.

▮ HEALTH

You may feel dizzy and weak and find yourself breathing heavily—signs that the thin mountain air isn't giving you your accustomed dose of oxygen. Take it easy and rest often for a few days until you're acclimatized. Throughout your stay, drink plenty of water and watch your alcohol consumption. If you experience severe headaches and nausea, see a doctor. It's easy—especially in a state where highways climb to 11,000 feet and higher—to go too high too fast. The rem-

FOR INTERNATIONAL TRAVELERS

CURRENCY

The dollar is the basic unit of U.S. currency. It has 100 cents. Coins are the penny (1¢), nickel (5¢), dime (10¢), quarter (25¢), half-dollar (50¢), and the very rare golden $1 coin and even rarer silver $1. Bills are denominated $1, $5, $10, $20, $50, and $100, all mostly green and identical in size; designs and background tints vary. You may come across a $2 bill, but the chances are slim.

CUSTOMS

Information U.S. Customs and Border Protection (⊕ www.cbp.gov).

DRIVING

Driving in the United States is on the right. Speed limits are posted in miles per hour (usually between 55 mph and 70 mph). Watch for lower limits in small towns and on back roads (usually 30 mph to 40 mph). Most states require front-seat passengers to wear seat belts; many states require children to sit in the backseat and to wear seat belts. In major cities rush hour is between 7 and 10 AM; afternoon rush hour is between 4 and 7 PM. To encourage carpooling, some free-ways have special lanes, ordinarily marked with a diamond, for high-occupancy vehicles (HOV)—cars carrying two people or more.

Highways are well paved. Interstates—limited-access, multilane highways designated with an "I–" before the number—are fastest. Interstates with three-digit numbers circle urban areas, which may also have other limited-access expressways, freeways, and parkways. Tolls may be levied on limited-access highways. U.S. and state highways aren't necessarily limited-access, but may have several lanes.

Gas stations are plentiful. Most stay open late (24 hours along major highways and in big cities) except in rural areas, where Sunday hours are limited and where you may drive for long stretches without a refueling opportunity. Along larger highways, roadside stops with restrooms, fast-food restaurants, and sundries stores are well spaced. State police and tow trucks patrol major highways. If your car breaks down on an interstate, pull onto the shoulder and wait for help, or have your passengers wait while you walk to an emergency phone (available in most states). If you carry a cell phone, dial *55, noting your location on the small green roadside mileage marker.

ELECTRICITY

The U.S. standard is AC, 110 volts/60 cycles. Plugs have two flat pins set parallel to each other.

EMBASSIES

Contacts Australia (☎ 202/797–3000 ⊕ www.austemb.org). **Canada** (☎ 202/682–1740 ⊕ www.canadianembassy.org). **United Kingdom** (☎ 202/588–7800 ⊕ www.britainusa.com).

EMERGENCIES

For police, fire, or ambulance, dial 911.

HOLIDAYS

New Year's Day (Jan. 1); Martin Luther King Day (3rd Mon. in Jan.); Presidents' Day (3rd Mon. in Feb.); Memorial Day (last Mon. in May); Independence Day (July 4); Labor Day (1st Mon. in Sept.); Columbus Day (2nd Mon. in Oct.); Thanksgiving Day (4th Thurs. in Nov.); Christmas Eve and Christmas Day (Dec. 24 and 25); and New Year's Eve (Dec. 31).

MAIL

You can buy stamps and aerograms and send letters and parcels in post offices. Stamp-dispensing machines can occasionally be found in airports, bus and train stations, office buildings, drugstores, and convenience stores. U.S. mailboxes are stout, dark-blue steel bins; pickup schedules are posted inside the bin (pull down the handle to see them). Parcels weighing more than a pound must be mailed at a post office or at a private mailing center.

Within the United States a first-class letter weighing 1 ounce or less costs 41¢; each additional ounce costs 24¢. Postcards cost 24¢. A 1-ounce airmail letter to most countries costs 84¢, an airmail postcard costs 75¢; a 1-ounce letter to Canada or Mexico costs 63¢, a postcard 55¢.

To receive mail on the road, have it sent c/o General Delivery at your destination's main post office (use the correct five-digit ZIP code). You must pick up mail in person within 30 days, with a driver's license or passport for identification.

Contacts **DHL** (☎800/225–5345 ⊕www. dhl.com). **Federal Express** (☎800/463–3339 ⊕www.fedex.com). **Mail Boxes, Etc./ The UPS Store** (☎800/789–4623 ⊕www. mbe.com). **United States Postal Service** (⊕www.usps.com).

PASSPORTS & VISAS

Visitor visas aren't necessary for citizens of Australia, Canada, the United Kingdom, or most citizens of European Union countries coming for tourism and staying for fewer than 90 days. If you require a visa, the cost is $100, and waiting time can be substantial, depending on where you live. Apply for a visa at the U.S. consulate in your place of residence; check the U.S. State Department's special Visa Web site for further information.

Visa Information Destination USA (⊕www.unitedstatesvisas.gov).

PHONES

Numbers consist of a three-digit area code and a seven-digit local number. Within many local calling areas you dial only the seven digits; in others you dial "1" first and all 10 digits—just as you would for calls between area-code regions. The same is true for calls to numbers prefixed by 800, 888, 866, and 877—all toll free. For calls to numbers prefixed by "900" you must pay—usually dearly.

For international calls, dial 011 followed by the country code and the local number. For help, dial 0 and ask for an overseas operator. Most phone books list country codes and U.S. area codes. The country code for Australia is 61, for New Zealand 64, for the United Kingdom 44. Calling Canada is the same as calling within the United States, whose country code, by the way, is 1.

For operator assistance, dial 0. For directory assistance, call 555–1212 or occasionally 411 (free at many public phones). You can reverse long-distance charges by calling collect; dial 0 instead of 1 before the 10-digit number.

Instructions are generally posted on pay phones. Usually you insert coins in a slot (typically 25¢–50¢ for local calls) and wait for a steady tone before dialing. On long-distance calls the operator tells you how much to insert; prepaid phone cards, widely available in various denominations, can be used from any phone. Follow the directions to activate the card (there's usually an access number, then an activation code), then dial your number.

CELL PHONES

The United States has several GSM (Global System for Mobile Communications) networks, so multiband mobiles from most countries (except for Japan) work here. Unfortunately, it's almost impossible to buy a pay-as-you-go mobile SIM card in the United States—which allows you to avoid roaming charges—without also buying a phone. That said, cell phones with pay-as-you-go plans are available for well under $100. The cheapest ones with decent national coverage are the GoPhone from Cingular and Virgin Mobile, which only offers pay-as-you-go service.

Contacts **Cingular** (☎888/333–6651 ⊕www.cingular.com). **Virgin Mobile** (☎No phone ⊕www.virginmobileusa.com).

edy for altitude-related discomfort is to descend into heavier air.

▌SAFETY

Although Colorado is considered to be generally safe, travelers should take ordinary precautions—unfortunate incidents can happen anywhere. At your hotel lock your valuables either in the hotel's safe or in the safe in your room, if one is available. Be aware of your surroundings, and keep your wallet and passport in a buttoned pocket, or keep your handbag in front of you where you can see it. At night, avoid dimly lighted areas and areas where there are few people. Consider a taxi ride to your hotel if it is a long walk or you are alone.

Regardless of the outdoor activity or your level of skill, safety must come first. When hiking or taking part in any other outdoor activity, it's best (and often more fun) to go in pairs or small groups. If you do hike, cycle, kayak, or backcountry ski alone, it is essential that you tell someone where you are going and when you plan to return, whether it's a park ranger or the host of your B&B. Let them know, of course, when you've returned safely.

Many trails are at high altitudes, where oxygen is scarce. They're also frequently desolate. Hikers and bikers should carry emergency supplies in their backpacks. Proper equipment includes a flashlight, a compass, waterproof matches, a first-aid kit, a knife, a space blanket, and a light plastic tarp for shelter. Backcountry skiers should add a repair kit, a blanket, an avalanche beacon, and a lightweight shovel to their lists. Always bring extra food and a canteen of water as dehydration is a real danger at high altitudes. Never drink from streams or lakes, unless you boil the water first or purify it with tablets. Giardia, an intestinal parasite, may be present.

Although you may tan easily, the sun is intense even at mile-high elevations

> ## WORST-CASE SCENARIO
>
> All your money and credit cards have just been stolen. In these days of real-time transactions, this isn't a predicament that should destroy your vacation. First, report the theft of the credit cards. If you bank at a large international bank like Citibank or HSBC, go to the closest branch; if you know your account number, chances are you can get a new ATM card and withdraw money right away. **Western Union** (☎ 800/325–6000 ⊕ www.westernunion.com) sends money almost anywhere. Have someone back home order a transfer online, over the phone, or at one of the company's offices, which is the cheapest option.

(which are relatively low for the state), and sunburn can develop in just a few hours of hiking or sightseeing. Coloradans slather on sunscreen as a matter of course. Be sure to pack plenty of it, and don't forget to put it on when skiing—there's nothing glamorous about a goggle tan. The state's dry climate and thin air can also dehydrate you quickly. Carry a couple of liters of water with you each day and sip frequently.

Flash floods can strike at any time and any place with little or no warning. The danger in mountainous terrain is heightened when distant rains are channeled into gullies and ravines, turning a quiet streamside campsite or wash into a rampaging torrent in seconds. Check weather reports before heading into the backcountry and be prepared to head for higher ground if the weather turns severe.

One of the most wonderful parts of the Rockies is the abundant wildlife. And although a herd of grazing elk or a big-horn sheep high on a hillside is most certainly a Kodak moment, an encounter with a bear or mountain lion is not. To avoid such an unpleasant situation while hiking, make plenty of noise and keep dogs on leashes and small children between adults. While camping, be sure to store all food, utensils, and clothing with food odors far away from your tent, preferably high in a tree. If you do come across a bear or big cat, do not run. For bears, back away quietly; for lions, make yourself look as big as possible. In either case, be prepared to fend off the animal with loud noises, rocks, sticks, etc. And, like the saying goes, do not feed the bears—or any wild animals, whether they're dangerous or not.

When in any park, give all animals their space. If you want to take a photograph, use a long lens rather than a long sneak to approach closely. Approaching an animal can cause stress and affect its ability to survive the sometimes brutal climate. In all cases, remember that the animals have the right-of-way; this is their home, you are the visitor.

▌ SPORTS & THE OUTDOORS

The Colorado Rockies are one of America's greatest playgrounds. Information about Colorado's recreational areas and activities is provided in each regional chapter; the following is general information.

FISHING

Fishing licenses, available at tackle shops and a variety of stores, are required in Colorado for anyone over the age of 16. The fishing season is year-round, though seasons for particular species vary. A few streams are considered "private," in that they are stocked by a local club; other rivers are fly-fishing or catch-and-release only, so be sure you know the rules before making your first cast.

Rocky Mountain water can be cold, especially at higher elevations. You'd do well to bring waterproof waders or buy them when you arrive in the region. Outfitters and some tackle shops rent equipment, but you're best off bringing your own gear. Lures are another story, though: Whether you plan to fish with flies or

other lures, local tackle shops can usually give you a pretty good idea of what works best in a particular region, and you can buy accordingly.

Most outfitters include lunch, flies, transportation, and waders. When booking, be sure to ask what equipment you're expected to bring or if there are extra charges for licenses and gear.

Information & Licenses Colorado Division of Wildlife (☎ 303/297–1192 ⊕ www.wildlife. state.co.us).

Instruction Orvis Fly Fishing Schools (☎ 800/548–9548 ⊕ www.orvis.com). **Telluride Outside** (☎ 970/728–3895 or 800/831–6230 ⊕ www.tellurideoutside.com).

KAYAKING

The streams and rivers of the Rockies tend to be better suited to kayaking than canoeing. Steep mountains and narrow canyons usually mean fast-flowing water in which the maneuverability of kayaks is a great asset. A means of transport for less-experienced paddlers is the inflatable kayak (it's easier to navigate and it bounces off the rocks). The Arkansas, Colorado, and Green rivers are the best rivers in Colorado for kayaking.

Outfitters provide life jackets and, if necessary, paddles and helmets; they often throw in waterproof containers for cameras, clothing, and sleeping bags. Bring bug repellent as well as a good hat, sunscreen, and warm clothing for overnight trips. The best footwear is either water-resistant sandals or old sneakers.

Outfitters Dvorak Expeditions (☎ 800/824–3795 ⊕ www.dvorakexpeditions.com).

MAPS

If you plan to go where trails might not be well marked or maintained, you'll need maps and a compass. Topographical maps are sold in well-equipped outdoor stores. Maps in several scales are available from the U.S. Geological Survey (USGS). Request a free index and catalog, from which you can order the maps you need. Many local camping, fishing, and hunting stores carry USGS and other detailed maps of their surrounding region. The U.S. Forest Service and the BLM also publish useful maps.

Maps U.S. Geological Survey (☎303/202–4700 or 888/275–8747 ⊕www.usgs.gov).

PACK TRIPS & HORSEBACK RIDING

Horsemanship is not a prerequisite for most trips, but it's helpful. If you aren't an experienced rider (and even if you are), you can expect to experience some saddle discomfort for the first day or two.

Clothing requirements are minimal. A sturdy pair of pants, a wide-brim sun hat, and outerwear to protect against rain are about the only necessities. Ask your outfitter for a list of items you'll need.

ROCK CLIMBING & MOUNTAINEERING

Before you sign on with any trip, be sure to clarify to the trip organizer your climbing skills, experience, and physical condition. Climbing tends to be a team sport, and overestimating your capabilities can endanger not only you but other team members. A fair self-assessment of your abilities also helps a guide choose an appropriate climbing route; routes (not unlike ski trails) are rated according to their difficulty. Novices may want to get some instruction at a climbing wall before a trip to the Rockies.

Guide services usually rent such technical gear as helmets, pitons, ropes, and axes; be sure to ask what equipment and supplies you'll need to bring along. Some mountaineering stores rent climbing equipment. As for clothing, temperatures can fluctuate dramatically at higher elevations. Bringing several thin layers of clothing, including a sturdy, waterproof, breathable outer shell, is the best strategy for dealing with weather variations.

**Instructional Programs & Outfitters
Colorado Mountain School** (☎800/836–4008 Ext. 3 ⊕www.totalclimbing.com).

Fantasy Ridge Mountain Guides (☎970/728–3546 ⊕www.fantasyridge.com).

▌TAXES

Colorado's state sales tax is 2.9%, but after that it gets a little tricky. City sales taxes around the state range from 0.25% to 4%. County sales tax is between 1% and 4.5%. On top of state, county, and city taxes, some areas have local sales and lodging taxes that range from 0.9% to 4%. Some jurisdictions do not impose sales tax on groceries, and in some areas alcohol served in bars is taxed at a different rate than alcohol served in restaurants or purchased at liquor stores. In Denver, sales tax adds up to 7.22%, you'll pay 8.22% on your bill at a restaurant, and lodging tax is 14.85%. In Colorado Springs, you'll pay only the sales tax—7.4%—at a restaurant, but lodging tax is 9.4%. In Boulder sales tax is 8.31%, restaurant tax is 8.46%, and lodging tax is 10.25%. At this writing, Aspen has the simplest system—8.6% tax across the board. *For regional tax ranges, see the What It Costs charts in each chapter.*

▌TIME

All of Colorado is in the Mountain Time Zone. Mountain Time is two hours earlier than Eastern Time and one hour later than Pacific Time, so Colorado is one hour ahead of California, one hour behind Chicago, and two hours behind New York.

▌TIPPING

It's customary to tip 15% to 20% at restaurants in cities; in resort towns, 20% is increasingly the norm. For coat checks and bellmen, $1 per coat or bag is the minimum. Taxi drivers expect 10% to 15%. In resort towns, ski technicians, sandwich makers, coffee baristas, and the like also appreciate tips.

INDEX

PHOTO CREDITS

8, *Robert Winslow/viestiphoto.com.* 9 (left), *Photodisc.* 9 (right), *Joe Viesti/viestiphoto.com.* 10, *Dan Peha/viestiphoto.com.* 11, *Richard Cummins/viestiphoto.com.* 12, *Ann Duncan/viestiphoto.com.* 13 (left), *Ann Duncan/viestiphoto.com.* 13 (right), *Joe Viesti/viestiphoto.com.* 14, *Loren Irving/age fotostock.* 15 (left), *Blaine Harrington/age fotostock.* 15 (right), *Dan Peha/viestiphoto.com.* 16, *Michael Javorka/viestiphoto.com.* 17 (left), *Robert Winslow/viestiphoto.com.* 17 (right), *Ann Duncan/viestiphoto.com.* 258–59, *National Parks Service.* 380–81, *National Parks Service.*

ABOUT OUR WRITERS

Jad Davenport, a freelance travel writer and photographer, grew up in Colorado where he lives with his wife and daughter. He enjoys backcountry skiing, ice climbing, white-water kayaking and hiking. His work has appeared in *Outside, National Geographic Adventure* and *Men's Journal* magazines.

Lois Friedland is a Colorado-based journalist and editor who specializes in travel, skiing, and golf. Her background includes authorship of travel- and ski-guide books, and stints as editor of a weekly newsletter about the winter sports industry's business side and as western editor of *Ski Magazine*.

Ann Miller is a travel and creative writer who grew up on a ranch in Colorado. She has published place-descriptive articles, poetry, and science fiction. She is also a columnist for the *Longmont Times-Call*.

Gregory Robl has lived on Colorado's Front Range for more than 40 years. He is a frequent traveler abroad, but Colorado remains his favorite destination for hiking, cycling, and the Takács String Quartet. His publications include travel articles and a genealogy handbook. He writes for the local newspaper about gardening in Colorado, and he has also contributed to a library journal and two reference works.

Kyle Wagner wrote about restaurants and food in Denver for 14 years, first for the alternative weekly *Westword* and then for the *Denver Post*, before being named travel editor for the Post in 2005. Her work also has appeared in the *Rocky Mountain News* and *Sunset* magazine. She lives in Denver with her two teenage daughters, who had their passports stamped before they started kindergarten and prefer sushi to McDonald's.